# The Nauvoo City and High Council Minutes

# The Nauvoo City and High Council Minutes

edited by

John S. Dinger

with a foreword by

Morris A. Thurston

Signature Books • Salt Lake City • 2011

*For Jessica, Ainsley, and Emmie*

Published in cooperation with the Smith-Pettit Foundation.


www.signaturebooks.com.

Jacket design by Ron Stucki

*The Nauvoo City and High Council Minutes* was printed on acid-free paper and was composed, printed, and bound in the United States of America.

2015 2014 21013 2012 2011 5 4 3 2 1

Library of Congress Cataloging-in-Publication Data
The Nauvoo City and High Council minutes / edited by
John S. Dinger.
pages cm
Includes bibliographical references and index.
ISBN-10: 1-56085-214-3 (alk. paper)
ISBN-13: 978-1-56085-214-8 (alk. paper) 1. Nauvoo (Ill.)—History—19th century—Sources. 2. Nauvoo (Ill.)—Church history—19th century—Sources. 3. Church of Jesus Christ of Latter-day Saints—History—19th century—Sources. 4. Church of Jesus Christ of Latter-day Saints—Illinois—Nauvoo—History—Sources. I. Dinger, John S., editor. II. Nauvoo (Ill.), author. III. Church of Jesus Christ of Latter-day Saints. Nauvoo High Council, author.
F549.N37N38 2011
977.3'43—dc23 2011032878

# CONTENTS

# FOREWORD

*Morris A. Thurston*

Since its early days, Mormonism has emphasized a structural similarity to the Church in Christ's day. For example, the fourth Article of Faith affirms a belief in "the same organization that existed in the Primitive Church." This does not mean, however, that today's organization emerged fully formed when the Church of Christ was established on April 6, 1830. Rather, the structure evolved gradually through the years.

Within the first few years after the Church was formed, informal groups were created on an ad hoc basis to organize events and resolve disputes. Then Joseph Smith put together the first permanent council at his home in Kirtland, Ohio, on February 17, 1834. He called it "the high council of the church of Christ" (D&C 102:1). Other councils were formed, but the high council "of the seat of the First Presidency of the Church" was to be the primary governing body for the Church, as well as the appellate court for other high councils that would be organized.[1]

Nearly six years later, on October 6, 1839, the Nauvoo High Council was formed, with William Marks presiding as stake president (339-40). Throughout its first sixteen months, the council governed both ecclesiastically and civilly. Since it had no official civil standing, however, the only means of enforcing its judgments was to withdraw fellowship from those found guilty of transgression. But in a city where religious standing was as important as civil standing, the threat of excommunication was a potent weapon.

---

[1]It was not until March 1835, more than a year after the organization of the Kirtland High Council, that the Council of the Twelve was formed. This council, whose members were called apostles, was responsible for governing in the far-flung mission fields, while the high councils were responsible for governance back home.

On February 1, 1841, shortly after the Nauvoo Charter was granted by the Illinois General Assembly, the city held an election to choose a mayor and city council. The mayor was given both executive and judicial duties, and the city council was given legislative duties. The high council would thereafter restrict itself more or less to religious issues, especially disputes between Church members.

The city council lost no time in exercising its parliamentary authority. It was headed by John C. Bennett, the mayor, with aldermen William Marks, Samuel H. Smith, Daniel H. Wells and Newel K. Whitney. The founding councilmen included three other Smith brothers (Don Carlos, Hyrum, and Joseph) and John T. Barnett, John P. Greene, Vinson Knight, Wilson Law, Charles C. Rich, and Sidney Rigdon. Although there were strong theocratic overtones to the structure of the council and its deliberations, the councilmen were not required to be Mormon. Daniel Wells would not join the Church until after Joseph Smith's death, for instance, although he later became a member of the First Presidency.

From the start, the city council took its law-making role seriously and began passing ordinances regarding the commercial and judicial make-up of the city, strengthening its autonomy from state government—something the council was particularly attentive to. The most contentious political issue involved a series of ordinances to expand the scope of habeas corpus powers held by the Nauvoo Municipal Court.

The chief beneficiary of these broad powers was Joseph Smith, who replaced Bennett as mayor on May 19, 1842. The fact that the president of the Church was now the mayor no doubt promoted bureaucratic efficiency. Even so, as I researched the background of attempts to extradite Smith to Missouri, in connection with my work on the Joseph Smith Papers Project, I was struck by the alacrity with which the city council met all threats against Smith's liberty.

For instance, on August 8, 1842, pursuant to a warrant issued by Illinois Governor Thomas Carlin, who was responding to an extradition request from Missouri, lawmen arrested Joseph Smith in Nauvoo. The main charge was being an accessory before the fact to an assassination attempt on Lilburn Boggs, the previous governor of Missouri. Smith's lawyers obtained a temporary release for their client under the Nauvoo habeas corpus ordinance. As the out-of-town lawmen returned to Quincy to seek further instructions from Carlin, the atmosphere in Nauvoo became highly charged. Before the day was out, the city council passed a revised and bolstered habeas corpus law (101-02). In an era before word processing programs or even typewriters, this was an impressive accomplishment!

The new law changed the rules of the game. Habeas corpus hearings typically had been understood to permit inquiry into the *procedures* utilized in obtaining an arrest warrant, but the new Nauvoo ordinance authorized the municipal court to "fully hear the *merits* of the case," a significant and controversial expansion of power. Furthermore, if the court–whose chief justice was Joseph Smith, or sometimes his brother Hyrum–determined after examining the merits that the warrant had been "issued either through private pique, malicious intent, religious or other persecution, falsehood, or misrepresentation," the court could quash the process. Since nearly everyone in Nauvoo believed the attempted extradition was motivated by Boggs's private pique, as well as by religious persecution, the outcome of such a hearing was foreordained.

This enlargement of habeas corpus infuriated Governor Carlin and proved irresistible to Nauvoo's municipal court; it was also easy fodder for anti-Mormon newspapers. Eventually, the perception that Smith and other Mormon leaders were beyond the reach of Illinois law contributed to the circumstances that led to the murder of the Smith brothers in Carthage.[2]

In this volume, John Dinger has assembled all the known minutes of Nauvoo's two highest governing bodies–ecclesiastical and civil. The book is well done, and makes a significant contribution to the canon of published primary sources in Mormon studies. Following the tradition of Signature Books, the documents are presented with care, along with interpretative annotation, for both a general reader and for scholars in history and religion, as well as researchers in other fields, such as jurisprudence, political science, and organizational behavior.

There is something about the exercise of studying primary doc-

---

[2]See my article, "The Boggs Shooting and Attempted Extradition: Joseph Smith's Most Famous Case," *BYU Studies* 48 (2009): 5-56, for a fuller discussion of these issues.

uments that makes history come alive for both the scholar and the casual reader. Sometimes it is just a matter of being able to better visualize how people interacted in historical times or how their institutions functioned. For instance, during much of the Nauvoo period, the high council meetings were held in the homes of various councilmen. As I read the minutes, I found myself wondering how the location was selected. Did it come down to whose house was large enough to accommodate everyone, or perhaps to whose house was most conveniently located, or was it something different, such as which councilman's wife served the best refreshments? (I hasten to add here that it was a man's world and the women cooked, as is painfully obvious from the minutes.)

Reading the unexpurgated transcripts helped me grasp things in a new light, even though I had spent time with other primary documents and several excellent histories. One idea that was brought home for me was the far-reaching authority of the high council. I was impressed and inspired by how motivated they were to promote the good of the city and Church. It was moving to learn of their effort to build a house for James Hendricks, who had been crippled in the Battle of Crooked River (358, Jan 19, 1840). I was amused when they voted that Joseph Smith and his family should "be exempt from receiving the crowded throng of visitors as have formerly thronged his house" (341n10, Oct. 20, 1839; please note that I have corrected and modernized the spelling and punctuation). How nice it would be if such things could be arranged by legislative fiat.

I found it interesting, too, that there are so many similarities between the Nauvoo High Council and modern councils at the stake level throughout the Church. This is because the procedures for hearing complaints against Church members were outlined early on in Section 102 of the Doctrine and Covenants. As confirmed by this volume, the rules include the following:

- When a high council is convened, the order in which the councilors speak is determined by lot.
- The high council conducts triage to determine which cases are most difficult and assigns two, four, or six councilors to cases depending on their complexity.
- In all instances, one half of the members of the high council

(those who draw even lottery numbers) are assigned to consider the case from the point of view of the accused.

- After all the evidence is heard and the councilors have had their say, the accused has the privilege of speaking.
- Finally, the president of the high council renders a decision and asks the councilors to sanction it.

The Nauvoo High Council conducted its business with appropriate solemnity, but the reader will smile at times at some unexpected comic relief. For instance, in January 1843, Henry Cook was summoned to appear for having sold his wife, Mary, to another man. From the evidence, it appears that Cook wed Mary not long after his first wife had died. He soon discovered that Mary "was in the habit of traveling about of nights when there was no need of it" and that she used "indecent language" around his children. She would also "insult him without cause," refusing "to be subject to him or be under his control, boasting that she would not be governed by no man."

Henry admitted that he had "whipped her pretty severely, ... thinking that might bring her to her duty." He also acknowledged that he had entertained an offer from someone interested in purchasing her but claimed it had been said in jest. Apparently, however, the "party making the offer held it as a bargain and so did she."

What did the high council do? "President Hyrum Smith spoke at some length on the subject and, after giving Cook a very appropriate and severe reprimand for whipping his wife, he thought that Cook had acted as well as could be expected under his circumstances and decided that he should be acquitted." The council affirmed the decision unanimously (438-39, Jan. 21,1843). As I read the Cook case, I couldn't help thinking how perfect it would be as a scene in a movie about the Nauvoo experience.

On another occasion I appreciated the counsel of Joseph Smith, who offered some remarks at a general conference in April 1843 about a high council inquiry into the beliefs of Pelatiah Brown. An elderly gentleman, Brown was charged with preaching false doctrine. Smith said:

> I did not like the old man being called up for erring in doctrine. It looks too much like the Methodist, and not like the Latter-day Saints. Methodists have creeds which a man must believe or be

> asked out of their church. I want the liberty of thinking and believing as I please. It feels so good not to be trammeled. It does not prove that a man is not a good man because he errs in doctrine (455n42).

Then there was the case of Amasa Bonney, who must win the award for inappropriate behavior before a high council. Cited on a charge of drunkenness, Bonney showed up "in a high state of intoxication, with a bottle in his pocket; and was soon in a state of ~~stupor~~ sleep, in the council room, whereupon it was voted unanimously that he be cut off from the Church of Jesus Christ of Latter Day Saints" (559, Sept. 6, 1845). You can almost see them helping him down the front steps, someone supporting him on either side. One wonders if he continued to deny the charge?

These are just a few random scenes that jumped off the page at me. There were other momentous and stirring occasions that would impact the future of the Restoration movement in profound ways, including the deliberations surrounding the destruction of the *Nauvoo Expositor*. Summarized in Dinger's excellent introduction, there is nevertheless no substitute for reading the full account in order to grasp the feverish emotions in the days leading to Joseph Smith's assassination (250-68, June 10-11, 1844). The issues seem as dramatically complex and tragic today as they were at the time.

As noted above, with the publication of *The Nauvoo City and High Council Minutes*, the library of readily accessible Mormon documents has been significantly enhanced. Looking at my own shelves, I notice a particularly strong contribution from Signature Books, which has emphasized the publication of documentary history. Their volumes are annotated in a way that is helpful to non-specialists, their editors merely providing context and letting readers draw their own conclusions. Here are a few of the titles from Signature that I notice in my own library from a quick scan of my shelves:

*An American Prophet's Record: The Diaries and Journals of Joseph Smith*, Scott H. Faulring, ed.

*The Autobiography of B. H. Roberts*, Gary James Bergera, ed.

*The Complete Discourses of Brigham Young* (five volumes), Richard S. Van Wagoner, ed., with the Smith-Pettit Foundation imprint

*Conflict in the Quorum: Orson Pratt, Brigham Young, Joseph Smith,* by Gary James Bergera

*The Development of LDS Temple Worship, 1846-2000: A Documentary History,* Devery S. Anderson, ed.

*Early Mormon Documents* (five volumes), Dan Vogel, ed.

*An Intimate Chronicle: The Journals of William Clayton,* George D. Smith, ed.

*Joseph Smith's Quorum of the Anointed, 1842-1845: A Documentary History,* Devery S. Anderson and Gary James Bergera, eds.

*Lucy's Book: A Critical Edition of Lucy Mack Smith's Family Memoir,* Lavina Fielding Anderson, ed.

*The Mormon Church on Trial: Transcripts of the Reed Smoot Hearings,* Michael Harold Paulos, ed.

*The Nauvoo Endowment Companies, 1845-1846: A Documentary History,* Devery S. Anderson and Gary James Bergera, eds.

*Waiting for World's End: The Diaries of Wilford Woodruff,* Susan Staker, ed.

*The William E. McLelllin Papers, 1854-1880,* Stan Larson and Samuel J. Passey, eds.

Each of these editions is a prized possession. I appreciate the efforts of the editors and the publisher to make them available outside the archive walls.

I have a personal interest in family and individual histories, and this pastime makes me sensitive to how people remember their forebears. In the Church we gather the names and vital statistics of our ancestors and preserve what inspirational stories we have of their lives. In a similar way, the narratives in the current volume, coming as they do from our spiritual ancestors, allow us to picture ourselves in their shoes. I can relate to the agony they felt in making difficult decisions. To a large extent, the dilemmas they faced are not unlike the perplexities we are confronted with today. Of course, we understand that our stalwart forebears, both genetic and spiritual, were not so perfect as they are sometimes made out to be, but we celebrate them for doing the best they could with what they were given. In reading this volume I found it fascinating to ruminate about how their actions helped determine what kind of people we would become.

# PREFACE

On June 27, 1844, Joseph Smith, the prophet and president of the LDS Church, was killed in jail in Carthage, Illinois, where he was being held for inciting a riot when the City of Nauvoo destroyed the *Nauvoo Expositor* newspaper. Earlier he had been exonerated of the charge by the Mormon-run municipal court but had subsequently agreed to submit to a non-LDS tribunal. He was killed, in part, because of actions, both religious and political, that many of his non-Mormon neighbors said they could no longer tolerate.

Much of what they found objectionable in him and his Church stemmed from the policies adopted by two high-profile governing bodies, the Nauvoo City Council and Nauvoo Stake High Council. The city council was created in early 1841 after the Illinois state legislature granted Nauvoo a city charter. This authorized the city council to hold elections and pass ordinances governing Nauvoo's citizens. The council passed traditional laws, such as specifying fines for people who let their dogs run free, and more controversial laws such as its expansive interpretation of *habeas corpus,* which was intended to make it virtually impossible for Church leaders to be arrested.

The high council, typically composed of twelve adult male priesthood holders, governed the religious life of the city. Mormons could come before the high council to charge others with dishonesty or immorality. The council heard evidence in these cases, appointed some councilmen to speak on behalf of the defendant and others to speak against him or her, ruled on the defendant's guilt or innocence, and imposed judgment. The range of penalties included confession, apology, and restitution to monetary fines and excommunication from the Church.

## The Sources

The minutes collected in this volume are a treasure trove of material relating to the religious and secular life of the early Latter-day Saints. These two sets of documents are, I believe, two of the most important primary sources for the period. Selected excerpts have previously appeared, most notably in Joseph Smith's *History of the Church* and Fred Collier's *Nauvoo High Council Minute Books,*[1] but this compilation gathers the most complete available material from sources Collier was unaware of and from documents the historians who compiled Joseph Smith's history used selectively. In preparing the minutes for publication, I relied on typescripts, photocopies, and photographs. In addition, as we were preparing to go to press, other researchers achieved access to some digital scans that helped clarify questions I had. Readers should know that I was not allowed to see the originals housed in the LDS Church History Library and Archives, where access to them is restricted.[2]

The evolution of the minutes is interesting. Typically the city council's scribe sat in on a meeting and took notes on loose sheets of paper, then translated his scribblings into full sentences and transferred them to a rough-draft minute book. There were four such books covering the period from November 1842 through December

---

[1]Joseph Smith, *History of the Church of Jesus Christ of Latter-day Saints,* 7 vols. (Salt Lake City: Deseret News, 1902-12); Fred Collier, ed., *The Nauvoo High Council Minute Books of the Church of Jesus Christ of Latter Day Saints* (Hanna, UT: Collier's Publishing Co., 2005).

[2]The reason the Church archivists usually cite for sequestering these documents, especially the high council minutes, is confidentiality. This makes sense today, and the rationale is also apparent in the documents Richard E. Turley included on the *Selected Collections from the Archives of the Church of Jesus Christ of Latter-day Saints,* 74 DVD discs (Salt Lake City: Intellectual Reserve, 2002), where the names of individuals have been blacked out; however, in Nauvoo, Church trials were public spectacles where curiosity seekers often packed the council room. If enough people showed up, the high council would pause the proceedings and move to a more commodious location such as the Seventies Hall. In some instances, the only settings that would accommodate the large crowds were outdoor "groves" (wooded areas on the outskirts of town) or "the stand" (an outdoor amphitheater). The high council usually specified, as part of the sentencing, that its ruling should be published in the *Times and Seasons,* public embarrassment being part of the punishment, and sometimes the full minutes were published to give the matter the airing the council thought it deserved.

1844. With input from others, the scribe corrected the minutes, struck out passages and added additional information above the line–indicated here by wording placed within caret marks (^like this^)–and transferred a final, approved version to a bound volume titled "A Record of the Proceedings of the City Council of the City of Nauvoo Hancock County, State of Illinois Commencing A.D. 1841." The Proceedings contained minutes from February 1841 through February 1845. Unfortunately, one rough-draft book is missing, the second of four. It is the book containing the transcript of the trial of the city's mayor, John C. Bennett.

On February 3, 1841, the style of the Proceedings changed from a narrative account to only the council's final resolutions and ordinances. Readers will be able to easily detect the underlying source in instances where I drew from the Proceedings. Even so, I have made it easy for readers by adding a dagger (†) each time I switched from an earlier source to the Proceedings. In addition, I added a double dagger (‡) to show when I switched to the rough-draft minute books, as well as two double daggers (‡‡) to indicate loose sheets of paper. At the end of the preface, I have placed a table summarizing the underlying sources by date and page number as Table 1: Identification of City Council Sources.

Although the pioneers did their best in preserving these documents, some of the papers and bound volumes were inevitably damaged or lost, as one can imagine for documents that were transported across the Great Plains by wagon. Add to the puzzle of incomplete sources the fact that I initially worked solely from typescripts, and you can see that a certain amount of detective work was necessary to assemble a full set of minutes. Before I fully understood the genealogy of the sources, I instinctively gave preference to the earlier, rough drafts. Along the way, I tried to keep the undulations from one source to another to a minimum, and my last task before going to press was to add the typographical glyphs to show where the sources change. For the high council meetings, I applied a similar technique as for the city council minutes, adding a double dagger (‡) to indicate rough-draft minutes, in this case one of the six extant books that were kept for the high council meetings, and two double daggers (‡‡) for loose sheets of paper. I drew one entry from the "Far West Record," indicating it with an inverted exclamation mark (¡). As with the city minutes, I summarized the high council documents in a list: Table 2: Identification of High Council Sources.

Much like the scribes who memorialized the city council meetings, those who took notes for the high council did so on loose sheets of paper and later transferred them to six bound volumes from October 1839 through October 1845. The first volume began as a diary titled "Oliver Cowdery's Sketch Book for 1836," which was converted to a minutes book after page 22, when the scribe drew a line across the page and wrote, "Nauvoo October 6, 1839," then "Book no 1" on the next page. (At the very end of the book is a recipe for making "stucco white wash," presumably added by high council scribe Hosea Stout.) Volume 2 in the series of six bound volumes was initially treated like the Record of Proceedings–a place to record the final, cleaned-up versions of minutes, beginning with the entry for March 8, 1840, which were transferred over from volume 1. However, the minutes soon become rough again as the scribe apparently began using the book for first or second drafts.

As I worked from various typescripts, I tried unsuccessfully to understand why there were duplicate, almost verbatim, repetitions in the transcripts and why the different transcripts were similar but not exactly alike. Later, colleagues with access to scans of the original documents helped me see that the duplications were, in fact, different versions drawn from the loose minutes, rough drafts, and the corrected "fair copy." I no longer felt like a blind man trying to detect the shape of an elephant.

Among those whose work and advice I have benefitted from are, first and foremost, the scholars who poured over the manuscripts years ago and transcribed the handwriting, which is difficult to do. I made use of typescripts prepared by Lyndon W. Cook, H. Michael Marquardt, D. Michael Quinn, and Edyth J. Romney, which are located at the J. Willard Marriott Library, University of Utah; the Quinn Papers at the Beinecke Rare Book and Manuscript Library at Yale University; and the Leonard J. Arrington Papers at the Merrill-Cazier Library, Utah State University. Photocopies and corroborating documents turned up in several locations, including the Valeen T. Avery Papers at Utah State University, the offices of the Smith-Pettit Foundation in Salt Lake City, and Richard Turley's 74 discs assembled as *Selected Collections from the Archives of the Church of Jesus*

*Christ of Latter-day Saints*. The original documents are housed in the Library, History Department, Church of Jesus Christ of Latter-day Saints, Salt Lake City.

## Editorial Style

In compiling this presentation, I tried to strike a balance between fidelity to the originals and readability where I thought minimal punctuation and paragraphing would be helpful. I placed missing or incomplete text within square brackets to alert readers to any extrapolations. It is sometimes difficult to interpret the scribes' intent regarding capital or lower-case letters or slight differences between commas and periods, and there were differences among the typescripts in these areas. I leaned in the direction of applying modern usage to such slight ambiguities to aid reader comprehension.

In the footnotes, I occasionally provided transcripts of additional primary source documents, which I hope will help explain the historical context. Occasionally I also mentioned basic facts I thought readers should be aware of. In such instances, I silently consulted dictionaries, encyclopedias, *Wikipedia,* and LDS reference sources such as the *Deseret News 2010 Church Almanac*, *FamilySearch*, *GospeLink*, the *New Mormon Studies CD-Rom*, and the *BYU Studies* and *Joseph Smith Papers* websites. I did the same when piecing together biographical information. Initially, I thought I could identify every person mentioned in the minutes, but as readers will readily notice, I had to lower my standard and just identify as many as possible.

I am greatly indebted to the prior work and suggestions of many other researchers and acquaintances, including Lyndon W. Cook, Alene Dinger, Scott H. Faulring, Joseph Johnstun, H. Michael Marquardt, Ardis E. Parshall, D. Michael Quinn, Edyth J. Romney, and Dan Vogel. I appreciated the constant support and encouragement of Gary James Bergera at the Smith-Pettit Foundation and Tom Kimball at Signature Books. I thank my wife, Jessica, and my daughter, Ainsley, for their patience throughout the project. As a concluding note, I should emphasize that this book is not endorsed by any of the individuals or organizations mentioned here and that I am alone responsible for any errors in the transcription or missteps in the interpretative annotations. I nevertheless hold to the hope that there will be few such unintentional errors.

**TABLE 1.** Identification of city council sources

| year | date | source | pages herein |
|---|---|---|---|
| 1841 | | | |
| | Feb 3–Dec 18 | Proceedings | 3–44 |
| 1842 | | | |
| | Jan 1–Nov 26 | Proceedings | 45–130 |
| 1843 | | | |
| | Jan 14–Jun 29 | Proceedings | 131–82 |
| | August 12 | Rough book, Proceedings | 183–84 |
| | Sep 9–Dec 29 | Rough book | 184–98 |
| 1844 | | | |
| | Jan 3–16 | Rough book | 199–220 |
| | January 17 | Proceedings | 221 |
| | February 10 | Rough book | 221 |
| | February 12 | Rough book, Proceedings | 221–27 |
| | March 1 | Proceedings | 227 |
| | March 5 | Rough book, Proceedings | 227–29 |
| | March 9 | Rough book, Proceedings | 230–34 |
| | April 13 | Rough book, Proceedings | 234–36 |
| | April 29 | Rough book, Proceedings | 236–37 |
| | May 11 | Rough book | 237–38 |
| | May 16 | Proceedings | 238 |
| | June 8 | Rough book, Proceedings | 238–50 |
| | June 10 | Rough book, loose minutes, Proceedings | 250–66 |
| | June 11 | Loose minutes | 266–68 |
| | June 21 | Rough book, Proceedings | 268–71 |
| | July 1 | Rough book, loose minutes | 271–75 |
| | July 2 | Rough book, Proceedings | 275–78 |
| | July 8 | Rough book, Proceedings | 278–81 |
| | July 13 | Rough book | 281–82 |
| | August 10 | Rough book, Proceedings | 282–89 |
| | September 14 | Rough book | 289–92 |
| | September 18 | Proceedings | 292 |
| | October 12 | Loose minutes, rough book, Proceedings | 292–96 |
| | November 1 | Proceedings | 296 |
| | November 9 | Loose minutes, rough book, Proceedings | 296–300 |
| | Nov 17–Dec 10 | Proceedings | 300 |
| | December 14 | Rough book, Proceedings | 301–08 |

TABLE 1. *(continued)*

| year | date | source | pages herein |
|---|---|---|---|
| 1845 | | | |
| | January 11 | Rough book, loose minutes, Proceedings | 309–18 |
| | January 13 | Rough book, Proceedings | 318–22 |
| | February 7 | Proceedings | 322–23 |
| | February 8 | Rough book, Proceedings | 323–36 |
| | March 8 | Rough book | 336 |

**Proceedings** = "A Record of the Proceedings of the City Council of the City of Nauvoo Hancock County, State of Illinois Commencing A.D. 1841"

**Rough book** = One of four bound, rough-draft minute books for the city council, Nov. 1842–Dec. 1844

**Loose minutes** = Loose sheets of first-draft versions of the minutes

TABLE 2. Identification of high council sources

| year | date | source | pages herein |
|---|---|---|---|
| 1839 | | | |
| | October 6 | Bound minutes | 339–40 |
| | October 20–27 | Loose pages | 340–44 |
| | Oct 28–Dec 1 | Bound minutes | 344–47 |
| | December 8–22 | Loose pages | 347–49 |
| | December 26 | Bound minutes | 349–50 |
| | December 29–30 | Loose pages | 350–53 |
| 1840 | | | |
| | January 5–12 | Bound minutes | 355–57 |
| | January 19 | Loose pages | 357–58 |
| | February 2–9 | Bound minutes | 358–59 |
| | Feb 23–Mar 1 | Loose pages | 359–61 |
| | March 8–16 | Bound minutes | 361–64 |
| | March 22–29 | Loose pages | 365–66 |
| | April 6 | Bound minutes | 366–67 |
| | April 12–May 2 | Loose pages | 367–69 |
| | Jun 12–Dec 20 | Bound minutes | 370–86 |
| 1841 | | | |
| | Feb 6–Oct 9 | Bound minutes | 387–97 |

TABLE 2. *(continued)*

| year | date | source | pages herein |
|---|---|---|---|
| 1842 | | | |
| | Jan 18–Dec 25 | Bound minutes | 399–434 |
| 1843 | | | |
| | January 1–21 | Bound minutes | 435–41 |
| | January 28 | Loose pages | 441–45 |
| | February 4–11 | Bound minutes | 445–47 |
| | February 18 | Loose pages | 447–48 |
| | Feb 19–Nov 11 | Bound minutes | 448–75 |
| | November 18 | Loose pages | 475–78 |
| | November 25 | Bound minutes | 478–80 |
| | December 9–23 | Loose minutes | 480–81 |
| | December 30 | Bound minutes | 481–82 |
| 1844 | | | |
| | Jan 6–27 | Bound minutes | 483–84 |
| | February 3 | Loose pages | 484 |
| | Feb 17–May 11 | Bound minutes | 485–92 |
| | May 18 | Loose pages | 492–94 |
| | June 1–15 | Far West record | 494–98 |
| | Aug 31–Sep 10 | Loose pages | 498–526 |
| | Sep 21–Dec 28 | Bound minutes | 526–39 |
| 1845 | | | |
| | Jan 4–Oct 18 | Bound minutes | 541–62 |

**Bound minutes** = One of six bound volumes of minutes for the high council, Oct. 1839–Oct. 1845

**Loose minutes** = Loose sheets of first-draft versions of the minutes

# INTRODUCTION

Joseph Smith Jr. was born on December 23, 1805, in Sharon, Vermont. He would later report that as a youth, he conversed with heavenly beings who called him to restore God's truth to the earth. After publishing the Book of Mormon in 1830, he organized the Church of Christ, later renamed the Church of Jesus Christ of Latter-day Saints, on April 6, 1830, and sent missionaries throughout New York and neighboring Pennsylvania, Ohio, and Canada. In 1831 he moved his small congregation to Kirtland, Ohio, and merged it with a group of recent converts there. But before long, he received a revelation (D&C 57:1-3)[1] naming Missouri as the proper gathering place to await Jesus's Second Coming.

Mormons settled in Jackson County, Missouri, where they clashed with the older settlers and were forced to move north across the Mississippi River into Clay County, Missouri, where there was more conflict. In the closing months of 1838, the Saints were told to leave the state under threat of an "extermination order" issued by Missouri Governor Lilburn W. Boggs. A large number headed east to cross the Missouri River into Quincy, Illinois, a small town fifty miles south of a settlement called Commerce, which the Mormons settled and renamed Nauvoo. Local residents seemed more tolerant there, and by April 1839, most Mormons had decided to relocate to Illinois.[2]

When Joseph Smith arrived, he made plans for a Mormon utopia on several hundred acres in and around Commerce, which he

---

[1]References to the Doctrine and Covenants (D&C) will be to the current edition published by the LDS Church.

[2]See Glen M. Leonard, *Nauvoo: A Place of Peace, a People of Promise* (Salt Lake City: Deseret Book, 2002), 30-33; Robert B. Flanders, *Nauvoo: Kingdom on the Mississippi* (Urbana: University of Illinois Press, 1975), 12-13.

and his followers platted on "a simple gridiron" with "150 squares of about four acres, each divided into four equal lots. The streets were, with two exceptions, three rods wide (49.5 feet) and ran north-south and east-west, regardless of the terrain."[3] Initially the First Presidency, composed of Smith and two counselors, and the Nauvoo High Council functioned as civic officials. In 1841 the high council decided to hold an election and allow Nauvoo's citizens to elect their first city council.

## The Nauvoo Stake High Council

The precedent for a "high council" was set in Kirtland when, on February 17, 1834, Smith conceived of having twelve elders function as the Church's primary judicial and legislative body responsible for finances, trials, disfellowshipments (suspension of membership privileges), and excommunications. As the Church spread to other areas, additional stakes would be created and given their own high councils, but the council at the "center stake of Zion" retained pre-eminence as a presiding council, its decisions setting policy for the entire Church. It took appeals from lesser high councils as needed.

When the Saints left Missouri for Illinois, the presiding high council was organized in Quincy, then in Nauvoo, convening for the first time on October 20, 1839, and for the last time six years later on October 18, 1845. A number of important events occurred when this august body met, including the formulation of responses to polygamy rumors and disputes about the Quorum of the Twelve Apostles and Brigham Young's rise to prominence. The Nauvoo High Council had a hand in establishing the city council and in electing the town's civic leaders.

## The Nauvoo City Council

An Illinois city could not legally govern itself without receiving authority to do so from the state. The legislature began chartering cities in 1837 with Chicago.[4] Springfield was chartered three years later[5] which was important because other cities, such as Nauvoo, modeled their charters on the example of the new state capital. All

---

[3]Flanders, *Nauvoo: Kingdom*, 42.

[4]Chicago was chartered on March 4, 1837.

[5]Springfield was chartered on February 3, 1840.

told, "more that 80 percent of [Nauvoo's] provisions closely followed franchises authorized for other Illinois cities."[6]

On December 16, 1840, Illinois legislators ratified Nauvoo's enabling charter.[7] Two months earlier, a recent Mormon convert, John C. Bennett, had been appointed to help write the charter and to "urge the passage of said bill through the legislature."[8] Bennett had arrived in Nauvoo the previous August or September,[9] but in December 1840 he was present as a Church lobbyist when the legislature was in session. He managed to attract the attention and support of the Illinois Secretary of State Stephen A. Douglas and state senator Sidney H. Douglas, a prominent Whig.[10] Historian Robert Flanders quotes from a government document describing the charter's passage:

> On December [November] 27 the Nauvoo charter bill was introduced in the Upper House by Senator Little, whose only comment was that it contained "an extraordinary militia clause" which he considered "harmless." Under a suspension of the rules, the bill was read the first and second times and referred to the Judiciary Committee; on December 5 it was reported back with an unspecified amendment; and on December 9 it was read the third time and passed, in company with other miscellaneous bills. In the House of Representatives the procedure was similar. Introduced from the Senate on December 10, it was read twice by title and referred to committee; two days later it was reported back without amendment, read again by title, and shouted through without calling for ayes and nays. It next went to the Council of Revision, a review body with

---

[6]Leonard, *Nauvoo,* 104-05. The standard histories of the city document are James L. Kimball Jr., "The Nauvoo Charter: A Reinterpretation," *Journal of the Illinois State Historical Society* 64 (Spring 1971): 66-78; James L. Kimball Jr., "'A Wall to Defend Zion': The Nauvoo Charter," *BYU Studies* 15 (Summer 1975): 491-97. See also Richard E. Bennett and Rachel Cope, "'A City on a Hill': Chartering the City of Nauvoo," *John Whitmer Historical Journal* 22 (Special edition 2002): 17-40.

[7]Bennett and Cope, "City on a Hill," 21.

[8]Joseph Smith, *History of the Church of Jesus Christ of Latter-day Saints,* 7 vols. (Salt Lake City: Deseret News, 1902-12) 4:205; hereafter *History of Church.*

[9]Flanders, *Nauvoo Kingdom,* 95.

[10]Ibid., 95-96.

> amending powers made up of Democratic Governor Thomas Carlin and the four supreme court justices, three Whigs and one Democrat. This group passed it without change on December 18 [16].[11]

Both political parties—Whigs and Democrats—viewed Mormons as a potential electoral boon they did not want to neglect, a fact Bennett was able to exploit. Illinois Governor Thomas Ford later wrote, "He [Bennett] flattered both sides with the hope of Mormon favor and both sides expected to receive their votes."[12]

Though the charter resembled those of other cities, it differed in important ways. Nauvoo's included the right to create a university,[13] a standing army,[14] and a municipal court.[15] It was specifically created to be both inclusive and powerful. As Joseph Smith wrote, "The City Charter of Nauvoo is my own plan and device; I concocted it for the salvation of the Church, and on principles *so broad,* that every honest man might dwell secure under its protective influence without distinction of sect or party."[16]

With the passage of its charter, Nauvoo was able to elect a mayor, city councilmen, and aldermen who were more powerful than councilmen. Like the mayor, aldermen could sit in as justices of the peace and municipal court judges, whereas councilmen were restricted to matters brought before the city council. Following the formation of a rudimentary municipal government, the council began passing laws and ordinances from the mundane to the exotic. Some of these contributed to Mormon/non-Mormon animosity and ultimately to Joseph Smith's death.

---

[11]Ibid., 96-97.

[12]Thomas Ford, *A History of Illinois: From Its Commencement as a State in 1818 to 1847* (Chicago: S. C. Griggs & Co., 1854), 264.

[13]Other charters allowed for the creation of "common schools" but not a university.

[14]Section 25 authorized creation of the Nauvoo Legion, a citywide militia, or standing army, controlled by Nauvoo's leaders.

[15]The municipal court was outlined in Section 17. It was especially powerful because it allowed the granting of writs of *habeas corpus.* No other city charter allowed this.

[16]*History of Church,* 4:249, emphasis added. Smith probably overstated his involvement in the composition of the charter, while Bennett was the primary architect.

## Members of the City Council

*Mayors*
John C. Bennett
Joseph Smith
Daniel Spencer
Orson Spencer

*Vice-mayors*
Hyrum Smith
Joseph Smith

*Aldermen*
Samuel Bent
George W. Harris
Gustavus Hills
Hiram S. Kimball
Wilson Law
Stephen Markham
William Marks
Charles C. Rich
Elias Smith
George A. Smith
Samuel H. Smith
Daniel Spencer
Orson Spencer
Daniel H. Wells
Newel K. Whitney

*Councilmen*
John T. Barnett
Samuel Bent
Sylvester Emmons
David Fullmer
John P. Greene
Edward Hunter
Orson Hyde
Aaron Johnson
Heber C. Kimball
Vinson Knight
William Law
Wilson Law
Amasa Lyman
Hugh McFall
George Miller
John Pack
William W. Phelps
Orson Pratt
Charles C. Rich
Levi Richards
Phineas Richards
Willard Richards
Sidney Rigdon
James Sloan
Don Carlos Smith
George A. Smith
Hyrum Smith
Joseph Smith
Samuel H. Smith
William Smith
Daniel Spencer
George P. Stiles
John Taylor
Benjamin Warrington
Lyman Wight
Wilford Woodruff
Jonathon Wright
Brigham Young

*Alternates*
George J. Adams
Reynolds Cahoon
Alpheus Cutler
Winslow Farr
Edward Hunter
James Ivins
John Lytle
William W. Phelps
Parley P. Pratt
Shadrach Roundy
Joseph Young

## Members of the Stake High Council

*Presidency*
William Marks
Austin Cowles
Charles C. Rich

*Councilmen*
James Allred
Ezra T. Benson
Samuel Bent
Seymour Brunson
Reynolds Cahoon
Daniel Carns
Austin Cowles
Alpheus Cutler
David Dort
David Fullmer
John P. Green
Thomas Grover
George W. Harris
Elias Higbee
William Huntington
Aaron Johnson
Newel Knight
Charles C. Rich
Shadrach Roundy
Henry G. Sherwood
Leonard Soby
Lewis D. Wilson

*Clerks*
Randolph Alexander
Joseph M. Cole
Calvin C. Pendleton

*Clerks* (continued)
Alonson Ripley
Henry G. Sherwood
Hosea Stout

*Alternates*
Alburn Allen
Isaac Allred
Erastus Bingham
Newman G. Blodget
James Brown
Philip H. Buzzard
Daniel Carns
James Carroll
Simeon Carter
Joseph M. Cole
Graham Coltrin
Zebedee Coltrin
Howard Coray
George W. Crouse
Erastus Derby
James G. Devine
Philo Dibble
Simeon A. Dunn
David Evans
William Felshaw
Thomas S. Gates
Reuben Hadlock
Edmond Harris
Peter Hawes
Hugh Herringshaw
Elias Higbee
Isaac Higbee
Joshua Holman
Dimick Huntington
Joseph Kingsbury
Andrew L. Lamoreaux
Tarlton Lewis
Stephen Markham
Duncan McArthur
Daniel S. Miles
Jacob Morris
Joseph Mount
Freeman Nickerson
Eli Norton
Harvey Omstead
Noah Packard
Abraham Palmer
Ezra Parrish
William C. Perry
Phineas Richards
Sidney Roberts
Shadrach Roundy
Daniel Shearer
James Sloan
Asa Smith
Joshua Smith
Josiah Smith
Samuel H. Smith
Abraham O. Smoot
John Snider
Charles Snow
Lorenzo Snow
William Snow
Richard D. Sprague
Sylvester B. Stoddard
Robert Stone
Hosea Stout
Jacob Suffitt
Andrew A. Timmons
Benjamin S. Wilber
Samuel Williams
Bushrod W. Wilson
Wilford Woodruf

The purpose of the city council was law-making, although sometimes Church doctrine and policies were discussed. For instance, for the council meeting of March 4, 1843, Joseph Smith recorded in his diary: "In debate on the bill, Geo[rge] A. Smith thought imprisonment better than hanging. Mayor [Joseph Smith] said he was opposed to hanging. If a man kill another[,] shoot him[,] or cut his throat[,] spilling his blood on the ground[,] and let the smoke thereof ascend up to God. If I ever have the privilege of Making a law on this point[,] I will have it so."[17] This is one of the earliest known references to the so-called blood-atonement doctrine.

---

[17]See Scott H. Faulring, ed., *An American Prophet's Record: The Diaries and Journals of Joseph Smith* (Salt Lake City: Signature Books and Smith Research Associates, 1989), 326-28.

## Plural Marriage

Beginning in 1842, Joseph Smith experienced a painful falling out with his former confidant, John C. Bennett.[18] On May 17, Bennett resigned as mayor (replaced by Smith), and on May 19 his resignation was accepted by the city council, which resolved to: "tender a Vote of Thanks to Gen[era]l John C. Bennett, for his great Zeal in having good & wholesome Laws adopted for the Government of this City, & for the faithful discharge of his Duty while Mayor of the same."[19]

Apparently, Bennett had secretly taught that worthy couples, married or not, could engage in sexual relations on the condition that they keep their behavior a secret. Rumors circulated that his doctrine had been authorized by Joseph Smith. In fact, Smith by this time had contracted several polygamous marriages and proposed to, and was rejected by, a handful of women.[20] Though some of the gossip regarding Smith was true, Bennett's teachings had not been sanctioned by Smith, and at his resignation as mayor Bennett signed an affidavit clearing Smith of moral impropriety.[21]

Though Bennett said he wanted to regain his Church membership, the situation turned ugly over the next several months. In mid-June 1842, Smith went public with his criticism, and Bennett left Nauvoo a few days later. On June 27, the nearby *Sangamo Journal* published a Bennett letter vowing to retaliate by exposing every secret he knew about Nauvoo. In fact, in successive letters, he explained what he knew of Smith's and other leaders' involvement in polygamy.

Smith's first documented plural marriage occurred in Nauvoo in April 1841. Two years later, on July 12, 1843, Smith recorded a revelation regarding polygamy (D&C 132) and the next month saw

---

[18]For more on Bennett and Smith, see Gary James Bergera, "John C. Bennett, Joseph Smith, and the Beginnings of Mormon Plural Marriage in Nauvoo," *John Whitmer Historical Association Journal* 25 (2005) 52-92. For a good biography, see Andrew F. Smith, *The Saintly Scoundrel: The Life and Times of Dr. John Cook Bennett* (Urbana: University of Illinois Press, 1997).

[19]Faulring, *American Prophet's Record*, 326-28.

[20]See Richard Van Wagoner, *Mormon Polygamy: A History* (Salt Lake City: Signature Books, 1986), 21-24; also George D. Smith, "Nauvoo Roots of Mormon Polygamy, 1841-1846: A Preliminary Demographic Report," *Dialogue: A Journal of Mormon Thought* 27 (Spring 1994): 13, which lists six of Joseph Smith's plural marriages entered into by May 1842.

[21]*History of Church*, 5:11.

his brother Hyrum broaching the topic with the high council. At that meeting, Councilman Dunbar Wilson "made inquiry in relation to the subject of a plurality of wives, as there were rumors about[,] respecting it, and he was satisfied there was something in those remarks, and he wanted to know what it was." Joseph was home ill, so Hyrum read the July 12 revelation to the group and stated, "Now, you that believe this revelation and go forth and obey the same shall be saved, and you that reject it shall be damned." Several high councilmen subsequently rejected the revelation, including William Law, William Marks, Leonard Soby, and Austin A. Cowles.[22]

Prior to being officially taught the doctrine of plural marriage, the high council had investigated rumors of various Church members accused of entering into multiple marriages. Beginning on May 21, 1842, the high council handled the first of twenty-three cases which arose, in large measure, from the nascent doctrine of plural marriage.[23]

## Presidential Succession

Another important doctrinal development to play out in meetings of the stake high council was the issue of presidential succession in the Church. After the deaths of Joseph and Hyrum Smith in June 1844, several individuals came forward asserting they were Joseph's rightful heir. The strongest claims were advanced by William Marks, president of the Nauvoo Stake and High Council; Sidney Rigdon, first counselor in the First Presidency; and Brigham Young, president of the Quorum of Twelve Apostles.[24] Other claimants included Lyman Wight and James Strang. In addition, William Clayton, Joseph Smith's personal secretary, remembered "Joseph has said that if he and Hyrum were taken away Samuel H. Smith [Joseph's brother] would be his successor."[25]

---

[22]See Van Wagoner, *Mormon Polygamy*, 63-64.

[23]For more, see Gary James Bergera, "'Illicit Intercourse,' Plural Marriage, and the Nauvoo Stake High Council, 1840-1844," *John Whitmer Historical Association Journal* 23 (2003): 64-67.

[24]See D. Michael Quinn, *The Mormon Hierarchy: Origins of Power* (Salt Lake City: Signature Books and Smith Research Associates, 1994), 155.

[25]George D. Smith, ed., *An Intimate Chronicle: The Journals of William Clayton* (Salt Lake City: Signature Books and Smith Research Associates, 1991), 138.

On August 8, 1844, six weeks after Joseph's and Hyrum's deaths, a meeting was held to determine who would lead the Church. Rigdon claimed he was shown by revelation that he should be the Church's guardian. Young stated that only the Twelve possessed all the necessary priesthood keys to lead the Church. The majority of the Saints sided with Young. Though Rigdon said he would yield to the Twelve, he instead recruited members to his own Church. In response, the Twelve met with Rigdon on September 3, 1844. Reportedly, "at this meeting ... Sidney said his authority was greater that than of the Twelve. He claimed to have many visions and revelations at variance with those given through Joseph Smith."[26] The apostles met again two days later and expelled Rigdon. Evidently, what most concerned the Twelve was that he had, without permission, ordained "prophets, priests and kings in secret meetings where he implied he had higher authority than any man in the Church."[27] Clayton recorded:

> Last evening the Twelve and some others met together with Elder Rigdon to investigate his course. He came out full against the Twelve and said he would not be controlled by them. They asked him for his license, and he said [if] he would give that[,][he] ... must expose all the works of the secret chambers and all the iniquities of the church. The Twelve withdrew fellowship from him[28] ...

Fearing that this would not stop Rigdon, on September 8 the Nauvoo Stake High Council publicly retried Smith's former counselor and concluded by endorsing the Twelve's actions.

### Habeas Corpus

The most controversial undertaking of the Nauvoo City Council was its passage of sweeping habeas corpus ordinances. Briefly, invoking habeas corpus (Latin: "you have the body") allowed courts to review the evidence against a suspect and free him if the evidence was deemed to be insufficient or illegal. The habeas corpus acts passed in Nauvoo were so expansive that the municipal court could

---

[26]Andrew F. Ehat, "Joseph Smith's Introduction of Temple Ordinances and the 1844 Mormon Succession Question," M.A. thesis, Brigham Young University, 1982, 214-15.

[27]Ibid., 215.

[28]Smith, *Intimate Chronicle,* 147-48.

review not only the legality of the arrest warrant but determine the guilt or innocence of the defendant, eliminating the possibility for a later trial regardless of where the crime occurred or where the warrant was issued. No other American city possessed such broad laws. This enabled Nauvoo's Mormon-dominated municipal court to try all cases against Joseph Smith and other LDS leaders.

The passage of habeas corpus acts stemmed from Joseph Smith's desire to protect himself from extradition to Missouri where he was charged with treason. Officers there told Illinois Governor Thomas Carlin to treat Smith and his inner circle as "fugitives from justice."[29] When Smith met with Carlin on June 4, 1841, the governor did not mention this but nevertheless commissioned "Thomas King, Sheriff of Adams county, Thomas Jasper, a constable of Quincy, and some others as a posse, with an officer from Missouri, to arrest [Smith] and deliver [him] up to the authorities of Missouri."[30]

The posse overtook Smith the next day on June 5, upon which Smith was returned to Quincy and presented to the master-in-chancery of Warren County. A master-in-chancery is a court-appointed official empowered to carry out an investigation or other task. Immediately, Smith asked for a writ of habeas corpus to prevent his extradition to Missouri.[31] On June 7, Smith and a group of supporters traveled to Monmouth, Illinois, for a hearing before Judge Stephen A. Douglas. The hearing began two days later. On June 10, Douglas determined that the original writ for Smith's arrest was "dead" and that a new writ should have been issued; Douglas chose not to rule directly on the evidence against Smith,[32] but his decision effectively freed the prisoner.

This was important to the development of habeas corpus acts in Nauvoo because it showed Mormons that there was a powerful legal device potentially at their disposal that could frustrate their enemies' plans. The first of several stronger, more expansive, versions of habeas corpus statutes in Nauvoo was adopted on July 5, 1842.

---

[29]*History of Church,* 4:198.

[30]Ibid., 4:364.

[31]See ibid., 365; Edwin Brown Firmage and Richard Collin Mangrum, *Zion in the Courts: A Legal History of the Church of Jesus Christ of Latter-day Saints, 1830-1900* (Urbana: University of Illinois Press, 1988), 94.

[32]See *History of Church,* 4:368-67, 369-70.

to convene when Joseph Smith, as mayor and chief justice, was indisposed. The fourth section put the ordinance into effect immediately.

Meanwhile, Smith was in hiding, and when the deputy sheriff returned on August 10, Mormon sources say he "endeavored to alarm [Smith's] wife and the brethren with his threats, if [Smith] was not forthcoming."[38] Smith left the city and camped on a small island in the middle of the Mississippi River, within the jurisdiction of the state of Iowa. When a sheriff from Lee County, Iowa, joined the search and rumors spread that Iowa's governor had issued a second arrest warrant for Smith and Rockwell, the Nauvoo City Council passed a third ordinance buttressing habeas corpus on September 9, 1842. Even so, Smith remained in hiding until the city passed an even stronger ordinance in early November, as discussed below, and with that, he felt secure enough to return to public life in Nauvoo.

*Threat of punishment for arresting officers*

On November 10-12, 1842, the Nauvoo City Council met in Joseph Smith's house to work on a new ordinance intended to facilitate Smith's return. Alderman and LDS Apostle Wilford Woodruff recorded: "We spent several days in the city Council passing a law relative to writ of Habus Corpus. After it was passed Joseph felt secure to stay at home as the law protected him as well as all other citizens."[39] The ordinance that passed two days later was composed of nineteen sections, some of which duplicated earlier sections or explained them in greater detail, as summarized here.

Section 1 specified that as soon as an arrest warrant was issued, the individual should be brought "before the Municipal Court of said City."

Section 2 added a penalty "not exceeding One thousand Dollars, nor less than five hundred Dollars, or in case of failure to pay such forfeiture, to be imprisoned not more than twelve Months nor less than six Months" for attempting, "through any false pretext to take or intimidate any of the inhabitants of this city." This applied spe-

---

against me as a religious teacher, and that it proceeds from a persecuting spirit" *(History of Church,* 5:90).

[38]Ibid.

[39]*Wilford Woodruff's Journal, 1833-1898,* ed. Scott G. Kenney, 9 vols. (Midvale, UT: Signature Books, 1983-85), 2:191.

cifically to "any officer, person, or persons knowing that he, or they, have an illegal Writ." This provided major hurdles for arresting officers from outside Nauvoo, and clearly, this was its purpose.

Section 3 stated that all hearings under habeas corpus were to take place within five days of the issuance of the writ. At a hearing, the "Prisoner or Prisoners may deny any of the material facts set forth in the return, or may alledge any fact to shew ... that the imprisonment or detention is unlawful," upon which the municipal court "shall proceed in a summary way to settle the said facts, by hearing the testimony & arguments, as well of all Parties interested civilly, if any there be."

Section 6 forbade Nauvoo's court from intervening if the defendant was "proven guilty of the charges" and if the offense was "clearly & specifically charged in the Warrant."

Section 7 addressed double jeopardy, stating: "No Person or Persons Who have been discharged by Order of the Municipal Court on a habeas Corpus, shall be again imprisoned, restrained, or kept in custody for the same cause." It was thought that this would end Missouri's attempts to arrest Smith and Rockwell because the municipal court had already reviewed the evidence and found it wanting. However, Section 7 did contain exceptions under which a person could be re-tried. If more evidence subsequently came to light, or if a defendant was let go on a technicality ("discharged for any illegality in the ... Process" or neglect of "any of the forms required by law"), the suspect could be detained a second time if the process and forms were re-done properly.

Section 11 imposed penalties upon any "Officer, Sheriff, Jailor, keeper, or other Person" who disregarded the provisions of an arrest warrant, apprehending someone after the warrant had expired, for instance, or beyond the time limit imposed by the ordinance. In such instances, the conniving sheriff was to be "committed to the City or county Jail ... there to remain without bail or mainprize [collateral], until he or they shall obey the said Writ," and "shall also forfeit to the Prisoner or Prisoners, party or parties, aggrieved a sum not exceeding One thousand Dollars, & not less than five hundred Dollars."

Section 12 levied similar penalties upon a sheriff or other officer who tried to "conceal" a prisoner "or change the place of his, her, or their confinement" to avoid the jurisdiction of the court. Such a sheriff would be fined "one Thousand Dollars, & may be imprisoned not less than one year, nor more than five years."

Section 14 imposed a penalty of "one thousand Dollars" upon anyone who arrested or detained a prisoner for a writ the court had already "discharged."

When this ordinance passed, Smith appeared in public, attending a religious meeting on November 21 and presiding as mayor at a city council meeting on November 26. Although he felt safe, his neighbors thought the new ordinance was evidence that he held himself above the law.

### *Third arrest and the Pope decision*

In early December 1842, an Illinois state representative named Davis urged the legislature to repeal the Nauvoo Charter, while another asked that the Mormons return any state-owned arms they had been loaned.[40] In response, William Smith, Nauvoo's representative to the legislature and Joseph Smith's younger brother, addressed the House of Representatives. He admitted that the "public mind has been heated in regard to what was supposed to be [Nauvoo's] chartered privileges" but stressed that Mormons just wanted "equal rights and equal provisions."[41]

While legislators were "in a high state of agitation," Joseph Smith sent a delegation to the new governor of Illinois, Thomas Ford.[42] The delegation consisted of several of Nauvoo's religious and

---

[40]*History of Church,* 5:201. The military hardware included "three cannon, six-pounders, and a few score of muskets, swords, and pistols, which were furnished by the United States to Illinois, for the supply of her militia for common defense." The *History of Church* identifies "Mr. Davis" as being from Bond County near St. Louis (201, 294); however, Jacob C. Davis, elected to the Illinois senate in 1842, was from Warsaw, Hancock County (where Nauvoo was also located), and may be the person in question. "Jake," as he was known, was an opponent of Mormon influence and became, in 1844, one of the accused assassins of Joseph and Hyrum Smith. He later served in the U.S. House of Representatives (*History of Church,* 7:314, 368, 373, 420; Dallin H. Oaks and Marvin S. Hill, *Carthage Conspiracy: The Trial of the Accused Assassins of Joseph Smith* [Urbana: University of Illinois Press, 1975], 48, 55, 217).

[41]*History of Church,* 203.

[42]Ibid., 204. Ford's election platform included revoking the Nauvoo Charter, which rankled Mormons.

civic leaders, including Joseph's brother Hyrum Smith and Josiah Butterfield, a U.S. District Attorney who opposed Missouri Governor Carlin's extradition order. The group met with Governor Ford on December 14 to submit an affidavit stating that Joseph Smith had been "in Illinois on the 6th of May [1841], and consequently could not have been concerned in the attempted assassination of ex-Governor Boggs" and to ask the governor to "revoke the writ and proclamation of Governor Carlin for [Smith's] arrest." Ford replied that he "had no doubt but that the writ of Governor Carlin was illegal; but he doubted as to his authority to interfere with the acts of his predecessor." He promised to submit the problem to the Illinois Supreme Court and abide by its decision.[43]

On December 16, convinced that Carlin's warrant was illegal and to prevent revocation of the Nauvoo Charter, Joseph Smith presented himself for arrest in Springfield. That morning, Wilson Law, a member of Nauvoo's city council and a general in the Nauvoo Legion, arrested Smith on Carlin's writ. While Smith was being arrested, he sent Nauvoo Sheriff and City Councilor Henry G. Sherwood and personal secretary William Clayton to Carthage, Illinois, to obtain a writ of habeas corpus issued by a non-Mormon. Law then released Smith into the custody of Willard Richards, a member of both the Nauvoo City Council and the Church's Quorum of Twelve Apostles.[44]

The next day, Smith received Ford's and the Supreme Court's opinions on the Missouri arrest warrant. Ford reported that the court was "divided as to the propriety and justice of my interference with the acts of Governor Carlin" and recommended that Smith "submit to the laws and have a judicial investigation of your rights." District Attorney Butterfield, who had spoken with the Supreme Court justices on Smith's behalf, wrote to his client: "The judges were unanimously of the opinion that you would be entitled to your discharge under a habeas corpus to be issued by the Supreme Court, but felt some delicacy in advising Governor Ford to revoke the order issued by Governor Carlin." Butterfield advised Smith to "come here without delay" so he could "stand by [Smith], and see [him] safely deliv-

---

[43]Ibid., 204-05.

[44]Ibid., 209.

ered from arrest." Smith received a brief letter from supreme court justice James Adams: "I will say that it appears to my judgment that you had best make no delay in coming before the court at this place for a discharge under a habeas corpus."[45]

Finding the letters "highly satisfactory," Smith left for Springfield on December 27, 1842. On December 31 he asked Governor Ford to issue a new arrest warrant, at which time Smith was immediately arrested. His attorney petitioned Nathaniel Pope of the U.S. District Court for Illinois for a writ of habeas corpus.[46] Pope issued the writ and set a time for a hearing on January 2, 1843.

On January 2, Illinois Attorney General Josiah Lamborn asked for a continuance of Smith's hearing, which was granted. Two days later, he urged that the case be dismissed, asserting that Pope's court did not have jurisdiction. Butterfield, who wanted the charges against Smith dealt with immediately, countered that jurisdiction was proper and that the court must "look into the depositions before the magistrate; and though the commitment be full and in form, yet, if the testimony prove no crime, the court will discharge *ex-parte.*" Butterfield claimed that Boggs's original affidavit "does not show that Smith was charged with any crime committed by him in Mo., nor that he was a fugitive from justice." Butterfield argued that "if the commitment be for a matter for which by law the prisoner is not liable to be punished, the court must discharge him," that "the executive of [Illinois] has no jurisdiction over the person of Smith to transport him to Missouri, unless he has fled from that state." Butterfield insisted that "the prisoner has a right to prove facts not repugnant to the return, and even to go behind the return and contradict it."[47] Butterfield asserted that the original arrest warrant was based on demonstrable lies. In closing, he directly appealed to the emotions of those present:

> I do not think the defendant ought, under any circumstances, to be given up to Missouri. It is a matter of history that he and his people have been murdered or driven from the state. If he goes there, it is only to be murdered, and he had better be sent to the gallows.

---

[45]Ibid., 205-06.

[46]Ibid., 207, 209-11.

[47]Ibid., 216, 221-22.

> He is an innocent and unoffending man. If there is a difference between him and other men, it is that this people believe in prophecy, and others do not.[48]

On January 5, 1843, Pope issued his opinion. He began by acknowledging the "importance of this case," which "affect[s] the lives and liberties of [Illinois] citizens."[49] He framed the issue before the court as a "question arising under the Constitution and laws of the United States,"

> whether a citizen of the state of Illinois can be transported from his own state to the state of Missouri, to be there tried for a crime, which, if he ever committed, was committed in the state of Illinois; whether he can be transported to Missouri, as a fugitive from justice, when he has never fled from that state.

Concluding that Illinois had jurisdiction in the case,[50] Pope stated: "The attorney-general seemed to urge that there was greater sanctity in a warrant issued by the governor than by an inferior officer. The court cannot assent to this distinction." He recounted the history of habeas corpus and found it "was indeed a magnificent achievement over arbitrary power." He found that it did not matter who issued a warrant, that "this munificent writ, wielded by an independent judge, reaches all."[51]

Pope next addressed Butterfield's claims, concluding that the initial arrest warrant was, in fact, improper:

> The [Boggs] affidavit ... furnished the only evidence upon which the Governor of Illinois could act. Smith presented affidavits proving that he was not in Missouri at the date of the shooting of Boggs. This testimony was objected to by the Attorney General of Illinois, on the ground that the Court could not look behind the return. The court deems it unnecessary to decide that point, inasmuch as it thinks Smith entitled to his discharge for defect in the affidavit. ...

---

[48]Ibid., 222.

[49]Ibid., 223.

[50]Ibid.

[51]Ibid., 225.

> Mr. Boggs having the "evidence and information in his possession," should have incorporated it in the affidavit to enable the Court to judge of their sufficiency to support his "belief." Again, he swears to a legal conclusion when he says that Smith was accessary before the fact. What acts constitute a man an accessary in a question of law are not always of easy solution. Mr. Boggs' opinion then, is not authority. He should have given the facts. He should have shown that they were committed in Missouri, to enable the court to test them by the laws of Missouri, to see if they amounted to a crime. Again, the affidavit is fatally defective in this, that Boggs swears to his belief.[52]

Pope therefore ruled: "Let an order be entered that Smith be discharged from his arrest." Vindicated, Smith returned to Nauvoo.

*Fourth arrest*

Though the U.S. District Court voided the arrest warrant, Ford issued a new one in response to another request from Missouri's governor.[53] At the time, Smith was preaching in Dixon, Illinois. Sheriff Joseph H. Reynolds of Jackson County, Missouri, and Constable Harmon T. Wilson of Carthage, Illinois, disguised themselves as Mormons, found Smith, and arrested him. Smith insisted that he had not been legally served and said, "Gentlemen, if you have any legal process, I wish to obtain a writ of habeas corpus." They replied, "G— d— you, you shan't have one." Smith then shouted to a passerby, "These men are kidnapping me, and I wish a writ of habeas corpus to deliver myself out of their hands." He assumed the officers intended to "drag [him] away immediately to Missouri, and prevent [him from] taking out a writ of habeas corpus."[54]

In fact, Smith was taken to an inn where eventually he was allowed legal council. His lawyers went to the nearest master-in-chancery to ask for habeas corpus. While there, they complained that Reynolds and Wilson had threatened to kill Smith, upon which the court issued an arrest warrant for the two officers. The tables turned, the master-in-chancery then ordered Reynolds, Wilson, and

---

[52]Ibid., 223-31.

[53]Justice Adams alerted Smith to this in a letter of June 16, 1843 (*History of Church,* 5:433).

[54]Ibid., 439, 441, 442.

Smith to appear before Judge John D. Caton of the Ninth Judicial Circuit in Ottawa, near Chicago. The writ prevented Smith's removal to Missouri. Smith, whose lawyers were unavailable to travel to northern Illinois, asked the famous attorney Cyrus Walker to represent their client. A candidate for U.S. Congress, Walker replied, perhaps tongue-in-cheek, that "he could not find time ... unless" Smith promised to vote for him. Smith said he would, at which Walker answered: "I am now sure of my election, as Joseph Smith has promised me his vote."[55]

Hours later, the Circuit Court of Lee County charged Reynolds and Wilson with "private damage and for false imprisonment." They were held on $10,000 bail and, ironically, sought a writ of habeas corpus in their own behalf.[56] When it was discovered that Judge Cato was in New York, the master-in-chancery issued new writs allowing Joseph Smith to return to Nauvoo, where he was exonerated by Nauvoo's municipal court on June 30.[57] Reynolds and Wilson were eventually released and returned to Missouri and Carthage, Illinois.

*Two new ordinances*

While Smith was en route to Nauvoo following his arrest by Reynolds and Wilson, the Nauvoo City Council moved to prevent future arrests by passing an ordinance dealing with strangers and contagious diseases. Adopted on June 29, 1843, it gave "the city council, marshal, constables, and city watch" authority to "require all strangers who shall be entering this city, or are already tarrying, or may hereafter be tarrying in said city, in a civil and respectful manner to give their names, former residence, for what intent they have entered or are tarrying in the city, and answer such other questions as the officer shall deem proper or necessary." Thus officers like Reynolds and Wilson would not be able to approach Smith without first stating their intent.

Five months later, on December 8, a special session of the city council convened to prepare "for any invasion" by sheriffs "from Missouri."[58] On December 2, a father and son residing in Nauvoo

---

[55]Ibid., 442-44.

[56]Ibid.

[57]Ibid., 461.

[58]Faulring, *American Prophet's Record,* 431.

were apprehended and taken to Missouri.[59] Though they were eventually released, people in Nauvoo worried that the same fate could befall the prophet. In response, the city passed, on December 8, a "Special Ordinance in the Prophet's Case, vs. Missouri." This ordinance provided, in part, that

> if any person or persons shall come with process, demand, or requisition, founded upon the aforesaid Missouri difficulties, to arrest said Joseph Smith, he or they so offending shall be subject to be arrested by any officer of the city, with or without process, and tried by the Municipal Court, upon testimony, and, if found guilty, sentenced to imprisonment in the city prison for life: which convict or convicts can only be pardoned by the Governor, with the consent of the Mayor of said city.

Though probably illegal, the ordinance revealed the extent to which the council would go to prevent Missourians from settling old scores going back to the Mormon War of 1838. On February 12, 1844, without explanation, the council repealed its special ordinance, deciding instead to rely on habeas corpus to protect Smith.[60]

*Joseph is arrested again*

On May 6, Joseph Smith used habeas corpus to defend himself in a civil suit. On this date, Francis Higbee sued him for $5,000 but failed to state explicitly what the grounds for the arrest were. The charge was slander. On May 8, Smith petitioned Nauvoo's municipal court for a writ of habeas corpus, even though Higbee's warrant had been issued in Carthage, Illinois. Before Nauvoo's municipal court, Smith claimed that

> the proceedings against him are illegal; that the said warrant of arrest is informal, and not of that character which the law recognizes as valid; that the said writ is wanting and deficient in the plea therein contained; that the charge or complaint which your petitioner is therein required to answer is not known to the law. ... Your petitioner further states that this proceeding has been instituted against him without any just or legal cause; and further that the

[59]*History of Church,* 6:145-48.

[60]Ibid., 212.

> said Francis M. Higbee is actuated by no other motive than a desire to persecute and harass.[61]

Smith called eight witnesses who testified to "(1) the very bad and immoral character of Francis M. Higbee; and (2) the maliciousness of his prosecution of Joseph Smith."[62] Higbee did not attend the proceeding. The court, after hearing the evidence, discharged Smith, ruled the suit malicious, and ordered Higbee to pay all costs.[63]

With the successful use of habeas corpus in a civil case, it must have appeared that Smith was completely immune from arrest from jurisdictions outside of the city. He had successfully evaded prosecution in both criminal and civil cases. His apparent invulnerability outraged even some of the residents of Nauvoo and formed one of the central themes in the *Nauvoo Expositor,* a short-lived newspaper published by disenchanted Mormons. In the concluding paragraph of the *Expositor*'s only issue of June 7, 1844, editor Sylvester Emmons, a member of the city council, called for the repeal of the Nauvoo Charter due to the Saints' abuse of habeas corpus:

> The city council have passed ordinances, giving the Municipal court authority to issue the writ of Habeas Corpus in all cases when the prisoner is held in custody in Nauvoo, no matter whether the offen[se] is committed in the State of Maine, or on the continent of Europe, the prisoner being in the city under arrest. It is gravely contended by the legal luminaries of Nauvoo, that the ordinances give them jurisdiction, not only jurisdiction to try the validity of the writ, but to enquire into the merits of the case, and allow the prisoner to swear himself clear of the charges.

The next day the city council met to decide how to respond to the newspaper. According to the minutes, Joseph Smith suggested "the propriety of purging the City Council" of its less supportive members. The council agreed that "counsellor Emmons be suspended ... for slandering the city ... and that the Recorder notify him of his suspension and that his case would be investigated at the next regular

---

[61]Ibid., 356-58.

[62]Ibid., 360. The eight witnesses were Heber C. Kimball, Joel S. Miles, Sidney Rigdon, Orrin Porter Rockwell, Henry G. Sherwood, Hyrum Smith, Cyrus H. Wheelock, and Brigham Young.

[63]Ibid., 361. The cost was $36.26½.

session of the Council." Smith then proposed that "the council pass an ordinance to prevent misrepresentation ~~of~~ & Libellous publication, and wanted a law passed to prevent all conspiracy against the peace of the city." He asserted that the *Expositor* was "calculated to ~~do~~ destroy the peace of the city—and it is not safe that such things should exist—on account of the Mob spirit which they tend to produce." The council decided to postpone acting on Smith's suggestion.

Two days later, on June 10, the council reassembled. After some discussion, Smith, according to the minutes, said that "if he had a city council who felt as he did, the establishment (referring to the Nauvoo Expositor) would be a Nuisance before night." He detailed his thinking and concluded that the newspaper should be "smashed." The council reviewed a proposed ordinance on libel, then unanimously passed it. The ordinance prohibited "any person or persons" from "writ[ing] or publish[ing], in said city, any false statement, or libel any of the Citizens, for the purpose of exciting the public mind against the chartered privileges, peace, and good order of said City, or shall slander, (according to the definition of slander or libel by Blackstone or Kent, or the act in the Statute of Illinois,) any portion of the Inhabitants of said City."

U.S. courts at the time relied on Blackstone's four-volume *Commentaries on the Laws of England,* with notes by Joseph Chitty and others, particularly for matters pre-dating American law. In this instance, the section cited by the city council read in part: "Whatsoever unlawfully annoys or doth damage to another is a nuisance; and such nuisance may be abated, that is, taken away or removed, by the party aggrieved thereby, so as he commits no riot in the doing of it."[64] The council also consulted James Kent's *Commentaries on American Law:* "A libel, as applicable to individuals, has been well defined to be a malicious publication, expressed either in printing or writing, or by signs or pictures, tending either to blacken the memory of one dead, or the reputation of one alive, and expose him to public hatred, contempt, or ridicule."[65] The council considered the Illinois constitution, Article 8, Section 22, to the contrary: "The print-

[64]William Blackstone, *Commentaries on the Laws of England,* 4 vols. (London: W. Walker, 1826), 3:5.

[65]James Kent, *Commentaries on American Law,* 4 vols. (New York: O. Halsted, 1826-30), 2:12-22.

ing presses shall be free to every person, who undertakes to examine the proceeding of the General Assembly or of any branch of government; and no law shall ever be made to restrain the right thereof. ..." Though the constitution supported freedom of the press in disagreeing with the state, the council found it did not prevent them from suppressing libel against the city.[66]

After the ordinance passed, the city had to determine if the *Expositor* was a nuisance. City councilmen examined its contents, and Joseph Smith declared it "treasonable against all chartered rights, privileges, peace, and happiness of the City." Hyrum Smith "spoke in favor of declaring the Expositor a Nuisance." Councilman John Taylor "said no city on earth would bear such slander and he would not bear it and spoke decidedly in favor of active measures." After more discussion, Hyrum moved to "smash the press all to pieces and pie [destroy][67] the type."

Councilman Benjamin Warrington did not like the idea of destroying the press and thought the council should not be hasty, recommending that they "assess a fine of $3000.00 for any libel. – & if they would not cease publishing [the] likes[,] declare it a nuisance." Joseph Smith replied that he had been threatened with death in Carthage and could not go there to prosecute the *Expositor.* After reasoning that the only way to stop the newspaper was to destroy it, the councilmen turned emotional, referring to past casualties in Missouri and the example of the Boston Tea Party. Finally the council voted to destroy the press. The motion read: "The Printing Establishment of the 'Nauvoo Expositor', was declared a nuisance, and ordered to be removed by the Mayor [Joseph Smith]." A little more than two weeks later, Smith lay dead on the ground outside Carthage Jail.

## Conclusion

The Nauvoo City Council and the Nauvoo Stake High Council

---

[66]See Dallin H. Oaks, "The Suppression of the *Nauvoo Expositor,*" *Utah Law Review* 9 (1964-65): 893.

[67]In printing, *pie* means to "make (type) into pie; mix up, muddle." As a noun, *pie* was "type in a confused mass, such as results from the accidental breaking up of a forme," and more generally "a collection of things made into a heap," as in a "heap of potatoes" (William R. Trumble and Angus Stevenson, eds., *Shorter Oxford English Dictionary,* 5th ed. [Oxford, Engl.: Oxford University Press: 2002], s.v. "pie").

contributed significantly to LDS history and theology. While both functioned for only a few years, each left a major impact inside and outside the Church. The minutes of the city council shed light on the John C. Bennett affair, the arrests and trials of Joseph Smith, the expansive habeas corpus ordinances, and how the city leaders ran a booming frontier city. The minutes of the high council provide insight into some of the most important developments in Mormonism: the beginnings of plural marriage, succession in the Church presidency, the trial of Sidney Rigdon, and the everyday governing of the Church. The minutes of these two councils are essential reading in understanding Nauvoo in a difficult decade of LDS Church history.

# CITY AND STAKE COUNCILMEN

**George J. Adams** was born in 1811 in Oxford, New Jersey. A Methodist preacher, he converted to Mormonism in New York City in 1840. In 1841–42, he served a mission to England. In 1843 he was called to serve in Russia but, because he was excommunicated, did not go. He was later rebaptized. In 1845 he was disfellowshipped on the charge of having taught false doctrine. He subsequently joined James Strang's Church, later to found his own rival denomination. He died in 1880 in Philadelphia.

**Alburn Allen** was born in Cornwall, Connecticut, in May 1802. He was baptized in New York in 1835 and moved to Nauvoo in 1840. He served in the Mormon Battalion during the War with Mexico, then briefly became involved with the Mormon settlement of Genoa, Nebraska, until the Utah War of 1857 prompted Brigham Young to recall the colonists. Allen died in June 1867 in Ogden, Utah.

**Isaac Allred** was born in 1788 in Pendleton County, Georgia. He married Mary Calvert in 1811 and settled in Tennessee, then in Missouri, where they converted to the LDS Church. Along with the rest of the Church, they relocated to Illinois in 1838. Isaac was one of the pioneer company that entered the Salt Lake Valley in 1847, thereafter settling Spring City, Utah, where he died in 1870.

**John T. Barnett** was a non-Mormon who was sympathetic to the LDS Church, lived among the Mormons in Nauvoo, and was a captain in the Nauvoo Legion. He was one of three county commissioners, two of whom were Mormons, who in October 1844 selected the grand jury in the murders of Joseph and Hyrum Smith.

**John C. Bennett** was born in August 1804 in Bristol, Massachusetts, and was baptized in September 1840. He helped obtain Nauvoo's city charter and was elected as the city's first mayor in February 1841. Two months later he was appointed Assistant President of the Church. He also helped found the University of Nauvoo and the Nauvoo Legion. After being charged with immoral conduct, he left the Church and attacked Joseph Smith in *The History of the Saints: Or, An Exposé of Joe Smith and Mormonism.* He died in Polk City, Iowa, in August 1867.

**Ezra T. Benson** was born in February 1811 in Mendon, Massachusetts. He was baptized in 1840 in Quincy, Illinois, where he was in the stake presidency. In 1846 he was ordained an apostle. He served several missions to the eastern states, Europe, and the Sandwich Islands. He also led the Church in the Winter Quarters, Nebraska, area in 1848, then immigrated to Utah the next year. He was a member of the provisional legislature in Utah and later a member of the Utah Territorial House of Representatives, while also presiding over the Church in Cache Valley. He died in September 1869 in Ogden, Utah.

**Samuel Bent** was born in July 1778 in Barre, Massachusetts. He was baptized in Michigan in 1833 and moved to a Mormon settlement in Missouri in 1836. Two years later, he became a member of the Far West, Missouri, high council. He moved to Nauvoo in 1839 after being expelled from Missouri. He was a member of the secret Council of Fifty and the Nauvoo Legion militia. During the migration to Utah in 1846, he was called to preside over the Church in Garden Grove, Iowa, where he died in August.

**Erastus Bingham** was born in March 1798 in Concord, Vermont. In 1833 he converted to Mormonism and moved to Kirtland, Ohio, three years later, then to Missouri, where he became a paramilitary Danite from June–October 1838. In the 1840s he lived twenty miles southeast of Nauvoo in Ramus, Illinois, and then on a farm a few miles south of Nauvoo. In September 1847 he arrived in Utah, right behind the original pioneer company, and settled in what became

Bingham Canyon. Later he helped settle Ogden and became a ward bishop, stake patriarch, and territorial legislator. He died in May 1882.

**Newman Greenleaf Blodget** was born in September 1800 in Chelsea, Vermont. He was baptized in 1832 and moved to Nauvoo in 1840. His wife, Sally, died there in childbirth in 1839. In 1850 he traveled to Utah with the Warren Foote Company and settled in North Ogden, building a flour mill and famously contending with Indians in the area who sometimes stole his sheep. He died in North Ogden in August 1882.

**James Brown** was born in September 1801 in Rowan County, North Carolina. On May 8, 1842, he served as an alternate high councilman in Nauvoo; the next year he was prominent in pushing for construction of the Nauvoo House hotel. During the Mexican-American War, he served as the captain of Company C in the Mormon Battalion. As the rest of the company continued west, he supervised the sick detachment in Pueblo, Colorado, for the winter of 1846–47, then continued on to Utah. When he acquired Fort Buenaventura from trapper Miles Goodyear in 1847, he became the first Mormon to settle in the Ogden area. He died in Ogden on his birthday in September 1863.

**Seymour Brunson** was born at Plattsburgh, New York, in September 1798. He was baptized in Ohio in 1831. In the mid-1830s he served as a major in the LDS militia in Missouri, then as a lieutenant colonel in the Nauvoo Legion. In 1839 he was appointed to the Nauvoo High Council. He died the next year in Nauvoo, and it was at his funeral that Joseph Smith introduced the doctrine of baptism for the dead.

**Philip Hammond Buzzard**, whose surname was apparently anglicized from the German "Buzhardt, was born in February 1814. He left Nauvoo in the late 1840s and settled in Des Moines, Iowa, where he stayed until 1859. He then immigrated to Utah and settled in the Mill Creek area south of Salt Lake City. A woman in his company of immigrants, Jennette Eveline Evans, commented that his "name did not inspire confidence." His date of death is unknown.

**Reynolds Cahoon** was born in Cambridge, New York, in April 1790.

He served in the War of 1812 and then settled in Ohio in 1825, where he became one of the early converts to Mormonism five years later. In Missouri, he was in the stake presidency of Adam-ondi-Ahman. After the expulsion from Missouri, he moved to Montrose, Iowa, across the river from Nauvoo, and became a counselor in the stake presidency there in 1839. He died in the South Cottonwood Ward near Salt Lake City in April 1862.

**Daniel Carn** (also Cairns) was born in December 1802 in St. Clair, Pennsylvania. He was baptized in 1830 and served as a Danite militiaman in Missouri and as a sergeant in the police department in Nauvoo. He was also bishop of Nauvoo's German-speaking ward. In 1852 he traveled to Hamburg to become the founding president of the German mission. In that capacity, he also worked on the original translation of the Book of Mormon into German. He died in 1872 near Salt Lake City.

**James Carroll** was born in June 1796 in Manchester, England. He was baptized in 1836 and ordained a Seventy. In Kirtland, he worked with Oliver Cowdery as a scribe and printer. In 1838 he served a mission to Kentucky. On returning home, he moved his family to Missouri, but they were forced out of their home in 1839 and spent part of the winter in an "open frame" exposed to the cold. It is possible that his wife died during that ordeal because he remarried in Walnut Grove, Illinois, in 1840. Three years later, he served a mission to Indiana. In 1845 he and Hiram Gates were excommunicated. Nothing more is known about Carroll.

**Simeon Carter** was born in June 1794 in Killingworth, Connecticut. Baptized in February 1831, he was called four months later to help settle Jackson County, Missouri. In 1833 he left his family in Missouri while he served a mission to Indiana; but the next year he was home and serving on the Far West high council. In Nauvoo he served as an alternate high councilman on September 4, 1842. After serving a mission in England from 1846–49, he immigrated to Utah in 1850. He helped settle Brigham City and died there in February 1869.

**Joseph M. Cole** was born in October 1797 in Royalton, Vermont, and converted to Mormonism in 1838. In Missouri, he was one of the scribes who kept the minutes of the Far West high council. In Illinois he was employed to teach grades nine through twelve at the University of Nauvoo, while also working as a scribe for Joseph Smith and recorder for baptisms for the dead, although in 1844 he moved some thirty miles away to the Mormon outpost of La Harpe, Illinois. In 1845 he followed Sidney Rigdon to Pittsburgh. He died in July 1875.

**Graham Coltrin** was born in December 1796 in Colrain, Massachusetts. A carpenter, he worked on the Kirtland and Nauvoo temples. He served as an alternate high councilor in Nauvoo on April 1, 1843. After immigrating to Utah in 1850, he helped settle the town of Bountiful. He died there in May 1851.

**Zebedee Coltrin** was born in September 1804 in Ovid, New York. His parents settled in Ohio in 1814. He converted to Mormonism in Ohio in 1831 and served a mission that year to Indiana. In 1834 he marched in the paramilitary campaign known as Zion's Camp and was called to the seventy in 1835. Although he moved to Illinois in 1839, he moved back to Kirtland as a member of the stake presidency in 1841, then returned to Nauvoo to served as an alternate high councilman in January, March, and April 1843. He arrived in Utah in 1847 and helped settle Spanish Fork in 1852, where he died in 1887.

**Howard Coray** was born in May 1817 in Dansville, New York. He was baptized in 1840 and served as a clerk for Joseph Smith, helping to compile his history. He taught school in Nauvoo. In 1842 he served a mission to Pennsylvania. Beginning in 1846, he spent four years farming at Fort Kearney, in what would become Nebraska, then he moved his family to Utah, settling in Provo. He served a mission to the southern states in 1882. In 1908 he died in Salt Lake City.

**Austin Cowles** was born in Brookfield, Vermont, in May 1792. He was a Methodist minister before being baptized in 1832 in New York. He moved to Kirtland, Ohio, in 1827, and by 1840 he was in Nauvoo. In 1841 he was called to be a counselor to William Marks in the Nauvoo stake presidency, while otherwise serving as the city's supervisor of streets. Later in the year, he was called on a mission to New England. When he was back in Nauvoo, he became an opponent of plural marriage, left the LDS Church, and wrote an article against polygamy in the 1844 *Nauvoo Expositor,* for which he was excommunicated. He moved to Burlington, Iowa, and became affiliated with Sidney Rigdon's Church and James Brewster's group before joining with the RLDS in the 1860s. He died in January 1872 in Hamilton, Iowa.

**George W. Crouse** was a member of the Quincy, Illinois, bishopric in 1840 and thereafter a policeman in Nauvoo, where he resided 1842–44. On September 15, 1844, he was excommunicated for following Sidney Rigdon. Nothing more is known of him.

**Alpheus Cutler** was born in Plainfield, New Hampshire, in February 1784. He served in the War of 1812. He was baptized in New York in 1833 and moved to Kirtland, Ohio, in 1834. As a stone mason, he was able to help build the Kirtland temple. He was ordained a high priest in 1836 and moved to Missouri, where he was appointed a master workman at the Far West site, although the planned temple there was never realized. In Illinois he helped supervise construction of the Nauvoo temple. He was also a member of the secretive Council of Fifty. He left Nauvoo in 1846 to preside over Cutler's Park in Nebraska, then Silver Creek, Iowa, until rejecting the leadership of Brigham Young and leading dissenters to a new settlement in Manti, Iowa, and founding "The True Church of Jesus Christ" in 1853. He died in Silver Creek in August 1864.

**Erastus H. Derby** was born in Hawley, Massachusetts, in 1810. He was living in Illinois when he converted to Mormonism in 1840. In 1842 he was an emissary to the governor of Missouri on behalf of Joseph Smith, but the next year he was found guilty of disturbing the peace in Nauvoo and resigned his membership in the Church. He relocated to Iowa, then to Chicago by 1855, and afterward to Ohio, serving in the 68th Ohio Infantry during the Civil War and then moving to Minnesota, where he died in 1890.

**Philo Dibble** was born in June 1806 in Peru, Massachusetts. He was baptized in 1830 and followed the Church to Missouri, where he was shot in a skirmish with the old settlers, then moved to Illinois, famously smuggling a pistol to Joseph Smith in the Carthage Jail in

1844. He is known for his lively storytelling about intervention by supernatural forces at critical times in Church history. He died in June 1895 in Springville, Utah.

**David Dort** was born in Surry, New Hampshire, in 1793. He married Joseph Smith's cousin, Mary ("Polly") Mack, and later her sister Fanny. He converted to Mormonism in 1831 in Rochester, Michigan, and moved from there to Kirtland, Ohio, where he participated in the Zion's Camp paramilitary march to Far West, Missouri, in 1834. He was a member of the high council in Kirtland, Far West, and Nauvoo until 1840 when he left the LDS Church to become a Methodist. He died in Nauvoo in March 1841.

**Simeon Adams Dunn** was born in August 1804 in Groveland, New York, and baptized in 1839 in Belleville, Michigan. He moved to Nauvoo in 1840 and served on the police force. His twenty-nine-year-old wife, Adaline, died in October 1841; he remarried the next year, but his second wife, Margaret, died in 1846. He arrived in Utah with a third wife in 1848 and soon helped settle Brigham City, where he died in February 1883. He served missions to Canada and Tahiti.

**Sylvester Emmons** was born in February 1808 in Readington, New Jersey, and lived in Philadelphia before moving to Illinois in 1840, where he practiced law. In 1843 he was elected to the Nauvoo City Council. He became the editor of the *Nauvoo Expositor* in 1844, thereafter moving to Beardstown, Illinois, to edit the *Beardstown Gazette*. He married Elizabeth Miller in 1847, became clerk of the circuit court in 1852, and died in Beardstown in November 1881.

**David Evans** was born in October 1804 in Cecil County, Maryland. He and his wife were living in Ohio when they converted to Mormonism in 1833. He marched with Zion's Camp in 1834, and the next year he became a president of the Seventies. He acquired a ten-acre farm southeast of Nauvoo and became bishop of the area in 1842, and on March 25, 1843, he served as an alternate on the Nauvoo High Council. Traveling to Utah in 1850 as the captain of a wagon train, he helped settle Lehi, Utah, the next year, becoming its bishop and mayor and eventually laying out blocks and property lines. He was also a member of the Utah territorial legistlature. He died in Lehi in June 1883.

**Winslow Farr** was born in January 1794 in Chesterfield, New Hampshire. He was baptized in 1832 in Vermont. As a member of Joseph Smith's Quorum of the Anointed in Nauvoo, he gave his sixteen-year-old daughter, Diantha, to William Clayton as a plural wife and acquired four plural wives for himself before leaving the city. He served as a temporary city councilman while Heber C. Kimball was away on Church business. In 1850 he moved to Salt Lake City and died in the Big Cottonwood settlement south of the city in August 1867.

**William Felshaw** was born in Granville, New York, in February 1800. He joined the LDS Church in Boston in 1832 and moved to Kirtland, Ohio, in 1833, where he helped build the temple. A carpenter, he also worked on the Nauvoo temple. He served as an alternate high councilman on October 22, 1842. One of the earliest polygamists in Nauvoo, he took a second wife in 1843, and on December 12, 1845, he was one of the first of the general Church membership to attend a session in the Nauvoo temple. He immigrated to Utah in 1851 and soon became a member of the territorial legislature. He was part of the rescue party for the snowbound handcart companies in Wyoming in 1856. For a time, he worked on the construction crew of the Salt Lake temple. He died in September 1867 in Fillmore, Utah.

**David Fullmer** was born in July 1803 in Chillisquaque, Pennsylvania. He was baptized in 1836 in Ohio, moved to Missouri and then Illinois, and was appointed to the Nauvoo High Council in October 1839. Later he was elected to the city council and assigned to the Council of Fifty. In 1844 he campaigned in Michigan for Joseph Smith's U.S. presidential run. Two years later he moved his family to Garden Grove, Iowa, for a year and then continued on to Utah, where he became a member of the Salt Lake Stake presidency and a member of the territorial legislature, as well as the city treasurer. He died in October 1879 in Salt Lake City.

**Thomas S. Gates** was ordained a seventy in February 1835. In August he served as an Assistant President of the general assembly held in Kirtland and testified to his belief in the soon-to-be-published Doctrine and Covenants. In 1836 he was one of the earliest members of the Church to receive a ministerial license. In 1838 he was excommunicated in Kirtland, but he was readmitted and served as an alternate on the Nauvoo High Council on October 5, 1844.

**John Portineus Greene** was born in Herkimer, New York, in 1793. He married Brigham Young's sister Rhoda and was living in Mendon, New York, at the time he was baptized in 1832. He was called to the Kirtland, Ohio, high council in 1836, but then presided over the Church in New York City in 1839. He served several missions for the Church. He moved to Quincy, Illinois, in 1839. In Nauvoo he was the city marshal who oversaw the destruction of the *Nauvoo Expositor*. He died a few months later in 1844.

**Thomas Grover** was born in July 1807 in Whitehall, New York, and grew up to be a riverboat captain. After he was baptized in 1834 in New York, he moved his family to Kirtland, Ohio, then to Far West, Missouri, and served on the high council in both locations. In Nauvoo he worked as a bodyguard for Joseph Smith and as his aide-de-camp in the Nauvoo Legion. In 1841 Grover filled a mission to the southern states; in 1844 he campaigned for Joseph Smith in Michigan. On the way west in 1846, Grover rejected a call to serve on the high council in Council Bluffs, Iowa. He reached Utah in 1847. Settling in Farmington, he came to be a legislator and judge before he died in Farmington in February 1886.

**Reuben Hadlock** (aka Hedlock) was born in 1809 and was trained as a printer. After joining the Church sometime before 1835, he showed himself to be overzealous in 1837 by bringing charges against people who had danced at a party hosted by a Church apostle. He served a mission to England in 1840. Two years later he carved the facsimile engravings in the printed Book of Abraham. On January 15, 1843, he served as an alternate on the Nauvoo High Council. He was called as president of the British Mission in 1843. While in England, he was excommunicated and decided to remain abroad. He died in Gravesend, Kent County, in July 1869.

**George Washington Harris** was born in April 1870 in Lanesboro,

Massachusetts. In 1830 he married Lucinda Morgan, widow of the famous anti-Masonic martyr, William Morgan. Four years later the couple were baptized by Orson Pratt in Indiana and moved to Missouri. He became a member of the Far West High Council. In 1842 in Nauvoo, Lucinda apparently became a plural wife of Joseph Smith even though she was still married to George. He died in Iowa, where he was serving as a bishop, in 1857.

**Peter Hawes** was born in February 1796 in Young Township, Ontario. After converting to Mormonism, he traveled to Illinois in 1839. He was a member of the Nauvoo Agricultural and Manufacturing Association, a trustee of the Nauvoo House hotel, and a member of the Council of Fifty. He operated a sawmill near the city. In 1848 he visited the former LDS apostle Lyman Wight in Texas and returned critical of the Quorum of the Twelve and a proponent of the Council of Fifty. For this, he was excommunicated in 1849. He subsequently moved to Nevada and then to California, where he seems to have joined the RLDS Church. He died in California in 1862.

**Hugh Herringshaw** was born in England. After immigrating to New York, he worked as a guard at Sing Sing Prison. When he converted to Mormonism, he moved to Nauvoo and bought a plot of land in the first ward neighborhood. He also experimented with a new design for a mill that apparently failed. After Joseph Smith's death, he dissented from Brigham Young's leadership and remained in the Midwest, following Sidney Rigdon, then James Strang, and finally Joseph Smith III.

**Elias Higbee** was born in Galloway, New Jersey, in October 1795. He was baptized in Ohio in 1832 and immediately moved to Jackson County, Missouri. He was driven from the county in 1833 and relocated to nearby Clay County, where he served on the high council. He moved to Kirtland, Ohio, in 1835 and attended the dedication of the temple in 1836. Later he made his way to Commerce (Nauvoo), and from there traveled with Joseph Smith to Washington, D.C., to petition Congress for redress for the Church's losses in Missouri. Higbee died of cholera in Nauvoo in August 1843.

**Isaac Higbee** was born in December 1797 in Galloway, New Jersey.

He was baptized in 1832 near Cincinnati and then moved to Far West, Missouri, where he served on the high council and fought with the Danite militia. After settling in Illinois in 1839, he became a Nauvoo bishop and justice of the peace. A year after traveling west in 1848, he was sent to Utah Valley by Brigham Young to found the first settlement there; he soon carried out an "extermination campaign" against the local Indians. He died in Provo in February 1874.

**Gustavus Hills** was born in January 1804, in Chatham, Connecticut, and trained as a watchmaker. In 1840 he was baptized in Ohio. He was a clerk to Joseph Smith in Nauvoo, as well as the assistant editor of the *Times and Seasons* and an associate justice of the municipal court. He was a professor of music, whom the city humorously commissioned to supervise four "wardens" "to prohibit the flat sound of notes" in the city. He was disfellowshipped in 1842 and died four years later in Iowa.

**Joshua Sawyer Holman** was born in April 1794 in Templeton, Massachusetts. He was issued a ministerial license in Kirtland, Ohio, in 1836, and two years later he moved his family of eight individuals to Missouri, then to Illinois. He was sent on proselyting missions to Indiana and New York in 1843 and 1844. In 1846 he traveled with the Church to Winter Quarters, Nebraska, and died there in November.

**Edward Hunter** was born in June 1793 in Newton, Pennsylvania. A prominent citizen, he was a county commissioner and cavalryman in the county militia. He was baptized by Orson Hyde in 1840 and moved a year later to Nauvoo, where he acquired several farms and served as a bishop. He was also introduced into the Nauvoo Masonic Lodge, commissioned as the herald and armor bearer of the Nauvoo Legion, and made a regent of the University of Nauvoo. Occasionally he provided a hiding place for Joseph Smith when the latter was on the lam. Hunter immigrated to Utah in 1857 and served as Presiding Bishop of the Church from 1851 to his death in Salt Lake City in October 1883.

**Dimick B. Huntington** was born in Watertown, New York, in May 1808. Trained as a blacksmith, he was nevertheless the constable (later deputy sheriff) of Far West, Missouri, and city marshal and coroner in Nauvoo. He was arrested in 1844 for the destruction of the *Nauvoo Expositor,* which he carried out on orders of the city council. He was a drum major in the Nauvoo Legion. He served in the Mormon Battalion during the Mexican-American War. After arriving in Utah in 1847, he helped settle the southern part of the territory and became adept as an interpreter for Native Americans. He died in Salt Lake City in February 1879.

**William D. Huntington Sr.** was born in March 1784 in Cheshire, New Hampshire, and served in the War of 1812. He was baptized in 1835 and moved to Kirtland, Ohio, becoming a member of the high council there. He later moved to Adam-ondi-Ahman, Missouri, until forced out. In Nauvoo he was the cemetery's sexton, commissary general of the Nauvoo Legion, a stone cutter at the Nauvoo temple construction site, and a fifer in the Nauvoo Band. He died in Mt. Pisgah, Iowa, in August 1846.

**Orson Hyde** was born in January 1805 in Oxford, Connecticut, and baptized in 1831 by Sidney Rigdon. He served a mission to the east coast with Samuel Smith and to Pennsylvania with Hyrum Smith. In 1833 he became clerk to the First Presidency. The next year, he was made a member of the Kirtland high council. In 1835 he was ordained an apostle. The next year, he served a mission to Canada, and in two years he left for England; in 1841 he traveled alone to Jerusalem to offer a zionist blessing on the land. In 1846 he returned to England. Upon returning to the U.S., he spent three years in Kanesville, Iowa, publishing the *Frontier Guardian* newspaper. He arrived in Utah in 1850. He was called to settle Carson Valley, Nevada, in 1855 and lived there for three years, then was called to help settle Sanpete Valley in central Utah. He died in Spring City in the northern part of Sanpete Valley in November 1878.

**James Ivins** was born in March 1797 in Cream Ridge, New Jersey, where he joined the Church in 1839. He moved to Nauvoo in 1842 and constructed three large brick buildings, one of which housed the *Times and Seasons.* He and his brother operated a successful store in one of the buildings and the families lived in the third structure. They also operated the Nauvoo ferry. James left the Church over polygamy in 1844 and moved to nearby Keokuk, Iowa, until John Taylor bought the family's three buildings in 1845, at which time James returned to New Jersey and died there in April 1877.

**Aaron Johnson** was born in June 1806 in Haddam, Connecticut, and learned the gun-making trade beginning at age fourteen. He was baptized in 1836 and moved to Kirtland, Ohio; to Far West, Missouri, two years later; and to Nauvoo in 1839. He was a justice of the peace in Nauvoo and a member of the Nauvoo Legion. In Garden Grove, Iowa, he was a bishop from mid-1846 to mid–1850, then immigrated to Utah. He settled Springville and was its first bishop, postmaster, and an appellate judge. He died in Springville in May 1877.

**Heber C. Kimball** was born in June 1801 in Sheldon, Vermont. He apprenticed as a blacksmith, then as a potter. He and his wife became Baptists in 1832 in New York, but three weeks later they read the Book of Mormon and converted to the LDS Church. They moved to Kirtland, Ohio; he participated in the paramilitary march on Missouri in 1834 and became a Church apostle in 1835. Two years later, he and two other apostles filled a successful mission to England, baptizing 1,500 people. He returned to England in 1839 with seven other apostles and converted 7,500 people. When Brigham Young claimed the Church presidency in 1847, Kimball became his first counselor. Kimball reached Utah as part of the pioneer company that year. He died in Salt Lake City in May 1868.

**Hiram S. Kimball** was born in West Fairley, Vermont, in May 1806. He was a resident of Commerce (Nauvoo) before the LDS arrival in 1839 and established a mercantile shop in the city. He was elected as an alderman and judge before he converted to Mormonism in 1843. He defended the city against outside attack in 1846, immigrated west in 1852, and oversaw the settlement of Las Vegas in 1856. He was killed in the Sandwich Islands in May 1863 when a ship's boiler exploded.

**Joseph C. Kingsbury** was born in Enfield, Connecticut, in May 1812. He was baptized in Kirtland, Ohio, in 1832, moved to Missouri in 1838, and settled in Montrose, Iowa, across the river from Nauvoo, in the early 1840s. He was a member of the high council at Montrose from mid-1841 and a clerk in Joseph Smith's Nauvoo store before migrating to the Salt Lake Valley in 1847. He also served two missions to the eastern United States in 1835 and 1843. In Salt Lake City he was a bishop, superintendent of the Tithing Office, and stake patriarch. He died in 1898 in Salt Lake City.

**Newel Knight** was born in Marlborough, Vermont, in September 1800. He met Joseph Smith when his father, Joseph Knight, hired him to dig for buried treasure in 1826 in Colesville, New York. Newel was baptized by David Whitmer in 1830 in New York, became president of the Colesville branch and led its members to Kirtland, Ohio, then to Jackson County, Missouri, in 1831. In Missouri in 1837, Newel was called to the high council. In 1839 he joined the exiled Saints in Illinois. He died in January 1847 while traveling from Nauvoo to the Salt Lake Valley.

**Vinson Knight** was born in Chester, New York, in March 1804. He converted in 1834 and moved to Kirtland, Ohio, in 1835, becoming a councilor in the bishopric, a founding member of the Kirtland Safety Society, and town clerk. In Missouri and Nauvoo he was a ward bishop and, in both locations, high councilman prior to being named Presiding Bishop in 1841. He was also the Nauvoo warden of common schools, a land agent, a trustee of the Nauvoo House hotel, and a member of the city council. He died in Nauvoo in July 1842.

**Andrew Losey Lamoreaux** was born in October 1813 in York, Ontario. He and his family were baptized in Canada in 1837 and moved to Kirtland in 1838. Joining the Kirtland Camp of immigrants to Missouri that year, they were nevertheless assigned to Dayton, Ohio, soon after they arrived in Missouri. They stayed in Dayton until 1840. Andrew was ordained a high priest in Nauvoo in 1843. In 1844 he was called on a mission to Indiana. In 1846, he and his brother David rescued the Nauvoo temple's bell, put it in a wagon, and proceeded to carry it with them across the plains. They arrived in Salt Lake City in 1848. Four years later, Andrew was called to be president of the French mission, and while overseas he translated the Doctrine and Covenants into French. Returning from the mission, he contracted cholera in St. Louis and died in June 1855.

**William Law** was born in Ireland in September 1809. His family immigrated to Pennsylvania in 1818, and he attended school in Philadelphia. In the 1830s he married and moved to Canada. John Taylor and Almon Babbitt arrived in 1836 and converted him and others. He led a company of Church members from Canada to Nauvoo in late 1839. Two years later, he was called to the First Presidency. Over the next few years, he built a saw mill in the city and sold real estate and merchandise. He opposed plural marriage in 1843–44 and was excommunicated for his opposition. He was involved in producing the dissident newspaper, *Nauvoo Expositor,* in June 1844. He moved to Wisconsin and died there in January 1892.

**Wilson Law,** a brother of William, was born in Ireland in February 1806. He followed his brother to Nauvoo in 1839 and was baptized there. He became a brigadier general and then major general in the Nauvoo Legion and a member of the Nauvoo Masonic Lodge. In April 1844, he was excommunicated after he joined with other dissidents in opposing plural marriage. Undeterred, he helped publish the *Nauvoo Expositor* in June, for which the city council retaliated by accusing him of having seduced a seventeen-year-old girl some years past. He and his brother William and Austin Cowles proposed organizing a reformed First Presidency in protest and launching a new Church, but their attempt was short-lived. William and Wilson ended up in Shullsburg, Wisconsin, where Wilson died in October 1876.

**Tarlton Lewis** was born in May 1805 in South Carolina. He was baptized in 1836 and moved to Missouri, where he became a survivor of the Haun's Mill Massacre. He moved to Nauvoo in 1839 and became a bishop there. In 1843 he was on board the *Maid of Iowa* riverboat in a skirmish with the *Chicago Belle,* its passengers comprising a posse intent on apprehending Joseph Smith. Tarlton was part of the 1847 pioneer company to the Salt Lake Valley. He became the first LDS bishop in Salt Lake City and then the bishop of Parowan in southern Utah. He died in November 1890 in nearby Teasdale.

**Amasa M. Lyman** was born in March 1813 in Lyman, New Hampshire. He was baptized in 1834 and moved to Kirtland, Ohio, where he participated that year in the aborted paramilitary attempt to rescue besieged Latter-day Saints in Missouri. He became an apostle in Nauvoo in 1842, a member of the First Presidency in 1843, and migrated to Utah with the pioneer company in 1847. On assignment from Brigham Young in 1851, he helped settle San Bernardino. From 1860–62 he presided over the European Mission. After returning home the next year, he moved to Fillmore, Utah, and was excommunicated there for heresy. He died in Fillmore in February 1877.

**John Lytle** was born in August 1803 in Turbotville, Pennsylvania, and baptized in 1836 in Kirtland, Ohio. Besides serving temporarily on the Nauvoo City Council, he was a policeman who was arrested for his involvement in destroying the *Nauvoo Expositor.* He migrated to Utah in 1848 and became bishop of the eleventh ward the next year. In 1856 he served a mission to Carson Valley. Then in 1861 he built a house in St. George and divided his time between there and Salt Lake City, where he was a member of the School of the Prophets. A smoker most of his life, he gave up the habit when he was eighty years old. He died in October 1892 in St. George.

**Stephen Markham** was born in February 1800 in Hartford, New York. He was baptized in 1837 in Kirtland, Ohio. In Nauvoo he was appointed the market master, a colonel in the Nauvoo Legion, and a body guard to Joseph Smith. He accompanied Joseph Smith to Carthage in 1844 but was run off at bayonet point. He was one of the first pioneers to arrive in the Great Salt Lake Valley in 1847. Ten years later he helped settle the town of Spanish Fork and played a role in the Walker Indian War. He died in Spanish Fork in March 1878.

**William Marks** born in Rutland, Vermont, in November 1792. He was baptized in Portage, New York, in 1835 and migrated with the Saints to Ohio, where he was called to the Kirtland high council and then appointed president of the Kirtland stake. In 1839, after moving with the Church to Illinois, he was called to be president of the Nauvoo stake. He later joined the Nauvoo Masonic Lodge and Council of Fifty, as well as becoming a city alderman, a trustee for the Nauvoo House hotel, and a regent of the University of Nauvoo. However, he was removed from all Church positions and responsibilities after he disagreed with the Quorum of the Twelve on presidential succession in 1844 after Joseph Smith's death. He leaned toward Sidney

Rigdon's right to lead, then became a counselor to James Strang in 1846 before embracing the Reorganization in 1859. He died in May 1872 in Plano, Illinois.

**Duncan McArthur** was born in May 1796 in Grafton, New Hampshire. He was baptized in 1835 and moved to Ohio the next year, to Missouri in 1838, and to Nauvoo the next year. In 1840 he left to serve a mission to New England. Back in Nauvoo in 1845, he served as a Nauvoo temple guard. He migrated to Utah in the late 1840s and was asked to help settle Mt. Pleasant in 1850. He died in Mt. Pleasant in October 1864.

**Hugh McFall** was born in Pennsylvania in 1799. A carpenter, he was useful in helping construct the temples as he settled in Kirtland in 1834 and Illinois in 1839. He became an adjutant general of the Nauvoo Legion in 1841. Although he moved out of the city the next year, he apparently remained nearby and continued to serve in the militia until 1847, when he moved to Mississippi. He was still in Mississippi in 1860, the last time he appears in the historical record.

**Daniel Sanborn Miles** was born in July 1772 in Sanbornton, New Hampshire. He was baptized in 1832 in New Hampshire and moved to Kirtland, Ohio, in 1836. He lived in Missouri for half a year in 1838 before becoming one of the first Mormon settlers of Commerce (Nauvoo), Illinois, and one of the seven presidents of Seventy in 1837 when four of the original presidents were released for having been mistakenly ordained high priests. He died in Nauvoo in October 1845.

**George Miller** was born in Standardville, Virginia, in November 1794. His parents moved to the Kentucky frontier when he was twelve, and when he was twenty he followed the Ohio River to Cincinnati, where he worked as a carpenter. He later returned to Virginia for construction work at the university in Charlottesville. He was twenty-seven years old when he married in 1822. Eleven years later, he and his wife moved to Illinois. They converted to Mormonism in 1839 and moved to Nauvoo in 1840. In the Mormon capital, Miller was appointed a bishop, a regent of the University of Nauvoo, a brigadier general of the Nauvoo Legion, president of the Nauvoo House (hotel) Association, and a member of the Council of Fifty. In 1844 he was called to be the Presiding Bishop. During the 1840s he served four missions to Iowa, Kentucky, Mississippi, and Wisconsin. Although he started west with the Saints in 1846, he soured on Brigham Young's leadership and gravitated first toward Lyman Wight and then toward James J. Strang. He was excommunicated in 1848. Two years later, he moved to Wisconsin to be with the Strangites. He died six years later in Meringo, Illinois.

**Jacob Morris** was born in Sussex County, Delaware, in August 1797. He moved with the Church to Missouri and Illinois and was ordained a seventy in 1844. He served as an alternate high councilor on December 28, 1844. He immigrated to Iowa by 1850 and on to Utah in 1852. He died in 1856 in Ogden.

**Joseph Mount** was born in 1806 in Middletown, New Jersey. He and his wife converted in Dayton, Ohio, and moved to Nauvoo in the early 1840s, although he would spend much of the decade away from Nauvoo on Church missions to New York, Tennessee, and Vermont. He served as an alternate high councilman on December 30, 1843. He and his family traveled to Utah in the fall of 1847. As he and others struggled to survive the next year, he became the first to launch a boat onto the Great Salt Lake when he became desperate in his search for game, thinking he could find food on Antelope Island. He nevertheless came back with only a few mud hens for his wife to cook. He moved to California in 1853 and died in Napa in 1876.

**Freeman Nickerson** was born in South Dennis, Massachusetts, in February 1779 and served in the War of 1812. He joined the Church in 1833, immediately visiting Joseph Smith and Sidney Rigdon at Church headquarters in Kirtland, Ohio, where he persuaded them to join him on a proselyting trip to Canada. He marched in the 1834 counter-assault on non-Mormons in Missouri. Five years later, he returned to Missouri, only to find that the Church had moved on to Nauvoo. He joined the Saints there and soon served a mission to New England, establishing a Church branch in Boston. He traveled west in 1846 but made it only as far as the Chariton River, midway across the Territory of Iowa, where he died in January 1847.

**Eli Norton** appears in LDS branch records in Joliet, Illinois, in 1841 and in the Nauvoo school records in 1842. He served as an alternate high councilman on four occasions in February and March 1843. Nothing more is known about him.

**Harvey Olmstead** was born in Sennett, New York, in February 1794. In Missouri in 1838, he was called to the Adam-ondi-Ahman stake high council despite the fact that he was a Danite operative fighting against non-Mormon neighbors. In Nauvoo in 1840 he officiated in the first baptisms for the dead in the Mississippi River. He served as an alternate high councilman on March 30 and July 4, 1841. He died in March 1879 in New York.

**John Pack** was born in May 1809 in St. John, New Brunswick. He was baptized in 1836 in New York and followed the Saints' peregrinations from Ohio to Missouri to Nauvoo, where he became a policeman and captain in the Nauvoo Legion. He was sent on several short missions to the eastern states. In 1847, he was a member of the pioneer exploration to the Salt Lake Valley and later built the first sawmill in Kamas, Utah. In 1849 he was one of the first missionaries to France. He died in 1885 in Salt Lake City.

**Noah Packard** was born in Plainfield, Massachusetts, in May 1796. He converted in Ohio in 1832 and moved to Missouri in 1838. The next year he was in Nauvoo, where he became a counselor in the high priests quorum. He filled several missions to the east coast. From 1846 to 1850 he worked in the Wisconsin lead mines, then immigrated to Utah. In 1851 he settled in Springville, where he died in February 1860.

**Abraham Palmer** was born in Sherbourne, New York, in December 1805 and converted to the LDS Church in 1834. As president of a Church branch in St. Lawrence County in 1838, he led a group of members to Missouri and had the bad luck of camping four miles south of Haun's Mill the night before the massacre, although they escaped unscathed. After settling in Nauvoo, he served a mission to Chicago in 1841 and Indiana in 1844 and served as an alternate high councilman on February 11, 1843. During the trek west, he stayed behind in Kanesville, Iowa, to help people gather provisions for the trip, then went himself, with his family, in 1852 and settled in Ogden. He later moved to Sanpete County and died in May 1875 in the Utah village of Fayette.

**Ezra Parrish** was born in May 1804 in Brownville, New York. He lived in Nauvoo's 4th Ward neighborhood and immigrated to Utah in 1850. In 1857 he moved to San Bernardino to be with his oldest daughter, Harriette Shepherd, despite the fact that Brigham Young had issued a travel ban during the Utah War. Ezra's brother William and nephew Beason tried to leave the territory that same year and were killed by people who thought they were enforcing Young's prohibition. Ezra died in San Bernardino in July 1883.

**Calvin C. Pendleton** was born in August 1811 in Hope, Maine. He clerked for Church conferences in Maine in 1841 and 1843 and then moved to Nauvoo. He and his wife built and furnished a log house in Nauvoo; he earned a living as an herbal doctor and school teacher. They moved to Utah in 1854 and settled in Parowan, where he died in May 1873.

**William C. Perry** was born in Madison, New York, in January 1812 and converted to Mormonism in 1832. He was a carpenter by trade and helped build the Kirtland, Ohio, temple. In fact, he received a special blessing in 1835 for his part in the construction of the temple. It was the same year he was also ordained a Seventy. In 1838 he migrated to Missouri with the Kirtland Camp, toppling his wagon at one point. The next year, he moved to Nauvoo, then returned to Missouri in the late 1840s, dying there in Stewartsville in May 1893.

**William W. Phelps** was born in February 1792 in Hanover, New Jersey. His parents moved to Homer, New York, when he was eight years old, and when he was twenty-nine he became editor of the town's newspaper, the *Western Courier.* In 1823 he moved to Ulysses, near Ithaca, on Cayuga Lake and edited the anti-Masonic newspaper called *Lake Light.* In 1830 he read the Book of Mormon and was baptized the next year. When he arrived in Kirtland, Ohio, in 1831, he became the Church Printer and was sent to Missouri to publish *The Evening and the Morning Star* and *Upper Missouri Advertiser.* In 1834 he was called to be a counselor to David Whitmer in the Missouri stake presidency. He moved to Nauvoo in 1841 and helped edit the *Times and Seasons* and *Nauvoo Neighbor.* Eventually he was also a clerk to Joseph Smith, a popular writer of new Church hymns, and the city fire warden. After migrating to the Salt Lake Valley in 1848, he died there in March 1872.

**Orson Pratt** was born in September 1811 in Hartford, New York. He was baptized in 1830, participated in the Zion's Camp march on Missouri in 1834, and became an apostle in 1835. He served missions to Austria, Canada, England, and New York. He taught at the University of Nauvoo. He was one of the first Mormon pioneers into the Salt Lake Valley, arriving three days before Brigham Young. He became the Church Historian in 1874. He served in the territorial legislature. He is most remembered today as a theological rival to Brigham Young, with whom Pratt publicly clashed and by whom he was often censored; as the husband of Sarah Pratt, who refused overtures from Joseph Smith while Orson was away on a foreign mission; and as the husband of ten wives, the last of whom he married when he was fifty-seven and she was sixteen. He died in Salt Lake City in October 1881.

**Parley Parker Pratt** was born in Burlington, New York, in April 1807. In 1826 he moved to Ohio. Three years later, he converted to Sidney Rigdon's reformed Baptist congregation, then to Mormonism the next year. He was one of its earliest missionaries, departing immediately for Missouri and thereafter filling six more missions in the 1830s to the British Isles, Canada, the eastern seaboard, and the Midwest. In 1835 he was ordained an apostle. In 1838–39 he spent nine months in jail after the Mormon conflict in Missouri. During much of the Nauvoo period, he was in England editing the *Latter-day Saints' Millennial Star,* but he returned in February 1843 to serve on the Council of Fifty and campaign for Joseph Smith's presidential candidacy. In 1844–45 he was sent to lead the Church in New York City, where he also became an influential Church pamphleteer. Soon after joining the Saints in the West in 1847, he was sent to South America. After he took a plural wife who was still married, her estranged husband tracked him down in Arkansas and murdered him there in May 1857.

**Charles C. Rich** was born in Campbell County, Kentucky, in August 1809. He was baptized in 1832 in Pleasant Grove, Illinois, and lived there intermittently until 1837 when he was made a member of the Far West, Missouri, high council. In Illinois he served as major general of the Nauvoo Legion and as a member of the Nauvoo stake presidency. He followed the Saints in the fall of 1847 to Utah, where he was made an apostle in 1849 and led the settlement party two years later to San Bernardino, California. He later became president of the British Mission. He explored and settled the Bear Lake Valley in Idaho in 1863. He died in Paris, Idaho, in November 1883.

**Levi Richards** was born in Hopkinton, Massachusetts, in April 1799. He converted to Mormonism in 1836, moved to Missouri in 1838, and left the state in the great exodus two years later. In Nauvoo he became Joseph Smith's personal physician and the surgeon-general of the Nauvoo Legion—this despite the fact that he was not in the city much of the time, serving two missions to England, 1840–43 and 1848–53. He afterward settled in Salt Lake City and died there in June 1876.

**Phineas Richards** was born in Framingham, Massachusetts, in November 1788. As with many of his generation, he fought in the War of 1812, earning the rank of sergeant. Afterward, he married and moved to Richmond, Massachusetts, and became the town's coroner. He converted to Mormonism in 1837 and moved to Kirtland, Ohio, where he was baptized by Brigham Young, ordained a high priest by Joseph Smith and Sidney Rigdon, placed on the Kirtland high council, and sent on a mission to the eastern states, all within six months. He moved to Nauvoo in 1843 and was appointed to the high council the next year. It was not long after he immigrated to Utah in 1848 that he was called to the Salt Lake high council. He was also elected to the territorial legislature and helped settle Sanpete Valley. He died in Salt Lake City in November 1874.

**Willard Richards,** a brother of Levi Richards (above), was born in June 1804 in Hopkinton, Massachusetts. He received training in Boston in 1834 in Thomsonian herbal medicine. He converted to Mormonism two years later and was baptized in Kirtland, Ohio, by Brigham Young. Before the decade was out, he had filled two missions: to the eastern states and to England. While abroad, he was ordained an apostle. After returning home and settling in Nauvoo, he became a secretary to Joseph Smith. Eventually he also became Church Historian, municipal court clerk, city council clerk, and temple recorder, and he was involved with the Council of Fifty and the Masonic lodge. He was with Joseph and Hyrum Smith when they were murdered in the Carthage jail. He migrated to Utah in 1847 as a counselor to Brigham Young and became editor of the *Deseret News,* territorial secretary, and Salt Lake City postmaster. He died in Salt Lake City in March 1854.

**Sidney Rigdon** was born in St. Clair, Pennsylvania, in February 1793. A Baptist minister, he helped Alexander Campbell found the Disciples of Christ denomination. After converting to Mormonism in 1830, Rigdon became Joseph Smith's "spokesman" in the First Presidency, 1833–44. Rigdon was the author of *Lectures on Faith* and many seminal theological concepts. He was present on nine occasions when Smith received revelations, sharing in his 1832 vision of the "three degrees of glory." They were also tarred and feathered together that year. In 1838 in Missouri, Rigdon gave the famous "salt sermon" in which he promised a "war of extermination" against non-Mormon Missourians. In 1842 Smith wrote a letter to Rigdon's daughter Nancy to persuade her to become Smith's plural wife. In 1844 Smith and Rigdon announced themselves running mates for the U.S. presidency; but before the year was out, Rigdon had withdrawn from the Church and gathered a group of separatists in Pittsburgh, where he eventually abandoned his followers. He died in Friendship, New York, in July 1876.

**Sidney Roberts** was born in August 1809 in Monroe, Connecticut. He was reprimanded in 1840 when he said God wanted a specified Church member to give him a suit of clothes and a gold watch, also in 1849 for preaching plural marriage. In 1841 he shared the podium with Joseph Smith in Nauvoo; three years later, Roberts became a Seventy. In Nauvoo he sold furniture and repaired wagons. In Iowa in 1849, he published a pamphlet, *To Emigrants to the Gold Region,* which gave detailed directions for traveling to California. In Utah, he became involved in manufacturing paper in the Big Cottonwood

Canyon area. When he died in Salt Lake City in April 1875, he was transported to Kanosh for burial.

**Shadrach Roundy** was born in January 1789, in Rockingham, Vermont. In early 1831 he was baptized. He moved to Kirtland, where he was ordained a Seventy in 1836. He was involved with the troubles in Missouri and notably helped the poorer refugees escape to Illinois. He became the chief of police in Nauvoo, as well as a bodyguard for Joseph Smith. He was also involved in two secret fraternities: the Masons and the Council of Fifty. He was in a bishopric in Nauvoo and was bishop of Winter Quarters, Nebraska, and a member of the first high council in the Salt Lake Valley. He was bishop of the Salt Lake Sixteenth Ward for seven years. He died in the city in July 1872.

**Daniel Shearer** was born in August 1791 in Stillwater, New York. In the Mormon War of 1838, he was active as a Danite insurgent and was taken as a prisoner in Richmond, Missouri. The next year, he helped assist the poorest Mormon refugees evacuate. By 1842, he was leading a branch of the Church in Edmeston and Crown Point, New York, and working as a travel agent for immigrants, as well as collecting donations for the Nauvoo temple. He was ordained a Seventy in 1845. In 1873 he was set apart as a patriarch. He died in April 1874 in Salt Lake City.

**Henry Garlic Sherwood** was born in Kingsbury, New York, in April 1785 and baptized sometime before August 1832. He helped construct the Kirtland temple, moved to Missouri and was driven out with the rest of the Church, and arrived in Commerce (Nauvoo), Illinois, in mid-1839, where he contracted malaria. He served as clerk of the Nauvoo High Council and as city marshal. From 1841–42 he served a mission to New Orleans. After sitting on the Salt Lake City high council, he was sent to San Bernardino to establish a ranch there. In the newfound freedom of California, he left the Church, dying in San Bernardino in 1867.

**James Sloan** was born in Donaghmore, Ireland, in October 1792. He was ordained an elder in Ohio in 1837 and moved to Missouri the next year. When he reached Nauvoo, he became the city recorder in 1840 and Church recorder in 1841, while also a secretary to Hyrum Smith. In 1843 he filled a mission to Ireland. During the trek west, he reached Council Bluffs, Iowa, where he stayed through 1851 as the county clerk and federal district judge. By 1860 he had arrived in Sacramento and settled down as a farmer, eventually converting to the RLDS Church. He died in Sacramento in 1886.

**Asahel Smith** was born in Windham, New Hampshire, in May 1773. He was baptized in New York in 1835 and moved to Kirtland, Ohio. He became a member of the Kirtland high council in 1837, the Iowa high council in 1839, and an alternate high councilman in Nauvoo on June 2, 1843. The next year, he was ordained a patriarch. He died in Iowaville, Iowa, in July 1848.

**Don Carlos Smith**, a younger brother of Joseph Smith, was named after the restorer of religious devotion in Spain, Don Carlos V, whose royal family had moved back to Madrid in 1814 after being displaced by the anti-Catholic armies of Napoleon. Don Carlos Smith was born in March 1816 in Norwich, Vermont. In Kirtland, he helped with the temple construction and edited the *Elders Journal* newspaper. In 1838 he travelled to Pennsylvania to gather donations for the extended Smith family as they were fleeing Missouri. After settling in Illinois, he edited the *Times and Seasons* newspaper. He was also a regent of the University of Nauvoo and a brigadier general in the city's militia. He died in the city in August 1841.

**Elias Smith,** a cousin of Joseph Smith, was born in September 1804 in Royalton, Vermont. He was baptized in 1835. In Kirtland he was employed as a school teacher. He worked on the staffs of two newspapers in Nauvoo: the *Nauvoo Neighbor* and the *Times and Seasons*. One day in 1843, his father, Asahel Smith, served with him simultaneously on the high council because Asahel was substituting for another, absent, member that day. In Utah, Elias worked at the *Deseret News*. He was also the postmaster and a county probate judge. He died in the city in June 1888.

**George A. Smith** was born in June 1817 in Potsdam, New York. A cousin to Joseph Smith, he was baptized in 1832, then left New York for Kirtland. He was part of the Zion's Camp march on Missouri in 1834. The next year, he was ordained a Seventy. In 1839 he became an apostle and served a mission with the rest of the Twelve to England. Returning to Church headquarters in Nauvoo, he became a member of the secret Council of Fifty and the Nauvoo Legion. In Utah, he was called to be the Church Historian, a counselor to Brigham Young, and a member of the Supreme Court of the Territory of Utah. He died in Salt Lake City in September 1875.

**Hyrum Smith,** older brother of Joseph Smith, was born in Tunbridge, Vermont, in February 1800. He was one of the eight spiritual witnesses to the gold plates of the Book of Mormon. In Ohio he was named to the First Presidency, first as an assistant counselor and then, in Missouri, as second counselor. He spent late 1838 and early 1839 in a Missouri jail along with other Mormon insurgents. In Illinois he became Church Patriarch and Assistant President of the Church. He was murdered with his brother in June 1844 in Carthage, Illinois.

**Joseph Smith** was born in Sharon, Vermont, in December 1805. A visionary prophet, he communed with God and angels and published the Book of Mormon, a guide to modern faith and practice couched in a history of ancient America. He founded and presided over the Church of Christ (later renamed the Church of Jesus Christ of Latter-day Saints) in 1830, received revelations establishing Church doctrine, initiated men into various degrees of priesthood, and married some thirty-five women in what he said was a restoration of the ancient order of polygamy. He was killed by a mob in Carthage, Illinois, in June 1844.

**Joshua Smith** was born in February 1788, the oldest of four pair of twins, in Nobleborough, Maine. He was baptized into the LDS Church in Kirtland, Ohio, in 1836. In Illinois he served in the Nauvoo elders quorum presidency and as an alternate high councilman. In November 1845, when he was subpoenaed to appear in court in Carthage, he tried to sneak in a knife and was apprehended and placed in jail, where he died that evening. According to the postmortem examination, his dinner was laced with poison.

**Josiah Smith** was born in November 1791 in Newry, Maine, and converted sometime between 1833, when the first LDS missionaries arrived, and 1839 when he was ordained a priest in his home town. On June 15, 1844, he served as an alternate Nauvoo high councilman. Five months later, his daughter, Lucy, married George A. Smith (above). Josiah returned to Maine sometime before 1875 when his daughter visited him there. He died in January 1880.

**Samuel Harrison Smith**, younger brother of Joseph Smith (above), was born in Tunbridge, Vermont, in March 1808. After the Church was founded in 1830, Samuel became the first proselyting missionary. He was a member of the Kirtland high council. In Missouri in 1838, he participated in the Battle of Crooked River. In Illinois he became bishop of the Nauvoo Ward and a member of the city's militia, the Nauvoo Legion. In mid-1844 he became sick after transporting the corpses of Joseph and Hyrum Smith from Carthage to Nauvoo and never recovered, dying on July 30.

**William Smith,** younger brother of Joseph Smith (above), was born in March 1811 in Royalton, Vermont. He was a member of the Quorum of Twelve Apostles from 1835 to 1845. Three years after moving to Illinois in 1839, he was elected to the Illinois State House of Representatives. He edited Nauvoo's short-lived, hard-hitting newspaper, *The Wasp*. He took several plural wives in 1845 after being called as the Presiding Patriarch, but by the end of the year, he had been excommunicated. Even though he joined with James Strang, he was soon excommunicated from Strang's Church. He affiliated with other small factions before going it alone and taking several more plural wives, then going a different direction altogether and joining the RLDS Church in 1878. In November 1893 he died in Osterdock, Iowa.

**Abraham O. Smoot** was born in February 1815 in Owenton, Kentucky. He was baptized in 1835 and then moved to Kirtland, Ohio, the next year. He was taken prisoner in Missouri during the Mormon War of 1838. On his release, he traveled to Quincy, then spent half a year settling in Nauvoo before departing on a mission to Charleston, South Carolina, where he later returned to help fellow Southerners immigrate to Winter Quarters, Nebraska. In the interim, he had become a policeman in Nauvoo. He arrived in Utah in 1847, freighted goods to the territory for four years, and served a mission to England in 1851. Back in Salt Lake City, he was elected mayor in 1856. Twelve years later, in 1868, he was called to help settle Provo, where he became the stake president, mayor, and president of the First National Bank of Provo, Provo Woolen Mills, and Utah County Savings Bank, as well as chair of the Brigham Young Academy (BYU) board. He died in Provo in March 1895.

**John Snider** (also Snyder) was born in Pleasant Valley, Nova Scotia, in February 1800. He was baptized in Toronto when he was thirty-six. He was ordained a Seventy in Far West, Missouri. In Illinois he became a regent of the University of Nauvoo and a trustee of the Nauvoo House, which was the Church-owned hotel. He was also an aide-de-camp to Joseph Smith in the Nauvoo Legion. He served missions to England in 1837 and 1842. After Joseph Smith's assassination in 1844, Snider returned to Toronto, then traveled to the California gold fields in 1850. He died in Salt Lake City in December 1875.

**Lorenzo Snow** was born in April 1814 in Mantua, Ohio. Prior to his baptism in June 1836, he attended a term at Oberlin College. After his baptism, he taught school in Shakersville, Ohio, then moved to LaHarpe, Illinois, twenty miles outside of Nauvoo. He was then called on a three-year mission to England. When he returned in 1843, it was at the head of a group of 230 convert immigrants. After the exodus from Nauvoo, he presided over the Church in Mt. Pisgah, Iowa, 1847–48. He was ordained an apostle in 1849 in Salt Lake City, then immediately called to Italy. On his return, he was called to settle in Brigham City, where he became president of the Box Elder Stake and the area's territorial representative. In 1873 he became a counselor to Brigham Young; in that capacity he traveled to Hawaii and Palestine. In 1886 he was found guilty of practicing polygamy and served eleven months in prison. He became Church president in 1898 and served three years until his death in October 1901.

**William Snow,** brother of Apostle Erastus Snow, was born in December 1806 in St. Johnsbury, Vermont. He was baptized in 1832 and the next year filled a mission to Charleston, South Carolina. In 1845 he became a member of the presidency of the Nauvoo high priests quorum. He took his family to Salt Lake City in 1850, and by the next year he was leading a weekly prayer circle in the city. He later became the bishop of Pine Valley in southern Utah, thirty miles north of St. George. He died in Pine Valley in May 1879.

**Leonard Soby** was born in 1810. He was living in Nauvoo by 1841 and was sent on a mission to Indiana in 1843. That was also the year he famously rejected the revelation on plural marriage when it was read to the Nauvoo High Council by Hyrum Smith. The next year, Soby helped publish the dissident *Nauvoo Expositor.* He was disfellowshipped in September 1844 for supporting Sidney Rigdon, whom he followed to Pennsylvania. Soby died in 1893 in Beverly, New Jersey.

**Daniel Spencer** was born in July 1794 in West Stockbridge, Massachusetts. When he was in his early twenties, he moved to Savannah, Georgia, and managed a store there for seven years, then returned to his home town in 1823 to marry Sophronia Eliza Pomeroy. They returned to Georgia, where she died nine years later. He returned home to marry Sarah Lester van Schoonover in 1834. When missionaries arrived in West Stockbridge in 1840, the Spencers converted and moved to Nauvoo. Daniel would often be away on proselyting missions (Canada, Massachusetts, Oklahoma) until 1844 when, after Joseph Smith's death, Daniel became the interim mayor. His wife Sarah died the next year, and Daniel married Mary Spencer, who died a year later. In Winter Quarters, where he was called to be a bishop, he married Emily Shafter Thompson, his fourth wife (and not yet a polygamist). He became a stake president and member of the territorial legislature in Salt Lake City, where he married three more women in 1856 and one more in 1857. He died in Salt Lake City in December 1868.

**Orson Spencer** was a younger brother of Daniel Spencer (above), born in May 1802 in West Stockbridge, Massachusetts. He was a Baptist minister from 1829 to 1841, when he was baptized into the LDS Church by his brother. He accepted an appointment that year as a professor at the University of Nauvoo. He served a mission to New Haven, Connecticut, in 1843, and became a high priest in 1844. He was elected mayor of Nauvoo in 1845. From 1847–49 he presided over the British mission. In Utah he became chancellor of the University of Deseret (University of Utah). He died in St. Louis, Missouri, while on a mission, in October 1855.

**Richard D. Sprague** was born in March 1807 in Junius, New York. He was baptized in 1840 in New York and was admonished two years later to "build up the church in the regions round about" his New York home. A stone mason, he was an asset in helping build the Nauvoo temple. He was also a police officer in Nauvoo and a drummer in the Nauvoo Legion. In 1847 he participated in the Mormon Battalion's march to San Diego during the War with Mexico. He died in December 1885 in Huntsville, Utah.

**George P. Stiles** was born in July 1816 in Watertown, New York. In Nauvoo he was the City Attorney. In Utah he became an Associate Justice on the Utah Territorial Supreme Court. He and fellow judge, William W. Drummond, were prominent in their criticisms of the LDS-dominated probate courts and actions by the territorial marshal. In response, Brigham Young's bodyguards intimidated the two justices, ransacking Stiles's office and running Drummond out of the territory. The justices' reports to Washington contributed to the Utah War. Stiles was excommunicated in 1856. In 1860 he was living in Ohio, but died in Belton, Texas, in 1885.

**Sylvester B. Stoddard** was born in February 1801, probably in Maine. After converting to the Mormon Church in 1830, he appears in the historical record as a clerk for a regional Church conference in Saco, Maine, in 1834. He returned to the state ten years later as a missionary. In 1836 he was ordained an elder in Kirtland, Ohio, and soon thereafter moved to Missouri. In 1839 he petitioned the state for reimbursement of $574 for losses during the Mormon War. He was appointed to the bishopric in Quincy, Illinois, in 1840. Within two years, he had moved to Nauvoo, where he was an alternate high councilman on May 9, 1842. His Nauvoo home and tinsmith shop have been restored for tourists. He died in Akron, Ohio, in August 1867 and was buried in Kirtland.

**Robert Stone** was born in June 1776 in Derby, England. He immigrated to New York City and married Maria Smith in Trinity Church in 1821. They settled down and had children in Brooklyn. Their conversion to Mormonism occurred in 1838. By 1846 they were in Nauvoo, where he served as an alternate stake high councilman. He died in November 1851 at Winter Quarters, Nebraska.

**Hosea Stout** was born in September 1810 in Danville, Kentucky. He was baptized in August 1838 in Caldwell, Missouri, and participated in the Battle of Crooked River two months later. He was ordained a Seventy and became a captain in the police force in Nauvoo, also a colonel in the Nauvoo Legion. He immigrated to Utah in 1848. In 1852 he was called on a mission to China, although he and two others stayed only a few months in Hong Kong in 1853 before determining that the Chinese weren't interested and returning home. He became a prosecuting attorney in Salt Lake City. He also served in the territorial legislature. In 1861 he helped found St. George. He died in March 1889 in the Big Cottonwood settlement outside of Salt Lake City.

**John Taylor** was born in November 1808 in Milnthorpe, England. He was baptized in 1836 by Parley P. Pratt in Toronto, Canada. He moved to Kirtland and then to Far West, Missouri, where he was made an apostle in 1838. In Nauvoo he served as a regent of the university, on the city council, and as editor of both the *Nauvoo Neighbor* and *Times and Seasons.* He was with Joseph Smith in Carthage Jail in June 1844. He went west with the Saints and became Church president after Brigham Young's death in 1877. He spent most of his administration in hiding from law enforcement officers because of his marriages to eighteen wives, the last a twenty-six-year-old who married him when he was seventy-eight. He died in Kaysville, Utah, in July 1887.

**Andrew A. Timmons** was born in 1798. He and his neighbors were visited by Mormon missionaries in southern Illinois in 1833, and Timmons was baptized the next year. In the 1840s he resided in Nauvoo. He was sent to Arkansas to campaign for Joseph Smith's U.S. presidential candidacy in 1844. In 1846, while living in Burlington, Iowa, he enlisted as a musician (drummer or fifer) with the Iowa Dragoon Volunteers in the War with Mexico. His company was transferred to Fort Atkinson in Prairie du Chien, Wisconsin, where it remained for a year. During that time, Timmons met Elizabeth Rowell, whom he married in 1848 in Nauvoo. They later moved to Montrose, Iowa. Nothing more is known about him.

**Benjamin Warrington** was born in October 1810 in New Jersey. By 1834 he was living in southeastern Ohio, then later in Nauvoo where, as a non-Mormon, he was a city councilman and quartermaster sergeant of the Nauvoo Legion. He was the lone dissenter in the council's decision to suppress the *Nauvoo Expositor* in 1844. He drowned in the Platte River in Nebraska in June 1850.

**Daniel H. Wells** was born in Trenton, New York, in October 1814. He moved to Commerce (later renamed Nauvoo) with his widowed mother in 1834 before the arrival of the Mormons. He married at age twenty-two in 1837. When Joseph Smith arrived, they became friends, and Wells served as a Nauvoo justice of the peace and a regent of the University of Nauvoo without converting to the faith until 1846, two years after Smith's death. After he migrated to Utah in 1848, Wells became a member of the First Presidency, as well as mayor of Salt Lake City. He served as president of the European mission from 1884–87 and president of the Manti temple from 1888–91. He died in Salt Lake City in March 1891.

**Newel K. Whitney** was born in Marlborough, Vermont, in February 1795. He was a member of Sidney Rigdon's Disciples of Christ congregation in Kirtland, Ohio, where he was co-owner of a successful mercantile store. He was baptized into the LDS faith in 1830 and became the bishop of Kirtland the next year. He accompanied Joseph Smith in 1832 to the cities of Boston and New York City. In Nauvoo he set up a retail store that rivaled his previous enterprise in Kirtland. He was called as the bishop of the Middle Ward in Commerce (Nauvoo) and was a member of the Council of Fifty. He immigrated to Salt Lake City in 1848, became bishop of the Eighteenth Ward, and died in the city in September 1850.

**Lyman Wight** was born in May 1796 in Fairfield, New York. He was stationed at Sackets Harbor during the War of 1812 and moved to Ohio in the mid-1820s. He was a member of Sidney Rigdon's Campbellite congregation before converting to Mormonism in 1830. He served on the high council and as a military leader in Missouri. While there, he drew considerable controversy for saying that all medical doctors are frauds and that sickness is the result of demonic influence. In Nauvoo in 1841, he was ordained an apostle. He traveled on the Mississippi River to Wisconsin in 1844 to supervise the Church's timber harvesting there. After Joseph Smith's death, he led 150 members to Texas to establish a religious colony. He was removed from the LDS Church rolls in 1848 and died in Dexter, Texas, ten years later in March 1858.

**Benjamin S. Wilbur** was born in 1811. In 1838 he was named one of the presidents of the Seventy and helped lead the Kirtland Camp, comprising 105 Mormon families, to land in the Far West, Missouri, area. Their resettlement was short-lived, however, since the Latter-day Saints were expelled from Missouri the next year. After escaping to Nauvoo, Wilbur and his family lived in the third-ward neighborhood. Nothing else is known of him.

**Samuel Williams** was born in March 1789 in Russell, Massachusetts. He was baptized before October 1839 and claimed damages, for which he wanted the state to reimburse him, when he was forced to move from Missouri to Illinois. While in Nauvoo, he was called as president of the elders quorum. He left the city in 1846, spent three years in Winter Quarters in Nebraska, and then continued on to Utah, where in 1850 the census showed him employed as a stonecutter. He died five years later in Ogden.

**Bushrod W. Wilson** was born in August 1808 in Willsboro, New York. He and his wife were baptized in 1836. He was included the next year in "a list of the names of ministers of the gospel, belonging to the Church of the Latter Day Saints." In Nauvoo he worked as a policeman. He was part of the counter-posse that traveled upriver in 1843 on the *Maid of Iowa* riverboat to rescue Joseph Smith from Missouri marshals. Wilson served a proselyting mission to England and a political mission to Ohio. He and his family traveled to Utah in 1852, settling in Spanish Fork, and the next year they continued farther west to San Bernardino. Over time, he became increasingly sympathetic with the dissidents in the Mormon colony. He may have joined them because when Brigham Young called the colonists back to Utah in 1857, Wilson stayed. He died there in November 1877.

**Lewis D. Wilson** was born in June 1805 in Milton, Vermont. He was baptized in 1836 in Ohio and ordained a Seventy in 1838. He moved to Illinois in 1839. In 1846 his wife died in childbirth, leaving him eleven living children. He and nine children left Nauvoo in 1846 for the Mormon settlement of Garden Grove, Iowa, where they stayed five years before moving on to Winter Quarters, Nebraska. They traveled to Utah and settled in Ogden in 1853, by which time he had married five more wives to replace the loss of his first one. He died in Ogden in March 1856.

**Wilford Woodruff** was born in March 1807 in Hartford, Connecticut, and baptized in 1833 in New York. After he served in the paramilitary march on Missouri in 1834 and filled missions to the southern states and New England, he was ordained an apostle in 1839, then immediately called on yet another mission, this time to Great Britain. In Illinois he raised funds for the Nauvoo House hotel and campaigned for Joseph Smith as president of the United States. In 1844 he crossed the Atlantic again, this time as president of the European Mission. He made his way to Utah in 1850. After John Taylor's death in 1887, he became the fourth president of the Church. He had ten known wives, although two of them, seventeen and eighteen years old at marriage (he was thirty-nine), were divorced for spending time during the exodus across Iowa in 1846 with "young men" in "evil and wickedness." He died on a business trip to San Francisco in 1898.

**Jonathan C. Wright** was born in November 1808 in Rome, New York. He was baptized by Hyrum Smith in the Mississippi River in 1843. While in Nauvoo, Wright worked on the *Nauvoo Neighbor* staff. From 1847–48 he traveled to various Midwestern locations to encourage Church members who "had been driven out of Nauvoo" to gather to Winter Quarters or to Utah—in other words, to accept the Quorum of the Twelve's leadership. Most of those who had stayed behind were unwilling to do so, and most of them expressed a strong distaste for polygamy. Wright died in Brigham City, Utah, in November 1880.

**Brigham Young** was born in June 1801 in Whitingham, Vermont. He was baptized in 1832, the same year he moved to Kirtland. In the Mormon capital, his skills as a professional carpenter were utilized in helping to construct and furnish the temple, although he also served missions in 1832 and 1835 to Canada and from 1835–37 to the eastern states. He marched on Missouri as part of the Zion's Camp campaign in 1834. The next year, he was made a member of the Twelve Apostles. He became president of the Twelve in 1838. In 1839 he oversaw the evacuation of Missouri. Over the next three years he traveled to England on a proselyting mission with the other Twelve. After the death of Joseph Smith, he directed the Church's departure from Nauvoo and the immigration to Utah, as well as the subsequent settlement of colonies from Canada to Mexico. He became president of the Church in December 1847. He was governor of the Territory of Utah, 1850–57, and Superintendent of Indian Affairs, 1851–57. He had some fifty wives. He died in Salt Lake City in August 1877.

**Joseph Young,** an older brother of Brigham Young (above), was born in April 1797 in Hopkinton, Massachusetts. Like his brother, he became a Mormon in 1832, and he was almost immediately called on a mission to New York and Canada. He participated in the 1834 Zion's Camp attempt to rescue besieged Mormons in Missouri. While there, he witnessed the Haun's Mill Massacre. In 1835 he became one of the presidents of the Seventy. In Nauvoo he was a member of the elite Council of Fifty. He spent four years at Winter Quarters in Nebraska, migrating to Utah in 1850. In Utah he was elected to the territorial legislature. He filled a mission to Britain in 1870 and died in Salt Lake City in July 1881.

# Minutes of the City Council

# 1.
# "A Feeble Testimonial"
# 1841

†*February 3, 1841; Wednesday.*[1] The City Council met at the House of Amos Davis at Six OClock P.M. on Wednesday the 3rd day of February 1841.[2] John C. Bennett Esq[uire], the Mayor, was Sworn into office, by Dan[ie]l H. Wells, J[ustice of the] P[eace]. Meeting opened by Prayer, by Joseph Smith. The Mayor gave Notice that H[enry] G. Sherwood had been appointed City Marshal, & requested the public to respect & obey him as such.[3]

---

[1]See also Joseph Smith, *History of the Church of Jesus Christ of Latter-day Saints,* 7 vols. (Salt Lake City: Deseret News, 1902-12), 4:288-95.

[2]On February 1, 1841, an election was held to determine who would comprise the Nauvoo City Council. The *Times and Seasons,* Feb. 1, 1841, 309, reported: "The following ticket was elected by majorities varying from 330 to 337 votes; to wit: REGULAR TICKET. For Mayor, John C. Bennett. Aldermen[:] William Marks, Samuel H. Smith, Daniel H. Wells, [and] N[ewel] K. Whitney. Counsellors[:] Joseph Smith, Hyrum Smith, Sidney Rigdon, Charles C. Rich, John T. Barnett, Wilson Law, D[on] C[arlos] Smith, J[ohn] P. Greene, [and] Vinson Knight. The Council will be organized on Wednesday the 3rd inst." An alderman held a municipal rank immediately below the mayor, doubling as a justice of the peace and adjudicator in the city court. Absent the mayor, an alderman could fill in as chief justice of the municipal court. According to the Nauvoo Charter, the councilmen discussed and voted on city ordinances and were not involved with the courts.

[3]Sherwood was the first city marshal in Nauvoo.

Aldermen,[4] Daniel H. Wells, William Marks, N[ewel] K. Whitney, & Samuel H. Smith, and Counsellors,[5] Joseph Smith, Don C[arlos] Smith, Hyrum Smith, Charles C. Rich, John P. Greene, John T. Barnett, Vinson Knight, & Wilson Laws, were sworn into office by the Mayor, having respectively subscribed their Oath of Office, & the Mayor, having duly subscribed his Oath of Office,[6] Co[unci]l[or] [Sidney] Rigdon, (who was Elected as the other City Co[unci]l[or]) not being present.[7]

H[enry] G. Sherwood was appointed City Marshal, & Sworn. & to continue for Two years ensuing. Robert B. Thompson appointed City Treasurer, & Sworn. & to continue for Two Years ensuing. James Sloan appointed City Recorder, & Sworn, and to continue for Two Years ensuing. Austin Cole appointed Supervisor of Streets, (not present,) to continue for Two Years ensuing. James Robison appointed City Assessor, & Sworn, & to continue for Two years.

The Mayor then addressed the Council, & Citizens, by an inaugural Speech of considerable length, and Read and[8] cited parts of the City Charter,[9] observing as to what he considered should be done in the City forthwith, &c, &c.[10]

---

[4]Elias Higbee, Isaac Higbee, and Alex Stanley also ran for alderman but were not elected. See the *Times and Seasons,* Feb. 1, 1841, 287.

[5]Hiram Kimball, Arthur Morrison, Robert D. Foster, James Robinson, William Huntington, Stephen Winchester, Titus Billings, Stephen Markham, Noah Packard, David Dort, and W. G. Wilson also ran for councilman but were not elected (ibid.).

[6]The oath of office was: "We ... do solemnly swear in the presence of almighty God that we will support the Constitution of the United States, and of the State of Illinois, and that we will well and truly perform the duties of councilors of the City of Nauvoo, according to law, and the best of our abilities" (*History of Church,* 4:295).

[7]Rigdon was probably ill. In a letter to John C. Bennett in late 1840, Joseph Smith wrote, "Rigdon is very sick, and has been for nearly twelve months, ... At present he is not able to leave his room." It was also reported in April 1841 that Rigdon's "normal body weight of 212 pounds had been reduced to 165 pounds" by sickness or stress. See Richard Van Wagoner, *Sidney Rigdon: A Portrait of Religious Excess* (Salt Lake City: Signature Books, 1994), 281-83.

[8]The scribe added a superfluous ampersand here, which I have deleted.

[9]For the text of the Nauvoo Charter, see Appendix A.

[10]The *Times and Seasons,* Feb. 15, 1841, 316-18, printed Bennett's speech in full, declaring it "a document of considerable interest, and is well

Counsellor Joseph Smith presented a Bill to Organize the Nauvoo Legion,[11] which was read three times, the Rules were dispensed with, & it passed Unanimously. To Wit.

An Ordinance Organizing the "Nauvoo Legion". –

Sec. 1. Be it Ordained by the City Council of the City of Nauvoo, that the Inhabitants of the City of Nauvoo, and such Citizens of Hancock County as may unite by Voluntary Enrollment, be, & they are hereby Organized into a Body of independent, Military Men, to be called the "Nauvoo Legion," as contemplated in the 25th Section of "An Act to incorporate the City of Nauvoo," approved December 16th, 1840.

Sec. 2. The Legion shall be, and is hereby, divided into two Cohorts, – the Horse Troops to constitute the first Cohort, & the foot Troops to constitute the second Cohort.

Sec. 3. The General Officers of the Legion shall consist of a Lieutenant General, as the Chief Commanding & reviewing Officer, & president of the Court Martial, & Legion; a Major General, as the second in Command of the Legion, the Secretary of the Court Martial, & Legion, & Adjutant & Inspector General; a Brigadier General, as Commander of the first Cohort; & a Brigadier General, as Commander of the second Cohort.

Sec. 4. The Staff of the Lieutenant General shall consist of two principal Aids-de-Camp, with the Rank of Colonels of Cavalry, & a guard of twelve Aids-de-Camp, with the Rank of Cap-

---

worth the perusal of our readers, and every one who loves the prosperity of our peaceable and improving city." Bennett touched upon three major themes: prohibition of liquor and suppression of all drinking establishments; education and the University of Nauvoo; and formation of the Nauvoo Legion as better for "the preservation of order ... than ... our military forces."

[11]The Nauvoo Legion was a private military force. It was set up, maintained, and run by the leaders of Nauvoo and the LDS Church. By 1842 it had over 2,000 soldiers. In comparison, the entire U.S. Army had 8,500. For more, see Hamilton Gardner, "The Nauvoo Legion, 1840-45: A Unique Military Organization," in Roger D. Launius and John E. Hallwas, eds., *Kingdom on the Mississippi Revisited: Nauvoo in Mormon History* (Urbana: University of Illinois Press, 1996), 48-61. For a general history of the city's militia, see Richard E. Bennett, Susan Easton Black, and Donald Q. Cannon, *The Nauvoo Legion in Illinois: A History of the Mormon Militia, 1841-1846* (Norman, OK: Arthur H. Clark, 2010).

tains of Infantry, & a drill officer, with the Rank of Colonel of Dragoons, who shall likewise be the Chief Officer of the Guard.

Sec. 5. The Staff of the Major General shall consist of an Adjutant, a Surgeon in Chief, a Cornet[ist], a quarter Master, a Pay Master, a Commissary, & a Chaplain with the Rank of Colonels of Infantry; a Surgeon for each Cohort, a quarter Master Sergeant, Sergeant Major, & Chief Musician, with the Rank of Captains of light Infantry; & two Musicians, with the Rank of Captains of Infantry.

Sec. 6. The Staff of each Brigadier General shall consist of One Aid-de-Camp, with the Rank of Lieutenant-Colonel of Infantry; provided that the said Brigadiers shall have access to the Staff of the Major General when not otherwise in Service.

Sec. 7. No Officer shall hereafter be elected by the various Companies of the Legion, except upon the nomination of the Court martial,[12] & it is hereby made the duty of the Court Martial to nominate at least two Candidates for each vacant Office, whenever such vacancies Occur.

Sec. 8. The Court Martial shall fill & supply all officers ranking between Captains & Brigadiers General by granting brevet Commissions[13] to the most worthy Company Officers of the Line, who shall thereafter take Rank & Command according to the date of their Brevets; provided that their Original place in the Line shall not thereby be vacated.

Sec. 9. The Court Martial consisting of all the Military Officers, Commissioned or entitled to Commissions, within the lim-

---

[12]Notice that the court martial served not only as a judicial body that tried soldiers for crimes but also as a military promotions board and supervisor of elections. As Hamilton Gardner observed in his seminal article on the legion: "Apparent at once to the military student is the incongruity of the provision that made the commissioned officers into a body with extensive law-making powers and called, inexactly, the 'court martial'" ("The Nauvoo Legion, 1840-45: A Unique Military Organization," *Journal of the Illinois State Historical Society* 54 [Summer 1961]: 184).

[13]In other words, the rank and file elected their officers (Sec. 7), but the court could also grant temporary commissions to fill vacancies until approved by the governor. The idea of a democratic militia came from the state constitution of 1818, which authorized an Illinois militia comprising "all free male ablebodied persons" (although explicitly excluding "negroes, mulattoes, and Indians"), divided into divisions and brigades, the members of which elected their own generals (Gardner, "Nauvoo Legion," 183).

its of the City Corporation, shall meet at the Office of Joseph Smith, on Thursday the 4th day of February 1841 at 10 o'clock A.M. & then, & there, proceed to elect the general officers of the Legion as contemplated in the 3rd Section of this ordinance.

Sec. 10. The Court Martial shall adopt for the Legion, as nearly as may be, & so far as applicable, the discipline, drill, Uniform, Rules & Regulations of the United States Army.

Sec. 11. This Ordinance shall take effect, & be in force from & after its Passage.

**Passed Feb[ruar]y 3rd. 1841. John C. Bennett, Mayor [and] Co[unci]l [member]. James Sloan, Recorder.**

Counsellor Joseph Smith presented a Bill to Organize the "University of the City of Nauvoo," which was read three times, the Rules were dispensed with, & it passed Unanimously.

An Ordinance Organizing
the "University of the City of Nauvoo."[14]

Sec. 1. Be it Ordained by the City Council of the City of Nauvoo, that the "University of the City of Nauvoo" be, & the same is hereby Organized, by the appointment of the following Board of Trustees; to wit: John C. Bennett, Chancellor, William Law, Registrar, & Joseph Smith, Sidney Rigdon, Hyrum Smith, William Marks, Samuel H. Smith, Daniel H. Wells, N[ewel] K. Whitney, Charles C. Rich, John T. Barnett, Wilson Law, Don C[arlos] Smith, John P. Greene, Vinson Knight, Isaac Galland, Elias Higbee, Robert D. Foster, James Adams, Robert B. Thompson, Samuel Bennett, Ebenezer Robinson, John Snider, George Miller, & Lenos M. Knight, Regents; who shall hereafter Constitute the "Chancellor & Regents of the University of the City of Nauvoo", as contemplated in the 24th Section of "An Act to incorporate the City of Nauvoo," approved December 16th 1840.

---

[14]The University of Nauvoo was authorized by the Illinois State Legislature through the Nauvoo Charter. Instructors included Gustavus Hill, John Pack, Orson Pratt, Sidney Rigdon, and Orson Spencer. Though some classes were held, the campus was never completed. It closed entirely when the Saints left Nauvoo in 1846. For more, see Donald Q. Cannon, "Joseph Smith and the University of Nauvoo," in *Joseph Smith: The Prophet, The Man,* eds. Susan Easton Black and Charles D. Tate Jr. (Provo: BYU Religious Studies Center, 1993), 285-300.

Sec. 2. The Board named in the 1st Section of this Ordinance shall hold its first Meeting at the office of Joseph Smith, on Tuesday, the 9th day of February 1841, at 2 OClock, P.M.

Sec. 3. This Ordinance shall take effect, & be in force, from & after its passage.

**Passed 3rd Feb[ruar]y 1841. John C. Bennett, Mayor. James Sloan Recorder.**

Counsellor Joseph Smith presented the following Resolution, which was unanimously adopted.

Resolved by the City Council of the City of Nauvoo, that ^the unfeigned^ ~~a Vote of~~ Thanks of this ~~Community of Nauvoo be~~ ^Community be respectfully^ tendered to the ~~Citizens of Quincy~~ Governor[,] Council of Revision, & Legislature, of the State of Illinois, as a feeble testimonial of their respect & esteem for noble, high minded, & patriotic Statesmen, & as an evidence of gratitude for the Signal powers recently conferred & that the Citizens of Quincy be held in everlasting remembrance for their unparall[el]ed liberality & marked kindness to our People, when in their greatest State of Suffering & want.[15]

That portion of the [the mayor's] Message respecting a Canal,[16] was referred to a Committee of three, namely, Co[unci]l[o]rs [Vinson] Knight, & Joseph Smith, & Alderman Wells. That portion of the Message respecting the vacating of the Town Plotts, & Town of

[15]In late 1838, Latter-day Saints living in Missouri were forced to leave, by order of Governor Lilburn W. Boggs. A large number headed east, crossing the Mississippi River into Quincy, Illinois, a small town south of Commerce (later Nauvoo). See Glen M. Leonard, *Nauvoo: A Place of Peace, A People of Promise* (Salt Lake City: Deseret Book, 2002), 30-33; Robert B. Flanders, *Nauvoo: Kingdom on the Mississippi* (Urbana: University of Illinois Press, 1975), 12-13.

[16]At the end of Bennett's inaugural address as mayor, he broached the idea of building a canal to create "water power for propelling any amount of machinery for mill and manufacturing purposes." The *Times and Seasons* editorialized on February 15, 1841, that "it is supposed that a [water] fall might be obtained by cutting a canal through the city, of from three to five feet, and water power to any amount obtained. This once accomplished would give an impetus to the prosperity of the City, and, with the natural advantages which it already possesses, it would soon take the lead of nearly all the cities in the west."

commerce,[17] was referred to a Committee, Messrs Joseph Smith, Wilson Law, & Cha[rle]s C. Rich. That Portion of the Message that relates to vending [selling] Spirituous Liquors, was referred to a select Committee, Viz Joseph Smith, W[illia]m Marks, & Hyrum Smith.

It was [also] referred to a Committee of five, to prepare a Cod[e] of City Ordinances. Joseph Smith, D[aniel] H. Wells, Don C[arlos] Smith, Wilson Law, & John P. Greene. It was adopted that the appointment of a Board of Health for the City, be referred to a Committee, to Wit: Joseph Smith, N[ewel] K. Whitney, & John T. Barnett.

It was unanimously adopted, that the inaugural Address, as also the proceedings of this Meeting, be published in the Times & Seasons. The Mayor made some remarks concerning the powers vested in him, also respecting the Duties of the several Officers.

Adjourned until Monday next, to meet at Mr. Daviss, at One Oclock P.M. February 3rd. 1841. John C. Bennett, Mayor. James Sloan, Recorder.

*February 8, 1841; Monday.*[18] City Council met pursuant to adjournment. Meeting opened by Prayer, by Counsellor, Hyrum Smith.

An ordinance in relation to the City Council was read the first time. – Counsellor [Sidney] Rigdon was Sworn, as Counsellor, & took his Seat. The Committee upon the Canal made their Report, & brought it in, which was read, & Co[unci]l[o]r Joseph Smith moved that it be accepted[;] after some discussion, a Committee of the whole was gone into, who rose and Reported, & the Report of the Committee was received.

The Committee upon the Vacation of the Town Plotts, & Town of Commerce, brought in their Report. It was moved, & Seconded, that it be laid upon the Table, which Motion was withdrawn after some discussion, & liberty was obtained to withdraw the Report, upon Motion, seconded, & Voted upon, and Report was withdrawn, with liberty to amend.

It was moved & seconded that Co[unci]l[o]r Joseph Smith be appointed to Contract for a Survey of the Canal, & to Report. Ald[er]m[a]n [Daniel H.] Wells moved that the Rules be dispensed with, &

---

[17]What is meant here is "plats" rather than "plots." The existing layout was being abandoned, not actual property.

[18]See also *History of Church,* 4:297.

to Report Progress. Co[unci]l[o]r Joseph Smith brought forward the Report of the Committee on Vending Spirituous Liquors, Poison, Gunpowder, &c, &c. and the Bill was read the first time.

An Ordinance in Relation to the City Council, & other Officers, Read the second time. A Clause was added to the second Section. Bill read the third time and Passed.

An Ordinance in relation to the City Council.

Section 1. Be it ordained by the City Council of the City of Nauvoo, That should any member of the City Council absent himself from, or neglect or refuse to attend, any Regular or special meeting of said Council, for more than thirty minutes after the time appointed, or should the Marshal or Recorder be guilty of a like offence, he shall ^be^ fined in the sum of two Dollars for each offence.

Sec. 2. Should any member of said Council neglect or refuse to attend said Meetings, for[th]with on a summons from the Mayor, served by the Marshal or special messenger of said Council, he shall be fined in the sum of Twenty five Dollars for each offence; Provided, that the City Council may on good cause shown, remit any fine herein, or by this ordinance Assessed.

Sec. 3. The above fines to be collected as other debts before the Mayor at the suit of the City Corporation. – This ordinance to take ^effect^ and be in force from and after its Passage.–

**Passed Feb[ruar]y 8th. 1841. John C. Bennett, Mayor. James Sloan Recorder.**

Austin Cole was Sworn as Supervisor of Streets. Adjourned until this day [next] Week, at 1 OClock P.M. To meet at same place. February 8th. 1841. John C. Bennett, Mayor. James Sloan, Recorder.

*February 15, 1841; Monday.*[19] City Council met pursuant to adjournment. Alderman [William] Marks called to the Chair in the absence of the Mayor. Meeting opened by Co[unci]l[o]r [Sidney] Rigdon, by Prayer. Proceedings of last Meeting Read.

Co[unci]l[o]r [John P.] Greene presented a Petition from Hiram Kimball accompanied with a Map, respecting his Kimballs property in the bounds of the City, known as Lotts in the Town Plott of Com-

---

[19]See also ibid., 208-09.

merce. It was Moved, seconded, & Carried, that Pet[itio]n & Map be laid on the Table.

An ordinance in Relation to Temperance read 1st time. Rules dispensed with, – Received [at] second Reading. Co[unci]l[o]r Joseph Smith moved, & it was adopted, that the Committee be relieved from further consideration as to the City Plott. The Committee on the Code of Ordinances for the City, reported progress, & obtained further time. A Pet[itio]n was presented on behalf of Newel Knight & others, for liberty to make a Dam or Pier out into the River, which was ordered to lie on the Table.

The Code of Laws & Ordinances for the City was read the second time. The Ordinance in Relation to Temperance was read [a] third ~~second~~ time, & discussed, & amended, & passed unanimously.

An Ordinance in Relation to Temperance.[20]

Sec. 1. Be it Ordained by the City Council of the City of Nauvoo, that all persons & establishments whatever, in this City, are prohibited from vending Whiskey in a less quantity than a Gallon, or other Spirituous Liquors in a less quantity than a Quart,[21] to any Person whatever, excepting on the Recommendation of a Physician duly accredited, in Writing, by the "Chancellor & Regents of the University of the City of Nauvoo," & any Person guilty of any act contrary to the prohibition contained in this Ordinance, shall, on conviction thereof before the Mayor, or Municipal Court, be fined in any Sum not exceeding twenty five Dollars, at the discretion of said Mayor, or Court; & any Person or Persons who shall attempt to evade this Ordinance by giving

---

[20]This was published in the *Times and Seasons* on February 15, 1841. The paper declared it a "Great Moral Victory!" because of the unanimous vote from "Aldermen [Daniel H.] Wells, [Samuel H.] Smith, [William] Marks and [Newel K.] Whitney [and] Councillors Joseph Smith, Hyrum Smith, Don C[arlos] Smith, [Sidney] Rigdon, [William] Law, [Charles C.] Rich, [John T.] Barnett, [John P.] Greene, and [Newel] Knight," along with the mayor, John C. Bennett, thus setting "a glorious example to the world."

[21]The intent of this statute was to keep saloons out of the city. The concept was borrowed from an 1838 state law in Massachusetts prohibiting the sale of intoxicating liquors in less than fifteen-gallon quantities. Even though the Massachusetts law was repealed two years after it passed, it influenced similar legislation across the country ("Prohibition," *Encyclopaedia Britannica Online,* 2011).

away Liquor, or by any other means, shall be considered alike amenable, and fined as aforesaid.

Sec. 2. This ordinance, to take effect, & be in force, from and after its Passage.

**Passed Feb[ruar]y 15th 1841. John C. Bennett, Mayor. Ja[me]s Sloan Recorder.**

Adjourned until Monday next at One oC[lock] P.M. to meet at same Place. February 15th 1841. John C. Bennett, Mayor. James Sloan, Recorder.

*February 22, 1841; Monday.*[22] City Co[unci]l met pursuant to adjournment, & adjourned by Vote, to the office at Co[unci]l[o]r [Sidney] Rigdons.

Co[unci]l[o]r [Charles C.] Rich presented a petition from Residents on that part of the City Plott known as Kimballs addition to Nauvoo, praying that it might be Surveyed according to the City Plott. Which Pet[itio]n was laid on the Table.

Alderman [Daniel H.] Wells brought forward that part of the ^Code^ of City Ordinances relating to City Officers, which was read the first time. Co[unci]l[o]r Joseph Smith moved The following Resolution which was unanimously adopted.

> Resolved by the City Council of the City of Nauvoo, that the freedom of the City be, & the same hereby is conferred on the present Governor, Lieutenant Governor, council of Revision, & Members of both Houses of the General Assembly, of the State of Illinois, as an evidence of Our Gratitude for their great liberality & kindness to this Community during the present Winter.[23]

Co[unci]l[o]r. Joseph Smith moved an Ordinance in Relation to the University, which was passed.

---

[22]See also *History of Church,* 4:300-01.

[23]Published in the *Times and Seasons,* Mar. 1, 1841, 334-35. The Freedom of the City Award, sometimes given to esteemed members of the community, was derived from a medieval tradition of bestowing vassals with the right to own land, engage in commerce, and enjoy the town's protection. By the nineteenth century, the award had come to have only a symbolic meaning.

An Ordinance in relation to the University.[24]

Sec. 1. Be it Ordained by the City Council of the City of Nauvoo, that all Matters & powers whatever in Relation to common Schools, & all other institutions of learning, within the City of Nauvoo, be, & the same hereby are, transferred from the City Council of the City of Nauvoo, to the Chancellor & Regents of the University of the City of Nauvoo.

Sec. 2. This ordinance to take effect, & be in force, from & after its passage.

**Passed Feb[ruar]y 22nd. 1841. John C. Bennett, Mayor. James Sloan, Recorder.**

Ald[er]m[a]n Wells brought forward an ordinance, to amend an Ordinance of the 15th Feb[ruar]y 1841, entitled an Ordinance in Relation to Temperance to grant Licences to Sell Spirituous & Vinous Liquors, which was Read the 1st. & 2nd time. A Committee of the whole was gone into, who rose & reported, & upon a Vote whether the Bill be Ordered to a third reading. It was LOST.

The 1st Division of a Bill, relating to the City Wards, was read the ^2nd &^ third time, & passed into the following Ordinance.

An Ordinance dividing the City into Wards.[25]

Sec. 1. Be it Ordained by the City Council of the City of Nauvoo, that the City be, & the same hereby is, divided into four Wards, as follows; to wit: all that District of Country, within the City Limits, North of the Centre of Knight Street, & West of the Centre of Wells Street, shall constitute the first Ward, – all North of the Centre of Knight Street, & East of the Centre of Wells Street, the second Ward; all South of the Centre of Knight Street, & East of the Centre of Wells Street, the third Ward, – & all South of the Centre of Knight Street, & West of the Centre of Wells Street, the fourth Ward of said City.

Sec. 2. Each Ward shall be entitled to the following representation in the City Council; to wit: One Alderman, & two Counsellors; Provided, that the fourth Ward shall be entitled to three Counsellors; & the Mayor for the City at large.

Sec. 3. The Aldermen, & Counsellors already elected by the

[24]Ibid.

[25]Ibid., 336-37.

general ticket system, shall be assigned as follows, for the first Term; to Wit: Samuel H. Smith, Alderman, & John P. Greene, & Vinson Knight, Counsellors, for the first Ward – N[ewel] K. Whitney, Alderman, & Sidney Rigdon, & Hyrum Smith Counsellors, for the second Ward – Daniel H. Wells, Alderman, & John T. Barnett, & Cha[rle]s C. Rich, Counsellors, for the third Ward – & W[illia]m Marks, Alderman, & Joseph Smith, Wilson Law, & D[on] C[arlos] Smith, Counsellors, for the fourth Ward of said City.

Sec. 4. This Ordinance [is] to take effect, & be in force, from & after its passage.

**Passed March 1st. A.D. 1841. (See p. 12.)[26] John C. Bennett, Mayor. James Sloan Recorder.**

The second division of a Bill, as relates to Streets & Bridges, was read a second time by the Title, & upon Motion was again referred to the former Committee.

The Pet[itio]n of C[harles] C. Rich & others was taken up, discussed, & amended, & the following Resolution adopted.

Resolved by the City Council of the City of Nauvoo, that the Citizens of Kimball's addition to Nauvoo be, and they hereby are, permitted to extend the survey of the original Plot over said addition, provided, that no survey shall ever be made therein, which does not conform to the City Plot of Nauvoo.

Co[unci]l[o]r Joseph Smith brought forward a Resolution relative to the County Road leading from Carthage to the late Town of Commerce, in order to have it Vacated, or changed[;] it underwent some discussion, & eventually carried, that it be laid on the Table.

Adjourned until One OClock on this day [next] Week, to meet at same place. February 22nd 1841. John C. Bennett, Mayor. James Sloan, Recorder.

*March 1, 1841; Monday.*[27] City Council met pursuant to adjour[n]-ment. – Meeting opened by Prayer. – Minutes of last Meeting read.

Co[unci]l[o]r J[oseph] Smith moved an Ordinance respecting

---

[26]This refers to a page in the Record of Proceedings.

[27]See also *History of Church,* 4:305-08.

roads & Town Plots, which went through the usual readings, (the rules being dispensed with) and passed as follow[s].[28]

An Ordinance ^in relation^ to Roads and Town Plots.[29]

Sec. 1. Be it ordained by the City Council of the City of Nauvoo, That all state and County roads within the limits of this City, excepting where they occupy the same grounds as the City Streets; and the original surveys and plots of the old Town of Commerce and Commerce City, be, and the same hereby are, vacated.

Sec. 2. This Ordinance, to take effect, and be in force, from and after its passage. –

**Passed March 1st. 1841. John C. Bennett, Mayor. James Sloan Recorder.**

Co[unci]l[o]r J[oseph] Smith moved an Ordinance respecting the surveying of any addition to the City Plot, which went through the usual readings (the Rules being dispensed with) and passed as follows. –

An Ordinance in Relation to the City Plot.[30]

Sec. 1. Be it ordained by the City Council of the City of Nauvoo. That no tract of Land ~~that~~ within the Limits of this City, shall hereafter be surveyed, plotted and laid out into City Lots, unless the same be surveyed and plotted, so as to correspond with the Original survey and plot of the City of Nauvoo. – and any survey, or plot, made in violation of this Ordinance shall be null & void.

Sec. 2. This ordinance to take effect, and be in force from and after its passage.

**Passed March 1st. 1841. John C. Bennett, Mayor. James Sloan Recorder.**

---

[28]The committee on "vacating of the Town Plotts, & Town of commerce," comprising Joseph Smith, Wilson Law, and Charles C. Rich, concluded: "We would therefore recommend to the council the passage of the following resolution – That the town plats of Commerce, and Commerce City be vacated, and that the same stand vacated from this time forth, and forever; and that the same be incorporated with the City of Nauvoo, from this time henceforth and forever" (ibid, 307-08). Thus, Commerce was absorbed into Nauvoo.

[29]See *Times and Seasons*, Mar. 1, 1841, 335.

[30]Ibid.

Co[unci]l[o]r J[oseph] Smith moved an Ordinance, to divide the City into 4 wards, and appoint the Aldermen and Co[unci]l[o]rs to their Respective Wards, the Bill received 3 readings and passed. Entitled – An Ordinance dividing the City into Wards[31] See This Ordinance, on Page 9.

Co[unci]l[o]r J[oseph] Smith brought forward an Ordinance relative to public Meetings which was read 3 times and Passed, to Wit:

An Ordinance in Relation to Public Meetings.[32]

Sec. 1. Be it Ordained by the City Council of the City of Nauvoo, That in order to Guarrantee the Constitutional right of free discussion upon all subjects, the Citizens of this City, may from time to time, peaceably assemble themselves together for all peaceable, or lawful, purposes whatever; and should any person be guilty of disturbing, or interrupting, any such Meeting or assemblage, he shall on Conviction thereof before the Mayor, or Municipal Court be considered a disturber of the public peace, and fined in any sum not exceeding five hundred Dollars, or imprisoned not exceeding Six Months or both at the discretion of said Mayor, or court.[33]

Sec. 2. Should any person be guilty of exciting the people to riot, or rebellion or of participating in a mob of any ^other^ unlawful riotous or tumultuous assemblage of the people, or of refusing to obey any civil officer executing the Ordinances of the City, or the general laws of the State or United States, or of neglecting or refusing to obey, promptly any military order for the due execution of said Laws or Ordinances, he shall on conviction thereof as aforesaid, be fined, or imprisoned; or both as aforesaid.

Sec. 3. this ordinance to take effect and be in force from and after its passage.

**Passed March 1st 1841. John C. Bennett, Mayor. James Sloan, Recorder.**

---

[31]It is not known why this ordinance was discussed and voted on a second time. It had passed at the previous meeting on February 22, though the *Times and Seasons* listed the date of passage as March 1.

[32]See *Times and Seasons*, Mar. 1, 1841, 336.

[33]At the time, the First Amendment right to association was not generally thought to apply to the states. Therefore, there was a need for such an ordinance.

Co[unci]l[o]r J[oseph] Smith moved an Ordinance in relation to religious Societies, [which was] read [the] first time, rules dispensed with, read [the] second and third times, and passed, as follows:

An Ordinance in relation to religious Societies.[34]

Sec. 1. Be it ordained by the City Council of the City of Nauvoo, That the Catholics, Presbyterians, Methodists, Baptists. Latter-Day Saints, Quakers, Episcopalians Universalists Unitarians, Mohommedans,[35] and all other religious sects and denominations whatever, shall have free toleration and equal Privilieges in this City, and should any person be guilty of ridiculing abusing, or otherwise depreciating another in consequence of his religion or of disturbing, or interrupting any religious meeting within the Limits of this City, he shall on conviction thereof, before the Mayor or Municipal Court be considered a disturber of the public peace, and fined in any sum not exceeding five hundred Dollars, or imprisoned not exceeding six months, or both at the discretion of said Mayor, or Court.

Sec. 2. It is hereby made the duty of all municipal officers to notice, and report to the Mayor any breach or violation of this or any other Ordinance of this City that may come within their Knowledge, or of which they may be advised; and any officer aforesaid is hereby fully authorized to arrest all such violators of rule, law, and order, either with or without process.[36]

Sec. 3. This Ordinance to take effect, and be in force from and after its Passage.

---

[34]See the *Times and Seasons*, Mar. 1, 1841, 335. Though this ordinance was passed, Smith still felt some resentment toward certain sects. He stated in a discourse less than two years later: "The pagans, Roman Catholics, Methodists and Baptists shall have place in Nauvoo – only they must be ground in Joe Smith's mill. I have been in their mill. I was ground in Ohio and York States, in a Presbyterian smut machine, and the last machine was in Missouri; and the last of all, I have been through the Illinois smut machine; and those who come here must go through my smut machine, and that is my tongue" (*History of Church*, 5:287). A smut machine removed fungi from grains.

[35]That is, Muslims.

[36]It is interesting that the council would pass an ordinance that specifically allowed detention "without process," which was forbidden by both the Fifth Amendment to the U.S. Constitution and Article VIII of the Illinois Constitution of 1818.

**Passed March 1st 1841. John C. Bennett, Mayor. James Sloan Recorder.**

Co[unci]l[o]r J[oseph] Smith moved and it was seconded and carried, that Kimball's petition and map, (which was laid on the Table) be taken up. It was then adopted that the Pet[itio]n[e]r be at liberty to withdraw his Petition, which was complied with, and the petition and Map were handed to Co[unci]l[o]r [John P.] Greene.

Co[unci]l[o]r J[oseph] Smith presented an Ordinance relative to additional City Officers which was read three times and passed, to Wit:

An Ordinance Creating certain additional City Offices therein named.[37]

Sec. 1. Be it ordained by the City Council of the City of Nauvoo. That in addition to the City officers heretofore elected, there shall be elected by the City Council, one High Constable for each Ward, one surveyor and engineer, one Market Master, one Weigher and Sealer and one Collector for the City, whose duties shall hereafter be defined by Ordinance.

Sec. 2. This ordinance to take effect, and be in force from and after its Passage.

**Passed March 1st 1841. John C. Bennett, Mayor. James Sloan Recorder.**

The following appointments were made (by the City Council) of High Constables for the City: Demick B. Huntington 1st Ward, Leonard Soby 3rd Ward, George Morey[38] 2nd Ward, James Allred 4th Ward. Leonard Soby was Sworn into office.

Co[unci]l[o]r J[oseph] Smith moved, that the office of Supervisor of Streets be declared vacant in consequence of Austin Cowles the Supervisor being neccessarily absent from the City, which was carried unanimously.[39] James Allred was appointed Supervisor of

---

[37]Published in the *Times and Seasons,* Mar. 1, 1841, 335.

[38]George Morey was born in 1803 in Pittstown, New York. He was a member of the Missouri high council and served as High Constable in Nauvoo. He left the LDS Church in 1844 and eventually became a leader in the Reorganized Church of Jesus Christ of Latter Day Saints. He died in 1875.

[39]Cowles's absence and removal are puzzling. Later in the month, on March 29, he was chosen to be a counselor to Nauvoo Stake President William Marks (*History of Church,* 4:323).

Streets. The City Marshal was then appointed to act as Supervisor of Streets in the absence of that officer, and was sworn in.

Co[unci]l[o]r J[oseph] Smith offered the following Resolution, which was seconded and Carried. –

> Resolved. That the Marshal give notice to the person having encumbrance on the Street at Co[unci]l[o]r [Sidney] Rigdon's House, and oblige him to have same removed within ten days.[40]

UPON MOTION of Co[unci]l[o]r [Wilson] Law, it was resolved, that all nuisances on the Street which runs along the River be removed by the Supervisor. Co[unci]l[o]r J[oseph] Smith moved that the council appoint some person to attend the County Commissioner's Court to procure an appropriation for Roads in this Section of Country, and it was resolved unanimously that Co[unci]l[o]r [Vinson] ^Knight^ be appointed for that purpose, and that he perform that duty.

A vote of thanks was tendered to, and the freedom of the City of Nauvoo conferred upon the Hon[orable] Richard M. Young[,][41] United States Senator for Illinois[,] by the City Council, Unanimously.

Adjourned until 1 oclock P.M. on Monday next March 8th to meet at the same place. March 1st 1841. John C. Bennett, Mayor. James Sloan, Recorder.

*March 8, 1841; Monday.*[42] City Council met pursuant to adjourment. – Meeting opened by Prayer. – Minutes of last Meeting read.

Co[unci]l[o]r J[oseph] Smith moved that the general Code of City Ordinances now before the Committee, be brought forward, seperately, for the convenience of discussion – which was seconded and Carried.

Upon Motion of Co[unci]l[o]r J[oseph] Smith, Alanson Ripley

---

[40]The owner of a saw mill was stacking logs in the street near Rigdon's house, blocking traffic. See further discussion below on March 8, 15.

[41]Richard Montgomery Young was born in Kentucky in 1796. He was admitted to the Illinois bar in 1817. He served as a circuit judge from 1825 to 1827 and 1829 to 1837. He later served as a U.S. Senator from 1837 to 1843, after which he sat on the Illinois Supreme Court. He died in 1853 in Washington, D.C.

[42]See also *History of Church,* 4:308.

was appointed City Surveyor. Upon Motion of Co[unci]l[o]r J[oseph] Smith, Theodore Turley was appointed Weigher and Sealer for the City. Upon Motion of Alderman [Daniel H.] Wells, James Robinson the City Assessor was appointed Collector of Taxes in the City. Upon Motion of Co[unci]l[o]r J[oseph] Smith, Stephen Markham was appointed Market Master for the City. Demick B. Huntington, and George Morey ^& James Allred,^ were Sworn into office, as High Constables for the City. James Allred was sworn in Supervisor of Streets.

Upon Motion of Co[unci]l[o]r J[oseph] Smith, Mr. [John C.] Annis[43] obtained liberty to address the Council respecting Nuisances, & he did so. Upon Motion of Co[unci]l[o]r J[oseph] Smith a further time of ten Days was extended to Mr. Annis for removing the obstruction upon the Street at the Mill. Upon Motion of Co[unci]l[o]r [John T.] Barnett, the Labour Tax for the Citizens of Nauvoo for this year was fixed at three Days.

Upon Motion of Alderman Wells, the following Committee, of four persons, were appointed to assertain where work is most needed upon the Streets, and to report: Ald[er]m[a]n S[amuel] ^H.^ Smith for the 1st Ward, Co[unci]l[o]r J[ohn] Barnett for the 3rd Ward, Ald[er]m[an]n D[aniel] H. Wells " 2nd Ward, Ald[er]m[a]n [William] Marks " 4th "

Adjourned until this day [next] Week to meet at One Oclock P.M. at the office of Co[unci]l[o]r Joseph Smith. March 8th 1841. John C. Bennett, Mayor. James Sloan, Recorder.

*March 15, 1841; Monday.*[44] The City Council met agreeable to adjour[n]ment. — Meeting opened by Prayer. — Upon Motion of Alderman [Daniel H.] Wells time was granted untill next meeting of Council for the Committee on Streets, to report.

Ald[erma]n Wells stated that Mr. [John C.] Annis wishes to know if the Council will decide, whether his Mill will be permitted to remain where it is; — Co[unci]l[o]r J[oseph] Smith moved, that the Mill be permitted to stand where it is, provided the Owner of the Mill shall not intrude upon the rights of the Ferry. — Several of

---

[43]John C. Annis was born in 1784 in Thetford, Vermont. He was a member of the Nauvoo Legion.

[44]See also *History of Church,* 4:310.

the Council spoke at length upon the subject matter of the motion. – It was then moved by Ald[e]r[man] Wells that the Mill be altogether removed, which was seconded by Co[unci]l[o]r D[on] C[arlos] Smith and fully discussed & finally prevailed. Co[unci]l[o]r J[oseph] Smith moved & it was unanimously carried that four months time be granted to the Owner of the Mill to remove the same, or in default that it be removed at the expence of the Owner.

Theodore Turley was sworn in [as] Weigher & Sealer. Adjourned untill 1 oclock on this day [in] two weeks to meet at the same place. March 15th 1841. John C. Bennett, Mayor. James Sloan, Recorder.

*March 29, 1841; Monday.*[45] City Council met pursuant to adjour[n]-ment. – Meeting opened by Prayer. – Reading of the Minutes of the last meeting dispensed with.

Co[unci]l[o]r J[oseph] Smith moved an ordinance respecting Dogs which was discussed & amended and finally passed as follows:

An Ordinance in Relation to Dogs.

Sec. 1. Be it ordained by the City Council of the City of Nauvoo, That all persons who keep a Dog within the City, be fined in a sum not less than one Dollar, nor exceeding ten Dollars, provided the Dog is set upon Cattle or Hogs or molests any person.[46]

Sec. 2. This ordinance to take effect, & be in force from and after its Passage. –

**Passed Mar[ch] 29th. 1841. John C. Bennett, Mayor. James Sloan Recorder.**

It was moved by Co[unci]l[o]r J[oseph] Smith & seconded & carried that the City Surveyor be ordered to survey the City of Commerce, and plots of Commerce, to accord with the City Plot of Nauvoo and make out a map to be recorded.

Co[unci]l[o]r J[oseph] Smith moved and it was seconded & carried that the Survey of the City Plot of the City of Nauvoo be recognised by this Council. – Ald[er]m[a]n [Daniel H.] Wells brought up the report of the Committee on Streets which was read so far as the same was prepared, and further time was obtained to report.

Adjourned to this day [in] two weeks, to meet at same place at 1

[45]See also ibid., 322-23.

[46]Joseph Smith stated: "I contended that it was right to fine individuals who would keep unruly dogs, to worry cattle, sheep, or the citizens" (ibid.).

OClock P.M. March 29th 1841. John C. Bennett, Mayor. James Sloan, Recorder.

*April 12, 1841; Monday.* City Council met pursuant to adjourment. – Reading of the Minutes of last Meetings dispensed with untill next Meeting.

Ald[er]m[a]n [Daniel H.] Wells brought forward the report of the Committee on Streets, which was accepted by vote. Upon Motion of Co[unci]l[o]r [John T.] Barnett, it was carried that the Supervisor be instructed & be exempt from working on Streets in the 3rd Ward untill the 1st of October next.

Adjourned untill this day [in] two weeks to meet at one O'clock P.M. at same place. April 12th 1841. John C. Bennett, Mayor. James Sloan, Recorder.

*April 26, 1841; Monday.*[47] Meeting opened and a majority of the Council being absent, it was moved by Co[unci]l[o]r J[oseph] Smith and seconded and carried that the Marshal be ordered to enforce the attendance of the Aldermen & Co[unci]l[o]rs who are absent[48] at one oclock on Saturday the 1st Day of May, next, to which time, the Meeting is adjourned, and to be held at same place. April 26th 1841. John C. Bennett, Mayor. James Sloan, Recorder.

*May 1, 1841; Saturday.*[49] City Council met pursuant to adjour[n]ment. – Meeting opened by Prayer. – It was carried by vote that the Marshal do notify the absent Co[unci]l[o]rs to attend forthwith: – [50] Minutes of the last three meetings were read. Upon Motion of Co[unci]l[o]r J[oseph] Smith it was resolved that the Sympathies of this Council be tendered to the relatives of James Robison deceased who was the Assessor for this City.[51] Lewis Robison was appointed Assessor ^& Collector^ in the place of James Robison deceased.

---

[47]See also ibid., 352-53.

[48]See "An Ordinance in relation to the City Council" on Feb. 8, 1842, which states that council members may be fined for being late or for missing meetings.

[49]See also the *History of Church,* 4:353-54.

[50]See April 26, 1841.

[51]The *Times and Seasons,* May 1, 1841, 404-05, reported: "Died, in this city ... on the 20th ultimo Mr. James Robison, aged 30 years. The deceased

Co[unci]l[o]r J[oseph] Smith moved and it was seconded and carried that a Bur[y]ing Ground be procured, out of the City, and purchased at the expence of the City. It was adopted that Alderman [Daniel H.] Wells, Co[unci]l[o]rs [Wilson] Law & [John T.] Barnett be a Committee to procure a Buring Ground. Upon Motion of Co[unci]l[o]r Law it was seconded & carried that ten acres be the quantity of Land to be procured for the Burying Ground.

Co[unci]l[o]r J[oseph] Smith moved, and it was seconded & carried that the Sexton be fined to the extent of the Charter if he refuses to act in his office & that the Marshal give him notice thereof. [52]

Alderman Wells presented a petition from John C. Annis for liberty to put his Mill upon the outside Butment. Co[unci]l[o]r Law moved that petition be accepted, which ^was^ seconded, & after being debated, the Motion was lost.

Upon Motion of Alderman Wells a petition was granted (from Elias Higby) that the supervisor be instructed to open that part of Wells Street which is North of Knight Street, as far North as Young Street & also that part of Young Street West of Knight Street to the next Corner by Mr. [Hugh] Herringshaw.

Co[unci]l[o]r J[oseph] Smith moved & it was adopted that the Citizens be protected for Killing all dogs running at large which are set upon Cattle, or Hogs, or molest any person.[53] Upon Motion of Co[unci]l[o]r Law, it was resolved, that all persons who keep a Slut,[54] & lets her run at large, while she has Dogs following her, be fined Twenty Dollars.

---

had resided in this county many years, and from his business habits and kind disposition he was highly respected. Previous to his death he held the offices of Quarter Master Sergeant in the Nauvoo Legion, and Assessor for the city of Nauvoo. In his death, this community has lost one of its most active and effective members, and his loss will not only be severely felt by his relations and friends, but by all who had the pleasure of his acquaintance."

[52]Apparently the sexton (grave caretaker and digger) did not improve his job performance. The council replaced him six months later (see entry for October 15 below).

[53]Apparently, the "Ordinance in Relation to Dogs" of March 29 did not adequately solve the problem.

[54]That is, a female dog, according to early nineteenth-century usage (*Shorter Oxford English Dictionary*, 5th ed. (Oxford: Oxford University Press, 2002), s.v. "slut."

Adjourned Sine Die.[55] May 1st 1841. John C. Bennett, Mayor. James Sloan, Recorder.

*May 21, 1841; Friday.*[56] City Council met pursuant to special appointment. The Mayor stated the object of the Meeting.

Co[unci]l[o]r [John T.] Barnett spoke on the Subject of the Streets leading into the State Road. Upon Motion of Co[unci]l[o]r Joseph Smith it was unanimously carried, that Parley Street be the Street to be improved, to meet the State Road.

Upon Motion of Co[unci]l[o]r [Vinson] Knight, it was carried, that the resolution of the 12th day of April last, (exempting the Supervisor from working upon the Streets in the third Ward, until the first of October next,) be rescinded.

Adjourned Sine Die. May 21st 1841. John C. Bennett, Mayor. James Sloan, Recorder.[57]

*July 12, 1841; Monday.*[58] City Council convened by special appointment. Meeting opened by Prayer. Minutes of last Meeting Read.

The Mayor produced an address,[59] recommending that this

---

[55]Though not stated in the minutes, the *History of Church,* 4:353, records another topic of discussion: "I [Joseph Smith] spoke at length on the rights and privileges of the owners of the ferry, showing that the City Council has no right to take away ferry privileges, once granted, without damages being paid to the proprietor."

[56]See also *History of Church,* 4:361.

[57]The minutes fail to mention the arrest of Joseph Smith on June 5, 1841, but his arrest and subsequent trial are important to the history of the council. On June 4 he visited Illinois Governor Thomas Carlin in Quincy. Carlin had been requested by the governor of Missouri to extradite Smith. Although the governor said nothing to his visitor about it, he sent Thomas King, sheriff of Adams County, to arrest Smith, which occurred on June 5. A few days later, Smith would be released because of errors in the arresting papers. While in Nauvoo, he would be arrested on three separate occasions for Missouri-related crimes, which would lead the Nauvoo City Council to pass laws dealing with habeas corpus.

[58]See also *History of Church,* 4:383.

[59]The text of this address on the death of Illinois Senator Sidney H. Little was published in the *Times and Seasons,* July 15, 1841, 480: "In this great calamity, this unexpected and most painful bereavement, the Whig party have lost a faithful friend and able advocate, and the Democratic an honorable opponent – one who stood high in the affections of this people,

Council cause Sunday the 18th Inst to be set apart throughout this City as a Day of public fasting, Humiliation, & Prayer. ^on account of the Death of Senator Little,[60]^ ~~as~~ a feeble Testimonial of our high regard, & great respect, for his public Services & private Virtues, as a Statesman & Citizen. – Upon Motion, the Address was received, & the recommendation unanimously adopted.

Alderman [William] Marks presented a Petition to have a publick Highway located, to Commence at the North East Corner of Section 7 in Range 6 N[orth] 8 W[est] & continue West on the Section Line to the River. Co[unci]l[o]r J[oseph] Smith opposed, in as much as it w[oul]d cause fractional Lots. – It was agreed to, upon discussion, that the proposed Highway be put on a line on either side of the proposed Location, that is to say, on the best Ground North, or South, as the City Surveyor may think proper. It was then <u>Resolved</u> that a Survey be taken forthwith, & the Road be opened hereafter.

The Mayor Read a Law relative to the granting of Licences; and reccommended the making of an Ordinance to License sellers of Vinous Liquors[61]: subject was discussed, and it was Moved seconded & <u>carried</u>, that any person or persons in the City of Nauvoo be at liberty to sell vinous Liquors in any quantity, subject to the City Laws heretofore made, & now in force.

The Mayor stated that the principal object of the Meeting was relative to an alledged variance between the survey of the City Plot of Nauvoo, & the map ^as^ recorded. Some discussion took place upon the subject, after which the Council adjourned Sine Die. July 12th 1841. John C. Bennett, Mayor. James Sloan, Recorder.

---

honored and beloved by all good men. As a feeble testimonial of our high regard, and great respect, for his public services and private virtues, as a statesman and citizen, I would recommend that this council cause Sunday, the 18th inst., to be set apart throughout this city as a day of public fasting, humiliation, and prayer. On this occasion we should 'mourn with those who mourn, and weep with those who weep.'"

[60]Little had been key in helping pass the Nauvoo Charter. See Flanders, *Nauvoo Kingdom,* 217.

[61]In the nineteenth century, *liquor* meant "a liquid or fluid ... water, milk, blood, sap, juice, &c." The word *vinous* meant "pertaining to wine" and a *vinous liquor* was simply wine, whereas a *spiritous liquor* was a distilled ("refined") liquid (Noah Webster, *An American Dictionary of the English Language* [New York: S. Converse, 1828], s.vv.).

*September 4, 1841; Saturday.*[62] City Council met by appointment. Brigham Young was elected Co[unci]l[o]r in the place of Don C[arlos] Smith deceased.[63] John Taylor and Heber C. Kimball were elected Regents of the university of the City of Nauvoo, in the places of D[on] C[arlos] Smith and R[obert] B. Thompson, both deceased.[64] Orson Pratt was elected Professor of Mathematics in the University of the City of Nauvoo, and master of Arts conferred upon him.

Alderman [Daniel H.] Wells moved & it was seconded & carried that the City Assessor do lodge the usual Bonds with the City Recorder and proceed ^with^ the Assessment.

It was unanimously adopted that Alderman [William] Marks be, and he is hereby appointed one of the Committee, (in the stead of Wilson Law) to procure a Burying Ground. Upon Motion it was carried that the Committee to procure a Burying Ground be at liberty to purchase two Blocks for that purpose, one on each side of the City, and so as to agree with the City Plot. Moved seconded & carried that the Committee to procure a Burying Ground be at liberty to lay off the same, in such form as they may consider most suitable.

William D. Huntington was appointed Sexton. A Petition was granted (preferred by D[aniel] Cathcart[65] and others) to open and grade that part of Partridge Street, North of Cutler Street.

Upon Motion the following Resolution was passed.

Resolved by the City Council of the City of Nauvoo, That the

---

[62]See also *History of Church,* 4:414.

[63]The *Times and Seasons,* Aug. 16, 1841, 503, carried the news of the death of Don Carlos Smith: "The deceased had been afflicted some time, but nothing serious was apprehended, and, not until a day or two before his death was he thought to be dangerous. It was then ascertained that disease had been preying upon his system in such a manner, as baffled all medical skill to check; and he gradually sunk in the arms of death." He reportedly died from "quick consumption," or tuberculosis. His partner at the *Times and Seasons,* Robert B. Thompson, died from this same disease a short time later.

[64]Thompson was eulogized in the September 1, 1841, issue of the *Times and Seasons* as someone who was "esteemed and much beloved" and who was "filled with that dignity and honor befitting a man of God; being always ready to pursue the ard[u]ous duties assigned him, with cheerfulness and pleasure" (519).

[65]Daniel R. Cathcart was born in 1803 in New Jersey. He was a member of Zion's Camp and later helped to assist people moving out of Nauvoo.

City Recorder, procure a Seal for the ~~City of Nauvoo~~ Corporation, and that orders be issued by Him under said Seal, to draw monies out of the City Treasury, signed by the Mayor, and Countersigned by the Recorder.

It was Resolved by ^the^ City Council of the City of Nauvoo that the Bonds of the Assessor, & Collector, be one thousand Dollars. John S. Fulmre [Fullmer][66] appointed City Treasurer, and Bond to be given by him ^for^ One thousand Dollars.

Adjourned Sine Die. September 4th 1841. John C. Bennett, Mayor. James Sloan, Recorder.

*October 16, 1841; Saturday.* City Council met pursuant to special Appointment. Minutes of last Meeting Read.

A petition from Jacob G. Bigler[67] & others was presented and Read representing inconvenience to several Citizens for the want of a Street to Wit: – Beginning at the North end of a Street near the Brick House of Br[other] Nurse, thence Running North across the half Section the distance of half a Mile. Alderman [William] Marks, Co[unci]l[o]r [Charles C.] Rich & Alderman [Daniel H.] Wells were appointed a Committee to inspect the Street ment[ione]d in the above mentioned Petition, and to report thereon. It was moved seconded & carried that the Committee above named receive instructions and act in viewing other Streets deemed neccessary to be opened.

Upon Motion of Co[unci]l[o]r [Vinson] Knight it was adopted that the Mayor be instructed to direct the Supervisor of Streets to have work done in the neighborhood of Gen[era]l [Joseph] Smith's dwelling House. Upon Motion of Alderman Wells it was carried that a Committee be appointed to view the best Ground to open a Street or Streets near the Temple Lot to run from where a Street was

---

[66]John Solomon Fullmer was born in 1807 in Huntington, Pennsylvania. He was baptized in 1839. He served as Nauvoo Treasurer and as a clerk to Joseph Smith. At the exodus from Nauvoo, he was appointed to stay behind to help dispose of Church property. He migrated to Utah in 1848, where he served in the territorial legislature. He died in 1883.

[67]Jacob G. Bigler was born in 1813 in Shinnston, West Virginia. He was baptized in 1838 in Far West, Missouri, and moved to Quincy, Illinois, the next year. He later served as a bishop and probate judge in Illinois before moving to Utah in 1852. He died in 1907.

opened to, until it would extend to the Eastern limits of the Corporation being a Continuous Route, and that they report at next Meeting. – Upon motion, Ald[er]m[a]n Marks, Ald[er]m[a]n Wells & Co[unc]l[o]r [John P.] Greene were appointed a Committee to view the last mentioned Ground. – Upon Motion of Co[unci]l[o]r [John T.] Barnett it was carried that some work be done on Parley Street, and the Street opened.

Upon Motion of Co[unci]l[o]r Rich it was carried that the Committee for Purchasing Burying Ground, be instructed to report at next meeting. Upon Motion of Ald[er]m[a]n Wells it was carried that the City Assessor procure necessary Documents to enable him to Assess the City Taxes. Upon Motion of Ald[er]m[a]n Wells, Leonard Soby was appointed to act as City Marshall in the absence and until the return of the City Marshall who intends to go ^to^ [New] Orleans.

Upon Motion it was carried that the Recorder be instructed to notify the High Constables of this City That unless each of them do lodge a Bond (with sufficient sureties) for five hundred Dollars each, with the City Recorder before the next meeting of this Council that they will be removed from said office for such neglect. It was adopted by the City Council that the Bond of the Marshal be one thousand Dollars, and that Leonard Soby do lodge a Bond with sufficient Sureties for that am[oun]t with the City Recorder before the next meeting of the City Council.

It was moved and unanimously carried that the thanks of this Council be given to H[enry] G. Sherwood the City Marshal for his good conduct, Zeal, and indefatigable exertions, for the welfare of this City and the peace & tranquility of its inhabitants and Citizens since his appointment to Office, and which is highly esteemed and appreciated by us. It was moved and carried that the vote of thanks of this Council to the City Marshal be copied and certified by the Recorder and given to the Marshall.

Adjourned until 1 oclock on Saturday next to meet at Co[unci]l[o]r H[yrum] Smith's Office. October 16th 1841. John C. Bennett, Mayor. James Sloan, Recorder.

*October 23, 1841; Saturday.*[68] City Council met agreeable to Appoint-

---

[68]See also *History of Church,* 4:439.

ment. – Meeting opened by prayer. – Minutes of last meeting read and amended.

Upon Motion of Co[unci]l[o]r Joseph Smith the following Resolution was adopted: after considerable discussion

> Resolved by the City Council of the City of Nauvoo that Certain Houses in the City of Nauvoo be, and the same are hereby declared to be Nuisances, to Wit: a small frame House upon the Hill, near the Temple Lot,[69] and Old Houses upon Kimball's Ground, namely the House wherein Mrs. Huntington Died, the House next to it on the North side, and the House wherein the family of Fisk Died, and that the House on the Hill be removed by Monday night, and the other houses in a week from this day; and that all vicious Dogs are declared to be a Nuisance and Counsellor J[oseph] Smith is hereby appointed to see that they be destroyed, also to see that all other Nuisances be removed. Given at the City Council House, which we Certify. Oct[ober] 23rd. 1841. John C. Bennett Mayor. James Sloan Recorder.

Alderman Wells brought forward the report of the Committee on the Petition of Jacob G. Bigler & others (Dated September 3rd 1841) for opening a Street. Petition granted & Route continued South to Mulholland Street. The committee appointed to view the ground to open a Street or Streets near the Temple lot brought in their Report, which was amended, and adopted. That the Street be

---

[69]The house in question was a "grog shop kept by Pulaski S. Cahoon." To destroy it, the mayor asked Joseph Smith to call up "two companies of the Nauvoo Legion" (*History of Church*, 4:442). Some people objected to such a drastic measure. Sympathetic to the mayor, the *Times and Seasons* reported (Nov. 15, 1841, 598-99) that "it is known to many of our patrons, that a certain young man[,] very injudiciously, and contrary to the remonstrancies of his friends, and in violation of the ordinances of this city, not long since erected a small building, near the Temple square, avowedly for the purpose of transacting the business of a Grocer. Said building was for a short time occupied for that purpose" but had since attracted graffiti as "a monument for every fool to write upon and exhibit his folly." People suspected it of being a building that sheltered illicit transactions, so the mayor, according to the paper, was justified in bringing the military in to demolish it. For a continuation of the controversy, see the entry for November 1, 1841, and Pulaski's return to ask for a "License to retail Spirits" on December 29, 1843, and January 13, 1844, along with a more general discussion on June 8, 1844.

opened around Speer's Field, to meet the Prairie, and Mulholland Street to be opened entirely through the Fields.

Moved Seconded & carried that the Street East of Warsaw Street between Mulholland, & Parley Streets, be opened. Co[unci]l[o]r [John T.] Barnett moved and it was carried that the Street West of Winchesters between Parley Street and Mulholland Street be opened, and continued North to Young Street. Upon Motion of Co[unci]l[o]r Barnett one of the Committee on Burying Ground[,] further time was granted to next ^Meeting of Council^ to report fully.

It was moved & carried that Leonard Soby's resignation as High Constable of the City & declining to accept of the office of City Marshal be accepted.[70] Demick B. Huntington ^appointed^ City Marshal, ad Interim, and was sworn accordingly, to Act in the place of H[enry] G. Sherwood. Lewis Robison appointed High Constable of the 3rd Ward in the place of Leonard Soby Resigned. George W. Harris appointed High Constable of the 4th Ward in the place of James Alred Resigned.[71]

Gustavus Hills and Orson Spencer were appointed Aldermen and added to the City Council. John Taylor, Orson Pratt, Hugh McFaul & Heber C. Kimball were added Co[unci]l[o]rs to City Council.

Adjourned to Saturday next at one Oclock at same place. October 23rd 1841. John C. Bennett, Mayor. James Sloan, Recorder.

*October 30, 1841; Saturday.*[72] City Council met pursuant to adjourment: – Meeting opened by Prayer. Co[unci]l[o]r Brigham Young, who was formerly appointed a Co[unci]l[o]r[,] subscribed [to] his oath of office & the Aldermen & Co[unci]l[o]rs who were appointed at last meeting, subscribed [to] their oaths & were sworn: – Minutes of last Meeting read, & amended.

Co[unci]l[o]r [John T.] Barnett, one of the Committee respecting

---

[70]It is not known why Soby resigned, but it was not due to unworthiness or duress because at the Church's general conference in April 1841, he was appointed to the Nauvoo Stake High Council and asked to "travel and collect funds for the ... building of the temple" (*Times and Seasons,* Apr. 15, 1841, 388). It seems reasonable that Soby resigned in order to join the high council.

[71]Allred was appointed to the high council at the same time as Leonard Soby.

[72]See also *History of Church,* 4:442.

the Burying Ground, reported orally, and the report was accepted. A Petition was presented on behalf of Isaac Hill[73] relative to a Pauper who had been at his House for a length of time[;] it was referred to a Committee viz: John P. Greene and C[harles] C. Rich to enquire into the Circumstances & report generally.

Upon Motion of Co[unci]l[o]r Rich, it was carried that the Street east of Warsaw Street be opened from Parley Street to the City Limits. It was unanimously adopted ^that^ Mr. Styles Counsellor at Law and Judge [Sylvester] Emmons be permitted to act as Lawyers in the discussion of the subject matter of the fine imposed upon Mr. [John] Eagle.[74]

It was moved & carried that the City Council have Jurisdiction and authority over all Fines imposed by the City officers whether in retaining or remitting them. Co[unci]l[o]r Joseph Smith moved & it was seconded that the Fine imposed upon Mr. Eagle be remitted. Mr. Styles spoke at considerable length, on the part of Mr. Eagle, to have the fine imposed upon him, remitted. Judge Emmons spoke at length upon the propriety of a Confirmation of the fine.

Several of the City Council spoke on the motion in debate, and it was carried that the Council adjourn for two Hours: —

Council met pursuant to adjourment. Lyman Wight, Willard Richards & Wilford Woodruff were appointed Counsellors, in the City Council.[75] Hiram Kimball, & George W. Harris were appointed

---

[73]Isaac Hill was born in 1806 near Brighton, Pennsylvania. He was baptized in 1833 in Ohio and moved to Kirtland the next year. He marched in Zion's Camp in 1834. Later he immigrated to Utah with the main body of Saints and died in Idaho in 1879.

[74]According to David Osborn, Eagle was selling hard liquor, and when Joseph Smith tried to hand him a summons to court, Eagle took a swing at him. Even though Osborn says this occurred when Joseph Smith was mayor, which would be later than 1841, the context may imply an earlier date and possible connection to Cahoon's grog shop. See the "Biography of David Osborn Senior," ca. 1879, David Osborn Sr. Collection, J. Willard Marriott Library, University of Utah, online typescript at "David Osborn, 1807-1893," *BOAP*, www.boap.org.

[75]Woodruff recorded: "The city council met in the evening[;] during their business they Appointed me a member of the City Council of the city of Nauvoo. I was notifyed of my appointment in the morning" (Scott G. Kenney, ed., *Wilford Woodruff's Journal: 1833-1898*, 9 vols. [Midvale, UT: Signature Books, 1983-85], 2:135).

Aldermen of the City. W[illia]m. D. Huntington was appointed High Constable in the place of George W. Harris resigned – for the 4th Ward.

The Freedom of this City ^was^ Conferred upon Silvester Emmons Esqr. & George P. Styles Esqr. Lyman Wight, Willard Richards & George W. Harris were sworn into office.

Judge Emmons spoke on the case of Mr. Eagle. George P. Styles Esq. spoke on the same Case. The Mayor spoke to a considerable length. Co[unci]l[o]rs J[oseph] Smith, & Lyman Wight both spoke at length.[76] It was carried by Vote, that the Fine stand, & be, not Mitigated.

W[illia]m. D. Huntington was sworn, as High Constable. Counsellor J[oseph] Smith moved, that One hundred & twenty five Dollars, be appropriated for Damages, for the Building which was removed on the Hill, as a Nuisance.[77] The Motion was laid upon the Table.

Adjourned until Ten OClock A.M. on Monday next. October 30th 1841. John C. Bennett, Mayor. James Sloan, Recorder.

*November 1, 1841; Monday.*[78] City Council met pursuant to adjournment. – Meeting opened by Prayer. – Minutes of last Meeting Read.

It was unanimously adopted, that the Swamp directly West of Counsellor B[righam] Youngs House, be drained, so soon as circumstances permit.

Upon Motion of Co[unci]l[o]r J[oseph] Smith, the Motion which was laid on the Table on Saturday Evening, (for Damages for the Building removed on the Hill) was taken up. It was then adopted, that Judge [Sylvester] Emmons & Geo[rge] P. Styles Esq. be permitted to take part in discussing the Motion. It was moved, & seconded, that the Council act, as if the Petition was on the part of Pulaski

---

[76]Originally Joseph Smith supported the remittance of the fine but later changed his mind. The *History of the Church* (4:442) records: "I attended the city council, and spoke against the council remitting a fine assessed against John Eagle by a jury of twelve men, considering that the jury might be as sensible men as any of the city council, and I asked the council not to remit the fine."

[77]See entry for October 23, 1841.

[78]See also *History of Church,* 4:444-45.

L. Cahoon.[79] Several of the Co[unci]l[ors] said they must know the Pet[itione]rs Name, before they could act.

Alderman [Hiram] Kimball signed his Oath, & was sworn. Counsellor [Willard] Richards Signed his Oath. It was Moved & carried that the amount of Wages for the Supervisor of Streets, be fixed at One Dollar per Day.

A Bill was presented, to empower the Mayor to cause the Supervisor of Streets to appropriate the Road labour on the Streets Ordered to be opened by the City Council, & other Streets already opened, as nearly equal, as the Condition of said Streets, & the Interests of the public may require.[80] After considerable discussion by sev[era]l of the Council, the Mayor stated that he had not power to appropriate equitably upon Streets already opened, & those to be hereafter opened, & that the passage of the Law in question is necessary to enable him so to do. It was moved & seconded, that the Words, "Mayor and Supervisor" be struck out of the Bill, as an amendment, which was opposed, & after long discussion, The Original Motion was withdrawn.

Adjourned until Six OClock this Evening. Council Met pursuant to adjournment. Sidney Rigdon sent in his Resignation as a Counsellor which was accepted.[81] William Law was unanimously appointed one of the City Council, in the stead of Sidney Rigdon.

Sidney Rigdon was duly appointed City Attorney. A Petition was presented from Pulaski ^S.^ Cahoon, claiming Damages for the House which was removed on the Hill as a Nuisance, which was Read, & liberty given to amend, which was done.[82] George P. Styles

---

[79]Pulaski Stephen Cahoon was born in 1820 in Harpersfield, Ohio, and died in 1892. He was the son of Reynolds Cahoon. For more, see Gary James Bergera, "John C. Bennett, Joseph Smith, and the Beginnings of Mormon Plural Marriage in Nauvoo," *John Whitmer Historical Association Journal* 25 (2005): 69.

[80]All male inhabitants of the city were required to devote three days per year to keeping the streets in repair. The wording of the city charter (Section 26) seemed to exempt citizens from the hard work of building new roads (*History of Church,* 4:244), which Smith wanted to change so the city could utilize its volunteer labor not just in road maintenance but also in new construction.

[81]Rigdon resigned "on account of ill health" (*History of Church,* 4:445), but was immediately sworn in as city attorney.

[82]See entry for October 23, 1841.

Esq. & Judge [Sylvester] Emmons both spoke in Support of the claim of the Pet[itione]r. Several of the Council also spoke at length. It was moved, seconded, & carried, that the Council approve of the Acts of the Mayor, as respects the removal & destruction of the Nuisance. A Motion was put, whether the Am[oun]t of Damages claimed, be paid to Pet[itione]r, which was Lost.

Adjourned until One OClock P.M. on Saturday next to meet at same place. Nov[embe]r 1st 1841. John C. Bennett, Mayor. James Sloan, Recorder.

*November 6, 1841; Saturday.*[83] City Co[unci]l met pursuant to adjournment. Meeting opened by Prayer. Minutes of last Meeting Read. Co[unci]l[o]r W[ilford] Woodruff was Sworn into office, and subscribed his Oath.

The Petition of James Sloan City Recorder relative to a Desk, Books, & Stationary, was presented, & upon Motion, referred to Committee, namely, Co[unci]l[o]rs Hyrum Smith, & John P. Greene. Upon Motion of Co[unci]l[o]r Greene, it was Resolved, that the City Recorder do lodge the usual Bond, with Surety, in the Sum of Five Hundred Dollars, as Recorder of this City.

The Committee on Isaac Hill's Petition brought forward their report which was received, and after discussion liberty was granted, to Pet[itione]r to withdraw his Petition.

Upon Motion of Co[unci]l[o]r Greene the following Resolution was agreed to

> Resolved by the City Council of the City of Nauvoo. That this Council meet on every Saturday Evening at Six Oclock to discuss the Laws of the City, and other business. – Nov[embe]r 6th 1841.

Upon Motion of Co[ounci]l[o]r [Charles C.] Rich the foll[owin]g resol[utio]n was agreed to.

> Resolved by the City Council of the City of Nauvoo. That this Council meet in Counsellor Hyrum Smith's Office and that he recieve pay for the use of the Room and for Fuel, & Candles, out of the City Treasury.

---

[83]See also *History of Church,* 4:445.

Upon Motion of Co[ounci]l[o]r [John T.] Barnett the foll[owin]g Resol[utio]n was agreed to.

> Resolved by the City Council of the City of Nauvoo. That the City Assessor be instructed to assess all property both real & personal within the City Limits, which is Taxable by the State, for state, or County purposes.

Adjourned to 6 oclock P.M. on Saturday next at same place. Nov[embe]r 6th. 1841. John C. Bennett. Mayor. James Sloan, Recorder.

*November 13, 1841; Saturday.*[84] Council met agreeable to adjourment: – Meeting opened by Prayer. – Minutes of last meeting Read.

Co[ounci]l[o]r W[illia]m Law sworn and subscribed his oath of office. Co[ounci]l[o]r Hyrum Smith Chairman of the Committee to whom the Recorders Petition was referred, presented their report which was accepted, and the following resolution was agreed to.

> It was unanimously adopted by the City Council of the City of Nauvoo, That the Recorder provide a Desk and suitable Books of Record, and also Stationary, and draw money from the City Treasury, to pay for the same and the above Property be kept at the Council House.

The Recorder presented his Bond which was accepted and it was adopted that it be lodged with the Treasurer & it was handed to the Marshal for that purpose.

Co[ounci]l[o]r Hyrum Smith presented a Petition from the City Surveyor, Claiming payment for surveying Young Street[,] Parley Street and other Streets: which was accepted &. It was unanimously adopted by the City Council of the City of Nauvoo that the Claim of the City Surveyor for a sum of Thirty two Dollars, be allowed.

Co[ounci]l[o]r J[oseph] Smith presented the following Ordinance which passed unanimously, after discussion

An Ordinance in relation to Appeals.

Sec. 1. Be it ordained by the City Council of the City of

[84]See also ibid., 447-48.

Nauvoo, that when an appeal is taken from any decision of the Mayor or Aldermen, to the Municipal Court, the person appealing shall give notice of his intention, immediately on the Rendition of the Judgment, and within five Days thereafter he shall file an approved Bond with the Treasurer of the City for all Costs & Costs that may accrue of which he shall give due Notice to the officer before whom the Judgment was obtained. – This act to take effect & be in force, from and after its Passage.
**Passed Nov[embe]r. 13th 1841. John C. Bennett, Mayor. James Sloan Recorder.**

Co[ounci]l[o]r J[oseph] Smith presented the following Ordinance which passed unanimously after discussion.

An Ordinance fixing the Compensation of
the Mayor and Recorder of the City of Nauvoo.

Sec. 1. Be it ordained by the City Council of the City of Nauvoo. That the Mayor & Recorder shall receive one hundred Dollars, each, for the current year, as a compensation for their Services. This Act to take effect and be in force, from and after its Passage. –
**Passed Nov[embe]r 13th. 1841. John C. Bennett, Mayor. James Sloan. Recorder**

Co[ounci]l[o]r J[oseph] Smith presented the following Ordinance. which passed Unanimously.

AN ORDINANCE CONCERNING
VAGRANTS AND DISORDERLY PERSONS.[85]

Sec. 1. Be it ordained by the City Council of the City of Nauvoo. That all ~~persons~~ vagrants, Idle or disorderly persons; Persons found ^drunk^ in or about the Streets; all suspicious persons; Persons who have no fixed place of Residence, or visible means of support, or cannot give a good account of themselves; persons guilty of Profane or indecent language, or behaviour; persons guilty of using indecent, impertinent, or unbecoming language towards any City officer when in the discharge of his duty, or of menacing, threatening, or otherwise obstructing, said

[85]This was published in *Times and Seasons,* Dec. 1, 1841, 622.

office, shall on conviction thereof before the Mayor, or Municipal Court, be required to enter into security for good behaviour for a reasonable time, and indemnify the corporation against any charge, and in case of refusal or inability to give security, they shall be confined to labour for a time not exceeding ninety days, or be fined in any sum not exceeding five hundred Dollars; or be imprisoned not exceeding six months; or all; at the discretion of ~~the~~ ^said^ Mayor or Court. This act to take effect, and be in force from and after its Passage. –

**Passed Nov[embe]r 13th. 1841. John C. Bennett, Mayor. James Sloan Recorder.**

Co[unci]l[o]r [Willard] Richards moved that the Resol[utio]n passed on the 6th Inst. relative to the Assessment of City Property, be reconsidered, & gave his Reasons therefor. The Mayor gave an explination of the Rights, & powers given by the City Charter, & the Right of the City Council to Tax the Citizens.[86] Co[ounci]l[o]r J[oseph] Smith spoke to considerable length, on the Subject of the right of Taxation, & the Taxation laid on by the Country, & so forth. Upon which the Motion was withdrawn.[87]

Co[unci]l[o]r Richards moved that all Dogs in the City, be assessed Five Dollars per Head.

Co[ounci]l[o]r J[oseph] Smith proposed an Amendment, that it be 12-2 each.[88] After considerable discussion, the amendment was lost by Vote. – Orig[ina]l Motion, also Lost.

Adjourned to Saturday next, at 6 Oclock, to same place. Nov[embe]r 13th 1841. John C. Bennett, Mayor. James Sloan, Recorder.

*November 20, 1841; Saturday.* City Council met pursuant to adjournment. – Meeting opened by Prayer. – Minutes of last Meeting Read.

Co[unci]l[o]r [John P.] Greene moved an Ordinance concerning Fire Arms, Parties litigant, & Witnesses, which upon discussion was amended, & ultimately referred to a Select Committee, to wit, Dan[ie]l H. Wells, Wilson Law, & William Marks.

---

[86]Bennett is referring to Section 8 of the Nauvoo Charter.

[87]The motion was withdrawn because Smith claimed "the expense of the City did not require [taxation] at present" (*History of Church,* 4:448).

[88]Presumably, Smith wanted to increase the dog tax to $12.20 per head.

Co[unci]l[o]r [Willard] Richards moved that it be the duty of the Recorder to keep a detached File of all City Ordinances for the benefit of the City Council. Co[unci]l[o]r [Lyman] Wight spoke in opposition. – Co[unci]l[o]r [Vinson] Knight wished the Res[o]l[utio]n to pass. The Recorder obtained liberty to speak, & explained the manner in which he intended to keep the City Records. Co[unci]l[o]r Wilson Law said, he considered an Index sufficient. Co[unci]l[o]r Richards withdrew his Motion.

The Mayor explained the Duties of the Mayor & Aldermen, in Criminal, & Civil Cases, as well as in their different capacities, of Justices, & Judges.

Adjourned to 6 oclock P.M. on Saturday next. Nov[embe]r 20th 1841. John C. Bennett, Mayor. James Sloan, Recorder.

*November 27, 1841; Saturday.*[89] City Council met pursuant to Adjournment. Meeting opened by Prayer. – Minutes of last Meeting Read.

Co[unci]l[o]r Hyrum Smith presented a Petition from the City Surveyor, upon which the following Resol[utio]n was adopted.

> Resolved by the City Council of the City of Nauvoo, that the Certificate of the City Surveyor, for Surveying the first Street South of Lumber Street, be received, & that he be allowed the Sum of Six Dollars and fifty Cents therein set forth.

Co[unci]l[o]r Wilson Law brought forward the Report of the Committee, to whom the Ordinance concerning firearms, Parties litigant, & Witnesses, was referred, which was adopted, in the following Ordinance, to wit.

> An Ordinance concerning Fire Arms, & Parties litigant.[90]
>
> Sec. 1. Be it ordained by the City Council of the City of Nauvoo That if any person will fire or shoot a Gun, Pistol, or other fire Arms (Idly or for sport or amusement) in the night or on Sunday, the person so doing shall forfeit and pay a fine not exceeding fifty Dollars: Provided that nothing herein contained shall be construed to affect any officer of this City, for ^firing or^ Shooting as aforesaid while in the ~~discharge~~ ^Execution^ of his duty.

---

[89]See also ibid., 461.

[90]This was published in the *Times and Seasons,* Jan. 1, 1842, 653-54.

Sec. 2. That if any person shall prosecute another before the authorities of this City (in a Criminal case) & fail to procure a Conviction said person shall be Taxed with the Costs of Suit if said authorities shall consider it a malicious prosecution, if not the City shall be liable for the costs thereof. This ordinance to take effect and be in force from and after its Passage.

**Passed Nov[embe]r 27th. 1841. John C. Bennett, mayor. James Sloan Recorder.**

Co[unci]l[o]r Joseph Smith presented the following Ordinance Which passed unanimously after being read three times, and the Rules dispensed with.

An Ordinance in Relation to
Hawkers,[91] Pedlars, & Public shows & Exhibitions.[92]

Sec. 1. Be it ordained by the City Council of the City of Nauvoo. That it shall not be lawful for any person or persons, usually denominated hawkers and Pedlars, to hawk or carry about from place to place in this City any goods, wares or merchandize, excepting such as are manufactored within the Limits of this Corporation. Who shall not, previously to selling or offering for sale, such goods wares or Merchandize have obtained a License therefor from this Corporation, signed by the Mayor & countersigned by the Recorder. for which he, she, or they shall at the time of obtaining the same, pay a sum not exceeding fifty Dollars nor less than ten Dollars; & such person or persons as aforesaid, who may be found hawking about any goods or merchandize, except as aforesaid & selling or offering the same for sale without a license therefor, shall forfeit and pay for each & every such offence the sum of twenty Dollars: and any person or persons who shall refuse to exhibit his, her, or their license so obtained, upon being required by any Citizen so to do, shall forfeit and pay the sum of five Dollars, for each & every such ~~off~~ refusal: provided, that nothing in the foregoing shall be construed to require a License for hawking about for sale any articles

[91]That is, someone who sells items by shouting in the public streets.

[92]This was published in the *Times and Seasons,* Dec. 15, 1841, 637. The authority to pass this ordinance was derived from Section 12 of the Nauvoo Charter.

of Poultry, fish, meat, bread stuffs, butter, cheese, Eggs, or vegatables; or such perishable merchandize as is used for food.

Sec. 2. That all Licenses granted by this corporation to Hawkers or Pedlars shall expire on the first Monday of November next following the date of such License.

Sec. 3. That any person or persons desiring to exhibit with this Corporation any curiosities of nature or art, not inconsistent with decency, or contrary to good morals, shall procure a License as aforesaid, for which he, she, or they shall pay a sum not exceeding fifty Dollars. Nor less than ten Dollars; and the said License shall continue in force for one week and no longer: and such person or persons as aforesaid, who may be found in open violation of this section, shall forfeit and pay for each & every such offence the sum of fifty Dollars: all exhibitions inconsistent with decency or contrary to good morals, are expressly prohibited under the penalty of one hundred Dollars for each offence.

Sec. 4. This Ordinance to take effect & be in force from & after its Passage.

**^Passed^ Nov[embe]r 27th 1841. John C. Bennett, Mayor. James Sloan Recorder.**

Upon Motion the following Resolution was adopted.

Resolved by the City Council of the City of Nauvoo that the City Treasurer be authorized by the City Council to procure seats for the use of said Council.

The Mayor informed the Aldermen last appointed that they are to represent the respective Wards Wherein they reside.

Upon Motion the following Resolution was adopted.

Resolved by the City Council of the City of Nauvoo that a majority of the entire City Council be considered requisite, and deemed necessary, to transact business in Council from time to time hereafter.

Upon Motion the foll[owin]g Resol[utio]n was unanimously adopted.

Resolved by the City Council of the City of Nauvoo, that the authorities of this City be authorized, to use a discretionary power in sending to a distance for Persons at the expence of the City, in order to ferret out the perpetrators of Crimes, or any secret combination against the peace of Society.[93]

Adjourned to 6 oclock next Saturday Evening at same place. Nov[embe]r 27th 1841. John C. Bennett, Mayor. James Sloan, Recorder.

*December 4, 1841; Saturday.*[94] City Council met pursuant to adjou^r^-ment: – Meeting Opened by Alderman [George W.] Harris by Prayer: Minutes of last Meeting read.

A Petition for the removal of the Marshal was presented & accepted containing a charge of Palpable omission of duty.[95] Ald[er]-m[a]n [Daniel H.] Wells ^moved^ that the Marshal be removed from Office. Mr. [Hiram] Kimball sworn and examined. – Cross Exam[ine]d by the Marshall.

Alderman Sam[ue]l H. Smith sworn & Examined. George Morey Sworn & exam[ine]d & Cross Exam[ine]d by the Marshall. Co[un-ci]l[o]r J[oseph] Smith sworn & Exam[ine]d, & Interrogated by the Marshall. W[illia]m D. Huntington Sworn & Exam[ine]d, & Inter[rogate]d by the Marshal.

Ald[er]m[a]n Wells, Smith, Harris, & [Orson] Spencer, & Counsellors [Charles C.] Rich, [Lyman] Wight, W[illia]m Law, Wilson Law, & O[rson] Pratt took part in the discussion, and a vote was taken ^by^ Ayes, ^for^ & Noes ^ag[ain]st removal,^ as follows. Ayes. Wells,

---

[93]Crime was a great concern to the city council. The apostles, in a published statement, said "we cannot and will not, countenance rogues, thieves, and scoundrels, knowingly; and we hereby warn them that the law will be as rigorously enforced against them in this place as in any other, as we consider such characters as a curse to society ... There is no poison that is and ought to be despised more than [that of] the thief" (*Times and Seasons,* Dec. 1, 1841, 616). One reason for this concern was because rumors were spreading that Joseph Smith and the Church "sanction and approbate the members of the said Church in stealing property from those persons who do not belong to the said Church" (ibid; see also *History of Church,* 4:460-62).

[94]See also *History of Church,* 4:467.

[95]The marshal, Henry Sherwood, had withdrawn when attempting to serve a warrant where his "life would have been endangered," for which Smith thought he should be forgiven (*History of Church,* 4:467).

Marks, Wilson Law, & [John T.] Barnett. 4. Noes. S[amuel] H. Smith, J[oseph] Smith, Rich, W[illia]m Law, Harris, Pratt, Wight, [Gustavus] Hills, Spencer, & the Mayor. 10.

Upon Motion of Ald[er]m[a]n Wells the following Resol[utio]n was adopted

> Resolved by the City Council of the City of Nauvoo, that the Resolution of this council of the 6th Instant (whereby the time of Meeting of this Council was appointed to be at Six Oclock on every Saturday ^Evening^ be rescinded.

Upon Motion of Co[unci]l[o]r Rich the foll[owin]g Resol[utio]n was adopted

> Resolved by the City Council of the City of Nauvoo, that this Council do meet in future, upon the 1st & 3rd Saturday of every Month.

The Council then sat with closed doors for some time & Adjourned until this day two weeks at the usual time & Place. Dec[embe]r 4th 1841. John C. Bennett, Mayor. James Sloan, Recorder.

*December 18, 1841; Saturday.*[96] City Council met pursuant to adjournment: – Meeting opened by Prayer. – Minutes of last Meeting read. The Mayor presented an address or communication from ^him to^ the City Council, respecting James Gordon Bennett,[97] Editor of the New York Weekly Herald. Whereupon.

Gen[era]l J[oseph] Smith offered the following Resolutions: to Wit.[98]

> Resolved by the City Council of the City of Nauvoo, that the high minded & honorable Editor, of the New York Weekly Herald –

---

[96]See also ibid., 477-78.

[97]James Gordon Bennett was born in 1795 in Scotland and came to America in 1819. He became a popular reporter at the *New York Enquirer*, then assistant editor for the combined *Enquirer* and *Courier*. In 1835 he launched his own daily newspaper, the *New York Herald*, which revolutionized reporting, selling 15,000 copies an issue. He died in 1872.

[98]The resolutions were published in the *Times and Seasons*, Jan. 1, 1842, 653.

James Gordon Bennett, Esq. is deserving of the lasting gratitude of this Community, for his very liberal & unprejudiced Course towards us as a People, in giving us a fair hearing in his Paper, – thus enabling us to reach the ears of a Portion of the Community, who, otherwise, would ever have remained ignorant of Our principles & practices.

Resolved, that, we recommend to our fellow Citizens to subscribe for the "New York Weekly Herald," & thus be found patronising true Merit, Industry, & Enterprize.[99]

Which Resolutions were carried as follows: to Wit. Yeas J[oseph] Smith, H[yrum] Smith, C[harles] C. Rich, B[righam] Young, H[eber] C. Kimball, Hugh McFall; J[ohn] Taylor, W[ilford] Woodruff, W[illia]m Law, W[illard] Richards, O[rson] Pratt, (Counsellors.) – W[illiam] Marks, N[ewel] K. Whitney, S[amuel] H. Smith, O[rson] Spencer, G[eorge] W. Harris, G[ustavus] Hills, H[eber] Kimball, (Aldermen,) John C. Bennett, (Mayor.) 19. – Nays None. –

Counsellor Kimball presented a petition from Alanson Ripley & others, to have a Street opened, which was referred to a Committee, viz, Co[unci]l[o]r J[oseph] Smith, H[eber] C. Kimball, and C[harles] C. Rich.

Co[unci]l[o]r J[oseph] Smith stated Circumstances respecting a communication he had received, relative to Mobocracy, & said he wished a Law made, that persons notifying others to leave their peaceable Homes, could be dealt with rigorously. The Mayor addressed the Council, & related a Circumstance which he stated had been told to some Person concerning him, the Mayor, & which statement, he declared to be false, & unfounded.[100]

Upon Motion of Co[unci]l[o]r J[oseph] Smith, it was Resolved

---

[99]The *Times and Seasons* boasted that, in frequently reprinting articles from the *New York Herald*, it had never "garbled" them. It praised the newspaper for being "free from the prejudices and superstitions of the age. That deservedly popular, and widely circulated paper, has been of incalculable benefit to us, as a people, by conveying to the ears of thousands, who would otherwise have remained in ignorance[,] correct information in relation to our doctrines and practices–our men and our measures" (ibid., 652-53).

[100]It is not known what rumor was circulating about Joseph Smith, but he had begun to take plural wives in April and by this time had five wives including his first, Emma (George D. Smith, *Nauvoo Polygamy: "... But We Called It Celestial Marriage"* [Salt Lake City: Signature Books, 2008], 621).

That the first St[reet] South of the Temple, (Mulholland St.,) be carried out to the extent of the City.

Adjourned until the first Saturday in Jany. next. December 18th 1841. John C. Bennett, Mayor. James Sloan, Recorder.

# 2.
# "Joseph Smith, Mayor" 1842

†*January 1, 1842; Saturday.*[1] City Co[unci]l met pursuant to adjournment, – Meeting opened by Prayer. – Minutes of last Meeting Read. – John S. Fulmer, Sworn as Treasurer.

Co[unci]l[o]r [Charles C.] Rich presented a Pet[itio]n from G. W. Hickerson & others, as a Remonstrance against opening Water Street, which was referred to (Co[unci]l[or]s J[oseph] Smith, [Heber C.] Kimball, & Rich,) the Committee to whom the Pet[itio]n for opening that St[reet], was heretofore referred.

The Council then Sat as a High Court of Impeachment in a Case, wherein Urial C. Nickerson was Complainant, and Gustavus Hills, (Alderman) was Defendant. Thomas Grover acted as Attorney or Assistant to Compl[ainan]t, Judge [Sylvester] Emmons on part of Def[endan]t – both by permission.

The Charges against Def[endan]t were for acting corruptly, partially, Erroneously, or through Error of Judgment, upon the hearing, & in the decision of Causes before him, as an Alderman of this City, & for refusing to give a Transcript of proceedings had before him as an Alderman, as will appear by the Charges filed. The following are the Names of Witnesses produced, Sworn, and examined.

---

[1]See also Joseph Smith, *History of the Church of Jesus Christ of Latter-day Saints,* 7 vols. (Salt Lake City: Deseret News, 1902-12), 4:490.

Thomas Grover. D. T. Smith, – Urial C. Nickerson, Hiram Dayton, Elias Higbee, Winsor P. Lyon, Stephen Markham, David Sessions,[2] & Levi Bracken.[3]

The Def[endan]t spoke briefly upon part of the Evidence. Judge Emmons spoke also upon part of Def[endan]t. Thomas Grover spoke to Evidence, on part of Compl[ainan]t. The Compl[ainan]t spoke upon the Testimony given – The following Counsellors spoke, & adverted to the Evidence. – (The Mayor made Observations,) To Wit, Joseph Smith, William Law, John Taylor, & B[righam] Young.

A Vote was then called for, by Ayes & Noes, whether Alderman Hills be guilty of all, or any, of the Charges, preferred against him. The number of the Council present was 17, who Voted in the Affirmative for his Acquittal, without a dissenting Voice.[4]

Adjourned until Saturday Ev[enin]g Jan[uar]y 15th. Inst. January 1st. 1842. John C. Bennett, Mayor. James Sloan, Recorder.

*January 15, 1842; Saturday.*[5] City Co[unci]l met pursuant to adjournment, – Meeting opened, by Prayer, – Minutes of last Meeting Read.

A Petition was presented on behalf of Dimick B. Huntington & Alanson Ripley, praying that Lumber Street be opened to the full extent, as it is obstructed by [a] Fence, which was referred to Ald[er]m[a]n [William] Marks, Co[unci]l[o]rs H[yrum] Smith, & W[illard] Richards. Ald[er]m[a]n Marks moved a Pet[itio]n from Joseph Fisher & others, for opening Back Street from Mulholland Street, to Munson Street, referred to a Committee of Ald[er]m[a]n Marks, Co[unci]l[o]r [John T.] Barnett, & Ald[er]m[a]n [Gustavus] Hills.

The Pet[itio]n of John Burscough[6] & others respecting a Street, was referred to a Committee, Viz Aldermen [George W.] Harris, & Marks, & Co[unci]l[o]r [Charles C.] Rich. The Pet[itio]n of Hyrum

---

[2]David Sessions was born in 1789 in Vershire, Vermont. He was baptized in 1835. In 1847 he migrated to Utah in one of the first companies to arrive in the Salt Lake Valley. He died in Utah in 1850.

[3]Levi Bracken was born in 1792 in Westmoreland, Pennsylvania. He was baptized in 1835 in Indiana and died in Nebraska in 1852.

[4]Whatever the issue was, it was sufficiently without merit that Nickerson would be fined on February 17 (see below) for "malicious prosecution" and charged the council's expenses for hearing the case.

[5]See also *History of Church*, 4:494.

[6]John Burscough was born in 1795 in Longton, England.

Smith for a Street, to be opened, was referred to Co[unci]l[o]rs [John P.] Greene, H[yrum] Smith & W[illia]m Law.

The Pet[itio]n of Jam[e]s Alred Supervisor of Streets, allowed, for a Sum of $36.12-½, for 35¼ days Work on Streets, & 87-½ ^c[en]ts^ Smith work included. The Petition of Alanson Ripley City Surveyor, was allowed, for Three Dollars, for Surveying the first Street East of Warsaw Street.

The Petition of Ebenezer Robinson for $52.50 was allowed, as per his Account [which was] furnished. The Petition of Dimick B. Huntington was allowed, for Five Dollars, for Summoning [the] City Council, & noticing Aldermen to lodge Bonds, noticing Assessor & Collector, & Leonard Soby to do the like, also the High Constables & posting up Ordinances, & Resolutions.

Co[unci]l[o]r Wilson Law moved a Resolution, that this Co[unci]l take it into consideration, whether this Co[unci]l shall have pay for their Services, & if so, what Amount. Co[unci]l[o]rs H[yrum] Smith, Barnett, & Wilson Law all spoke in favour of the Motion, Co[unci]l[o]r B[righam] Young said he would wish to have a full Meeting, or at least, another Meeting, before a Law would be passed, & stated, he considers the People are Poor. Ald[er]m[e]n Harris & [Samuel H.] Smith spoke, the latter to great length, & Co[unci]l[o]r H[yrum] Smith spoke again, all in support of the Motion, &, It was Resolved, that the City Council shall have pay for their Services.

Co[unci]l[o]r Wilson Law Moved a Resol[utio]n that the City Council & Committees, shall be paid the sum of Two Dollars per day, each, for their Services as Co[unci]l[o]rs & Committees of this Council, & spoke in support of it, Co[unci]l[o]r Hyrum Smith, Ald[er]m[e]n Smith & Marks, as also others of the Co[unci]l spoke in favour of the Resol[utio]n. An Amendment was moved, that the Sum be made One Dollar each per day, which was lost by Vote, & the Original Resolution carried.

Co[unci]l[o]r H[yrum] Smith applied on the part of Theodore Turley, that he be instructed in his Duty as Weigher & Sealer. Mr. Turley was permitted to speak, & he gave an Idea of the mode of adjusting & Sealing Weights & Measures. This matter was discussed at some length by the Co[unci]l but no decision made.

The Mayor appointed the following Committees. Committee of Ways & Means – Joseph Smith, D[aniel] H. Wells, & B[righam]

Young. On Claims – C[harles] C. Rich, W[illia]m Law, & H[eber] Kimball. On public Grounds – W[illia]m Marks, H[yrum] Smith, & W[illard] Richards. On Finance – Wilson Law, H[eber] C. Kimball, & G[ustavus] Hills. On Municipal Laws – J[oseph] Smith, O[rson] Pratt, & John Taylor.

Upon Motion of B[righam] Young, It was Resolved, that the City Marshal receive the same pay for his Time as one of the City Counsellors. Upon Motion of Ald[er]m[a]n Marks, It was Resolved that the Sexton have Two Dollars for digging each Grave, & interring a Body, & that no other Person or Persons shall have the priviledge so to do, in any Case, unless by permission of the Sexton, and that the Sexton do keep a Record of all the Interments.

Upon Motion of Co[unci]l[o]r Wilson Law, that this Council procure a complete plot of the City, for their use, the same was referred to the Committee of Ways & Means. Upon Motion of ^Co[unci]l-o]r^ B[righam] Young, that this Co[unci]l appoint a Committee to buy a Lot for, & prepare a House for the Council, It was Ordered that the Resolution be laid on the Table. The Subject Matter of the burying Ground was spoken upon, as regards the obtaining of a Title Deed for same.

Adjourned until Saturday next, to hold a Special Meeting at Six Oclock P.M. at the Co[unci]l Room. Jan[uar]y 15th 1842. John C. Bennett, Mayor. James Sloan, Recorder.

*January 22, 1842; Saturday.*[7] The City Council met pursuant to adjournment. Meeting opened by Prayer. Minutes of last Meeting Read.

The Mayor presented a Communication to the City Council Containing several Rules & Regulations for the City Council, embracing the Order of proceeding in Council, the Rights & priviledges of the Members, & Duties of the Officers &c, which was read, & referred to the Committee on Municipal Laws.

The Committee to whom a Petition was referred, respecting a Street which Co[unci]l[o]r Hyrum Smith, Petitioned for, & wished to be opened, brought in their Report, which was received, & the Petition granted, by the following Resol[utio]n.

---

[7]See also *History of Church,* 4:501. As mentioned in the preface, the "Record of Proceedings of the City Council" begins to change its format here from a narrative account to a more limited record of resolutions and ordinances. The new format will continue through August 12, 1843.

Resolved by the City Council of the City of Nauvoo, that Harris Street be opened from the River, running East till near Mr. Baties West Line, thence South One Block thence East to the East Line of Mr. Moffitts Farm, thence South two Blocks to the North Line of Sam[ue]l Bents Farm, thence East to the Eastern Bounds of the City.

**Passed Jan[uar]y 22nd 1842. John C. Bennett, Mayor. James Sloan — Recorder.**

The Committee to whom was referred the Petition for the opening [of] a Street running on the South Side of the City, between Hibbard & Doil, from the River East to the limits of the City, brought in their Report, upon which Co[unci]l[o]r [John T.] Barnett, Ald[er]m[a]n [George W.] Harris, Co[unci]l[o]r [Charles C.] Rich, Ald[er]m[e]n [Daniel H.] Wells & [William] Marks spoke in debate, & same was adopted as follows.

Resolved ^by^ the City Council of the City of Nauvoo, that the Street Seven Rods North of the Line running on the South Side of the City, (between Hibbard & Doil from the River East to the limits of the City,) be opened, as it has been Surveyed, & is on the best Ground, & that it vary a little where it is now laid, from the Creek by Caspers East, and to extend no further West at this time, than the first Street East of Warsaw Street.

**Passed Jan[uar]y 22nd. 1842. John C. Bennett, Mayor. James Sloan Recorder.**

The Committee on the Petition for the opening of Back Street, brought in their Report, which was accepted. Co[unci]l[o]r Barnett, Ald[er]m[e]n Wells & [Gustavus] Hills spoke in discussion & the following Resolution was adopted.

Resolved by the City Council of the City of Nauvoo, that Back Street be opened from Mulholland Street to Munson Street.

**Passed Jan[uar]y 22nd. 1842. John C. Bennett, Mayor. James Sloan Recorder.**

The Committee of Ways & Means brought forward their report respecting a Plot of the City, which was accepted, & adopted by the following Resol[utio]n.

Resolved by the City council of the City of Nauvoo, that a complete Plot of the City be procured for the use of the City Council. **Passed Jan[uar]y 22nd. 1842. John C. Bennett, Mayor. James Sloan Recorder.**

The Mayor presented an Ordinance for fixing the Compensation of the City Council, & for other purposes, which rec[eive]d the first & second Readings, & was ordered to be Engrossed.[8] Co[unci]l[o]r H[yrum] Smith spoke in support of the Bill. The Mayor spoke in explination of the Views with which he prepared the Bill. Ald[er]m[a]n Wells moved an Amendment to strike out the second Saturday in each Month, & insert the first Monday in each Quarter, commencing on the first Monday in March next, – Which Amendment was lost on Vote. The Bill received the third Reading, & passed, by the above Title, to Wit.

An Ordinance fixing the Compensation of the City Council, and for other purposes.[9]

Sec. 1. Be it Ordained by the City Council of the City of Nauvoo, that from & after the passage of this Ordinance, the City Council shall meet on the 2nd Saturday of every Month at 10 OClock A.M. & shall continue in Session during the day, & evening, if the business of the City requires it, allowing one hour for Dinner, and One for Supper;[10] & the said Monthly Meetings shall be called "The Regular Meetings of the City Council."

Sec. 2. Each Member of the City Council & the Recorder, & Marshal, shall be allowed Two Dollars per Day for attendance, Co-operation, & Services, at said Regular Meetings: & each Person aforesaid shall be fined in the Sum of Two Dollars for neglecting to attend at any such regular Meeting, without an

---

[8]In this context, *engross* meant "to copy in a large hand; to write a fair, correct copy, in large or distinct, legible characters, for preservation or duration; as records of public acts, on paper or parchment" (Noah Webster, *An American Dictionary of the English Language* [New York: S. Converse, 1828], s.v. "engross").

[9]This was published in the *Times and Seasons,* Feb. 15, 1842, 701.

[10]In nineteenth-century America, dinner was still, as in Europe, "the meal taken about the middle of the day; or the principal meal of the day, eaten between noon and evening," while "supper" was "the evening meal" (Webster, *American Dictionary,* s.vv. "dinner," "supper").

excuse satisfactory to the City Council, & for each part of a Day so attended, or neglected, a proportionate allowance, or fine, shall be granted, or assessed, as the case may be.

Sec. 3. It is hereby made the duty of the Recorder to keep a just & accurate Record of the Members present, including the Recorder & Marshal, at every such regular Meeting; together with a full list of Absentees, which list shall be returned to the Mayor for collection of Fines quarterly.

Sec. 4. Special Meetings of the City Council, called by order of the Mayor, by Summons or otherwise, shall be governed by the aforesaid Regulations.

Sec. 5. All Ordinances, or parts of Ordinances, contrary to the Provisions of this ordinance, are hereby repealed. This Ordinance to take effect & be in force, from & after its Passage.

**Passed Jan[uar]y 22nd 1842. John C. Bennett, Mayor. James Sloan Recorder.**

The following were this Day appointed to be the Committee of Ways & Means. Gen[era]l Joseph Smith 4th Ward, Ald[er]m[e]n [Orson] Spencer 2nd Ward, Dan[ie]l H. Wells 3rd Ward, Ald[erm[a]n [Heber C.] Kimball 1st [ward]

The Committee on the Mayors Communication, brought in their Report, which was ^accepted, &^ discussed, so far as regards amendments or Alterations made by them. The Communication as amended, was Adopted by a Vote of Ayes & Noes. to Wit Ayes 21. — Noes, none. — Absent 4. —

The following is the Mayors Comm[unicatio]n as Adopted. Mayors Office, City of Nauvoo, Illinois, Jan[uar]y 22nd A.D. 1842:

Gentlemen of the City Council, Aldermen, & Councillors, I have carefully selected & prepared the following "Rules of Order of the City Council of the City of Nauvoo," & present them for your adoption. To Wit.

Rules of the Order of the City Co[unci]l. of the City of Nauvoo.

Duties of the Mayor.[11]

1st. The Mayor, or President pro tempore, shall take the Chair & Organize the Council, within thirty Minutes after the

[11]Published in the *Times and Seasons,* Feb. 1, 1842, 683-86.

arrival of the Hour to which it shall have been adjourned, and, while presiding, shall restrain all Conversation irrelevant to the business then under Consideration.[12]

2nd. The Mayor having taken the Chair, & a Quorum (which shall consist of a Majority of the entire Council) being present, the Council shall be opened by prayer, after which the Journal of the preceding Meeting shall be read by the Recorder, to the end that any mistake may be corrected that shall have been made in the Entries; after which no alteration of the Journal shall be permitted, without the unanimous consent of the Members present.

3rd. The Mayor shall decide all questions of Order – subject, nevertheless, to an appeal to the council, by any Member.

4th. When the question is taken on any Subject under consideration, the Mayor shall call on the Members in the affirmative to say, Aye, – those in the negative to say, No, – & he shall declare the result. When doubts arise on the decision, he may call on the Members voting to rise, or take the Yeas and Nays – the Yeas and Nays, likewise, may be taken on the Call of any four Members.

5th. The Mayor shall have a right to Vote on all Occasions; & And when his Vote renders the division equal, the question shall be lost.

6th. The Mayor shall sign his Name to all acts, addresses. & resolutions of the Council.

Of the Vice Mayor.[13]

7th. The Council shall Elect a Vice Mayor, to serve as Presi-

---

[12]In other words, the mayor has thirty minutes to take his chair and call the session to order, after which it is his duty to keep the council from digressing from matters at hand. Notice some confusion here and elsewhere about the meaning of *adjournment*, the mayor apparently using the word to refer to times when the council was in session rather than when not. In nineteenth-century usage, "an *adjourned* session of a court" referred to a session that was not "*stated* or *regular*." However, the general usage was otherwise the same as today, meaning "to put off, or defer to another day," "a formal intermission," "to suspend business," or "to close a session" (Webster, *American Dictionary*, s.vv. "adjourn," "adjourned," "adjourning," "adjournment").

[13]The Nauvoo Charter did not specify such a position.

dent pro tempore, who shall preside during the absence of the Mayor, & who shall be chosen by Ballot, & a majority of the votes of the Members present shall be necessary to a choice.

8th. If at any Meeting when a Majority shall be assembled, neither the Mayor, nor the president pro tempore, shall be present, the council shall proceed to the Election of a President for that Meeting.

Of the Recorder.

9th. The Recorder shall keep a Journal of the Proceedings of the Council, & shall enter therein whatever a Majority of the Members shall Order; & in all Cases, the Yeas & Nays, or dissent of any Member, when required to do so.

10th. The Recorder shall read whatever is laid before the council for the consideration of the Members, and shall Countersign every Act, address, or resolution, passed by the Council, noting the Date of its Passage.

11th. When the Yeas & Nays are called upon any Question, The Recorder shall read over distinctly, first, the Names of the members who voted in the Affirmative; & next, the names of those who Voted in the Negative.

Of the Marshal.

12th. The Marshal shall serve as Door Keeper, and Sergeant at Arms, to the Council.

Order of Business.

13th. After the reading of the Journal of the preceding Meeting, the Mayor shall call for Petitions, & no Petition shall be received thereafter unless by unanimous consent.

14th. Petitions having been called for & disposed of, Reports of standing Committees shall next be received, then Reports of Select Committees, & then any miscellaneous Business shall be in Order.

DECORUM.

15th. The Mayor shall always be at liberty to deliver his Sentiments in debate, on any question before the Co[unci]l, but when the Mayor speaks, it shall be from his Chair.

16th. In cases of disorderly conduct in Spectators, The

Mayor may either Order the persons out, committing the disorder; have the Room cleared; or fine or commit the offenders to Prison, for Contempt.

Of Order and Debate.

17th. When any Member is about to speak in Debate, or offer any Matter to the council, he shall rise from his Seat, & address the Mayor as "Mr. President" & avoid Personalities.[14]

18th. When two Members rise at the same time, the Mayor shall Name the person to speak, but in all other Cases the Member first rising shall speak first, No Member shall speak more than three times to the same question, without leave of the Council, nor speak more than twice without leave, until every Person, choosing to speak shall have spoken.

19th. Any Member may call another to Order, & when a Member is so called to Order, he shall immediately desist speaking, until the Mayor decide whether he is in order, or not; & every question of Order shall be decided without debate; but any Member may appeal from his decision, to the Council; if the decision be in favour of the Member called to Order, he shall be at liberty to proceed; if otherwise, the council shall determine upon the propriety of his proceeding with his Observations.

20th. When a question has been taken & carried in the Affirmative or Negative, it shall be in order for any Member of the Majority to move for the reconsideration thereof; but no Motion for the reconsideration of any Vote shall be in Order, after the paper upon which the same shall have been taken, shall have gone out of the Poss[essio]n of the Co[unci]l.

21st. No Motion, or proposition, shall be received as an Amendment which shall be a substitute for the proposition before the council; but nothing shall be considered a Substitute which shall have relation to the subject Matter under consideration.

---

[14]To "avoid personalities" meant to keep one's comments relevant and not to slander opponents. The term came from Thomas Jefferson's 1801 *Manual of Parliamentary Practice for the Use of the Senate of the United States*, Section 361, "Personalities in debate forbidden," which drew from the 1604 version of British parliamentary procedures for the House of Commons ("Jefferson's Manual," *Government Printing Office Access,* www.gpoaccess.gov).

22nd. When the Yeas & Nays are called, every Member shall Vote, unless specially excused; and in Voting by Yeas & Nays, the Councillors shall be called first, the Aldermen next, & the Mayor last.

23rd. When a Motion is made & seconded, it shall be reduced to writing, & shall be first read aloud before any Order be taken thereon; but the question, "Will the Council now consider it," shall not be put unless called for by a Member, or is deemed necessary by the Mayor: & on Motions to amend, the question of Consideration shall in no Case be p[u]t.

24th. Any Motion may be withdrawn or modified by the Mover,[15] at any time before a final decision or Amendment.

25th. When a question is under debate, no Motion shall be received but to adjourn, to lie on the Table, for the previous question, to postpone indefinitely, to postpone to a Day certain, to Commit, or to amend; which several Motions shall have precedence in the Order they stand arranged. A Motion to strike out the enacting Words of a Bill, shall have precedence of a Motion to refer to a standing Committee, shall have precedence of one to refer to a select Committee. A Motion to Adjourn shall always be in Order: that, & a Motion to lie on the Table, shall be taken without debate.

26th. The previous question shall be in this Form, "Shall the Main Question be now put?" It shall only be admitted when demanded by a Majority of the Members present; until it is decided, shall preclude all Amendment & further debate on the Main Question, & upon said Question there shall be no debate.

27th. Any Member may call for the division of a Question where the sense will admit of it, but a question to strike out & insert, shall be indivisible.

28th. When a Question is carried in the Affirmative by Yeas & Nays any member may enter on the Journal, his reasons for dissenting.

29th. It shall not be in Order to introduce a Bill, unless by

---

[15]A mover is one who proposes something for consideration in a meeting, as in, "I move the previous question." The 1828 dictionary stated that a mover was "one that offers a proposition, or recommends any thing for consideration or adoption; as the *mover* of a resolution in a legislative body" (Webster, *American Dictionary*, s.v., "mover").

way of Report from Committee, or leave [to do so should] be previously asked & obtained.

30th. Every Bill or Resolution requiring the Signature of the Mayor & Recorder, shall receive three se[parate] Readings previous to its Passage.

31st. The first reading of a Bill shall be for information, & if Opposition be made to it, the question shall be, "Shall this Bill be rejected?" If no opposition be made it shall go to the second Reading without a question, when it shall be open for discussion and amendment, or such Order as the Council may think proper to take, except the question on the Passage thereof, which can only be taken, on the day of the introduction of the Bill, by the Consent of two thirds of the Members present.

32nd. Before any Bill or Resolution requiring the Signature of the Mayor & Recorder, shall be read a third Time, the Question shall be put "Shall this Bill be read a third time?" & if a Majority of The Members present shall not Vote in the Affirmative, the same shall be declared to be rejected.

33rd. On the third Reading of a Bill, the question shall be on its passage, but it may be committed [to committee] at any Time previous to its Passage.

34th. When a Blank is to be filled, & different Sums or Dates are proposed, the Question shall be first taken on the highest Sum or longest Date, & thence downwards.

35th. The Council may at any time suspend any of its Rules by a majority of three fourths of the Members Present.

36th. After the arrival of the Hour to which the Council may stand adjourned, no Member who may have appeared, shall absent himself without leave of those Present, or of the Council when formed.

Of Committees.

37th. All standing & Select Committees shall be appointed by the Mayor, unless otherwise directed, & the first named Member shall be the Chairman. The following Standing Committees shall be appointed, to Wit:

A Committee of Ways & Means, to consist of One Member from each Ward, to whom shall be referred all Subjects of Taxation & Revenue.

A Committee of Improvement, to consist of One Member from each Ward, to whom shall be referred all Subjects relative to Repairs and opening of Roads & Streets, & other Subjects of a similar nature.

A Committee of Claims, to consist of three Members to whom shall be referred all Matters of claims against the City, & applications for remission of Penalties.

A Committee of Unfinished Business to consist of two Members, who shall examine the Journal of the preceding Council, & report such business as may have remained unfinished.

A Committee of Elections, to consist of Three Members.

A Committee of Police, to consist of One Member from each Ward, who are empowered to call upon any Officer of the Corporation, for any information, report, paper or other matter relative to the Police.

A Committee of Municipal Laws, to consist of five Members, to whom shall be referred all Bills for Ordinances presented to the Council.

A Committee of Public Grounds, to consist of One Member from each Ward.

A Committee of Public Works, to Consist of three Members.

Of Amendment to Rules.

38th. All Motions for amendment of the Rules shall be submitted One Month previous to a final determination thereof, Unless three fourths of the Members present shall assent that it shall be finally acted on the day on which it is submitted.

Of Balloting.

39th. In Balloting for Committees, a plurality of Votes shall be sufficient to make a Choice, but in other Cases a majority of the whole number of Votes shall be required to decide.

**All of which is respectfully submitted. Passed Jan[uar]y 22nd. 1842. John C. Bennett, Mayor. James Sloan, Recorder.**

The Assessor brought in his Book of Assessment of the Property of the Citizens, as a Report, which was referred to the Committee of Ways & Means, who [were] appointed to meet at the council Room on Thursday next, to investigate the Assessment, & ascertain the expences of the City for the Current Year &c. The Mayors Communication as amended & reported upon, was Ordered to be published in the Times & Seasons, & 30 Extra copies to be got for the use of the Council.

Gen[era]l J[oseph] Smith was Elected Vice-Mayor, by Ballot, Viz. Gen[era]l J[oseph] Smith 18[,] Willard Richards 1. For Hyrum Smith 1[,] Wilson Law 1. It was unanimously adopted, that Gen[era]l H[yrum] Smith be allowed One Dollar per Day for the use of the Room & Fuel & Candles, for twelve Days, amounting to Twelve Dollars. Gen[era]l J[oseph] Smith, Sworn in Vice Mayor of the City.

The Mayor then announced the following Committees, to Wit:[16]

> [Printed sideways: "Committee of ———"] Ways and Means. – Joseph Smith, Daniel H. Wells, Orson Spencer, & Hiram Kimball. Improvement – Samuel H. Smith, N[ewel] K. Whitney, Charles C. Rich, & William Marks. Claims – William Law, Vinson Knight, & Hugh McFall. Unfinished Business – Wilson Law, & Lyman Wight. Elections – John T. Barnett, John P. Green & Gust[avu]s Hills. Police. – Willard Richards, J[ohn] Taylor, Heber C. Kimball, & George W. Harris. Municipal Laws – Hyrum Smith, Brigham Young, W[ilford] Woodruff, Orson Pratt, & Joseph Smith. Public Grounds – W[illia]m Marks, D[aniel] H. Wells, Hyrum Smith & Hiram Kimball. Public Works. – Joseph Smith, J[ohn] T. Barnett, & W[illia]m Law.
>
> **John C. Bennett, Mayor. James Sloan, Recorder. Jan[uar]y 22nd 1842.**

Co[unci]l[o]r Rich presented an Ordinance in relation to Dogs, which was rejected. The Recorder was instructed to make out a list of Expences granted by the City Council, & have same ready for the use of the Committee of Ways & Means, on Thursday next. – Adjourned to 2nd Sat[ur]d[a]y in Feb[ruar]y next.

*February 12, 1842; Saturday.*[17]

> The City Council of the City of Nauvoo do hereby allow the Claim of Silvester B. Stoddard, for a sum of Eleven Dollars & fifty Cents, for Measures furnished by him.

---

[16]The committee assignments were printed in the *Times and Seasons,* Feb. 1, 1842, 686.

[17]See also *History of Church,* 4:514.

**Feb[ruar]y 12. 1842. John C. Bennett, Mayor. James Sloan Recorder.**

Resolved by the City Council of the City of Nauvoo That the Streets of the City running East & West, North of North Street, be called North first Street. North Second Street, North Third Street, and so forth, numerically, to the extent of the City limits North, and that the Streets South of South Street, running in the same direction, be called South first Street, South second Street, South third Street, and so forth to the extent of the City Limits South.

**Passed Feb[ruar]y 12th 1842. John C. Bennett, Mayor. James Sloan, Recorder.**

Resolved by the City Council of the City of Nauvoo, that Young Street be opened through to the Eastern Boundary of the City of Nauvoo, & that Mulholland Street be not opened further than Alderman [Daniel H.] Wells's Farm ^at^ present.

**Passed Feb[ruar]y 12th. 1842. John C. Bennett, Mayor. James Sloan — Recorder.**

Resolved by the City Council of the City of Nauvoo, that the Select Committee be released, & the business of the burying Ground be transferred to the standing Committee on public Grounds.

**Passed Feb[ruar]y 12th 1842. John C. Bennett, Mayor. James Sloan, Recorder.**

Resolved by the City Council of the City of Nauvoo, that Water Street be not opened at this time.

**Passed Feb[ruar]y 12th. 1842. John C. Bennett, Mayor. James Sloan, Recorder.**

Resolved by the City Council of the City, of Nauvoo, that the Road labour Tax[18] be assessed at Three Days for the Year of A.D. 1842.

**Passed Feb[ruar]y 12th, 1842. John C. Bennett, Mayor. James Sloan, Recorder.**

---

[18]The labor tax applied to male citizens between twenty-one and fifty years of age. If someone neglected to help maintain the streets, they were fined one dollar per day, or three dollars total (Nauvoo Charter, Sec. 26).

An Ordinance regulating Auctions in the City of Nauvoo.[19]

Sec. 1. [Printed sideways: "Repealed May 14th 1842"] Be it ordained by the City Council of the City of Nauvoo, that no Person or Persons whatsoever shall, after the publication of this Act, sell or expose to sale by way of vendue,[20] or Auction, any Property, Real of Personal, within the City of Nauvoo, unless such Person or Persons shall reside within the said City, & first obtain a License for the purpose from the Mayor, for which such Person or Persons shall pay to the Corporation, not exceeding One hundred Dollars, and give Bond to the Mayor and Council, with two good Securities, in the Sum of One Thousand Dollars, for the honest and due performance of all the Duties required by Law.

Sec. 2. That if any Person or Persons shall be found selling or disposing of any Property real or personal within the City of Nauvoo, by way of Vendue, or Auction, without having obtained such License, & given such Security, as aforesaid, such person or Persons so Offending, & being thereof lawfully convicted, shall forfeit & pay to the Corporation, the sum of Twentyfive Dollars for every Lot which he or they shall have ^so^ Sold.

Sec. 3. That the Auctioneer or Auctioneers licensed as aforesaid, shall receive all Articles which he or they shall be required to sell at Auction, giving his or their Receipt for the same, if required, and within Ten Days after any Sale made, shall deliver a fair Account of the same, & pay the amount thereof to the Person or Persons entitled thereto, deducting therefrom the Fees & Commissions hereafter allowed, that is to say, on the amount of the sale of personal Property of every description, a Commission of five per Cent, except public Securities, & Bank or other incorporated Stocks, respecting which a different Rate is hereinafter prescribed, & on the Amount of Sale of Real Estate, public Securities & Bank or other incorporated Stocks, two per Cent on the first Two hundred Dollars, & One per Cent on the next One Thousand three hundred Dollars; & if the amount of Sales shall exceed fifteen hundred Dollars, then One fourth of One per Cent on such excess; & when the said Auctioneer or Auction-

---

[19]Printed in the *Times and Seasons,* Mar. 1, 1842, 716-18.

[20]*Vendüe* was a nineteenth-century word meaning *auction* (Webster, *American Dictionary,* s.v. "vendüe").

eers shall let by Auction any Real Property, on ground Rent, he or they shall be entitled to receive a Commission on a Sum equal to Ten Years amount of such Rent; & in all Cases when any Article shall be actually exposed to sale, which shall not be sold, by reason of its not producing the price at which it may be limitted, it shall be lawful for the Auctioneer or Auctioneers to demand & receive, on the Sum at which such Article shall have been struck off, one fourth of the Commission which he or they would have been entitled to receive, had it been actually sold; & every Auctioneer who shall demand or receive any Fees or Commissions not allowed by Law, or greater Fees or Commissions than are so allowed, shall forfeit four Times the amount of Fees & commissions so demanded or received, to the use of the Person or Persons on whom such demand shall be made, or from whom such Fees or Commissions shall be received, provided that nothing herein contained shall be construed to prevent any Auctioneer from charging and receiving a reasonable compensation for extra trouble for services rendered.

Sec. 4. That no Person or Persons, licensed as aforesaid, shall receive Goods for Sale, of any Servant or Minor, unless accompanied by a Certificate from the Owner or Owners thereof, nor expose to public Sale any Real or personal Property, without first making out in writing, & signing, & publicly reading the Conditions of Sale, nor without advertising the property intended for Sale, & the time & place of Sale in a Newspaper, or by posting up Notices in three public Places in the City; & also giving Notice of the same by a Crier & the Ringing of a Bell.

Sec. 5. That no auctioneer or Auctioneers shall, either directly or indirectly, purchase at Auction any article or articles put up to sale by him or them, except for his or their own use, & not to sell again, under a penalty of Twenty five Dollars, for every such offence.

Sec. 6. [Printed sideways: "Repealed April 9th. 1842"] That no Auctioneer or Auctioneers shall Sell by Auction dry Goods or Groceries, in Lots or Parcels of less Value than five Dollars, or Liquors of any kind in less quantities than five Gallons, under the Penalty of Five Dollars for every offence.

Sec. 7. That in no Case where two or more Persons shall take out a joint License as Auctioneers, shall it be lawful for any of them, under colour thereof, to hold seperate Auctions, or to sell at more than one Place at one & the same time; but the said License shall be construed to confer no greater privilege or Authority than if the same were granted to a Single Person; & that if any of the Persons who may have taken out a joint License as aforesaid, shall violate this Provision, he or they shall forfeit & pay the same Penalty for every offence, as is imposed on any Person who shall Sell as an Auctioneer, without having taken out a License & given Security, as hereinbefore required.

Sec. 8. That from & after the passage of this Act, there shall be levied & paid to this Corporation, a duty on the amount of all Sales at Auction by the Auctioneers licensed pursuant to the Laws thereof, at the following Rates, that is to say: upon all real Estate, public securities, Bank & other incorporated Stocks, at the Rate of One fourth of One per Cent; upon all Watches, Jewelry, Cutlery, perfumery, & Stationary, at the Rate of five per Cent; & upon all other Goods, Articles, or Things, of whatever sort or kind, whether in the Raw or manufactured State, at the Rate of One per Cent, except on Sales of any Property at Auction, made under any Order, Decree, Sentence, or Judgment of any Court of the United States, or of any Justice of the Peace, or by Virtue of any Distress for Rent, all of which are hereby exempted from the Duties imposed by this Act.

Sec. 9. That it shall be incumbent on every Auctioneer, licensed as aforesaid, to deduct from the proceeds of all Sales made by him, the Duties herein before directed to be levied, & to pay over the same to the Treasurer of this Corporation, for its use & benefit once in every three Months; & in accounting for such Duties, it shall also be incumbent on every such Auctioneer to make his return under the Solemn Sanction of an Oath or Affirmation, & to exhibit to the Treasurer aforesaid whenever required by him, the Books of Sales of such Auctioneer, in Order to enable the Treasurer to ascertain the Correctness of the Returns aforesaid; & in Case any such Auctioneer shall fail strictly to perform the Duties hereby imposed on him, or to account accurately for, & pay over, as above prescribed, the Revenue payable to this Corporation on Sales at Auction by him, or to exhibit the Books, as aforesaid, he shall forfeit his License, & be, moreover, liable to a Penalty of Fifty Dollars, & to a further

Penalty of Twenty Dollars for every Day which shall elapse after a default shall be made in payment of the said Duties, or in rendering his Returns, or in exhibiting his Books, agreeably to this Section, until he shall comply with the directions it contains; & all Penalties accruing under it shall be for the Sole use & benefit of this Corporation.

Sec. 10. That in Case any Person or Persons who shall have become the Surety or Sureties for the faithful performance of the Duties of any Auctioneer or Auctioneers, licensed as aforesaid, shall Die, remove from the City of Nauvoo, or become Insolvent, the Mayor shall, & he is hereby authorized & empowered, to demand other satisfactory Security or Securities, for the due performance of such Duties; & in case such satisfactory security or securities shall not be given within Eight Days, the License taken out by such Auctioneer or Auctioneers shall thenceforth become, & is hereby declared to be, null & Void, to all intents & purposes as if the same had never been granted; & whenever the Mayor shall have been informed that the License of any Auctioneer or Auctioneers shall have expired, or that he or they shall have failed to comply with the requisitions of the Law, so that such license be no longer in force, the Mayor shall, at the expiration of eight days, give public notice thereof.

Sec. 11. That the Auctioneer or Auctioneers licensed as aforesaid, shall constantly keep a fair Copy of this Law in some conspicuous Place in his or their Auction Room, for the inspection of the public; & if he or they shall fail so to do, he or they shall forfeit & pay a Penalty of Twenty Dollars.

**Passed February 12th 1842. John C. Bennett, Mayor James Sloan, Recorder.**

*February 17, 1842; Thursday.*[21]

Resolved by the City Council of the City of Nauvoo, that the

[21]According to *History of Church,* 4:515, this was a "special session of the city council," during which "Joseph the seer made many interesting remarks concerning our priviliges" (Scott G. Kenney, ed., *Wilford Woodruff's Journal: 1833-1898,* 9 vols. [Midvale, UT: Signature Books, 1983-85], 2:154). The next day (see entry for February 18 below), Smith spoke on the "great privileges of the Nauvoo Charter," probably continuing his topic from the day before. However, Smith often referred to the "privileges" of marriage, and in light of the ordinance passed on February 17, he may have

Committee of public Grounds be Authorized to proceed forthwith & do all Acts & things that they may consider necessary, in Relation to the Burying Ground, or Grounds, & that the Mayor & Recorder be directed to Consummate such acts, of said Committee, all of which to be Reported to the next Council.

**Passed February 17th 1842. John C. Bennett, Mayor, James Sloan. Recorder.**

Resolved by the City Council of the City of Nauvoo, that the City Tax for 1841, be assessed at One half of One per Cent, on all Taxable Property.[22]

**Passed 17th Feb[ruar]y 1842. John C. Bennett, Mayor. James Sloan, Recorder.**

Resolved by the City Council of the City of Nauvoo, that the Claim of Carlos Gove for Lumber, Nails, Butts, Screws, & labour, in making Desks & Seats for the City Council, be allowed, for Nine Dollars & thirty seven & one half Cents, being the balance due him.

**Passed Feb[ruar]y 17th. 1842. John C. Bennett, Mayor. James Sloan, Recorder.**

Resolved by the City Council of the City of Nauvoo, that the case of Urial C. Nickerson Versus Gustavus Hills, is a malicious Prosecution, & that said Nickerson be Taxed with the Costs of Suit.[23]

**Passed Feb[ruar]y 17th. 1842. John C. Bennett, Mayor. James Sloan, Recorder.**

Resolved by the City Council of the City of Nauvoo, that the Monies resigned by the City Council, or any part of them, if not disposed of by themselves, become a poor Fund, to be appropriated hereafter for the benefit of the Poor of the City of Nauvoo.

**Passed Feb[ruar]y 17th 1842. John C. Bennett, Mayor. James Sloan Recorder.**

---

discussed marriage on this day. For Smith's use of "privileges" as a code word for plural marriage, see George D. Smith, *Nauvoo Polygamy: "... But We Called It Celestial Marriage"* (Salt Lake City: Signature Books, 2008), 55, 178, 183, 186-87, 244-47, 424, 453.

[22]This is in accordance with Section 8 of the Nauvoo Charter.

[23]See the entry for Nov. 27, 1841.

It was Ordered, upon Motion of the Vice Mayor, that Bluff Street be opened from Mulholland Street to Munson Street.

**Feb[ruar]y 17th 1842. John C. Bennett. Mayor. James Sloan, Recorder**

The Vice Mayor, Councillors B[righam] Young, W[illard] Richards, H[eber] C. Kimball & W[ilford] Woodruff Assigned their Fees as Councillors for the City, in favor of the City, until further Notice. Ald[er]m[a]n [Samuel H.] Smith resigned up his Fees for the past Year. Co[unci]l[o]r Wilson Law resigned his Claim to pay [compensation], as a City Councillor, up to this time, in favour of the Blind Inhabitants of the fourth Ward of this City, to be equally divided amongst them. Co[unci]l[o]r W[illia]m Law resigned his pay as Co[unci]l[o]r for the time past, and the present year, except any Fines which may be levied on him.

**Feb[ruar]y 17th 1842. John C. Bennett, Mayor. James Sloan, Recorder.**

Upon Report of the Comittee it was Adopted, that the City Assessment, amounting to $140,128.00, be accepted.

**Adopted Feb[ruar]y 17th 1842. John C. Bennett, Mayor. James Sloan, Recorder.**

An Ordinance concerning Marriages.

Sec. 1. Be it Ordained by the City Council of the City of Nauvoo, that all Male Persons over the Age of seventeen years, and Females over the Age of fourteen years,[24] may contract and be joined in Marriage: Provided in all Cases where either Party is a Minor, the consent of Parents or Guardians be first had.

Sec. 2. Any Persons as aforesaid wishing to Marry, or be joined in Marriage, may go before any regular Minister of the Gospel, Mayor, Alderman, Justice of the Peace, Judge or other Person authorized to Solemnize Marriages in this State, and Celebrate or declare their Marriage, in such manner and form as shall be most agreeable; either with or without License.

Sec. 3. Any Person solemnizing a Marriage as aforesaid shall

[24]The age of consent in late nineteenth-century Illinois was ten—even though the actual average age of marriage was twenty-six for men and twenty-two for women (Mary E. Odem, *Delinquent Daughters: Protecting and Policing Adolescent Female Sexuality in the United States* [Chapel Hill: University of North Carolina Press, 1995], 14-15; Table MS-2, "Families and Living Arrangements: Historical Time Series," *U.S. Census Bureau,* www.census.gov).

make return thereof to the City Recorder, accompanied by a recording Fee of Fifty Cents, within thirty days of the Solemnization thereof, And it is hereby made the Duty of the Recorder to keep an accurate Record of all such Marriages. The Penalty for a Violation of either of the Provisions of this Ordinance shall be twenty Dollars, to be recovered as other Penalties or Forfeitures. **Passed February 17th 1842. John C. Bennett, Mayor. James Sloan, Recorder.**

*March 5, 1842; Saturday.*[25]

Resolved by the City Council of the City of Nauvoo, that when Property is sold at Sheriffs, Marshals, or Constables Sale, under the Ordinances of this City, the Persons having their Property Sold shall have the privilege to redeem the same, by paying

---

[25]A meeting of the city council, not recorded in the official minutes, took place on February 18. "After some business on roads was performed," Wilford Woodruff recorded, "Joseph the Seer took the floor & followed Gen[eral] [John C.] Bennet Concerning law[,] our rights &c. His speach was truly interesting and powerfull" (2:154). The *History of the Church* has: "I [Joseph Smith] attended an adjourned city council, and spoke at considerable length in committee of the whole on the great privileges of the Nauvoo Charter, and especially on the registry of deeds for Nauvoo, and prophesied in the name of the Lord God, that [neither] Judge [Stephen A.] Douglas [nor any] other judge of the Circuit Court will ever set aside a law of the city council, [and spoke of the need for] establishing a registry of deeds in the city of Nauvoo" (4:516).

Stephen Douglas was mentioned because of his visit to Nauvoo in May 1841 as a circuit judge and state supreme court justice. The next month, when Smith was arrested near Quincy, Illinois, Douglas granted Smith release from custody. As seen here, their relationship took a strange turn, Smith seeming to think the judge was in his pocket, as again in 1843 when they dined together in Carthage, Illinois, and Smith told Douglas if he ever opposed the prophet, the judge would "feel the weight of the hand of the Almighty on him." Douglas would later say, when campaigning for the U.S. presidency, he would like to "apply the knife" to Mormonism "and cut out this loathsome disgusting ulcer" (Robert Bruce Flanders, *Nauvoo: Kingdom on the Mississippi* [Urbana: University of Illinois Press, 1965], 224, 286; Edwin Brown Firmage and Richard Collin Mangrum, *Zion in the Courts: A Legal History of the Church of Jesus Christ of Latter-day Saints, 1830-1900* [Urbana: University of Illinois Press], 94; William P. Mackinnon, "'Like Splitting a Man Up His Backbone': The Territorial Dismemberment of Utah, 1850-1896," *Utah Historical Quarterly* 71 [Spring 2003]: 108).

the Principal, and fifteen per Cent on Principal, with Cost and Charges, within thirty days after Sale.[26]

**Passed March 5th 1842. John C. Bennett, Mayor. James Sloan, Recorder.**

Adopted by the City Council of the City of Nauvoo, that the Street running South from Parley to Lumber Street, between Charles Hubbard,[27] Bently, Taylor &c., be opened, and that said Street be called Rich Street.

**Adopted March 5th 1842. John C. Bennett, Mayor. James Sloan, Recorder.**

Upon Report of the Committee, It was Adopted that the Delinquents for labour Tax upon the Streets, be required to pay, or work out the Amount on the Streets by the first of July next, in this Year.

**Adopted March 5th 1842. John C. Bennett, Mayor. James Sloan, Recorder.**

Resolved by the City Council of the City of Nauvoo, that those Wells in or near the Centre of Streets, be Ordered to be filled up by the Owners, within thirty Days, otherwise to be done by the Authorities of the City at the owners expence, and that no Well shall hereafter be dug in any Street, except by Order of the City Council, and also that all Wells on the Sides of Streets shall be well and sufficiently curbed within twenty Days, or be filled up as aforesaid, and that all excavations be filled up as aforesaid.

**Passed March 5th 1842. John C. Bennett, Mayor. James Sloan, Recorder.**

It is hereby Adopted by the City Council of the City of Nauvoo, upon the Report of the Committee, that the Street running South East of Warsaw Street, heretofore ordered open, be discontinued at its Junction with Knight Street, instead of Mulholland Street.

**Adopted March 5th 1842. John C. Bennett, Mayor. James Sloan, Recorder.**

Adopted by the City Council of the City of Nauvoo, upon a Report, that the following Names be given to the following numbered Streets, from Warsaw Street Eastward, to wit, 1 Fulmer. 2

---

[26]The *History of the Church* reports, apparently incorrectly, that this resolution passed on Friday, March 4, 1842 (4:543).

[27]Charles Wesley Hubbard was born in 1810 in Sheffield, Massachusetts. He was baptized in 1833 and died in 1903.

Rich. 3 Green. 4 Barlow. 5 Winchester. 6 Brigham, 7 Bagby, 8 Spears, 9 Bennett, 10 Richards, 11 Sloan, 12 Marks. –

**Adopted March 5th 1842. John C. Bennett, Mayor. James Sloan Recorder.**

Resolved by the City Council of the City of Nauvoo, that the Inhabitants of this City who shall not keep their Children at Home (except on lawful business,) on Sundays, and from skating on the Ice, and from marauding upon their Neighbours Property, and any Persons refusing to do the same, shall pay five Dollars Fine for every offence for the same.

**Passed March 5th 1842. John C. Bennett, Mayor. James Sloan, Recorder.**

AN ORDINANCE to regulate Weights and Measures.[28]

Sec. 1. Be it Ordained by the City Council of the City of Nauvoo, that there shall be appointed biennially, on the fourth Monday of June, and whenever a Vacancy shall Occur, a suitable Person to be Sealer of Weights and Measures, who shall before he enters on the Duties of his Office, enter into Bond, with security to the satisfaction of the Mayor in the Sum of One hundred Dollars, for the faithful discharge of his Duty, and take and Subscribe the following Oath or Affirmation before the Mayor or other Justice of the Peace: "I do solemnly Swear (or Affirm) that I will diligently, faithfully, and impartially execute the Duties of my Office, without favor or affection."

Sec. 2. That the Sealer of Weights and Measures shall keep an Office near the Centre of the City, and shall have the keeping of such Standard Weights and measures as now are, or hereafter shall be provided by the Corporation; which shall be used only as the Standards for Weights and measures.

Sec. 3. That the Sealer of Weights and Measures shall rectify, and brand or Seal with the Letter W all Scale Beams,[29] Weights, and Measures, that may be brought to his Office for that purpose, as near the upper edge or ends thereof as possible; for each of which he shall receive, from the respective Owners thereof, twenty Cents, and double that Sum if rectified, branded

---

[28]Published in the *Times and Seasons,* Mar. 15, 1842, 732-33.

[29]A scale beam refers to a T-shaped balance with weighing pans suspended from either end of a horizontal beam, which itself balances at a fulcrum point on an upright beam.

or Sealed at any other place. And if he shall neglect to rectify, brand or Seal any Scale Beams, Weights or Measures, within three days after the same shall have been brought to his office, he shall incur a Penalty of Five Dollars for every such neglect.

Sec. 4. That the Sealer of Weights and measures shall, under a Penalty of twenty Dollars for each neglect, at least once in every Six Months, between the rising and setting of the Sun, enter every Store, Shop, Market, or other Place where Goods are Sold within this City, and examine the Scales, Weights, and measures, if any therein; and if any Scale Beams, Weights, or Measures should be found without the Official Stamp, brand, or Seal, of the Sealer of Weights and Measures, or deficient, or exceeding in Weight or Measure, the same shall be forfeited to the Corporation, and Seized by the Sealer of Weights and Measures; and the Person in whose Possession such Scale Beam, Weight, or Measure shall be found, shall pay a fine of One Dollar for each and every such Scale Beam, Weight or Measure: Provided, that nothing herein contained shall be construed to prevent any Manufacturer, or other Person, from keeping Scale Beams, Weights, and Measures for Sale, in which Case, such Person shall previously give information thereof to the Recorder, on failing to do which, he shall incur the said Penalty.

Sec. 5. That if any Person shall refuse to produce his or her scale Beams, Weights, or Measures for examination, when required by the Sealer of Weights, and Measures, or refuse to relinquish the same, when found forfeited to the Corporation, the Person so refusing shall pay a fine of not less than One, nor more than Ten Dollars, according to the discretion of the Magistrate.

Sec. 6. That any Person who shall sell [products] by any Scale Beam, Weight or Measure, not rectified and Stamped, branded, or sealed, by the Sealer of Weights and Measures, shall, upon Conviction thereof, pay a fine of One dollar for each and every Offence; and any Person is hereby Authorized to prosecute for this Penalty. And if the Sealer of Weights and Measures shall pass any Scale Beam, Weight or measure that shall not correspond with the Standards prescribed by Law, he shall, for each offence, forfeit and pay a Fine of Ten Dollars.

Sec. 7. That if any Person shall sell by the Steel Yard,[30] the

---

[30]A steelyard, also known as a roman balance, has a hook from which

Sealer of Weights and Measures, (who is hereby Authorized to examine any Steel Yard which he may see in use,) if he shall, on examination, find the same not to agree with the Standard aforesaid, shall seize the same; and the Person found selling therewith, or the Owner, shall incur a Penalty of Two Dollars.

And the said Sealer of Weights and Measures shall, twice in every year, examine, and cause the Owners thereof to adjust, every Hay Scale in this City; and he shall be entitled to receive, for every such examination, two Dollars, to be paid by the owner of such Scales.

Sec. 8. That the Sealer of Weights and Measures shall keep a Book, wherein he shall enter the Names of the Persons who shall have Scale Beams, Weights and Measures adjusted, the number and description of the same, and the times when adjusted: and return to the Mayor, halfyearly, to be laid before the City Council, a Copy of said Entries, together with a Statement of all Weights and Measures seized and forfeited to this Corporation, with the Names of the Persons forfeiting the same.

Sec. 9. That all Weights and Measures which have been heretofore seized and forfeited to this Corporation shall be adjusted, where practicable, and delivered to their original Owners, upon their paying the legal Fees for Sealing, stamping or branding the same.

Sec. 10. That the Mayor be, and he is hereby Authorized, to cause to be procured the necessary Seals, avoirdupois Weights,[31] and Measures, of such form and Materials as he may think proper, to be regulated by the Standards adopted by Authority of the Legislature of the State of Illinois, as the Standards by which the Weights and Measures, to be used in this City, shall be regulated.

Sec. 11. That all Fines incurred under this Act shall be recovered and disposed of as are other small Fines for infractions of the Laws of this Corporation.

**Passed March 5th, 1842. John C. Bennett, Mayor. James Sloan, Recorder.**

---

an item is hung, as well as a counterweight that is moved along a measured arm to find a point of equilibrium.

[31]That is, weights based on the British pound (16 ounces) and used on steelyards.

Adopted by the City Council of the City of Nauvoo, upon report, that Wells Street be opened from the Temple, North.
**Adopted, March 5th 1842. John C. Bennett, Mayor. James Sloan, Recorder.**

Resolved by the City Council of the City of Nauvoo, upon Motion of Gen[era]l Hyrum Smith, that the City Collector be authorized to collect the City Tax.
**Passed March 5th 1842. John C. Bennett. Mayor. James Sloan, Recorder.**

Resolved by the City Council of the City of Nauvoo, that so much of Warsaw Street as has been heretofore located, be removed farther Eastward, to correspond with the City Survey –
**Passed March 5th 1842. John C. Bennett, Mayor. James Sloan, Recorder.**

Adopted by the City Council of the City of Nauvoo, upon the report of a select Committee, that Kimball Street be opened from Hibbards East Line, East to Barlow Street.
**Adopted March 5th 1842. John C. Bennett, Mayor. James Sloan, Recorder.**

Resolved by the City Council of the City of Nauvoo, that it be the Rule of this Council to grant all Petitions from the Citizens of this City, for the opening of Streets, at the expence of said Petitioners, if there is no remonstrance against ^the^ same by more than an equal number of Names.
**Passed March 5th 1842. John C. Bennett, Mayor. James Sloan Recorder.**

Resolved by the City Council of the City of Nauvoo, That all Carrion be removed without the Bounds of this City, or buried three feet under the surface of the Ground, by, or at the expence of the Person or Persons owning the Animal when it Died.
**Passed March 5th 1842. John C. Bennett, Mayor. James Sloan, Recorder.**

An Ordinance in relation to the
Registry of Deeds, and other Instruments of Writing.

Sec. 1. Be it Ordained by the City Council, of the City of Nauvoo, that there shall be appointed by the City Council a City Register whose duty it shall be to Record all Deeds and other Instruments of Writing presented to him for that purpose, for which he shall be entitled to such Fees as the City Council shall hereafter Enact.
**Passed March 5th 1842. John C. Bennett — Mayor. James Sloan Recorder.**

The Vice Mayor was appointed Register by Vote, by Ballot, To Wit, For William Law, One, Willard Richards One, Orson Spencer three, and Joseph Smith Vice Mayor Eighteen, who was then declared duly Elected.

**March 5th 1842. John C. Bennett, Mayor. James Sloan Recorder.**

Resolved by the City Council of the City of Nauvoo that the Fees of the Recorder of Deeds and other Instruments of Writing shall be, for Recording One Hundred Words fifteen Cents, – For Copies of the same twelve and one half cents, – For every search of [a] Record twelve and one half Cents, – Official Certificate of Seal, when requested, thirty seven and one half Cents, – For each Certificate without Seal, twenty five Cents, – Payable in all Cases in advance.

**Passed March 5th 1842. John C. Bennett, Mayor. James Sloan Recorder.**

*April 9, 1842; Saturday.*[32]

Adopted by the City Council of the City of Nauvoo, that Bagbee Street be opened from Parley Street North to Kimball Street, at the expence of Reuben Atwood and others [of the] petitioners.

**Adopted April 9th 1842. John C. Bennett, Mayor. James Sloan, Recorder.**

Resolved by the City Council of the City of Nauvoo, that a right Angle be made on Harris Street, two Blocks to the South, said Angle to be made on the East Line of Thomas Beattys Farm, & thence to go East according to the former Ordinance, to the East End of the City Limits.

**Passed April 9th 1842. John C. Bennett, Mayor. James Sloan, Recorder.**

Resolved by the City Council of the City of Nauvoo, that in all Cases before the Authorities of this City, Costs of Suit shall be Taxed against the unsuccessful Party.

**Passed April 9th 1842. John C. Bennett, Mayor. James Sloan, Recorder.**

Nelson Higgins,[33] Complaint. The Complainant having made

---

[32]See also *History of Church,* 4:586.

[33]Nelson Higgins was born in 1806 in Milford, New York. He was baptized in 1834 and served in Zion's Camp. He was ordained a Seventy in

[charges against] Lewis Robinson[,] City Constable[,] [and] filed an Affidavit containing ... charges of Impeachment against the Defendant [who][,] as such Constable, the same came on for [the] hearing. The Complainant, as also Gustavus Hills, Robert D. Foster, & Benjamin Warrington were Sworn, the Compl[ainan]ts Affidavit having been first Read, & Def[endan]t pleaded not Guilty. – The Witnesses were examined, & Cross examined, & the Case was Dismissed.

**April 9th 1842. John C. Bennett, Mayor. James Sloan, Recorder.**

Resolved by the City Council of the City of Nauvoo, That H[enry] G. Sherwood, the City Marshal do enter upon his Duties, and [will] lodge his Bond with Security, at next Meeting.

**Passed April 9th 1842. John C. Bennett, Mayor. James Sloan, Recorder.**

Resolved by the City Council of the City of Nauvoo, that the City Collector do make his Returns the second Saturday in June next.

**Passed April 9th 1842. John C. Bennett, Mayor. James Sloan, Recorder.**

Resolved by the City Council of the City of Nauvoo, that the City assessors Fees for Assessment, for the Year 1841, amounting to Seventy Dollars, for thirty five days Assessing, be, and the same is hereby allowed.

**Passed April 9th 1842. John C. Bennett, Mayor. James Sloan, Recorder.**

Adopted by the City Council of the City of Nauvoo, that Gen[era]l H[yrum] Smith & Ald[er]m[a]n N[ewel] K. Whitney be, and they are hereby instructed to Contract with Newel Knight & another, for liberty for them (Knight & ano[the]r) to run a Wing into the River, for a Dam,[34] and the Mayor and Recorder are instructed to Confirm the same.

**Adopted April 9th 1842. John C. Bennett. Mayor. James Sloan, Recorder.**

---

Kirtland and later called to the first Quorum of Seventy. He served in the Mormon Battalion, immigrated to Utah, and died in 1890.

[34]A wing dam extends partway into a river. In this case, it was meant to divert water to the center of the river to eliminate the rapids, protect the harbor, and feed a canal that would power several mills (Glen M. Leonard, *Nauvoo: A Place of Peace, A People of Promise* [Salt Lake City: Deseret Book, 2002], 491-95).

Adopted by the City Council of the City of Nauvoo, that the following Names Viz, first, Wilson Street, second Law Street, be given to the two Streets which are the only ones now without Names, & these being the Names reported by the Committee appointed to select Names for said Streets.
**Adopted April 9th 1842. John C. Bennett, Mayor. James Sloan, Recorder.**

An Ordinance amending an Ordinance entitled "An Ordinance regulating Auctions in the City of Nauvoo"[35]

Sec. 1. Be it Ordained by the City Council of the City of Nauvoo, that the 6th Section of "an Ordinance regulating Auctions in the City of Nauvoo" be, and the same is hereby Repealed.
**Passed April 9th 1842. John C. Bennett, Mayor. James Sloan. Recorder.**

Resolved by the City Council of the City of Nauvoo, that the City Recorder procure a Copy of the Times and Seasons, to be furnished for the use of the City Council, to commence at the beginning of the present Volume.
**Passed April 9th 1842. John C. Bennett. Mayor. James Sloan, Recorder.**

Adopted by the City Council of the City of Nauvoo, upon the Report of a Committee, that the Well be permitted to remain open for Eight Months, which is on the first Street West of Wells Street.
**Adopted April 9th 1842. John C. Bennett, Mayor. James Sloan, Recorder.**

Adopted by the City Council of the City of Nauvoo, upon the Report of a Committee, that the Well dug in the Street, at the Junction of Partridge Street with Carlos Street, shall be permitted to remain open for Eight Months.
**Adopted April 9th 1842. John C. Bennett, Mayor. James Sloan, Recorder.**

Adopted by the City Council of the City of Nauvoo, upon the Report of a Committee, that a Bridge be erected on Carlin Street, at the Junction of Joseph Streets across the Ravine.[36]
**Adopted April 9th 1842. John C. Bennett, Mayor. James Sloan, Recorder.**

---

[35]Published in the *Times and Seasons,* Apr. 15, 1842, 765. See February 12, 1842, for the entire ordinance.

[36]The ravine was at the northern edge of the city. The Mississippi River backed up into it (Flanders, *Nauvoo Kingdom,* 151).

Adopted by the City Council of the City of Nauvoo, upon the Report of a Committee, that Hibbard Street be opened running eighty Rods, across Kimballs Addition only, and to be done at the expence of the Petitioners.

**Adopted April 9th 1842. John C. Bennett, Mayor. James Sloan, Recorder.**

AN ORDINANCE to regulate
Taverns and Ordinaries in the City of Nauvoo.[37]—

Sec. 1. [Printed sideways: "Repealed May 14th 1842"] Be it Ordained by the City Council of the City of Nauvoo, that no Tavern or Ordinary shall be kept in the City of Nauvoo, without a License being first had and obtained therefor, which License and the Person or Persons by whom such License shall be obtained, shall be subject to such Conditions, regulations, and Penalties, as shall be provided for by Law, at the date of such License, or at any time thereafter, during the period for which it shall be obtained.

Sec. 2. That all Licenses for Taverns or Ordinaries shall expire on the first Monday in November in each year, and the Mayor shall not charge less than Ten, nor more than One hundred Dollars for any such License.

Sec. 3. That every Person who shall apply for a Tavern or Ordinary License, shall produce to the Mayor, a Certificate signed by six respectable Freeholders, of the Ward in which such Person resides, which Certificate shall set forth, that each of said Six respectable Freeholders have personally examined the Premises, for which application for a License is made, and that they are satisfied that the Person making application hath provided on the said Premises suitable and proper accomodations for Travellers or Guests, and that such applicant hath provided a good and sufficient Stable.

Sec. 4. That before any License for a Tavern or Ordinary

---

[37]An *ordinary* was a tavern with fixed prices (Webster, *American Dictionary,* s.v. "ordinary"). "Puritan ordinaries," the earliest American inns, were allowed for "the convenience of travellers, ... the comfort of the townspeople, the interchange of news and opinions, the sale of solacing liquors, and the incidental sociability," but all under a town's strict supervision (Alice Morse Earle, *Stage-coach and Tavern Days* [New York: Macmillan, 1900], chap. 1, online at *Project Gutenberg,* www.gutenberg.org). This ordinance was printed in the *Times and Seasons,* Apr. 15, 1842, 765-66.

shall be granted, the Person making application for the same, shall, in addition to the Certificate required by the third Section of this Act, produce also to the Mayor, a Certificate Signed by Six respectable Freeholders residing in the neighbourhood of the Premises, for which application for a License is made, that the public convenience requires a Tavern or Ordinary to be established in such neighbourhood.

Sec. 5. That if any Person shall falsely Certify that any Applicant for a Tavern or Ordinary License hath the accomodations required by the third Section of this Act, such applicant not having provided the same, he shall, upon conviction thereof, be fined in the Sum of Twenty Dollars.

Sec. 6. That it shall be the duty of each of the High Constables in the several Wards, (and of each of the Persons Acting as such,) from time to time & whenever he may be informed or suspect, that the accomodations required by the third Section of this Act, are not kept by any Person having a License to keep a Tavern or Ordinary, to Visit, in company with the police officer of the Ward, or with some other citizen, any Tavern or Ordinary, and ascertain whether the said accomodation continue to be kept, and if he finds that the said Accomodations are not kept, he shall forthwith report the same to the Mayor, whose duty it shall be, upon being satisfied in such Case, that the aforesaid Accomodations are not kept as required by the third Section of this Act, to annul the License which had been granted for such Tavern or Ordinary, which License shall from that time cease & termin[at]e.

Sec. 7. That if any Person or Persons keeping a Tavern or Ordinary, shall refuse to permit a High Constable, (or Person acting as such,) to make the examination required by the Sixth Section of this Act, or if any other Person or Persons shall prevent or attempt to prevent the High Constable (or Person acting as such,) as aforesaid, from making such examination, the Person or Persons so refusing, preventing or attempting to prevent, shall each, upon conviction thereof, be fined in the Sum of Twenty Dollars, and the License for such Tavern or Ordinary, shall cease & termin[at]e, & be annulled by the Mayor.

Sec. 8. That all keepers of Ordinaries or Taverns, shall be, & they are hereby prohibited from Selling Spirituous Liquors; & any keeper of a Tavern or Ordinary, who shall sell or permit to be sold, any Spirituous Liquors, in violation of this Prohibition, shall, on Conviction, for the first offence, be fined in the Sum of Twenty Dollars, & for the second offence, forfeit his License, which shall be annulled by the Mayor.

Sec. 9. That in all Cases where the Mayor shall annul the License of any Tavern or Ordinary keeper, under the provisions of this Act, he shall notify the Person whose License shall be annulled, of the facts in Writing, to be left at the Tavern or Ordinary of such Person, by the High Constable, or Person acting as high Constable, or a Police officer of the Ward in which the Tavern or Ordinary of such Person may be, & any Person who, after having been so notified, shall sell Spirituous Liquors, or keep a Tavern or Ordinary without having obtained a new License, shall, for each & every Offence, incur the same Fine.[38]

Sec. 10. That all Fines under this Act shall be recovered and distributed as is by Law provided for the recovery and distribution of Fines.

**Passed April 9th 1842. John C. Bennett. Mayor. James Sloan, Recorder.**

*April 22, 1842; Friday.*

An Ordinance fixing the
Size of Brick Moulds in the City of Nauvoo.[39]

Sec. 1. Be it ordained by the City Council of the City of Nauvoo, that from and after the passage of this ordinance, all Bricks made in the City of Nauvoo, for Sale, shall be made in Moulds of the following size & demoninations, that is to say: nine Inches and one quarter long in the clear, four Inches and a half wide in the Clear, & two Inches & a half deep in the clear; but Stock Bricks shall be made in Moulds, two Inches & five eighths deep in the clear.

Sec. 2. That if any Person or Persons shall Sell, or expose to Sale, within the City of Nauvoo, Bricks hereafter made in Moulds of any other dimensions, than those given & described in the first Section of this Ordinance; Arch Bricks, cornice Bricks, & water-

[38]It should be kept in mind that taverns served wine and beer and that citizens had stronger alcohol at home (see, e.g., the *Nauvoo Neighbor*, Oct. 29, 1845).

[39]Published in *The Wasp*, Apr. 30, 1842.

table Bricks excepted, or in Moulds not tested & stamped as Correct, with the Letter N, by the Sealers of Weights & Measures, (by which Letter all Articles passed upon by him shall hereafter be Stamped, who shall receive as a Compensation therefor, from the owner of such Moulds the Sum of twelve & a half Cents for such Mould[)] for three Bricks, so stampled[,] they shall forfeit and pay, upon conviction thereof, from one to Twenty Dollars, for each and every offence as aforesaid, at the discretion of the Mayor or Municipal Court.

**Passed April 22nd 1842. John C. Bennett, Mayor. James Sloan, Recorder.**

An Ordinance in relation to Stores and Groceries.[40]

Sec. 1. Be it Ordained by the City Council of the city of Nauvoo, that from & after the passage of this ordinance no Person shall be permitted to keep a Store or Grocery within the city of Nauvoo, without a License for that purpose, which License shall be granted for the same amount, and under the same regulations, as that for Taverns & Ordinaries contemplated in the 2nd Section of the Ordinance entitled "An Ordinance to regulate Taverns & Ordinaries in the City of Nauvoo," & any Person who shall without such License Sell, or offer for Sale, any Goods, Wares, Merchandize, or Groceries, shall, upon Conviction thereof, incur a Penalty of Ten Dollars for every Months delay.

Sec. 2. Nothing herein contained shall be so construed as to Authorize the Violation of "An Ordinance in relation to Temperance."[41]

**Passed April 22nd. 1842. John C. Bennett, Mayor. James Sloan, Recorder.**

An Ordinance altering the
Names of certain Streets therein named.[42]

Sec. 1. Be it Ordained by the City Council of the City of Nauvoo, that the Names of certain Streets in the City of Nauvoo be, and the same hereby, are changed as follows: to Wit: Carlin to Hyde; Bluff to Woodruff; Back to Page; Warsaw to Mulholland; Bennett to Cahoon; Wilcox to Green; Mulholland to Bennett;

---

[40]Published in ibid.

[41]See entry for Feb. 15, 1841.

[42]Published in ibid.

Lumber to Rich; Water to Hills; Hill to Water; Barlow to Arlington; Green to James; Rich to Gordon; & Wilson to Barlow; & that the Square or Block North of Bennett & West of Arlington Street, be called Park Place.

**Passed April 22nd. 1842. John C. Bennett, Mayor. James Sloan, Recorder.**

An Ordinance to amend an Ordinance entitled "An ordinance to regulate Taverns and Ordinaries, in the City of Nauvoo."[43]

Sec. 1. [Printed sideways: "Repealed May 14th 1842"] Be it ordained by the City Council of the City of Nauvoo, that every Tavern or Ordinary keeper, within the City of Nauvoo, who may neglect to take out a License according to the provisions of the Ordinance to which this is an amendment, shall upon conviction thereof, be fined in the Sum of twenty Dollars for every Month so neglected or refused.

**Passed April 22nd. 1842. John C. Bennett, Mayor. James Sloan, Recorder.**

Resolved by the City Council of the City of Nauvoo, That the Freedom of the City be, & the same hereby is conferred on Gen. James Arlington Bennett, of Arlington House; James Gordon Bennett Esq[ui]re,[44] Editor of the New York Herald; & Col. John Wentworth,[45] Editor of the Chicago Democrat; & they are hereby declared free Citizens of the City of Nauvoo.

**Passed April 22nd 1842. John C. Bennett, Mayor. James Sloan, Recorder.**

Adopted by the City Council of the City of Nauvoo, upon the

---

[43]Published in ibid., this amendment added a penalty but did not otherwise change the ordinance passed earlier in the month.

[44] James Gordon Bennett was born September 1, 1795, in Banffshire, Scotland. He immigrated to North America in 1819, where he worked as a schoolmaster, a proofreader, and then as the assistant editor of the *New York Courier and Enquirer.* In 1835 he started his own newspaper, the *New York Herald.* He turned the paper over to his son in 1866. He died in 1872.

[45]John Wentworth was born March 5, 1815, in New Hampshire. In 1836 he became managing editor of the first newspaper in Chicago, the *Chicago Democrat.* He was also a two-time governor of Illinois and six-time member of the U.S. House of Representatives. He died in 1888. Best remembered by Mormons as the recipient of what is known as "the Wentworth Letter," it was a letter to him from Joseph Smith that contained a history of the Latter-day Saints and the Articles of Faith. It was published in March 1, 1842, in the *Times and Seasons.*

Report of a Committee, "that Wells Street be opened, running from the Temple Lot South to the River" at the expence of Aaron Fare[46] & o[the]rs [of the] Pet[itione]rs.

**Passed April 22nd 1842. John C. Bennett, Mayor. James Sloan, Recorder.**

Resolved by the City Council of the City of Nauvoo, that the Act ordering that part of Hibbard Street which runs through Kimballs addition 1-2 block North of the Old La'Harp Road, be annulled, unless the Damages be paid before the Street be opened.

**Passed April 22nd. 1842. John C. Bennett, Mayor. James Sloan, Recorder.**

Resolved, that this Council shall not have or make any claim for pay, for their services, at this Meeting of the City Council of the City of Nauvoo.

**Passed April 22nd 1842. John C. Bennett, Mayor. James Sloan, Recorder.**

*May 14, 1842; Saturday.*[47]

An Ordinance concerning Brothels and disorderly Characters.[48]

---

[46]Aaron Freeman Farr was born in Caledonia, Vermont, in 1818. He was baptized in 1832.

[47]See also *History of Church,* 5:8. Wilford Woodruff stated, "It was the most interesting council I ever attended in some respects" (Kenney, *Woodruff's Journal,* 2:175).

[48]The ordinance was published in *The Wasp* on May 14. Joseph Smith explained that the ordinance was intended "to suppress houses & acts of infamy in the city; for the protection of the innocent & virtuous & [for the] good of public morals" and said he demonstrated "clearly that there were certain characters in the place who were disposed to corrupt the morals & chastity of our citizens & that houses of infamy did exist" (Dean C. Jessee, ed., *The Papers of Joseph Smith,* 2 vols. [Salt Lake City: Deseret Book, 1992-2002], 2:382). At the time, allegations were circulating that Smith and the mayor were involved with the brothels. Bennett would resign his mayoral post in three days and would be accused of "adultery, fornication, ... buggery" and miscegenation (*The Wasp,* July 27, 1842). For his part, Joseph Smith had, by now, married twelve women (Smith, *Nauvoo Polygamy,* 621-22), which is the presumed source of the rumors.

In two years, testimony would come from a young man, Francis Higbee, that Bennett had introduced him to "a woman on the hill," with whom Higbee had sex (*Times and Seasons,* May 15, 1844, 538-39, qtd. in Andrew F. Smith, *The Saintly Scoundrel: The Life and Times of Dr. John Cook Bennett*

Sec. 1. Be it Ordained by the City Council of the City of Nauvoo, that all Brothels or Houses of ill Fame, erected or being in the City of Nauvoo, be, and the same hereby are henceforth prohibited, and by Law declared public nuisances, and that the owner or keepers of such Houses, be fined in a Sum of not less than five Hundred, nor more than fifty Thousand Dollars,[49] and imprisoned for Six Months for each offence of one Days continuance of such establishment; and that any Person frequenting such establishment (except on lawful business) shall be fined in the Sum of five hundred Dollars, and Six Months imprisonment for each Offence: and further, that for every Act of Adultery, or Fornication, which can be proved, the Parties shall be imprisoned Six Months, and fined, each, in the Sum of from five hundred to fifty thousand Dollars, and that the individual's own acknowledgment shall be considered sufficient Evidence in the case.

**Approved May 14th 1842. John C. Bennett, Mayor. James Sloan, Recorder.**

Resolved by the City Council of the City of Nauvoo, that the Petition of Thomas I. Brandon & others to have Hotchkiss Street opened from Arlington Street East, to Winchester Street, be, and the same is hereby rejected.

**Passed May 14th 1842. John C. Bennett, Mayor. James Sloan Recorder.**

Resolved by the City Council of the City of Nauvoo, that the claim of H[enry] G. Sherwood as City Marshal for notifying the City Council, and other services from Feb[ruar]y 3rd 1841, until October 15th 1841, amounting to Twelve Dollars, be, and the same is hereby allowed.

**Passed May 14th 1842. John C. Bennett, Mayor. James Sloan Recorder.**

---

[Urbana: University of Illinois Press, 1997], 112-13). Fifty years after that, in testimony in the famous Temple Lot Case, John Taylor (not the LDS Church president) testified that Bennett had run a brothel in Nauvoo and that the authorities had pushed it off a cliff into a gully (qtd. in Richard Price, *Joseph Smith Fought Polygamy* [Independence, MO: Price Publishing, 2001], chapter 11, online at http://restorationbookstore.org/jsfp-index.htm), but this is probably confused with later legends of a grocery-store "grog shop" that was destroyed in 1841.

[49]This was comparable to about $1.4 million in today's dollars, an 1842 dollar being equal to $27.60 today ("Purchasing Power of Money in the United States from 1774 to Present," *Measuring Worth,* www.measuringworth.com).

Resolved by the City Council of the City of Nauvoo, that the Petition of Thomas Grover & others, to have the highway Taxes of the City altered, & to Tax every Man according to the Property he Possesses, be, and the same is hereby rejected.
**Passed May 14th 1842. John C. Bennett, Mayor. James Sloan, Recorder.**

An Ordinance repealing certain
Ordinances respecting Licenses in the City of Nauvoo.[50]

Sec. 1. Be it Ordained by the City Council of the City of Nauvoo, that the several Laws & Ordinances heretofore enacted, to wit: An ordinance entitled "An ordinance in relation to Hawkers, Pedlars, & Public Shows and Exhibitions" passed November 27th 1841; So much of an Ordinance entitled "An ordinance regulating Auctions in the City of Nauvoo" passed February 12th 1842, as has not been repealed by an Ordinance passed April 9th 1842, entitled "An Ordinance amending an Ordinance entitled 'An Ordinance regulating Auctions in the City of Nauvoo;'" an Ordinance entitled "An ordinance to regulate Taverns & Ordinaries in the City of Nauvoo," passed April 9th 1842; an Ordinance entitled "An Ordinance in relation to Stores and Groceries," passed April 22nd 1842; and an Ordinance entitled "An Ordinance to amend an Ordinance entitled 'An Ordinance to regulate Taverns & Ordinaries in the City of Nauvoo,'" passed April 22nd 1842, & every part ^thereof^ be & the same are hereby repealed.[51]
**Passed May 14th 1842. John C. Bennett, Mayor. James Sloan, Recorder.**

Resolved by the City Council of the City of Nauvoo, that Alanson Ripley be, and he hereby is allowed, Six Dollars, for Surveying Harris Street, & extending Young Street.
**Passed May 14th 1842. John C. Bennett, Mayor. James Sloan Recorder.**

---

[50]Published in *The Wasp,* June 4, 1842, Joseph Smith said, "I also spoke at length for the repeal of the ordinance of the city licensing ... desiring that this might be a free people, and enjoy equal rights and privileges" (see also *History of Church,* 5:8).

[51]Two of these ordinances would soon be passed again in almost identical form ("An Ordinance in relation to public Shows and Exhibitions," July 5; "An Ordinance regulating the duties and fees of City Auctioneers," July 12), but the ordinances regulating "taverns and ordinaries" and "stores and groceries" were removed and not replaced.

An Ordinance to amend an Ordinance
entitled "An Ordinance to regulate Weights & Measures."[52]

Sec. 1. Be it Ordained by the City Council of the City of Nauvoo, that from & after the passage of this Ordinance, the following Sums shall be paid to, and received by the Weigher & Sealer of the City of Nauvoo, for the Duties herein prescribed, that is to say, for rectifying, Branding, and Sealing the following Articles, to Wit: all Scale Weights & Measures of Metal, Six and one fourth Cents each; all Measures of Wood, ten Cents each; and all Scale Beams & Steelyards, twelve & a half Cents each; which Sums shall be in full lieu & satisfaction of the Sums allowed for the like Services, in & by the Ordinance of which this is an Amendment, and it shall not be lawful for the Weigher & Sealer to ask, demand, receive, or take any greater Sum or Sums, or other compensation for such Services, under the Penalty of Five Dollars for every offence, & to be recovered & disposed of, in like manner as are other small Fines & Forfeitures of a like nature.

**Passed May 14th 1842. John C. Bennett, Mayor. James Sloan, Recorder.**

Resolved by the City Council of the City of Nauvoo, that William Law & Wilson Law have [the] privilege of erecting Butments & Piers in the Mississippi River, between Locust Street & the next Street North, for the indispensable use and convenience of the Steam Mill now being erected between said Streets, on the River Beach, not infringing upon the Rights of the Ferry.

**Passed May 14th 1842. John C. Bennett, Mayor.**

Resolved by the City Council of the City of Nauvoo, that Winchester Street be opened South from Parley Street to Hills Street, at the expence of the Petitioners, Benjamin Brown and others.

**Passed May 14th 1842. John C. Bennett, Mayor. James Sloan, Recorder.**

Resolved by the City Council of the City of Nauvoo, that Councillor Wilson Law be, and he is hereby authorized to Sell a Portion of the Lots of the Burying Ground, the Terms of Sale to be, One third part of the price or purchase Money to be paid down in hand, One third part to be paid in Six Months from the time of Sale, and the remaining third to be paid in Twelve Months

[52]This was published in *The Wasp,* June 4, 1842.

from the Time of Sale, the obtaining of Security for such payments to be at the discretion of the said Wilson Law, & he to give Bonds or other necessary Documents to insure the due performance & fulfilment by the Mayor & Recorder, of all ^Sales and^ Agreements he may so make.

**Passed May 14th 1842. John C. Bennett, Mayor. James Sloan, Recorder.**

*May 19, 1842; Thursday.*[53]

Resolved by the City Council of the City of Nauvoo, that the res-

---

[53]There are no minutes for the first half of the meeting, but Joseph Smith's scribe recorded some notes about it in Smith's diary, as quoted below. Two days earlier, John Bennett had resigned as mayor and swore an affidavit before Alderman Daniel H. Wells, stating that "he never knew [Joseph] Smith to countenance any improper conduct whatever either in public or private; and that [Smith] never did teach to me in private that an illegal, illicit intercourse with females, was under any circumstance justifiable, and that I never knew him to so teach others" (Jessee, *Papers of Joseph Smith,* 2:384-85; *History of Church,* 5:11).

> 1. oclock P.M. City Council. The Mayor John C. Bennet having resigned his office, Joseph [Smith] was Elected Mayor & Hyrum Smith Vice Mayor of Nauvoo. While the election was going forward in the council, Joseph recieved & wrote the following Rev[elation] – & threw it across the room to Hiram Kimball one of the [city] Councillors. [According to Hiram's wife, Sarah, Joseph had asked her to be one of his plural wives; see Andrew Jenson, *The Historical Record,* May 1887, 232].
>
> "Verily thus saith the Lord unto you my sevant Joseph by the voice of my Spirit, Hiram Kimball has been insinuating evil & forming evil opinions against you with others, & if he continue[s] in them he & they shall be accursed, for I am the Lord thy God & will stand by thee & bless thee. Amen."
>
> After the Election Joseph spoke at some length concerning the evil reports which were abroad in the city concerning himself – & the necessity of counteracting the designs of our enemies, establishing a night watch &c, whereupon the mayor was authorized to establish a night watch by city ordinance.
>
> Dr. John C. Bennet, Ex mayor, was then called upon by the mayor to state if knew ought against him. – when Dr. Bennet replied "I know what I am about & the heads of the church know what they are about, I expect. I have no difficulty with the heads of the church. I publicly avow that any one who has said that I have stated that General Joseph Smith has given me authority to hold illicit intercourse with women is a Liar in the face of God. Those who have said it are damned Liars: they are infernal Liars. He never (either) in public or private gave me any such authority or license, & any person who states it is a scoundrel & a Liar.

ignation of the office of Mayor of this City, by John C. Bennett, which has been presented & Read by the City Recorder, be, and the same hereby is unanimously Accepted.

**Passed May 19th 1842. Joseph Smith, Vice Mayor, & President, Pro Tempore. James Sloan, Recorder.**

The Vice Mayor was duly Elected Mayor, by Ballots, to wit, for Alderman William Marks One, and for Joseph Smith vice Mayors Eighteen, upon which Gen[eral]l Smith was declared duly Elected Mayor of the City of Nauvoo.

**May 19th 1842. James Sloan, Chairman, Pro Tempore. James Sloan, Recorder.**

General Hyrum Smith was duly Elected Vice Mayor, by Ballot, to wit, for Alderman William Marks One, for Councillor Willard Richards one, and for Hyrum Smith Eighteen.

**May 19th 1842. Joseph Smith, Mayor. James Sloan, Recorder**

Resolved by the City Council of the City of Nauvoo, that the place of Hugh McFall, as one of the City Council of this City, be, and the same is hereby declared Vacant, in consequence of his becoming a nonResident of this City.

**May 19th 1842. Joseph Smith, Mayor. James Sloan, Recorder.**

George A. Smith was duly elected a Member of the City council of the City of Nauvoo, in the place of Hugh McFall, whose place had been declared Vacant.

**May 19th 1842. Joseph Smith, Mayor. James Sloan, Recorder.**

The following Ballot took place for the Election of a Member for the City Council of this City, in the place of Gen[era]l Joseph Smith, elected Mayor, to wit, For Thomas Grover One, Aaron Johnston two, Ebenezer Robinson two, Robert Stone four, & William Smith ten, whereupon W[illia]m Smith was declared duly Elected.

**May 19th 1842. Joseph Smith, Mayor. James Sloan, Recorder.**

The following Appointments were made upon Vote. George A. Smith to the Committee of Claims, in the place of Hugh McFall. William Smith to the Committee of Public Works, in place of Joseph Smith. Willard Richards to the Committee of Municipal

Laws, in place of Joseph Smith. N[ewel] K. Whitney to the Committee of Ways & Means, in place of Joseph Smith.
**May 19th 1842. Joseph Smith, Mayor. James Sloan, Recorder.**

Resolved by the City Council of the City of Nauvoo, that this Council tender a Vote of Thanks to Gen[era]l John C. Bennett, for his great Zeal in having good & wholesome Laws adopted for the Government of this City, & for the faithful discharge of his Duty while Mayor of the same.[54]
**Passed May 19th 1842. Joseph Smith, Mayor. James Sloan, Recorder.**

Resolved by the City Council of the City of Nauvoo, that a Night Watch be, and the same is hereby ordered to be established in this City, & that the number of Persons to compose said Watch, & the regulations & Duties connected therewith, be at the sole appointment & discretion of the Mayor.
**Passed May 19th 1842. Joseph Smith, Mayor. James Sloan, Recorder.**

Resolved by the City Council of the City of Nauvoo, that the Petition of Alanson Ripley and others, to have their Wages answer on their Taxes for the year 1841, be, and the same hereby is rejected.
**Passed May 19th 1842. Joseph Smith, Mayor. James Sloan, Recorder.**

Resolved by the City Council of the City of Nauvoo, that the Claim of Alanson Ripley City Surveyor, for a Sum of Twenty four Dollars, for Surveying the Burying Grounds, be, and the same is hereby allowed.
**Passed May 19th 1842. Joseph Smith, Mayor. James Sloan, Recorder.**

Resolved by the City Council of the City of Nauvoo, that the Military Officers do make such Arrangements as they deem proper

---

[54]Though the council thanked Bennett, who stepped down gracefully, things turned ugly in mid-June when Smith made allegations against the former mayor. After he left town, Bennett wrote an exposé about the city for the area's non-Mormon newspapers, including information about polygamy, accusations about the May 1842 attempted assassination of Missouri Governor Lilburn Boggs, rumors about inappropriate conduct in the Masonic lodge, and tension over whether or not to allow private ownership of property. His writings were published in book form that same year as *The History of the Saints: Or an Exposé of Joe Smith and Mormonism* (Boston: Leland and Whiting, 1842).

for the preservation of the Cannon belonging to the Nauvoo Legion.
**Passed May 19th 1842. Joseph Smith, Mayor. James Sloan, Recorder.**

*May 23, 1842; Monday.*[55]

Resolved by the City Council of the City of Nauvoo, that the office of Coroner be, and the same hereby is created for this City of Nauvoo.
**Passed May 23rd 1842. Joseph Smith, Mayor. James Sloan, Recorder.**

Samuel H. Smith was elected Coroner by Vote, but he having requested that it be rescinded, it was done, accordingly.
**May 23rd 1842. Joseph Smith, Mayor. James Sloan, Recorder.**

Dimick B. Huntington was duly Elected Coroner, by an Unanimous Vote.
**May 23rd 1842. Joseph Smith, Mayor. James Sloan, Recorder.**

Resolved by the City Council of the City of Nauvoo, that it be, and it hereby is referred to the Committee of Municipal Laws, to prepare a draft of the Duties of the Coroner to lay before this Council.
**Passed May 23rd 1842. Joseph Smith, Mayor. James Sloan, Recorder**

Resolved by the City Council of the City of Nauvoo, that the Resignation of Samuel H. Smith, of the office of Alderman of this City, be, and the same is hereby accepted.
**Passed May 23rd. 1842. Joseph Smith, Mayor. James Sloan, Recorder.**

Resolved by the City Council of the City of Nauvoo, that a Vote of approbation and thanks of this Council, be and the same hereby is tendered to Samuel H. Smith, for his praiseworthy Conduct, as an Alderman of this City, while holding that office.
**Passed May 23rd. 1842. Joseph Smith, Mayor. James Sloan, Recorder.**

Samuel H. Smith was duly elected a Councillor, and added to the City Council.
**May 23rd 1842. Joseph Smith, Mayor. James Sloan, Recorder**

---

[55]See also *History of Church,* 5:18.

*June 11, 1842; Saturday.*[56]

Samuel H. Smith was duly appointed Chairman of the Committee of Improvement, by an Unanimous Vote.
**June 11th 1842. Joseph Smith, Mayor. James Sloan, Recorder.**

Resolved by the City Council of the City of Nauvoo, that a City Pound be established in this City, and that it be, and it is hereby referred to Councillor William Law, to prepare the Duties of Poundkeeper, to be laid before the Council at next Meeting.
**Passed June 11th 1842. Joseph Smith, Mayor. James Sloan, Recorder.**

Resolved by the City Council of the City of Nauvoo, that the time for Lewis Robison the City Collector, to complete the Collection of the City Taxes, be, and the same is hereby extended until the second Saturday in September next, and that he do now lodge with the City Treasurer the amount of Taxes already Collected, and in his Hands, not duly appropriated.
**Passed June 11th 1842. Joseph Smith, Mayor. James Sloan, Recorder.**

Resolved by the City Council of the City of Nauvoo, that the publication of the City Charter, and Ordinances of the City Council, and Nauvoo Legion, be procured to be done before the first day of July next, and the proceedings until that time, to be included.
**Passed June 11th 1842. Joseph Smith, Mayor. James Sloan, Recorder.**

Resolved by the City Council of the City of Nauvoo, that the Bond executed by William Marks, (Alderman,) binding him to make a Deed for the Property purchased of him for a Burying Ground for the use of this City, be put on Record in the Office for the Registering of Deeds &c in the City of Nauvoo, and that the City Recorder procure same to be done.
**Passed June 11th 1842. Joseph Smith, Mayor. James Sloan, Recorder.**

Resolved by the City Council of the City of Nauvoo, that the office of City Auctioneer be, and the same hereby is, Created for this City.
**Passed June 11th 1842. Joseph Smith, Mayor. James Sloan, Recorder.**

---

[56]See also ibid., 25.

Charles Warner was unanimously, duly Elected City Auctioneer, for the City of Nauvoo.

**June 11th 1842. Joseph Smith, Mayor. James Sloan, Recorder.**

*June 22, 1842; Wednesday.*[57]

Resolved by the City Council of the City of Nauvoo, that the petition of Alderman [William] Marks, to have Two Dollars and fifty-five Cents granted to him, for his Services for 1842, to a satisfy his City Tax of 1841, be, & ^hereby is,^ ordered to be laid on the Table.

**Passed June 22nd 1842. Joseph Smith, Mayor. James Sloan, Recorder.**

An Ordinance repealing all Ordinances, Laws, and Resolutions, relative to the changing of the Names of Streets.

Sec. 1. Be it Ordained by the City Council of the City of Nauvoo, that all Ordinances, Laws, and Resolutions, that have been passed by the City Council, changing the Names of Streets, be, and the same are hereby repealed.

Sec. 2. That the Names of all Streets in the City of Nauvoo, that were named at the time that the City Plot was drawn out; and as the Plot stands Recorded in the Recorders office, retain their Original Names.

Sec. 3. That those Streets that have been named since the Plot was recorded, and have not had their Names changed, also retain the Names that were first given to them.

**Passed June 22nd. 1842. Joseph Smith, Mayor. James Sloan, Recorder.**

*July 5, 1842; Tuesday.*[58]

An Ordinance in Relation to Writs of Habeas Corpus.[59]

Sec. 1. Be it, and it is hereby Ordained by the City Council of the City of Nauvoo, that no Citizen of this City shall be taken out of the City by any Writs, without the privilege of investigation before the Municipal Court, and the benefit of a Writ of Habeas

---

[57]*History of Church,* 5:35, describes this as a "special session."

[58]See also *History of Church,* 5:57.

[59]Published in *The Wasp,* July 16, 1842.

Corpus, as granted in the seventeenth Section of the Charter of this City. Be it understood that this Ordinance is enacted for the protection of the Citizens of this City, that they may in all Cases have the Right of Trial in this City, and not be subjected to illegal Process by their Enemies.

Sec. 2. This Ordinance to take effect, and be in force, from and after its passage.

**Passed July 5th 1842. Joseph Smith, Mayor. James Sloan, Recorder.**

An Ordinance creating certain further additional City Offices therein named.[60]

Sec. 1. Be it Ordained by the City Council of the City of Nauvoo, that in addition to the City Officers heretofore Elected, there shall be elected by the City Council, One City Coroner, One City Poundkeeper, and One City Auctioneer, whose Duties and Fees shall hereafter be severally defined; by Ordinance.

Sec. 2. That all Laws and parts of Laws, inconsistent with this Ordinance, be, and they hereby are repealed.

Sec. 3. This Ordinance to take effect, and be in force, from and after its passage.

**Passed July 5th 1842. Joseph Smith, Mayor. James Sloan, Recorder.**

An Ordinance in relation to public Shows and Exhibitions.[61]

Sec. 1. Be it Ordained by the City Council of the City of Nauvoo, that any Person or Persons who shall at any time hereafter, bring into, and desire to exhibit within this Corporation, any Curiosities of nature or Art,[62] not inconsistent with decency, or contrary to good Morals, shall previously to the exhibition

---

[60]Published in ibid.

[61]Published in ibid. This replaced the ordinance of November 27, 1841, that had been repealed on May 14, 1842. It was the same ordinance except the restrictions on "hawkers" and "pedlers" had been removed.

[62]The kinds of shows the city anticipated were exhibits of human deformities, stuffed animals, skeletons, animal tusks, insects preserved in amber, and related biological and anthropological oddities. In fact, the first museum in the United States to include oil paintings in its art exhibits was the Peale Museum in Baltimore. When the museum opened in 1786, it was devoted exclusively to mastodon fossils, and when it added paintings of famous Americans thirty years later, the images were considered to be instructional rather than art for its own sake.

thereof, procure a License for that purpose from this Corporation, Signed by the Mayor, and Countersigned by the Recorder, for which he she or they shall at the time of obtaining the same, pay a Sum not exceeding Fifty Dollars, at the discretion of the Mayor, with a Fee of One Dollar to the Recorder, for making out the same, and the said License shall Continue in force for one Week, and no longer; And such Person or Persons as aforesaid, who may be found in open Violation of this Section, shall forfeit and pay for each and every such offence, a sum not exceeding Fifty Dollars.

Sec. 2. That all exhibitions inconsistent with decency, or contrary to good Morals, are expressly prohibited under the Penalty of One hundred Dollars for every Offence, and said Penalties are to be recovered and applied in the same manner, as are Penalties of a like nature within this City.

**Passed July 5th 1842. Joseph Smith, Mayor. James Sloan, Recorder.**

Resolved by the City Council of the City of Nauvoo, that an Order be, and the same is hereby granted to James Alred, upon the Treasury of this City, for fifteen Dollars, towards his Labour.

**Passed July 5th 1842. Joseph Smith, Mayor. James Sloan, Recorder.**

*July 12, 1842; Tuesday.*[63]

An Ordinance regulating the duties and fees of City Auctioneers, in the City of Nauvoo.[64]

Sec. 1. Be it Ordained by the City Council of the City of Nauvoo, that there shall be one or more City Auctioneers appointed by this Council, who shall after the passage of this Act, and within thirty days after his or their appointment, produce and give Bond to the Mayor and Council, with two good Securities, in the Sum of two Thousand Dollars, for the honest and due performance of all the duties required by Law.

Sec. 2. That no Person or Persons whatsoever, save and except as set forth in the sixth Section of this Ordinance, shall,

[63]See also *History of Church,* 5:60.

[64]This replaced the ordinance that was passed on February 12, amended on April 9, and rescinded on May 14. The new version was published in *The Wasp* on July 23, 1842.

after the passage of this Act, sell or dispose to Sale, by way of Vendue, or Auction, any property, real or personal, within the City of Nauvoo, except he or they be Authorized by the Mayor or City Council, and subject to the same Laws that refer to the City Auctioneer, or Auctioneers, and that if any Person or Persons shall be found selling or disposing of any Property, real or personal, within said City, by way of Vendue or Auction, otherwise than as in manner herein prescribed, such Person or Persons so offending, and being thereof lawfully Convicted, shall forfeit and pay to the Corporation, a sum not exceeding twenty-five Dollars for every lot which he or they shall have so sold, as also the Auctioneers fees, and duties, specified in this Act, upon any Sale or Sales which may have been made by such Person or Persons before detection, one half to go to the corporation, and the other half to the informer.

Sec. 3. That every Auctioneer or Auctioneers who may be appointed for this City, shall receive all Articles which he or they shall be required to sell at Auction, giving his or their receipt for the same, if required, and within two days after any Sale made, shall deliver a fair account of the same, and pay the Amount thereof to the Person or Persons entitled thereto, deducting therefrom the duties, fees, Commissions and charges hereafter allowed, that is to say, to said Auctioneer or Auctioneers, on the Amount of every Sale of Property of any description, where the Amount of Sales shall not exceed the sum of fifty Dollars, a Commission, fee, or sum at the rate of ten per Cent, where the Amount of Sales shall exceed fifty Dollars, and not exceed one hundred Dollars, five per Cent on the amount over the first fifty Dollars, and where the Amount of Sales shall be over one hundred Dollars, three per Cent on the amount so over; and when any Auctioneer shall let by Auction or Vendue, any real property, on ground Rent, he shall be entitled to receive for his use a Commission or fee on a Sum equal to ten Years Amount of such Rent, and in all cases when any Article or Articles, or property whatever, shall be actually exposed to Sale, which shall not be sold by reason of its not producing the price at which it may be limited, it shall be lawful for the Auctioneer, so exposing the same, to demand and receive, on the sum at which such Article, Articles, or property shall have been struck off, one fourth of the Commission or fee which said Auctioneer would have been entitled to receive for his use had it been actually sold; and every Auctioneer who shall demand or receive any fees or Commissions not allowed by law, or greater fees or Commissions than are so allowed, shall forfeit four times the Amounts of fees and Commissions so demanded or received, one half to go to the use of the Person or Persons on whom such demand shall be made, or from whom such fees or commissions shall be received, and the other half to the use of this Corporation, provided that nothing herein contained shall be construed to prevent said Auctioneer from charging and receiving for his use repayment of expenditures or advances made, and a reasonable compensation for storage, and extra trouble, for services rendered.

Sec. 4. That no Auctioneer shall wilfully & knowingly receive Goods for Sale, of any Servant or minor, unless accompanied by a Certificate from the owner or owners thereof, nor expose to public Sale any Real or personal Property, without first making out in Writing, and signing, and publicly reading the Conditions of Sale, nor without advertising the property intended for Sale, and the time and place of Sale in a Newspaper, or by posting up notices in three public places in the City; and also giving notice of the same by a Crier and the ringing of a Bell.

Sec. 5. That no Auctioneer of this City shall put up or sell by Vendue, or Auction, Liquors of any kind in less quantities than five Gallons, under the penalty of five Dollars for every offence.

Sec. 6. That from and after the passage of this Act, there shall be levied and paid to this Corporation, a duty on the amount of all Sales at Auction by the City Auctioneer or Auctioneers, at the following rates, that is to say, upon all Real Estate public Securities, Bank & other incorporated Stocks, at the rate of one half of one per cent, upon all Watches, Jewelry, Cutlery, perfumery, and Stationary, at the Rate of five per Cent; and other Goods, articles, or things, of whatever sort or kind, whether in the Raw or manufactured state, at the rate of one per Cent, except on Sales of any Property at Auction, made under any Order, Ordinance, Decree, Sentence, or Judgment of any Court, of the United States, or of any Justice of the Peace, or by Virtue of any distress for Rent, all of which are hereby exempted from the duties imposed by this Act and may be sold by All public Officers legally Authorized so to do; Provided that nothing herein contained shall be so construed as to prevent any Administrator, Executor, Guardian, or persons by them employed in due course of Law from selling by Vendue or Auction.

Sec. 7. That it shall be incumbent on said City Auctioneer or Auctioneers to deduct from the proceeds of all Sales made by him or them, the duties hereinbefore directed to be levied, and to pay over the same to the Treasurer, of this Corporation, for its use and benefit, once in every three Months; and in Accounting for such duties, it shall also be incumbent on said City Auctioneer or Auctioneers to make his or their return under the solemn sanction of an Oath or Affirmation, and to exhibit to the Treasurer aforesaid whenever required by him, the Books of Sales of such Auctioneer or Auctioneers, in order to enable the Treasurer to ascertain the correctness of the returns aforesaid, and in case any Auctioneer shall fail strictly to perform the duties hereby imposed on him, or to account accurately for and pay over, as above prescribed, the Revenue payable to this Corporation on Sales at Auction by him, or to exhibit his Books as aforesaid, he shall forfeit his office, and be moreover, liable to a penalty of fifty Dollars, and to a further penalty of fifteen Dollars for every two days which shall elapse after a default shall be made in the payments of the said duties, or in rendering his returns, or in exhibiting his Books, agreeable to this Section, until he shall comply with the directions it contains; and all penalties accruing under it shall be for the sole use and benefit of this Corporation.

Sec. 8. That in Case any Person or Persons who shall have become the surety or sureties for the faithful performance of the duties of any City Auctioneer shall die, remove from the City of Nauvoo, or become Insolvent, the Mayor shall and he is hereby Authorized and empowered, to demand other satisfactory security or securities for the due performance of such duties; and in case such satisfactory security or securities shall not be given within eight days, the appointment of said Auctioneer shall thenceforth become, and is hereby declared to be null and void, to all intents and purposes as if the same had never been granted; and whenever the Mayor shall have been informed that the said Auctioneer shall have so failed to comply with the requisitions of the law, the Mayor shall, at the expiration of eight days, give public notice thereof.

Sec. 9. That every City Auctioneer within this City shall constantly keep a fair Copy of this Law in some conspicuous place in his Auction Room, for the inspection of the public, and if he shall fail so to do, he shall forfeit and pay a penalty not exceeding twenty Dollars, at the discretion of the Mayor, Alderman, or Municipal Court, before whom the same may come for Trial.
**Passed July 12th 1842. Joseph Smith, Mayor. James Sloan, Recorder.**

An Ordinance, to amend an Ordinance entitled "An Ordinance Organizing the Nauvoo Legion, passed Feb[ruar]y 3rd 1841."[65]

Sec. 1. Be it, and it is hereby Ordained by the City Council of the City of Nauvoo, that the Lieutenant General of the Nauvoo Legion shall not be required to act as the President of any Court Martial, or of the Legion; also, that he may add to his Staff a Chief Chaplain, with the Rank of Colonel.[66]

Sec. 2. That officers may be elected without being nominated by the Court Martial, and that all vacancies shall be filled by lawful elections, and not by granting Brevet Commissions.

Sec. 3. That the General Officers may appoint such officers in their respective Staffs as may be in Conformity with the rules and regulations of the United States Army.

Sec. 4. That so much of the 3rd Section of the Ordinance Organizing the Nauvoo Legion, approved Feb[ruar]y 3rd, 1841, as Authorizes the Major General to act as the Secretary of the Court Martial and Legion, and Adjutant, and Inspector General, is hereby repealed.[67]

---

[65]Published in ibid.

[66]As documented by Richard E. Bennett, Susan Easton Black, and Donald Q. Cannon in *The Nauvoo Legion in Illinois: A History of the Mormon Militia, 1841-46* (Norman, OK: Arthur H. Clark, 2010), 168-69, 173, the legion wanted to downplay its image as the strong arm of the LDS Church. If Joseph Smith no longer presided at court martials or preached to the troops, it would temper the impression left by the recent laying of the cornerstone of the Nauvoo temple, at which the prophet appeared on horseback in full military regalia (117-18).

[67]John C. Bennett was no longer the mayor and had been excommunicated in May, but he was still a general in the Nauvoo Legion and presided over a court martial on June 3. The difficulty in removing him from office

Sec. 5. This Ordinance shall take effect and be in force from and after its passage, notwithstanding any thing to the contrary heretofore enacted.
**Passed July 12th 1842. Joseph Smith, Mayor. James Sloan, Recorder.**

An Ordinance, authorizing the
publication of additional Laws and Ordinances.[68]

Sec. 1. Be it ordained by the City Council of the City of Nauvoo, That all Laws and Ordinances passed by the City Council, until the Laws are printed, be inserted in the Book that is now being printed, all Ordinances to the contrary notwithstanding.
**Passed July 12th 1842. Joseph Smith, Mayor. James Sloan, Recorder.**

Dimick B. Huntington was duly elected City Coroner, by an unanimous Vote. Charles Warner was duly elected a City Auctioneer, by an unanimous Vote.

It is hereby Ordered by the City Council of the City of Nauvoo, that a sum of Fifty Dollars be appropriated towards the printing of the Laws and Ordinances of this City, and that the usual Order be drawn upon the Treasury for that purpose.
**Passed July 12th 1842. Joseph Smith, Mayor. James Sloan, Recorder.**

It is hereby Ordered by the City Council of the City of Nauvoo, that the City Recorder do draw from the City Treasury, in the usual manner, Fifty Dollars, in part pay for his Services in the present Year.
**Passed July 12th 1842. Joseph Smith, Mayor. James Sloan, Recorder.**

*July 20, 1842; Wednesday*

We, the undersigned, members of the city council, of the city of Nauvoo,[69] testify that John C. Bennett was not under duress

---

in mid-June probably inspired the need for this section of the ordinance (Bennett et. al, *Nauvoo Legion,* 156-57).

[68]Published in *The Wasp,* July 30, 1842.

[69]According to *History of Church,* 5:68, the affidavit was signed by all but one councilman in the presence of Daniel H. Wells, a Hancock County justice of the peace, on July 20, and Newel Whitney signed it the next day. Wells was a "jack Mormon," which at the time meant a sympathetic non-Mormon.

at the time he testified before the city council, May 19, 1842, concerning Joseph Smith's innocence, virtue and pure teaching. His statements that he has lately made concerning this matter are false; there was no excitement at the time, nor was he in anywise threatened, menaced or intimidated. His appearance at the city council was voluntary; he asked the privilege of speaking, which was granted. After speaking for some time on the city affairs, Joseph Smith asked him if he knew anything bad concerning his public or private character. He then delivered those statements contained in the testimony voluntarily, and of his own free will, and went of his own accord, as free as any member of the council. We further testify that there is no such thing as a Danite Society in the city, nor any combination, other than the Masonic Lodge of which we have any knowledge. WILSON LAW, GEO[RGE] A. SMITH, JOHN TAYLOR, GEO[RGE]. W. HARRIS, WILFORD WOODRUFF, NEWEL K. WHITNEY, VINSON KNIGHT, BRIGHAM YOUNG, HEBER C. KIMBALL, CHARLES C. RICH, JOHN P. GREENE, ORSON SPENCER, WILLIAM MARKS

*July 22, 1842; Friday.*[70]

Resolved by the City Council of the City of Nauvoo, that Co[unci]l[o]rs [John] Taylor, W[illia]m Law, & [Brigham] Young be, and they hereby are appointed[,] a special Committee, ^with the Recorder to assist,^ to prepare a Petition to lay before the Governor of this State, praying that he will protect Lieut[enant] Gen[era]l Joseph Smith from Arrest under any Writ from Missouri, and the Inhabitants of this City and its Vicinity from the intrigues of evil designing Men.[71]

**Passed July 22nd. 1842. Joseph Smith, Mayor. James Sloan, Recorder.**

To his Excellency, Thomas Carlin,[72] Governor of the State of

---

[70]See also *History of Church*, 5:68-70.

[71]Bennett had recently claimed that Joseph Smith prophesied the death of Governor Lilburn Boggs prior to the assassination attempt on Boggs. Fearing that Smith would be extradited to Missouri, the Nauvoo City Council sought the protection of a heightened ordinance.

[72]Thomas Carlin was born in Kentucky in 1789 and moved to Illinois in 1812. He served in the War of 1812 and the Black Hawk War. He was twice elected to the state senate, serving from 1825 to 1833. In 1838 he

Illinois. – We the undersigned Citizens of the State of Illinois, having heard that many Reports are in circulation prejudicial to the interest, happiness, peace, wellbeing, & safety of the Inhabitants of the City of Nauvoo & Vicinity, have thought proper to lay before your Excellency the following statements.

Whereas the latterday Saints having suffered much in the State of Missouri, in time past, through the hand of oppression, brought upon them by the falsehoods & misrepresentations of wicked & designing Men, whose hands are yet dripping with the Blood of the innocent, & whose fiendish rage has sent many a Patriot to his long home, leaving in our midst many Widows & Orphans, whose sorrows & tears even time cannot wipe away.[73]

We would respectfully represent to your Excellency, that we broke no law, violated no constitutional Rights, nor trampled upon the privileges of any other People in Missouri, yet we had to suffer banishment, exile, the confiscation of our Properties, & have diseases, distress, & misery entailed upon us & our Children, the effects of which we bear about in our Bodies, & are indelibly engraven on our Minds, & we appeal to your Excellency at the present time that you will not suffer an occurrence of such heart rending scenes to take place under your Administration.

Whilst we have been in this State we have behaved as good peaceable Citizens, we have availed ourselves of no priviledges but what are strictly Constitutional, & such as have been guaranteed by the Authority of this State, we have always held ourselves amenable to the Laws of the Land, we have not violated any Law, nor taken from any their rights.

---

became Illinois's governor on the Democratic ticket. He retired from public life in 1842 and died ten years later.

[73]Mormons moved into Jackson County, Missouri, in 1831 and announced that God would give them the land of the old settlers, who had to leave. When conflict resulted, the Mormons moved north across the Missouri River into Clay County. Violence continued, and in 1836 the Missouri legislature created Caldwell County for the Mormons, where the latter founded the town of Far West. Eventually the Mormons moved into Davies and Carroll Counties, where opposition from neighbors again led to violence and Governor Lilburn Boggs eventually called out the state militia with the order that Mormons had to be "exterminated or driven from the state." By April 1839, most Mormons had fled to Illinois. For a general discussion of Mormon troubles in the state, see Stephen C. LeSeuer, *The 1838 Mormon War in Missouri* (Columbia: University of Missouri, 1987).

Your Excellency must be acquainted with the false statements & seditious designs of John Cook Bennett with other political Demagogues, pertaining to us as a People. We presume Sir, that you are acquainted with the infamous Character of that individual, from certain statements made to us by yourself, pertaining to him, but lest you should not be, we forward to you documents pertaining to this affair which will fully shew the darkness of his Character, & the infamous course that he has taken.

Concerning those statements made by him against Joseph Smith, we know that they are false; Joseph Smith has our entire confidence, we know that he has violated no Law, nor has he in any wise promoted sedition, or Rebellion, nor has he sought the injury of any Citizen of this or any other place[;] we are perfectly assured that he is as loyal, patriotic, & virtuous a Man as there is in the State of Illinois, & we appeal to your Excellency if in three years acquaintance with him, you have seen any thing to the contrary.

In as much as this is the Case, we your Pet[itione]rs knowing that Joseph Smith could not have Justice done him by the State of Missouri, that he has suffered enough in that State unjustly already, & that if he goes there it is only to be murdered, Pray, Your Excellency not to issue a Writ for him to be given up to the Authorities of Missouri, but if your Excell[enc]y thinks that he has violated any Law, we request that he may be tried by the Authorities of this State, for he shrinks not from investigation. We furthermore Pray, that our Lives & the Lives of our Wives & Children may be precious in your sight, & that we may have the priviledge of following our avocations, of living on our Farms, & by our own firesides in peace, & that John C. Bennett[,] nor any other Person[,] may not be able to influence your Excell[enc]y either by intrigue, or falsehood, to suffer us as a people to be injured by Mob or Violence, but if in the estimation of your Excell[en]cy we have done wrong, we appeal to the Laws of this State.

Having heard a report that your Excellency had called upon several companies of Militia to prepare themselves & be in readiness, in case of emergency, we would further ask of Your Excellency, that if the State or Country should be in danger, that the Nauvoo Legion may have the priviledge of shewing their loyalty in the defence thereof.

We have the fullest confidence in the honor, Justice, & integrity of your Excellency, & feel confidence that we have only to present our case before you to ensure protection, believing that the cries of so many peaceable & patriotic Citizens will not be disregarded by y[ou]r Excell[en]cy.

We therefore ask you, as the Chief Magistrate of this State, to grant us our requests, and we as in duty bound will ever Pray.

[(]Signed by the Vice Mayor, & the Majority of the City Council, to wit: all who were present, unless Orson Pratt,[74]) & also signed by about eight hundred, or upwards, of the Inhabitants. July 22nd. 1842.

*August 5, 1842; Friday.*[75]

Amasa Lyman was duly elected, & sworn, a Member of the City Council, in the stead of Vinson Knight Deceased.[76]

**August 5th 1842. Joseph Smith, Mayor. James Sloan, Recorder.**

---

[74]After returning from a mission to England in 1841, Orson Pratt had heard rumors about Joseph Smith's conduct toward his wife, Sarah Pratt, while he was away. According to Sarah, Joseph had asked her to become his plural wife in the fall of 1840 and again in the spring of 1842. She told her husband about this, and Joseph recorded in his journal that he was "conflicting with O[rson] P[ratt]." John Bennett knew something about the episode and broadcast it to the world upon leaving the city. The *Times and Season* reported that there was nothing to the rumor, that Joseph had asked Orson, "Have you personally a knowledge of any immoral act in me toward the female sex, or in any other way?" Pratt answered, not very persuasively, "Personally, toward the female sex, I have not." Orson and Joseph eventually reconciled, but Sarah continued to harbor resentment. See Jessee, *Papers of Joseph Smith,* 2:400; *Times and Seasons,* Aug. 1, 1842, 869; Richard S. Van Wagoner, "Sarah M. Pratt: The Shaping of an Apostate," *Dialogue: A Journal of Mormon Thought* 19 (Summer 1986), 69-99; Gary James Bergera, *Conflict in the Quorum: Orson Pratt, Joseph Smith, Brigham Young* (Salt Lake City: Signature Books 2002), 17-23.

[75]See also *History of Church,* 5:84.

[76]The *Times and Seasons,* Nov. 15, 1841, 894, reported Vinson Knight's death: "DIED. In this city, on Sunday the 31st day of July last, VINSON KNIGHT, aged 38 years. Brother Knight was one of the bishops of this church, and a man favored of God, and respected by all good men. He had been long in the church and had always adorned his life, works and profession, with that decorum virtue and humility, which ever characterizes the true followers of our blessed Jesus."

*August 8, 1842; Monday.*[77]

An Ordinance regulating the mode of proceeding in cases of Habeas Corpus, before the Municipal Court.[78]

Sec. 1. Be it Ordained by the City Council of the City of Nauvoo, that in all cases, where any Person or Persons, shall at any time hereafter, be arrested or under arrest in this city, under any Writ or process, and shall be brought before the Municipal Court of this City, by virtue of a Writ of Habeas Corpus, the Court shall in every such Case have power and authority, and are hereby required to examine into the Origin, validity, & legality of the Writ of Process, under which such arrest was made, & if it shall appear to the Court, upon sufficient testimony, that said Writ or Process was illegal, or not legally issued, or did not proceed from proper Authority, then the Court shall discharge the Prisoner from under ^said^ arrest, but if it shall appear to the Court that said Writ or Process had issued from proper Authority, and was a legal Process, the Court shall then proceed and fully hear the merits of the case, upon which such Arrest was made, upon such evidence as may be produced and sworn before said Court, & shall have power to adjourn the hearing, and also issue process [serve warrants] from time to time, in their discretion, in Order to procure the attendance of Witnesses, so that a fair & impartial trial, & decision may be obtained, in every such case.

Sec. 2. And be it further Ordained, that if upon investigation it shall be proven before the Municipal Court, that the Writ or Process has been issued either through private pique, malicious intent, religious or other persecution, falsehood, or misrepresentation, contrary to the constitution of this State, or the constitution of the United States, the said Writ or Process shall be

---

77See also *History of Church,* 5:87-88. On August 8, 1842, Joseph Smith and Orrin Porter Rockwell were arrested for shooting Governor Boggs. Because of the July 5 "Ordinance in Relation to Writs of Habeas Corpus," the officers were unable to take Smith out of the city. See Jessee, *Papers of Joseph Smith,* 2:402-03. The Nauvoo Charter, Section 17, gave the city council this authority.

78Published in *The Wasp,* Aug. 13, 1842, this ordinance, passed in response to the attempted arrest of Joseph Smith, strengthened the power of habeas corpus by allowing the city to review the writ process.

quashed, & considered of no force or effect, & the Prisoner or Prisoners shall be released & discharged therefrom.

Sec. 3. And be it also further Ordained, that in the absence, sickness, debility, or other circumstances disqualifying or preventing the Mayor, from Officiating in his office, as Chief Justice of the Municipal Court, the Aldermen present shall appoint one from amongst them, to act as chief Justice, or president pro tempore.[79]

Sec. 4. This Ordinance to take effect, and be in force, from and after its passage.

**Passed August 8th 1842. Hyrum Smith, Vice Mayor, & President pro tempore.[80] James Sloan, Recorder.**

*August 20, 1842; Saturday.*[81]

Resolved by the City Council of the City of Nauvoo, that Hugh McFall be paid seven Dollars, out of the City Treasury, for his services while a City Councillor of this City.

**Passed August 20th 1842. Hyrum Smith Vice Mayor, & Pres[i]d[en]t pro-tem. James Sloan, Recorder.**

Resolved by the City Council of the City of Nauvoo, that the City Sexton be, and he hereby is required, to make a weekly report for publication to the Editor of some Newspaper published in this City, of the number of interments, and the names and Ages of the persons deceased, with the nature of the Diseases of which they died.

**Passed August 20th 1842. Hyrum Smith, Vice Mayor, & pres[i]d[en]t pro tem. James Sloan, Recorder.**

---

[79]This was passed to give authority to another in the event Joseph Smith should be arrested.

[80]Joseph Smith had gone into hiding. Illinois Governor Thomas Carlin and Missouri Governor Thomas Reynolds responded by offering rewards of $200 and $300 respectively for his capture. But on the outskirts of Nauvoo, he enjoyed "frequent visits from friends and relatives [to] bring comforts, and from the devoted Emma, who came often, despite the fact that she was watched, followed and harassed by the sheriffs" (Donna Hill, *Joseph Smith: The First Mormon* [Garden City, NY: Doubleday, 1977], 311-12).

[81]See also *History of Church,* 5:120.

Resolved by the City Council of the City of Nauvoo, that John C. Bennett be, and he hereby is discharged, from the office of Chancellor of the University of the City of Nauvoo, he being unworthy to hold said Office.

**Passed Aug[us]t. 20th 1842. Hyrum Smith, Vice Mayor, & pres[i]d[en]t pro tem. James Sloan, Recorder.**

Amasa Lyman was duly elected a Regent of the University of the City of Nauvoo, in the place of Vinson Knight deceased.

**August 20th 1842. Hyrum Smith, Vice Mayor, & Pres[i]d[en]t pro tem. James Sloan, Recorder.**

Resolved by the City Council of the City of Nauvoo, that the City Recorder be, and he hereby is instructed to procure for the Corporation, a sealing Press, for the use of the Corporation Seal, the price whereof is not to exceed five Dollars.

**Passed Aug[us]t 20th 1842. Hyrum Smith, Vice Mayor & Pres[i]d[en]t pro tem. James Sloan, Recorder.**

Resolved by the City council of the City of Nauvoo, that the Recorder procure a Book to keep an Account of the Orders drawn upon the Treasury, and so forth.

**Passed Aug[us]t 20th 1842. Hyrum Smith, Vice Mayor, & Pres[i]d[en]t Pro tem. James Sloan, Recorder.**

*September 9, 1842; Friday.*[82]

Resolved by the City Council of the City of Nauvoo, that on any Member or Members of the City Council of the City of Nauvoo leaving, or reporting that he or they is or are about to leave the City, with the intention of being absent for three Months or longer, the City Council may elect a member or Members to fill his place or their places, until his or their return.[83]

---

[82]See also ibid., 160-61.

[83]This allowed council members to travel to other states with the Mormon side of the Bennett controversy. As the *History of Church*, 5:160, explained: "Brigham Young, Heber C. Kimball, Amasa Lyman, George A. Smith, and Charles C. Rich declared to the city council their intention of absence for three months or more, and others were appointed to fill their places during their absence. John P. Greene, Lyman Wight, and William Law were absent, and their places were filled. The object of the absence of

**Passed Sept[ember]. 9th 1842. George W. Harris President pro tem.[84] James Sloan, Recorder**

The following Elections took place for Persons to Act in the place & absence of some of the City Councillors, to wit: Shadrach Roundy for Brigham Young, – Winslow Farr for Heber C. Kimball, – Edward Hunter for Amasa Lyman, – John Lytle for George A. Smith, – Joseph Young for Charles C. Rich, – Alpheus Cutler for John P. Green, – Reynolds Cahoon for Lyman Wight – & James Ivins for William Law.

**Sept[embe]r 9th 1842. George W. Harris Pres[i]d[en]t Pro tem. James Sloan, Recorder.**

Dimick B. Huntington was elected City Marshal pro tem, in the place & absence of H[enry] G. Sherwood.

**Sept[embe]r 9th 1842. George W. Harris Pres[i]d[en]t pro tem. James Sloan, Recorder.**

William H. Clayton was elected City Treasurer, to fill the vacancy occasioned by the removal of John S. Fullmer, the former incumbent, and it was Ordered that said Clayton appear and give Bond at the next meeting of this Council.

**Sept[embe]r 9th 1842. George W. Harris Pres[i]d[en]t pro tem. James Sloan, Recorder.**

An Ordinance relative to
the return of Writs of Habeas Corpus.[85]

Sec. 1. Be it, and it is hereby Ordained by the City Council of the City of Nauvoo, that the Municipal Court, in issuing Writs of Habeas Corpus, may make the same returnable forthwith.

---

these brethren was to preach the gospel in different states, and show up the wickedness and falsehood of the apostate John C. Bennett."

[84]Hyrum Smith joined the exodus out of Nauvoo. On August 29, Joseph Smith had said: "I will send Brother Hyrum to call conferences everywhere throughout the states, and let documents be taken along and show to the world the corrupt and oppressive conduct of [Lilburn] Boggs, [Thomas] Carlin, and others, that the public may have the truth laid before them" (*History of Church,* 5:138-39). On September 4, Hyrum was joined by Wilson Law on a trip to the eastern states. They returned on November 4 and reported "that John C. Bennett's exposé has done no hurt, but much good" (ibid., 183).

[85]Published in *The Wasp,* Sept. 17, 1842.

Sec. 2. This Ordinance to take effect, and be in force from and after its passage.

**Passed Sept[embe]r 9th 1842. Geo. W. Harris President pro tem. James Sloan, Recorder**

*September 26, 1842; Monday.*[86]

An Ordinance creating the
office of Notary Public in the City of Nauvoo.[87]

Sec. 1. Be it ordained by the City Council of the City of Nauvoo, that in addition to the City Officers heretofore elected, there shall be elected by the City Council One Notary Public, whose duties and fees shall hereafter be defined by Ordinance.

Sec. 2. This Ordinance to take effect and be in force from and after its passage.

**Passed Sept[embe]r 26th 1842. Wilson Law Pres[i]d[en]t Pro tem. James Sloan, Recorder.**

An Ordinance respecting
Mad Dogs, and other Animals.[88]

Sec. 1. Be it, and it is hereby Ordained by the City Council of the City of Nauvoo, that all Dogs or other Animals known to have been bit or worried by any rabid Animal shall be immediately killed or confined by the owner under a penalty not exceeding One thousand Dollars, at the discretion of the Court, and also no Dog shall be permitted to run at large in the City for thirty days after the passage of this Ordinance, under a penalty of twenty five Dollars to be paid by the owner or owners of said Dog or Dogs, and all Dogs during said thirty days shall be liable to be killed if found twenty Rods from their Masters, and such penalty or penalties shall be recoverable and applied in like manner as are other penalties within this City.

Sec. 2. this Ordinance to take effect and be in force from and after its passage.

**Passed Sept[embe]r 26th 1842. Wilson Law Pres[i]d[en]t pro tem. James Sloan, Recorder.**

---

[86]See also *History of Church,* 5:165.

[87]Published in *The Wasp,* Oct. 1, 1842.

[88]Published in ibid.

An Ordinance to regulate proceedings by and under Writs of attachment in the municipal Courts.[89]

Sec. 1. Be it, and it is hereby Ordained by the City Council of the City of Nauvoo, that the Municipal Court of said City be, and said Court hereby are, authorized and empowered to issue Writs of Attachment against all and every Person or Persons who may commit a contempt of said Court, by disobedience to any Writ or Order of said Court, and to fine to such amount, or imprison for such length of time, or both fine and imprisonment, as to them in their discretion may seem proper.

Sec. 2. This Ordinance to take effect and be in force from and after its passage.

**Passed Sept[ember] 26th 1842. Wilson Law Pres[i]d[en]t pro tem. James Sloan, Recorder.**

James Sloan, the City Recorder, was duly and unanimously elected Notary Public for this City.

**Passed Sept[ember] 26th 1842. Wilson Law, Pres[i]d[en]t pro tem. James Sloan, Recorder.**

Theodore Turleys claim of five Dollars, for making a City Seal, was allowed.

**Sept[embe]r 26th 1842. Wilson Law Pres[i]d[en]t pro tem. James Sloan, Recorder.**

The City Recorder was instructed by the City Council, to procure a Seal for the Municipal Court.

**Sept[ember] 26th 1842. James Sloan, Recorder.**

*October 8, 1842; Saturday.*

The Report of the Committee on the claim of Dimick B. Huntington was accepted, & adopted, allowing him a Sum of Twelve Dollars, for summoning Council, & attending their Meetings.

**Oct[obe]r 8th 1842. James Sloan, Recorder.**

Resolved by the City Council of the City of Nauvoo, that the Act of the Mayor & Recorder in drawing upon the City Treasury

---

[89]Published in ibid. A writ of attachment enforces obedience to a court order. Often this requires the person who fails to comply with the original order to be brought back to answer for their neglect.

for a sum of $538.50, being the claim of the City Watch up to the 27th day of August last, inclusive, be, & the same is hereby approved.
**Passed Oct[obe]r 8th 1842. James Sloan, Recorder.**

Resolved by the City Council of the City of Nauvoo, that the City Treasurer be, & he hereby is Ordered, to not make any further payment out of the City Funds, upon the Order heretofore drawn upon him, for payment of the City Watch, unless [by] further Order of this Council.
**Passed Oct[obe]r 8th 1842. James Sloan, Recorder.**

Resolved by the City Council of the City of Nauvoo, that the Supervisor be, and he hereby is instructed to proceed & recover payment of the Arrears due by delinquents for Road labour Tax, for the year 1841.
**Passed Oct[obe]r 8th 1842. James Sloan, Recorder.**

*October 25, 1842; Tuesday.*

An Ordinance respecting Carrion.[90]

Sec. 1. Be it Ordained by the City Council of the City of Nauvoo, that all Carrion be removed without the bounds of this City, or buried three feet under the surface of the Ground, by or at the expense of the Person or Persons owning the Animal when it died; & if said Person or Persons shall neglect or refuse to comply with this Ordinance, he or they shall be liable to pay a fine not exceeding ten Dollars, at the discretion of the Court, one half of the fine to go to the informer, & the other half to be paid into the City treasury, & to be recoverable in the same manner as fines of a like nature within this City. And if the owner or owners of such dead Animals cannot be ascertained, or if known, refuse to comply with this Ordinance, the Marshal shall cause the Animals to be removed or buried at the expense of the City Corporation.

Sec. 2. This Ordinance to take effect, & be in force, from & after its passage, all other Acts to the contrary notwithstanding.
**Passed Oct[obe]r 25th 1842. Wilson Law, Pres[i]d[en]t pro tem. James Sloan, Recorder.**

---

[90]Published in *The Wasp*, Oct. 29, 1842.

An Ordinance respecting absent Members.[91]

Sec. 1. Be it Ordained by the City Council of the City of Nauvoo, that in case a less number than a quorum of the City Council shall convene, they are hereby Authorized to send the Marshal or any other Person or persons by them Authorized, for any or all absent Member or Members, as the majority of such Members present shall agree, who shall take him or them into his or their custody, & bring him or them forthwith before the Council, at the expense of such absent Member or Members, respectively, unless such excuse for non-attendance shall be made as the Council[,] when a quorum is convened, shall judge sufficient; & in that case, the expense shall be paid out of the City Treasury.

Sec. 2. That the same fees be allowed the City Marshal or other Persons employed by the City Council, as are awarded to the City Marshal for like services, & that they shall be collected as all fines are, of a similar kind.

Sec. 3. This Ordinance shall take effect, and be in force, from & after its passage.

**Passed Oct[obe]r 25th 1842. Wilson Law, Pres[i]d[en]t pro tem. James Sloan, Recorder.**

Wilford Woodruff one of the Councillors gave notice of his not rendering services as a Councillor, any longer, Gratis.[92]

**October 25th 1842. James Sloan, Recorder.**

*October 31, 1842; Monday.*

It is hereby Ordered by the City Council of the City of Nauvoo, that the City Marshal shall receive fifteen Dollars from the Treasury, to apply towards his services as Marshal.

**Oct[obe]r 31st 1842. James Sloan, Recorder.**

An Ordinance concerning
the public Revenue of the City of Nauvoo.[93]

Sec. 1. [Printed sideways: "Sec[ond] amendment, p[age] 193[")]

---

[91]Published in ibid.

[92]On February 17, Woodruff had waived his $2.00 payment for attending a council meeting, but now, in the face of having to pay for the city marshal to compel his attendance, he no longer felt so magnanimous.

[93]Published in ibid., Nov. 12, 1842.

Be it Ordained by the City Council of the City of Nauvoo, that all Lands, tenements, & hereditaments, situated in this City, claimed by individuals, or bodies politic or corporate, shall be subject to taxation, except such lands as may be owned by the City Corporation, societies, or Corporations, for the purpose of burying Ground, the Temple Lot, unimproved Church Lands, and Grounds for the use of literary institutions; the following personal Property shall also be taxed, Viz: Stud Horses, Asses, Mules, Horses, Mares, Cattle, Clocks, Watches, Carriages, Waggons, Carts, money actually loaned, Stock in trade, & all other description of personal Property, & the Stock of incorporated companies, so that every Person shall pay a Tax in proportion to the value of the property he or she has in his or her possession[;] the aforesaid property declared subject to taxation shall be valued according to the true value thereof as hereinafter directed.

Sec. 2. The Recorder is hereby required to obtain from the most correct sources either within this City or elsewhere, abstracts containing a description of all City Lots & other Lands, so as to enable him to make a list of the same, & the name of the owner, which list with the name of the owner he shall cause to be made out in the form of a Book having sufficient space between the lines to insert the description of subdivision of every lot or tract, & shall keep the same in his Office. The aforesaid description of Lots and Lands shall be arranged in regular Order beginning with the lowest number on the Original Plot of the City of Nauvoo, & proceed in the same manner with each of the additions, & then the other Lands, beginning at the South West extremity of the City limits, taking notice in which Ward of the City the same may be found.

Sec. 3. There shall be appointed one Assessor & Collector in each Ward of the City, whose duty it shall be to take lists of the taxable property and Assess the value thereof, within his Ward[;] each Assessor & Collector before entering upon the duties of his appointment shall give Bond with security to be approved by the Mayor & filed in the office of the Recorder, in the sum of One Thousand Dollars, & take & subscribe an Oath or Affirmation, as follows: I A.B.[94] do solemnly swear (or affirm,) that I will faith-

[94]The initials "A.B." implied what we would call "John Doe." In the

fully & impartially perform the duties required of me as Assessor & Collector of the Ward of the City of Nauvoo, according to the best of my skill & Judgment.

Sec. 4. Within ten days after the appointment of Assessors & Collectors in any Ward, the Recorder shall cause to be delivered to each Assessor & Collector, a copy of his appointment & a transcript from the Book described in the 2nd Section of this Ordinance, containing a list & description of all taxable Lots & lands lying within the Ward of said Assessor & Collector, with the names of the Owners of the same, provided the name of the present owner shall be given when known.

Sec. 5. Every Assessor & Collector upon being notified of his appointment as aforesaid, shall provide a Book in which to take down the list of taxable property within his Ward, the names of the Owners, & the value of the property; which Book shall be ruled & headed in the following form, viz: list of property in the Ward in the City of Nauvoo, with the names of the Owners, & the Value of the property assessed by A.B. for the year 18--.

Sec. 6. It shall be the duty of each Assessor & Collector to proceed without delay[,] after being furnished with a list of taxable Lands lying within his Ward, to take a list of taxable Lands & City Lots, & all other taxable property within his Ward, [and] he shall call at the place of residence of each owner of taxable property for a list of the same, & it shall be the duty of each & every Person when called on or applied to by the Assessor & Collector to deliver to such Assessor & Collector, a list & description of all Lands & City Lots, & all other Property in his or her possession, subject to taxation, & the Assessor & Collector shall in the presence of such Person list the same in his Book & value the same according to the true value thereof, placing the description & value in figures opposite the name of the owner or Person listing the same, in the columns of the Book marked for that purpose. Lands & Lots shall be valued according to their true value without regard to the kind ^&^ character of Title, or any conflicting claims to the same, & to enable Assessors & Collectors more effectually to discharge the duties required of them, they are Authorized to administer an Oath or Affirmation to

---

entry for Nov. 14, where "A.B." is said to be "in the custody of C.D.," the principle is evident.

every Person listing taxable property, in words following. "You do solemnly Swear (or affirm) that you will true answers make to all such questions as may be propounded to you on the present occasion touching the quantity & description of taxable property now possessed or owned by you." If any Assessor & Collector shall be unable to find the owner of any Lands or Lots contained in the list furnished him by the Recorder, he shall value the same according to the best information that ^he^ can ~~be~~ obtain~~ed~~, & shall enter the same on his list in the name of the Original, or present owner if known: provided the Assessor & Collector shall not be required to enumerate any other kind of personal Property than is enumerated in the first Section of this Ordinance, but shall ascertain the aggregate value thereof, & shall set down the same in said list.

Sec. 7. If any Person shall be absent or refuse to deliver to any Assessor, when called on for that purpose a list of his or her taxable property as required by law, the Assessor & Collector shall list the same from the best information which he can obtain, & such Person shall for such refusal be liable to a penalty of twenty Dollars which may be sued for in an Action of Debt in the name of the City Corporation, before the Mayor or any Alderman of the City, & when collected shall be paid into the City Treasury, & the Testimony of the Assessor & Collector shall be sufficient evidence in the premises.

Sec. 8. Assessors & Collectors shall finish taking in the list of taxable Property within sixty days after receiving the list from the Recorder, & shall return the same together with the Original list to the Clerk of the Municipal Court, which original list he shall file and preserve in his Office, & shall deliver a Copy of the same over to the Assessors & Collectors as hereinafter provided.

Sec. 9. Upon the return of the list of taxable property by the Assessors & Collectors to the Clerk of the Municipal Court, it shall be the duty of the Clerk aforesaid to cause written notice to be posted up in three of the most public places in the City, stating that the Assessment of the City is taken, & that any Person feeling aggrieved by the valuation of their property may apply before the Municipal Court at their next sitting, for redress stating the time when and where they will sit, which Notice shall be posted up at least ten days previous to the sitting of the Court aforesaid, and have then and there the lists or Books of Assessment aforesaid.

Sec. 10. If the Court shall be satisfied either from their own knowledge or from the testimony of others, that the valuation of the Assessors & Collectors was too high[,] considered in reference to the actual value of the property, or in reference to the valuation fixed upon the property of others, they shall revalue said Property, & fix the value which ought to have been fixed by the Assessor & Collector, but applications under this Section shall be made at the time stated in the notice provided for in the preceding section, unless the Court shall adjourn for the purpose of giving longer time, and not afterwards.

Sec. 11. Assessors & Collectors shall be required to Value and assess any City Lots and other Lands not included in the list furnished them by the Recorder aforesaid, which they may ascertain to be liable to Taxation.

Sec. 12. Within ten days after the sitting of the Municipal Court aforesaid it shall be the duty of the Clerk aforesaid to make out & deliver to each Assessor & Collector alphabetical lists of taxable property returned by them as corrected by the Municipal Court aforesaid, and take receipts for the aggregate amount of Taxes to be collected upon the Lands contained in the lists, and also upon personal Property; one of which shall be filed in the Office of the City Recorder, and the other shall be delivered to the City Treasurer.

Sec. 13. For the purpose of defraying the necessary expences attendant upon the enactment, administration, & execution of the laws of this City, it is hereby declared & Ordained that a Tax of fifty Cents upon every hundred Dollars worth of taxable property shall be levied & collected from the owners thereof, or the Persons in whose names the same may be listed & assessed for taxation.

Sec. 14. The Assessors & Collectors of the City shall, so soon as they receive the lists of taxable property delivered to them by the Clerk of the Municipal Court, proceed to collect the Taxes charged upon said lists, by calling upon each & every person residing in their respective Wards, at his or her usual place of residence, & requiring payment thereof; if any person shall be absent from home when the Assessor & Collector shall call upon him or her for payment of taxes, the Assessor & Collector shall leave a Written or printed notice at the residence of every such Person stating the amount of taxes due from such Person, & requiring him or her to make payment of the same within ten days from the date of such notice, specifying the place where said payment shall be made, & such notice shall be considered a demand for the Taxes within the meaning of this Ordinance.

Sec. 15. If any Person shall fail to pay his or her taxes within ten days after the expiration of the time stated in said Notice, the Assessor & Collector is authorized & required to seize and levy upon a reasonable portion of personal property of such Person, of value sufficient to pay the Taxes & Cost, & to advertize & sell the same [property] at public vendue; he shall give ten days notice of the time & place of sale by posting up notices in three of the most public Places in his Ward, & if the property shall sell for more than sufficient to satisfy said Taxes & Cost, the remainder shall be refunded to the owner.

Sec. 16. Upon the receipt or payment of Taxes the Assessors & Collectors shall give a receipt therefor stating in such receipt the Amount paid & the value of the property taxed, & also describing each lot or tract of land by its numbers as described in the Tax list.

Sec. 17. The Assessor & Collectors shall receive in payment of taxes, City scrip, Gold & Silver Coin, but for all other funds taken by them they shall be allowed the specie value thereof only. Provided the Assessors & Collectors shall keep an accurate account of the amount of City Scrip received by them in payment of taxes, and shall endorse the name of the Person from whom he receives the same on each Bill so received, & the Treasurer, on settlement with said Assessors and Collectors shall not receive any City scrip which was not received in payment for Taxes.

Sec. 18. The Assessors and Collectors shall account for & pay over all Taxes due the City, deducting from the same the amount of all Taxes which he shall have been unable to collect on account of the insolvency, removal, or non-residence of persons charged with Taxes.

Sec. 19. It shall be the duty of the Assessors & Collectors to note upon their lists opposite the name of each Person whether such Person has paid his or her tax, and if not, the reason why, if nonresident, removed, or any other cause, & shall be required to make Oath or affirmation that the same is correct according to the best of his information & belief[;] & if upon investigation by the Municipal Court there shall be found no errors or mistake, or if found, when corrected, the Court aforesaid shall make an allowance for all Taxes he shall have been unable to collect for good & sufficient cause. Provided the Court shall be satisfied that such taxes could not have been collected by reasonable & proper diligence, & that such diligence has been used without success.

Sec. 20. If any Person shall fail to pay the taxes due upon any city lots or other lands belonging to them, & the Assessor shall be unable to find any personal property of such Person in this City whereon to levy of value sufficient to pay said taxes & Costs, it shall be his duty to make report thereof to the Clerk of the Municipal Court of the City on the first Monday of December of each year, unless a longer time be granted by the City Council, which Report shall be in the following form[:] List of Lands and City Lots situated within the limits of the City of Nauvoo and State of Illinois, on which taxes remain due & unpaid for the Year A.D. 18--. Wards. description. valuation. Amount of Tax. Costs Other Lands. City Lots. Names of Owners.

Sec. 21. Before making the report to the Municipal Court referred to in the preceding section, the Assessors & Collectors shall publish in some Newspaper within the City, if any such there be, & if there be no such paper printed in the City, then by putting up a written notice in each Ward at least four Weeks previous to reporting to said Court, & the said advertisement shall contain a list of the delinquent Lands & City Lots to be reported to said Court, the names of the owners if known, the amount of taxes due, & costs due thereon, & the year for which the same are due, & shall give notice that application will be made to the Municipal Court for Judgment against said lands & City lots for said taxes & costs thereon, & for an Order to sell the said lands or city lots for the satisfaction thereof: & shall also give notice that on the day next succeeding the said term of the said Court all the lands against which Judgment shall be pronounced & for the sale of which such Order shall be made, will be exposed to public Sale at the Recorders Office for the amount of said taxes

& Costs due thereon, & the Assessor & Collector shall obtain a certificate from the Printer of said publication, or if notice be given, by putting up written notice in each Ward, then the Collector shall certify to the same, & a copy of said advertisement together with the certificate of the due publication & report provided for in the 20th Section of this Ordinance shall be filed in the office of the Clerk of the Municipal Court.

Sec. 22. The Clerk of the municipal Court upon the filing of such Report & certificate aforesaid, shall receive & record the same in a Book to be kept for that purpose, in which he shall enter all Judgments, Orders, and other proceedings of the Court in relation thereto, & shall keep & preserve the same as a part of the Records of his Office, & shall docket all Suits brought for Taxes in the usual form of Debt, stating that the same is for Taxes.

Sec. 23. It shall be the duty of said Court to hear and determine, if any defence be made, all Suits brought for Taxes, & if no defence be made, the said Court shall pronounce Judgment against said City lots or other lands, & shall thereupon issue an Order for the sale of the same, which shall be in the following form, to wit:

State of Illinois, } Set.[95]
City of Nauvoo }

Whereas A.B. Assessor & Collector of the Ward in the City of Nauvoo, returned to the Municipal Court of this City on the __ day of ____ 18__, the following city lots & tracts of land as having been assessed for Taxes by the Assessor & Collector of said ____ Ward, for the year 18__, & that the Taxes thereon remained due & unpaid on the day of the date of the Assessors & Collectors return, & that the respective owner or owners have no Goods & Chattels within this City on which the said Assessor & Collector can levy for the taxes & Costs due thereon and unpaid on the following

[95]"Set" seems to indicate that what follows is a model–a blank form–rather than an actual document. The legal definition of *set* was "to recite," and the usage of "recite" included copying a written document (Webster, *American Dictionary,* s.vv. "set," "recite"). However, it is also possible that "set." was an abbreviation or that the authors thought so.

described lands & City lots, to wit: And whereas due notice has been given of the application for Judgment against said city lots or other lands, & no owner hath appeared to make defence or shew cause why judgment should not be entered against the said City lots & other lands or the Taxes & Costs due thereon & unpaid for the year herein setforth. Therefore it is considered by the Court that Judgment be & is hereby entered against the aforesaid tract or tracts of Land, or city lots, or parts thereof (as the case may be) in the name of the City of Nauvoo for the sum annexed to each tract of land or City lot, being the amount of taxes & Costs due severally thereon; & it is ordered by the Court that the several tracts of Land or city lots, or so much thereof as shall be sufficient of each of them, to satisfy the amount of taxes & Costs annexed to them severally, be sold as the law directs.

Sec. 24. It shall be the duty of the Clerk within five days after the adjournment of said Court to make out under the Seal of said Court a copy of the Assessors & Collectors report together with the Order of the Court thereon, which shall constitute the Process on which all lands & city lots shall be sold for Taxes, & deliver the same to the City Marshal, & the Marshal thereupon shall cause the said Lands to be sold on the day specified in the notice given by the Assessors & Collectors, & make return thereof to the Clerk aforesaid within ten days after the day of Sale.

Sec. 25. Any Person or Persons owning or claiming lands advertised for sale as aforesaid may pay the taxes & Costs due thereon, to the Assessor & Collector at any time before Judgment be pronounced against said lands or city lots, or to the Clerk at any time before the report of the Assessor & Collector shall be delivered to the Marshal, & to the Marshal at any time before the Sale of the same.

Sec. 26. The Clerk of the Municipal Court shall attend all sales of Lands or city Lots, made by the Marshal, under the provisions of this Ordinance, & shall keep a Register of the sales in a Book to be provided for that purpose, in which he shall enter each lot or parcel of land exposed to sale by the Marshal, copying the description of the same from the advertisement, & when a sale is made he shall enter the name of the purchaser, his place of residence, the quantity of land sold, & when any tract or parcel of land is run down, shall designate what part of said tract is sold, & the amount of the sale, & give certificates of Purchase to the Purchaser.

Sec. 27. Sales of City lots or other lands under this Ordinance shall be made between the hours of ten OClock A.M. & three OClock P.M., & continue from day to day if necessary, until all is sold & if no Person offers to pay the said amount of tax & cost due thereon for the whole tract of land or city lot offered by the Marshal, the same shall be struck off to the City, & the City set down as the purchaser thereof.

Sec. 28. When a portion of any such city lot or tract of land shall be struck off on any bid, it shall be taken off from an average quality of the same, considered without the building that may be found thereon.

Sec. 29. Lands or city lots sold under the provisions of this Ordinance may be redeemed at any time before the expiration of two years from the date of the sale by any person who will pay double the amount for which the same was sold, & all taxes accruing after such sale, together with six per cent interest on the amount of each subsequent years tax.

Sec. 30. Immediately after the expiration of two Years from the date of the sale of any land for taxes under the provisions of this Ordinance, the Marshal shall make out a Deed for each City lot or tract of land sold & remaining unredeemed & deliver the same to the purchaser upon the return of the certificate of Purchase. Deeds executed by the Marshal shall be in the following form:

> Know all Men by these presents that whereas on the day of ____ A.D. 18__ before the Municipal Court of the City of Nauvoo a judgment was obtained in said Court in favor of the City of Nauvoo against the (here insert the description of the land) for the sum of Dollars and Cents, being the amount of taxes & Costs assessed upon said tract of land (or city lot) for the year 18__. And whereas on the ____ day of 18__, I, A.B. Marshal of the city aforesaid by virtue of a pre-

cept issued out of the Municipal Court of the City aforesaid, dated the ____ day of __, & to me directed, did expose to public sale at the ______ in the City aforesaid, in conformity with all the requisitions of the Ordinances & laws in such cases made & provided, the tract of land (or city lot) above described, for the satisfaction of the judgment so rendered as aforesaid, And Whereas at the time & place aforesaid, C.D. of the ______ and State of ______ having offered to pay the aforesaid Sum of ____ Dollars and ____ Cents[,] for ____ which was the least quantity bid for, the said tract of land (or city lot) was stricken off to him at that price. Now therefore I, A.B. Marshal as aforesaid[,] for & in consideration of the sum of ____ Dollars and ____ Cents to me in hand paid by the said C.D. at the time of the aforesaid Sale, and by virtue of the ordinance in such case made & provided, have granted, bargained, & sold, & by these Presents do grant, bargain, & sell, unto the said C.D.[,] his Heirs & assigns[,] the ____ to have & to hold unto him[,] the said C.D.[,] his Heirs & Assigns[,] for ever, subject however to all the rights of redemption provided by law. In Witness whereof I, A.B. Marshal as aforesaid, by virtue of the authority aforesaid have hereunto subscribed my name and affixed my Seal this __ day of _____18__. ____ Marshal.

Sec. 31. The Clerk of the Municipal Court shall as City Recorder keep a correct account of all Monies or Treasurers Receipts that shall come to his Hands, so as to enable him to give a correct statement of the finances of the City at the end of each Municipal Year.

Sec. 32. The following fees & compensation shall be allowed to the several Officers & Persons herein named for services rendered under the provisions of this Ordinance. Viz. To each Assessor & Collector a sum of two Dollars per day for every day necessarily employed in the performance of his duty. To the City Treasurer for receiving & paying out the City Revenue two per Cent upon all sums paid out. To the City Recorder & Clerk of the Municipal Court for making out transcripts from his Record of Lands & City Lots, & Lands sold for taxes, two Cents per lot for each list. For assisting the Marshal in the selling Lands & City

Lots for Taxes, twenty five cents for each certificate of purchase. And he shall also be allowed the sum of ten Dollars for the strict performance of his duties as herein setforth, & making a complete exhibit of the state of the finances of the City, annually, to be paid out of the City Treasury. There shall also be allowed for publishing the advertisement for the sale of lands or city lots the sum of four cents for each lot or parcel of land contained in the list of Sales, & also to the Assessor & Collector the sum of two cents for each city lot or parcel of land in said list, & ten per cent for selling personal property for taxes, & the sum of twentyfive cents for advertising the same. Provided he shall not reckon the time so expended in making out said list & advertising & selling, in his settlement. And to the Marshal for selling said Lands or city Lots, the sum of six cents for each lot or tract sold, to be collected from the sale of said property.

Sec. 33. Any Person who may accept the appointment of Assessor & Collector in any Ward in this City, & shall fail to perform the duties required of him, shall forfeit & pay the sum of One hundred Dollars for the use of the City to be recovered by action of Debt in the name of the City, and shall moreover be liable for all damages sustained by the City by reason of such failure. Provided if any Assessor & Collector is unable from sickness or any other unavoidable casualty to discharge his duties, he shall forthwith tender his resignation to the City Recorder, which shall fully discharge him from the penalty aforesaid, & the City Council shall fill such vacancy.

Sec. 34. This Ordinance to take effect & be in force from & after its passage.

**Passed October 31st 1842. Joseph Smith, Mayor. James Sloan, Recorder.**

*November 12, 1842; Saturday.*[96]

Resolved by the City Council of the City of Nauvoo, that Kimball Street be opened from Barlow Street East to Bagby Street, at the expence of George McKinzie & others [of the] Petitioners.

**Passed Nov[embe]r 12th 1842. Joseph Smith, Mayor. James Sloan, Recorder.**

---

[96]See also *History of Church,* 5:184.

*November 14, 1842; Monday.*[97]

An Ordinance regulating the proceedings on Writs of Habeas Corpus.[98]

Sec. 1. Be it ordained by the City Council of the City of Nauvoo, that if any Person or Persons shall be or stand committed, or detained for any criminal or supposed criminal matter, it shall & may be lawful for him, her, or them, to apply to the Municipal Court, when in Session, or to the Clerk thereof, in vacation, for a Writ of Habeas Corpus, which application shall be in writing, & signed by the Prisoner, or some Person on his, her, or their behalf, setting forth the facts concerning his, her, or their imprisonment, & in whose Custody he, she, or they are detained, & shall be accompanied by a Copy of the Warrant or Warrants of commitment, or an Affidavit that the said Copy had been demanded of the Person or Persons in whose custody the Prisoner or Prisoners are detained, and by him or them refused or neglected to be given; the said Court or Clerk to whom the application shall be made shall forthwith award the said Writ of Habeas Corpus, unless it shall appear from the Petition itself, or from the documents annexed that the party can neither be discharged nor admitted to Bail, nor in any other manner relieved. Which said Writ shall be Issued under the hand of the Clerk, & the Seal of the Court; which seal may be a Written one, until another shall be obtained, & shall be in the following Words, to wit: "Seal of the Municipal Court of the City of Nauvoo." & said Writ shall be in substance as follows, to wit:

State of Illinois } The People of the State of Illinois, to
} the Set.
City of Nauvoo } Marshal of said City, Greeting:

Whereas application has been made before the Municipal Court of said City that the Body (or Bodies) of A.B. &c. is or are in the custody of C.D. &c. of &c. These are therefore to

---

[97]See also ibid., 185-92.

[98]Published in *The Wasp,* Dec. 3, 1842. After this ordinance was passed, Joseph Smith felt "secure enough" to come out of hiding and "stay at home as the law protected him as well as all other citizens" (Kenney, *Woodruff's Journal,* 2:192).

command the said C.D. &c. of &c. to safely have the body (or Bodies) of said A. B. &c in his custody detained as it is said, together with the day and cause of his (her or their) capt[ure] & detention, by whatsoever name the said A.B. &c. may be known or called, before the Municipal Court of said City, forthwith, to abide such Order as the said Court shall make in this behalf, and further, if the said C.D. &c. or other Person or Persons having said A.B. &c. in custody, shall refuse or neglect to comply with the provisions of this Writ, you, the Marshal of said City, or other Person authorized to serve the same, are hereby required to arrest the Person or Persons so ^refusing or^ neglecting ~~or refusing~~ to comply as aforesaid, & bring him or them, together with the Person or Persons in his or their custody, forthwith, before the Municipal Court aforesaid, to be dealt with according to law; & herein fail not, & bring this Writ with you. Witness J[ames] S[loan] Clerk of the Municipal Court, at Nauvoo, this __ day of ____ in the Year of our Lord One thousand eight hundred and ____. [Signed by] J[ames] S[loan], Clerk. And [the prisoner will] be directed to the City Marshal, & shall be served by delivering a Copy [of the writ] thereof to the Person or Persons in whose custody the Prisoner or Prisoners are detained, & said Writ shall be made returnable forthwith, & the form & substance thereof, as hereinset forth, & be taken & considered as part & parcel of this Ordinance; To the intent that no Officer, Sheriff, Jailor, Keeper, or other person, or persons, upon whom such Writ shall be served, may pretend ignorance thereof, every such Writ & copy thereof served shall be endorsed with these Words, "By the Habeas Corpus Act;" & whenever the said Writ shall by an[y] Person be served upon the Sheriff, Jailor, Keeper, or other Person or Persons whomsoever, holding said Prisoner or Prisoners, or being brought to him or them, or being served upon any of his or their under officers or deputies at the Jail, or place where the Prisoner or Prisoners are detained, he or they or some of his or their under officers or deputies shall, upon payment or tender of the charges of bringing the said Prisoner or Prisoners, to be ascertained by the Court awarding the said Writ, & indorsed thereon, not exceeding ten cents per mile; & upon sufficient security given to pay the charges of carrying him, her or them back, if he, she, or they shall be remanded, make return of such Writ, & bring, or cause to be brought the Body or Bodies of the Prisoner or Prisoners before the Municipal Court forthwith, & certify the true cause of his, her, or their imprisonment, unless the commitment of such Person or Persons shall be to the County Jail, in Hancock County, in which case the time shall be prolonged till five days after the delivery of the Writ as aforesaid, and not longer. Provided, nevertheless, that in case any Person or Persons may at any time hereafter be taken & lodged in the City or County Jail, under any Writ or process, as provided by the City Charter of the City of Nauvoo, & shall require a Writ of Habeas Corpus to issue, to bring him, her, or them before the Municipal Court of said City, said Writ shall issue to bring him, her, or them before said Court, & be directed to the city Marshal to be served upon the person or persons in whose custody such Prisoner or Prisoners may then be detained.

Sec. 2. Where any Person or Persons not being committed or detained for any criminal, or supposed criminal matter, shall be confined, or restrained of his, her or their liberty, under any color or pretence whatever, he, she, or they may apply for a Writ of Habeas Corpus, as aforesaid, which application shall be in writing signed by the Party, or some person on his, her, or their behalf, setting forth the facts concerning his, her, or their imprisonment, & wherein the illegality of such imprisonment consists, & in whose custody he, she, or they are detained; which application, or Petition, shall be verified by the Oath or affirmation of the party applying, or some other Person on his, her, or their behalf; if the confinement or restraint is by virtue of any judicial Writ or Process, or Order, a copy thereof shall be annexed thereto, or an affidavit made that the same had been demanded & refused: the same proceedings shall thereupon be had in all respects, as are directed in the preceding Section, & any officer, person, or persons knowing that he, or they, have an illegal Writ, or not having any Writ, who shall attempt through any false pretext to take or intimidate any of the inhabitants of this City, through such pretext, shall forfeit for every such offence a sum not exceeding One thousand Dollars, nor less than five hundred Dollars, or in case of failure to pay such forfeiture, to be imprisoned not more than twelve Months nor less than six Months.

Sec. 3. Upon the return of the Writ of Habeas Corpus, a day shall be set for the hearing of the Cause of imprisonment or detainer, not exceeding five days thereafter unless the Prisoner or Prisoners shall request a longer time. The said Prisoner or Prisoners may deny any of the material facts set forth in the return, or may alledge any fact to shew, either that the imprisonment or detention is unlawful, or that he, she, or they is or are then entitled to his, her, or their discharge, which allegations or denials shall be made on oath. The said return may be amended by leave of the Court; before or after the same is filed, as also may all suggestions made against it, that thereby material facts may be ascertained. The said Court shall proceed in a summary way to settle the said facts, by hearing the testimony & arguments, as well of all Parties interested civilly, if any there be, as of the Prisoner or Prisoners, & the Person or Persons who holds him, her, or them in custody, & shall dispose of the Prisoner or Prisoners as the case may require. If it appear that the Prisoner or Prisoners are in custody by Virtue of Process from any Court, legally constituted, he, she, or they can be discharged for the following causes: First, where the Court has exceeded the limits of its Jurisdiction, either as to the matter, place, sum, Person or Persons; second, where though the original imprisonment was lawful, yet by some Act, omission or event which has subsequently taken place, the party has become entitled to his, her, or their discharge; Third, where the process is defective in some substantial form required by law; Fourth, where the process though in proper form has been issued in a case, or under circumstances where the law does not allow Process, or orders for imprisonment or arrest, to issue; Fifth, where, although in proper form, the process has been issued or executed by a Person or Persons, either <un>Authorized to issue or execute the same, or where the Person or Persons having the custody of the Prisoner or Prisoners under such Process is not the person or Persons empowered by law to detain him, her, or them; Sixth, where the process appears to have been obtained by false pretence or bribery; Seventh, where there is no general law, nor any judgment, order, or decree of a Court to authorize the process, if in a civil suit, nor any conviction, if in a criminal proceeding. In all cases where the imprisonment is for a criminal or supposed criminal matter, if it shall appear to the said Court that there is ~~a~~ sufficient legal cause for the commitment of the Prisoner or Prisoners, although such commitment may have been informally made, or without due authority, or the process may have been executed by a Person or Persons not duly authorized, the Court shall make a new commitment, in proper form, & directed to the proper Officer or Officers, or admit the party to Bail, if the case be bailable.

Sec. 4. When any Person or Persons shall be admitted to Bail, on Habeas Corpus, he, she, or they shall enter into Recognizance with one or more securities in such sum as the Court shall direct, having regard to the circumstances of the Prisoner or Prisoners, & the nature of the offence, conditioned for his, her or their appearance at the next Circuit Court to be holden in & for the County where the offence was committed, or where the same is to be tried: Where the Court shall admit to bail, or remand any Prisoner or Prisoners brought before the Court, on any Writ of Habeas Corpus, it shall be the duty of said Court to bind all such Persons as do declare any thing material to prove the offence with which the Prisoner or Prisoners are charged, by recognizance to appear at the proper Court having cognizance of the Offence, on the first day of the next Term thereof, to give evidence touching the said offence, & not to depart the said Court without leave: which Recognizance so taken, together with the Recognizance entered into by the Prisoner or Prisoners, when he, she or they are admitted to Bail, shall be certified & returned to the proper Court on the first day of the next succeeding term thereof. If any such Witness or Witnesses shall neglect or refuse to enter into a Recognizance as aforesaid, when thereunto required, it shall be lawful for the Court to commit him, her, or them to Jail until he, she, or they shall enter into such recognizance, or be otherwise discharged by due course of law; if the Court shall neglect or refuse to bind any such Witness or Witnesses, Prisoner or Prisoners, by recognizance as aforesaid, or to return any such recognizance, when taken as aforesaid, the Court shall be deemed guilty of a misdemeanour in office, & be proceeded against accordingly.

Sec. 5. Where any Prisoner or Prisoners brought up on a Habeas Corpus, shall be remanded to Prison, it shall be the duty of the Municipal Court remanding him, her, or them, to make out & deliver to the Sheriff, or other Person or Persons to whose Custody he, she, or they shall be remanded, an Order in writing, stating the cause or causes of remanding him, her, or them. If such Prisoner or Prisoners shall obtain a second Writ of habeas Corpus, it shall be the duty of such Sheriff or other Person or Persons upon whom the same shall be served to return therewith the Order aforesaid; & if it shall appear that the said Prisoner or Prisoners were remanded for an offence adjudged not bailable, it shall be taken & received as conclusive, & the Prisoner or Prisoners shall be remanded without further proceedings.

Sec. 6. It shall not be lawful for the Municipal Court on a second Writ of Habeas Corpus obtained by such Prisoner or Prisoners to discharge the said Prisoner or Prisoners if he, she or they are proven guilty of the charges clearly & specifically charged in the Warrant of Commitment with a criminal offence, but if the Prisoner, or Prisoners shall be found guilty, the Municipal Court shall only admit such Prisoner or Prisoners to bail, where the offence is bailable by law, or Ordinance, or remand him, her, or them to Prison where the offence is not bailable; or being bailable, if such Prisoner or Prisoners shall fail to give the Bail required.

Sec. 7. No Person or Persons Who have been discharged by Order of the Municipal Court on a habeas Corpus, shall be again imprisoned, restrained, or kept in custody for the same cause, unless he, she, or they, be afterwards indicted for the same offence, or unless by the legal Order or Process of the Municipal Court wherein he, she or they are bound by recognizance to appear; the following shall not be deemed to be the same cause, First, if after a discharge for defect of proof, or any material defect in the commitment in a criminal case the Prisoner or Prisoners should be again arrested upon sufficient proof & committed by legal process, for the same offence; Second, if in a civil suit the Party or Parties have been discharged for any illegality in the judgment or Process & are afterwards imprisoned by legal process, for the same cause of Action; Third, generally, whenever the discharge has been ordered on account of the non-observance of any of the forms required by law the Party or Parties may be a second time imprisoned if the cause be legal & the forms required by law observed.

Sec. 8. If any Person or Persons shall be committed for a criminal matter in case of the absence of a Witness or Witnesses whose testimony may be considered to be of importance in behalf of the People, the Municipal Court may adjourn from time to time at its discretion, provided they decide upon the Case within thirty days, if it shall appear by Oath or affirmation that the witness or Witnesses for the people of the State are absent, such Witness or Witnesses being mentioned by name & the Court shewn wherein their testimony is material.

Sec. 9. Any Person or Persons being committed to the City or County Jail, as provided in the Charter of the City of Nauvoo, or in the custody of any Officer, Sheriff, Jailor, keeper, or other Person or Persons, or his or their under officer or deputy for any criminal, or supposed criminal matter shall not be removed from said Prison or custody, into any Prison or custody unless it be by Habeas Corpus, or by an Order of the Municipal Court, or in case of sudden Fire[,] infection[,] or other necessities; if any Person or Persons shall after such commitment as aforesaid, make out, sign, or countersign any Warrant or Warrants, for such removal, then he or they shall forfeit to the Prisoner or Prisoners, aggrieved, a sum not exceeding five hundred Dollars, to be recovered by the Prisoner or Prisoners aggrieved in the manner hereinafter mentioned.

Sec. 10. If any Member of the Municipal Court, or the Clerk of said Court shall corruptly refuse or neglect to issue Writ or Writs of Habeas Corpus, when legally applied to, in a case where such Writ or Writs may lawfully issue, or who shall for the purpose of oppression unreasonably delay the issuing of such Writ or Writs, shall for every such offence forfeit to the Prisoner or Prisoners, party or Parties aggrieved a sum not less than five hundred Dollars, and not exceeding One thousand Dollars, & be imprisoned for six Months.

Sec. 11. If any Officer, Sheriff, Jailor, keeper, or other Person or Persons upon whom any such Writ shall be served, shall neglect or refuse to make the returns as aforesaid, or to bring the Body of the Prisoner or Prisoners according to the command of the said Writ, within the time required by this Ordinance, all & every such Officer, Sheriff, Jailor, keeper, or other Person or Persons shall be guilty of a contempt of the Municipal Court who issued said Writ; Whereupon the said Court may, & shall, issue an attachment against said Officer, Sheriff, Jailor, keeper, or other Person or persons & cause him or them to be committed to the City or county Jail as ~~an~~ provided for by the City Charter of the City of Nauvoo; there to remain without bail or mainprize, until he or they shall obey the said Writ; such Officer, Sheriff, Jailor, keeper, or other Person or Persons shall also forfeit to the Prisoner or Prisoners, party or parties, aggrieved a sum not exceeding One thousand Dollars, & not less than five hundred Dollars.

Sec. 12. Any Person or Persons having a Prisoner or Prisoners in his or their custody, or under his or their restraint, power or control, for whose relief or Writ ^or Writs^ of Habeas Corpus is issued who with ~~the~~ intent to avoid the effect of such Writ or Writs, shall transfer such Person or Persons to the custody of, or place him, her or them under the control of any other Person or Persons, or shall conceal him, her or them, or change the place of his, her, or their confinement, with intent to avoid the operation of such Writ or Writs, or with intent to remove him, her or them out of the state, shall forfeit for every such offence one Thousand Dollars, & may be imprisoned not less than one year, nor more than five years. In any prosecution for the penalty incurred, under this section, it shall not be necessary to shew that the Writ or Writs of Habeas Corpus had issued at the time of the removal, transfer or concealment therein mentioned, if it be proven that the Acts therein forbidden were done with the intent to avoid the operation of such Writ or Writs.

Sec. 13. Any Sheriff, or his deputy, any Jailor or Coroner, having custody of any Prisoner or Prisoners, committed on any civil or criminal Process, of any Court or Magistrate, who shall neglect to give such Prisoner or Prisoners a copy of the process, order or commitment by virtue of which he, she, or they are imprisoned, within six hours after demand made by said Prisoner or Prisoners, or any one on his, her, or their behalf shall forfeit five hundred Dollars.

Sec. 14. Any Person who knowing that another has been discharged by Order of the Municipal Court, on a Habeas Corpus shall contrary to the provisions of this Ordinance, arrest or detain him or her again for the same cause, which was shewn on return of such Writ, shall forfeit one thousand Dollars, for the first offence & two thousand Dollars for every subsequent one.

Sec. 15. All the pecuniary forfeitures incurred under this Ordinance shall be and inure to the use of the Party for whose benefit the Writ of Habeas Corpus was issued, & shall be sued for & recovered with Costs, by the City Attorney, in the name of the City, by information, & the amount when recovered, shall without any deduction, be paid to the Parties entitled thereto.

Sec. 16. In any Action or suit for any Offence against the provisions of this Ordinance, the Defendant or Defendants may plead the general issue, & give the special matter in evidence.

Sec. 17. The recovery of said Penalties shall be no bar to a civil suit for Damages.

Sec. 18. The Municipal Court upon issuing a Writ of Habeas Corpus, may appoint any suitable Person to serve the same, other than the Marshal, & shall endorse the appointment on the back of said Writ.

Sec. 19. This Ordinance to take effect & be in force from & after its passage, any act heretofore to the contrary thereof in any wise notwithstanding.

**Passed Nov[embe]r 14th 1842. Joseph Smith, Mayor. James Sloan, Recorder.**

The Assessor and Collector is hereby required to lodge all Funds received by him for City Taxes, & now in his Hands, with the City Treasurer, & lay a statement of the Arrears due for city Taxes, before the City Council.

**Nov[embe]r 14th 1842. James Sloan, Recorder.**

The City Council of the City of Nauvoo, do hereby approve of the Act of the Recorder, in drawing upon the City Treasury for a sum of fifty Cents for a Block for a Seal for the Municipal Court, which sum was included in an Order drawn upon the Treasury for $5.00, for a City Seal.

**Nov[embe]r 14th 1842. James Sloan, Recorder.**

*November 19, 1842; Saturday.* [Although there was a city council meeting on this date, there are no extant minutes.[99]]

*November 26, 1842; Saturday.*[100]

<u>An Ordinance</u> regulating the erection & removal of Slaughter Houses within the City of Nauvoo:[101]

<u>Sec. 1.</u> Be it Ordained by the City Council of the City of Nauvoo, that any establishment, House, or Houses, now erected, or which may hereafter be erected within the limits of the Corporation of said City, for the purpose of Slaughtering Cattle, Sheep, Hogs, or other Animals, said Establishment, House, or Houses being situated within one half Mile of any dwelling House within said City, shall be considered public Nuisance or Nuisances, & shall be removed according to the Ordinances in such Case made ~~made~~ & provided, said Nuisances to be removed at the expence of the Owner.

<u>Sec. 2.</u> If the owner of any such establishment, house or houses, shall, on being duly warned by the Mayor, or an Officer appointed by him, refuse to remove such nuisance or nuisances, he shall be fined in the sum of One hundred Dollars for each House or establishment, for every Week that he continues to use such establishment, house, or houses for the purpose of Slaughter.

<u>Sec. 3.</u> If such nuisance is not removed within one month of the time that the Person or Persons received warning thereof, the Mayor shall have power to remove such nuisance at the expence of the offending party, in addition to the above named fines, & the Mayor shall draw from the City Treasury all necessary expences incurred by such removal, which said fines & expences shall be collected before an Alderman, or the Mayor, as in other cases of Debt.

<u>Sec. 4.</u> This Ordinance to take effect, & be in force, from & after its passage.

**Passed Nov[embe]r 26th 1842. Joseph Smith, Mayor. James Sloan, Recorder.**

---

[99]Kenney, *Wilford Woodruff's Journal,* 2:192.

[100]See also *History of Church,* 5:194-95.

[101]Published in *The Wasp,* Dec. 10, 1842.

The following Elections took place by Ballot, for Assessors & Collectors, for this City, John S. Higbee[102] for the first Ward, – Elijah Fordham for the second Ward, – Jonathan H. Hale for the third Ward, – & Henry G. Sherwood for the fourth Ward, for the Assessment for the year 1842.

**Nov[embe]r 26th 1842. James Sloan, Recorder.**

Resolved by the City Council of the City of Nauvoo, that the Seal to be procured for the Municipal Court of this City, shall consist of a Circle, including the Words, "Municipal Court. – City of Nauvoo," within which is to be a Book circled with Rays, on which is to be inscribed the Words "Constitution and Charter."

**Passed Nov[embe]r 26th 1842. James Sloan, Recorder**

---

[102]John Somers Higbee was born in 1804 in Tate, Ohio. He was baptized in 1831. He moved to Illinois in 1840 and died in 1877.

3.

# "Regarding the Protection of the Citizens" 1843

†*January 14, 1843; Saturday.*

Resolved by the City Council of the City of Nauvoo, that the balance of Cash now reported to be in the Treasury, and which will be remaining therein after paying Alderman [William] Marks the balance due him on the purchase of the burying Ground, be paid over by the Treasurer to the City Recorder, in part payment for his services as Recorder.

**Passed Jan[uar]y 14th 1843. James Sloan, Recorder.**

An Ordinance regulating
Municipal Elections in the City of Nauvoo.[1]

Sec. 1. Be it Ordained by the City Council of the City of Nauvoo, that all general Elections for Mayor, Aldermen, and Counsellors in the City of Nauvoo shall be held, conducted, and returns thereof made in the manner hereinafter prescribed.

Sec. 2. The City Council may divide the City into as many Wards as they may think proper, not exceeding eight; and shall designate the House or place in each Ward at which Elections are to be held; and the Wards and places of holding Elections so

[1]Published in *The Wasp,* Feb. 1, 1843.

established, shall so remain, until changed by Order of the City Council; and all general Elections shall be held at the places so designated, until changed as aforesaid, provided that the City Council may Order that the said election of Mayor, Aldermen, and Counsellors, shall be held at one place if they shall deem it expedient.

Sec. 3. On the first Monday of February next, and every two years thereafter, an election shall be held for the election of One Mayor, four Aldermen, and nine Counsellors; and the City Council shall, at least twenty days previous to any election, appoint three capable and discreet Persons possessing the qualifications of Electors, to act as Judges of election, in each place of election; and the Recorder shall make out and deliver to the Marshal of the City, immediately after the appointment of said Judges, a notice thereof in writing, directed to the Judges so appointed; and it shall be the duty of the Marshal, within five days after the receipt of said notice, to serve the same on each Judge of election. The said Judges of election shall choose two Persons having similar qualifications with themselves, to act as Clerks of the election.

Sec. 4. Previous to any votes being taken at any election, the Judges and Clerks thereof shall severally take an Oath in the following form, to wit: "I A.B. do solemnly swear (or affirm as the case may be) that I will perform the duties of Judge, (or Clerk as the case may be,) according to Law and the best of my ability; that I will studiously endeavour to prevent fraud, deceit, and abuse in conducting the same:" which Oath may be administered by any Person having authority to administer the same, or by any of the Judges of the election.

Sec. 5. If any person appointed to act as Judge or Clerk of the Election ^as^ aforesaid, shall neglect, or refuse to be sworn or affirmed to act in such capacity, the place of such person shall be filled by nomination of the other Judge or Judges of the Election; and if there be no Judge of the Election present to fill such vacancy or vacancies by nomination, at the time of holding said Election, then the three Judges shall be chosen viva voce[2] by the Electors present.

[2]Latin for "by mouth," which means to give vocal assent.

Sec. 6. The City Council shall at least twenty days previous to any general election determine the number of Aldermen and Counsellors and otherwise designate the offices to be filled at the ensuing election, and the place or places at which such election shall be held; and the Recorder shall immediately make out and deliver to the Marshal four written notices thereof (or as many as there are City Wards;) and the Marshal shall post up in some public place in each Ward, the proper notice as aforesaid, at least ten days previous to any general election. The Notices as aforesaid shall be, as nearly as circumstances will admit, as follows, to wit:

Notice.

> Is hereby given, that on Monday the __ day of next ____ at the house of ____ in the Ward, in the City of Nauvoo, a general election will be held, for the election of One Mayor, four Aldermen, and nine Counsellors, for said City, which election will be opened at eight O clock in the morning and will continue open until Six O Clock in the afternoon of the same day. Dated at Nauvoo this __ day of ____ A.D. 18 __. By Order of the City Council. J[ames] S[loan], Recorder.

Sec. 7. At all elections to be held under this Ordinance the polls shall be open at the hour of eight in the morning, and continue open until Six O Clock in the afternoon of the same day, at which time the polls shall be closed: Provided, however, that if no Judge shall attend at the hour of eight in the morning, and it shall be necessary for the electors present to appoint Judges to conduct the election, as hereinbefore prescribed, the election may in that case commence at any hour before the time for closing the Polls shall arrive, as the Case may require: and provided also, that the Judges of the Election may, if they shall deem it necessary, for the purpose of receiving the votes of all the electors wishing to vote; postpone the closing of the Polls until twelve O Clock at night. And upon opening of the Poll, one of the Clerks, under the direction of the Judges, shall make proclamation of the same; and thirty minutes before the closing of the Polls, proclamation shall be made in like manner that the Poll will be closed in half an hour.

Sec. 8. All free white Male inhabitants who are of the Age of twentyone Years, who shall have resided within this State six Months next preceding any election, and who shall have been actual residents of the City of Nauvoo sixty days next preceding said Election, shall be entitled to vote for City Officers.[3]

Sec. 9. The manner of voting shall be by the Electors approaching the bar, in the election room, at any time when the poll is open, and addressing the Judges of the election in his proper Person, and with an audible voice, to be heard by the Judges and Clerks of the election, to mention by name the Persons he intends to vote for to fill the different offices which are to be filled at the said election, and the Clerks shall enter his name and vote accordingly, and he shall then withdraw[4]: Provided that a Voter may Vote by presenting an open Ticket to the Judges, containing the names of the persons for whom he votes, and the Offices; and the said Judges shall read the same to the voter, and the Clerks with the assent of the voter, shall set the same down in their Books, as in other cases.

Sec. 10. When any person shall present himself to give his vote, and either of the Judges shall suspect that such person does not possess the requisite qualifications of an elector, or if his Vote shall be challenged by an elector who has previously given his Vote at such election, the Judges of the election shall tender to such person an Oath or affirmation in the following form, to wit: "I A.B. do solemnly swear, (or affirm as the case may be,) that I am a resident of the City of Nauvoo; that I have resided in said City for the period of sixty days next preceding this election; that I have resided in the State of Illinois, for the period of Six Months immediately preceding this Election; that I have to the best of my knowledge and belief, attained to the age of twenty one Years; and that I have not voted at this Election." And if the person so offering his vote shall take such Oath or affirmation, or shall consent to take the same, his vote shall be received,

---

[3]The Illinois Constitution of 1818 had almost identical language: "In all elections, all white male inhabitants above the age of 21 years, having resided in the state six months next preceding the election, shall enjoy the right of an elector."

[4]In other words, they did not have secret ballots, which was also true for state elections.

unless it shall be proved by evidence satisfactory to a majority of the Judges, that said Oath or Affirmation is false; and if such Person refused to take such Oath or Affirmation, his Vote shall be rejected. And if any person shall take the said Oath or affirmation knowing it to be false, he shall be deemed guilty of wilful and corrupt perjury, and shall on conviction be punished accordingly. And it any Person shall vote at any election, knowing himself not to be a qualified Voter he shall forfeit and pay any sum not exceeding fifty Dollars, nor less than twenty five Dollars, to be recovered in the same manner as other penalties under this Ordinance.

Sec. 11. For the preservation of Order, as well as the security of the judges and Clerks of the election from insult and abuse, it shall be the duty of the Marshal and the high Constables, when called upon by the Judges of the Election, to attend at all elections within their respective Wards; and should neither the Marshal nor any Constable be present at such election, the Judges of Election are hereby authorized and empowered to appoint one or more special Constables to assist in preserving Order, during the election; and the Judges are hereby empowered to impose a fine, not exceeding twenty Dollars, on any person or persons, who shall conduct [himself] in a disorderly and riotous manner, and should he refuse to pay said fine, or persist in such Conduct after having been warned of the consequences or fined as aforesaid, the Judges may cause such person or persons so offending, to be arrested and committed to the common Jail of the City or County, for any time not exceeding twenty days, or until the fine shall be paid, or he or they discharged by due course of law; and the Marshal or Constable to whom the Order shall be directed, and the Jailor of the City or County are hereby required to execute such Order, and receive such person or persons so committed, as though it had been issued or delivered by a Magistrate in due form of law.

Sec. 12. When the Votes shall have been examined and counted, the Clerks shall set down in their Poll Books, the name of every person voted for, written at full length, the office for which such Person received such Vote or Votes, and the number he did receive, the number being expressed in words at full length, such entry to be made as nearly as circumstances will admit, in the following form, to wit: "At an election held at the House of ____ in ____ Ward in the City of Nauvoo in the State of Illinois on the __ day of ____ in the Year of Our Lord One thousand eight hundred and forty ____ the following named Persons received the number of Votes annexed to their respective names, for the following described Offices, to wit:

A—B— had sixty three Votes for Mayor.<br>
C—D— had thirty four Votes for Mayor.<br>
E—F— had sixty one Votes for Alderman.<br>
G—H— had sixty Votes for Alderman.<br>
I—K— had forty Votes for Alderman.<br>
L—M— had seventy Votes for Counsellor.<br>
(And in the same manner for any other names or offices [and] votes for.)

Certified by us A—B— }<br>
C—D— } Judges of the Election<br>
E—F— }<br>
Attest G—H— } Clerks of the Election.<br>
I—K— }

The Judges of the election shall then enclose and Seal one of the Poll Books, under cover, directed to the Recorder of the City, and the packet thus sealed shall be conveyed by one of the Judges or Clerks of the Election, to be determined by lot if they cannot otherwise agree, and delivered to the said Recorder at his office, within two days from the close of the Polls, and the other Poll Book shall be deposited with one of the Judges of the election to be determined as aforesaid, and the Poll Book shall be subject to the inspection of any elector who may wish to examine it.

Sec. 13. On the third day after the election, or sooner if all the returns be received, the Recorder, taking to his assistance two Aldermen of the City, shall proceed to open the returns and make out his abstract of the same; and shall make out a certificate of election, under the Seal of the Corporation, to each of the Persons having the highest number of Votes for Mayor, Aldermen, and Counsellors, and shall deliver the same to the person entitled thereto, on his making application for that purpose to the Recorder at his Office. And it shall be the duty of the

Recorder, on the receipt of the election returns of any general election, to make out his certificate, stating therein the compensation to which the Judges and Clerks of each election may be entitled, for their services, and to lay the same before the next City Council, and the City Council shall Order the compensation aforesaid to be paid out of the City Treasury.

Sec. 14. If, by reason of any two or more persons having an equal and the highest number of Votes for one and the same Office, the requisite number of Officers shall not be elected, the Recorder shall give notice to the several Persons so having an equal and the highest number of Votes, to attend at his Office, at a time to be appointed by the said Recorder, who shall then and there proceed publicly to decide by lot which of the Persons so having an equal number of Votes shall be declared duly elected; and the Recorder shall make out and deliver to the Person thus declared duly elected, a Certificate of his election, as herein before provided.

Sec. 15. The Recorder, immediately after making out the abstracts of Votes given at any general election, shall make out his Certificate, under Seal of the Corporation, certifying the names of the Persons duly elected Mayor, ^and^ Aldermen, and the time and place of said election, and shall transmit the same by Mail, to the Secretary of State; and upon the receipt of their respective Commissions shall require of each the Oath of Office, now required by law of Justices of the peace, [who] shall Certify the same upon their respective Commissions, and deliver the same to each Person entitled thereto.

Sec. 16. When any Candidate shall desire to contest the validity of any Election, or the right of any Person declared duly elected to hold and exercise the office of Mayor, Alderman, or Counsellor, such Candidate shall give notice of his intention, in writing, to the Person whose election he intends to contest, or leave a notice thereof at his usual place of residence, within ten days after the day of election; expressing the points on which the same will be contested, the name of One Alderman of the City, who will attend at the Trial of such contest, the time, and the place, when and where said Trial will be held, which time shall not exceed thirty days from the day of the election. And the Person whose election is contested, shall, within five days after receiving said notice, select another Alderman to attend said Trial: Provided however, that should the party whose election is contested, refuse or neglect to select an Alderman as aforesaid, the Alderman chosen by the person contesting the election as aforesaid, shall make such selection; and the two Aldermen so selected shall make choice of a third Alderman; and if they cannot agree upon a third Alderman to act with them, they shall make such selection by lot; and the three Aldermen thus selected, or either of them, shall have power, and they are hereby authorized and required to issue Subpoenas and such other Process as may be necessary to secure the attendance at such Trial of all persons whose testimony may be required by either party, in the same manner as is provided in other cases of proceedings before Justices of the Peace. The said Aldermen shall meet at the time and place appointed for the trial of said Contest as aforesaid, and after hearing and examining the evidence offered by both parties, they shall decide which of the said Candidates shall have been duly elected, and shall certify the same to the Recorder, who shall thereupon make out and deliver to the successful party a certificate of his election as hereinbefore provided. The said Aldermen shall enter judgment against the unsuccessful party. Either party may appeal from the decision of said Aldermen to the municipal Court as in other Cases, and the decision of said Court shall be final. And the unsuccessful Party shall pay all Costs incurred before either or both of said Courts, as the Case may be.

Sec. 17. There shall be allowed out of the City Treasury to the several Judges and Clerks of election, such compensation, not exceeding two Dollars per day; as the City Council shall deem proper to allow; they shall also allow to the Clerks of election such compensation as they may deem just, for any stationary such Clerk may have furnished for the purposes of election.

Sec. 18. If any Judge of the election, or Clerk, or any other officer or person, in any manner concerned in conducting the election, shall wilfully neglect, improperly delay, or refuse to perform any of the duties required by this Ordinance, after having undertaken to perform such duties, he shall, on conviction thereof before the Mayor or municipal Court, be fined in any sum not exceeding One hundred Dollars; and if any such Judge of the election, Clerk, or other Officer or person, in any wise concerned in conducting the election, shall knowingly admit any person to vote, [who is] not qualified according to law; or shall knowingly receive and count more than one Vote for one person, at the same election for one office; or shall be guilty of fraud, corruption, or partiality, or manifest misbehaviour in any matter or thing relating to said election; or shall refuse to receive the Vote of any elector, who has a right according to law to vote at the Polls; each and every person so offending, shall upon conviction thereof before the Mayor, or municipal Court, be fined in any sum not exceeding One hundred Dollars, for each and every offence; each of the aforesaid fines to be collected and appropriated in the name of, and for the benefit of the City; together with Costs of Suits, provided, that nothing in this Ordinance shall be so construed as to prevent the Judges of election from refusing to receive the Vote of any person, when it shall be proved to the satisfaction of a majority of them, that in taking the said Oath he shall have sworn falsely.

Sec. 19. This Ordinance to take effect and be in force from and after its passage.

**Passed Jan[uar]y 14th 1843. Joseph Smith, Mayor. James Sloan, Recorder.**

Resolved by the City Council of the City of Nauvoo, that the next general election to take place in this City, be held in the Office of General Hyrum Smith, in the fourth Ward of this City.

**Passed Jan[uar]y 14th 1843. Joseph Smith, Mayor. James Sloan, Recorder.**

Alderman [George W.] Harris, Benjamin Warrington, and Daniel Spencer, were duly elected by the City Council of the City of Nauvoo, Judges to act at the next general Election to be held in this City, for the election of Mayor, Aldermen, and councillors for said City.

**Passed Jan[uar]y 14th 1843. Joseph Smith, Mayor. James Sloan, Recorder.**

An Ordinance regulating the Fees and compensation of the several Officers and persons therein mentioned.[5]

Sec. 1. Be it Ordained by the City Council of the City of Nauvoo, that the Salaries, Fees, and compensation of the several

[5]Published in *The Wasp,* Jan. 28, 1843.

Officers and persons hereinafter mentioned, are established as follows: to wit:

The City Council.

| | |
|---|---|
| The Mayor shall be allowed a Salary per Annum | $500.00 |
| The Vice Mayor, or president pro tem, presiding in the absence of the Mayor, per day, | 3.00 |
| The Aldermen and Counsellors, each, for every days attendance | 2.00 |
| The Recorder, as Secretary of the Council, per Annum | 100.00 |
| The Recorder shall in addition to his Salary, be allowed to claim the following Fees, to Wit: | |
| For copies or exemplification of Records or Ordinances, for every seventy two Words | .12½ |
| For recording each Marriage | .50 |

The Treasurer shall be allowed two per Cent on all monies or funds paid out by him, as full compensation for his services.

The Salaries and Compensation aforesaid shall be due semi-annually, and on the Certificate of the Recorder, (except in his own case, then on the Certificate of the President of the Council,) shall be paid out of any monies in the Treasury not otherwise appropriated.

The Municipal Courts.

| | |
|---|---|
| Sec. 2. The Chief Justice shall be allowed, per day, | 3.00 |
| The associate Justices shall each be allowed, per day | 2.50 |
| The Clerk of the municipal Court shall be entitled to the following fees, to wit. | |
| For each Warrant, Summons, Subpoena, and other process not herein specified, and sealing the same | .25 |
| Filing papers on Appeals from the Mayor or Aldermens Court, taking appeal Bond[,] and issuing supersedeas[6] | .50 |

[6]A *supersedeas* suspends a legal judgment, usually in the case of an appellate court in reconsidering a lower court's decision. In Nauvoo, the mayor and aldermen presided over the courts of first resort as justices of the peace, and their decisions "could be appealed to Nauvoo's municipal court, consisting of the mayor as chief justice and the aldermen as associate justices–in other words, all of the city's justices of the peace sitting

| | |
|---|---|
| Docketing each suit. | .12½ |
| Entering each Order or Rule of Court for continuance, default, discontinuance, retraxit,[7] nonsuit &c. | .25 |
| For each dedimus[8] or commission to take depositions | .50 |
| Calling and swearing each Jury | .12½ |
| Administering each oath | .06¼ |
| Swearing person to Affidavit | .12½ |
| For each Venire[9] to summon Jury | .25 |
| Receiving and entering Verdict of Jury | .12½ |
| Entering each Decree or final Judgment, | .25 |
| Issuing Writ of Habeas Corpus, Certiorari,[10] or procedendo,[11] | .50 |
| Entering special Bail on Record | .25 |
| Issuing Execution[12] | .25 |
| Entering Marshals return of the same | .12½ |
| For each Certificate and Seal, other than ^the^ process of Court | .50 |
| For each License under Seal granted by Ordinance | .50 |
| For each Certificate of Magistracy under Seal[13] | .25 |

The unsuccessful Party in any suit before the Municipal Court shall be taxed a docket fee of three Dollars, to be collected with the Costs of Suit, and paid over, in proportionate sums, to the Justices sitting on said Suit, as compensation, or part compensation for their services, and the deficit, if any, in the compensation of the Justices shall be paid semi-annually, on the Certificate of the Clerk, out of any monies in the treasury not otherwise appropriated.

---

together" (Glen M. Leonard, *Nauvoo: A Place of Peace, a People of Promise* [Salt Lake City: Deseret Book, 2002], 103).

[7]*Retraxit* is the withdrawal of a suit by a plaintiff.

[8]A *dedimus* authorizes an individual to act in place of a judge.

[9]*Venire facias* is a summons for a potential juror.

[10]When an appellate court grants *certiorari,* it accepts an appeal.

[11]A writ of *procedendo* orders a lower court to stop delaying.

[12]This means to authorize a judgment, as through the collection of funds or property.

[13]A *certificate of magistracy* informs someone in another jurisdiction that an action was approved by a judge.

Mayor and Aldermens Fees.

| | |
|---|---|
| Sec. 3. For taking each complaint in writing under Oath, | .25 |
| For each Warrant, Summons, or Subpoena, | .25 |
| For each Venire or Jury Warrant, | .25 |
| Swearing Jury in each Case, | .25 |
| Entering verdict of Jury | .12½ |
| Administering each Oath | .06¼ |
| Issuing dedimus to take depositions | .25 |
| Taking each deposition when required for each 100 Words | .12½ |
| Entering security on Docket | .25 |
| Levie facias[14] to be served on Security | .25 |
| Notification to each Referee [arbiter] | .25 |
| Entering Award of Referees | .25 |
| Each Order or Judgment and entering the same | .25 |
| Docketing each Suit | .12½ |
| For each precept on forcible entry and detainer | .50 |
| Issuing process of attachments and taking Bond and security | .75 |
| On Trial, per day | 2.00 |
| Entering appeal to the Municipal or Circuit Court | .25 |
| For each transcript of Judgment and proceedings | .25 |
| For each Execution, or mittimus[15] | .25 |
| Taking the acknowledgment of a Deed or other Indenture | .25 |
| For each Marriage Ceremony performed | 1.00 |
| For Certificate of the same | .25 |
| For each continuance of a Case | .12½ |

Marshal and Constables Fees.

| | |
|---|---|
| Sec. 4. For serving a Warrant or summons on each person named therein | .25 |
| Serving each Subpoena | .12½ |
| Serving and returning each execution | .50 |
| Serving and returning [a] Jury Warrant in each Case | .50 |
| Serving each Mittimus | .25 |
| Each day's attendance on the City Council, or Municipal Court when required | 2.00 |
| Each day's attendance on the Mayors or Alderman's Court when required | 1.00 |

[14]*Levari Facias* entails the seizure of property.

[15]A *mittimus* is an order to convey an individual to jail.

Advertising property for sale .25

Commission on all Sales not exceeding ten Dollars, ten per centum; and on all Sales exceeding that sum, six per centum.

Mileage when serving a Warrant, Summons, or subpoena, from the Justices or Clerks office to the residence of the Defendant, Juror, or Witness, per mile .05

Mileage when serving a mittimus, from the office of the Justice or Clerk to the Jail, per mile .06¼

For guarding Jail, or other similar service, for every twenty four hours, 1.00

Jurors Fees.

Sec. 5. To each Juror sworn in a case before the Mayor or Aldermen .25

To each Juror sworn in a case before the Municipal Court .25

To each Juror attending a Coroners inquest .25

Witnesses Fees.

Sec. 6. Each Witness attending the Mayors, Aldermen or Municipal Court, or attending for the purpose of having his deposition taken, in each case, .50

Arbitrators Fees.

Sec. 7. To each Arbitrator for every day he shall be necessarily employed in performing the duties of his appointment, where the Award is to be made the Judgment of the municipal Court 1.50

To each Arbitrator or referee, for each day he shall be necessarily employed in making up his Award in Cases before the Mayor or Aldermen 1.00

Coroners Fees.

Sec. 8. For holding an inquest over a dead body when required by law, 5.00

For summoning a Jury. .75

For Burial expences, &c. 10.00

All of which fees shall be certified by the Coroner, and paid out of the City Treasury, when the same cannot be collected out of the Estate of the deceased. And whenever the Coroner shall be required by law to perform any of the duties appertaining to the office of Marshal, he shall be entitled to the like fees and compensation.

Registers Fees.

Sec. 9. For recording all Deeds, Mortgages, and other instruments of writing, for every 100 Words .15

For copies of the same, when requested, for every 100 Words .12½

For every search of Record. .12½

Official Certificate under Seal. .37½

Notary Public's Fees.

Sec. 10. For noting a Bond, promissory note, or Bill of exchange for Protest, .25

For protesting and recording the same. .50

For noting without Protest. .25

For notice to endorsers &c each, .25

For affixing the Seal notorial, .25

For each Certificate, .25

For taking acknowledgement of [a] Deed or other Indenture .25

Assessor and Collectors Fees.

Sec. 11. The Assessors and Collectors shall be allowed for every day they are necessarily employed in the business of their appointment, 2.00

The City Watch.

Sec. 12. The City Watch shall be allowed for services in guarding the City for every day 1.50

Sec. 13. The fees of the several Officers and persons aforesaid, where not otherwise designated or provided for, shall be due, and if demanded, paid by the party claiming said services, upon the rendition of said services.

Sec. 14. The Mayor, Aldermen, and Clerk of the Municipal Court, shall keep an exact Account of all Costs that may accrue in the progress of each and every suit in their respective Courts, specifying the particulars of each charge, and upon the rendition of Judgment, shall charge the unsuccessful Party with the Costs of Suits.

Sec. 15. When Execution shall issue against the unsuccessful Party, for the recovery of the Judgment rendered, a Bill of the Costs as aforesaid shall be included in such execution, and if said Costs are not recovered from the unsuccessful Party by execution as aforesaid, it shall and may be lawful, and it is hereby made the duty of the Mayor, Aldermen, or Clerk, as aforesaid, to issue a fee Bill against the successful Party for all Costs that remain unsatisfied; which fee Bill shall contain the particulars for which Fees are charged; [and shall] be directed to the Marshal; and shall have all the force of an execution.

Sec. 16. There shall be a Clerk of the Mayors Court who shall be appointed from time to time by the Mayor, as he shall deem expedient, whose compensation of services shall be the usual perquisites of the Mayors office as set forth in the third Section of this Ordinance, excepting the compensation "on trial per day $2.00" and "for each Marriage ceremony performed $1.00."

Sec. 17. This Ordinance to take effect, and be in force, from and after its passage.

**Passed Jan[uar]y 14th 1843. Joseph Smith, Mayor. James Sloan, Recorder.**

The Report of the City Collector for the year 1841, as adopted by the City Council, upon the Report of a Committee. "to wit": Lewis Robison City Collector dr. [debit] to the City of Nauvoo Seven hundred Dollars and sixty four Cents ($700.64) the amount of Tax to be collected for the year A.D. 1841.

Contra

| | |
|---|---|
| Paid over to the City Treasurer in City Scrip | $ 430.50 |
| d[itt]o d[itt]o in Cash | 43.06 |
| Cash Paid on Order to William Marks | 126.26 |
| Scrip endorsed and not taken in | 15.00 |
| Tax due and not collected for want of a law to collect | 34.10 |
| " " from delinquents by Removal | 12.51 |
| Per Cent for collecting | 39.24 |
| $39.24 retained as my Fees. Total | $ 700.67 |

I hereby certify that the above is a true and correct account of all monies collected by me as City Collector. Also of Scrip endorsed, and a true statement of the amount due from delinquents, as appears from my Books.

**Adopted Jan[uar]y 14th 1843. Lewis Robison, City Collector. James Sloan, Recorder. Joseph Smith, Mayor.**

~~Resolved by the City Council of the City of Nauvoo, that the City Council, having business of importance to transact at all times when met, be not treated as though they were a Cattle Show, by people running in and out of the Council Room, & the Marshal is hereby required to prevent such intrusions~~

~~**Passed, Jan[uar]y 14th 1843. Joseph Smith, Mayor. James Sloan, Recorder**~~

[Printed sideways: "Ordered to be stricken out, Jan[uar]y 31st 1843."]

*January 30, 1843; Monday.*[16]

It is hereby Ordered by the City Council of the City of Nauvoo, that the opening of the first Street east of Warsaw Street, from Water Street South to the River, be discontinued.

**Passed Jan[uar]y 30th 1843. Joseph Smith, Mayor. James Sloan, Recorder.**

It is hereby Ordered by the City Council of the City of Nauvoo, that Harris Street be opened, running on the north line of Hyrum Smiths land & Kreymers land, running east through the Widow Beatties farm, & from thence to the Prairie, at the expence of Samuel Bent and other Petitioners.

**Passed Jan[uar]y 30th 1843. Joseph Smith, Mayor. James Sloan, Recorder.**

It is hereby Ordered by the City Council of the City of Nauvoo, that the claim of James Allred Supervisor, for a sum of thirty four dollars, and eighty seven and one half Cents, being the balance due him by the City, to this date, be, and the same is hereby allowed ^and ordered to be paid to^ him, and that the amount of money intended to be appropriated to[ward] payment of the balance [of the] purchase of the burying ground as mentioned in the resolution passed upon the 14th day of January instant, (and then supposed to be due to Alderman [William] Marks,) be paid to said James Allred, as part of his said claim, the said balance being sixteen dollars & fifty six and one fourth Cents, and that amount having been retained by the Collector for the purpose of paying over the same (prior to the passing of said resolu-

---

[16]See also *History of Church,* 5:263.

tion, & prior to the adoption of the Collectors account upon the same day,) the said Collector having been Ordered to pay said purchase money previous thereto.

**Passed Jan[uar]y 30 1843. Joseph Smith, Mayor. James Sloan, Recorder.**

The Claim of H[enry] G. Sherwood City Marshal, for services done for the City, commencing May 14th 1842, up to this date, was laid before the City Council, who referred it to the committee on claims, who reported, recommending that he be allowed fifty dollars, and that the fifteen Dollars received by him on account of said services, be deducted therefrom, and also that the fines against him be remitted. Which report was received and adopted.

**Adopted Jan[uar]y 30th 1843. Joseph Smith, Mayor. James Sloan, Recorder.**

Resolved by the City Council of the City of Nauvoo, that all delinquents up to this time, have privilege to work out their road labour tax, any time prior to the first day of May next.

**Passed Jan[uar]y 30th 1843. Joseph Smith, Mayor. James Sloan, Recorder.**

It is hereby Ordered by the City Council of the City of Nauvoo, that Gustavus Hills be paid the sum of three dollars, for engraving a Seal for the Municipal Court, he having warranted that it would make a good impression, so that it would hold fast where it was soldered.

**Passed Jan[uar]y 30th 1843. Joseph Smith, Mayor. James Sloan, Recorder.**

It is hereby Ordered by the City Council of the City of Nauvoo, that James Sloan be paid the sum of four dollars, for a Press procured by him for the use of the City Seal.

**Passed Jan[uar]y 30th 1843. Joseph Smith, Mayor. James Sloan, Recorder.**

Resolved by the City Council of the City of Nauvoo, that Councillor Wilson Law who was appointed to sell lots in the burying ground, be, and he hereby is instructed, to pay over the proceeds of Sales made by him, to Alderman Marks and others, the Committee upon the burying Ground.

**Passed Jan[uar]y 30th 1843. Joseph Smith, Mayor. James Sloan, Recorder.**

Resolved by the City Council of the City of Nauvoo, that the surplus funds, if any, arising from the Sales of lots in the new burying ground, after paying for fencing & improving the same, be applied towards fencing the old burying ground.

**Passed Jan[uar]y 30th 1843. Joseph Smith, Mayor. James Sloan, Recorder.**

An Ordinance in relation to Interments.[17]

Sec. 1. Be it Ordained by the City Council of the City of Nauvoo, that all graves for the interment of human Bodies in the burying ground or grounds belonging to the City of Nauvoo, shall be dug fully six feet deep from the surface, and in covering the same it shall be left well filled, raised up, and rounded upon the top, and the Sexton shall receive the sum of two dollars for digging the grave and interring the Body of every Person, and shall keep a regular Record thereof in a Book set apart for that purpose, as hereinafter set forth.

Sec. 2. Any Person who has not procured a lot or place in the City burying ground, and who wishes to dig a grave, and inter therein without the assistance of the Sexton, shall call upon the Sexton, whose duty it shall be to point out the place where such interments shall be made, for which he shall receive the sum of twenty five Cents.

Sec. 3. Any person having a lot or place in the City burying Ground may inter their dead without the assistance of the Sexton, and they are hereby required to make a due return to the Sexton of each case of interment so made, within three days thereafter.

Sec. 4. The City Sexton shall keep a Book of Record in which he shall Record the names and ages of all Persons deceased, coming to his knowledge, & the nature of the diseases of which they died, & to enable him the better so to do, he is to procure such information as he may require from the Persons referred to in Section two (2) of this Ordinance, & he shall also make a weekly report for publication, to the Editor, of some Newspaper, published in this City.

Sec. 5. Should the City Sexton be unable to procure his pay from the relatives or assetts of the deceased, or from the Over-

[17]Published in *The Wasp,* Mar. 1, 1843.

seers of the Poor, upon substantiating these facts to the satisfaction of the City Council, he shall receive pay therefor out of the City Treasury.

Sec. 6. Any person acting in violation of this Ordinance, respecting the manner and Order of interments, shall be fined in any sum not exceeding fifty dollars, to be recovered before the Mayor or Aldermen of this City, at their discretion.

Sec. 7. This Ordinance to take effect, & be in force from and after its passage, all laws or Ordinances to the contrary thereof in any wise notwithstanding.

**Passed Jan[uar]y 30th 1843. Joseph Smith, Mayor. James Sloan, Recorder.**

Laws & Ordinances of the City of Nauvoo.[18]

The City Council do Ordain as follows: The several Sections following are declared Laws & Ordinances of the said City, and any Person who shall be guilty of any of the offences hereinafter mentioned shall be subject to the penalty hereinafter to be prescribed to be sued for & collected before the Mayor, the Municipal Court, or any Alderman of said City.

Of City Officers.

There shall be appointed by the City Council of the City of Nauvoo, biennially, the following Officers for the City of Nauvoo, in addition to those provided for in the City Charter of said City, to wit: an engineer, market master, weigher & sealer of weights & measures, a fire warden in each Ward of the City, a Sexton, & a police Officer to act under the direction of the Mayor as Captain of the Watch, & a supervisor of Streets and Alleys.

First Division.

Sec. 1. Of the preservation of good Order. No Person shall keep a billiard Table, pharo Bank,[19] or any other instrument of gaming, where, or on, or with which, money, liquor, or other

[18]Published in ibid., Feb. 8, 1843.

[19]Faro was a casino game played against a dealer, the "faro banker," who stood at an oval table and drew cards from a dealing box, placing them face-up on the table. A survey of crime in Nauvoo showed that gambling was not a major problem compared to theft, post office fraud, counterfeiting, murder, and other offenses. See Kenneth W. Godfrey, "Crime and

Articles, shall in any manner be played for, or if any person shall keep a disorderly or gaming house, such person shall for every offence forfeit & pay a penalty of twenty five dollars, & also the further penalty of twenty five dollars for every forty eight hours, during which such person shall continue to keep the same, after the first conviction for any violation of this section.

Sec. 2. Any Person or Persons who shall make, aid, countenance, or assist in making any improper noise, riot, disturbance, or diversion in the Streets, or elsewhere; & all persons who shall collect in bodies or crowds, for unlawful purposes, to the annoyance or disturbance of Citizens or travellors, shall for each offence forfeit & pay a penalty not exceeding fifty dollars, in the discretion of the Court convicting.

Sec. 3. No person shall use any abusive, indecent, or threatening words to another individual without being deemed a disturber of the peace, & shall forfeit & pay a penalty of not less than one dollar & not exceeding twenty dollars, and shall moreover be bound to keep the peace in the discretion of the Court.

Sec. 4. If any person shall injure another by quarrelling, fighting, assaulting, beating, or otherwise, the person so offending shall on conviction forfeit & pay a penalty not less than three dollars, & not exceeding one hundred Dollars, and moreover may be imprisoned not exceeding six Months, in the discretion of the Court convicting.

Second Division.

Sec. 1. Of Streets and Alleys. No person shall place or cause to be placed, any Stones, timber, lumber, plank, boards, or other materials for building, in or upon any Street, lane, alley, or public Square, without a written permission for that purpose first obtained from the Mayor, or one of the Aldermen, under the penalty of two dollars for each offence, & the further penalty of two dollars for each & every forty eight hours during which the articles or materials aforesaid shall be or remain in any such Street, lane, Alley, or public Square, (without permission as aforesaid,) after notice from the Mayor, any Alderman, the supervisor of Streets, or any police officer to remove the same.

---

Punishment in Mormon Nauvoo, 1839-1846," *BYU Studies* 32 (1992), 195-228.

Sec. 2. The Mayor or any of the Aldermen, is authorized to grant to any person permission in writing to place & keep any building materials in any of the public Streets, for a period not exceeding four months, but such permission shall not Authorize the obstructing of more than one half the side walk, & one half the Streets, on the side next the lot on which a building is to be or being erected, by the person to whom such permission is granted, & such permission may be revoked at any time by the City Council, in their discretion.

Sec. 3. Every person to whom permission is granted as aforesaid, shall cause all the timber, building materials, & rubbish arising therefrom to be removed from the Street by the expiration of the time limited in such permission, as aforesaid, under the penalty of One dollar for every forty eight hours the timber, materials, or rubbish aforesaid shall be and remain in such Street after the expiration of the time limited in the permission granted, but no single recovery shall exceed the sum of twenty five dollars.

Sec. 4. All ornamental or shade trees hereafter placed or set out in any street, shall be placed within one foot of the outer line of the side walk of such Street, under the penalty of five Dollars for each offence, & the further penalty of one dollar for each week any such tree shall be suffered to remain contrary to the prohibition contained in this section.

Sec. 5. All side walks in said City shall be at least eight feet in width where the Streets are three Rods wide,[20] but where the Streets shall exceed that width, ten feet shall be the width.

Sec. 6. Any person who shall injure or tear up any pavement side or cross walk drain or sewer or any part thereof, or who shall dig any hole, ditch, or drain in any street, without due authority, or who shall hinder or obstruct the making or repairing any pavement, side or cross walk, which is or may be [in the]

---

[20]No longer in common use, the rod, 16.5 feet long, was one of the standard units of measure into the nineteenth century. Three rods, or 49.5 feet, was wider than most of today's two-way city streets, which hover around 40 feet in width. For comparison, the famously wide streets of downtown Salt Lake City are 132 feet in width ("Salt Lake City History," online at *Utah.com*). Showing the Mormon love for spacious roads, notice the anticipation in the ordinance for the potential need of even larger streets and wider sidewalks for proportionality's sake.

making under any law or resolution of the City Council, or who shall hinder or obstruct any person employed by the City Council, or the supervisor of Streets, or the person employed by him in making or repairing any public improvement, or work ordered by the City Council, shall for every offence forfeit & pay a penalty of ten dollars.

Sec. 7. No person shall cast or throw, or cause to be cast or thrown into any of the drains or sewers within the City, any straw, shavings, Wood, Stones, shells, rubbish or any filthy or other substances, or any obstructions nuisance or injury in or to the same by diverting or stopping the course thereof, or otherwise, under a penalty not exceeding ten dollars, nor less than one dollar for every offence, in the discretion of the Court convicting.

Sec. 8. No person shall without permission from the City Council, dig, remove, or carry away or cause the same to be done, any Stone, Earth, sand, or gravel from any public Street, highway, Alley, or public ground in this City, under the penalty of five dollars for each offence.

Third Division.

Sec. 1. Nuisances. No person shall throw, place, or deposit, or suffer any person in his or her employ to place or deposit any dead animal, carrion, putrid meat, or fish, or decayed vegetables, or nuisances of any kind in any Street, Alley, public square, in said City. Any person who shall violate any of the prohibitions contained in this Section, shall for each offence forfeit and pay a penalty of two dollars.

Sec. 2. No owner or occupant of any lot or tenement in said City, shall cause or permit any nuisance to be or remain in or upon the same lot or tenement or between the same & the centre of the street adjoining, upon the pain of forfeiting the penalty of two dollars for each and every twenty four hours during which the same nuisance shall be or remain on the same lot or tenement, or on such part of the Street, adjoining as aforesaid, but [for which] no single recovery shall exceed the sum of twenty five dollars.

Sec. 3. Every Butcher or other person immediately after killing any beeves,[21] Calves, Sheep, or other animals shall destroy

---

[21]*Beeves* was the nineteenth-century plural of "quadrupeds of the bo-

the offal, garbage, & other offensive & useless parts thereof, or convey the same into some place where the same shall not be injurious or offensive to the inhabitants, under a penalty of twenty dollars for every offence.

Sec. 4. Whenever any dead carcass, putrid or unsound meat of any kind, fish, hides or skins of any kind, or any other putrid or unsound substance, shall be found in any part of the City, it shall be the duty of [the] Supervisor of Streets to cause the same to be destroyed or to be disposed of in such other manner as may be equally secure as regards the public health, & if any person shall resist the supervisor of Streets in the execution of the duties hereby imposed, or shall disturb, hinder, molest or resist him or any person, or persons by him employed in the execution thereof, such offender shall forfeit the penalty of twenty five dollars.

Sec. 5. It shall be the duty of the supervisor of Streets to cause any stagnant waters to be drained off, or removed from any lot, or out of any Street or other place within said City, and he is hereby authorized to call upon such persons as owe road labour to assist him therein, & also to abate or remove ^every^ ~~evey~~ nuisance whatever within the City.

Sec. 6. It shall be the duty of the supervisor of Streets to report to the City Council, with respect to any other nuisances that may exist in the City, such as may be caused from Vats, pits, or pools of stationary water, whether from tanners, skinners, dyers, or other Persons, as he may deem injurious or dangerous to the public health; for their order thereon, & shall carry the Order of the City Council into effect in the Premises.

## FOURTH DIVISION.

Of the prevention of Fires.

Sec. 1. No pipe of any Stove or franklin[22] shall be put up,

---

vine genus." A distinction was made between an animal, in which case, in "the original sense, the word has a plural," and the flesh of an animal, "in [which] sense, the word has no plural" (Noah Webster, *An American Dictionary of the English Language* [New York: S. Converse, 1828], s.vv. "beef," "beeves").

[22]A Franklin was a metal stove, said to have been invented by Benjamin Franklin and used for heating a room rather than for cooking.

unless it be conducted into a chimney made of brick or stone, except where the Mayor or any Alderman shall deem it equally safe if otherwise put up, to be certified under his hand.

Sec. 2. It shall be the duty of the fire Wardens of each Ward to examine carefully under the direction of the City Council any cause from which immediate danger of fire may be apprehended, & to remove or abate with the consent of the Mayor or any Alderman (in case of neglect or refusal of the owner or occupant,) any cause from which danger may be apprehended, & to cause all buildings, chimneys, Stoves, pipes, hearths, Ovens, boilers, Ash houses, & apparatus used in any building which shall be found in such condition as to be considered unsafe, to be without delay, at the expense of the owner thereof, or occupant thereof, put in such condition as not to be dangerous in causing or promoting fires.

Sec. 3. If any Person shall obstruct, or hinder any person under the direction of the Warden aforesaid, in the performance of his duty under the preceding Section, such person shall, for every such offence, forfeit the penalty of twenty five dollars.

FIFTH DIVISION

Of the City Watch.

Sec. 1. Be it Ordained by the City Council of the City of Nauvoo, that there be established in said City a night Watch or patrol to be composed of a Captain of the police & such watchmen as may from time to time be appointed by the City Council, & who shall be governed by such laws & regulations, & endowed with such powers & authority as may be given or imposed upon them by the City Council.

Sec. 2. It shall be the duty of the Captain of the police to keep a general superintendance of the Watch; direct the manner of keeping Watch, & the times & Rounds of the Watchmen; & to perform such duties as are necessary & proper for the discharge of his duty & office; he shall keep a Register of the Watchmen, & have a house or building for the use of the same, & shall appoint a Lieutenant who shall discharge his duties in his absence.

Sec. 3. To the said Watch shall be intrusted the peace & safety of the City during the night, & they shall arrest all persons who may be found in said City at unusual hours & under suspicious circumstances, & bring such Person or Persons before the Captain of the Police, who may, in his discretion, detain such Person or Persons until such time as the Mayor or some Alderman can examine into the nature of the charges against him or them; they shall also stop all riotous or improper noises during the night, & may arrest offenders as aforesaid, & exercise such a discretion in preserving the peace & quiet of the City as may be proper & salutary; & for such or other services there shall be allowed them such reasonable compensation as the Council may agree upon.

SIXTH DIVISION.

Public Market.

Sec. 1. All persons keeping fresh meat or fish in this City, shall at all times keep the building in which such meat or fish is exposed for sale, clean & free from any disagreeable smell; & if any Person [is found] neglecting to comply with this or the next succeeding Section, [he] shall for each offence forfeit & pay the sum of five dollars.

Sec. 2. It shall be the duty of the supervisor of Streets to inspect the state of all places within this City, in which fresh meat or fish is exposed for sale, once in each Month, between the first of November & the first of April, & once in each week between the first of April & the first of November, & if he shall find the foregoing Section to be not complied with, he shall Order the said buildings to be cleansed; & it shall be the duty of the Person or Persons in charge of said building or buildings, to facilitate such examination, & when directed as aforesaid, to cause such place or places to be cleansed and put in a healthy condition.

**Passed Jan[uar]y 30th 1843. Joseph Smith, Mayor. James Sloan, Recorder.**

It is hereby Ordered by the City Council of the City of Nauvoo, that the following named Persons be paid the Sums respectively annexed to their names, for their services in the City Council, up to this date, inclusive: to wit:

| | $ ¢ | | $ ¢ |
|---|---|---|---|
| Hyrum Smith | 20.00 | John Taylor | 21.50 |
| N[ewel] K. Whitney | .50 | Wilford Woodruff | 2.00 |
| Orson Spencer | 21.00 | Poor fund, p[e]r Wm. Law | 20.00 |

| | | | |
|---|---|---|---|
| George W. Harris | 32.00 | Orson Pratt | 20.50 |
| Gustavus Hills | 16.50 | Sam[uel]l H. Smith | 6.00 |
| Charles C. Rich | 22.50 | Amasa Lyman | 6.50 |
| John P. Green | 16.00 | Vinson Knight | 13.50 |
| John T. Barnett | 11.50 | H. G. Sherwood (see his claim allowed page 148.) | |
| Wilson Law | 24.50 | | |
| George A. Smith | 17.50 | James Sloan | 34.50 |

**Passed Jan[uar]y 30th 1843. Joseph Smith, Mayor. James Sloan, Recorder.**

It is hereby Ordered by the City Council of the City of Nauvoo, that the persons whose names are hereinafter mentioned do pay the sums annexed to their respective names, the same being the fines incurred by them for neglect of attendances in the City Council, up to this date inclusive, to wit.

| | $ ¢ | | $ ¢ |
|---|---|---|---|
| Daniel H. Wells | 1.50 | Hiram Kimball | .50 |
| William Marks | .50 | Lyman Wight | 9.00 |
| William Smith | 14.00 | | |

**Passed Jan[uar]y 30th 1843. Joseph Smith Mayor. James Sloan, Recorder.**

Resolved by the City Council, that the Council will not claim any pay for this meeting.
**Jan[uar]y 30th. 1843. Joseph Smith, Mayor. James Sloan, Recorder.**

*February 11, 1843; Saturday*

The following City Officers were elected for the ensuing two years,[23] to wit.

---

[23]Five days earlier, on Monday, February 6, elections were held in Hyrum Smith's office. Hyrum won his election to the city council. Joseph Smith ran unopposed and returned from lunch to find he had been "elected mayor by unanimous vote" by 424 citizens. The city council met on Saturday, February 11, to swear in new members and elect new city officers (*History of Church,* 5:264-65, 270-71).

As covered by *The Wasp,* the February 6 election resulted in the following wins for aldermen's seats, followed by vote tallies: Orson Spencer, 423; Daniel H. Wells, 420; George A. Smith, 221; and Stephen Markham, 212. The losers were William Law, 205; and Samuel Bennet, 205. On February 25, Stephen Markham would resign because he was "elected without his knowledge," to be replaced by Samuel Bennett on March 4 (see below).

James Sloan, City Recorder
William Clayton, City Treasurer
Dimick B. Huntington, City Constable
Lewis Robinson, ditto
W[illiam] D. Huntington, ditto
James Sloan, Notary Public
H[enry] G. Sherwood, Market Master
Sidney Rigdon, City Attorney
Samuel Bennett, Market Inspector
H[enry] G. Sherwood, City Marshall
W. W. Phelps, ^approved as^ Mayors Clerk
Alanson Ripley, City Surveyor
James Allred, Supervisor of Streets
Dimick B. Huntington, Coroner
Theodore Turley, Weigher & Sealer
W. W. Phelps, Fire Warden of the 4th Ward
John D. Parker, City Constable

**Passed. Joseph Smith, Mayor. James Sloan, Recorder.**

A Board of Health was established, to consist of Joseph Smith (the Mayor), William Law, William Marks, & Samuel Bennett, M.D. **Feb[ruar]y 11th 1843. Joseph Smith, Mayor. James Sloan, Recorder.**

The following Committees were then Appointed, to be standing Committees, in this Council: to wit.

| Of Ways & Means | Of Police. |
|---|---|
| Daniel H. Wells. | Orson Spencer. |
| Orson Spencer. | Daniel H. Wells. |

---

The winners of nine city councilmen seats were Hyrum Smith, 422; John Taylor, 422; Orson Hyde, 421; Orson Pratt, 421; Sylvester Emmons, 418; Heber C. Kimball, 216; Benjamin Warrington, 215; Daniel Spencer, 214; and Brigham Young, 213. The losers were William Marks, 212; Wilson Law, 211; Albert P. Rockwood, 211; and Samuel Bent, 209 (*The Wasp,* Feb. 8, 1843).

In the council meeting, Joseph Smith asked the officers "not to attempt to improve the city but [to] enact such laws as will promote peace and good order," saying "the people will improve the city. Capitalist[s] will come in from all quarters and Mills, factories, and machinery of all kind and buildings will arise on every hand [and] this will become a great city" (Scott H. Faulring, ed., *An American Prophet's Record: The Diaries and Journals of Joseph Smith* [Salt Lake City: Signature Books, 1989, 302).

| | |
|---|---|
| Orson Pratt. | Samuel Bennett. |
| Of Improvements. | Of Municipal Laws. |
| Hyrum Smith. | Sylvester Emmons. |
| George A. Smith. | Orson Hyde. |
| Samuel Bennett. | Daniel H. Wells. |
| Of Claims. | Of Public Grounds. |
| Heber C. Kimball. | George A. Smith. |
| Brigham Young. | Benjamin Warrington. |
| Benjamin Warrington. | Samuel Bennett. |
| Of Unfinished Business. | Of Public Works. |
| John Taylor. | Orson Pratt. |
| Sylvester Emmons. | Orson Hyde. |
| Daniel Spencer. | Heber C. Kimball. |
| Of Elections. | Of Finance. |
| Hyrum Smith. | Daniel Spencer. |
| Orson Hyde. | Orson Hyde. |
| John Taylor. | Orson Spencer. |

**Feb[ruar]y 11th 1843. Joseph Smith, Mayor. James Sloan, Recorder.**

It is hereby unanimously adopted, by the City Council of the City of Nauvoo, that a Market be, and hereby is, established in this City.

**Feb[ruar]y 11th 1843. Joseph Smith, Mayor. James Sloan, Recorder.**

It is hereby unanimously adopted, upon the report of the Committee of public Grounds, that the rising ground upon Main Street, opposite or near to Ivin's brick House, be the site for a Market House.

**Feb[ruar]y 11th 1843. Joseph Smith, Mayor. James Sloan, Recorder.**

It is hereby unanimously adopted, that the kind of a Market House, & size thereof, be at the discretion of the Mayor, & that he also procure the same to be built at the expence of the City.

**Feb[ruar]y 11th 1843. Joseph Smith, Mayor. James Sloan, Recorder.**

It is hereby Ordered by the City Council of the City of Nauvoo, that the Ordinance in relation to interments, passed Jan[uar]y 30th 1843, be amended, by making it to read, "that the Sexton is to receive two Dollars for digging each Grave & interring a Body, in cases where he performs that duty."

**Feb[ruar]y 11th 1843. Joseph Smith, Mayor. James Sloan, Recorder.**

It is hereby Ordered by the City Council of the City of Nauvoo, that Alanson Ripley be, & he hereby is[,] allowed the following sums; to wit: for surveying back Street from Mulholland Street to Munson Street, Two dollars, – for surveying Bluff Street, from Mulholland Street to Munson Street, Two dollars. – for surveying the Street East of Warsaw Street, from parley Street South to the City limits, four dollars. – for surveying the Street running South from Parley Street to lumber Street, between Charles Hubbard, Bently, & Taylor &c. Two dollars, Amounting in all to ten dollars.
**Feb[ruar]y 11th 1843. Joseph Smith, Mayor. James Sloan, Recorder.**

Alderman Harris, & Councillors Warrington & Spencer, do hereby resign their claim to pay, as Judges of the Election of [the] City Council, held upon the 6th day of feb[ruar]y inst.[24]
**Feb[ruar]y 11th 1843. Joseph Smith, Mayor. James Sloan, Recorder.**

*February 25, 1843; Saturday.*[25]

Resolved by the City Council of the City of Nauvoo, that the resolution passed on the 15th day of Jan[uar]y 1842, respecting the pay of City Council & Committees, be, & the same is hereby[,] repealed & abolished, so far as it respects remuneration of Committees.
**Feb[ruar]y 25th 1843. Joseph Smith, Mayor. James Sloan, Recorder.**

The City Council of the City of Nauvoo, do hereby approve of the Bond of the City Recorder, & instruct him to lodge it with the Treasurer.
**Feb[ruar]y 25th 1843. Joseph Smith, Mayor. James Sloan, Recorder.**

It is hereby Ordered by the City Council of the City of Nauvoo, that the Ordinance in relation to interments be further amended, by striking out the part thereof which granted pay for keeping a Record & making a return of interments for publication.
**Feb[ruar]y 25th 1843. Joseph Smith, Mayor. James Sloan, Recorder.**

---

[24]Joseph Smith had reprimanded the election judges at this council meeting "for not holding the poll open after 6 o'clock when there were many wishing to vote. The judges were Geo[rge] W. Harris, Daniel Spencer, and [Benjamin] Warrington" (Faulring, *American Prophet's Record,* 302-03).

[25]See also *History of Church,* 5:288-90.

An Ordinance in relation to the duties of City Attorney.[26]

Sec. 1. Be it Ordained by the City Council of the City of Nauvoo, that it shall be the duty of the City Attorney to defend the interests of the Corporation in all Suits instituted by or against this Corporation, to make such returns to the Mayor, of the State & condition of the said Suits, at such periods and in such manner as he shall prescribe, & generally to give such legal advice on matters pertaining to the interests of the Corporation, as the Mayor and Aldermen shall from time to time require.

Sec. 2. Be it Ordained, that a Salary of fifty dollars per Annum, be, and the same is hereby allowed to the said Attorney, in full for such legal advice and services as the Mayor and Aldermen are authorized to require of him by the first section of this Act, payable semiannually out of the general fund.

Sec. 3. This act to take effect from and after its passage.

**Passed February 25th 1843. Joseph Smith, Mayor. James Sloan, Recorder.**

An Ordinance, concerning a Market on Main Street.[27]

Sec. 1. Be it Ordained by the City Council of the City of Nauvoo, that the Mayor of the City be, & he hereby is authorized to contract with any competent person, to furnish materials for, and erect and finish a good, substantial, & convenient market house for this City, on the ground that shall be selected for that purpose by the City Council, which said building shall be built on the most approved plan, and Cost not less than five hundred dollars.

Sec. 2. When said Market House shall be finished, the Mayor is hereby Authorized to make, execute, and deliver unto the competent person building the market house aforesaid, a lease of the same for five Years, for and as a full consideration to him for the materials furnished, and labor bestowed in and about the erection & finishing said building by said Person as aforesaid; and that said competent person may lease out the Stalls thereof at public auction in this City, to the highest bidder; for such period of time as he may think best, within the five Years above men-

---

[26]Published in *The Wasp,* Mar. 1, 1843.

[27]Published in ibid., Mar. 8, 1843. It does not appear that a "good, substantial" market costing "not less than five hundred dollars" ever materialized.

tioned; and the rents and profits arising from the same during the said five Years shall be payable to, and for the sole uses of the said competent person aforesaid, for the consideration aforesaid; and at the expiration of said term said competent person shall surrender the possession of said Market House, in good Order, to the Market Master of this City, or to such other Person as the City Council shall direct.

Sec. 3. That as soon as said Markethouse shall be completed, and the Stalls thereof leased & furnished with good wholesome meats for sale and delivery, that from & after that time a Market shall be established in this City, and no person or persons shall vend sell or buy any fresh meat or meats at any other place in this City than at the Markethouse aforesaid, and every person offending against this section shall forfeit and pay to this City twenty dollars for each offence, with Costs, provided however, any person may sell by the quarter in this City at any other place,[28] and that nothing in this Ordinance or in the lease to be given to said competent person as may be contracted with by the Mayor as aforesaid, shall be so construed as to prohibit or in any manner obstruct the right of the City Council of this City from building an addition to said market house, and leasing the Stalls thereof, or from establishing in this City any other market or markets whenever the City Council shall be of Opinion that the interest of the inhabitants of this City shall require either to be done, and this proviso, shall be inserted in the lease to be given by the Mayor to the competent person contracted with aforesaid.

Sec. 4. That the market shall be held in said market house every Monday, Wednesday, and Friday, or every day except Sunday, to be regulated by the City Council.

Sec. 5. There shall be a passage lengthwise through the entire market house ten feet in width, & the space between the Piers or Pillars shall be deemed Stalls for Butchers, which Stalls may extend from each side of the building towards the cent[er] thereof, so as to leave the space for passage aforesaid.

Sec. 6. That all that space of ground outside the market

---

[28]Just like with whiskey, which individuals could sell by the gallon but not by the drink, it was conceived that individuals could sell sides or quarters of beef but not individual cuts, except out of a city-owned stall.

house & under the Eaves of the same, may be used free of charge, for the Sale of Fish, Poultry, butter, eggs, and vegetables, and that the roof of said building shall extend over the outside of the house so as to cover about four feet of ground on each side thereof.

Sec. 7. No vegetables, eggs, or poultry of any kind shall be sold or bought within this City during market hours, except at the market or markets in this City, every person who shall violate this section shall forfeit and pay to this City two dollars with Cost of suit.

Sec. 8. No person or persons shall obstruct the passages of the market with Wheelbarrows or other Articles during market hours under the penalty of two dollars, to be recovered with Cost of Suit for this City.

Sec. 9. That all Lessees or Occupiers of Stalls shall keep the same clean and free from any disagreeable smell, and shall cleanse the same as often as necessary, and every person for a failure to comply with the provisions of this section shall forfeit and pay to the City the penalty of two dollars for each offence.

Sec. 10. It shall be the duty of the market master of this City to superintend the market and put in force all the Ordinances of this City concerning markets, or having relation thereto; he is hereby Authorized, if required by any one, to weigh, measure, try and examine all butter, lard, fruit, and other articles of provision offered for sale, in lump, parcels, tubs, or other Vessel, or Vessels, and all weights and measures in said market; and in case the same are less than the required weight or measure, then to seize the butter lard weights or measures or other articles aforesaid so found deficient, and sell the same at Auction, and pay the avails thereof into the City Treasury, provided, that the owner of the Article or Articles so seized may appeal to the Mayor of the City who shall hear try & determine the same, making such disposition of the matter as he shall deem just and right in the premises, the market master shall do and perform all things belonging to the Office of Clerk of markets or market masters, within this City, he shall enforce obedience to all rules and regulations herein contained, and to such others as from time to time shall be ordained respecting the market; he shall prevent all unsound and unwholesome provisions from being sold or exposed for sale, by seizing the same and making such disposition thereof as the Mayor shall Order or direct; and shall try all Seals weights and measures used in market, and shall enforce the payment & recovery of all penalties and forfeitures which by any law or ordinance are inflicted on any Person offending against the rules and regulations of the market, and shall decide all disputes that may arise between buyer and seller, touching the weight, measure, or quality of things bought and sold.

Sec. 11. That the market aforesaid shall be open of a morning at day light, and during summer months shall close at 11 OClock in the morning, and in the Winter at one OClock afternoon each market day, nothing herein contained shall prohibit the butchers from opening market and selling meats between sun set and nine OClock at night to Steamboats, and also selling to Citizens every Saturday night to ten OClock at night, if they shall think necessary.

**Passed Feb[ruar]y 25th 1843. Joseph Smith, Mayor. James Sloan, Recorder.**

Resolved by the City Council of the City of Nauvoo, that the resignation of Stephen Markham, of the Office of Alderman of this City, be, and the same is hereby accepted, by reason of his name having been used, and he elected, without his knowledge.

**Passed Feb[ruar]y 25th 1843. Joseph Smith, Mayor. James Sloan, Recorder.**

General Wilson Law is hereby declared, by the City Council of the City of Nauvoo, to be duly elected by them, an Alderman of this City, to fill the vacancy occasioned by the resignation of Stephen Markham.

**Feb[ruar]y 25th 1843. Joseph Smith, Mayor. James Sloan, Recorder.**

James Sloan the City Recorder, took the Oath of Office, administered by Alderman [Daniel H.] Wells. The following named Persons were sworn to the Offices hereafter mentioned, by the Recorder; to wit: Henry G. Sherwood, Marshal. – Henry G. Sherwood, Market Master. – Dimick B. Huntington, John D. Parker, & Lewis Robison, Constables. – Theodore Turley, Weigher & Sealer. – Dimick B. Huntington, Coroner.

**Feb[ruar]y 25th 1843. Joseph Smith, Mayor. James Sloan, Recorder.**

*March 4, 1843; Saturday.*[29]

An Ordinance, regulating the Currency.

Sec. 1. Be it Ordained by the City Council of the City of Nauvoo, that from and after the passage of this Bill, Gold and Silver Coin only [will] be received as lawful tender in payment of City Taxes, and of debts, and also of fines imposed under the Ordinances of the City.

Sec. 2. That City Scrip shall not hereafter be emitted as moneyed Currency; provided however that nothing in this Bill shall be so construed as to prevent the redemption of previous emissions.

Sec. 3. That any Person passing counterfeit Gold, or Silver,

---

[29]Joseph Smith's diary adds color to the minutes: "10 o'clock, opened City Council. Prayer B[y] Geo[rge] A. Smith. Bill regulating currency read. The Legislature of Illinois have long been trying to repeal the Charter of Nauvoo. Upon which the Mayor made some [comments] as he had done on former occasions to shew the council and others that the Legislature cannot repeal a charter where there is no repealing clause. Upon which he read a letter from James Arlington Bennet to confirm his decision. Letter dated Arlington House Feb[ruary] 1st 1843.

"Spoke against [*USS Somers* Captain Alexander S.] Makenzie's murdering [executing] those boys [Midshipman Philip] Spencer &c. [for mutiny in November 1842] as stated in Arlington's letter. Called it murder. The boys had the malary [malaria] on the coast of Africa and did not know what they did. [The captain learned that Secretary of War John C. Spencer's son Philip, a crew member, had spoken about mutiny, apparently as part of an adventure story to pass the time, and had Philip and two others hanged.]

"In debate on the bill, Geo[rge] A. Smith thought imprisonment better than hanging. Mayor said he was opposed to hanging. If a man kill another[,] shoot him or cut his throat[,] spilling his blood on the ground and let the smoke thereof ascend up to God. If I ever have the privilege of Making a law on this point I will have it so.

"In reply to councillors who thought it impolitic to stop circulating uncurrent Bank notes at once, [the] Mayor said he would use a figure and talk like a father to his children. If you want to kill a serpent, don't cut off his head for fear he will bite you, but cut off his tail piece by piece and perhaps you won't get bit. So with this bill. If paper currency is an evil put it down at once. Stop the circulation at once.

"When councillors get up here[,] let them talk sense. Great God[,] where is common sense and reason? Is there none in the Earth? Why have the [c]anker lingering to sap our life? Get a 5 dollar bill[.] [You] can get nothing with it. ...

or copper Coin, or counterfeit or spurious paper currency, or aiding and abetting therein, or holding the same with intent to pass it; knowing it to be such: shall be liable to a fine not exceeding five thousand dollars, or to imprisonment or hard labour in the City, for a term not exceeding fourteen years, or all these penalties at the discretion of the Court.[30]

Sec. 4. That any person passing a paper currency, or aiding and abetting therein, or holding the same with intent to pass it within the bounds of this City Corporation, shall be liable to a fine of one dollar for every dollar thus offered or passed, to be recovered as in Action of debt, one half of said fine to be paid to the complainant, the other half to said Corporation.[31]

**Passed March 4th 1843. Joseph Smith, Mayor. James Sloan, Recorder.**

---

"I wish you had my soul long enough to know how good it feels. It is expedient[,] when you strike at an enemy, [to] strike the most deadly blow possible. ([Orson] Hyde asked what the editer would do)? Mayor said advertise in the next paper to your agents to send you gold and silver as we take no paper here.

"Prisoners may be kept in the city as safe as in the Prison of the state by chaining to a block with a guard and labor in blacksmith shops or any where else and never have a prisoner sent out of the city for imprisonment.

"Bills passed to stop circulation of paper currency in the city, punish counterfeiting &c. by unanimous vote. Dr. Samuel Bennet[t] chosen Alderman, A[lbert] P. Rockwood fire warden for 1st ward, Elijah Fordham fire warden 2d ward, Charles C. Rich fire warden 3d ward. ^Voted^ [to] open an alley north and south through block 126. 1½ P.M., adjourned (Faulring, *American Prophet's Record*, 326-28; see also *History of Church*, 5:296-98.).

[30]"There were among us [in Iowa] those who were passing counterfeit money and had done it all the time since we left Nauvoo," Brigham Young said in 1846 (Joseph Smith, *History of the Church of Jesus Christ of Latter-day Saints*, 7 vols. [Salt Lake City: Deseret News, 1901-12] 7:23). Young said coins were counterfeited "by wagonloads" in Nauvoo by non-Mormons (Leonard, *Nauvoo*, 570). Rumor had it that a member of the Council of Fifty was involved, that he had a printing press to manufacture currency (D. Michael Quinn, *The Mormon Hierarchy: Origins of Power* [Salt Lake City: Signature Books, 1994], 650).

[31]Published in *The Wasp*, Mar. 8, 1843. In *History of Church*, 5:288-89, we learn that the council reconvened after mid-day dinner because of doubts about whether they had the authority to regulate currency. The Church had previously encountered trouble with banking in Kirtland, Ohio (see Donald Q. Cannon, Richard O. Cowan, and Arnold K. Garr, eds., *Encyclopedia of Latter-day Saint History* [Salt Lake City: Deseret Book, 2001], s.v. "Kirtland Safety Society").

But Joseph Smith remained confident: "I have read the Constitution

Samuel Bennett was duly elected an Alderman of this City, by the City Council, and is hereby declared to be so duly elected, to fill the vacancy occasioned by the resignation of Stephen Markham, and also by reason of Wilson Law, (who was elected on the 25th day of July last, to fill that Office,) having declined to act.
**March 4th 1843. Joseph Smith, Mayor. James Sloan, Recorder.**

The following named Persons were duly appointed to the Offices annexed to their names; to wit: Albert P. Rockwood[32] fire Warden for the 1st Ward. Elijah Fordham fire Warden for the 2nd Ward. Charles C. Rich fire Warden for the 3rd Ward.
**March 4th 1843. Joseph Smith, Mayor. James Sloan, Recorder.**

Gen[era]l Joseph Smith, was reelected Register of Deeds, & so forth.
**March 4th 1843. Ja[me]s Sloan Rec[orde]r.**

It is hereby Ordered by the City Council of the City of Nauvoo, that an Alley be opened sixteen feet wide, running from North to South, through the Cent[er] of Block number One hundred and twenty six (126), in the City of Nauvoo, at the expence of the Petitioners, Brigham Young and others.
**March 4th 1843. Joseph Smith, Mayor. James Sloan, Recorder.**

*March 11, 1843; Saturday.*

It is hereby Ordered by the City Council of the City of Nauvoo, that Knight Street be opened from the Temple square, East, to

---

and find my doubts removed. The Constitution is not a law, but empowers the people to make laws. ... We will make a law for gold and silver. ... ^I am a Lawyer^. I am big lawyer and comprehend heaven, earth, and hell to bring forth knowledge which shall cover up all Lawyers and doctors." Following Smith's speech, "O[rson] Spencer said he could have wished [that U.S. Senator] Daniel Webster[,] the Lion of the East[,] had heard the Lion of the west in the choir," at which "the Mayor gave another speech" (Faulring, *American Prophet's Record*, 312-13).

[32]Albert Perry Rockwood was born in Holliston, Massachusetts, in 1805. He converted to Mormonism in 1837 and later moved to Nauvoo. He was an officer in the Nauvoo Legion and member of the First Council of Seventy. He died in 1879.

Alderman [Daniel H.] Well's Farm, at the expence of A[lonzo] W. Whitney[33] and others, Petitioners.

**March 11th 1843. John Taylor President pro tem.[34] James Sloan, Recorder.**

It is hereby Ordered by the City Council of the City of Nauvoo, that Ripley Street be opened from the New York Store unto Heringshaws Land, at the expence of J[ohn] S. Workman & others Petitioners.

**March 11th 1843. John Taylor, Pres[i]d[en]t pro tem. James Sloan, Recorder.**

The claim of Gen[era]l Hyrum Smith, for the use of his Office as a Council Room, & fuel & Candles, up to this date, amounting to thirteen dollars & twenty five Cents, is hereby allowed by the City Council of the City of Nauvoo.

**March 11th 1843. John Taylor, Pres[i]d[en]t pro Tem. Ja[me]s Sloan, Recorder.**

The Claim of James Sloan for three dollars, as a Clerk of the municipal Election in 1843, is hereby allowed by the City Council of the City of Nauvoo.

**March 11th 1843. John Taylor, Pres[i]d[en]t pro tem. Ja[me]s Sloan, Recorder.**

The Claim of John A. Forsgens for three dollars, as a Clerk of the municipal Election in 1843, is hereby allowed by the City Council of the City of Nauvoo.

**March 11th 1843. John Taylor, Pres[i]d[en]t Pro tem. Ja[me]s Sloan, Recorder.**

The sum of seventy five Cents is hereby granted, by the City Council of the City of Nauvoo, for stationary furnished for the last municipal Election.

**March 11th 1843. John Taylor, Pres[i]d[en]t Pro tem. Ja[me]s Sloan, Recorder.**

Resolved by the City Council of the City of Nauvoo, that the Res-

---

[33]Alonzo Wells Whitney was born in 1818 in Canandaigua, New York. He died in 1845.

[34]The mayor was out of town, visiting Saints in Ramus, Illinois.

olution of this Council of the 8th day of October last, (whereby the Treasurer was Ordered to not make any further payments out of the City funds, upon the Order theretofore drawn upon him for payment of the City Watch, unless further Order of this Council,) be and the same is hereby rescinded.

**March 11th 1843. John Taylor, Pres[i]d[en]t Pro tem. Ja[me]s Sloan, Recorder.**

An Ordinance to amend an Ordinance regulating the currency, passed March fourth A.D. 1843.[35] Be it Ordained by the City Council of the City of Nauvoo, that nothing in the Ordinance regulating the Currency shall be so construed, as to prevent the receiving of City Scrip or Treasury Orders, for Taxes or City dues.

**Passed March 11th 1843. John Taylor, Pres[i]d[en]t pro tem. Ja[me]s Sloan, Recorder.**

*April 14, 1843; Friday.*[36]

Office of Secretary of State
Springfield 14th April 1843.

Sirs,

Yours, certifying the Election of certain Officers of your City, came to hand to day.

Whatever may have been the practice heretofore, I am compelled with my views of the 16th section of the Charter of your City to state – that hereafter no Commissions will be issued to any City Officers but on the Certificate of the Clerk of the County Commissioners Court, certifying that such persons elect, have filed in his Office, bond as required by law of Justices of the Peace.

All Elections of Militia Officers who are to be commissioned, should be directed to the "Adjutant General" at this place, such returns will then be properly attended to.

---

[35]Published in *The Wasp,* Mar. 15, 1843.

[36]In 1843 the Illinois state government wanted to see Nauvoo more fully integrated into the county and state hierarchy, for which the letter from Secretary Campbell might be cited as evidence. The provision cited by Campbell placed the commission of justices of the peace, who in Nauvoo were the mayor and aldermen, at the discretion of the governor and subject to state law. The Nauvoo city council responded on June 6, 1843 (below), that they disagreed.

Respectfully &c.
Thompson Campbell Sec[retary] of State.
James Sloan Esq. Recorder
Nauvoo, Illinois.

You will see farther, the propriety of the position taken, by reference to the 6th section of "An Act declaring what shall be evidence in certain Cases" approved Jan[uar]y 10 1827 – See revised Laws page 281 – Sec[tion] 6. Sec[retary] of State.

*April 15, 1843; Saturday.*

It is hereby Ordered by the City Council of the City of Nauvoo, that Granger Street be made wider than the Original Survey, in manner following, that is, eight feet to be taken from the lots of each side of the Street, from Water Street to the North end of Granger Street, and from Water Street to the River at the South end of Granger Street, on the West side of said Street only, and that this Order is not to interfere with Houses that are already built, but that those persons who have Houses on the Street shall have the privilege of moving them at their discretion, and those Persons who have fences made shall have one year from this date, to remove them, also that all improvements that may be hereafter made shall be put eight feet back from the original Survey. ~~and the widening of said Street to be at the expence of Petitioners, John Taylor and others~~

**April 15th 1843. Hyrum Smith, Pres[i]d[en]t Pro. T[em.] Ja[me]s Sloan, Recorder.**

The Petition of Stephen Winchester[37] and others, for the opening of Winchester Street, is hereby rejected, by the City Council of the City of Nauvoo.

**April 15th 1843. Hyrum Smith Pres[i]d[en]t Pro tem. Ja[me]s Sloan, Recorder.**

It is hereby Ordered by the City Council of the City of Nauvoo, that Brigham Street be opened, running from Young Street one

[37]Stephen Winchester was born in 1795 in Vershire, Vermont. He was baptized in 1833 in Pennsylvania. He was a member of Zion's Camp and fought in the battle of Crooked River. He moved to Illinois after being expelled from Missouri in 1839. He died in 1873.

half mile North, at the expence of Petitioners, John M. Finch and others.

**April 15th 1843. Hyrum Smith, Pres[i]d[en]t Pro tem. Ja[me]s Sloan, Recorder.**

It is hereby Ordered by the City Council of the City of Nauvoo, that Wight Street be opened from Warsaw Street, East to Winchester Street, at the expence of John Pack and others Petitioners.

**April 15th 1843. Hyrum Smith, Pres[i]d[en]t Pro tem. Ja[me]s Sloan, Recorder.**

Councillor Brigham Young obtained leave to retract the assignment made by him, upon the 17th day of February 1842, of his pay as a member of this Council, so far as the Amount which will pay his City Taxes for the year 1842, and he retracted same accordingly.

**April 15th 1843. Hyrum Smith, Pres[i]d[en]t Pro tem. Ja[me]s Sloan, Recorder.**

It is hereby Ordered by the City Council of the City of Nauvoo, that the Collectors of the City Taxes, do receive the Certificate of the City Recorder when presented to them, in payment of City Taxes, due by Brigham Young for the Year 1842, and endorse such payments thereon, and the City Treasurer will Accept said Certificate in the payments and Settlements to be made with him by the said Collectors.

**April 15th 1843. Hyrum Smith, Pres[i]d[en]t Pro tem. Ja[me]s Sloan, Recorder.**

*May 12, 1843; Friday.*

An Ordinance in relation to Swine running at large.

Sec. 1. Be it Ordained by the City Council of the City of Nauvoo, that from and after the passage of this Act, it shall not be lawful for any Person or Persons owning Hogs or Swine to allow the same to run at large within the limits of said City.

Sec. 2. And it is hereby further Ordained that a fine of five dollars for every Hog or Swine shall be imposed upon any person or persons suffering their Swine to run at large within the limits of said Corporation; said fine to be imposed by the Mayor or any Alderman of said City upon the complaint of any person or persons aggrieved, and to be collected of the Goods and Chattels of the Defendant as in common Action of Debt.

Sec. 3. And be it further Ordained, that from and after the passage of this Act, it shall be lawful for any Citizen or Constable to take up any Swine found running at large within the bounds of said City, and convey them to the Marshal of said City, who shall give three days notice, posted up in three public places in the City, in writing, and if no owner shall appear and pay all expences incurred by virtue of this Act, said Swine shall be sold at public Auction to the highest bidder, and after deducting all necessary expences, the proceeds shall be paid into the City Treasury.

Sec. 4. And be it further Ordained, that the Marshal of said City be allowed twenty five cents per day for keeping such Hogs or Swine, and ten per Cent of the proceeds of Sales made by him in accordance with the provisions of this Ordinance.

Sec. 5. This Ordinance to take effect, and be in force from and after its passage.

**Passed May 12th 1843. Hyrum Smith, Pres[i]d[en]t pro. tem. Ja[me]s Sloan, Recorder.**

It is hereby Ordered by the City Council of the City of Nauvoo that Samuel H. Smith be, and he is hereby allowed the sum of nine dollars and fifty Cents, (in addition to the sum of six dollars heretofore allowed him, & for which he received an Order on the City Treasurer,) being the amount deducted from his pay as a Member of the City Council, for fines, for the Year 1842.

**May 12th 1843. Hyrum Smith, Pres[i]d[en]t pro. tem. James Sloan, Recorder.**

It is hereby Ordered by the City Council of the City of Nauvoo, that the claim of Alexander Mills for eight dollars, for boarding and lodging several Prisoners and their keepers, up to this date, be, and the same is hereby allowed.

**May 12th 1843. Hyrum Smith, Pres[i]d[en]t pro. tem. James Sloan, Recorder.**

It is hereby Ordered by the City Council of the City of Nauvoo, that the claim of [John] Taylor & [Wilford] Woodruff, for a sum of three dollars and seventyfive cents, for stationary got for the use of the City Council, up to this date, be, and the same is hereby allowed.

**May 12th 1843. Hyrum Smith Pres[i]d[en]t pro. tem. James Sloan, Recorder.**

*June 1, 1843; Thursday.*[38]

An Ordinance to establish a Ferry across the Mississippi River at the City of Nauvoo.[39]

Sec. 1. Be it Ordained by the City Council of the City of Nauvoo, that Joseph Smith is authorized and licensed to keep a Ferry for the term of perpetual succession across the Mississippi River,[40] within the limits of said City, on said River, bounded north near the north West corner of Section No. thirtyone, township seven north, of range eight west, of the fourth principal meridian; and South near the south east corner of fractional

---

[38]The *History of Church,* 5:415-16, has the council meeting twice on May 31, at 10:00 a.m. and 6:00 p.m., to "draft the ordinance in relation to the ferry."

[39]Section 13 of the Nauvoo Charter granted the city council "exclusive power within the city, by ordinance, to license, regulate, and restrain, the keeping of ferries." The same section granted the city the authority to "regulate the police of the city; impose fines," and any "other legislative powers as are conferred on the City Council of the City of Springfield," which of course indicated the source for much of what is found in the Nauvoo Charter. Springfield's charter was granted in February 1840, Nauvoo's in December the same year. Although Springfield is more-or-less land-locked, the narrow Sangamon River connects to the Illinois River, which connects to the Mississippi, and the town received a visit from the steamship *Talisman* in 1832, accompanied by axmen clearing the way for it.

[40]In May the LDS Church bought half interest, with riverboat captain Dan Jones, in the *Maid of Iowa* steamboat. The current ordinance gave Joseph Smith hypothetical control of the docks where the *Maid of Iowa* and other boats would bring passengers and goods from Montrose, Iowa. However, there were no docks, only "landings" on private property, which would soon become a point of contention (see minutes for March 5, 9, 1844). One other boat shuttled between Nauvoo and Montrose, the *Iowa Twins,* a barge owned by Daniel Davis that hauled freight, propelled by two horses on treadmills. The *Maid of Iowa* not only ferried people to Iowa, it "transported Latter-day Saint immigrants from New Orleans or St. Louis, ... hauled corn and wheat, ... served for pleasure excursions, and at times became a police patrol boat." The mayor had once invested in a steamboat called the *Nauvoo,* which operated three months and sank (Leonard, *Nauvoo,* 149-51).

section No twelve, in township six north, of Range nine West, of the fourth principal meridian, according to the Charter of said City of Nauvoo, (which Charter was granted by the State of Illinois, on the 16th day of December A.D. 1840,) embracing all Ferries heretofore authorized by the State of Illinois, if any there be, within the aforesaid limits.

Sec. 2. And be it further ordained, that the said Smith shall furnish said Ferry with a good flat boat, or a good Boat to be worked by Steam or horse power, and skiff or yawl in such case, sufficient for the speedy and safe transportation of all passengers, together with their teams, animals, goods and effects; and further, that said Boat or Boats shall be furnished with a suitable number of Men, to manage them with skill and ability.

Sec. 3. And be it further Ordained, that if any Person or persons, except those whose Ferry is established and confirmed by this Ordinance, shall, at any time, run any boat, or boats, or other craft, for the purpose of conveying passengers or their property across said River as aforesaid, within said boundaries as aforesaid, he, she, or they, so offending, shall forfeit every such boat, or boats, or other Craft, to the owner or proprietor of the Ferry, and the owner or proprietor of the Ferry aforesaid, may at any time, after such forfeiture shall have accrued, enter upon and take possession of such boat, or boats, or other Craft, to his, or her own use, without precept; and such offender shall, moreover, pay to the owner or proprietor of the ferry aforesaid, who may be aggrieved as aforesaid, the sum of fifteen dollars for each person who may be thus unlawfully carried or conveyed across said ferry as aforesaid, to be recovered on motion, before any Alderman, or any Magistrate within said City competent to try the same, upon giving to such offender five days notice of the time and place of making such motion, which notice may be served on such person or persons, either in or out of the State, by delivering or tendering a Copy thereof, or leaving a Copy at their last place of residence: Provided, that nothing herein contained, shall be so construed as to prevent any person crossing said River, at said Ferry as aforesaid, on his or her own boat or other craft, on his or her own business; and also to take in and cross his or her neighbours, when the same is done without fee, and not with intention to injure said ferry, as aforesaid.

Sec. 4. And be it further Ordained, that the said Smith shall be governed in his rates of toll, and in the general management of said ferry, by Ordinance of said City Council.[41]

Sec. 5. This Ordinance to take effect, and be in force, from and after its passage.

**Passed June 1st 1843. Joseph Smith, Mayor. James Sloan, Recorder.**

The City Council of the City of Nauvoo, do hereby allow James Sloan, City Recorder, One hundred and fortyseven dollars and forty cents, for business done by him for the City in the Year 1842.[42]

**June 1st 1843. Joseph Smith, Mayor. James Sloan, Recorder.**

An Ordinance respecting mad Dogs and other Animals.

Sec. 1. Be it Ordained by the City Council of the City of Nauvoo, that all dogs or other animals known to have been bitten or worried by any rabid Animal, shall be immediately killed or confined by the owner, under a penalty not exceeding One thousand dollars, at the discretion of the Court.

Sec. 2. No dog shall be permitted to run at large in this City for five months after the passage of this Ordinance, under a penalty of twentyfive dollars, to be paid by the owner or owners of said dog or dogs, and all dogs during said five months shall be liable to be killed if found twenty Rods from their masters, and such penalty or penalties shall be recoverable and applied in like manner as other penalties within this City.

Sec. 3. This Ordinance to take effect and be in force from and after its passage.

**Passed June 1st 1843. Joseph Smith, Mayor. Ja[me]s Sloan, Recorder.**

The City Council of the City of Nauvoo, do hereby allow the claim of [John] Taylor & [Wilford] Woodruff, ^of^ nine dollars and seventy five Cents, for printing City Script, & for Newspapers &c furnished the City, up to this date.

**June 1st 1843. Joseph Smith, Mayor. James Sloan, Recorder.**

The City Council of the City of Nauvoo, do hereby allow the fol-

---

[41]For the regulated prices, see the entry for June 10, 1843, below.

[42]Joseph Smith nevertheless criticized Sloan for "charging for room, candles, fuel, etc., etc., as extras" (*History of Church,* 5:416).

lowing claims, to wit: Henry G. Sherwood twelve dollars, Alexander Mills twelve dollars, Shadrach Roundy twelve dollars, for services rendered as Watchmen, commencing Nov[embe]r 8th 1842, & ending Feb[ruar]y 23rd 1843, & the sum of Six dollars & fifty cents is to be deducted from Sherwood & Roundys claims, (one half from each,) being for Lime bought by them under Sale by Execution, at suit of the City against W[illia]m Niswanger, for Costs.

**June 1st 1843. Joseph Smith, Mayor. James Sloan, Recorder.**

The City Council of the City of Nauvoo, do hereby allow the claim of Alanson Ripley for three dollars, for services rendered to the City, by assisting the Recorder in the making out of the Original List of City Lots and other Lands.

**June 1st 1843. Joseph Smith, Mayor. James Sloan, Recorder.**

Edward Hunter, Parley P. Pratt, George J. Adams, & William W. Phelps were elected Members of the City Council, pro tem, for the City of Nauvoo, by the City Council of said City.

**June 1st 1843. Joseph Smith, Mayor. James Sloan, Recorder.**

*June 6, 1843; Tuesday.*[43]

Copy Letter from a Committee of vigilance, to Thomas Ford Governor of Illinois. The Undersigned, a Committee of the City Council of Nauvoo, appointed to address your excellency on the subject of Commissions for the Mayor and Aldermen of said City, beg leave to state.

On a careful and attentive perusal of the Act of incorporation for said City we are of the opinion your excellency will clearly perceive that the inhabitants of said City are invested with plenary powers to govern themselves by their representatives in Council assembled, and to make ordain and establish such laws as they may deem requisite for the peace benefit welfare and convenience of the inhabitants of said City, not inconsistent with the laws of this State or of the United States, Vide Sec. 11.[44]

---

[43]The following letter was in reply to the letter received from Thompson Campbell, Illinois Secretary of State, on April 14, 1843, above.

[44]Section 11 of the Nauvoo Charter gave the city council authority

By reference to Sections 4. 9. & 10 and from the whole tenor and general Spirit of the instrument your excellency we think cannot fail to conclude that it formed no part of the design of the Grantors to impose a single onerous or irksome obligation upon the inhabitants of said City, and that it could never have been designed by the general Assembly who granted the Charter, that the bonds of the Mayor and Aldermen required by the 16th Section of that instrument, should be filed at the office of the Clerk of the County Commissioners Court, is, we think abundantly manifest by the provision for a Recorder, the prescription of his duties, and the express provision of the 10th Section, that the bonds of all Officers created by this act shall be exacted by the City Council as they may deem expedient.

The Mayor and Aldermen acting under the laws of the State are by the 16th Section required to give the same Bonds to the State as are by law enjoined, but it by no means follows we humbly conceive that those Bonds should be lodged with the County Officers, indeed we would repeat that it appears in our estimation such was not the design of the Legislature nor is it fairly deduceable from the clause in the 16th Section to which the Secretary of State has referred but that the Rule in all such Cases is to take into consideration the general scope and design of the instrument. We would moreover state that the view we have taken of the matter was that which [has] universally prevailed so far as we know [and] was never questioned until the Secretary of State has raised the objection. If your Excellency should persist in refusing to act on the precedent of your predecessor which on a careful reconsideration of the matter we cannot believe you will, the Citizens of this State[,] inhabitants of Nauvoo[,] will be thereby placed in a very embarrassing and vexatious position[,] such an one as the executive officers of this State would not be so suicidal as to inflict upon one of the most flourishing and rapidly increasing Cities in the State embracing a population of 15 thousand and one which is at least adding as much to the strength and resources of the State as any other. The Clerk of the County Commissioners Court has already refused to receive the Bonds at his Office as being out of his jurisdiction deciding

---

to make laws for "the peace, benefit, good order, regulation, [and] convenience" of the city.

that the proper place to file them was at the Recorders office of the City of Nauvoo, and the Secretary of State has refused to forward the Commissions because the Bonds were not filed there. Will your Excellency take this matter into serious consideration, and Act as to you shall seem just and equitable in the premises.

Respectfully Yours, John Taylor. Sylvester Emmons. Samuel Bennett.

City of Nauvoo, June 6th 1843.

To Thomas Ford, Governor of Ill[inoi]s[,] Springfield.

*June 7, 1843; Wednesday.*

The Mayor signed an Order upon the City Treasury, in favour of James Sloan City Recorder, for twentythree dollars and fifty Cents, being the balance due him of his Salary of One hundred dollars, as Recorder, for the Year 1842, after deducting fifty dollars for which he received an Order upon the 12th day of July 1842, and twentysix dollars & fifty Cents by an Order dated Jan[uar]y 14th 1843, for the balance of Cash then remaining in the Treasury.

**James Sloan, Recorder.**

*June 10, 1843; Saturday.*[45]

The Members elected on the 1st instant, to act in the absence of those whose vacancies they fill, were arranged as follows, to wit; Edward Hunter for Brigham Young, Parley P. Pratt for Orson Pratt, George J. Adams for Heber C. Kimball, and William W. Phelps for Orson Spencer.[46]

**June 10th 1843. John Taylor, Pres[i]d[en]t pro. tem.[47] James Sloan, Recorder.**

---

[45]See also *History of Church,* 5:421.

[46]Brigham Young, Heber C. Kimball, Orson Pratt, Orson Hyde, Wilford Woodruff, and George A. Smith were called as "legal agent[s] to collect funds for the purpose of building the Nauvoo House and Temple of the Lord," as well as "messenger[s] of peace and salvation, as ... the Lord's noble men" (ibid., 5:274).

[47]Joseph Smith was at home the entire day.

Three Petitions were presented, and moved upon, for a Repeal of the Hog Law, and the motion was seconded by Hyrum Smith, for the purpose of having it discussed, and upon discussion, the Petitions were rejected.[48]

**June 10th 1843. John Taylor, Pres[i]d[en]t pro. tem. James Sloan, Recorder.**

An Ordinance to regulate the
rates of toll at the Ferry in the City of Nauvoo.

Sec. 1. Be it Ordained by the City Council of the City of Nauvoo, that from and after the passage of this Ordinance, the following shall be the rates of toll for crossing the Mississippi River at the City of Nauvoo; Viz:

| | ¢ |
|---|---|
| One Horse Waggon, with contents, and driver, | $ .75 |
| Two Horse Waggon, d[itt]o d[itt]o. | 1.00 |
| Four Wheel Carriage, for 2 or 4 horses, d[itt]o. d[itt]o. | 1.50 |
| Two Wheel Carriage for 1 horse, d[itt]o. d[itt]o. | .50 |
| Cart d[itt]o. d[itt]o. | .50 |
| Horse, Ass, Mule, or Jenny | .25 |
| Foot Passenger | .12½ |
| Horse, or other Animal with Rider | .37½ |
| Oxen per Yoke | .25 |
| Every head of Stock one year old | .18 |
| Under one year, and Sheep, Hogs, &c. | .06¼ |

Whatever is not herein specified shall be calculated by agreement.

Sec. 2. Be it further Ordained that there shall be a list of the above rates of toll posted up at a conspicuous place at the Ferry, and Boats of the Ferry, for the benefit of the public.

Sec. 3. Be it further Ordained that the keeper of the Ferry shall at all reasonable hours, when Wind and Weather will permit, keep his Craft of Conveyance, and skil[l]ful hands to manage the same, ready for the conveyance of passengers and effects, under a Penalty of fifteen dollars, to be recovered before any competent Authority, for each offence.

**Passed June 10th 1843. John Taylor, Pres[i]d[en]t pro. tem. James Sloan, Recorder.**

---

[48]See "An Ordinance in relation to Swine running at large," passed May 12, 1843.

It is hereby ordered by the City Council of the City of Nauvoo, that Fundy Street be opened from South Street to the burying Ground, and that the Supervisor be instructed to open it, and make it passable.

**June 10th 1843. John Taylor. Pres[i]d[en]t pro. tem. James Sloan, Recorder.**

*June 29, 1843; Thursday.*[49]

An Ordinance concerning Strangers and contagious diseases, and for other purposes.[50]

Sec. 1. Be it Ordained by the City Council of the City of Nauvoo, "for the peace, benefit, good Order, convenience, cleanliness, health and happiness,"[51] of said City agreeably to the Charter of the same, that the City Council, Marshal, Constables and City Watch are hereby Authorized, and empowered and required, to require all strangers who shall be entering this City, or are already tarrying, or may hereafter be tarrying in said City, in a Civil and respectful manner to give their names, former residence, for what intent they have entered or are tarrying in the City, and answer such other questions as the Officer shall deem proper or necessary for the good order, health, or convenience of the said City; and for a failure or refusal on the part of strangers to give the desired information, or for giving false names or

---

[49]See also *History of Church,* 5:457-58.

[50]This ordinance was not meant to prevent contagious disease, but rather to keep people from arresting Joseph Smith. In his *History of Church,* 5:439-41, Smith describes his arrest on June 23 and the need for an ordinance: "Mr. Joseph H. Reynolds, the sheriff of Jackson county, Missouri, and Constable Harmon T. Wilson, of Carthage, Illinois, ... arrived at Mr. Wasson's while the family were at dinner, about two p.m. They came to the door and said they were Mormon elders, and wanted to see Brother Joseph. ... They then hurried me off, put me in a wagon without serving any process, and were for hurrying me off without letting me see or bid farewell to my family or friends, or even allowing me time to get my hat or clothes, or even suffer my wife or children to bring them to me." Days later, Smith's journal records the presence of other strangers in Nauvoo: "Tuesday, June 27th Reported to be many strangers in the city. Watch doubled in the city this night. Wednesday, June 28th Some anxiety about so many strangers and suspicious characters in this city. New ordinance proposed by some Aldermen" (Faulring, *American Prophet's Record,* 288).

[51]See Nauvoo Charter, Section 11.

information, they shall be subject to the penalty of the Ordinance concerning "Vagrants and disorderly persons" passed November 13th 1841.

Sec. 2. And be it further Ordained, that the aforesaid Authorities of the said City, are further Authorized and empowered, and required to hail and take all persons found strolling about the City at night, after nine OClock and before sunrise, and to confine them in [the] ward [jail] for trial according to the aforesaid Ordinance concerning "Vagrants and disorderly persons," unless they give a good and satisfactory account of themselves, or offer a reasonable excuse for being thus caught out after nine OClock.

Sec. 3. And be it further Ordained that the aforesaid Authorities are further authorized, and empowered, and required, to require all such persons as they may suspect, to give information whether they have recently had, or have been exposed to any contagious disease or diseases from whence they came, under the same penalties as are annexed to the two preceding sections of this Ordinance.

Sec. 4. And be it further Ordained that the aforesaid Authorities are further authorized, and empowered and required to enter all Hotels, or houses of public entertainment, and such other habitations as they may judge proper, and require the inmates to give immediate information of all persons residing in said Hotel or habitation, and their business, occupation or movements; and for a failure noncompliance, or false information, their license shall be a forfeit, if it be a public House, and they and the transient Persons subject to the penalties of the three preceding Sections.

Sec. 5. And be it further Ordained that if any of the aforesaid officers shall refuse, or neglect, to do their duty as required by this Ordinance, they shall be fined One hundred dollars, and be broke of Office.

Sec. 6. This Ordinance to take effect and be in force from and after its passage.

**Passed June 29th 1843. Daniel H. Wells[52] Pres[i]d[en]t Pro. Tem. James Sloan, Recorder.**

---

[52]Joseph Smith was in hiding.

An Ordinance concerning
confining or keeping Animals in the City of Nauvoo.

Sec. 1. Be it Ordained by the City Council of the City of Nauvoo, that if any person shall confine any Animal in any manner, or place, within the limits of said City for the purpose of increasing the passions, or ferocity of said Animal, for any purpose, or keep any animal knowing the same to be possessed of ferocious or evil habits, whereby the life or limb of any person or Animal, may be put in jeopardy, or in danger of life or limb, by the Acts of such Animal, such person shall be subject to a fine of twenty five dollars, and the Animal may be killed by any Person, in any place, without notice.

Sec. 2. If any person shall keep any animal for exhibition or for any purpose whereby passions are excited, and modesty, decency, or virtue are affected, such Person shall be fined twenty five dollars, and the Animal disposed of by the Marshal, for the benefit of the City.[53] The fines to be recovered before the Mayor or any Alderman of the City.

Sec. 3. And be it further Ordained that no Animals except Cows, Calves, Sheep, Goats, and harmless and inoffensive dogs, shall be suffered to run at large, as free Commoners, within the limits of this City, under a penalty of from five to twentyfive dollars, at the discretion of the Mayor or Alderman, and the Animals liable for the penalty unless redeemed.

Sec. 4. And be it further ordained, and empowered, and required to carry the foregoing ordinance into effect, and to provide a good and sufficient yard or Pound suitable for the confinement of disorderly Animals, or such as may be actionable under the Ordinances; and he is further Authorized to draw on the treasury for and use any monies in the treasury (except the Recorders Orders,) to defray the expences of erecting the before mentioned Yard or Pound, and for a failure or neglect of duty

---

[53]This seems to be in reference to coaxing animals to fight, drawing from the previous paragraph about "increasing the passions, or ferocity of said Animal." Notice the language of the next paragraph about free-range animals being "free commoners" (cf. Martin J. Hershock, "'Free Commoners by Law': Tradition, Transition, and the Closing of the Range in Antebellum Michigan," *Michigan Historical Review* 29 [Fall 2003], 97-123, suggesting that the term offered protection for livestock).

he shall be subject to the same fine of the Offender in the three preceding Sections.

Sec. 5. And be it further Ordained that the Marshal shall furnish keeping for said Animals so impounded, and immediately give notice of the same by Posting three handbills in some of the most public places in the City, and if the owner appear not for the redemption of such Animal or Animals within three days he shall sell the same at Auction to the highest bidder and pay expence and fines from the avails of said sale, (the fees and compensation for his services to be the same as in the Ordinance respecting Swine, passed in this City,) and the remainder shall go into the City treasury unless claimed by the owner of said Animals within one Year.

Sec. 6. Be it further Ordained that the Marshal shall carry this Ordinance into effect under the penalty of the loss of Office. This Ordinance to be in force from and after its passage.

**Passed June 29th 1843. Daniel H. Wells. Pres[i]d[en]t Pro. Tem. James Sloan, Recorder.**

An Ordinance, concerning bathing and swimming.

Sec. 1. Be it Ordained by the City Council of the City of Nauvoo, that if any person shall bathe or swim in any Waters, within the limits of said City, whereby such Person shall be exposed to public view, in a state of nudity, such Person shall be subject to a fine of three dollars, for the first offence, to be recovered on complaint before any Court competent to try the same; and for the second offence, to the penalty of the Ordinance concerning Vagrants and Disorderly Persons, passed November 13th 1841.

Sec. 2. This Ordinance to be in force from and after its passage.

**Passed June 29th 1843. Daniel H. Wells, Pres[i]d[en]t Pro. tem. James Sloan, Recorder.**[54]

[54]From here to the end of the chapter, the transcription will draw almost exclusively from the rough minute books, as discussed in the preface and indicated by a double dagger at the beginning of an extended passage. Loose pages of minutes will be consulted beginning midway through chapter 4

‡*August 12, 1843; Saturday.*[55] Regular Meeting 10. A.M. A minority of the City Council [had] assembled, and issued an order to ^Alderman^ Samuel Bennett, to bring the Marshall, H[enry] G. Sherwood, before the council, forthwith and the order [was] returned, with the Marshall.

Counsellor John Taylor was appointed President Pro. tem. Prayer by O[rson] Hyde. [The] Names of [the] members [were] called. A communication ^was^ read from James Sloan ^Recorder^ to ~~Willard Richards~~ whom it may concern, ^stating his absence^ [upon which] it was voted that Willard Richards be the Recorder of the City – and [he was] sworn accordingly by the President of the Council.

Minutes of [the] previous council [were] read and ~~approved. Petition of Horace S. Eldridge was mentioned by Alderman Bennett, petition lost, unknown where~~ [the] committee on public grounds reported favorably on the petition of Horace S. Eldridge. [The] Report [was] accepted. ~~passed an ordinance to remunerate Horace S. Eldridge for land occupied by a Street~~ A bill was presented for An Ordinance to remunerate Horace S. Eldridge for land occupied by a street, which ~~passed~~ received the usual readings, and passed into a law, entitled as above.

The ^semiannual^ report of the Recorder, concerning the pay of Members of the Council was presented, ~~a~~ and approved. Adjourned to next regular meeting.

†Willard Richards was Elected Recorder of the City of Nauvoo,
in place of James Sloan, who was absent; and sworn.
W[illard] Richards, Recorder. John Taylor Pres[i]d[en]t Pro-tem.[56]

An Ordinance to remunerate
Horace S. Eldridge[57] for land occupied by a street.

Sec. 1. Be it ordained by the City Council of the City of Nauvoo that the Mayor be, and he is hereby authorized to make unto

[55]See also *History of Church,* 5:528.

[56]Joseph Smith was "sick at home" (ibid., 528).

[57]Horace Eldredge was born in 1816 in Brutus, New York. He was baptized in 1836 while residing in Indiana. He moved to Missouri in 1838 but returned to Indiana after the Mormons were forced out of Missouri. In 1840 he moved to Nauvoo and was present at the groundbreaking of the temple. He died in 1888.

Horace S. Eldridge, a good and sufficient deed for the land lying on the river side of Lot No 4, in Block No. 151, and occupied as a street in the original survey of the town plot of the City of Nauvoo, on condition that the said Horace S. Eldridge make a good and sufficient deed to the City of Nauvoo, for the land which the street now occupies.

**Passed August 12th 1843. John Taylor Pres[iden]t Pro Tem. W[illard] Richards, Recorder.**

It is hereby ordered by the City Council of the City of Nauvoo, that the following named persons be paid the sums respectively annexed to their names for their services in the city council, ^from Feb[ruary] 11, 1843^ up to this date, exclusive. To Wit:

| | $ | cts | | $ | cts |
|---|---|---|---|---|---|
| Hyrum Smith | 4 | 0 | Heber C. Kimball | 1 | 50 |
| John Taylor | 5 | 50 | Benjamin Warrington | 11 | |
| Orson Pratt | 7 | 50 | Brigham Young | 9 | |
| Sylvester Emmons | 11 | | Orson Spencer | 5 | |
| Daniel H. Wells | 4 | | Gustavus Hills | 50 | |
| George A. Smith | 11 | | George J. Adams | 1 | 50 |
| George W. Harris | 4 | | Edward Hunter | 1 | |
| Samuel Bennett | 5 | 50 | W[illia]m W. Phelps | 1 | 50 |
| N[ewel] K. Whitney | | 50 | H[enry] G. Sherwood, Marshall | 7 | |

out of any money in the treasury not otherwise appropriated; and it is further ordered that the persons hereafter named pay the sums annexed to their names, restively,[58] the same being fines incurred by them for non-attendance during the same period of time. to Wit:

| | $ | cts | | $ | cts |
|---|---|---|---|---|---|
| Orson Hyde | 5 | | Parley P. Pratt | | 50 |

**Passed August 12th 1843. John Taylor, Pres[i]d[en]t Pro. Tem. W[illard] Richards, Recorder.**

‡*September 9, 1843; Saturday.* 10 o clock A.M. Regular Meeting. A

---

[58]By "restively," they seem to be saying the fines will not be dismissed. *Restive* meant unyielding; *restiveness* meant "obstinate reluctance or indisposition to move" (Webster, *American Dictionary*, svv. "restif," "restifness").

minority of the Council assembled, and adjourned until Monday the 18th instant at 10 o-clock A.M.

*September 18, 1843; Monday.* 10 A.M. [An] Adjourned Meeting. ~~10 A~~ A minority of the council issued a~~n~~ warrant to Alderman N[ewel] K. Whitney to bring the Marshall which was immediately executed, and the Marshall notified absent members [that their presence was required]. – At 11 oclock & 30 minutes a majority were assembled. John Taylor was ^chosen^ president Pro Tem. Prayer by Orson Spencer. Names of [the] Members [were] called. Minutes of the two last councils [were] read and approved. Alderman W[illiam] W. Phelps, (who had acted in place of Orson Spencer,) was appointed in place of Geo[rge] A. Smith who was absent.

Petition was read from Eldridge Tufts,[59] and others to open an alley through Block 124. – which was refered to the committee on ~~Public Grounds~~ Improvements, who reported favorably, and [the] report was accepted.

A bill ^was presented^ for "an Ordinance for the inspection and measurement of lumber in Nauvoo and other purposes[,] which was twice read. – Alderman [George W.] Harris spoke[.] Alderman Phelps replied. Alderman Whitney spoke ^by query,–^ followed by Aldermen Harris & [Samuel] Bennett, and replied to by Alderman Phelps. Alderman [William] Marks spoke. ~~Bill~~ [The bill was] referred to a special Committee (viz) W[illiam] W. Phelps, W[illia]m Marks, & N[ewel] K. Whitney.

A bill ^was presented^ for ["]an ordinance concerning the inspection of ~~flower~~ flour &c in Nauvoo & for other purposes." Read twice. Alderman Phelps spoke, in favor of the bill. ~~three~~ The number three was added to the blank – with other amendment as shewn on the bill – with its title, as above.

A Bill ^was presented^ for An ordinance to authorize the city constables to execute and enforce the ordinances, relating ~~to ways and means~~ to Hogs and beasts, and to build a pound in the city of Nauvoo. Read twice – and the third time by its title, and passed into a law with its title, as above. 1. P.M. Council adjourned to next regular Meeting.

[59]Eldridge Tufts was born in 1812 in Farmington, Maine. He moved to Nauvoo in 1839 and died in 1850.

*October 14, 1843; Saturday.*[60] 10 Oclock A.M. Regular Meeting. A Minority of the council issued a warrant to the Marshall to call absent Members at half past eleven. [The] names of members [were] called. Prayer by W. W. Phelps, – Minutes of last Council read and approved.

A Bill was presented By Alderman Phelp[s] for "an Ordinance concerning the measurement of stone[,] coal, and Lime, which was read twice. ^On motion to insert the number 1 in [the] blank^ [the council heard from] [John] Taylor, [William] Phelps[,] [Edward] Hunter, [John] Taylor, [and George W.] Harris. [On] the Amendment[,] Hunter, the President[,] [and] Phelps, [who] replied. [Then] Phelps, O[rson] Spencer, Taylor, [and] Harris. The President spoke in objection to regulating the bushel by weight. – Motion lost. [The] Bill [was] Laid on the table.

W[illia]m E. Horne[61] was appointed inspector of flour in the City of Nauvoo. The ordinance concerning the inspection of flour in the city of Nauvoo, passed Sept[ember] 18th 1843, ^was read^ [and] followed with remarks by A[lderman] Harris[,] the President & A[lderman] Phelps[.] Council adjourned at 1-Oclock P.M.

*November 11, 1843; Saturday.*[62] 2 past 11. oclock A.M. Names of members called. Quorum Present, ^Hyrum Smith chosen Pres Pro tem^ [and] Alderman W[illiam] W. Phelps was added to the council in place of Al[der]m[an] [Daniel H.] Wells who was absent. Prayer by Alderman Phelps. Minutes of last council read and approved.

Elijah Fordham, present[ed] an account of $60.00 for Assessing and collecting[,] [which was] referred to the committee on Claims[.] J[onathan] H. Hale [presented a] Bill, for assessing and collecting in [the] 3rd Ward, [which was] referred to [the] committee on Claims. $65.00, [and] Josiah Arnold, [for] $13.50 as city watch, [to the] Committee of Claims[.]

Shadrack Roundy $48, as city Watch. Referred to Com[mittee] on Claims
James Alred $63.00 as supervisor Referred "

[60]See also *History of Church,* 6:56.

[61]William Eaton Horner was born in 1807 in Adams, Pennsylvania. He was baptized in 1834. He resided in Nauvoo's 3rd Ward neighborhood. He died in 1876.

[62]See also *History of Church,* 6:71.

H[enry] G. Sherwood $30.00 as City watch. Referred "
Quick $13.50 as city Watch. Referred "
Alexander Mills 28.50 as city watch Referred "
[The] Committee reported favorably on the foregoing Accounts.
H[enry] G. Sherwood['s] Bill for sundry services, $67.05, [was] referred "
[This was] reported favorably – and [the] Report accepted – and allowed
Johnathan H. Hale ^was appointed by nomination^ assessor & collector [in the] 3rd Ward for 1843

| | | | | |
|---|---|---|---|---|
| H[enry] G. Sherwood | " | " | 4 | " |
| Daniel Hendricks | " | " | 2 | " |
| A[lbert] P. Rockwood | " | " | 1 | " |

[A] Petition of Eldridge Tufts ^and others^ [was] granted ~~and others~~ to lay out an alley through block 124, North & South from Parly to Kimball St[reets]. Willard Richards [posted a] Bond as city Recorder & W[illia]m E. Horner [a] Bond as Inspector of flour. [These were] read and approved & given to the Marshall to deposite in the Treasury. [A] Bill for [John] Taylor & [Wilford] Woodruff for printing, was read and referred to [the] Committee on Claims, $117, deducting 1/3 = $78.00[.] [The] Report [was] accepted – account ^with the aforesaid claims^ allowed. 2 past 1 oclock P.M. adjourned.

*December 8, 1843; Friday.*[63] Special Session. December 8 – 1843, 4 oclock P.M. Names of members called. Prayer by the Mayor. Minutes of [the] last ~~conf~~ council read and approved.[64]

"An extra Ordinance for the extra case of Joseph Smith and

---

[63]See also *History of Church,* 6:105-07.

[64]The purpose of this special session was to be "prepared for any invasion from Missouri." Just previous to the meeting, Daniel and Philander Avery, father and son, were apprehended as horse thieves by a Missouri posse, held briefly, and then released. The incident struck alarm into the hearts of Mormons who feared that Joseph Smith could be abducted. However, one interesting detail about the posse is that one of its members was a school teacher. See Faulring, *American Prophet's Record,* 431; Dallin H. Oaks and Marvin S. Hill, *Carthage Conspiracy: The Trial of the Accused Assassins of Joseph Smith* (Urbana: University of Illinois Press, 1975), 58; *History of Church,* 6:145.

others," was read twice, & the third time by its title and passed by unanimous vote.[65] Also "An ordinance to erect a dam in the Mississippi River and for other purposes" was read & the rules dispensed with & read twice by its title and passed unanimously. The Mayor suggested the idea ^that the council might pass^ ~~of passing~~ an ordinance to suspend the operation of the [illegible] in this city, also the idea of petitioning congress to receive the ~~Nauvoo Legion~~ ^City^ under their protection, and acknowledge the Legion as United States troops and assist in fortification ^and other purposes^ and a messenger be sent to Congress for this purpose at the expence of the City. – A[lderman] [William W.] Phelps & [George W.] Harris approved, also C[ouncillor] O[rson] Pratt.

Mess[ieurs] [John] Taylor, O[rson] Spencer, & O[rson] Pratt were appointed a committee to draft a Memorial according to the Mayors Suggestion as above. Resolved that the Citizens of this City be called together tomorrow morning to hear read the ^extra^ ordinance for the extra care of Joseph Smith & others, also that the same be printed immediately.[66] Adjourned till Monday ^morning next^ at 10 A.M.

*December 12, 1843; Tuesday.*[67] 10. A.M. Special Session, according to adjournment. [The] Names of [the] Members [were] called, [and a]

---

[65]The ordinance, alternately referred to as the "Special Ordinance in the Prophet's Case, vs. Missouri," reads that "if any person or persons shall come with process, demand, or requisition, founded upon the aforesaid Missouri difficulties, to arrest said Joseph Smith, he or they so offending shall be subject to be arrested by any officer of the city, with or without process, and tried by the Municipal Court, upon testimony, and, if found guilty, sentenced to imprisonment in the city prison for life: which convict or convicts can only be pardoned by the Governor, with the consent of the Mayor of said city" and that "the trial shall be conducted according to the fifth [due process] and sixth [fair trial] articles of the amendment to the Constitution of the United States" (*History of Church,* 6:105-06.)

[66]The *Nauvoo Neighbor* printed the "special ordinance" and elaborated that the Illinois Attorney General had said the Nauvoo Legion was unauthorized and "disconnected from the military communities of the whole State." "General Joseph Smith" disputed this, insisting that "his commission declared that he (General Smith) was the Lieutenant-General of the Nauvoo Legion and of the Militia of the State of Illinois" (Ibid., 6:107-08).

[67]See also ibid., 6:110-11.

quorum [was] present. Prayer by the Mayor. Minutes of last council read and approved.

Resolutions passed by the inhabitants of the 3d Ward regarding the protection of the Citizens ~~of the~~ & Nauvoo. Read also some [suggestions] of the 2d Ward[.] Alderman [George W.] Harris spoke. A[lderman] [William W.] Phelps replied. [There was a] Petition of W[illia]m Clayton in behalf of Temple committee praying exemption from taxation [of] all property belonging to the Temple, which was [considered] and [the] peti[ti]on granted & A[lderman] O[rson] Spencer instructed to write an amendment to the ordinance. A[lderman] Harris spoke of the petitions of the 2d. & 3d Wards. A[lderman] G[eorge] A. Smith replied. A[lderman] Phelps spoke. The Mayor spoke.

[A] Petition of [the] Assessors and Collectors for [a] continuance of time in advertising [the] lots for sale for taxes [was] read, and [the] ^Petition^ granted by ~~Amendment to the~~ a[n] ordinance ~~for assessing and collecting taxes~~ to amend an ordinance concerning the public revinue[,] [originally] passed [on] Nov 31, 1842, read twice & [a] 3d time by its title and passed. An ordinance for selecting forty policemen & for other purposes [was] read. [The] ^rules [were] dispensed with^ & [it was read] twice by its title & passed.[68]

Councillor [John] Taylor on the committee for writing a Memorial to congress asked [for an] extension of time to report and [was] granted till saturday next [at] 10 oclock A.M. – "An ordinance for the health and convenience of travellers and other purposes" [was] read. The Mayor spoke in explanation. A[ldermen] Phelps & Harris spoke[.] ~~Ordinance passed~~ [The ordinance was] read again and the third time by its title & passed.[69]

---

[68]The ordinance reads: "Section 1. Be it ordained by the City Council of the City of Nauvoo that the Mayor of said city be, and is hereby authorized to select and have in readiness for every emergency forty policemen, to be at his disposal in maintaining the peace and dignity of the citizens, and enforcing the ordinances of the said city, for ferreting out thieves and bringing them to justice, and to act as daily and nightly watchmen, and be under the pay of said city" (Ibid., 6:110-11).

[69]The ordinance allowed the mayor to sell alcohol to non-citizens: "Be it ordained by the City Council of Nauvoo, that the Mayor of the city be and is hereby authorized to sell or give spirits of any quantity as he in his wisdom shall judge to be for the health and comfort, or convenience of such

[The] Petition of H[enry] G. Sherwood, S[hadrack] Roundy, [and] J[onathan] H. Hale that the Recorder issue his certificat for payment of all bills that have been allowed by the council [was] read & passed. Claims of Theodore Turly for Shackles, $2.50, [were] read. [The] Rules [were] dispensed with and [the] claims allowed. The Recorder stated to the council that he had furnished the old tax list to the new assessors as their directory ~~With some other~~ instead of a new list, which the council approved. 12½ noon. Adjourned till Saturday[,] 16th inst.[,] 10 A.M.

*December 16, 1843; Saturday.*[70] Special Session. Saturday Dec[ember] 16th 1843, 10 oclock A.M. [The] Names of [the] Members [were] called. Prayer by B[righam] Young. Minutes of last council read and approved. W[illia]m W. Phelps was added to the council to supply the place of counsellor [Sylvester] Emmons who was absent. [Phelps was] notified and took his seat.

The Mayor, Aldermen, and counsellors signed the Memorial to petition congress for redress of Missouri Losses, officially. [The] Memorial [was] Read.[71] Counsellor P[arley] Pratt, on the committee for Memorializing Congress for protection, read the Memorial. Counsellor Phelps suggested an amendment. Counsellor [John] Taylor suggested additions. [The] Mayor spoke. C[ouncillor] O[rson] Pratt spoke. [The] Mayor spoke in reply, stating [that] we wished to ask the privilege of calling on U.S. troops to protect us as is our privileges, which is not unconstitutional – but lays in the breast of congress.

[The] City Attorney spoke – on legal and constitutional points. C[ouncillor] Phelps read from the U.S. constitution – & spoke suggesting the propriety of referring [this to] the Men [on the committee]. ~~Counsellor Phelps was added to the committee on the Memorial~~ Moved by Coun[cilo]r Young, 2d and carried that Cou[ncilo]r

travelers or other persons as shall visit his house from time to time" (Ibid., 6:111).

[70]See also ibid., 6:116-17.

[71]At this meeting, Joseph Smith predicted: "I prophecy by virtue of the Holy Priesthood vested in me in the name of Jesus Christ that if Congress will not hear our petition and grant us protection they shall be broken up as a government and God shall damn them. There shall nothing be left of them, not even a grease spot" (Faulring, *American Prophet's Record,* 432).

Phelps be added to the committee, and the memorial [was] referred back to the committee for revision on Motion of A[lderman] G[eorge] A. Smith.

Coun[cilo]r Pratt read from the constitution. The Mayor spoke that the state had ceded to us the power which they possessed[,] therefore we have a claim on congress. All th[e] right[s] ceded by Congress to the Legislature [are] now ceded to us – and [he] continued his speech at considerable length. A[lderman] [Daniel H.] Wells spoke by [blank]. – The Mayor replied at length. C[ouncillor] Phelps spoke. Counsellor Taylor spoke. O[rson] Pratt spoke. An Ordinance regulating merchants & grocers Licences was twice read. A[lderman] Wells spoke by objection. C[ouncillor] Phelps replied. C[ouncillor] Taylor spoke. The Mayor spoke.

[A] Motion [was made] by Co[unci]l[or] Phelps and carried that Charles Warner be removed from the office of City Auctioneer. Heber C. Kimball was duly elected City Auctioneer in place of Charles Warner[,] [who was] removed. Resolved by the City Council of the City of Nauvoo that the Recorder Notify C[harles] Warner that he is removed from office. Cou[nci]l[or] [Benjamin] Warrington & A[lderman] Wells had leave of absen[ce].

The ordinance Regulating Merchants and Grocers Licences [was] amended [and] read by its title & passed. [The] Title [was] approved. [At] Twenty[-]five Minutes past 2[,] [the council] adjourned for 1 hour.

[At] Twenty[-]five minutes past 3 oclock [the] council assembled pursuant to adjournment. [The] Names of [the] members [were] called. [The] Minutes of [the] last council [were] read and approved. Notice of Charles Warners discontinuance of office was given to the Marshal. Counsellor Young – spoke of the measures of the City – that he had tried a pint cup by measuring it twice in a quart measure, and found it larger in proportion than the quart. Counsellor Pratt spoke in explanation.[72]

An ordinance concerning wharfage and for other purposes in Nauvoo [was] read twice & amended by erasing the word stop, and ~~inject~~ "land" inserted. – The number [of] ton[s] was erased & fifty

[72]It would be interesting to know what explanation Pratt gave for why two pints did not equal a quart. Perhaps in Nauvoo anything was possible! However, Pratt likely knew that a British pint was 20 percent larger than an American pint and that both were in use at the time.

added. [It was] read [a] third time and Passed. Its Title, An Ordinance concerning the landing of Steam boats in Nauvoo, passed. Johnathan Dunham[73] was ~~duly~~ appointed wharf Master, for one year.

Counsellor Kimball was appointed a committee to wait on Mr. Davidson Hibbord to solicit a block of land on which to build a Jail. – A[lderman] G[eorge] A. Smith was added to this Committee. [A] Petition of [the] City Attorney ~~read~~ for claims [against] city [was] read & refered to committee on claims[.] [The] Committee reported favorably – and the council refered the bill back to the committee[.] [The] committee reported to [the] attorney 25 dollars – and the report was accepted, and twenty five dollars was allowed. – Resolved that the office of City attorney be vacated for the time being and that the recorder give notice accordingly. [At] 5 oclock PM [the] council adjourned to next Thursday 10. A.M.

*December 21, 1843; Thursday.*[74] 12 oclock. [A continuance of an] Adjourned Council. [The] Names of [the] members [were] called. C[ouncillor] B[righam] Young was chosen pres[i]d[en]t protem ~~in Mayors absence~~[.][75] Prayer by A[lderman] [Orson] Spencer. Minutes of [the] last council [were] read and approved.

The committee appointed to visit Mr Hibbard[76] concerning a site for a Jail Reported that Mr Hibbord ~~nev~~ would give 3/4 of a Lot on parly St[reet] or 1 lot on Sidney & Back St[reet] for the purpose of building a jail. [He agreed to] deeding the same to the [city] on conditions the city should occupy said lot for ~~sad~~ said purposes. [The council] voted that the same committee proceed to select the Lot & procure a title for the same. Counsellor Young moved [that] the com-

---

[73]Jonathan Dunham was born in Paris, New York, in 1800. He was appointed captain of the Nauvoo police in 1843 and wharf-master in 1844. He was Acting Major General in June 1844 and among those arrested for the destruction of the *Nauvoo Expositor.* He died in 1845.

[74]See also *History of Church,* 6:124.

[75]According to his journal, Joseph Smith was present at the city council meeting. It is not known why Brigham Young served as temporary president.

[76]Davidson Hibbard was born in New Hampshire in 1786. He was one of the first settlers in the Commerce area, having moved there in 1829. Lands he sold to the Mormons were surveyed and added to Nauvoo in 1841 and 1842. He died in 1852.

mittee ^be instructed to^ select the ~~whole~~ Lot on Sidney and Back Street. A[lderman] [Samuel] Bennet preferd the 3/4 lot. [The] Mayor said that would depend on the Location. The object was to keep prisoners, and had better be in the most public place.

A[lderman] Spencer proposed the most valuable Lot, C[ouncillor] [Heber C.] Kimball thought the fractional Lot was the most valuable. C[ouncillor] Young thought the full lot was equally valuable with a stone quarry thereon. [The] Motion carried for selecting the full lot. [The] Claims of W[illiam] D. Huntington for Burying certain individuals ~~&c~~ ^and furnishing a coffin^ to the amount of $29.00 [was] read and refered to the Committee on claims. The Committee Reported favorably and [recommended] that the account be allowed. [The] Report [was] accepted and [the] claim allowed, to be paid out of any money in the treasury not otherwise appropriated.

An ordinance was reported by the committee to Memorialize Congress. [It was] read & ~~accep~~ [the] Report accepted. And the report ~~of the~~ ordered to a second reading. Read by C[ouncillor] O[rson] Pratt. C[ouncillor] Phelps moved an amendment, [that] "the" [be] erased and this inserted. C[ouncillor] Pratt proposed an additional Section to the ordinance requiring the U.S. Troops to obey the orders of the Mayor in case of insurrection.[77]

A[lderman] Bennet ~~made~~ raised a query, to which C[ouncillor] Phelps replied and the 4th Section was added to the ordinance. The mayor suggested an amendment of perpetual succession. A[lderman]

---

[77]The memorial to Congress asked for independence from the State of Illinois and the authority to command federal troops:

"Be it ordained ... that all the rights, powers, privileges, and immunities belonging to Territories, and not repugnant to the Constitution of the United States, are hereby granted and secured to the inhabitants of the city of Nauvoo ...

"And be it further ordained ... that the mayor of Nauvoo be ... empowered ... to call to his aid a sufficient number of United States forces, in connection with the Nauvoo Legion, to repel the invasion of mobs, keep the public peace, and protect the innocent from the unhallowed ravages of lawless banditti ...

"And be it further ordained that the officers of the United States army are hereby required to obey the requisitions of this ordinance" (*History of Church,* 6:125-32). See the city council minutes for February 12, 1844, for Joseph Smith's sanguine instructions to Orson Pratt, who was instructed to take the memorial to Congress, that "we must have that document passed, – and we will have it."

Bennet proposed an amendment to add "the nearest troops." C[ouncillor] Phelps related an anecdote of concerning Owens, and objected to the word contiguous[,] & [the] Mayor concurred. ~~in~~ C[ouncillor] Phelps suggested that we ^will^ have a right to a garrison assured &c ~~when~~ if the ordinance pass[es]. [It was] motioned by G[eorge] A. Smith & carried that the Memorial & ordinance be forwarded to Congress. Motioned & seconded ^and carried^ that C[ouncillor] P[arley] Pratt be delegated to present the same to Congress. [The] Mayor proposed a combined delegation of the Representatives of Illinois, in presenting the bill.

An Ordinance to prevent unlawful Search or seizure of person or property by foreign process in the city of Nauvoo [was] read twice, – [then a] 3 time by its title & passed, [all] satisfied with its title.[78] [The] Mayor suggested the propriety of making all coloured people free – so that they cannot be carried out of the City unless guilty of crime.[79] C[ouncillor] Phelps suggested the propriety of giving instructions to the committee to bring in an Ordinance concerning the Registry of deeds.

Charles Warner had leave & spoke, enquiring the reason of his removal from the Office of City auctioneer.[80] The Mayor explained,

---

[78]By "foreign," the council meant any process initiated outside the City of Nauvoo. Despite the phrase "unlawful search or seizure," outsiders assumed it meant impunity for Nauvoo citizens. Bowing to outside pressure on January 10, 1844 (see next chapter in this volume), the city council passed an amendment to clarify that the ordinance would not be "so construed as to prevent, hinder, or thwart the designs of justice," although this carried the weight of an opinion rather than a clear directive about how to proceed in such cases (Ibid., 174).

[79]Joseph Smith, an abolitionist, held to these views and published them as part of his U.S. presidential platform: "Petition, also, ye goodly inhabitants of the slave states, your legislators to abolish slavery by the year 1850, or now, and save the abolitionist from reproach and ruin, infamy and shame. Pray Congress to pay every man a reasonable price for his slaves out of the surplus revenue arising from the sale of public lands, and from the deduction of pay from the members of Congress. Break off the shackles from the poor black man, and hire him to labor like other human beings; for 'an hour of virtuous liberty on earth, is worth a whole eternity of bondage!'" (*General Smith's Views of the Powers and Policy of the Government of the United States* [Nauvoo: John Taylor, 1844], 7).

[80]Whatever the reason was, the discussion would conclude with Warner's reinstatement.

also C[ouncillor] Phelps. Warner asked leave to pay action tax in ~~treasury~~ orders[.] A[lderman] Spencer objected; C[ouncillor] Phelps spoke, [saying he] thought Warners claim had priority. C[ouncillor] Taylor thought there was no action called for. [A] Motion [was made] and carried that the Treasurer be instructed to give ~~C[harles] Warners~~ James Sloans Orders ^for services rendered [to] the city ~~priority~~^ priority in payment. H[eber] C. Kimball resigned his ~~appointment~~ office ^Elect^ as City Auctioneer, Charles Warner was ~~duly~~ reelected City auctioneer

~~Motiond & Seconded that carried that John P. Greene be Marshal of the city for the city~~ Marshall [Henry G.] Sherwood [was] expecting soon to leave ^the city.^ John P. Green was duly elected Marshall of the city. Counsellor Young spoke of the duties of a Marshal &c. Counsellor Phelps spoke. The Mayor gave instruction to the Marshall & policemen – to see that all carrion is removed, that all ~~public~~ houses are kept in order. [A policeman] stops boys fighting, prevent[s] children floating off on the ice, [and] correct[s] any thing out of order; like a father.

H[enry] G. Sherwood resigned his office as assessor & collector to J[ohn] P. Green[,] with the approbation of the Council. The Mayor offered to build a jail if they would leave it to him and he was authorized so to do. The Mayor referred to the statutes – and the criminal code of the City. B[righam] Young moved & [it was] carried unanimously that ~~the Old committee on the Criminal code be dropped~~ Counsellor [Sylvester] Emmons be dropped [from] the Committee on the Criminal code & C[ouncillor] W[illiam] W. Phelps Substituted.

The Mayor proposed as soon as opportunity presents we vote for our own Court house &c. [At] 3 oclock [the council] adjourned to [the] next regular meeting.

*December 29, 1843; Friday.*[81] Special Session[,] Dec[ember] 29, 1843. [At] 4 oclock P.M. [the] Names of [the] Members [were] called. Prayer by W W Phelps[.] Minutes of last council [were] read and approved.

Capt[ain] [Jonathan] Dunham & 40 Policemen were sworn into office to support the constitution of the U.S. & the State of Illinois and obey the ordinance[s] of this city and the Mayor according to the

[81]See also *History of Church,* 6:149-53.

best of their ability, by Counsellor ~~the~~ W[illiam] W. Phelps clerk of the Mayors Court.[82] [The] Names ^of [the] police^ [were] called by Capt[ain] Dunham.[83] A[lderman] G[eorge] W. Harris admonished the police to do their duty.

The Mayor ~~spoke~~ said that it was expected that a part [of the force] would be on duty while [the] others rest – that it might be expected that thieves had crept into the Church, that it would be an abominable thing to se[nd] a thief to catch a thief, & [he] would look upon men in their situation[,] [who were] guilty of a mean or cowardly act[,] with the utmost contempt. – Capt[ain] Dunham [was] to be called High policeman.

Men have strange ears, [he said][,] transformed [by flattery], – altogether different from what they were [intended for]. ^We will^ be forbearing until we are compelled to strike, then [you should] do it decently and in good order & break the yoke so that it cannot be mended. The ~~mob~~ mob [that pursued us in Missouri] has been so repulsed[,] they stand in fear. ~~Let us~~ We will be at peace with all men so long as they will let us alone" shall be the Motto of the C[hurch] of J[esus] C[hrist] O[f] Latter D[ay] Saints from this time forth.

In relation to Missouri, Let them alone. – They stink in the nose of the Almighty. Let them alone. – [Orrin] Porter Rockwell has gone clear and that proves me clear of being accessory of [the] shooting [of Missouri Governor Lilburn W.] Boggs.[84] ~~that~~ Our difficulties from the State of M[iss]o[uri] are hurled on us through the influence of our neighbors around us. – The Gov[ernor] [of Illinois] has boasted of being a law abiding man. It is our best policy to acquaint

---

[82]Part of this entry appears in the Record of Proceedings, signed by "W[illard] Richards Recorder."

[83]The forty members of the force included "High Policeman" Jonathan Dunham; Lieutenants Charles C. Rich (1st), Hosea Stout (2nd), and Shadrack Roundy (3rd); Ensign John Pack; Sergeants Jesse P. Harmon (1st), John D. Lee (2nd), Daniel Carn (3rd), and Josiah Arnold (4th); Corporals James Emmett (1st), Alexander Mills (2nd), Steven H. Goddard (3rd), and William Pace (4th); "pioneer" Abraham C. Hodge; "filers" Levi W. Hancock and Daniel M. Repsher; and twenty-four officers. In addition, Richard D. Sprague and Samuel Billings were drummers.

[84]A Missouri grand jury decided not to bring charges against Rockwell in August 1843, but he was not released until December 13. See Harold Schindler, *Orrin Porter Rockwell: Man of God, Son of Thunder* (Salt Lake City: University of Utah Press, 1983), 94-102.

the Gov[ernor] by affidavits &c so that when the onset comes he will be obliged to send the Militia to our support. Let us keep cool as a cucumber in a frosty morning. Say nothing about M[iss]o[uri]. Soft words turn away wrath "in the heart of a fool," therefore ^we will^ [be gentle][.] Poor pussy this generation.

Keep time, – have the ordinances in [your] possession and study them, & ferret out all brothels and disorderly conduct, and if a transgressor resists[,] cuff his ears. – If any one lifts a weapon [or] presents a pistol &c [you must] take his life if needs be. Take care of your~~selves~~ own lives. Let no horse be taken away – or any thing stolen. – Let M[iss]o[uri] alone, stay at home, [and] if any man attempt to bribe you[,] tell me. Let us have a reformation. The speculators are in this state & wanting to sell revolving pistols to us to fight the M[iss]o[urians] & the M[iss]o[urians] to fight us. I think my life more in danger from some little do[ugh] head[85] of a fool in this city than from all the co[nsta]bular[ies] of enemies abroad, and [if] I can escape the ^the hand of an ~~as~~^ assassin[,] ~~of a Brutus~~ I can live ~~as like~~ as ^might^ Caesar ^have lived if [it] had not been for a Brutus.^ I have ^had^ pretended friends who have betrayed me[,] as I am informed.

Then [the mayor] blessed the police. – It may be said in time to come [by those whom you have assisted,] where is our ^of[ficer]^ old policeman[?] ^If^ [you do well][,] ~~you magnify you office~~ [people will say][,] Let us have one of our policemen. ^If you will magnify you[r] office^ [that] shall be the blessing that shall be conferred on you in time to come. Counsellor Hyrum Smith spoke – of the importance of the Police office. The Mayor said that if any one offered a bribe to a policeman[,] the city will pay that Policeman twice the amount offered for the information [after being] reported to the Mayor.

[The] Petition of Pulaski S. Cahoon to have [a] Licence to retail Spirits [was] read & ordered to be laid on the table. [The] Petition of B[enjamin] Warrington & others for opening a part of the Street called Mulholland St[reet] as far east as the Corporation line & [related] pet[it]ion [were] ordered to be granted.[86] [The] Petition of

[85] A dough head was a person who was intellectually slow or whose loyalties were easily manipulated.

[86] The Record of Proceedings has this: "Granted by the City Council of the City of Nauvoo the Petition of Benjamin Warrington and fifty six

R[euben] H Loomis[87] for a Licence to Retail spiritous Liquors [was] read and ordered to be laid upon the table. [The] Council Adjourned to [the] next regular Meeting.

---

others, for opening a part of the Street called Mullholland Street as far East as the Corporation line," witnessed by "W[illard] Richards, Recorder."

[87]Reuben H. Loomis was born in 1809 in New York. He was still in Nauvoo, along with his wife and son, when the 1860 census was taken. He was aligned with the dissenters in Nauvoo.

# 4.
# "The Greatest Nuisance" 1844

‡*January 3, 1844; Wednesday.*[1] Special Council. Jan[uary] 3rd 1844 [at] 12 oclock. [The] names of [the] members [were] called. The Mayor directed the Marshal to bring W[illia]m Law & John Snider before the Council and [Joseph] said Bro[ther] Hiram [Smith] told him last evening that W[illia]m Law had said that some of the police had told him that they have been sworn by the Mayor secretly to put him (Law) out of the way.[2] – [The mayor said he] has had no private

---

[1]In Joseph Smith, *History of the Church of Jesus Christ of Latter-day Saints,* 7 vols. (Salt Lake City: Deseret News, 1902-12), 6:162-65, references to plural marriage–the main issue of contention–were removed from these minutes, and other changes were made to make the witnesses appear uncertain, the Missouri Danites seem to be acting on their own, and the prophet appear to be unwaveringly heroic.

[2]On January 2, 1844, William Law recorded the events leading up to this meeting: "This day I learned from remarks made by J[oseph] Smith before the city council and police, I am suspected of being a Brutus, and consequently narrowly watched, and should any misconceive my motive, my life would be jeopardized[.] [I] went to Hyrum Smith and told him how matters were going [and] he seemed astonished, and said he would see Joseph and have it put down; he went to him and returned to me again, and I went with him to Joseph; he said he never intended any such idea to be conveyed and that he would have the Council and the Police together tomorrow" (in Lyndon W. Cook, *William Law: Biographical Essay, Nauvoo Diary, Correspondence, Interview* [Orem, UT: Grandin Book, 1994], 38).

conversation with any of the Police but High Policemen [Jonathan] Dunham and that [was] to have special care [for] his [Joseph's] ^personal^ safety. Called on the policemen to say no if they had received ~~my~~ no private oath from the Mayor & they all said no.

Coun[cilor] Hiram Smith said Bro[ther] Law said that the policeman swore [to] him[,] Law[,] ^according to Masonic degradation[3]^ to keep the secret, that he was to be put out of the way in 3 months. [The] Mayor wanted policemen to understand forever that all he wanted was they should execute the law [not William Law], & his orders according to the law. Policemen [were] called for the individual police [to testify]. [The] Mayor said he thought proper [that] Bro[ther] Law should come before the council and make his statement on oath.

Mayor[:] If you see a man stealing and you have told him to stand 3 times, and warned him that he is a dead man if he does not stand, ^& he runs^ [then] shoot [at] his leg. – The object of the police is to stop theiving, but an enemy should not be harmed until he draws weapons upon you.

W[illia]m Law come in and was sworn to tell the truth, touching the case before the council, by W[illiam] W. Phelps[,] C[lerk of] M[ayor's] Court. W[illia]m Law ~~oath before the~~ said he had been informed that some of the policemen ~~that~~ had had another oath ~~had been~~ administered ^beside the one administered publicly^ [and] that [in this] one [they were told] there was a Judas in the Gen[eral] Smith['s] cabinet, one who stood next to him[4] and he must be taken care of, and that he ^must^ not be allowed to go into the world but must be taken care of ^and not only^ a do[ugh] head & Judas, but a Brutus, ^that the idea had been advanced^ that the scriptures support such a doctrine.

A[lderman] [George W.] Harris[:] Who is the person, & who told you.

[William] Law[:] I am under obligations not to tell.

Harris[:] That is immaterial. You are bound to disclose by your oath here.

Law[:] One oath is as good as another.

---

[3]The word *degredation* alludes to the promise of a painful death for revealing the Masonic secrets.

[4]That is, Smith's counselor in the First Presidency, William Law.

[The] Mayor said he would protect him – he was bound to tell.

Law Said he would tell who told him ^& he might tell the name of the police^ [because it was] Eli Norton [who] told me.

The Marshal ^was^ sent to bring Eli Norton. Counsellor Phelps enquired [into some of the details]. [The] Mayor said ^to the police[,]^ on conditions I have had no private conversation with any of you[,] ~~that they~~ will [you please] rise up & change the breech of your guns upwards[,] & all arose & changed ~~butt of~~ their guns.

Counsellor Hyrum Smith [said he] consider[ed] the things very alarming when he heard it [and] referred to Dr [Sampson] Avard & John Carls doings in M[iss]o[uri][5] – and stated what was said by the Mayor [at] a former council [meeting].

[The] Mayor said the reason why he made the remarks he did [at the last meeting] was on account of the reports brought from Jail by [Orrin Porter] Rockwell – that they wanted to get me & thus ~~to~~ put down Mormonism – so that they might organize upon their old principles – on the Orthodox system. [They] did not design to try me[,] but [to] hang me, that they had a man in our midst who would ~~deliver me up~~ fix me out if they could not get me without, and [thus] related his remarks at the previous council. [The] Minutes of [the] last council [meeting were] read.

Eli Norton [was] Sworn to testify the truth the whole & nothing but the truth – by counsellor W[illiam] W Phelps[,] Clerk of [the] Court. [Norton said][:] All I know about a private oath i[s] on intimation. Bro[ther] [Daniel] Cairns said all that I have heard – [and the mayor] probably refered to what has been stated, about a doe head &c.

^By Mayor^[:] Did he sa[y] he ^I^ had administered a private oath?

---

[5]Hyrum Smith is referring to the Danites, a secret society that was formed in Far West, Missouri, in 1838. Their purpose was to defend Mormons by any means necessary and to terrorize the perceived enemies of the Church. Joseph Smith denied any involvement in the group and claimed to have cut off Sampson Avard when he learned of the organization. Avard, on the other hand, said Smith was the "prime mover and organizer of the ... band." By 1844, Smith had publicly denounced the group (Harold Schindler, *Orrin Porter Rockwell: Man of God, Son of Thunder* [Salt Lake City: University of Utah Press, 1983], 28-33). Avard was born on the Isle of Guernsey in 1803 and was baptized in Pennsylvania when he was thirty-two. He was excommunicated in 1839 for testifying against Joseph Smith. He died in 1869.

^Norton[:]^ No! [He] said not much about Law, did not say you had ever ministered any private oath. Cairns never intimated Law must be put out of the way. [He] did not call W[illia]m Laws [by] name nor no other name, did not say the policemen had a private oath. – ~~did~~ [I] underst[oo]d Cairns to say there was private instructions, and if a man could not keep a secret[,] [he] was not worthy of a place in the Church. [Cairns] did not say the Mayor had given him a charge, did not tell where. [He] told me there were doe heads about, did not say the doe heads were in danger. The Mayor was in danger from the doe head.

By W[illia]m Law[:] Did you not understand from Bro[ther] Cairns that [Joseph] was suspicious of one near him as a doe head, & must be taken care of. – [Were you not] satisfied he had reference to me?

E[li] N[orton][:] Yes. He mentioned a doe head standing near Joseph. [He said he] had [a] conversation on Spiritual wifes.[6] – I did not believe [it].[7] – [I] knew Bro[ther] Law was opposed [to polygamy], and in this conversation the doe head came in. Cairns did not say Joseph had anything to do with spiritual wifes or had ~~not~~ taught any such things, did not say Bro[ther] Law had any thing to do with it. – ^There was^ no chain to the conversation, – ^He suggested^ there was another Law, the Law of God, [and] d[id] not know who administered the ^other^ oath.

Mayor[:] Tell what you know that made you so alarmed about Bro[ther] Law.

Eli Norton[:] Cairns told me several times Daniteism was not down, never said [the] Mayor had any thing to do about Daniteism. Cairns said it was a good system, said ~~Q~~ every ~~department~~ Quorum had their teachings and they must not tell another quorum, did not say I must take an oath to remain his counsellor. – I drew the inference that Bro[ther] Law was the doe head from Cairns conversation, but Cairns did not name Law.

---

[6]Spiritual wives, in this context, refers to plural marriage. By January 1844, at least sixty-five plural marriages had been performed in Nauvoo. The doctrine was being taught secretly, but rumors were rampant (George D. Smith, "Nauvoo Roots of Mormon Polygamy, 1841-46: A Preliminary Demographic Report," *Dialogue: A Journal of Mormon Thought* 27 [Spring 1994]: 14).

[7]Law never accepted Joseph Smith's doctrine of plural marriage.

Bishop Cairns[8] said[:] I told him we were sworn & our duties [were] specified. I said by the covenant we have made in Baptism we are bound to protect each other in righteousness. Daniteism is to stand by each other[,] that is all I know about Daniteism. – [The] Mayor said he was not afraid of any thing but a doe head in our midst. ^In our conversation we^ referred to spiritual wifes and one thing brought on another. – I was asked who can that man be? I gave my opinion that certain men had been required to give their property to certain purposes & then went & built a mill & sowed a hundred acres of hemp & lost it in the river. – Norton said Bro[ther] Law knew about the Spiritual wife system. I never intimated that Bro[ther] Law['s] life was in danger. I intimated that Bro[ther] Law might be the doe head, previously Bro[ther] Law and me had [a] conversation about stories afloat on spiritual wifes. He thought it was from the devil – and we must put it down[,] that he knew such a thing was in existence & [was] breaking up ~~of~~ families &c.

By Law[:] Did I ~~said~~ not say we have a good foundation [for believing so] because Joseph blowed it all up before the [Nauvoo Stake] High Council & Hyrum before the Elders Quorum?[9]

Yes said Cairns, [confirming that] Law did not[,] [in their conversation][,] speak disrespectfully of Joseph or of the Church. [Cairns said he] had no secret conversation with [the] Mayor. Nor [had he received a] charge except before the council [and people had] never heard any thing from me to endanger the life of any man.

[The] Mayor spoke on [the] Spiritual wife system and explained, The man who promises to keep a secret and does not keep it he is a liar and not to be trusted. [He said][:] Esq[ui]r[e] [Daniel H.] Wells came to me the other night and said that he was satisfied & pleased with all I had said[,] [that] I did say[,] [also to] A[lderman] Wells.

Counsellor H[yrum] Smith spoke at considerable length.[10]

---

[8]Cairns (aka Carn) was bishop of the German-speaking ward. He was also a Danite.

[9]See the entry for July 12, 1843, in chapter 10 for Hyrum Smith's introduction of plural marriage to the high council. One of the elders, Charles Smith, confirmed that in the winter of 1843-44, Hyrum also visited the elders quorum to inform them of "the Revelation given 12 July 1843" on "the doctrine of Plurality of Wives" (qtd. in Richard S. Van Wagoner, *Mormon Polygamy: A History* [Salt Lake City: Signature Books, 1989], 55).

[10]Law wrote that "Hyrum Smith made a speech very much in my favor

Gen[eral] W[illia]m Law Spoke [and] said there was no man in the city more zealous to support Mormonism than himself. I have ever been ready to stand forth one against 9 for the defense of Joseph and am yet [willing to]. If he lives till I shed his blood or strike a hair from his head[,] he will live till he is as old as Methuselah – and I firmly believe if I live till Joseph kills me or sets any one to kill me I shall live as long as I shall want to.

Mayor [to Law][:] Did I ever tell you that any body had told me that you would sell your property [and] you would blow up Mormonism?

Law[:] Hyrum told me that.

Bishop Cairns said he had never conveyed the idea to father Norton that Joseph ^had^ said that Mr Law was the Doe head.

Mayor[:] Where a man becomes a traitor to his friend or country who is innocent, treacherous to innocent blood, I consider it right to cut off his ~~innocent~~ influence so that he could not injure the innocent, but [it is] not right to meddle with that man without testimony, law & trial. [I] suggested the propriety, since Rockwell is clear & Avery &c & we have promise of protection from the Govern[or] &c[,] of the policemen laying up their guns and carrying only small arms – and that the [City] Council pass such an order. The Danite system never had any existence. The term grew out of a term I made [in] an off[ice] when the brethren prepared to defend themselves from the mob in Far West [Missouri]. [It was] ~~the~~ in reference to the stealing of Macaiah images, [that] if the enemy comes[,] the Danites will be after them, meaning the brethren in self defense.[11] [The] Mayor instructed the police to lay up their arms till further orders. 4 [minutes past] 2 P.M.[,] Council Adjourned.

*January 5, 1844; Friday.*[12] 11 AM. Special Session. Names of Members called. Prayer by O[rson] Spencer. Minutes of the last 2 Councils

---

and Wilson Law's. Said we and all our people were high minded and noble and no one ought to have an[y] suspicions against us" (Cook, *William Law,* 41).

[11]This is in reference to six hundred warriors from the biblical tribe of Dan who stole a silver idol from a bedouin named Micah, then "went on to Laish, against a people at peace and secure. They attacked them with the sword and burned down their city." The rationale for stealing the silver was that it had been consecrated to God (Judges 17:1-3; 18:14-27).

[12]See also *History of Church,* 6:166-70.

read and approved. – [The] Object of the Council [was] stated by Mayor [as] similar to the last Council wherein W[illia]m Marks considered himself & W[illia]m & Wilson Law ~~are~~ in danger. – When [the mayor] heard the report he was unwilling to believe any thing about it from the course the thing took in the last council. – But for the sake of others he had called this council.[13]

Bro[ther] [Leonard] Soby [was] going home the other night [and] was hailed by a policeman ~~and~~ who ~~and~~ frightened him. ^A^ Policeman told Soby that Marks & Law must not cross his tracks, that Warren Smith[14] said at another ^time^ that W[illia]m Marks & W[illia]m Law were enemies to Joseph – &c – I have never thought[,] [said the mayor][,] not even [dared] to dream[,] of doing any thing against the peace of this City. [I] did not know I had any

---

[13]Joseph Smith recorded the reason for this meeting: "Another Tempest in a tea pot about nothing at all. W[illia]m Marks thought somebody had concluded he was the Brutus or doe head. Leonard Soby made [an] affidavit that Warren Smith had said something about Law and Marks" (Scott H. Faulring, ed., *An American Prophet's Record: The Diaries and Journals of Joseph Smith* [Salt Lake City: Signature Books, 1989], 437).

William Law recalled the situation differently: "This morning a new rumor is afloat. Leonard Sobey states that Warren Smith[,] one of the Police men[,] said he believed that I was the Brutus and that W[illia]m Marks was an other, and that we had better keep out of his way or he would pop us over. Wilson Law, Hyrum Smith and I went to Joseph Smith and told him; he became very angry that any should have any fears or suspect that he would encourage such a thing, and said that he had a good mind to put them (the police) on us any how, we were such fools, or words to that effect. It produced an indignation in my heart, that I could not control, to find the mayor of the City, threaten two innocent men, with forty armed police, because they complained to him of threats having been made by them, against their lives; some hard words passed between us, and so the affair passed off for that day" (Cook, *William Law*, 41-42).

[14]Warren Smith was a blacksmith and member of the Nauvoo police force. He was born in June 1809 in Nashville, Tennessee. He and his wife, Lydia Alexander Smith, joined the LDS Church in 1836 and lived in Far West, Missouri, for a time; but when they were forced to move to Illinois, she died there in 1839. Warren then married Amanda Melissa Barnes Smith, the widow of his namesake, Warren Smith, who had been killed at Haun's Mill in Missouri. They later separated and Warren married Rachel Blackburn and Mahala Dudley. Warren died in American Fork, Utah, in May 1886 (Joni Kesler and Julia Roberts, "Warren Smith," "History of Benjamin Mark Smith," www.jnjtreeclimbers.com; "Warren Smith," *Find a Grave*, www.findagrave.com).

enemies. [I] have been at home. [I have] heard but little [and] did not know there was so much evil surmising in the city. My long forbearance to my enemies ought to be sufficient testimony of my ~~d~~ peaceful Disposition towards all. It occurred to my mind that it was not fear, but got up for effect, but I do not know it. — I want the council to investigate.

W[illia]m Marks [was] sworn [and] testified [that] Monday evening Bro[ther] Soby came up & said are you aware of the danger you are in? [I said] No! [He told me my] life [wa]s threatened, — A policeman [had] stopped [Soby] in the dark [to say this, and Soby] was alarmed. —

Marks[:] [At first] I supposed the threats were from that policeman — but I was mistaken. Another policeman said last Sunday that Joseph had enemies, that Law & Myself were Josephs enemies & if [we] came in his way, ~~a~~ [we] might be popped over. A fire was kindled in the street near my house, and I thought I was watched. Francis Higby told me, — and a man in the east part of town told me, and a man came from the other side of the river [came] & told the story ^to that man[,] as he said[.]^ [And] yesterday morning Hiram [Smith], Wilson Law & William Law met in [the] street & I told [them] the story, as before related.

Mayor[:] Did ever any body tell you I was the one who directed you to be watched? W[illia]m Marks[:] No!

[The] Marshall went for Francis ^M^ Higby — & — [George W.] Crouse. Leonard H. Soby [was] sworn[:] On Sunday, 31 Dec[ember] — I met Warren Smith in Crouses Store [and] asked him if he knew who the Brutus was. [Warren] Smith said he believed W[illia]m Law was one & Marks another. [He said] they had better not come in ~~my~~ his way. — ~~my impression was if they were coming in~~ [He] did not say he would shoot them or endanger their lifes [in] any way. — [I] did not know whether there [had been] any private instructions — or what — [but I] believed Bro[ther] Marks was in danger. [I] did not think Marks [was] in danger from Joseph. [I] thought [Warren] Smith was under a wrong impression with regard to Marks. — W[arren] Smith said he ^(Marks)^ had better not come in my way. — I gathered the idea there was something wrong with Bro[ther Warren] Smith — [I] dont recollect any person present. —

Mayor[:] Did Mr [Warren] Smith give you to understand that I had authorized him to believe there was any difficulty between us, or any other policeman?

Soby[:] No! – [I] did not think W[arren] Smith would transcend his official duties, towards Marks. [I] felt at the time Marks & Law was in danger [but] did not think they were in danger if they did not rise up against the authority. – [He] did not say he had any instruction – [I] said to Mr Marks[,] you have enemies. – My impression was that somebody had been to Joseph to make a bad impression on his mind. – W[arren] Smith did mention Bro[ther] Marks name, ^I think^ ~~according to the best of my recollection~~

30 Policemen [were] Sworn ^all who were present^ [and] Testified that Gen[eral] Smith had never given them any private instruction concerning the case before the council.

Warren Smith[:] Soby asked my opinion. I [responded that] from rumor I would suspect W[illia]m Law. [I do] not believe [I] mentioned Marks name. – My opinion was founded on rumor. Bro[ther] ^coun[cillor]^ I[saac] Hill said [to me that] Bro[ther] Law was in a bad situation, was kicking [against the pricks], and if he did not mind [his behavior][,] he would go over the board. If he had his property & was away [from the city][,] he would feel better. – [I] have heard it talked of that Bro[ther] Law was not going to stand &c &c. ^Hill^ did not tell [me] what [William Law] was kicking at. [I] think he mentioned [the] spiritual wife system, &c. I understood a Brutus to mean a treacherous man. – Bro[ther] Hill did not believe in the ^Spiritual wife system^ & Law did not believe in it.

G[eorge] W. Crouse [was] sworn. [He said he] does not recollect any conversation between W[arren] Smith & L[eonard] Soby. [He was] at his office relative to the case in question. – [He] had a discussion about the duties of policemen.

Counsellor [John] Taylor said it was customary for policemen to go armed, in time of danger. C[ouncillor] [Orson] Hyde confirmed [this]. Counsellor Taylors observation [was made]. C[ouncillor] H[yrum] Smith spoke, told the story of that old Dutchman & the Divil.[15]

---

[15]According to *History of Church,* 6:168, Hyrum said that "Soby makes me think of an old Dutchman that had an ox" and wanted to see if it was broken. He asked his son to jump out and say boo. "The son did accordingly. The ox was frightened, and threw the old man off. 'Father,' said the son, 'I did as you told me.' 'Yes,' said the old man; 'but you made too big a boo.'"

Francis M. Higby [was] sworn[:] [I] have ~~heard~~ received the impression from some source that Mr. Law, Mr Marks & probably one or two others could not subscribe to all things in the church, and it might make trouble, [but I] dont know of any ones being endanger[ed]. No one told me the police had received any ^private^ instruction – [I] could not tell of one who even had mentioned the subject to [me].

W[illia]m Law spoke, – said he had no personal feeling against Warren Smith. Some 2 or 3 years since he sued Bro[ther] Warren & staid the suit &c [and] was suspicious ~~his~~ Warren Smiths feelings might have risen from that source. C[ouncillor] H[yrum] Smith spoke. Daniel Cairns spoke. Warren Smith spoke. Leonard Soby spoke. – W[illia]m Marks spoke.

[The] Mayor spoke, said no one had come to him with tales about Marks to prejudice his mind against him, was totally ignorant of it. ~~if any thing had been revealed to him he had kept it to himself~~ I said to Bro[ther] [Jonathan] Dunham if any man approach my house with arms or attempt to ~~force open~~ disturb ~~my~~ my house, I wanted him to take care of him. Never could bring my feelings to take revenge on my enemies. The [city] council did not concoct the Idea of having a police. The several wards petitioned for a police to protect them against invasion [and] wanted citizens to pass the streets at any time of night without molestation, but if the police see a man breaking [into] my house or barn, ^or any bodys house or barn^ tell him to stand and enquire his business. Thought it possible some one had been practicing fraud on the police. – & upon individuals.

[He] proposed ~~Let~~ that Daniel Cairns & W[arren] Smith be dropped from the police if the council consent ^lest they scare some body^ – Dont guard Bro[ther] Marks house any more. Men must ^not^ pervert the power entrusted to them[.] [He] referred to [Lilburn W.] Boggs, [adding that] Bro[ther] Soby does not know that it was a policeman who stopped ^him^. Bro[ther] Marks does not know that the police kindled the fire before his house[.] Let the police have canes. Let the citizens pass & repass at all times of night.

C[ouncillor] H[yrum] Smith spoke. [He] thought the conclusion drawn upon by Bro[ther] Soby th[at] ~~right~~ Joseph or somebody was going ^to^ get revenge by setting the guard to kill Marks was the most contemptible [thing] that could be imagined and if Bro[ther]

Soby had had the respect for Bro[ther] Joseph he ought to have had, he would not have done [him the disservice of repeating] it.

Marks and Higby retired. [Printed sideways: "Ordered to be crossed Jan[uary] 16, 1844"] ~~Mayor referred to Francis Higbys testimony. Thought Francis Higby had better stay at home & hold his tongue, lest rumor turn upon him. Did not believe there was any rumor of the kind afloat. Thought the young men of the city had better withdraw from him & let him stand on his own merits [and] not consider him the Standard. of the city~~[16]

[The mayor said] there is a system of things which has been from the beginning[,] which this has grown out off – and ~~from~~ these individuals are those who do not want a police, they want to prowl at pleasure. [The] H[igh] Policeman spoke. A[lderman] [Orson] Spencer spoke in objection to dropping the 2 police mentioned by the Mayor. C[ouncillor] [George W.] Harris – said the police were in the hands of the Mayor.

Gen[eral] Wilson Law spoke. Gen[eral] William Law said ~~Bro[ther] Joseph~~ I am Joseph's friend, he has no better friend in the world[.] I am ready to lay down my life for him, & upon that the Mayor & Gen[eral] William Law shook hands.[17]

[The] high policeman said the fire was kindled before Marks by some men from the North part of the city and not the policemen. Gen[eral] Law spoke again, expressed of his good feelings. Council-

---

[16]William Law recorded this speech made by Joseph Smith: "Joseph made another speech, and in it said that F[rancis] M. Higbee had better be careful or a train of facts would be disclosed concerning him that he would not like; gave us to understand that [Francis] was conniving with Missouri &c., and that [Joseph] ... denied [Francis] the privilege of his house (or words like that) and would not allow him to associate with his females &c; that he had been called on to lay hands on him when he stank from a cause that he did not name (or such a saying). I did not believe the story at all, and cannot see why he should tell it" (Cook, *William Law,* 45-46).

Francis ("Frank") had become a confidant of Nancy Rigdon, who rejected Joseph Smith's written proposal that famously began with, "Happiness is the object and design of our existence" (George D. Smith, *Nauvoo Polygamy: '... But We Called It Celestial Marriage"* [Salt Lake City: Signature Books, 2008], 149-54, 429). See the temporary reconciliation with Higbee below during the meeting of January 16.

[17]Law wrote: "I made some remarks, said Joseph had nothing to fear from me, I was not his enemy (I did not say I was his friend)" (Cook, *William Law,* 45).

lor [William W.] Phelps [said the] policemen have always had to learn their duty. [He] hoped no~~t~~ one would get up another tempest in a tea pot. C[ouncillor] H[yrum] Smith apologized –

[The] Ordinance concerning the 40 policemen [was] read twice.[18] [The] Mayor objected to assuming the ~~whole~~ entire disposal of the police, [which he said was] beyond the definition of the ordinances – C[ouncillor] Taylor ~~Spoke~~ thought the difficulties with W[arren] Smith & D[aniel] Cairns w[ere] of a private nature, and did not belong to the council. A[lderman] Smith said he could sleep with a fire by his house.

On Motion of W[illiam] W. Phelps, voted that the 2 police be retained and the police received the thanks of the Council. Bro[ther] Soby – said W[arren] Smith did not say he would pop a hole through [Marks] – did not say anybody would pop a hole through him. [He] never heard such a thing. [The] Council adjourned [at] 25 m[inutes] past 4 PM.

*January 10, 1844; Wednesday.*[19] [A] 7 oclock P.M. Special Session. – [The] names of [the] members [were] called. – [The] Mayor state[d] that Lawyer Backman, officer Hamilton and ^Lawyer^ Sherman had called on him from Carthage [Illinois] and told ^him^ that the occasion of the excitement at Carthage, and the resistance to the law in [the] case of the [attempted] arrest of [Milton] Cook[20] was the late ordinance of this council to ["]prevent ~~illi~~ unlawful search or seizure of person or property by foreign process in the city of Nauvoo." [It was this] that [had incited resistance to arrest in Carthage][.] They considered said ordinance [to be] designed to hinder the execution of the [county's] Statutes in the City [of Nauvoo], ~~by county officers~~ consequently they[,] the old citizens[,] felt disposed to stop the execution of [legal] processes issuing from the city, in the county

---

[18]This was an ordinance to disband the police force.

[19]See also *History of Church,* 6:173-74.

[20]The Mormon Constable Horace S. Eldredge, who would later become a President of the Seventy, attempted to arrest non-Mormon Milton Cook at a grocery store in Carthage on the charge of "bastardy," or fathering a child out of wedlock. Cook lived in the county outside the city's jurisdiction. When Eldredge arrived, Cook's friends intervened to prevent his arrest. Eldredge returned with a posse of eleven, who were repulsed by twenty armed men (*History of Church,* 6:171-73).

– and also, they raised objections against the process issued by Justice [Robert D.] Foster because it was made returnable to him alone, when the statute required it to be made returnable before himself or some other Justice.

The Mayor explained to the delegation from Carthage the nature and reason of the ordinance, that it was to prevent kidnapping under the pretense of Law, or process, & to further the apprehension of theives &c in this city by throwing ~~the~~ all foreign processors into the hands of the marshall who would be most likely to know the hiding places of fugitives from Justice who might seek to secrete themselves in ~~their~~ our Midst. – and if any wrong impression had gone a broad with regard to the motives of the council in passing said ordinance, he would call the council immediately that they might have the opportunity of giving any explanation necessary – so that the public might understand the ordinance in its true light – and had called the council accordingly.

The Mayor also referred the Lawyers from Carthage to the Statute which requires all processors issued in cases of Bastardy to be returnable alone to the Justice issueing the same. After ~~Mature~~ Deliberation, ~~the council~~ an additional Section ~~bars the~~ relative to the foregoing ordinance was read 3 times, and passed by way of Amendme[n]t [as] Sec[tion] 3a. Council adjourned.

> Section 3 Be it ordained by the City Council of the City of Nauvoo, that nothing in the foregoing ordinance shall be so construed as to prevent, hinder or thwart the designs of Justice, or to retard the civil officers of the State or County in the discharge of their official duties, but to aid and assist them within the limits of this City.
>
> **Passed January 10, 1844. Joseph Smith Mayor. Willard Richards, Recorder.**

*January 13, 1844; Saturday.*[21] Regular Session[,] January 13th 1844. [At] 11 oclock [the] names of members [were] called. Prayer by Alderman [George W.] Harris. – Minutes of the 2 last Councils [were] read and approved. –

[The] Petition of Aaron Johnson and four others, for a continu-

---

[21]See also *History of Church,* 6:175.

ance of Water St. &c [was] Read. [The] Mayor observed that Water Street was continued where the road is now worked. – Counsellor [William W.] Phelps moved the petition be referred back to the Petitioners. [The] Mayor explained that he [had] made a contract with [Horace S.] Eldridge & [William] Law, that Water Street should be where the street is now worked, and the council had sanctioned the same. [The] Mayor instructed the Recorder to make a deed to H[orace] S. Eldridge for all the Land opposite said Eldridge [and] let [it extend] to [the] high water mark. [It was] referred back to the Petitioners –

An ordinance concerning the Recording of deeds [was] read twice [and an] amendment [was] offered by A[lderman] Phelps [so that] the word ~~Recorder crossed and~~ "Registery" ^of Deeds^ [was] inserted – ^also said conveyance shall be null & void. –^ [It was] read the third time, as amended. Counsellor [Brigham] Young objected to the penalty. [The] Mayor explained. Counsellor Young continued his objections. [The] Mayor spoke in favor of the penalty.

Coun[cillor]r Young spoke again. C[ouncillor] H[yrum] Smith spoke in favor. Counsellor [John] Taylor enquired who would own the land, if not recorded. [The] Mayor explained concerning the Statute on Registry of Deeds. Coun[cillor] Phelps read ^from the^ statutes. Alderman [Daniel H.] Wells, spoke. [The] Mayor spoke. A[lderman] Wells spoke[.] Counsellor Young spoke again. – Counsellor Taylor offered an amendment, in full. C[ouncillor] Phelps spoke. –

C[ouncillor] [Benjamin] Warrington moved the bill be refered to ~~a~~ ^the standing^ committee and [the motion] carried – [The] Mayor spoke [to say] that the object of an ordinance on Registry was to keep our own papers & not be obliged to send them to Carthage.

[The] Petition of H[enry] G. Sherwood for an intelligence office [was] read Twice & refered to the committee on Municipal Laws. [The] Petition of Robert Campbell[22] & 72 others to tax dogs [was] read – A[lderman] [Samuel] Bennet spoke in favor. ~~O[rson] Spencer spoke by objection~~ A[lderman] Bennet spoke again in favor. C[ouncillor] Young moved the Petition be granted – & seconded. – [The] Mayor objected. – Said he would never pay a tax on his dog in this city.[23] [The] Petition [was] laid on the Table.

---

[22]Robert Campbell was born in 1810 in Cambridge, England. He was baptized in June 1838 and immigrated to Nauvoo. He died in 1890.

[23]Joseph Smith had come full circle on dogs. In 1841 he had led the

[The] Petition of J. S. Wild & 21 others for ~~an~~ John ~~H~~ Glovers to be appointed Inspector of flour [was] read, petition granted. And on Motion[,] John ~~Gl~~ Glovers[,] [who] was elected 2nd inspector of flour in this city[,] [was required] to give the same bonds as the [previous inspector] ^and be governed by the same rules^ of [the former] inspector – & be sworn in office. [At] 10 minutes before 2 Oclock [the council] adjourned [for] one hour.

[At] 10 minutes before 3 [the council] assembled according to adjournment. [The] Names of [the] members [were] called. ~~Mayor introduced~~ The ordinance in relation to [a] Merchants Licence was conversed upon at considerable length, and the words "Auctioneers or drugists" were ordered to be inserted in the ordinance Regulating Grocers and Merchants Licences, passed Dec[ember] 16, 1843, [with the words "auctioneers or drugists" added] immediately after the words Merchants and grocers in the third line on the Record.

Policemen Benjamin Boyce, Josiah Arnold,[24] Richard D. Sprague, Howard Egan,[25] Geo[rge] W. Clyde,[26] Davis McOlney,[27] Alexander Mills, Shadrach Roundy, James Emmet, [and] Dwight Harding[28] were sworn to tell the truth[,] the whole truth, ^and nothing but the truth^ in the matter between W[illia]m Law & W[illia]m

---

charge to fine owners for unruly behavior (see entries for March 29, May 1, Oct. 23). After Willard Richards suggested on November 13, 1841, "that all Dogs in the City, be assessed Five Dollars per Head," Joseph Smith immediately moved to increase the tax to $12.20 each. As mayor on June 1, 1843, he signed a bill into law authorizing the city to put down dogs found running free, although this was tempered on June 29 to allow for "harmless and inoffensive dogs." But in 1844 he is opposed to the tax and able to say by March 9 that "God withdrew his spirit from the earth ... because the people were so ready to take the life of animals."

[24]Josiah Arnold was born in 1800 in Hoosick, New York. He was baptized in 1837, was residing in Nauvoo by 1841, and was present when Joseph Smith and Governor Thomas Ford met in Carthage, Illinois. Arnold died in 1859.

[25]Howard Egan was born in 1815 in Montreal, Canada. He immigrated to Nauvoo immediately after being baptized in 1842. In Nauvoo he was a policeman and member of the Nauvoo Legion. He died in 1878.

[26]George Washington Clyde was born in Shelburne, Vermont, in 1798. He was baptized in 1844 in Nauvoo.

[27]Davis McOlney was born in 1796 in Fairhaven, Vermont. He lived in Nauvoo's First Ward neighborhood.

[28]Dwight Harding was born in 1807 in Worcester, Massachusetts. He

Marks & the City Council, and they all testified they had received no private instructions from the Mayor.

[The] Petition of Pulaskie S. Cahoon ^for Retailing spirits^ was called up and read – and the Mayor spoke proposing that said petition be granted on the principle of equal rights and on condition the petitioner give bond for security to the city that he keep an orderly house. ~~Alderman~~ Counsellor Phelps ~~spoke by way~~ proposed to disannul the ordinance now in force rather than take up the time in discussion. [He said they] should record his vote against granting the petition. Alderman Harris spoke against the petition, and requested that the Mayor rather give up ~~the~~ his licence than grant more. [The] Mayor thus ~~resigned his L~~ [agreed to] give up his licence.[29] A[lderman] Spencer – concurred, and spoke against the petition.

Alderman G[eorge] A Smith thought there should be one place to sell spirits [but] did [not] wish to intrude on the Mayors Licence. [They] should vote against granting any licence to [anyone to sell] retail spirits. [The] Mayor said he was willing to give up his licence if that ^was^ thought the best way, but wanted some ordinance passed to prevent drunkards ~~gam~~ coming to his house to stay over night. [He] said[:] I'd give up my licence. I would ^not^ have it any how since being admonished by ~~father~~ counsellor Harris. Counsellor Phelps proposed a special committee be appointed to draft an ordinance concerning the sale of spirits.

P[ulaski] S. Cahoon asked leave to withdraw his petition [and was given] leave. [The] Mayor directed his Licence be entered as repealed. [The] Council decided not [to]. – C[ouncillor] [Brigham] Young spoke in favor of the Mayor retaining his licence. – A[lderman] Wells spoke in objection to all Licences for spirits. –

[The] Mayor spoke [and] suggested that if Lewis & Butler could have the privilege to [sell distilled drinks] retail, he would give up

---

was baptized in 1833. After being expelled from Missouri, he moved to Quincy until 1840 and then to Nauvoo. He died in 1871.

[29]In September 1843, Joseph Smith employed Orrin Porter Rockwell to establish a bar in the Smith family's Mansion House which doubled as a hotel, and three months later the city council granted Smith the exclusive right to sell hard alcohol (Robert Bruce Flanders, *Nauvoo: Kingdom on the Mississippi* [Urbana: University of Illinois Press, 1975, 246-47; see also chapter 3, note 68, in the current volume).

his licence, & not be obliged to go to Amos Davis. – [He said] the Council has not the constitutional power to prohibit the selling by the Lo[d]ge ~~R. H. Loomis Petition for retailing read~~ [and] wanted his friends to have the same chance [to sell alcohol] as his enemies. [He] was willing to transfer his Licence to Lewis & Butler [and] grant the honorable portion of community the privilege which the dishonorable take & he would call it equal Rights.

A [comment was made by John] Taylor [that he] was sorry the Mayor had offered to give up his Licence. C[ouncillor] B[righam] Young concurred, & proposed the Mayor continue his Licence and use Gentlemen Lewis & butler as clerks [to procur whiskey for the bar]. A[lderman] Harris concurred – Counsellor Spencer wished the Mayor might retain his Licence.

Alderman Wells said if we are to have Licences~~ee~~ [he] would think the Mayor [would be] the proper person to give [a] licence for a certain season. [The] Mayor said the reason why he asked for a Licence ~~were asking~~ was, that others were selling [whiskey] and he wanted the privilege lawfully which others took unlawfully – was willing to hold my licence if the council says so & have men appointed in each ward. [A hotel that is a] temperance house cannot support itself, and if any body needs those profits, I do.

Orson Spencer – moved an Amendment [with] "or such person or persons as he shall depute" to be added to the Mayors Licence. – Alderman Wells propose[d] an ordinance [and] C[ouncillor] Warrington proposed [that it be] referred to a committee. A[lderman] Spencer spoke in favor of the amendment [and] refered [it] to a Committee, [followed by remarks by] A[lderman] Wells, ^Counsellor^ W[illiam] W. Phelps [and] A[lderman] Spencer. [At] 10 mi[nutes] before 6 [the council] adjourned to next Tuesday[,] 10 o clock AM.

> Granted by the City Council of the City of Nauvoo the Petition of J. S. Wild and twenty-one others to have John Haven[30] appointed second Inspector of Flour for the City – and he to give the same bonds, and be governed by the same regulations as the other Inspector.
>
> **January 13, 1844. Joseph Smith Mayor. Willard Richards, Recorder.**

---

[30]John Haven was born in 1794 in Holliston, Massachusetts. He was baptized in 1838 and died in 1853.

The Ordinance in relation to merchant's Licences was conversed upon at considerable length – and the words "Auctioneers or Druggists" were ordered to be inserted in the Ordinance regulating Grocers and Merchants Licenses, passed December 16, 1845, immediately after the words Merchants and Grocers in the third line on the Record.

**January 13, 1844. Joseph Smith Mayor. Willard Richards, Recorder. [Marginal note: "see page 195"]**

*January 16, 1844; Tuesday.*[31] [An] Adjourned Session, Tuesday, January 16th 1844, 24 minutes past 11. – [The] Names of [the] members [were] called. Prayer by O[rson] Pratt. Minutes of [the] last council [were] read and approved. – [A] Petition of E[benezer] Robinson & Aaron Johnson concerning Robinsons Lot in relation to Water St[reet] [was] read & referred to the committee on Public grounds. An ordinance concerning the Registry of deeds [was] read by Counsellor Phelps. – [It was] read [a] 2d time by counsellor Phelps.

[The] Mayor objected to having any thing to do with things out of the City. C[ouncillor] Phelps explained. – [The] Mayor explained [that] the terms should be explicit. – Counsellor Phelps explained [that] it is customary in all countries to make ~~exceptions to~~ regulation[s] for foreign deeds. – Coun[ci]l[lor] H[yrum] Smith took exceptions – to requiring a seal. Coun[cil]l[or] Phelps corrected [this by saying that] no seal [is] required in the city. – [The phrase] "Or Justice of the Peace" – was inserted on motion. [The] Mayor objected to saying any thing about qualifications out of the city. – C[ouncillor] H[yrum] Smith, thought further investigation necessary – and motioned the bill [to] lay on the table, for further investigation and [the motion] carried.

~~Ordinance concerning Report~~ An Ordinance concerning the sale of spirituous Liquors [was] Read twice by Alderman [Orson] Spencer, and [his] report [was] accepted. [It was] read twice [and a] third time by its title & passed.[32] – [The council was] satisfied with its

---

[31]See also *History of Church,* 6:178-79.

[32]The Record of Proceedings," has the following:

An Ordinance concerning the Sale of Spirituous Liquors

Whereas, the use and sale of distilled and fermented Liquors for all purposes of Beverage and drink by persons in health are viewed by this City Council with unqualified disapprobation; Whereas, neverthe-

[passage by] title. A[lderman] [George W.] Harris [was] called to the chair [because of the] Mayors absen[ce].

A[lderman] [Daniel H.] Wells read a Report on the petition of H[enry] G. Sherwood. – [It was suggested that the] Report be accepted. – An ordinance Regulating a City Directory and an Intelligence office [was] read.[33] – C[ouncillor] [Brigham] Young moved an

---

less the aforesaid Liquors are considered highly beneficial for medical and mechanical purposes and may be safely employed for such uses under the counsel of discreet persons, Therefore,

Section 1st. Be it ordained by the City Council of the City of Nauvoo, That the Mayor of this City is hereby authorized to sell said Liquors in such quantities as he may deem expedient.

Section 2nd. Be it further ordained that other persons not exceeding one to each Ward of the City may also sell said Liquors in like quantities for Medical and Mechanical purposes, by obtaining a license of the Mayor of the City.

The above ordinance to be in full force and effect immediately after its passage, all ordinances to the contrary notwithstanding.

**Passed January 16, 1844. Joseph Smith Mayor. Willard Richards, Recorder.**

[33]As it appeared in the Record of Proceedings, it read:

<u>An Ordinance regulating a City Directory and an Intelligence Office</u>

Section 1. Be it ordained by the City Council of the City of Nauvoo that Henry G. Sherwood shall be authorized to make out a City Directory and also establish a[n] Intelligence Office in this City.

Section 2. The said Henry G. Sherwood shall make out a complete Directory stating therein in Alphabetical Order the names of any and every householder in said City with a convenient and easy reference to his place of residence and business together with his profession or occupation.

Section 3. He shall also keep an office for the purpose of giving Intelligence or information to all such Citizens, Strangers or others that may call upon him for that purpose and shall take especial care to obtain from the most authentic sources all information necessary for the benefit of the Citizens of said City.

Section 4. The said Henry G. Sherwood shall be allowed to receive a fee of not exceeding twenty five cents from each applicant for each information so given as a compensation for his trouble in obtaining such information and for keeping said office. He shall also be allowed the sole and entire benefit of whatever may be obtained by the use or sale of the said City Directory for the space of three years from the first of April next.

Section 5. The said Henry G. Sherwood shall procure the printing of the said City Directory so soon as he shall be able to complete the same Providing he shall be able to obtain subscribers sufficient to justify the expense.

amendment [by suggesting that] "&" be stricken out & "5" inserted. A[lderman] Wells spoke in objection to the amendment. C[ouncillor] Young spoke in favor of the amendment, and moved ^as^ ~~an~~ ^further^ amendment that the whole be under the supervision of the ^City^ council. [A] Counsellor concurred. C[ouncillor] [John] Taylor – spoke of the difficulty of finding a persur [purser] in this city – and considered it would be [a] lucrative business to keep an intelligence office. [He] thought 3 years long enough. – C[ouncillor] [William] Phelps ^spoke^ against the amendment – and suggested the addition of a Lithographic Map connected with the directory. – ^P[helps] pro[posed that after]^ making those allowances[,] [he] would be in favor of the bill.

Alderman Harris spoke standing – concerning the papers of the Intelligence office. C[ouncillor] Taylor spoke, [also] C[ouncillor] Phelps. On Motion, H[enry] G. Sherwood had leave & spoke – suggested an amendment. [He asked if it should say] "3 full years" – "or full years" [without specifying the number][.] C[ouncillor] Phelps ~~spoke 3~~ again referred to the Map[.] ~~again~~ C[ouncillor] Taylor, said he should go against the amendment. H[enry] G. Sherwood spoke again. – C[ouncillor] Young spoke [and said he] should go against the bill till it was qualified – so as ~~that~~ to make it a charter. [He] thought 5 years little time enough. [The] Question on [the] amendment [was] lost. – C[ouncillor] Phelps moved an amendment. – Alderman [Orson] Spencer moved the bill be recommitted ^to the [committee]^ & counsellor[s] Young & Taylor be added to that committee.

---

Section 6. The said Henry G. Sherwood shall furnish the City Council, Mayor, and City Marshall one copy each of the said City Directory Providing he shall be able to procure the printing of the same and also give any and all information in his possession connected with the business of the City at all times when called upon for that purpose, free of expense.

Section 7. He shall have until the first day of April next to make out and complete the said Directory and shall correct and make such additions as may be necessary annually thereafter between the first day of February and the first day of April next following. This ordinance to be in force from and after its passage.

Section 8. That if the foregoing requisitions are not complied with by Henry G. Sherwood the office shall revert back to the City Council. **Passed January 16, 1844. Joseph Smith Mayor. Willard Richards Recorder**

[The] Mayor resumed his seat. [The] Blank Bond of Davison Hibbard [was] read.[34] [The] Mayor suggested the propriety of laying aside all as person[alities] in this council. Councillor ^?^ ~~spoke~~ spoke. Co[uncillor] Young considered the bond an insult. A[lderman] Wells moved ^the Bill be^ refered to a special committee & referred [to] Wells, [Benjamin] Warrington & [Samuel] Bennett.

[The] Mayor announced that all difficulties between him & Francis M. Higby were eternally buried ~~up~~ – and he was to be his friend forever & F[rancis] M. Higby said he will be his friend forever ^and his right hand man[35]^ – And C[ouncillor] Hiram Smith stated that all aspersions which may have been [or were] supposed to have been cast up [by Francis] Higby – are ~~false~~ a mistake – tis not so. [The] Mayor explained at length respecting what, in substance, he had said at previous councils on the same subject. – C[ouncillor] O[rson] Pratt spoke. F[rancis] M. Higby spoke, stating his distraction of mind the past week. – [He said he was] glad the difficulties are settled [and that Joseph Smith] shall be his friend as said before[.] The ~~Minu~~ observations of the mayor before the council on the 5th inst[ant] concerning F[rancis] M. Higby – were ordered to be stricken from the Minutes & [were] stricken accordingly.

[An] Ordinance concerning Witnesses fees [was] read by A[lderman] Spencer – who explained & spoke in favor. A[lderman] Harris spoke in favor [of] amendments ^[that were] offered & carried^ [regarding which] "criminal["] cases [were to be] accepted – also [to have] "Jurors" added.

[The] Account[s] of Shadrach Roundy [for 8 days guarding the

---

[34] On December 21, 1843, Hibbard agreed to sell the city land for a jail. He now apparently wanted to be guaranteed that the city would be able to finance the construction.

[35] Earlier in the day, Nauvoo's municipal court had met on a complaint of Orson Pratt, who claimed that Francis M. Higbee had not appeared, as summoned, as a witness but had used slanderous and abusive language toward city council members. During the council meeting, Smith's diary noted the reconciliation which "took place with Francis M. Higby who had written a slanderous letter concerning me and said many hard things which he acknowledged and I forgave him. I went before the Council and stated that all difficulties between me and Francis M. Higby are eternally buried and I am to be his friend forever. To which F[rancis] M. Higby replied I will be his friend forever and his right hand man" (Faulring, *American Prophet's Record*, 440-41).

city], $12.00; Alexander Mills [for 7 days], $10.50; Josiah Arnold [for 7 days], $10.50; H[enry] G. Sherwood [for 8 nights], $12.00; [were] read and allowed. H[enry] G. Sherwoods Bill for sundry services [was] read & referred to the committee on Claims. A[lderman] Harris [was] called to the chair. [The] Mayor [was] absent. [The] Committee reported [and] the account of H[enry] G. Sherwood [for] $39.50 [was voted on, to] be allowed. [The] report [was] accepted, and [the] account allowed.

[A] Committee reported again ^the ordinance^ on the Intelligence Office, ^with^ amendment[,] [and the] Report [was] accepted – amended from [the] date [given] to first of April next.

[The] Mayor suggested the propriety of having a city attorney connected with the Marshall so that all business may be brought up before the aldermen in due form. C[ouncillor] Phelps moved the subject be refered to a ~~special~~ committee. – Carried. – C[ouncillor] Phelps ~~Pratt~~ refered [it] to the committee on Municipal laws. C[ouncillor] Young moved an amendment, "with a map to be added" [attached][.] A[lderman] Wells expressed doubts, Counsellor Young spoke in favor. O[rson] Spencer proposed it be left [out] to [consider later][.] [The council] voted [and] the bill pass[ed], [the council being] satisfied with [the] title.

An Ordinance concerning Witnesses & Jurors fees [was] read ~~twice~~ once [and then a] 2d. time by its title. A[lderman] Wells objected to .50 [cents because he] thought .25 c[en]t[s] [was] sufficient. A[lderman] Spencer objected. C[ouncillor] Young objected. A[lderman] Wells moved an amendment of 25 instead of 50 c[en]ts. – [The] Motion lost, no second. – A[lderman] Harris approved the bill. C[ouncillor] Phelps approved the bill. B[righam] Young approved. [It was] read [a] third time & passed.[36] [At] 6 minutes before Two [the council] adjourned to [the] next regular meeting.

---

[36]The Record of Proceedings reads:
An Ordinance concerning Witnesses and Jurors fees.

Be it ordained by the City Council of the City of Nauvoo, That hereafter all persons subpoen[a]ed and attending upon Courts of Trial as witnesses or as Jurors in Civil Cases, shall not be compelled to testify or be held in attendance either as Witness or Juror unless they shall first be tendered the sum of fifty cents per day for each witness and each Juror subpoenaed.

**Passed January 16, 1844. Joseph Smith Mayor. Willard Richards, Recorder**

†*January 17, 1844; Wednesday.* John Haven took the Oath of Office as second Inspector of Flour in the City and gave [a] bond with Surety[,] according to the Ordinance, at my Office in Nauvoo [on]January 17, 1844. [Signed] W[illard] Richards, Recorder[37]

‡*February 10, 1844; Saturday.* [At] 10 oclock A.M. [the council met in] Regular Session. [The] Names of [the] members [were] called. – [There was] not a quorum present. [The council] adjourned until Monday next [at] 10 oclock – to wit Feb[ruary] 12th 1844, [as an] Adjourned Session.

*February 12, 1844; Monday.*[38] 10 oclock. A.M. Nauvoo Mansion. [The] Names of [the] Members [were] called. [There was a] Quorum Present. Prayer by O[rson] Pratt. [The] Minutes of [the] last Council [were] read – and approved. [A] Petition of Thomas Moss[39] for remuneration for damage done his ~~a fr~~ cellar by a change in the location of ~~water street~~ Water Street [was] read and referred to [the] Committee on Claims. [The] Mayor suggested that the rise of [the] property [value] was sufficient to indemnify the petitioner.

A[lderman] [Daniel H.] Wells objected to any action on the bill. [The] Mayor agreed with A[lderman] Wells [and] said ~~that~~ Laws' Mill stood where the road was originally located & should have been made [to run there] – and it was altered to accomodate the Laws – and they agreed to ~~and must~~ satisfy all who were injured by the alteration, and they must do it. The order ~~T Moss~~ for committment to ~~recommended the committee~~ [have the bill] reconsidered [was issued][,] the petition [set aside] & ordered to be laid on the table.

The select Committee on (to whom was previously reported ~~the blan~~ a blank bond of Davidson Hibbards ~~bond reported that the council~~ to the Agent of the city of Nauvoo, for Lot 3 – in Block 4 0 of Hibbards Addition for use of the City of Nauvoo, for ^the erection

---

[37]Aside from the fact that incomplete copies of the various versions of the minutes survive, it is interesting to see that occasionally, as here, the scribe added information that was absent from at least the intermediate version.

[38]See also *History of Church,* 6:212.

[39]Thomas Moss was born in 1808 in Lancashire, England. He resided in Nauvoo's Fourth Ward neighborhood. He died in 1872.

of^ public buildings by said city, [was discussed][.] [It was] reported that though the Lot was desireable for the City to erect public buildings upon, yet ~~the committee~~ they did not Judge it wisdom to accept the Lot on the conditions mentioned in said other Bond, as the city might not think it best to erect a hall more than 38 f[ee]t or 39 square or might prefer some other form. [The] report [was] accepted & the Bond ordered to be laid on the table. [The] Committee on City Attorney [matters] reported [that] they had not time to draft the bill [and] ordered the committee [to] have further time.

A[lderman] Wells, reported. The criminal code was probably with Counsellor [Sylvester] Emmons, and he was expected to return to the city soon. C[ouncillor] H[yrum] Smith moved [the] committee have further time & [the motion] carried. [The] petition of J[onathan] H Hale [was] ordered to be laid on the table.

An ordinance to amend certain ordinances [was] read twice. [The] 2d [time, the word] Sir [was] added. [It was] read [a] third time [and] passed. [The] Title [of the] ordinance [was] an ordinance to repeal certain ordinances therein mentioned. [It was] read & ~~approved~~ approved.

An ordinance to repeal an ordinance regulating the currency [that was originally] passed March 4th 1843 [was] read twice[,] [the] rules dispensed with[,] & [it] passed.[40] [At] 15 minutes before 12 [we] adjourned to [the] next regular meeting.

At 12 oclock the Mayor ordered the council to be recalled. [At] 1 Oclock P.M. [the] Council re-assembled. [The] Names of [the] members [were] called. [A] Quorum [was] present. The compendium of the 6th Census of the United States was received by the city council from Mr [Joseph P.] Hoge[41] –

A Memorial To the Honorable Senate and Representatives ^of the United States of America in Congress assembled^ passed Dec[ember] 21, 1843, ~~was~~ was read & signed by the counsellors[,] Aldermen, Mayor, & Recorder[,] & Marshall.[42] 2 counsellors & 1 Alderman [were] absent.

---

[40]In keeping with the repeal of this ordinance, Smith "Burned $81 [in] Script of the city" (Faulring, *American Prophet's Record,* 446).

[41]Joseph P. Hoge, a Democrat, was Illinois's U.S. Representative from 1843 to 1847.

[42]See chapter 3, note 76.

[It was] voted th[at] Thomas Bullock[43] receive an order of $25.00 on the treasury for engrossings[44] Petitions &c. Voted that the Treasurer procure $50 on the credit of the City for to pay O[rson] Pratt['s] passage to Washington [D.C.] as special Messenger from the Council to carry the Memorial. The Mayor intrusted Counsellor Pratt to call all the Representatives of Illinois [and] tell them our suffering[s] have been such that we must have that document passed, – and we will have it. You must go in for it. Go to John Quincy Adams[45] and call a delegation from his State, separate from [the] Ill[inois] Delegation, [and] Demand the same. [Talk to] Henry Clay,[46] and other prominent men. – Call public meetings in the city of Washington, take [to] the Saloon [and rent one, then] publish so much [for a] Ticket [to an event with food and drinks and] invite the members & [when they are assembled][,] roar upon them. – Take all my writing[s] you think any thing of. – Send [reports] &c and you shall prosper in the name of God. Amen.

[The] Report of the Recorder, of the attendance of the City Council, Marshall[,] Recorder &c – from Aug[ust] 12, 1843 to Feb[ruary] 9 inclusive Total[ed] $828.11. [The] Fines [totaled] 4.50[.]

---

[43]Thomas Bullock was born in 1816 in Leek, England. He was baptized in 1841 and immigrated directly to Nauvoo two years later, along with his wife and three small children. In Nauvoo he served as a clerk during the writing of Joseph Smith's history. He was part of the pioneer company of 1847. In Utah he became the Salt Lake City and County Recorder and Chief Clerk in the LDS Historian's Office. He died in Coalville, Utah, in 1885.

[44]*Engrossment* was 'the appropriation of things in the gross, or in exorbitant quantities," in order to "raise the price, by diminishing the supplies in open market, and taking advantage of an increased demand" (Noah Webster, *An American Dictionary of the English Language* [New York: S. Converse, 1828], svv. "engrossment," "engross," "engrossing"). It is also possible that the scribe meant *engravings*.

[45]John Quincy Adams was born in 1767, the son of U.S. President John Adams and Abigail Adams, and was himself U.S. president from 1825 to 1829. Prior to that, he was the U.S. Secretary of State and U.S. Ambassador to England. In 1844 he was a U.S. Congressman representing Massachusetts. His political career included leaving the Federalist Party for the Republicans and then the Whigs. He died in 1848.

[46]Henry Clay was born in 1777 in Hanover County, Virginia. During his political career, he served in both the U.S. House of Representatives and U.S. Senate and founded the Whig Party; he unsuccessfully ran for president five times between 1824 and 1848. He died in 1852 in Washington, D.C.

[The] Report [was] accepted. [The] Mayor spoke in favor of the Marshalls proceedings.

Alderman Wells spoke in favor of the Marshall & of the Report of the Recorder. A[lderman] [William W.] Phelps spoke – [The] Mayor offered to give the 60 dollars ^out of his salary^ for Co[uncillor] Pratt's passage to Washington, if the city would raise the funds immediately. C[ouncillor] Pratt nominated Geo[rge] P. Stiles as counsellor in his absence which was confirmed by the council[.] Mr. Stiles accepted the appointment.

[The] Marshall spoke on reciprocation of the good feelings which had be[en] manifested by the Mayor & others. [The] Report of the city council ~~adjourned~~ [on] attendance [was] accepted, and [the council] ordered to be paid out of any money in the treasury not otherwise appropriated [the amount due the councilmen for their attendance][.] [The] disbursements of the City [were] read and accepted ^[regarding the] council for the past year[.] [All was] read & accepted[.]^ [The] Docket of the Municipal Court for Feb[ruary] 5th 1844 [was] read. Attendance of the Municipal court [was] read. [The] Council adjourned to [the] next regular Session.

†An Ordinance entitled an Ordinance to repeal certain Ordinances therein mentioned

Whereas an Ordinance entitled "An extra ordinance for the extra case of Joseph Smith and others[,"] passed December 8th 1843[47] – and whereas the Ordinance entitled "An Ordinance to prevent unlawful Search and Seizure of person or property by

[47]The "Extra Ordinance for the Extra Case of Joseph Smith and Others" began by stating:

> Whereas, Joseph Smith has been three times arrested and three times acquitted upon writs founded upon supposed crimes or charges preferred by the State of Missouri, which acquittals were made from investigations upon writs of *habeas corpus*–namely one in the United States Court for the district of Illinois, one in the Circuit Court of the State of Illinois, and one in the Municipal Court of Nauvoo:
>
> And whereas, a *nolle prosequi* [a prosecutor's decision to withdraw a case] has once been entered in the courts of Missouri upon all the cases of Missouri against Joseph Smith and others:
>
> And whereas, there appears to be a determined resolution by the State of Missouri to continue these unjust, illegal, and murderous demands for the body of General Joseph Smith:
>
> And whereas, it has become intolerable to be thus continually

foreign process in the City of Nauvoo[,] Passed Dec[embe]r 21, 1843," have had their desired effect in preserving the peace, happiness, persons and property of the Citizens of Nauvoo according to their intent and meaning, Therefore

Section 1. Be it ordained by the City Council of the City of Nauvoo, that the aforesaid ordinances are hereby repealed.

Section 2. And be it further ordained that nothing in the first section of this Ordinance shall be so construed as to give license or liberty to any foreign officer or other person or persons to illegally disturb the peace happiness or quiet of any citizen of said City, any ordinance to the contrary notwithstanding, under a penalty of not less than five dollars, nor more than five hundred dollars, or imprisonment not more than six months in the City Prison.

**Passed February 12, 1844. Joseph Smith Mayor. Willard Richards, Recorder**

An Ordinance to repeal an Ordinance entitled "An Ordinance regulating the Currency["]

Be it ordained by the City Council of the City of Nauvoo that "An Ordinance regulating the Currency[,]" passed March 4th 1843[,] be and the same is hereby repealed.

**Passed Feb[ruary] 12, 1844. Joseph Smith Mayor. Willard Richards, Recorder.**

A memorial "To the Honorable Senators and Representatives of the United States of America in Congress assembled[,]" passed December 21st 1843[,] was read, and signed by the Councillors, Aldermen, Mayor[,] Recorder[,] and Marshall, and the Treasurer was ordered to procure Sixty Dollars for the purpose of paying

---

harassed and robbed of our money to defray the expenses of these prosecutions:

And whereas, according to the Constitution of Illinois, "all men are born equally free and independent, and have certain inherent and indefeasible rights, among which are those of enjoying and defending life and liberty, and of acquiring, possessing, and protecting property and reputation, and pursuing their own happiness":

And whereas, it is our bounden duty, by all common means, if possible to put a stop to such vexatious lawsuits an[d] save expense ..."

The ordinance then disallowed any arrest warrant stemming from the 1838 Mormon War in Missouri (*History of Church,* 6:105).

the passage of Councillor Orson Pratt as a Special Messenger from the Council to the City of Washington to present said Memorial to the Senators according to the vote of the City Council on said 21st December 1843. The Treasurer was ordered to procure the Sixty Dollars on the credit of the City, if needs be. The Mayor afterwards offered to give the Sixty Dollars out of his Salary if the Council would raise the money now. The foregoing Memorial is now on Record in the Recorder's office.

**Passed February 12, 1844. Joseph Smith Mayor. Willard Richards, Recorder**

The Recorder's [blank] Semi annual Report of the attendance of the City Council, Marshall[,] and Recorder from August 12th 1843 to February 9th 1844 inclusive was read and the City Council of the City of Nauvoo ordered that the following named persons be paid the sums respectively annexed to their names for their services in the City Council during the above named period: to wit –

| | $ | Cts | | $ | Cts |
|---|---|---|---|---|---|
| Hyrum Smith | 12 | 50 | Daniel Spencer | 11 | 00 |
| John Taylor | 15 | 50 | Brigham Young | 12 | 00 |
| Orson Pratt | 13 | 00 | Orson Spencer | 13 | 00 |
| Orson Hyde | 1 | 00 | Daniel H. Wells | 2 | 50 |
| Heber C. Kimball | 9 | 00 | George A. Smith | 13 | 00 |
| Benjamin Warrington | 11 | 50 | George W. Harris | 13 | 50[48] |
| Samuel Bennett | 12 | 50 | W[illiam] W. Phelps | 16 | 50 |
| William Marks | 4 | 00 | Edward Hunter | 2 | 00 |
| H[enry] G. Sherwood[49] | 6 | 00 | Willard Richards | 50 | 00 |
| John D. Parker | 1 | 00 | Joseph Smith | 601 | 61 |
| John P. Green | 7 | 00 | | | |
| | | | Total | $828 | 11 |

and ordered that the same be paid out of any money in the Treasury not otherwise appropriated. And it was further ordered that

48There is a note here that reads "Continued up," alerting the reader to the fact that the column continued on the next page.

49Sherwood, Parker, and Green are identified as "Marshall." The words "½ years Salary" are written after Willard Richards's name, and after Joseph Smith's name "Salary as Mayor" appears, all removed from this list for the sake of simplicity.

the following named person pay the sum annexed to his name, the same being a fine incurred by him for non attendance during the same period of time to wit:

| | $ | Cts |
|---|---|---|
| Sylvester Emmons | 4. | 50 |

**Passed February 12, 1844. Joseph Smith Mayor. Willard Richards, Recorder.**

The Recorder's report of the Annual Disbursements of the City council from January 30th 1843 to February 9th 1844 inclusive amounting to $1342.322 was read and accepted as was also the Docket of the Municipal Court for February 5th, 1844. George P. Stiles Esq[ui]re was nominated, and chose[n] as Councillor in the room of [in place of], and during the absence of[,] Councillor Orson Pratt.

**Passed February 12, 1844. Joseph Smith Mayor. Willard Richards, Recorder**

*March 1, 1844; Friday.*[50] Jonathan Dunham filed his bond in the Recorder's office and took his Oath as Wharfmaster of the City of Nauvoo [on] March 1st 1844. [Signed] Willard Richards, Recorder.

‡*March 5, 1844; Tuesday.*[51] [A] Special Session [convened at] 2. P.M. [The] Names of [the] members [were] called. [A] Quorum [was] present.

[The] Mayor stated that he had called the council because that when the wharf master called on the steam boats for wharfage the ^officers of the^ boats declined paying, ~~because~~ ^assigning as a reason that^ Hiram Kimball & [Arthur] Morrison[52] had told them that they owned the land and they need pay no wharfage to the city. And [Joseph Smith] called the Council to know their views on the subject,

---

[50]See also *History of Church,* 6:229.

[51]See ibid., 234-36.

[52]Arthur Morrison was "a friendly non-Mormon who greatly assisted the Saints in Clay County, Missouri, 1834-36" and "subsequently moved to Nauvoo" (Andrew F. Ehat and Lyndon W. Cook, eds., *Words of Joseph Smith* [Provo: BYU Religious Studies Center, 1980], 388). He is said to have been born in Virginia in about 1802, married Keziah Ann Voorhees in Ohio in November 1825, and died in Keokuk, Iowa, in about 1850 ("Arthur Morrison," *Family Search,* www.familysearch.org).

as he had told H[iram] Kimball that he should see the Ordinances executed and if the~~y~~ ^boats^ did not ^pay^ he should blow them up, and [also] all those who uphold them in resisting the ordinances. – And every measure is taken to palsy the hands of the officers of the city and I want to know how to remedy the evil or whether he should abandon the ordinances, &c.[53]

Al[derman] [George W.] Harris said that it was the mayor's duty to Enforce the ordinances of the City and that no man has a right to build a wharf without leave from the City. Coun[cillor] [William W.] Phelps suggested the propriety of Licencing ~~those~~ those who owned ~~land on~~ wharfs to collect a tax for the landing of the boat. Ald[erman] [Daniel H.] Wells, concurred.

[The] Mayor said the land on the waters edge was a street. Ald[erman] Wells suggested the propriety of having the street worked, as soon as may be. Co[uncillor] Phelps ^said^ that if Water Street ~~was existed~~ ^[was to run]^ all round the city [and] there [was interference with it, then] Kimball had been constructing a nuisance.

[The] Mayor spoke ~~by~~ in explanation and said that Kimball said if the city would make a wharf he would give up what he had done[.] C[ouncillor] O[rson] Spencer said – he wished the mayor to execute the laws of the city. C[ouncillor] B[righam] Young concurred. C[ouncillor] W[illiam] W. Phelps – proposed that Water Street be worked the whole length. C[ouncillor] [John] Taylor said ~~he~~ "I go in for executing the laws of the city.["]

[The] marshal stated that Morrison said he had a Bond for a deed to low water mark – and the city could not take his personal rights and he objected to the boats paying wharfage – C[ouncillor] O[rson] Pratt said if Kimball or Morrison or any one else has built wharfs since that street was laid out they could get no damage[.] C[ouncillor] Daniel Spencer considered the ordinance passed [and] good & [thought it] ought to be enforced. C[ouncillor] H[yrum] Smith believed it was our duty to stand up to the ordinances.

Motioned ~~that~~ by B[righam] Young ^See Motion^ ~~that water street be~~ that the city council instruct the Mayor to order the supervisor

---

[53]Smith wrote in his diary on this day: "I saw Hiram Kimball at Bryants' Store an[d] gave him a lecture on his resisting the ordinances of the city by [Kimball] telling the Capt[ains] of the boats they need not pay wharfage &c." (Faulring, *American Prophet's Record,* 451).

to open Water Street from [the place specified] &c. Joseph Smith [agreed]. Co[u]n[cillor] Phelps approved the ~~resolution~~ Motion that the road might be cleared from Rafts – and the rafts might also pay licence [fees]. Coun[cillor] [Benjamin] Warrington said the upper steam house was in the street.[54] – [The] Mayor said that was the greatest nuisance there was in the street. A[lderman] O[rson] Spencer was in favor[.] [The] Motion carried unanimously. [William W.] Phelps said he had read ^the decision [of] the post master general^ that a letter has no right to go out of a vessel until it has passed the Post office.

The question arose by N[ewel] K. Whitney & W[illia]m Marks, who were Aldermen[,] [whether elected officials should wait for the state's blessing before assuming office]. – [The] Mayor explained that if the governor refused to grant a commission, it does not disqualify the officer elect to act in his office, consequently there was no virtue in the commission – but the virtue of the office consists in the election. Counsellor Young thought they were alderman all the time, or none of the time. [The] Mayor said he wanted all the Aldermen to be added to the city council. Moved by O[rson] Spencer that a committee ~~of~~ be appointed to revise the list of members – of this Council.

B[righam] Young spoke. Cou[ncillor] Taylor spoke of the corruption of the Clerk, or Governor[,] in granting one commission & denying the other [his] Elect[ion]. Counsellor Phelps ~~spoke~~ proposed to add all the old Alderman and save litigation. [Parley] P. Pratt read from the Charter. [It was] motioned & carried that all ~~all~~ the old aldermen [should] be added to the list of members of this Council. Alderman Wells said he considered the election made the Aldermen and not the commission. [The] Mayor said if he had been Elected Alderman and filed his bond he would act as councillor & Magistrate. Adjourned to the next Regular Meeting – 4 P.M.

> †<u>Moved</u> by Councillor Brigham Young "that the City Council instruct the Mayor to order the Supervisor to open Water Street from Joseph Smith's brick Store to the Upper Steam Mill in the City of Nauvoo," and it was carried unanimously.
> **March 5th 1844. Joseph Smith Mayor. Willard Richards, Recorder**

---

[54]William and Wilson Law had a steam-powered mill on Water Street where they ground flour and cut lumber (Glen M. Leonard, *Nauvoo: A Place of Peace, a People of Promise* [Salt Lake City: Deseret Book, 2002], 144-45).

‡*March 9, 1844; Saturday.*[55] 10 A.M. – Regular Session. – [The] Names of [the] members [were] called. [There was] no quorum present. [At] 22 minutes past 10 oclock [a] Quorum [was] present. C[ouncillor] John Taylor was chosen president pro Tem. – Prayer by Alderman [George W.] Harris – [The] Minutes of [the] last council [were] read and approved.

[The] Petition of Geo[rge] W Prouse and about 170 others to open Knight St[reet] [was] read and refered to the committee on public grounds. [The] Petition of Job E. Green and about 20 others to have Fulmer Street from Mulholland to Parly St[reet] worked [was] read: – and referred to the Mayor.

[The] Petition of Amos Davis & 18 others ^for the repeal of the Hog law^[56] [was] read. B[righam] Young moved to lay [the] petition on the table. C[ouncillor] W[illiam] W. Phelps – would rather the petition be refered to a committee. C[ouncillor] Taylor – would rather give 10 bu[shels] of corn – per hog than have them run at large. – A[lderman] O[rson] Spencer – thought it a bone of contention.

[The] Mayor offered some ~~of his~~ reasons in favor: he was afraid no man in the city would ever make a fence round his garden unless the hogs are suffered to run at large, and if the people think there is a hog law, they will not fence – and consequently will be eat[en] up by Hogs &c from the county &c. – The hog law has made more contention than all the hogs would, if they had been let alone[.] Let the hogs run in the streets and the people make good fences, and physicians have given as their opinion that a hog mud hole is the most healthy of any damp place. And if we do not let the hogs run at large, the hogs & cattle from the country will eat the grass &c of the city & we suffer all the evils & lose all the benefit. – Impound the county Hogs & the owner will damn the impound[ing] & the City – and fight against us. Let the city council [step back and] let the Hog & dog laws alone. That man that grumbles a deal about a days bo[a]rding of him ~~he~~ is a great coward. – This is a reason why God withdrew his spirit from the earth, is because the people were so ready to take the life of animals.

A[lderman] Harris had not much to say about [the] hog law.

---

[55]See also *History of Church,* 6:248.

[56]See the minutes for May 12, 1843, "An Ordinance in relation to Swine running at large."

J[ohn] Taylor acknowledged the coun[cil] [and] approved [of] the Mayor['s] remarks. C[ouncillor] H[yrum] Smith would like a law to prevent keeping any hogs but the grass breed.[57] A[lderman] [William] Mark thought hogs ought to be free commoners. C[ouncillor] Phelps – spoke, suggested to take time to look up the laws before granting [the] petition. A[lderman] Wells said we have had the hog law and tried it, and is not aware there is any less hogs.

[The] Mayor – remarked [that an] improvement in [the] breed of hogs should ~~should~~ be made as in other cases, by public opinion. – Coun[cillor] Phelps said he [a hog] was so much meaner than a dog [to] a dog – A[lderman] [Samuel] Bennett [said he] was certain the voice of the inhabitants of the City were in favor of the hog law and of having ~~them~~ it enforced, that it was the poor who suffered from the richer class keeping hogs. C[ouncillor] B[righam] Young said, he thought there was 8/10th of the people were in favor of having hogs shut up.

[The] Mayor said it was the principles of democracy[,] that the peoples voice should be heard when the voice was just, but when it was not just[,] it was no longer democratic. But if the minority views are more just, then Aristarchy[58] ~~would be~~ should be the governing principle, i.e. the wisest & best laws should be made. When S[amuel] Bennet & C[ouncillor] Young will call caucuses & explain the subject to them – then we will hear them & they can petition understandingly, and [he] believed if he could explain the subject, that 99 of a hundred would vote to have no hog law in this city from its birth to its death. Cannot believe in the doctrine of exalting the Majority when it must be brought about by depressing the Minority. In a greater degree[,] [he] spoke at considerable length – and [said he] would rather not tax a saddle horse [any more] than tax a dog – or shut up a hog. [At] 25 minutes before 1, [the council] adjourned 1 hour.

[At] 1 O clock P.M. [the] Council [was] called [to order][.] [A]

---

[57]What farmers called the "grass breed" came from Massachusetts and had "short legs and noses, white sleek hair, small bones, and may be called a very comely, fat, indolent, good natured sort of swine–a race of animals in which the devil would never think of entering for any mischievous purposes" (*The Plough Boy,* Dec. 23, 1820, p. 231; *The American Agriculturist,* May 1848, pp. 151-52).

[58]Aristarchy meant "a body of good men in power, or government by excellent men" (Webster, *American Dictionary,* s.v. "aristarchy").

Quorum [was] present. [A] Motion to lay the Petition on the table [was] withdrawn ~~Motio it be~~ [and the] petition rejected. [The] Petition to grade River Hill [at the] North end of Well St[reet] [was] ref[erred] to [the] Mayor.

[A] Petition for opening an alley through 118, North & South, [by] H[enry] G. Sherwood & other owners [was considered]. – [The] Mayor suggested that the owners could open it at pleasure by agreement. A[lderman] Harris objected and spoke in favor of the petition. C[ouncillor] [Heber C.] Kimball said he presumed the parties could agree. – Leave [was given] to withdraw [the] Petition.

[The] Mayor Spoke – on various subjects. [The] W[illia]m Clayton dr [debit] to John Taylor [for] [$]375. passed. [The] Petition of H[enry] G. Sherwood [regarding] his endorsement on city scrip for taxes [was] ordered to be allowed by the Treasurer[.] [It was] read twice[.] [An] Explanation [was given] by H[enry] G. Sherwood, Marshall[,] [who] explained [the need for the resolution]. – J. H. Flake ^Hake?^ said he was in the same situation, & ^it was ordered^ [that] all the assessors['] endorsements on scrip shall be allowed by the Treasurer. Bill of Hud [Theodore] Turly['s] acc[oun]t [of] $4.00 [was] refered to [the] Com[mittee] on Claims.

[The] Mayor proposed to licence Hiram Kimball [and Arthur] Morrison &c ^who own the land opposite [Water Street]^ to make wharfs and collect wharfage – & dispensed with [the] wharf master, [saying] that Kimball [could] pay a tax of ~~so~~ [an amount to be determined] for the landing of every boat and he could tax the boat or not.

| | | |
|---|---|---|
| Alderman Harris | spoke | no motion before the house |
| C[ouncillor] John Taylor | spoke | D[itt]o |
| A[lderman] Marks | spoke | D[itt]o |
| N[ewel] K. Whitney | " | D[itt]o |
| B[righam] Young | " | D[itt]o |
| J[ohn] Taylor | " | D[itt]o |

[A] Bill of J[onathan] H. Hale, for printing Blank tax receipts & assessing [forms] &c – $45.85c [was] allowed. [It was] motion^ed^ and carried, that the committee on Municipal laws, be instructed to examine the wharf tax relative to Boats, and report a bill, for an ordinance to suit the case.[59]

---

[59]On March 7, at a general meeting held near the Nauvoo temple, Joseph Smith again mentioned the wharfage issue:

[The] Account of Tarlton Lewis for burying a horse [was] read [and] referred to [the] Mayors Court. [It was] motioned & carried that the Recorder be authorized to audit [John] P Green, Marshall['s] ~~an order~~ account to pay for his services on the Treasurer. [The council] adjourned till next regular Meeting

†The Recorder has allowed J[ohn] P. Green ~~Marshal~~ $64.25 for sundry services as Marshal and Collector in 4th Ward.[60]
**Willard Richards Re[corder]**

The claim of John Taylor against William Clayton for three dollars and seventy five cents for the printing of Treasurers Blanks is hereby allowed by the City Council of the City of Nauvoo.
**March 9th 1844. Joseph Smith Mayor. Willard Richards, Recorder.**

The claim of Jonathan H. Hale for printing Blank Tax receipts and for assessing twenty days in the third ward amounting to forty five dollars eighty five cents [was] also allowed by the City Council.
**March 9th 1844. Joseph Smith Mayor. Willard Richards, Recorder**

---

There is another person I will speak about ... the two first letters of his name are Hiram Kimball. When a man is baptized and becomes a member of the Church, I have a right to talk about him, and reprove him in public or private, whenever it is necessary, or he deserves it.

When the city passed an ordinance to collect wharfage from steamboats, he goes and tells the captains of the steamboats that he owned the landing, and that they need not pay wharfage.

I despise the man who will betray you with a kiss; and I am determined to use up these men, if they will not stop their operations. If this is not true, let him come forward and throw off the imputation.

When they appeal to Carthage, I will appeal to this people, which is the highest court. I despise the lawyers who haggle on lawsuits, and I would rather die a thousand deaths than appeal to Carthage. Kimball and Morrison say they own the wharves; but the fact is, the city owns them, sixty-four feet from high water mark. From the printing office to the north limits of the city is public ground, as Water street runs along the beach, and the beach belongs to the city and not to individuals" (*History of Church*, 6:238).

[60]This entry is repeated a second time in the Proceedings, clarifying that the amount cited was for services rendered "between January 3rd and March 5th 1844." The entry also appears a third time, crossed out.

Motioned and Carried that all the Old Aldermen be added to the List of Members of this Council.

**Passed March 9th 1844. Joseph Smith Mayor. Willard Richards Recorder**

Voted by the City Council, that the Treasurer allow[,] [on] the accounts of the Collectors of the different Wards[,] for their endorsements of Taxes on outstanding City Scrip.

**Passed March 9th 1844. Joseph Smith Mayor. Willard Richards Recorder**

‡*April 13, 1844; Saturday.*[61] [At] 10 AM, [the council met in] Regular Session[.] [The] Names of [the] Members [were] called. Geo[rge] P. Stiles [was] sworn [in] as [a city] counsellor. [A] Quorum [was] present. Alderman [George W.] Harris [was] elected Pres[iden]t Protem. [The] Minutes of [the] last council [were] read and approved. [The] Mayor took his seat.

[The] bill of A[lbert] P. Rockwood [for] $22.00 [was] refered to [the] committee on claims[.] [The] bill of H[orace] S. Eldridge [was] read. Hyrum Smith moved that Geo[rge] P. Stiles esq[ui]r[e] be appointed city Attorney. A[lderman] Harris proposed an ^house [discussion] on^ ordinance on this subject. A[lderman] G[eorge] A. Smith – spoke – by explanation &c. A[lderman] Harris suggested that the City attorney have his office with the Marshal.

[The] President of [the] council proposed to the council to stick to the Motion before the house for the future. – [The] Motion carried. Geo[rge] P. Stiles [was] elected City Attorney. [An] Ordinance on [the] duties of [the] City Attorney [was] read. G[eorge] Stiles proposed that the City Attorney hold his office with the Marshal and ^that^ all papers originate with the Attorney, [but] thought the salary [was] not a sufficient inducement [and] suggested the ordinance be repealed. C[ouncillor] [John] Taylor suggested the Idea of the parties litigant paying the Attorney or the one who breaks the ordinance.

[The] President remarked that the counsel take such a course as will protect the innocent, – that in many cases, he would get his pay of the individual employing [him], that the appointment would be a valuable ~~considerable~~ consideration, and for 1 year perhaps a salary

[61] See also *History of Church,* 6:331-32.

of $100 would be sufficient – perhaps 120 the next year &c increasing as the city increases, and if $100 would not satisfy, we had better have no attorney [or one who] would rather give his services as [a] counsellor &c then levy a tax [to help] the people [who] are not able to pay, and that every man ought to be willing to help prop the city by bearing a share of the burden till the city is able to pay a higher salary. – His opinion was that the officers of the City be satisfied with a very small salary. – [He] had never received $25.00 for his services, but the peace he had enjoyed in the rights & liberties of the city had been ample compensation[.] [He] suggested the propriety of a clause in the ordinance to be made of authorizing the city Attorney to claim fees of parties in certain cases, and the small salary satisfy the attorney in cases where he can get no fees from his client[,] [that he] would rather be docked $100 in his [own] salary [as mayor] than have the 2d hundred dollars given to the city Attorney by the city.

C[ouncillor] Phelps had attended almost all the cases of the city for the past 2 yrs and asked nothing for it [and] approved the remarks of the Mayor – that every moment of the Mayor['s] [time in court] had [not] cost one hundred dollars. C[ouncillor] H[yrum] Smith supposed there were ^or should be^ fixed duties for the C[ity] Attorney and would like to have an understanding of those duties in the proposed ordinances – thought $1.50 cts might be compensation for Assessors, considering the bargains they might make abroad.

A[lderman] Marks proposed curtailing some of the city officers [and] fees. G[eorge] Stiles ~~spoke~~ said that it was not the amount of salary he [was] anxious for, but for the honor of the city there should be ~~an~~ a city Attorney, & [he] would be satisfied with [$]100 or any sum which the council think[s] proper.

C[ouncillor] Phelps moved that the ordinance on [the] city Attorney be refered to the Committee on Municipal Laws – with the addition of 1 member [to the committee] and that [the] committee report on the duties & fees of the city Attorney. G[eorge] Stiles on motion was added to the committee.

C[ouncillor] Phelps was fined $5.00 for not rising when He addressed the house. [The] Mayor Decided that all cost arising in a Habeas Corpus be collected as in other suits. [The] Mayor proposed [that] the council take into consideration the payment of the police

[and] proposed a public meeting ~~for the pay~~ in each ward to see if the people will pay the police & if they will not then the council will take the case into consideration. C[ouncillor] [Brigham] Young moved the assessors and collectors be a committee to get up their meeting & make collections. [The] President suggested we should then have another bill of particulars – and [asked if anyone] objected. [It was] moved & sec[onde]d & carried that the Mayor & Marshal be authorized to call Meetings in the different wards and collect funds to pay the police for their services the past season.

[The] Mayor said he would get up meetings – until the people would pay the whole – that he had called upon the Marshal to do this thing but the Marshal would not serve until it was acted upon by the council, & [he] told the Marshal to do this and he came back & said he would not do it. [The council] adjourned till [the] next regular session, at ½ past 12.

> †George P. Stiles Esq[ui]re was elected City Attorney when the duties of the City Attorney were read.
> **April 13th 1844. Joseph Smith Mayor. Willard Richards, Recorder.**
>
> Motioned and carried that the Mayor and Marshall be authorized to call meetings in the different wards, and collect funds to pay the police for their services the past season.
> **April 13th 1844. Joseph Smith Mayor. Willard Richards, Recorder.**

‡*April 29, 1844; Monday.*[62] [A] Special Session [was] called by the Mayor [at] 3 oclock P.M. [The] Members [were] called[,] [but there was] no quorum. [At] 2 [minutes] past 3 a Quorum [was] present. Alderman [George W.] Harris was chosen President Pro tem. [The] reading of the minutes dispensed with.

[A] Petition of Christopher Keegan for opening Green St[reet] from his house [to the] south [was] read & granted. [A] Report of the Committee on claims of A[lbert] P. Rockwood for $22.00 for his services in ~~Listing~~ assessing property &c in 1st Ward [was] accepted and the account allowed.

[It was] moved[,] seconded[,] and carried that W[illiam W.] Phelps take the place of John Taylor during his absence this season, also: Aaron Johnson the place of Orson Hyde, Phinehas Richards the

---

[62]See also ibid., 347.

place of Heber C. Kimball, Edward Hunter the place of Daniel Spencer, [and] Levi Richards the place of Brigham Young as councillors in the City Council – And Elias Smith as Alderman in place of Geo[rge] A. Smith.

Daniel Spencers fine for absence last summer was remitted. [The] Bills of Theodore Turly & H[orace] S. Eldridge were laid over to next council. Willard Richards the Recorder was permitted to change his surety[63] [from] W[illia]m Law [to] Ebenezer Robinson. [The] Petition of Elizabeth Taylor[64] & six others for opening Lumbard St[reet] from Golden St[reet] to Horner St[reet] [was] granted. At 5 [the] Council adjourned.

> †[The] Petition of Christopher Keegan, for the opening of Green Street, from its intersection with Young Street, [to] be opened one half block north, to the Petitioners line - [was] granted.
> **April 29th 1844. Joseph Smith Mayor. Willard Richards, Recorder**
>
> The claim of A[lbert] P. Rockwood for twenty two dollars, for his service as Assessor, Collector &c in first ward was allowed.
> **April 29th 1844. Joseph Smith Mayor. Willard Richards, Recorder.**[65]

‡*May 11, 1844; Saturday.* [At] 5 minutes past 10 AM [a] Regular May Session [was held]. [The] Names of [the] members [were] called. – No ~~Member~~ one [was] present[.] ~~except the Recorder~~ [At] 11 oclock [and] 20 minutes[,] [the] names of [the] members [were] called[.]

---

[63]Law had co-signed a loan to Richards, and now Robinson was assuming responsibility for the guarantee. See the minutes for May 16, 1844.

[64]Elizabeth Patrick Taylor was born in 1793 in Mecklenburg, Virginia. She married William Taylor in Bowling Green, Kentucky, in March 1811, and by 1831 when they moved to Missouri, she had born eleven children. The next year in Missouri, she and her husband converted to Mormonism. Tragically, her husband died while the family was escaping Missouri for Illinois in 1839. She married James Allred in Nauvoo in 1846. They immigrated to Utah, where she died in Ogden in 1880 ("William Taylor, 1787-1839," *The Joseph Taylor Sr. Family Association,* www.taylorassociation.org; "Elizabeth Patrick," *Family Search,* www.familysearch.org).

[65]The mayor and recorder re-confirmed the substitutions on the council, the remittance of the fine against Daniel Spencer, the change in guarantee of Ebenezer Robinson's loan, and Elizabeth Taylor's request to extend a street, all in the same wording as already appears in the minutes.

[There was] no quorum – [The] Council adjourned to [the] next Regular session [at] 11.20 oc[loc]k AM.[66]

†*May 16, 1844; Thursday.* Willard Richards took up his bond as Recorder of the City which was signed by William Law, and substituted a bond signed by Ebenezer Robinson as Surety. Willard Richards, Recorder [67]

‡*June 8, 1844; Saturday.*[68] [At the] Regular Session, June 8th 1844, 10 oclock A.M.[,] Phinehas Richards and Levi Richards recorded their oath of office & took their seats. [The] names of [the] Members [were] called [and there was a] Quorum present. [The] Mayor [was] presiding. [The] Prayer [was given] by N[ewel] K. Whitney. [The] Minutes of [the] last 3 councils [were] read and approved.

[The] account of Theodore Turly [for] $4.00 [was] read. [It was] moved seconded and carried that the Marshal call Theodore Turly. [The] marshal said he had loaned [borrowed] a portion of [the] money [he needed] to pay the police[,] so far [as] Mr Lewis was con^cerned[.]^

[A] Petition of Edson Whipple[69] & 25 others [was] read. Mr [Christopher] Keegan explained [his views] by way of objection – and said it was A[lderman] [George W.] Harris [who] asked if the street [at Keegan's farm] had been surveyed. C[ouncillor] H[yrum] Smith said there was no need of a street across [from the] Keegans farm, [and] there [has been] no street surveyed. A[lderman] Harris said if the street had ~~not~~ been surve[ye]d, the council had [had] no Jurisdiction [over it]. C[ouncillor] H[yrum] Smith said there was no

---

[66]In his diary, the mayor acknowledged that he arrived late for the meeting at 11:30 a.m. (Faulring, *American Prophet's Record,* 478). One of the distractions was that "a prospectus of the *Nauvoo Expositor* was distributed" the day before by "apostates" (*History of Church,* 363).

[67]This short entry is not in the rough minute book.

[68]See also *History of Church,* 430, 434-39. On June 7, the day before this council meeting, the first issue of the *Nauvoo Expositor* was published. Sylvester Emmons was the editor. It was the brainchild of the dissenting Church members Charles A. Foster, Robert D. Foster, Chauncey L. Higbee, Francis M. Higbee, Charles Ivins, William Law, and Wilson Law. Its main main purpose was to get the Nauvoo Charter repealed.

[69]Edson Whipple was born in 1805 in Dummerston, Vermont. He was baptized in 1840 in Philadelphia, Pennsylvania, and moved to Nauvoo in 1842. He died in 1894.

street laid out. Keegan said he had left open 2 streets, voluntarily. C[ouncillor] H[yrum] Smith moved [and] it was ~~said to~~ ordered to be layed on the table ~~& carried~~.

[A] Petition of Josiah Butterfield[70] & 51 others [was] ^read and ordered to be^ laid on [the] table. [A] Petition of W[hitford] G. Wilson[71] and 55 others [was] read[.] C[ouncillor] H[yrum] Smith moved to lay it on the table – W[illiam] W. Phelps proposed some action be had on said bill. The petition^ers^ were respectable – and if spirits w[ere] to be sold [in] the city[,] [we] might have the benefit of [it] &c [as] some would have grog [shops]. C[ouncillor] H[yrum] Smith was opposed to drink shops – would not have any one licenced. – If the officers would do their duty[,] there would be no trouble[.] [The] Mayor said the marshal could do no more[,] [that] Capt[ain] [Jonathan] Dunham ought to attend to it.

C[ouncillor] W[illiam] W. Phelps referred to the speech of the Indian in the council chamber – advising His brethren to drink no strong drink – &c & compared it with the proceedings of the citizens of this city and told the story of the Devil and the Drunken Deacon[72] – & said ~~said~~ let the Marshal speak to all the police & have them do their duty. – [He] referred to the boys playing, swimming & visiting shops on the sabbath – and urged the Council to rise up against it, and spoke at considerable length – on the principles of government & good order in the city.

A[lderman] O[rson] Spencer – referred to an ordinance authorizing the Mayor to regulate the sale of spirits[73] and spoke against

---

[70]Josiah Butterfield was born in Dunstable, Massachusetts, in 1795. He was baptized in Maine in 1833 and soon moved to Kirtland, Ohio, then to Bear Creek, Illinois, in 1839. He was excommunicated in 1844 but was later rebaptized. He died in 1871.

[71]Whitford Gill Wilson was born in 1799 in St. Albans, Vermont. He was baptized in 1836 in Kirtland, Ohio, and moved to Nauvoo in 1839.

[72]Nathaniel Hawthorne's 1835 short story, "Young Goodman Brown," told of a Salem resident who went for a midnight walk, against his wife's protest, and encountered everyone else from the town at a witches' feast, his wife about to be initiated into the group. "The deacons of many a church have drunk the communion wine with me," the devil tells Goodman Brown; "the selectmen of divers towns make me their chairman" ("Young Goodman Brown," *The Literature Network*, www.online-literature.com).

[73]See "An ordinance for the health and convenience of travellers and other purposes," December 12, 1843.

selling spirits by the small [quantity] by every one who was disposed to make a picayune[74] [and] urged that the people sustain the Mayor in the exercise of a wholesome opinion on this subject.

[The] Mayor said he had granted no licence in the city to sell Liquors, each ward petitioned that no Licences be granted in their wards. [The] Mayor had sold some Liquor at the ^Barbers^ shop – to accommodate those who needed [it] and [to] oblige O[rrin] P[orter] Rockwell in his suffering condition after being imprisoned in M[iss]-o[uri] – had sold none in his house [Nauvoo Mansion] – since the passage of the last ordinance. Mayor has heard complaints [from some individuals] about certain houses & when he has called them to make [a public] complaint, they have run away. [He] believes it is generally the case that when a man goes to law he has an unjust case & wants to go before an unjust Judge or one who wants [his] business – [He] has very few suits on his docket.

[The] Mayor referred to Councillor [Sylvester] Emmons – and suggested the propriety of purging the City Council ~~first. of Nuisan of Nuisances~~ The man who steps forward to put down iniquity is the first to be put down by the people of the city. ~~Mayor said if he had kept a whore from Canada here and since & had done every thing [he] would have been as good a man as William & Wilson Law. T[heodore] Turly~~ Theodore Turly [was] sworn [in and] said [William and Wilson] Laws had brought ^Bogus^ dies[75] to him to fix –

H[yrum] Smith: referred to Dr. [Robert D.] Foster, his brother [Charles A. Foster] & the [Chauncey and Francis M.] Higbys & asked what good they had ever done? Where is the ^first^ act of goodness and greatness in Wilson & William Law? While Joseph [Smith] was under arrest, [the] Laws & Foster[s] would have been rode [out] on a rail if he had not ~~have~~ stepped forward to prevent it.[76]

---

[74]That is, a few pennies–literally, a Spanish coin worth about six cents. The standard medium of exchange in the western hemisphere at the time was the *ocho real* ("piece of eight"), upon which the American silver dollar was fashioned and eight times that of a *real,* while a picayune was worth half a *real* ("Spanish Silver Reales Coinage," *Metal Detecting World,* http://metaldetectingworld.com).

[75]This refers to metal dies for printing counterfeit money.

[76]The version of the minutes that was published in the *Nauvoo Neighbor Extra* of June 17, 1844, continued this sentence with "on account of their oppressing the poor."

[The] Mayor – said [that] at the time he was under arrest W[illia]m Law pursued him for $40.00 he was owing Law, and it took the last expense money he had, to pay it. C[ouncillor] H[yrum] Smith continued and referred to J[oseph] H. Jackson – coming to this place, &c. [The] Mayor said W[illia]m L[aw] had offered Jackson $5.00 dollars to kill him.[77]

C[ouncillor] H[yrum] Smith continued [that] Jackson told him he me[a]nt to have [Hyrum's] daughter.[78] Jackson laid a plan with 4 or 5 persons to kidnap his daughter & threatened to shoot any man that should come near after he got her in the skiff[.] [He] was engaged in trying to make Bogus [currency][,] which was his principle business. – [Hyrum] referred to the revelation [he] read to the [Nauvoo Stake] High council[79] – that it was in answer to a question concerning things which transpired in former days & had no reference to the present time[80] – that W[illia]m Law[,] when sick[,] [confessed

[77]Wilford Woodruff recorded in his journal that a plot was underway to kill Joseph Smith: "I have been informed by two gentleman that a conspiracy is got up in this place for the purpose of taking the life of President Joseph Smith his family and all the Smith family & the heads of the Church. One of the gentleman will give his name to the public & the other wishes it to be hid for the present. They will both testify to it on oath & make an affidavit upon it. The names of the persons revealed at the head of the conspiracy are as follows: Chanc[e]y [L.] Higby[,] Dr [Robert D.] Foster, Mr [Joseph] Jackson, [and] W[illia]m & Wilson Law ... Jackson said [that] Smith should not be alive 2 weeks[,] [or] not [in] over two months any how" (Scott G. Kenney, *Wilford Woodruff's Journal, 1833-1898,* 9 vols. [Midvale, UT: Signature Books, 1983-85], 2:368).

[78]That is, Hyrum Smith's seventeen-year-old daughter, Lovina. Hyrum's mother wrote that "a man by the name of Joseph Jackson, who had been in the city several months, being desirous to marry Lovina Smith, Hyrum's oldest daughter, asked her father if he was willing to receive [Joseph Jackson] as a son-in-law. Being answered in the negative, he went and requested Joseph [Smith] to use his influence in his favour. As Joseph [Smith] refused to do so, he next applied to Law, who was our secret enemy, for assistance in stealing Lovina from her father, and, from this time forth, [Joseph Jackson] continued seeking out our enemies, till he succeeded in getting a number to join him in a conspiracy to murder the whole Smith family" (Lucy Smith, *Biographical Sketches of Joseph Smith the Prophet and His Progenitors for Many Generations* [Liverpool: Orson Pratt, 1853], 275).

[79]This was Joseph Smith's revelation on the plurality of wives, which Hyrum Smith read to the Nauvoo Stake High Council on August 12, 1843.

[80]Hyrum Smith married four plural wives in 1843: Mercy Fielding, Catherine Phillips, Lydia Dibble, and Louisa Sanger. His first wife, Jerusha

and] said ^he had been guilty of adultery &^ he was not fit to live or die, had sinned against his own soul[81] &c. Who was Judge Emmons[?] When he come here he had scarce 2 shirts – was dandled[82] by the authorities of the city. – Now [he is] Editor of the [Nauvoo] Expositor – His right hand man [is] Francis Higby who confi[d]ed to ~~him~~ the speaker he had had the Pox[83] – &c – Emmons had lifted his hand against the Municipality of God Almighty and the curse of God shall rest upon him.

Washington Peck[84] [was] sworn – [and] said [that] soon after J[oseph] H. Jackson come here[,] Jackson come to him and wanted [Peck] to loan [him] some money[.] ~~I~~ [The] Witness let him have some and took some jewelry as security. Soon after[,] a man from across the river come after the jewelry [saying] Jackson had stolen it from him. ~~or loaned it of him~~ At another time [Jackson] wanted to get money [and] ~~he should enlist in bogus making~~ asked ~~me when~~ [the] witness if he would do any thing dishonorable to get a living – [Peck] said he would not. – Jackson said ~~he~~ [the] witness was a damned fool [because] he could get a living a [good] deal easier than ~~work~~ [doing what] he was then doing ^by making Bogus [currency] -^ [and that] some men high in the church were engaged in the business – ^[The] witness asked if it was Joseph [Smith] – No said Jackson. I dare not tell it to Joseph[,] [he said][.] ~~but not Joseph~~^ [The] Witness understood [from Jackson that] the Laws were engaged in it. ^Jackson said he^ would be the death of [the] witness if [Peck] ever went to Joseph or any one to tell of what he had said.

---

Barden, died in 1837, and he married Mary Fielding (Mercy's sister) two months after his first wife's death for a total of five living wives at the time he denied a present-day relevance to the revelation (Smith, *Nauvoo Polygamy,* 620-21).

[81]It is not known if this is true. For a discussion, see Cook, *William Law,* 25-27.

[82]"Dandled," the past participle of "dandle," meant to be bounced and burped: "danced on the knee, or in the arms; fondled; amused by trifles or play" (Webster, *American Dictionary,* s.v. "dandled").

[83]That is, syphilis (Webster, *American Dictionary,* s.v. "pox"). Although the word could be used to refer to small pox or chicken pox, when it was unqualified it signified "the venereal diseases." The word was so shocking that the editors of the June 17 *Nauvoo Neighbor Extra* softened it to "P**," while the *History of the Church* replaced it with "–!" (6:435).

[84]Washington Peck was born in 1820.

[The] bill of Theodore Turly for $4.00 [was] read & $1.50 allowed thereon. [At] 1 oclock & 12 min[utes] [the] council adjourned [for] 1 hour. [At] 2 [o'clock and] 12 mi[nutes][,] [the] names [were] called. [There was] no quorum[.] [The] Council adjourned for one hour [until] 3 oclock 7 minutes.

Edward Hunter received his oath of office & took his seat in the Council. W[illiam] W. Phelps moved that ~~counsellor Sylvester~~ counsellor Emmons be suspended ~~from his office as city councillor~~ until his case can be investigated for slandering the city [council.] [The motion] carried and [also] that the Recorder [should] notify him of his suspension and that his case would be investigated at the next regular session of the Council – 2d. [seconded] by N[ewel] K. Whitney – and carried.

~~Moved~~ Counsellor [John] Taylor – expressed his feelings that Counsellor Emmons had helped make the ordinances of the city and never lifted his voice against them in the council – and was now trying to destroy those ~~same~~ ordinances & the charter. Lorenzo Wasson[85] [was] sworn [and] said Joseph H Jackson told [the] witness that Bogus ~~Business~~ Making was going on in the City, but it was too damned small [a] business. He wanted [the] witness to help him to procure Money[,] ^for the Gen[eral] [Joseph Smith] was afraid to go into it[,] &^ with $500.00 he could get an engraving ^for bills^ on the Bank of M[iss]o[uri] and one on the Nati[onal] [Bank] of New York and could make money. – [He] said many times [the] witness did not know him. ~~Mayor~~ Said he believed the Gen[eral] had been telling ~~me~~ [the] witness something [against him]; God Damn him[,] if he has I will kill him – ^& swore he^ would kill any man that should prove a traitor to him. – [He] said if he could get a company of men to suit him he would go onto the frontier and live by highway Robbery – for he had got sick of the world.

W[illiam] W. Phelps moved that the Marshal & police be instructed to investigate the selling of Liquor in the city. C[ouncillor] Taylor objected to calling [out] names before the council. [The] marshal said 50 had complained of houses and persons &c – but [he] has told them to enter legal complaint[s]. C[ouncillor] Taylor ex-

---

[85]Lorenzo D. Wasson was born in Amboy, Illinois, in 1818. He was a son of Emma Smith's sister, Elizabeth. He converted to Mormonism in Illinois in 1842 and was appointed to the Council of Fifty in 1844. He died in 1857.

plained [the law] to [the] Marshal. [The] Mayor called for the Marshal to report.

[The] Marshal said he knew where the grog shops were. Upon Stone House [was] one [that] has decanters and glasses. – [At the] Gordon & Allen Nauvoo Store – men come away drunk. – [There is the] Grubb & Ritchie City Bakery [and] Snows or Ashbys brick house [where, he] said[,] they were selling candy & wine. [He] believes a good deal ^of Liquor^ [is] drunk at [the] Morris Store. – [I] have never seen any sold at Masonic Hall, – no appearance of it. And [there is] gambling going on at all these places or most of them[,] as [the] Marshal believes. – [The] lynching of the Negro originated in drinking.[86] – [The marshal said he] saw a glass poured out at Thompsons but saw none drunk, believed they drink and gamble [at] Morris's House – [also that] on Mulholland St. Beeches sells by [the] swall[ow] ~~I am~~ as [I am] informed.

A[lderman] Harris called for the reading of the ordinance on Spiritous Liquors[.] [The] ordinance [was] read. – A[lderman] Harris suggested that [the] complaint have 2 [double] the fine. C[ouncillor] Phelps had not weighed the measure, [was] not ready to go for the measure[,] did not want to do any thing to create [a] quarrel among men & thought the police might bring up the ordinance of the city without fee or reward. ~~Mayor asked if Co[uncillor] Phelps~~ [The] Mayor queried Phelps [and] explained [his feelings][.] A[lderman] Harris argued his motion that a house div[id]ed against itself cannot stand – & [the] drunkard[s] will betray each other.

Coun[cillor] Phelps – moved that the petition of W[hitford] G. Wilson & others be laid on the table and the police be instructed to watch the house & learn if the ordinance [is] be[ing] broken – [The] Mayor suggested that there might be a mistake about the upper stone house being [a grog shop]. [The] Petition [was] ordered to be laid on the table forever.

---

[86]Newspapers in Delaware, Iowa, Louisiana, Maryland, Ohio, and Tennessee reported this for April 1844: "The following shows what a law-abiding people Joe Smith's minions are. A negro was recently found with some stolen goods at Nauvoo, and, to make him divulge the names of those who committed the theft, he was taken by the Mormons to the woods and lynched. They did not succeed, however, in their object" (qtd. in Paul D. Ellsworth, "Mobocracy and the Rule of Law: American Press Reaction to the Murder of Joseph Smith," *BYU Studies* 20 [1979], 10-11).

John S. Higbee['s] [claim for] $38.00 [was] read [and] refered to [the] Com[mittee] on claims. [The] Petition of B[enjamin] Warrington & 4 others [was] read, referred to the Mayor. An ordinance concerning the City Attorney and his duties [was] read twice.[87] C[ouncillor] Taylor objected to [the] 3d Section – ~~thought~~ A[lderman] Spencer concurred with C[ouncillor] Taylor that complainant ought not to be compelled to pay for [legal] Council. [The] Mayor concurred – and spoke at length. C[ouncillor] Phelps spoke in concurrence[.] [The] Mayor suggested – that a bill be got up to give a portion of the fine to the complain[an]t – a portion to ~~Council~~ the Attorney & the rest to the City. Counsellor Stiles – explained [his feelings].

[The] Mayor called A[lderman] Harris to the chair. [The] Mayor remarked [that] the Attorney might have the privilege of occupying the Mayors office – and suggested that 1/3 fine go to Attorney 1/3 to complain[an]t [and] 1/3 to [the] city - so far the Mayor has had to be complainant, witness, Mayor – & every thing else[.] A[lderman] Spencer spoke. G[eorge] Stiles explained [his views]. [The] 3d Section was erased and a new one inserted. [The] Mayor Moved that the rules be dispensed with & the bill pass[,] [which] carried. – [The council was] satisfied with [the] Title[:] An Ordinance concerning the City Attorney and his duties.

[A] Report on J[ohn] S. Higbees account [was] accepted – [the] acc[oun]t allowed. W[illiam] W. Phelps and Geo[rge] P. Stiles were appointed a committee to draft an ordinance. [The] Mayor suggested that the council pass an ordinance to prevent misrepresentation ~~of~~ & Libelous publication, and wanted a law passed to prevent all conspiracy against the peace of the city.[88] – ~~ord[in]an[ce] read~~

[The] Mayor said he had never made any proposals to [Robert D.] Foster to come Back. Foster proposed to come back[,] come to his home[,] and wanted a private interview[.] [The] Mayor told him he would have no private interview – [He] had some conversation with Foster in the hall, in [the] presence of several. ~~Mayor~~ [He] related to [the] Council [his] conversation with Dr. Foster and read a letter from Dr Foster – dated June 7th[,] and when he left my house he went to a ^s[hoe]^ shop on the hill – and said that Joseph

---

[87]See below.

[88]This, of course, refers to the *Nauvoo Expositor,* published the day before.

[Smith] said if he would come back he would give him Laws place in the church & a [bag] full of specie[89] – and then wrote the Letter just read.[90]

Lucien Woodworth,[91] sworn[,] stated that the conversation as stated by the mayor was correct - [Woodworth] was present May 7th[,] AM 10[,] at [the Nauvoo] Mansion. Dr Foster rode up [and] enquired if Gen[eral] Smith was at home [and the] witness told him

---

[89]The missing words are interpreted to be *shoe* ("shoe shop") and hat ("hat-full") in *History of Church,* 6:437.

[90]Smith's journal reads: "R[obert] D. Foster called professidly to make some concessions and return to the Church. [He] wanted a private interview which I declined. Told him I would choose individuals and he might choose others and we would meet and I would settle any thing on righteous principles. Report was circulated in the evening that Foster said I would receive him on any terms and give him a hat full of dollars into the bargain" (Faulring, *American Prophet's Record,* 488).

According to the *Nauvoo Neighbor,* June 19, 1844, the letter from Robert Foster of June 7, 1844, read:

To Gen[eral] J[oseph] Smith

> Sir, I have consulted my friends in relation to your proposals of settlement, and they as well as myself are of [the] opinion that your conduct and that of your unworthy, unprincipled, clan, is so base that it would be morally wrong & detract from the dignity of Gentlemen to hold any conference with you[.] [T]he repeated insults, and abuses, I as well as my friends have suffered from your unlawful course towards us demands honorable resentment, [and] we are resolved to make this ["honorable resentment"] our motto[.] [N]othing on our part has been done to provoke your anger but [we] have done all things as become men, [while] you have trampled upon everything we hold dear and sacred[.] [Y]ou have set all law at defiance and profaned the name of the most high to carry out your damnable purposes – and I have nothing more to fear from you than you have already threatened, & I as well as my friends will stay here & maintain and magnify the law as long as we stay – and we are resolved never to leave until we sell or exchange our property that we have here[.] [T]he proposals made by your agent D[i]mic[k] Huntington as well as the threats you sent to intimidate me, I disdain and despise[,] as I do their unhallowed author[.] [T]he right of my family and my friends demand at my hand a refusal of all your offers[.] [W]e are united in virtue and truth, and we set hell at defiance and [bid] all her agents adieu.

R[obert] D. FOSTER

Gen[eral] J[oseph] Smith

[91]Lucien Woodworth was born in 1799 in Thetford, Vermont. He was the principal architect of the Nauvoo House. He died in 1867.

he believed he was. Dr Foster went in to the house, [then the] witness went in. Dr [Foster] was there, the General & others [were there] [,] looking at some specimen of penmanship. Something was said respecting a conversation at that time, between the Gen[eral] & Dr. [Foster]. Gen[eral] Smith observed to Foster, if he had a conversation [with him][,] he would want others present. [The] Dr said he would have a [quick] word with him by himself and went into the Hall. [The] witness [said he] went to the door, that he might see and hear what was passing. They still continued to talk on the subject of a conversation that they might have afterward with others present, that Mr Smith might choose [witnesses] and ~~there~~ that Dr Foster might choose [witnesses]. Foster left, and went for those that he said he wanted present, and would return soon with them. – [Woodworth] thinks he heard all the conversation. – [He] heard nothing about Gen[eral] Smith making any offers to Foster to settle [their dispute]. – [The witness] was present all the time. – [Woodworth sent] Dimick Huntington ~~asked Dr Foster to talk with him me and reported foster was~~ [to Foster. The] Mayor said he wanted it distinctly understood that he knew nothing about Dimick Huntingtons going to see Dr. Foster.

Woodworth Continued – and said he sent Dimick Huntington to Dr Foster and Joseph knew nothing about it. H[yrum] Smith said Dimick Huntington come to him on the 7th ~~&~~ [and] said he had had an interview with Dr Foster & thought he was almost ready to come back – and a word from [the] Witness or Joseph would bring it about, &c.

[The] Mayor said the conduct of such men & such [news]papers are calculated to ~~do~~ destroy the peace of the city – and it is not safe that such things should exist – on account of the Mob spirit which they tend to produce – and he had made the statements he had [been quoted saying], and called the witnesses to propose [to] the Council to act in the case.

[The mayor said] Emmons was blackguarded[92] out of Philadelphia and dubbed ~~him~~ with [the ironic] title of Judge. ^(As he had understood from citizens of Phila[delphia],)^ ~~he~~ [Emmons] was poor,

---

[92]That is, "reviled," treated as "the lowest menial of a household" (*Shorter Oxford English Dictionary* [Oxford: Oxford University Press, 2002], s.v. "blackguard").

and [the] Mayor helped him to [purchase] cloth for a Coat before he went away ^last fall^ & [Emmons] labored all winter to get the post office [job] from Mr [Sidney] Rigdon (as informed). [The] Mayor referred to a writing from Dr [W. G.] Go-forth[93] – showing that the Laws presented the commendation from the female Relief Society in the ^Nauvoo^ Neighbor to Dr Goforth ~~be~~ as the bone of contention[.] [The mayor] said If God ever spoke by any man[,] it will not be 5 years before this city [is] in ashes and we [will be] in our Gore unless we go to Oregon ^California^ or some ^other^ place, if the city does not put down every thing which tends to mobocracy – and put down these murders, Bogus Makers and scoundrels[.] All the sorrow ~~I~~ he had ever had in his family, has arisen through the influence of W[illia]m Law.

C[ouncillor] H[yrum] Smith spoke – in relation to the Laws, Fosters, Higbees, ~~[Thomas] Sharpe~~ Editor of the [Warsaw] Signal[94] &c – and of the importance of suppressing that spirit which has driven us from M[iss]o[uri] &c. [He said] that he would go in~~to~~ for an effective ordinance.

[The] Mayor said at the time Gov[ernor] [Thomas] Carlin was pursuing him with his writs – W[illia]m Law come to my house with a band of Missourians for the purpose of betraying me – come to my gate – and was prevented ~~with~~ by Daniel Cairns who was set to watch[.] [They] had come within his gate, and [Cairns] called [the] Mayor ~~after~~ and the Mayor reproved Law for coming at that time of night.

Daniel Cairns [was] sworn [and] said – about 10 Oc[loc]k at night – a boat come up the river with about a Doz[en] men. W[illia]m Law come to the gate with them when [he] was on guard – and [he] stopped them. Law called Joseph to the door, and wanted an inter-

---

[93]Though little is known about Dr. W. G. Goforth, he served under Andrew Jackson in the Battle of New Orleans. He was probably a Mason because on April 5, 1844, he addressed the Masonic Lodge in Nauvoo. On May 15, 1844, he introduced Smith to a son of John Quincy Adams, and on April 8, 1845, he was baptized by Brigham Young.

[94]The *Warsaw Signal* was a newspaper run by Thomas Sharp, who was hostile to Mormons. It was the only non-Mormon newspaper in Hancock County, Illinois, and it regularly published letters and editorials by dissenting Mormons. The *Nauvoo Expositor* described it as "rich with anti-Mormon matter."

view. Joseph said Bro[ther] Law you know better than to come here at this hour of the night – & Law returned. [The] next morning Law wrote a letter to apologize – which [Cairns] [had] heard read – which was written apparently to screen himself [Law] from the censure of a conspiracy, and the Letter betrayed a conspiracy on the face of [it] –

Peter Haws [was] sworn [and] said [he would answer some questions]. [The] Mayor proposed an adjournment. C[ouncillor] Phelps – read an ordinance concerning libels. [The] Mayor suggested the propriety of having a preamble to said ordinance. [The] Chairman said he would add C[ouncillor John] Taylor to the committee to draft a preamble. C[ouncillor] P[hineas] Richards suggested an addition to the ordinance [that was] read to prevent attempts to take away our Charter, &c – [and] would go for an effective ordinance. [The] Chairman instructed the committee to go all lengths to ^make a^ full report on the preamble & ordinance. [At] 6.30 mi[nutes] [the council] adjourned till Monday next [at] 10 oclock AM.

†Phinehas Richards, and Levi Richards received their oath of Office and took their seats as Councillors in this City Council.
**June 8th, 1844. Willard Richards Recorder.**

The claim of Theodore Turley for four dollars was read, and the Council allowed the sum of one dollar and fifty cents thereof.
**June 8th 1844. Joseph Smith, Mayor. Willard Richards, Recorder.**

Edward Hunter received his Oath of Office and took his seat as one of the Councillors of the City.
**June 8th, 1844. Willard Richards, Recorder.**

[It was] motioned and carried that Councillor Sylvester Emmons be suspended, until his case can be investigated, for slandering the City Council, and that the Recorder notify him of his suspension, and that his case would be investigated at the next regular Session of the City Council.
**June 8th 1844. Joseph Smith, Mayor. Willard Richards, Recorder.**

An Ordinance concerning the City Attorney and his duties

Be it ordained by the City Council of the City of Nauvoo.

Sec. 1. It shall be the duty of the City Attorney to council and advise with any officer of said City in any matter pertaining to the Municipal affairs of said City w[h]en called upon so to do.

Sec. 2. It shall be the duty of the City Attorney to prosecute as Attorney in all cases for breach of City ordinances, when [a] complaint is regularly and duly made.

Sec. 3. When any individual shall complain of a breach of ordinance and shall prosecute any individual to final judgment, said Complainant shall receive one third; ~~and the remaining thir~~ of the fine so collected; the City Attorney shall receive one third; and the remaining third of said fine shall be paid into the City Treasury.

Sec. 4. The City Attorney shall have and receive a salary of one hundred dollars per annum for his services as City Attorney.

Sec. 5. All ordinances conflicting with the provisions of this ordinance are hereby repealed.

Sec. 6. This ordinance to take effect and be in force from and after its passage.

**Passed June 8th 1844. Geo[rge] W. Harris, pres[ident] pro tem. Willard Richards Recorder.**

Allowed the claim of John S. Higbee amounting to thirty eight dollars as Assessor and Collector of First Ward.

**June 8th, 1844. Willard Richards Recorder.**

‡*June 10, 1844; Monday.*[95] [The] adjourned session [resumed], Monday June 10th 1844, 10 AM. [The] names of [the] Members [were] called [and a] Quorum [was] present[.] Prayer by J[ohn] P. Green. [The] Minutes of [the] last council [meeting were] read and approved.

[The] Mayor called Alderman [George W.] Harris to the chair. [The] Mayor made some observations in reference to [Robert D.] Foster & read the Letter written by Foster on the 7th instant which was read to the council on the 8th which is as follows [blank][96]

Elias Smith [was] sworn into office as [an] Alderman, and took his seat. Cyrus Hills [was] Sworn [and said that] one day last week I believe it Wednesday a gentleman whom I did not know come into the sitting room of the Nauvoo Mansion and requested the Hon[orable] Mayor to step aside[,] he wanted to speak with him –

---

[95]See also *History of Church,* 6:439-48.

[96]See note 87 above.

[The visitor] stepped through the door into the entry by the foot of the stairs and the Gen[eral] asked him what he wished. Foster ^as [the] witness learned the gentlemans name [was]^ said he wanted some conversation on some business which [the] witness did not understand at that time. The Gen[eral] refused to go any further – & said he would have no conversation in private. What should be said[,] he would have in public. They had some conversation which [the] witness could not repeat. Witness then heard the General tell [the] witness if he would choose 3 or 4 men he would meet him with the same number of men (among whom was his brother Hyrum [Smith]) and they would have a cool and calm investigation of the subject – and by his making a proper satisfaction things should be honorably adjusted. [As he] witnessed [it, he] judged from the manner which Foster expressed himself that he agreed to the Mayors proposals and would meet him the same day. – [The] Witness heard no proposals made by [the] Mayor to Foster for a settlement, heard nothing about any offers of dollars or money or any other offers except those mentioned before. – Nothing [was] said about W[illia]m Law. – [The] Witness was within hearing of the parties all the time [the] conversation was going on.

O[rrin] P[orter] Rockwell [was] sworn [and] said some day last week [he] saw Dr Foster ride up to the Nauvoo Mansion & go in. [The] Witness went in & found the Gen[eral] Mayor & Dr Foster talking as he went in. Gen[eral] Smith was naming the men he would have present [at a meeting] – among whom [were] Hyrum Smith, W[illia]m Mark[s], [Lucien] Woodworth, & [Peter] Hawes – and that Dr Foster might call an equal number of his friends[.] As [the] witness understand[s] it[,] [it] was for the purpose of having an interview on some matters in contention. Foster asked the Gen[eral] if he had any objections to his brothers coming down. – The Gen[eral] replied he had not, but [in fact] wanted [him to] be present. Dr Foster started and said he would be back shortly. Before Dr Foster left[,] the men whom the General had named to be present at the conversation were sent for. – [Rockwell said he] went in as the Mayor & Dr Foster were coming out of the Bar room into the Hall. Nothing [was] said by the Mayor to Foster about his coming back. [The] Mayor made no offers to Foster about a settlement.

[The] Mayor said the first thing that occurred when he stepped into the Hall with Foster, he saw something shining below his vest. – [The] Mayor put his finger on it, and said what is that. Foster replied it is my pistol and immediately took out the pistol and showed it fairly & openly – & wanted [the] Mayor to go with him alone. [The] Mayor said he would not go alone. – [He had] never s[een] the pistol before. [It] had a hook on the side to hang on his ~~suspender~~ waistband.

Andrew L. Lamereaux [was] sworn – [and] read his statements, marked A. No 1. on File.[97] [He was followed by] Peter Haws[,] ~~who was sworn at the last council~~ [who had been sworn in] on Saturday[,] [and] said [he would continue]. – [He] stated that ~~he~~ he came to Nauvoo before the Laws and brought ~~much~~ considerable property [with him]. It was just ~~before~~ after the Church was driven from Missouri & [when he] arrived in this place, the families, having been robbed of all in M[iss]o[uri][,] were in a starving condition. By council of the presidency[,] [the] ~~witness~~ witness converted his funds to feeding the poor, bringing in meat & flour &c, and while thus engaged, [he] drew upon the [store of William and Wilson] Laws – who were then engaged in merchandiz[ing] – to the amount of some six hundred Dollars which, on account of his expenditures for the poor[,] he was not able to pay [in full.] [He was] within some 70 or 80 dollars[,] [and could not pay] as soon as [the] Laws wanted it, though he offered them good property ~~property~~ at considerable less than market value [in exchange for what he owed]. – As [the] witness was obliged to leave the city a little season, on church business, W[illia]m Law ~~oppressed his~~ worried therefore [about the account] & intimidated [the] witness['s] family in his absence for said pay. When Dr Foster made a public dinner on the 4th of July, [the] witness ^was obliged to be absent &^ deposited ~~funds~~ meat [and] flour &c with W[illia]m Law to feed the poor at that dinner, and Law handed it out as his own property.

‡‡Haws[,] sitting before [the] City Council – June 10 – 1844 [continued his testimony]. [He said he had] come to [Nauvoo to] purchase lands. Joseph [Smith had] reminded [the Nauvoo Stake] High Coun-

[97]The *Nauvoo Neighbor,* June 19, 1844, published the transcript of Lamereaux's testimony, in which he said he received a visit in Dayton, Ohio, in 1839 or 1840 from Joseph Smith, Elias Higbee, Orrin Porter Rockwell, and Robert D. Foster and that at a social event during the visit, he saw Robert Foster put his hand on a woman's knee. He said Foster later "confessed it was true, and promised to reform."

cil [to] look to [the] poor. [The] Witness purchased hogs. [The] Laws purchased goods [and] Haws bought flour and meal [from them] for [the] fut[ure] winter. In June [he] went to W[illia]m Law [and said] take the flour [I] have on hand to pay ~~600 dollar Haws owed~~ what [I] owed him [and Law said he] would do it at [a] reduced price – so as to make [a] 2 per cent [profit] – While [the] witness was gone – by council, to get some pine lumber, ~~Have~~ Law ~~then~~ told [his] family [he] would attach my property. – When [the] witness was about to go again, [Law] said he would confine [the] witness. – [I said] go ahead – [and] told Bro[ther] Joseph – [who said Haws] was as good [a] man as W[illia]m Law – [and] did not Capias [arrest him][.][98]

Last Summer [the] witness went south[.] [He] had 24½ bu[shels] [of] wheat [brought to the] Laws mill[.] [Haws had] ground up [the] wheat and owned it [himself]. – [Law] put me off &c [by saying he could not grind it immediately] – with [a] notice in [my] hand [regarding] what is to be done about flour. – Law [said][:] Bro[ther] Haws[,] upon the honor of a gentleman & saint I will get it [done] this week [and] will lodge it in your house. When [Haws] came back [in town, his] family had been without funds [and had] 7½ [bushels of flour] only – [and] must have starved if they had not [borrowed money from] some place right off – [Haws said he] could not say one word[,] [he] was boiling over. [99]

---

[98]Haws then repeats his story about having engaged William Law, a store owner, to deliver food to a Fourth of July party hosted by Robert Foster, where Law let people assume that the store had paid for the food. The transcript has something incomprehensible about "nails to co----r cabin" and adds that Law "preached punctuality [and] charged 2 per cent, pressed the poor." Haws says that he went east and that Law's wife gave his family $50 credit for meal, for which William reduced the credit to $40.00. The transcript is, again, garbled and reads: "gone East reined up by sis Law. – he did not not know it. – Allowed $50. for meal Law allowed $40.00." A "writ of capias" is an arrest warrant.

[99]There is an indecipherable portion here: "some Wilson said we have done the best we could. built mills – bot farms – and oppressed the poor. Some other God beside the one I served. hitched on to bro Green. – acknowledge his fault – Law gulled N[auvoo] House $500. – blocked the wheels & locked the guns." "Green" may refer to Younger Green, who was excommunicated on June 1 and joined William Law as a counselor in his new Church (Lyndon W. Cook and Donald Q. Cannon, *Far West Record: Minutes of the Church of Jesus Christ of Latter-day Saints, 1830-1844* [Salt Lake City: Deseret Book, 1983], 245. According to Webster's *American Diction-*

‡C[ouncillor] H[yrum] Smith said he recollected the time Haws referred to. [The] Mayor said Haws gave him his Notes & he destroyed them[.] Hawes was the first man to step forward and help save the poor from Missouri.

G[eorge] P. Stiles [presented a] bill [for] $40, [which was] read & referred to [the] committee on Claims[.] [A] Special Committee reported on [a] Bill – on [an] Ordinance on Libels & for other purposes – with preamble[.] [The] Mayor said – if he had a city council who felt as he did, the establishment (referring to the Nauvoo Expositor) would be [declared] a Nuisance before night – and read an Editorial from the 2d No. of the Nauvoo Expositor.[100] Who ever said a word vs Judge [Sylvester] Emmons until he has attacked this council – or against J[oseph] H. Jackson or the Laws until they have come out against the City? – & here is a paper (Nauvoo Expositor) that is exciting our enemies abroad.

[The mayor said] Joseph H. Jackson has been proved a murderer before this Council[101] and [the mayor] declared the paper a nuisance, a greater nuisance ~~greater~~ than a dead carcass. – They make [it] a criminality ~~of~~ for a man to have a wife on the earth while he has one in heaven – according to the keys of the holy priesthood, and [the mayor] read the statement of W[illia]m Law in the Expositor, where the truth of God was transformed into a lie. [He] read [the] statements of Austin Cowles – & said he had never had any private conversation with Austin Cowles on these subjects, that he preached on the stand from the bible showing the order in ancient days[,] having nothing to do with the present time.

What the opposition party wanted was to raise a mob on us and take the spoil of us as they did in Missouri. Said that he had as much as he could do to keep his clerk [Robert B.] Thompson from publishing the proceedings of the Laws and causing the people to [amass

---

*ary, gull* means "to deceive; to cheat; to mislead by deception; to trick; to defraud." Thank you to Joseph Johnstun for helping analyze this and a few other difficult passages.

[100]This counts the prospectus as the first number of the *Expositor.*

[101]In fact, nothing in the minutes of the city council indicated that Joseph Jackson had committed murder. Joseph Smith had alleged an intent on Jackson's part, and Washington Peck may have felt intimidated by Jackson; there was fear that Jackson might elope with Hyrum Smith's daughter, but he had not eloped and had not killed anyone either.

against them] – said he would rather die tomorrow and have the thing smashed, than live and have it grow.

Peter Hawes referred to Mr A Smith who came from England, and was taken sick and died. [His] children had no one to protect them. There was one girl 16 or 17 years old – & a younger sister. [The] Witness took in these girls out of pity. Wilson Law was familiar with the oldest daughter. [The] Witness cautioned the girl. – Wilson was soon there again and out [with the older girl] in the evening. [The witness] charged the girls [with carelessness] & she confessed to [the] witness['s] wife [that] Wilson had seduced her. [The] Witness told her he could not keep her – [The] Girls wept and made much ado – made many promises[.] [The] Witness told her if she would do right she might stay, but she did not keep [her promise.] Wilson came & she went [out with him] again. [The] Mayor said certain women came to complain to his wife that they had caught Wilson Law with the girl on the floor – at Mr Hawes – in the night.

C[ouncillor] H[yrum] Smith – spoke to show the falsehood of Austin Cowles in relation to the revelation referred to – that it referred to former days [and] not the present time as stated by Cowles. [The] Mayor said he had never preached the revelation in private as he had in public – had not taught it to the ~~highest~~ anointed in the Church ^in private^ which many confirmed.

[The mayor said][,] on enquiring [of God regarding] the passage in [the Bible that in] the resurrection they neither marry &c[:] I received for [an] answer, Men in this life must be married in view of Eternity, [and that] was the [full] amount of the [content of the] revelation,[102] otherwise [in the resurrection] they must remain as

---

[102]In fact, the revelation included this:

> And let mine handmaid, Emma Smith, receive all those that have been given unto my servant Joseph, and who are virtuous and pure before me; ... for I am the Lord thy God, and ye shall obey my voice, ... And again, verily I say, let mine handmaid forgive my servant Joseph his trespasses; and then shall she be forgiven her trespasses, wherein she hath trespassed against me; ...
>
> And again, as pertaining to the law of the priesthood–if any man espouse a virgin, and desire to espouse another, and the first give her consent; and if he espouse the second, and they are virgins, and have vowed to no other man, then is he justified; he cannot commit adultery for they are given unto him; for he cannot commit adultery with that that belongeth unto him and to no one else; and if he have ten virgins

angels ~~only~~ in heaven, and [the mayor] spoke at considerable length in explanation of the[se] principles[.] [He] was willing[,] for one[,] to subscribe his name to declare that paper [*Nauvoo Expositor*] & the whole establishment as a nuisance. [At] 1 Oclock & 19 min[utes], [the council] adjourned for one hour.

[At] half past 2 oclock P.M. [the] council [was] called [and a] Quorum [was] present. The Clerk bore testimony of the good character & high standing of Mr Smith's family – whose daughter was seduced by Wilson Law, as stated in the morning council. C[ouncillor] H[yrum] Smith concurred.

[The] ~~Bill on Libels~~ Bill ~~Ordinance~~ on Libels was read the 2d time. [It was] moved by [the] Mayor that the words, "and Statute of Illinois" be added to the 1st Section of the ordinance, immediately after Kent.[103] – [It was] seconded and carried – and the words added. C[ouncillor] Phelps proposed the addition of a word. [The] Mayor – ~~mentioned~~ said no man would join the clique who ~~is~~ was not guilty – and objected to [the addition]. [It was] read [a] 3d time by its title. [It was] motioned by [the] Mayor [and] 2d. [seconded] by C[ouncillor] H[yrum] Smith that the bill pass[,] and [the motion] carried unanimously – [all] satisfied with [the] title "An Ordinance concerning libels and for other purposes."[104]

[The] Mayor said the Constitution did not authorize the press

---

> given unto him by this law, he cannot commit adultery, for they belong to him, and they are given unto him–therefore is he justified. ...
>
> If any man have a wife ... and he teaches unto her the law of my priesthood, as pertaining to these things; then shall she believe and administer unto him, or she shall be destroyed, saith the Lord your God; for I will destroy her (Doctrine and Covenants, 132:52-53, 56, 61-62, 64).

[103]The specific passage in James Kent's *Commentaries on America Law,* 4 vols. (New York: O. Halsted, 1826-30), is unknown. A probable candidate is: "Expressions which tend to render a man ridiculous, or lower him in the esteem and opinion of the world, would be libelous if printed, though they would not be actionable if spoken. A libel, as applicable to individuals, has been well defined to be a malicious publication, expressed either in printing or writing, or by signs or pictures, tending either to blacken the memory of one dead, or the reputation of one alive, and expose him to public hatred, contempt, or ridicule. A malicious intent towards government, magistrates, or individuals, and an injurious or offensive tendency, must concur to constitute the libel" (2:12-22).

[104]See below.

to publish Libels – and proposed the council make some provision for putting down the Nauvoo Expositor. C[ouncillor] H[yrum] Smith moved that the Marshall procure a prospectus of the Nauvoo Expositor. [This was] 2d [seconded] by C[ouncillor] Phelps. C[ouncillor] Phelps [then] read Art[icle] 8 1[st] S[ection] [of the] Illinois Constitution.[105]

[The] Mayor called for the [Nauvoo] charter. [The] Prospectus of the Nauvoo Expositor was read[106] – [The] Mayor read statements of Francis M. Higbee from the "Expositor."[107] Is it not treasonable against all chartered rights, privileges, peace, and happiness of the City? And [the mayor] spoke at great length an[swering] [this question].

C[ouncillor] H[yrum] Smith spoke in favor of declaring the Expositor a Nuisance. C[ouncillor] [John] Taylor said no city on earth would bear such slander and he would not bear it, and spoke decidedly in favor of active measures. [The] Mayor made a statement of what W[illia]m Law said before the Council concerning his friendship ^[and] if he knew any thing against the Mayor [and he said no]^ – and [asked if anyone remembered the exchange, to which] scores responded to the question – Yes.

C[ouncillor] [Edward] Hunter said W[illia]m Law stated before [a] grand Jury that he did not say before the Council that he was Josephs friend.[108] C[ouncillor] Taylor continued [that] Wilson Law was president of this Council – [that] W[illia]m Law & [Sylvester] Emmons were members – & Emmons has never objected to any ordinance – [and] has been More like a cypher – And [Taylor] read from the constitution of the U.S. on freedom of the press. – We are willing they should publish the truth – but the paper is a nuisance – and stinks in the nose of every honest man.

[The] Resolution on nuisances [was] read. [The] Mayor read

[105]"That the general, great and essential principles of liberty and free government may be recognized and unalterably established, we declare that all men are born equally free and independent, and have certain inherent and indefeasible rights; among which are those of enjoying and defending life and liberty, and of acquiring, possessing and protecting property and reputation, and of pursuing their own happiness" (1818).

[106]See Appendix 2.

[107]Ibid.

[108]See Law's comment at the January 5, 1844, council meeting, also note 17 in this chapter.

Article 8, sec[tion] 22, page 365, [of the] Constitution of Illinois.[109] C[ouncillor] [George P.] Stiles spoke[,] [saying a] Nuisance is any thing [that] disturbs the peace of [the] community – & Read [James] Chitty's [1826 edition of] Blackstone['s] [*Commentaries on the Laws of England*][,] page 4.[110] – [He] said the whole community [would] have to rest under the stigma of these falsehoods[111] – If we can prevent the [*Expositor* from the] issuing of any more slanderous communications[,] he would go in for it. – It is right for this community to shew a proper resentment – I would go in for suppressing all further publications of the kind.

C[ouncillor] H[yrum] Smith believed the best way [would be] to smash the press all to pieces and pie[112] the type. C[ouncillor] A[aron] Johnson concurred ~~whith~~ with what other counsellors had said. A[lderman] [Samuel] Bennet refered to the statement of the Expositor relative to the Municipal Court in [the] case of Jeremiah Smith[113] – and considered [the paper] a public Nuisance.

---

[109]The section reads: "The printing presses shall be free to every person, who undertakes to examine the proceeding of the General Assembly or of any branch of government; and no law shall ever be made to restrain the right thereof. The free communication of thoughts and opinions is one of the invaluable rights of man, and every citizen may freely speak, write, and print on any subject, being responsible for that liberty."

[110]William Blackstone's *Commentaries on the Laws of England* (London: W. Walker, 1826) was a four-volume historical treatise that was used as a source for common law. The section read by the council stated:

> A fourth species of remedy by the ... party injured, is the *abatement,* or removal of *nuisances* ... [W]hatsoever unlawfully annoys or doth damage to another is a nuisance; and such nuisance may be abated, that is, taken away or removed, by the party aggrieved thereby, so as he commits no riot in the doing of it. ... And the reason why the law allows this private and summary method of doing one's self justice, is because injuries of this kind [such as the erection of a gate across a public highway], which obstruct or annoy such things as are of daily convenience and use, require an immediate remedy; and cannot wait for the slow progress of the ordinary forms of justice. (3:4-5)

A footnote read: "As to private nuisances, they may also be abated. ... So it seems that a libelous print or paper, affecting a private individual, may be destroyed, or, which is the safer course, taken and delivered to a magistrate."

[111]Stiles cited "Priest wrongs Vol 2," probably in reference to volume 2 of Blackstone's *Commentaries,* but the relevance is unknown.

[112]That is, to scatter or spill.

[113]Jeremiah Smith was born in 1782 in New Ipswich, New Hampshire,

B[enjamin] Warrington [said he was] convinced [t]his [was] a peculiar ^situation^ for the city council to pass this a[ction][,] [to declare a newspaper] a nuisance[,] [and] would [not] be hasty & [he] propose[d] giving a few days limitation & assess a fine of $3000.00 for any libel – & if they would not cease publishing [the] libels[,] [then] declare it a nuisance.[114] C[ouncillor] Warrington said the ~~counsellor~~ State made provisions [for such instances]. – [They could] fine [the paper] 500.00.

[The] Mayor replied [that] they threatened to shoot him when at Carthage & the women and others dare not go to Carthage to [confront the] prosecute[rs] – and read a libel from the Expositor concerning Jeremiah Smith – and explained and showed the falsehood of the Expositor. [Jeremiah] Smith was openly in the streets of the city daily[,] [he said]. C[ouncillor] H[yrum] Smith spoke of the [libelous content of the] Warsaw Signal.

[The] Mayor was sorry to have one dissenting voice[.] – C[ouncillor] Warrington did not mean to be understood to go [against the proposition][115] but [would] not be in haste. C[ouncillor] [Hyrum] Smith – spoke of the Mortgages on the property of the proprietors of the Expositors [and thought the city could not collect fines against them]. A[lderman] E[lias] Smith considered there is but one course to pursue[.] They were out of the reach of the law. – [There is] one course[,] to put an end to the thing at once. – [He] believed if the city did not do it others would – by what he had heard.

C[ouncillor] Hunter believed it to [be] a Nuisance – and refered to the Opinion of Judge Pope on Habeas Corpus[116] and spok[e]

---

and was a relative of Joseph Smith (*History of Church,* 6:416). The *Expositor* explained that Jeremiah was a federal fugitive accused of embezzling $4,000. When a U.S. marshal asked Joseph Smith to help locate the man, Joseph said he "knew nothing about him," to which the marshal promised to bring federal troops to conduct a search. In light of this, Joseph immediately produced the fugitive, along with a writ of habeas corpus, and the city let the man go free.

[114]Here the transcript reads "Mayor – Quincy," the meaning of which is unknown. The mayor, John Wood, is referred to in the minutes for July 1, 1844 (not to be confused with Joseph Smith's attorney, James W. Woods).

[115]Instead of "against the mayor," the transcript reads "vs. the mayor."

[116]On January 4, 1843, Judge Nathaniel Pope ruled in Springfield, Illinois, that an arrest warrant for Joseph Smith from December 1842 was invalid. Since the judge did not address the Nauvoo Charter or nuisances,

in favor of our charter – &c. [He had] asked F[rancis] M. Higbee, before the Grand Jury, if he was not the man he saw at Joseph's making professions of friendship[.] [Higbee] said he was not. – [He] asked Dr Foster if he did not state before hundreds of people that you believe Joseph a Prophet? No! said Foster. – They were under oath when they said it.

A[lderman] [Orson] Spencer accorded with the views expressed, that this paper is a nuisance. [He] did not consider it wise to give them ~~time~~ [liberty] to trumpet a thousand lies their property could not pay for. If we pass only a fine or imprisonment, have we any confidence that they will desist? None at all. – [He] found these men [to be] covenant breakers with God [and] with their wives, &c. Have we any hope of their doing better[?] – Their [moral] characters have gone before them.

Counsellor [John] Taylor said [that] when [he was] at Quincy the people said no body cared for [Joseph Smith] – they all believed him to be a scoundrel [like] Higbee. A[lderman] Spencer Continued. – Shall they be suffered to go on[?] No[,] I had rather my blood would be spilled – and would like to have the press removed as soon as the ordinance will allow. [He] wished the matter [to] be put in the hands of the Mayor and every body stand by him – in the execution of his duties – and hush every murmur.

C[ouncillor] L[evi] Richards said he had felt deeply on this subject, and concurred fully in Gen[eral] Smiths views as expressed ~~by him~~ this day. – [He] considered private interest as nothing in comparison with the public good. – Every time a line was formed in Far West

---

his opinion seems irrelevant to the current deliberation. However, his discussion of natural law is interesting, wherein he argued that "man in a state of nature is a sovereign, ... But when he unites himself with a community, he lays down all the prerogatives of sovereign (except self defense,) and becomes a subject. He owes obedience to its laws and the judgments of its tribunals, which he is supposed to have participated in establishing, either directly or indirectly. He surrenders also, the right of self-redress. In consideration of all which, he is entitled to the aegis of that community to defend him from wrongs. He takes upon himself no allegiance to any other community, so owes it no obedience, and therefore cannot disobey it. None other than his own sovereign can prescribe a rule of action to him. Each sovereign regulates the conduct of its subjects, and they may be punished upon the assumption that they know the rule and have consented to be governed by it" (qtd. in *History of Church,* 5:227).

[Missouri] he was there, for what[?] To defend themselves against such scoundrels as are now fighting against us. [He] considered the doings of the council this day of immense Moment, not to this city alone but to the whole world. [He] would go in to put a stop to the thing at once. – Let the thing be thrown out of this city – and have the responsibility off his shoulder & let it fall on the state of Illinois.[117]

[The] R[ecorder] [Phineas] Richards – refered to the scenry at Haun Mill [Missouri] – & the death of his son [George S. Richards] at that place[118] & said he could not sit still when he saw the same spirit arising in this place, and he considered the publishers of the Expositor as much murderers at heart as David was before the death of Uriah.[119] ^[He] was for making a short work of it –^ [He] was prepared to take his stand by the Mayor & whatever he propose[d,] [Richards] would stand by ~~by~~ him to the last – the quicker it is stopped the better.

C[ouncillor] Phelps [said he] had investigated the constitution, [Nauvoo] Charter, & laws. – The power to declare that [newspaper] office a nuisance is granted to us in the Springfield Charter, and a resolution declaring it a nuisance is all that is required.

John Birney [was] sworn [and] [claimed that] Francis M. Higbee & William Law said they had commenced their operations and would carry them out law or no law. Stephen Markam [was] sworn [and testified that] F[rancis] M. Higbee said the nihilation of this city is done[,] the Moment a hand is laid on this press.

C[ouncillor] Phelps continued – and refered to Wilson Law in destroying the Character of a child – who had the ~~Child~~ charge of another child. Warren Smith [was] sworn [and said that] F[rancis] M Higbee [had] come to me and proposed to have me go in as a partner Making Bogus Money – [that he] would not work for a living. [Hig-

---

[117]Here the transcript has a stray partial word, "Ge."

[118]Haun's Mill was a Mormon settlement of a dozen families in Caldwell County, Missouri. During the Mormon troubles, the little town was attacked on October 30, 1838, by over 200 mounted, non-Mormon militia who killed eighteen individuals and pillaged the town. It became a rallying point for Mormons as an example of Missouri cruelty. See Stephen C. LeSueur, *The 1838 Mormon War in Missouri* (Columbia: University of Missouri Press, 1987), 162-68.

[119]For the story of David's sending Uriah to his death so that he could take Uriah's wife, see 2 Sam. 11.

bee said the] Witness might go in with him if [the] Witness would advance $50, and [he] shew[e]d me 2 [twice] a dollar he said was made by his dies.

C[ouncillor] Phelps continued [that he] had felt deeper this day than he ever felt before. – [He] wanted to know by yes if there was any one here who wanted to avenge the blood of that Innocent female.[120] Yes resounded from every quarter of the room. – [He] referred to the Tea plot at Boston[.] Are we offering[,] or have we offered[,] to take away the right of any one [by] this [action] 2 day [today]? No!!! from every quarters. – N[o] – Refered to [the] Laws grinding the poor[121] – and spoke at great length – in support of active measures to put down iniquity.

Alderman [George W.] Harris spoke from the Chair [and] expressed his feelings that the press ought to be demolished. [The] Resolution on the printing press [was] read and passed.[122]

[The] Petition of Samuel Gully[123] & 9 others [was] read[,] [the] rules dispensed with[,] and [their] Petition ordered to be granted. – [The] Committee on Petitions of E[dwin] D. Wooley reported unfavorabl[y] – [The] report [was] accepted and [the] Petition ordered to be laid on the table indefinitely.

[The council] voted that the collector of the 4th Ward have an

---

[120]This seems to be in reference to the testimony that morning about the seventeen-year-old girl Wilson Law was allegedly seeing–the blood being in reference to virginity rather than murder.

[121]In contrast to this dim view of the Laws, they ran an ad in the *Nauvoo Expositor* offering to grind flour for the poor.

[122]The *Nauvoo Neighbor Extra,* June 17, 1844, reported that the resolution "passed unanimously, with the exception of Councellor Warrington." It read: "*Resolved* By the City Council of the City of Nauvoo, that the printing office from whence issues the 'Nauvoo Expositor' is a public nuisance, and also all of said Nauvoo Expositors, which may be, or exist in said establishment, and the Mayor is instructed to cause said printing establishment and papers to be removed without delay, in such manner as he shall direct. Passed June 10th, 1844. GEO[RGE] W. HARRIS, Pres[iden]t pro tem. W[illard] Richards, Recorder."

[123]Samuel Gully was born in 1809 in Smithfield, North Carolina, and was residing in Nauvoo by 1843. For his petition, see "To the honerable Mayor Aldermen and counsellors" below. The city council had just declared the *Nauvoo Expositor* a nuisance, and now the council was granting these petitioners the right to destroy Robert Foster's barn in what was clearly a sychronized action. Foster was one of the publishers of the *Expositor.*

extension of 60 days for the collection of taxes for 1843. [At] 10 minutes past 6[,] [the] Council adjourned. Truman Gillet[124] offered his name in testimony vs W[illia]m Law.

‡‡Nauvoo June 10th 1844

To the honerable Mayor Aldermen and counsellors, of the City of Nauvoo. – We the undersigned citizens of s[ai]d City respectfully represent, that we are deeply interrested in the health, and improvement of S[ai]d City. We therefore represent To your Honerable Body, that We deem it expedient that the Old Barn Belonging to Dr [Robert D.] Foster on Hyde Street, Opposite the City Surveyers Office should Be removed, in consequence of the filth in and around s[ai]d Barn[.] We your Petitioners Believe it to be a Perfect Nuisance, and dangerous to the health of the citizens in the vicinity, and pray your Honerable Body will so ordain[.] We your Petitioners as in duty Bound will ever Pray.

**Signers Names[:] A[lanson] Ripley[,] John Scott[,] Sam[ue]l Gully[,] Thomas Hatfield[,] Henry Thomas[,] John F I Allred[,] John Hatfield[,][125] John M. Clark[,] Joseph W Coolidge[,] Albert Clark**

†An ordinance concerning Libels, and for other purposes

Whereas the Saints in all ages of the world, have suffered persecution and death, by wicked and corrupt men under the garb of a more holy appearance of religion; and whereas the Church of Jesus Christ of Latter Day Saints from the moment that its first "truth sprang out of the Earth" till now, has been persecuted with death, destruction and extermination; And whereas men, to fulfill the Scriptures, that a man's enemies are they of his own household, have turned traitors in the Church and combined and leagued with the most corrupt scoundrels and villains that disgrace the Earth unhung,[126] for the heaven[-] daring and damnable purpose of revenge on account of disap-

---

[124]Truman Gillet was born in Schyler, New York, in 1811. He was a missionary in New York and Iowa in 1840 and 1841 and immigrated to Iowa in 1846.

[125]John Hatfield was born in 1819 in Washington, Indiana. He accompanied Joseph Smith to Carthage Jail in June 1844.

[126]"The greatest scoundrel unhung" was an idiomatic reference to an alleged criminal who had managed to escape execution. For a variation,

pointed lust, disappointed projects of speculation, fraud, and unlawful designs, to rob and plunder mankind with impunity, and whereas such wicked and corrupt men have greatly facilitated their unlawful designs; horrid intentions and murderous plans by polluting, degrading and converting the blessings and utility of the press, to the sin[-]smoking and blood[-]stained ruin of innocent communities, by publishing lies, false statements; coloring the truth, slandering men, women, children, societies, and counties, by polishing the characters of black legs,[127] highwaymen[128] and murderers, as virtuous. And whereas a horrid, bloody, secret plan, upheld, sanctioned, and largely patronized by men, in Nauvoo and out of it, who boast that all they want is for the word "go", to exterminate or ruin the Latter day Saints is, for them to do "one" unlawful act, and the work shall be done, is now fostered, cherished, and maturing in Nauvoo, by men too, who helped to obtain the very charter they would break; and some of them drew up and voted for the very ordinances they are striving to use as a "scare crow" to frighten the surrounding country in rebellion; mobbing and war; and whereas, while the blood of our brethren, from wells, holes, and naked prairies, and the ravishment of female virtue, from Missouri, and the smoke from the altars of infamy, prostituted by J[ohn] C. Bennett and continued in the full tide of experiment and disgraceful damnation, by the very self[-]called fragments of a body of degraded men that have got up a press in Nauvoo, to destroy the Charter of the City, to destroy Mormonism, men, women, and children, as Missouri did, by force of arms, by fostering laws that emanate from corruption, and betray with a kiss; wherefore to honor the State of Illinois, and those patriots who gave the Charter, and for the benefit, convenience, health, and happiness of said City.

Sec. 1. Be it ordained by the City Council of the City of Nauvoo, That if any person or persons shall write or publish, in said

---

see "the damndest scoundrel unhung" in John Y. Simon, ed., *The Papers of Ulysses S. Grant: January 1-October 31, 1876,* 27 vols. (Carbondale: Southern Illinois University Press, 2005), 27: 99.

[127]A *blackleg* was "a swindler" or "bookmaker" (Webster, *American Dictionary,* s.v. "blackleg"), not to be confused with a *blackguard* (see note 91).

[128]A *highwayman* was "a mounted man who robbed passengers on the highway" (ibid., s.v. "highwayman").

city, any false statement, or libel any of the Citizens, for the purpose of exciting the public mind against the chartered privileges, peace, and good order of said City, or shall slander, (according to the definition of slander or libel by Blackstone[129] or Kent, or the act in the Statute of Illinois,[130]) any portion of the Inhabitants of said City, or bribe any portion of the Citizens of said City, for malicious purposes; or in any manner or form excite the prejudice of the Community against any portion of the Citizens of said City, for evil purposes, he, she, or they, shall be deemed disturbers of the peace, and upon conviction before the Mayor, or Municipal Court, shall be fined, in any sum not exceeding five hundred dollars, or imprisoned six months, or both, at the discretion of said Mayor or Court.

Sec. 2. Be it further ordained that nothing in the foregoing section shall be so construed as to interfere with the right of any person to be tried by a jury of his vicinage [vicinity]; with the freedom of speech or the liberty of the press, according to the most liberal meaning of the Constitution, the dignity of freemen; the voice of truth; and the rules of virtue.

Sec. 3. And be it further ordained that this ordinance shall be in force, from and after its passage.

**Passed June 10, 1844. Geo[rge] W. Harris, pres[iden]t pro tem. Willard Richards, Recorder.**

---

[129]Joseph Smith, in defending the city's action to Illinois Governor Thomas Ford, stated: "Upon consulting Blackstone upon what might be considered a nuisance, that distinguished lawyer, who is considered authority, I believe, in all our courts, states, among other things, that a libelous and filthy press may be considered a nuisance, and abated as such. ... [O]ne of the most eminent English barristers, whose works are considered standard with us, declares that a libelous press may be considered a nuisance: and our own charter, given us by the legislature of this State, gives us the power to remove nuisances; and by ordering that press abated as a nuisance, we conceived that we were acting strictly in accordance with law. We made that order in our corporate capacity, and the City Marshal carried it out. It is possible there may have been some better way, but I must confess that I could not see it" (*History of Church,* 6:581-82).

[130]Dallin H. Oaks has written that the government could not exercise "prior restraint" against a forthcoming publication, but that according to the understanding at the time, it could censor an existing publication ("The Suppression of the *Nauvoo Expositor,*" *Utah Law Review* 9 [1964-65]: 893).

Elias Smith received his oath of Office, and took his Seat as an Alderman of the City
**June 10, 1844. Willard Richards, Recorder.**

The Printing Establishment of the "Nauvoo Expositor," was declared a nuisance, and ordered to be removed by the Mayor.[131] June 10, 1844.

[The] petition of Samuel Greely and nine others [was] granted, declaring the old Barn on Hyde Street a nuisance, and ordering it to be removed.
**June 10, 1944. Willard Richards, Recorder**

Voted that the Collector of the Fourth Ward have an extension of sixty days to enable him to collect the Taxes for 1843.
**June 10, 1844. Willard Richards Recorder**

‡‡*June 11, 1844; Tuesday.*

Jason R. Luce said [he heard] Ianthus Rolf[132] said while the [*Nauvoo Expositor*] press was burning last eve[ning] [that] before 3 weeks [were out] the [Nauvoo] Mansion House[133] would be strung [pulled] to the ground & he would help do it. And Tall-

---

[131]Before the city council had adjourned at about 6:00 p.m., the police had already entered the *Expositor* offices on Mulholland Street and, as described by Francis Higbee, "tumbled the press and materials into the street and set fire to them, and demolished the machinery with a sledgehammer, and injured the building" (Leonard, *Nauvoo,* 364-66). The police were backed up by two companies of the Nauvoo Legion–about 100 soldiers (Richard E. Bennett, Susan Easton Black, and Donald Q. Cannon, *The Nauvoo Legion in Illinois: A History of the Mormon Militia, 1841-1846* [Norman: Arthur H. Clark Company, 2010], 108, 235-36).

[132]Ianthus Jerome Rolfe was seventeen years old at the time and had recently been arrested for stealing tools. He was born in September 1826 in Rumford, Maine. Soon he would travel west with his parents, Samuel and Elizabeth, to Utah Territory, then on to Nevada City in 1853 to co-found the *Nevada Democrat* with his brother Tallman, who had learned the printing trade under Samuel Brannan at San Francisco's *California Star*. Ianthus returned east to marry his one-time girlfriend, Emily Lindsey, and took her west to Nevada (Maria E. Brower, *Nevada City* [Charleston, SC: Arcadia Publishing, 2005], 18).

[133]The Joseph Smith family lived in the Mansion House.

man Rolf[134] said the city would be strung to the ground within 10 days (Moses Leonard[135] heard it. Joshua Miller[136] was present[)]. ^Henry Redfield[137] said^ Matthias Spencer[138] said that [store-owner David] Bryant said before he would see such things[,] he would wade to his knees in blood. (Others were present).

The day Joseph [Smith] went to Carthage[,] ^[I] was at^ [the] Finch[139] & Rollason Key Stone [store]. [Abner] Powers ^[a] taylor^ was talking with Mr ^N. N.^ Davis–about Joseph's going [to Carthage]. Powers ^of Potsdam N.H.–^ said they would attempt to kill Joseph. Mr Davis replied ["]O[h] no, I think not.["] – Yes says Powers[,] "they will by God & you know it[,] by God."[140]

---

[134]Tallman (also spelled Tolman) Rolfe was fifteen at the time. He was born in September 1824 in Romford, Maine. His father was president of the Nauvoo priests quorum and would soon become a bishop in Winter Quarters. There were eleven children in the family. See note 127.

[135]Moses Leonard was seventeen–born in 1827 in Bradford County, Pennsylvania. He lived with his parents in Nauvoo's 4th Ward neighborhood.

[136]Joshua Miller was also seventeen–born in 1827 in Monroe County, Tennessee. He also resided in Nauvoo's 4th Ward.

[137]David Harvey Redfield was born in Herkimer, New York, in 1807 and joined the Church in 1831. After helping destroy the *Nauvoo Expositor,* he was charged in Carthage, Illinois, with rioting, along with Joseph Smith and sixteen others. He died in 1879.

[138]Matthias Freeman Spencer was born in May 1806 in New Jersey, married Amelia Brown in 1827, and died in Salt Lake City in February 1884.

[139]John M. Finch lived in Rock Island, Illinois, before he opened a store in Nauvoo in 1840. A non-Mormon immigrant from Liverpool who sometimes lectured on socialism, he moved to Dallas City, Illinois, and opened a new store there after the destruction of the *Nauvoo Expositor.* He later moved to Kearney, Nebraska, where he died in 1888 (Samuel Clay Bassett, *Buffalo County, Nebraska, and Its People,* 2 vols. [Chicago: S. J. Clarke, 1916], 110).

[140]This is a difficult paragraph. In the case of Finch, Rollason, and Powers, "N. W.," and Davis, it is an educated guess that they were John Finch, William Rollason (the handwriting could be "Robison"), and Abner Powers (a tailor, but perhaps John Taylor was intended). I have not been able to identify N. N. Davis. In any case, the policeman, Addison Everett, who submitted the statement of "Luther W." to the council, was collecting the kind of gossip that he felt was representative of what people were saying.

On the hill last night just before the police arrived, [I] was talking with ~~Chauney L.~~ Francis M. Higbee[141] [who] said if they lay their hand ~~if they destroy the press~~ upon it (the press) or touch it[,] they may date their downfall from that very hour. In ten days there will not be a Mormon left in Nauvoo. What they – the Mormons do[,] they may expect the same in return.

**Addison Everet,[142] received of Luther W**

Recorders Office. June 11. 1844. Summons was issued for Sylvester Emmons to attend the City Council on the 2d. Saturday of July 10. AM. to answer charges then & there to be prefered vs him for slandering said city council agreeably to the order of said council.

**Passed June 8 1844. W[illard] Richards Recorder & C. C. C. C N.[143]**

‡*June 21, 1844; Friday.*[144] [A] Special Session, June 21, 1844, [was] called by the Mayor. [At] ½ past ~~from~~ 4 oclock P.M. [a] Quorum [was] present. Prayer by W[illiam W.] Phelps.

[The] Council accepted the minutes published in the [Nauvoo] Neighbor of the 19th inst[ant] as true. Affidavit[s][145] [were accepted] of

Hiram B. Mount,[146] & John Cunningham June 20, 1844

---

141Chauncey L. Higbee, younger brother of Francis M. Higbee, was born in Tate, Ohio, in 1821. He was twenty-three years old when he assisted in publishing the *Nauvoo Expositor,* two years after being excommunicated in May 1842 for sexual promiscuity. An attorney, he went on to become a prominent lawyer, state senator, banker, and judge in Pittsfield, Illinois, where in 1908 a high school was named after him. He died in Pittsfield in 1884 (John M. Palmer, ed., *The Bench and Bar of Illinois: Historical and Reminiscent,* 2 vols. [Chicago: Lewis Publishing, 1899), 1051-52).

142Addison Everett was born in 1805 in Walhall, New York, where he was baptized in 1837. He was a policeman in Nauvoo. He died at eighty years of age.

143Probably "City Councillor, City Council of Nauvoo." The same notice of a summons was recorded in the Record of Proceedings.

144See also *History of Church,* 6:521-22.

145Most of these affidavits are in *History of Church,* 6:505-16.

146Hiram B. Mount was born in 1809 in Ontario, New York. He was residing in Nauvoo by 1845. He testified, along with John Cunningham, that non-Mormons arrived at the Morley Settlement outside of Nauvoo on

| | |
|---|---|
| Cyrus Canfield[147] & Gilbert Belnap[148] | " 18 " |
| David Evans & William E. Horner[149] | " 19 " |
| Isaac Morley,[150] Gardner Snow,[151] John Edmiston, [and] Ed[war]d Durphy | " 20 " |
| Solomon Hancock,[152] W[illia]m Garner, & John G. Lofton | " 20 " |
| Allen Wait[153] | " 20 " |

---

June 15 and demanded the Mormons' guns, telling them to either join the county militia or retreat to Nauvoo (ibid., 6:508).

147Cyrus Culver Canfield was born in 1817 in Columbus, Ohio. He was a member of the Mormon Battalion. He died in 1889. In his affidavit, he stated that he and Gilbert Belknap overhead Joseph H. Jackson say "the Governor of Illinois was as big a scoundrel as Joseph Smith" and that "the mob were coming to Nauvoo with sufficient force to take Smith" (ibid., 6:502).

148Gilbert Belnap was born in 1821 in Ontario, Canada. He was baptized in 1842 and died in 1899.

149Along with Anson Call, Evans and Horner stated that they were sent as city representatives to consult with Hancock County Militia Colonel Levi Williams, who on orders from the governor was assembling a regiment to keep the peace. However, while in the colonel's camp, they overheard plans being talked of to tar and feather Joseph Smith (*History of Church,* 6:505-06).

150Isaac Morley was born in Montague, Massachusetts, in March 1786, and moved to Ohio sometime before his service in the War of 1812. He and his family were members of Sidney Rigdon's Campbellite congregation in Kirtland, Ohio, and were baptized, along with him, into the LDS Church in 1830. He was a bishop's counselor in Independence, Missouri; bishop of Morley's Settlement, twenty-five miles south of Nauvoo in Lima Township; and president of the Lima Stake which straddled Adams and Hancock Counties. He immigrated to Utah Territory in 1848 and helped settle Sanpete Valley, which is where he died in 1865. His testimony, along with Snow, Edmiston, and Durfee, was essentially the same as from Hiram Mount and John Cunningham (ibid., 6:509-10).

151Gardner Snow was born in Chesterfield, New Hampshire, 1793. He was baptized in 1833. He died in 1889.

152Solomon Hancock was born in 1793 in Springfield, Massachusetts. He was baptized in 1830 in Ohio and moved to Illinois in 1839, then to Iowa in 1846. He died on the way to the Salt Lake Valley in 1847. In his affidavit, he testified, along with William Garner and John Lofton, to the same as was stated by Hiram Mount and John Cunningham (*History of Church,* 6:510-11).

153Allen T. Wait was told by Colonel Levi Williams that he needed to surrender his arms or join the county militia against Nauvoo.

| | |
|---|---|
| James Guyman[154] | " 20 " |
| Alvin Tippets | " 20 " |
| Obadiah Bowers | " 20 " |
| Thomas G. Wilson[155] | " 16 " |
| Stephen Markham[156] | " 17 " |
| John P. Green & John M Bernhisel[157] | " 20 " |
| Truman Gillet Jr. | " 18 " |
| Carlos W. Lyon[158] | " 20 " |
| H. P. Hugins[159] | May 21 " |

Dr Bernhisel, John Taylor, [and] Willard Richards were appointed to meet the Governor [Thomas Ford] in council[.] John P. Green's affidavit [of] June 21st [was] read[.] Joseph Smiths affidavit [of June]

---

[154]James Guymon was born in 1816 in Jackson, Tennessee. He was baptized in 1836 and was living in Nauvoo by 1840. He died in 1912.

[155]Wilson said that a certain Robert Johnson told him that "the arms of the Quincy Greys had been sent up to Warsaw; that they had five cannon at Warsaw; ... and the Quincy Greys and other companies from Adams county were to meet the Missourians in Carthage ... and if Joseph and Hyrum and the City Council were not given up they would blow up the city" (*History of Church,* 6:480).

[156]In his affidavit, Markham stated that he read in "the public papers, especially the Warsaw papers," that Nauvoo was about to be attacked. This was not something he knew independently (ibid., 6:492).

[157]John M. Bernhisel was born in Tyrone, Pennsylvania, in 1799 and graduated from the University of Pennsylvania Department of Medicine prior to being baptized in New York in 1842. He moved to Nauvoo in 1843 and became an influential member of the Council of Fifty. After he immigrated to Utah in 1847-48, he served as the territorial delegate to the U.S. Congress, 1851-59, 1861-63. He died in September 1881 in Salt Lake City.

In his affidavit, he and John P. Greene swore that "a body of citizens, in a mass meeting convened on the 13th instant at Carthage, resolved to exterminate the Latter-day Saints of the said city of Nauvoo" and that "bodies of armed men are coming from the State of Missouri, and also from the territory of Iowa," bringing "cannon and ammunition" by way of "steamboats." Like Stephen Markham, he did not seem to learn these facts on his own but read them in the June 15 extra of the *Warsaw Signal* (ibid., 6:516).

[158]In Carlos W. Lyon's affidavit, he stated that while in St. Louis, the gossip on the street was that arms were being sent to Warsaw, Illinois, on steamers (ibid., 6:507).

[159]Huggins stated that Thomas B. Johnson, former U.S. Marshal of Iowa Territory, said at the end of May that he intended to bring U.S. dragoons from Iowa to Nauvoo (ibid., 6:423).

21 [was read].[160] [A] Letter from Sylvester Emmons [was] Read. Alderman [George W.] Harris considered it a good letter & moved it be ~~published~~ accepted – carried. [It was] voted that Counsellor Emmons resignation be accepted.

[The] Clerk of the council was instructed to prepare all necessary papers and affidavits [to be] ready for the Governor in the morning. [The] Council adjourned.

> †Voted that the Resignation of Counsellor [Sylvester] Emmons be accepted.
> **June 21, 1844. Willard Richards, Recorder**

‡*July 1, 1844; Monday.*[161] 12 am. At a meeting of the City Council of the City of Nauvoo, [the following were present][:] Councillor[s] W[illiam] W. Phelps[,] George P. Stiles[,] Aaron Johnson[,] Phinehas Richards[,] [and] Levi Richards[;] Aldermen Orson Spencer[,] N[ewel] K. Whitney[,] Samuel Bennett[,] George W. Harris[,] William Marks[,] Elias Smith[,] [and] Hiram Kimball[;] Willard Richards Recorder[;] [and] John P. Green Marshall[.] Alderman Harris was appointed President of the Council.

W[illard] Richards ~~read~~ prayed. He then read a communication from Gov[erno]r [Thomas] Ford by Col[one]l [Hart] Fellowes[162] and

---

[160]Joseph Smith said he was in a tavern in Carthage, Illinois, on May 27, when Charles A. Foster took him aside and told him there was a conspiracy against his life and that he "had not better go out of doors. If he did, his blood would be shed. Foster said he was deponent's friend, and did not want to see bloodshed" (ibid., 6:523).

[161]Joseph and Hyrum were shot and killed in the Carthage jail on June 27, 1844. After the destruction of the *Nauvoo Expositor,* Joseph Smith was arrested, then used habeas corpus to arrange to be tried in Nauvoo, where he was acquitted by the municipal court on June 17. This outraged non-Mormons in surrounding areas. While both sides prepared for conflict, Illinois Governor Thomas Ford went to Carthage to try to diffuse the situation. While there, he demanded that Smith come to Carthage to be tried. On June 24, Smith arrived in Carthage with Hyrum Smith, John Taylor, Orrin Porter Rockwell, William W. Phelps, Willard Richards, and thirteen members of the Nauvoo City Council. Joseph and Hyrum Smith, John Taylor, and Willard Richards were told the jail was the safest place for them; the others returned to Nauvoo. On June 27, after Ford left, a group of men stormed the jail. Taylor and Richards were wounded, the Smiths killed.

[162]Hart Fellows was born in Cincinnati, lived in Indiana, and helped

A[braham] Jonas[163] Esq[ui]re.[164] – also a communication from them to this City Council[165] – also at the request of Ald[erman] Harris[,] [Richards] read a letter from Gov[erno]r Ford to Gen[era]l Deming at Carthage [Illinois][166] – [Harris] then addressed the City Council – and read a series of Resolutions – [It was] motioned by W[illiam] W. Phelps that they pass – & by Ald[erman] Harris to pass by sections[.]

---

settle the town of Rushville in the northeastern corner of Illinois. He served in the Black Hawk War of 1831-32. In the post office in Rushville, there is a New Deal mural, *Hart Fellows, Builder of Rushville,* that commemorates his life ("Rushville Township History," *Schuyler County,* http://schuyler.ilgenweb.net).

[163]Abraham Jonas was born in Devonshire, England, in 1801. He moved to Illinois, where he served in the legislature. He was the first Masonic Grand Master of Illinois and helped establish Nauvoo's lodge in 1841. He served as the postmaster of Quincy, Illinois. He died in 1864.

[164]Ford's communication read: "Colonel Fellows and Captain Jonas are requested to proceed by the first boat to Nauvoo, and ascertain what is the feeling, disposition, and determination of the people there, in reference to the late disturbances; ascertain whether any of them propose in any manner to avenge themselves, whether any threats have been used, and what is proposed generally to be done by them.

"They are also requested to return to Warsaw and make similar inquiries there; ascertain how far false rumors have been put afloat for the purpose of raising forces; what is the purpose of the militia assembled, whether any attack is intended on Nauvoo.

"Ascertain also, whether any person from Missouri or Iowa intends to take part in the matter, and in my name forbid any such interference, without my request, on pain of being demanded for punishment" (*History of Church,* 7:150).

[165]Fellows and Jonas wrote: "Gentlemen, – With this you will receive a copy of instructions from Governor Ford to us. You will understand from them what we desire from you in action on your part, as the only authorities of your city now known to the country, of such a character as will pacify the public mind and satisfy the governor of your determination to sustain the supremacy of the laws, which will, we are sure, be gratifying to him" (ibid.).

[166]Miner R. Deming was born in February 1810 in Sharon, Connecticut. A teacher in Cincinnati before moving to Illinois, he was appointed brigadier general and commander-in-chief of the Illinois State Militia in 1842. Sympathetic to Mormons, he would receive their votes two months later when he successfully ran for the office of county sheriff. Unfortunately, he would die of a fever the next year (Judson Keith Deming, ed., *Genealogy of the Descendants of John Deming of Wethersfield, Connecticut* [Dubuque: Mathis-Mets, 1904], 438).

Ford's letter to Deming stated: "It is my present opinion that the Mor-

[The] 1st carried[,] [the] 2nd carried, 3rd carried, 4th carried, 5th carried.[167]

Councillor Phelps stated that there would be a meeting this evening at four oclock of the Inhabitants of the City, so that they may approve of these resolutions. Councillor Phelps moved an adjournment. Some letters from Carthage [were read]. Dr. [Willard] Richards read a letter from state legislator W[illiam] A. Richardson,[168] another from [the same person], [and letters from] E. A. Conger, [Quincy Mayor] John Wood, & another from F[rancis] M. Higbee[.] Councillor Orson Spencer said [he] ought to mention for [the benefit of] all [present] the whole [history of the] establishment [of the Nauvoo Expositor].

Coun[cillor] Phelps thanked all the writers but one, [then suggested that the council] respond to the others and do what is right. "Resolved that we tender our thanks to ~~Messrs~~ W[illiam] A. Richardson Esq[ui]re for his proposition to settle for the "Nauvoo Exposi-

---

mons will not commit any outbreak, and that no further alarm need be apprehended. I regret to learn that the party in Hancock, who are in favor of violent measures have circulated a thousand false rumors of danger, for the purpose of getting men together without my authority, hoping that when assembled, they may be ready to join in their violent councils. This is a fraud upon the country, and must not be endured.

"I am afraid that the people of Hancock are fast depriving themselves of the sympathy of their fellow citizens, and of the world. I strictly order and enjoin on you that you permit no attack on Nauvoo or any of the people there without my authority. I think it would be best to disband your forces, unless it should be necessary to retain them to suppress violence on either side: of this you must be the judge at present.

"I direct that you immediately order all persons from Missouri and Iowa to leave the camp and return to their respective homes without delay.

"I direct, also, that you cause all mutinous persons, and all persons who advise tumultuous proceedings to be arrested; and that you take energetic measures to stop the practice of spreading false reports put in circulation to inflame the public mind" (ibid., 146).

[167]See below.

[168]William A. Richardson was born in Lexington, Kentucky, in January 1811 and moved to Illinois in 1831. He became a state's attorney for the circuit court, Speaker of the House in the Illinois legislature, a U.S. Congressman, and eventually U.S. Senator. He fought in the War with Mexico. In 1857 President Buchanan appointed him governor of Nebraska Territory. He died in December 1875 (David F. Wilcox, ed., *Quincy and Adams County History and Representative Men* [Chicago: Lewis Publishing, 1919), 2:834.

tor" Printing Press, and also tender our thanks to Mess[ieu]rs Richardson[,] Wood[,] & Conger for their endeavors to restore peace. As to the press[,] we will do whatever is right towards a remuneration "whenever we ascertain the minds of all the Proprietors of the Expositor." Moved by Ald[erman] Phelps that the resolution pass – and it was carried. Moved that Hiram Kimball be appointed to [make an] [en]treat[y] with the Proprietors of the said Expositor – and carried.

W[illard] Richards moved that Mr. James be heard on the subject of the ~~mob~~ citizens at La Harpe[169] and he spoke accordingly. He [had] attended [the session] at the [town] meeting – & spoke on the protection of the peace, and support of the laws. They looked on the outrage with detestation and abhorrence, & ^they would^ use ^none but lawful^ all means to bring to Justice the assassins and ^they would^ sustain the laws, & keep the peace, was the opinion of the general meeting [at La Harpe]. Ald[erman] Harris moved an adjournment and [it] carried.[170]

> ‡‡At a meeting of the City Council held in the Council Room in the City of Nauvoo on the first day of July A.D. 1844, having received instructions from Governor Ford through the Agency of A[braham] Jonas Esq[ui]r[e] and Col[onel] [Hart] Fellows, it was unanimously
>
> Resolved. For the purpose of ensuring peace and promoting the welfare of the County of Hancock and surrounding country, that we will rigidly sustain the laws and the [directions of the] Governor of the State so long as they and he sustain us in all our constitutional rights.
>
> Resolved secondly. That to carry the foregoing Resolution into complete effect, that inasmuch as the Governor has taken from us the Public Arms, that we solicit of him to do the same by all the rest of the Public Arms of the State.

---

[169]At La Harpe, twenty miles east of Nauvoo, "eight or ten men, in a warlike attitude, in company with two teams," were heard bragging that they had shot at two Mormons and thought they may have "killed them both" (*History of Church,* 6:530).

[170]At this point, the minutes repeat (omitted here) with the added wording shown in italics: "Councillor Orson Spencer said it ought to mention for all the whole establishment *of the Nauvoo Expositor*"; "the opinion of the General Meeting *at La Harpe*"; "*^would^* do what is right."

Resolved thirdly. To further secure the peace, friendship and happiness of the people, and allay the excitement that now exists, ~~that no~~ we will reprobate [denounce] private revenge on the assassinators of General Joseph Smith and General Hyrum Smith ~~shall be made~~ by any of the Latter Day Saints. That instead of an appeal to arms, we appeal to the majesty of the law, and will be content with whatever judgement it shall award, and should the law fail, we leave the matter with God.

Resolved unanimously. That this City Council pledges themselves for the City of Nauvoo, that no aggressions by the citizens of said City shall be made ~~on the Citizens of said City shall be made~~ on the Citizens of the surrounding country, but we invite them as friends, and neighbors, to use the Saviors Golden rule, and do unto others as they would have others do unto them, and we will do likewise.

Resolved lastly that we highly approve of the present public pacific course of the Gov[erno]r to allay excitement and restore peace among the citizens of this country – ~~munity~~ and while he does so and will use his influence to stop all vexatious proceedings in law until confidence is restored[,] so that the citizens of Nauvoo can go to Carthage or any other place for trial without exposing themselves to the violence of assassins[,] ~~he~~ we will uphold him and the law by all honorable means.[171]

‡*July 2, 1844; Tuesday.* 6 oclock PM. Special Session. Alderman Orson Spencer – was elected President Pro tem. Prayer by W[illiam] W Phelps. [Some] special business of the council [was] called for by vote.

W[illard] Richards ^spoke^ [and said][:] I took~~en~~ the liberty of calling this Council for the purpose of setting before them the state of the people & the [Nauvoo] Legion for the purpose of Securing Means, as provisions are scarce indeed, and as there is some Murmuring amongst the Soldiers for some of them only can get one Meal in a day or two days and in such a state of things it will not last long[,] for if a Man has the spirit of a soldier it will rise and of course they will take where they can get – therefore I thought it was best to send

[171]The Record of Proceedings has three of these five resolutions, signed by recorder Willard Richards and temporary council president George W. Harris.

some people to the Territory of Iowa for there we can get plenty of provision as will put us ~~pu~~ over till the harvest. Gen[eral] [Jonathan] Dunham [confirmed that the Nauvoo Legion was wanting].

Mr. [Isaac] Morley said that they had a few acres of wheat which would soon be ready if peace was obtained[,] and he calculated to bring it here to supply the inhabitants. Geo[rge] W. Harris [said] all donations given into the City should go to the Bishops for the support of the poor for we are commanded to look after the poor. And what is obtained by loan should go to the support of the Legion –

The Legion was called together to take Measures for the sustenance of the poor till the Twelve [Apostles] come.[172] Motioned, seconded & carried that the high Council be a Committee to collect Means to provide for the support of the poor, for the present. Motioned secd & carried that the inhabitants sustain them in this calling and give them all information in their power[.] This was carried unanimously –

Moved & Seconded ^& carried^ that Cha[rle]s Patton[173] & W[illia]m H. Jordan[174] ~~go to Iowa & L. S. Dalrymple~~ & L[ewis] S. Dalrymple[175] were appointed [a] committee for [seeking aid from] Iowa[.] Moved & Carried that A. Morrison & D[aniel] M. Repsher[176]

---

[172]At this time, most of the Twelve Apostles were on missions for the Church.

[173]Charles W. Patten was born in November 1811 in Newport, New York. In 1841 he was living across the river from Nauvoo in Iowa, but he soon moved to Nauvoo to become a crane operator at the temple site. He and his wife had eleven children. They were together at Winter Quarters, although Charles disappears from the record after heading west, presumably dying along the trail. Peggy later joined the RLDS Church.

[174]William H. Jordan was born in 1802. As a non-Mormon in 1841, he attended a high council meeting in Nauvoo with the intent to badger Joseph Smith and was so unexpectedly impressed, he converted to the Church. He lived nearby in Iowa, and it was at his house that Joseph Smith hid in June 1844 before deciding to submit to arrest in Carthage.

[175]Lewis S. Dalrymple was born in 1809 in Saratoga County, New York. He was baptized in 1840 and was living in Nauvoo by January 1842.

[176]Daniel M. Repsher was born in 1804 in Philadelphia. In Nauvoo he was a policeman, a fife player for the legion, and a Seventies Quorum president. His wife, Roxena, left him in July 1843 to become a plural wife of James Adams (Gary James Bergera, "Identifying the Earliest Mormon Polygamists, 1841-44," *Dialogue: A Journal of Mormon Thought* 3 [Fall 2005], 5). What became of him after the fall of Nauvoo is unknown.

& Capt[ai]n Ross be appointed [a] Committee for [seeking aid from] the North. Moved & carried that Benjamin Clapp go to the east & Sam[ue]l James[177] also Bro[ther] Hyrum Clark[178] were appointed [a] Committee for the east.

Moved & Carried that a Committee be appointed to negociate to get Means for the present emergency of the army[.] Moved & carried that L[ucius] N. Scovil,[179] E[dwin] D. Wooley, & W[illia]m A. Gean[180] be the committee. N[ewel] K. Whitney [said] as for myself I think it would [be important] to look after the provision[s] [generally] as there are many poor people in this city besides the Soldiers.

P[hineas] Richards [said] I think it would be necessary to give these [people] some instructions [on] how to get provisions whether by contribution or any other way or by loan. I know there are more people [who are] more so in want than many of the soldiers out in my part [to the] east. John P. Green [said] I would like to know if it is for the poor or for the Legion entirely that the provisions is for. I am aware & have a knowledge that there is a great Many in want, besides the Legion, & they would require something to keep them or else they will have to leave this place.

W[illiam] W. Phelps [said] that when these Men go for the provisions[,] that they [need to know if it should] go through the hands of the City Council or the Marshall or Maj[or] Gen[eral] Dunham & then [perhaps] to the officers of the different Regi[men]ts to dis-

---

[177]Samuel James was born in Pennsylvania in 1814. He was baptized by 1836 and became a member of the high council in Kirtland, Ohio. After Joseph Smith's death, he became a counselor to Sidney Rigdon in Pittsburgh. He died in Ohio in 1876.

[178]Hiram Clark was born in Wells, Vermont, in 1795. He joined the Church in 1835. He served two missions to England and was president of the Hawaiian mission in 1850-51. He committed suicide in San Bernardino in 1853.

[179]Lucius N. Scovil was born in March 1806 in New Haven, Connecticut. Baptized in 1836 in Kirtland, Ohio, in Nauvoo he established a bakery and was warden of the Masonic lodge. In 1848 he was sent to New Orleans to assist Church members emigrating from Great Britain. In 1860 he served a mission to New York. He died in February 1889 in Springville, Utah.

[180]William Gheen was born in Downingtown, Pennsylvania, in 1798 and was raised a Quaker. He moved to Nauvoo after being baptized into the LDS fold in 1840. He was ordained a high priest the next year. He died in Nauvoo in 1845.

tribute amongst their Men so that there Might be no murmuring amongst them. As there is prospects of peace now[,] let some of the people go to harvest, for it will open up a communication amongst the inhabitants round about so that they might be enabled to support themselves.

Coun[cillor] [George P.] Stiles [said] I concur with Bro[ther] P[hineas] Richards in what he has stated. Notwithstanding that Many of the Legion, especially the Artillery, [who] said they had no Means at present to obtain any provisions, I though[t] it was the duty of the Bishops to look after the poor and endeavor by all means to get some little [help] for them. [It was] moved & carried that the council adjourn.

> †Motioned, seconded, and carried that the [Nauvoo Stake] High Council be a committee to collect means to provide for the support of the poor for the present, and that the Inhabitants sustain them in this calling, and give them all information in their power.
>
> **July 2, 1844. Orson Spencer Pres[iden]t pro tem. Willard Richards Recorder.**
>
> Motioned and carried that Charles Patten & W[illia]m H. Jordan & L[ewis] L. Dalrymple be a committee for Iowa Territory. Motioned and carried that A. Morrison, D[aniel] M. Repsher and Capt[ai]n Ross be a committee for the North. That Benjamin Clapp, Samuel James, & Hyrum Clark be a committee for the East. That L[ucius] N. Scovil, E[dwin] D. Woolley, & W[illia]m A. Gean be a Committee to get means for the present emergency of the army.
>
> **July 2, 1844. Orson Spencer Pres[iden]t pro tem. Willard Richards, Recorder**

‡*July 8, 1844; Monday.* 1 o clock PM. Special Session. [The] Names of [the] Members [were] called. D[aniel] H. Wells, Ald[erman][,] [was] chosen Pres[ident] pro Tem. Prayer [was offered] by Geo[rge] W. Harris. W[illiam] W. Phelps request[ed] the Recorder to Read the communication of Gov[ernor] [Thomas] Ford to Dr. [Robert D.] Foster.

W[illard] Richards said you all know the circumstance which was occassioned yesterday at the Stand by some persons on acc[oun]t of

Dr Foster Coming to this City.[181] Mr [Hiram] Kimball was deputed by this Council to transact business on their behalf – & he pledged his all that he would be responsible for Dr Foster & see that he ~~was~~ [would] be protected till he sees about his property here &c & gets it exchanged or leave[s] it in the hands of ~~or~~ some one to act as proxy for him. W[illard] Richards then read a letter from Dr R[obert] D. Foster to the City Council.

W[illiam] W. Phelps said I used all the influence I had & [even with] the statement [guaranteeing Foster's safefy] being there & Gen[eral] Deming [being] here[,] I think an Agent can transact all his business & as there is debts owing to the Mayors office[,] it also can be arranged & put in [order] and an Agent can do all that is wanted & he can go away and not be assassinated & there is ~~so~~ Many Men here which is so exasperated that I think his life would not be in safety.

H[iram] Kimball. I would just state what I know in the first place[.] I went to Carthage to see the Higbees & then to Dr Foster & had some conversation ^with^ him concerning the Matter, [and] he said he had a letter from the Gov[erno]r to Cap[tai]n Dunn as he wanted to come here to settle himself as a citizen and transact his own business & [see] if he can Not leave here in peace & go away & if he can not sell [his home] he is willing to exchange it for other property[.] I tried all I could to get him here on my own pledge ~~of~~ for his safety & not have a company from Carthage to come in with him ~~from~~ for his protection & it was with much difficulty [that] he con-

---

[181]The *History of the Church* is silent on "what occasioned yesterday at the Stand" but does state that "R[obert] D. Foster arrived in the city. His presence produced some excitement in consequence of the saints believing he was accessory to the murder of the Prophets" (7:169). William Clayton recorded: "I was told on the way that R[obert] D. Foster is in Nauvoo having a permit from the Governor [Thomas Ford] to come and settle business. O[rrin] P. Rockwell, M[erinus] G. Eaton and Theodore Turley are raging and threaten his life if he tarry here, consequently the City Council have sent a guard to take care of him. I reasoned with Rockwell and tried to show him the folly of his conduct inasmuch as the Governor had said that if one of those men were assassinated the whole city would be held responsible, and that President Joseph [Smith] gave himself up into the hands of his murderers for the express purpose of saving the City from being Massacred. But no reasoning seemed to touch him. He swore bitterly he would have revenge and that Foster should not tarry here. I feel grieved at this conduct, for there is now a little prospect that the public sympathy will turn in our favor if we keep still" (qtd. in Smith, *Intimate Chronicle*, 137-38).

sented to come here under My charge. – F[rancis] M. Higbee is Now in Warsaw waiting for an answer to see what is to be done.

Coun[cillor] [George P.] Stiles – said he ^Dr Foster^ is ~~the one is~~ ^was^ the first who brought on all this trouble & the enormous expense which this Community has been under & I think it is giving him too Much honor to give him any More protection[,] More than any other person, for he has been the person who has brought up all this excitement of this people (& not only so) but all the work [we have to do to make things right]. D[anie]l H. Wells concurred fully in Coun[cillor] Stiles statement [and] said if he looses his property he has brought it on by his own conduct & of course he Must suffer the loss.

S[amuel] Bennett sustained the conduct & [thought the council should] approve of the course of Hiram Kimball & discharge him from all censure [in] bringing Dr Foster to this City & that he [should] still continue to undertake & try & make a settlement with the proprietors. W[illiam] W. Phelps – again – spoke a great length on the conduct of Dr Foster and the course he has taken. [It was] moved by Mr Bennett & Seconded & carried that Ald[erman] Kimball [should] receive a Vote of thanks for the honorable course he has pursued in reference to Dr. Foster – & that he be requested to continue his agency relative to [settling for] the press of the Nauvoo Expositor –

Geo[rge] W. Harris [said that] relative to the [loss of the] press[,] when we sat in Council & let that suit be [brought and] put [ordinances] into the law [that were favored] by either party[,] [we incurred liabilities] & I think it would cost $1500 or 2000 [in reimbursement] cost & paying their attorney & it is My opinion that H[iram] Kimball['s] duty is not done –

O[rson] Spencer [agreed] in regard to the press & the agency of Ald[erman] Kimball & [agreed] that he [should] receive our thanks for what he has done & let him Negociate with the proprietors [but] when we declared that [the] printing Press [was] a Nuisance[,] I never thought we would have to pay for destroying it – but whatever the laws is, we will be amenable to the laws & we will settle for it.

Elias Smith – said it had never entered his head that he would have to pay it & he concurred in the statement of Couns[illor] Stiles. D[aniel] H. Wells – said it was in his Mind that we would have to pay for the press & perhaps More, & damages. If Men would take the right way of it, the easiest way is the best[.] [It would be best] if we pay for it & not let it go into law – for doing so [settling out of court] we will find it all the best.

Geo[rge] W. Harris spoke again relative to the payment of that Press. – These Nuisances, or any other house, or slaughter house if they take it away or removes it, they are under the necessity of paying for it. W[illiam] W. Phelps – said the Marshall can do as he pleases ^about keeping a watch about Foster^ & that we the City Council had nothing to do with it, that if he chooses to appoint his own agent to look after his affairs we will look after his property just the same as we have done heretofore –

Ald[erman] [Edward] Hunter – said I am well ~~pallas~~ pleased with the conduct of Ald[erman] Kimball & as for Fosters property some time ago Bro[ther] Joseph said to me that I had better buy it & I bought his property at that time for he was in a very ragged condition & not fit to travel with & Bro[ther] Joseph give him the loan of $100 –

> †Motioned and carried that Alderman [Hiram] Kimball receive a vote of thanks for the honorable course he has pursued in reference to Dr. Foster, and that he be requested to continue his agency relative to the press of the Nauvoo Expositor.
>
> **Passed July 8th, 1844. Daniel H. Wells Pres[iden]t pro tem. Willard Richards, Recorder.**

‡*July 13, 1844; Saturday.* [At] 2 [minutes] p[ast] 10, [the] Names [were] called. Ald[erman] N[ewel] K. Whitney [was] appointed chairman[.] [The] reading of the Minutes [was] dispensed with, [and with] no business being brought forward[,] [the] meeting [was] adjourned until [the] next regular meeting. [The] meeting [was] again called to order by J[ohn] P. Green [and] W[illiam] W. Phelps spoke as to keeping up the Police[.] The Marshall wants the authority of this Council to provide food for them.

Coun[cillor] [George P.] Stiles enquired if there was any ordinance to pay the police – [and said] if there is no provision of that sort made[,] it ought to be. The Recorder knows of no ordinance regulating pay of the police. Ald[erman] [Orson] Spencer thought there was some resolution, authorizing the mayor to employ the Police and to regulate their pay. [The] Resolution [was] made by the Recorder.

"Resolved by the City Council of the City of Nauvoo that John P. Green Marshal of said city, be and is hereby authorized to draw on the Treasury, for any sum not exceeding two hundred dollars of any monies not otherwise appropriated, or if necessity require, make a loan of the same, for the purpose of supplying the City Police with food.["]

**Moved & seconded that it be adopted & [was] adopted accordingly.**[182]

Willard Richards spoke in regard to an abundance of food passing our doors while a number of persons are starving to death. – Why not extend our powers to catch the fish and feed the poor – dont let the people cry aloud for food while thousands are passing [by] daily [with food]. I simply thr[ew] out this as a suggestion – will there be any more harm to take advantage of the resources of the river – than sending the committees all round the world to gather in food for the city[?]

Levi Richards [said] this is not an idle suggestion – if a little exertion is made it will be of great benefit. W[illiam] W. Phelps said the committees were sent out while we had 500 troops under arms – as we have [left] the police to find food for [themselves] – they can speak.

[The] Recorder handed in a bill of G[eorge] P. Stiles to the amount of $40 which was allowed.[183] [The] Counsel then adjourned until the next regular Session [on the] Second Saturday in Aug[us]t[,] Willard Richards Recorder.

*August 10, 1844; Saturday.*[184] Regular Session, August 10th 1844, 10 Oclock AM. [The] Names of [the] members [were] called [and] Quorum Pres[iden]t Geo[rge] W Harris [was] Elected president Pro tem. [The] Prayer [was given] by O[rson] Pratt. – [The revisions] of [the] preceding unaccepted minutes [were] read & accepted.

John C. Annis [presented a] Petition to erect a water Mill opposite C[harles] Ivins. O[rson] Pratt moved [that] it lie on the table [because] C[ouncillor] [William] Phelps objects to granting [it]. C[ouncillor]

---

182This resolution also appears in the Record of Proceedings, dated and signed by Newel K. Whitney, temporary council president, and Willard Richards, Recorder.

183This allowance also appears in the Record of Proceedings.

184See also *History of Church,* 7:247-48.

[Brigham] Young proposed granting the petition. Al[derman] [William] Mark pleaded the Motion & it was ordered to lie on the table.

[A] Petition of Reuben Atwood[185] ~~granted~~ & 14 oth[ers] for opening Ann St[reet] from Water Street to [the] corporation line [was] read & granted. [It was] voted that ~~the Recorder~~ the Estate of Gen[eral] Joseph Smith be allowed the sum of $15.70 to satisfy for Col[onel] Brewers Road bill. An ordinance concerning Brothels & disorderly characters [was] read twice [and a] 3rd time by its title & passed. – [The members were] satisfied with its title.[186]

A Report [was given] of the attendance of the City Council &c from Feb[ruary] 10th 1844 to Aug[ust] 9, 1844 inclusive. [The] Total [due is] $429.15, [which was] accepted & ordered to be paid. John P. Green, Marshall, stated that he had made a settlement with Amos Davis – on an ~~action~~ suit &c and the council voted to sanction the proceeding of the Marshal.

Ald[erman] O[rson] Spencer referred to settling for the Nauvoo Expositor. Ald[erman] [Hiram] Kimball said he had been told by Charles Ivins that the whole could be settled for $800 if the money could be forth coming – or security to be paid soon. A[t which] Counsellor Phelps – wished [to dispute whether] the [whole matter with the] press might be settled. C[ouncillor] B[righam] Young said if they were to proceed with the riot part, he would go in for their waiting till they could get it [ruled on in court], but if they would take $800 or 1000 and stop all proceedings they [sh]ould go in for it.

~~Alde~~ Councillor Phelps explained [his view] and spoke of the good character of the city and [agreed with] Council[or] B[righam] Young [in that he] wanted counsellor Kimball to settle for the press if the parties will indemnify the city [and] council from all further suits. [It was] Moved & Second that Alderman Kimball be instructed to settle for the Nauvoo Expositor so soon as the proprietors of the press will indemnify the city council from all ~~all further suits~~ suits commenced or to be commenced by them or their influence in future time or the pres[en]t instance.

C[ouncillor] Phelps referred to Esq[ui]r[e] [James W.] Woods – [a] bill also for attending to suits of Gen[eral] [Joseph] Smith at

---

[185]Reuben Atwood was born in May 1797 in Mansfield, Connecticut. He died in February 1863 in Iowa.

[186]See below.

Carthage. Esq[ui]r[e] Wood[s] said he did not feel disposed to bring in a bill but leave it to the generosity of the Council, and requested the Council to consider Mr Reed's Acc[oun]t. C[ouncillor] Young moved [that] Mess[ieurs] Read & Woods present their Bills to the committee of claims [and] send [them] by [way of] Ald[erman] Spencer, ^to be reported at the next regular meeting.^ [This was] carried unanimously. [The meeting was] adjourned till 2 oclock.

[At] 2 P.M. [the] Council assembled according to adjournment. [The] Names of [the] Members [were] called. [A] Quorum [was] present. [The council] voted to reconsider the vote of the morning on the petition of John C. Annis. [It was] moved by C[ouncillor] B[righam] Young to grant the petition of John C. Annis if it interfere with no other rights or privileges. Mr Annis explained [himself]. – Coun[cillor] Phelps replied. [It was] 2d.d. [seconded] and carried.

[The] Petition of Davis McOlney & 20 others of the police [was] read. C[ouncillor] Phelps proposed that an action be had, and was ready to enter into any measures which were wise & would be necessary[.] Coun[cillor] B[righam] Young – would pay the Police Gold & Silver if the ^city^ were able – but they were not – and suggested that certain men might be found to buy the scrip if they could have an interest attached to it, also suggested a voluntary tax of the people to be collected by the bishops.

O[rson] Pratt Moved that some of the council propose to the people a voluntary ~~tax on the~~ [subscription] on the manual [labor] tax. C[ouncillor] Daniel Spencer enquired the amount due the police[.] A[lderman] Geo[rge] A. Smith – said the present taxation amounted to the extent of the [Nauvoo] Charter – and that a voluntary tax or contribution was the only means [available][,] according to Coun[cillor] Pratts Motion.

Counsellor Young proposed to commence [a collection for the police] in the council and said [he would head the list].

| | | | |
|---|---|---|---|
| [Brigham Young] | $ 5.00 paid | Daniel Spencer | 5.00 paid |
| Willard Richards | 5.00 paid | Daniel Repshon | 10.00 |
| H[eber] C. Kimball | 5.00 paid | W[illiam] W. Phelps | 1.00 |
| O[rson] Pratt | 2.00 | N[ewel] K. Whitney | 1.00 paid |
| ~~Amasa Bonnya~~ | ~~coat & hat~~ | O[rson] Spencer | 1.00 paid |
| Daniel Avery | 5.00 | Geo[rge] A. Smith | 1.00 paid |
| John P. Green | 5.00 paid | | $46.00 |

O[rson] Spencer suggested the propriety of changing the plan of having a police[man] [guard the city] by voluntary watch, and exchange [the assignments] from night to night. Coun[cillor] Young ~~said he~~ spoke in favor of relieving the present distress of the Police for what they have served &c

| | |
|---|---|
| Joseph Kingsbury | $ 1.00 paid |
| Amasa Bonney | 2.00 note[187] |
| Charles Shumway | 1.00 paid |

J[ohn] P. Green Marshal reported that there was no money in the Treasury and that he had loaned about $70 for the police. H[eber] C. Kimball spoke. C[ouncillor] Young enquired if the Marshall had not been instructed to get up meetings in the wards to raise funds for the police. Marshall Green said he had been so instructed & done what he could but could raise nothing.

B[righam] Young ~~said~~ proposed giving an interest on Scrip for 1 year. A[lderman] ~~Bennet. Bennett.~~ Kimball – proposed lowering salaries[.] C[ouncillor] ^H[eber] C.^ Kimball offered his dues as [a] council[or]. B[righam] Young[,] d[itt]o[;] Geo[rge] A. Smith[,] d[itt]o[;] H[eber] Kimball[,] d[itt]o[;] W[illiam] W. Phelps[,] $10 on his salary[;] O[rson] Pratt[,] 10–[;] Geo[rge] W Harris[,] 10 " [.]

Hosea Stout, of the police, said the police had considered the subject that they were willing to watch the City while it was necessary & all they wanted was to live while they did it. W[illiam] W. Phelps thought high salaries were good to ~~prevent~~ try men – ~~it was a~~ & learn their liberality – Did not want the old police broken up – It was established by the former Mayor.

Daniel Cair was willing to serve as [a] police[man] if he could only live[,] and they were going to guard the City till they got all [their resources spent], then the rest might guard it till they got it back again. W[illiam] W. Phelps Moved that the council pass a resolution to ~~add~~ pay 10 per cent interest on scrip sufficient to pay the police. B[righam] Young concurred. Col[onel] [Jonathan] Dunham thought interest added to the scrip would not give any relief to the police.[188]

---

[187]This line continues with "of [illegible] paid," maybe "of note paid," which could mean that he paid $2.00 toward a larger note.

[188]Dunham's skepticism was warranted. The municipal scrip already in circulation had little street value. This is why the city stopped issuing it back in March 1843 (see chapter 3; also note 40 in this chapter). The federal

B[righam] Young nominated Daniel Spencer for Mayor till Next election. 2d. [seconded] by H[eber] C. Kimball & carried unanimously – and he accepted. A bill for an ordinance concerning city scrip to pay the police [was] read twice. O[rson] Pratt objected to the bill. Daniel Spencer proposed to defer action on the bill till the subscription [for the police could] go through[.] [The] Bill [was] ordered to be laid on the table. [It was] moved by Daniel Spencer that the Bishops offer the subscription to the different Wards – Coun[cillor] Spencer ~~proposed~~ suggested [an] examination [of the police]. C[ouncillor] Phelps said we have a Mayor and he has charge of the police – and referred to the unruly boys swimming & Kiting.

[A] Bill [was presented for] an Ordinance to amend an ordinance entitled an ordinance regulating the fees and compensation of the several officers & persons therein mentioned[,] [originally] passed Jan[uary] 14th 1843. [It was] read. [It was] moved by O[rson] Pratt that the blank be filled with 2.00. C[ouncillor] Phelps – moved [that it be changed to] $1.00 & [this] carried. [It was] moved by Daniel Spencer [the interim] Mayor that W[illiam] W. Phelps be Clerk of the Mayors court. [It] Carried.

> I, Daniel Spencer, do solemnly swear in the presence of Almighty God that I will support the constitution of the United States & the state of Illinois and execute the duties of the Mayors office in the City of Nauvoo according to the best of my ability.[189]
> **Nauvoo Aug[ust] 10, 1844, Daniel Spencer.**

The Mayor [was led] to his seat as President of the council. [A] bill regulating the salary of [the] Mayor & Aldermen & Councellors passed. [The] Resignation of Geo[rge] A Smith as [an] Alderman of the city [was] accepted.[190]

---

government had not yet begun printing paper money, and people tended to only trust silver coins. But in Nauvoo, the economy ran largely on promissory notes and tithing office credit, while private bank notes and municipal scrip were often discounted up to 55 percent (Leonard, *Nauvoo,* 161-65, 311-12). The council will continue its discussion of how to pay for its police force at its next meeting on September 14. The city will print and distribute $900 worth of scrip (see the minutes for October 12), realize that it was not a good plan because of its effect on the scrip's value, and try to recall it.

[189]This oath is set out in the Nauvoo Charter, Section 5.

[190]It is not known why George A. Smith resigned his position as an

[It was] voted that the ^present^ assessor & Collectors of the city of Nauvoo for 1843 be the assessors & collectors for 1844[.] [It was] voted that the Recorder return the books of 1843 to the assessor & collector & instruct them to proceed immediately to assess the property of the city and levy a tax of one half per cent for the year 1844. [All] voted [and] the council adjourned.

†Voted that the Estate of the late Gen[era]l Joseph Smith be allowed the sum of sixteen dollars and seventy cents to satisfy the Board Bill of Colonel Brewer.[191]

**August 10th 1844. Geo[rge] W. Harris Pres[iden]t pro tem. Willard Richards Recorder**

An Ordinance concerning brothels and disorderly characters[192]

Sec. 1. Be it ordained by the City Council of the City of Nauvoo, that all brothels or houses of ill fame erected or being in the City of Nauvoo, be, and the same hereby are henceforth, prohibited and by law declared public nuisances, and that the owners or helpers of such houses be fined in a sum of not less than fifty, nor more than two thousand five hundred dollars, and imprisoned for six months for each offence of one days continuance of such establishment, and that any person frequenting such establishment (except on lawful business) shall be fined in any sum of not less than fifty, nor more than five hundred dollars, and six months imprisonment for each offence; and further, that for every act of adultery or fornication, which can be proved, the parties shall be imprisoned six months and fined each in the sum of not less than fifty or more than two thousand five hun-

---

alderman, but the next month he would be nominated to replace Daniel Spencer in a councilman seat that Spencer vacated when he became acting mayor. George A. would be sworn into office on November 1.

191Brewer must have been a guest of the city. At this point, the minutes repeat the resolution to allow Reuben Atwood to extend Ann Street, deleted here because of the redundancy.

192This seems to be window-dressing, perhaps to counteract rumors about polygamy. As one LDS historian confirmed, "Actually, there is no record of a brothel in Nauvoo even though Palaskie Cahoon was accused of operating one. There were bars and some women sold sexual favors" (Kenneth W. Godfrey, "Crime and Punishment in Mormon Nauvoo, 1839-1846," *BYU Studies* 32 [1992]: 228).

dred dollars, and that the individuals own acknowledgment shall be considered sufficient evidence in the case.

Sec. 2. Be it ordained that the ordinance concerning brothels, and disorderly characters passed May 14, 1842, be, and the same is hereby repealed.

Sec. 3. Be it further ordained that this ordinance shall take effect, from and after its passage.

**Passed Aug[us]t 10th 1844. Geo[rge] W. Harris Pres[iden]t pro tem. Willard Richards[,] Recorder**

The Recorder's semi annual report of the attendance of the City Council, Marshall[,] and Recorder from February 10th 1844 to August 9th 1844 inclusive, was read, and the City Council ordered that the following named persons, be paid the sums, respectively set opposite their names for their services in the City Council during the above named period, to wit,

| | | | |
|---|---|---|---|
| Hyrum Smith | 12.00 | Samuel Bennett | 6.00 |
| John Taylor | 8.00 | William Marks | 3.50 |
| Orson Pratt | 6.00 | N[ewel] K. Whitney | 11.00 |
| W. W. Phelps | 16.00 | Gustavus Hills | 1.00 |
| Heber C. Kimball | 5.00 | Hiram Kimball | 2.00 |
| Benj[ami]n Warrington | 14.50 | Elias Smith | 4.00 |
| Daniel Spencer | 8.50 | George P. Stiles | 10.00 |
| Brigham Young | 5.00 | Aaron Johnson | 9.50 |
| Orson Spencer | 11.50 | Phinehas Richards | 8.00 |
| Daniel H. Wells | 2.00 | Edward Hunter | 2.00 |
| George A. Smith | 6.00 | Levi Richards | 7.00 |
| George W. Harris | 17.00 | John P. Green (Marshall) | 14.50 |
| | | | 190.00 |

| | |
|---|---|
| Willard Richards Recorder one half year's Salary | 50.00 |
| Joseph Smith Mayor Salary to June 27th 1844 | 189.15 |
| Total | $429.15 |

and ordered the same to be paid out of any money in the Treasury not otherwise appropriated. Allowed August 10th, 1844. George W. Harris Pres[iden]t pro tem. Willard Richards Recorder

Granted the Petition of John P. Anis to erect a Water Mill on the old site near Charles Ivins', if it do[es] not interfere with any other rights and privileges.

**Passed Aug[us]t 10th 1844. Geo[rge] W. Harris Pres[iden]t. pro tem. Willard Richards, Recorder**[193]

Councillors Heber C. Kimball, Brigham Young, Aldermen George A. Smith and Hiram Kimball relinquished their pay as Members of the Council, and W. W. Phelps, Orson Pratt and George W. Harris relinquished Ten dollars each of their pay.
**August 10th 1844. Geo[rge] W. Harris Pres[iden]t pro tem. Willard Richards Recorder**

An Ordinance to amend an Ordinance, entitled An Ordinance regulating the Fees and Compensation of the several officers and persons therein mentioned[,] [originally] passed January 14th 1843

Sec. 1. Be it ordained by the City Council of the City of Nauvoo That the Mayor shall be allowed a Salary per annum of one hundred dollars and that the Aldermen and Councillors shall receive each one dollar per day while in Session, also [a] fine for absence [of] one dollar per day.[194]

Sec. 2. This ordinance to be in force from and after its passage, any other ordinance to the contrary notwithstanding.
**Passed Aug[us]t 10th, 1844. Daniel Spencer Mayor. Willard Richards Recorder.**[195]

‡*September 14, 1844; Saturday.*[196] Regular Session, Sept[ember] 14th 1844. At Eleven oclock – A.M. [the] Names of [the] Members [were] called. [A] Quorum [was] Present. Prayer by Daniel Spencer Mayor.

[A] Petition [was] presented by P[hillip] B. Lewis[197] for the Sum

---

[193]The minutes also repeat the decisions for Marshall John Green to settle with Amos Davis, for Alderman Hiram Kimball to settle with the proprietors of the *Nauvoo Expositor,* and for Daniel Spencer to serve as mayor until the next election.

[194]This was $400 less per year than Joseph Smith had received as mayor and one dollar less per day (down from two dollars a day) for aldermen and councilmen (see the minutes in chapter 3 for January 14, 1843).

[195]Three decisions have been removed because of redundancy: the nomination of William W. Phelps as the mayor's court clerk, the resignation of Alderman George A. Smith, and the retention of existing assessors and collectors, who are instructed to levy a ½ percent tax for the year.

[196]See also *History of Church,* 7:271.

[197]Phillip Bessom Lewis was born in 1804 in Marblehead, Massachusetts. He was an early convert in Massachusetts, who boarded with Joseph

of $34.504[198] which was lent for the benefit of the City – H[eber] C. Kimball [said] there was a Matter presented before us, that is, the claims of Mr Wood[s] for his Services to Joseph Smith. Moved & seconded, that the committee w[as] dismissed from any further ~~claims~~ action on the claims of Mr Wood[s]. Moved & Seconded that the council have Nothing to do with the petition for it belongs to the Recorder. Moved & sec[onde]d that the Bill be allowed.[199]

[It was] moved & seconded that Jonathan C. Wright be elected Marshall[;] moved & seconded that Jonathan C. Wright act as assessor & collector in the place of John P. Green[;] moved & Seconded that W[illiam] W. Phelps be ^elected^ Recorder of Deeds.

[The] Mayor [said] Col[onel] [Jonathan] Dunham stated that the old police was about to be broken up (see last Council). Geo[rge] W. Harris [said][:] I still hold the same idea that the old police be kept up as they have been on duty for a long time, the same as I stated at last council Meeting. B[righam] Young said that there is one or two of the police [who] sleeps at his house at Nights while he is on watch & I say to them there is My house & My bed for you & also My table is read[y] for them if required. [It was] motioned & seconded that there be a committee of three ^[to] be^ appointed to confer with the trustees[200] ^of the church^ relative to paying the police. Moved & seconded that Daniel Spencer & John Taylor & Alderman [Orson] Spencer be the committee appointed for that purpose.

John Taylor [asked to] speak of the police[,] [saying] that it is of Natural importance that this body should be kept up & I think if the inhabitants of ^the^ different wards would have Meetings in their Neighborhoods to see if they would allow themselves [to vote] for a small tax put on each of them for the purpose of keeping up the police[,] [they would respond favorably] for it is right that these Men are sustained & they are willing to go any length for the Safety of the

---

Smith in Nauvoo. He reburied Joseph and Hyrum Smith following their removal from their first burial place in the cellar of the Nauvoo House. He died in 1879.

198Sums were sometimes figured to a fraction of a cent, which were paid with a copper half penny that was in circulation until 1857.

199These were the legal fees for defending Joseph Smith in Carthage prior to his assassination.

200The Church trustees were Presiding Bishops Newel K. Whitney and George Miller (Leonard, *Nauvoo,* 480, 495-96).

city. [It was] moved & Seconded that the committee of three that was appointed [by the] Council [to act] together for the best Means of sustaining the police or of choosing new police [coordinate their actions with the heads of the Church].

B[righam] Young said all that the City [has] is worth Nothing [without the police] & it would be a good plan to see if [the Church] trustees could donate any things or a piece of land ^or property^ that could be sold for the support of the police. Hiram Kimball said that he would like to see the City clear of debt & that if the trustees ~~for~~ would donate a piece of property he was willing to give half a lot for the support of the police.

H[iram] Kimball reported[:] I called on the Higbees & one of the Fosters ^at Appanoose[201]^ but I dont see that any thing can be done with the Laws & Fosters [to avoid going to court over the *Nauvoo Expositor*] but I am going to Carthage on Thursday & I will see Francis Higbee when I can lay before him what this council decides on.

An ordinance concerning the
Register of Deeds ~~& for other purposes~~

Sect. 1. Be it ordained by the City Council of the City of Nauvoo that the Register of deeds before entering upon the duties of his office ^shall be sworn and^ shall give a bond with security to the City in a penalty of ~~two~~ Five hundred dollars that he ~~he~~ will faithfully execute & perform the duties of said office & deliver over the books & papers ~~of~~ belonging to the said office to his successor in office without defalcation or delay.

**Passed Sept[ember] 14th, 1844. Daniel Spencer Mayor.**

[It was] moved & Seconded that Hiram Kimball & Edmund D. Wooley be appointed to prosecute a settlement as far as possible for the [*Expositor*] press[.] It was also Moved & Sec[on]ded that he have discretionary power. [It was] moved & Seconded that the assessors & collectors of taxes be allowed one dollar p[e]r day. [It was] moved & Seconded that Geo[rge] A. Smith be elected councillor in place of Daniel Spencer.

Moved & seconded that this Meeting adjourn until the Next general session. [After the] Report on J[oseph] S[mith] [and the] Hig-

---

[201]Appanoose is six miles northeast of Nauvoo, next to Pontoosuc and across the river from Fort Madison.

bees[,] [the] Acc[ou]nt [was] accepted [and] allowed. [The] Mayor suggested that [the] council pass an [amended] ordinance to prevent misrepresentation of and libelous publications [and that a] Committee be appointed to attend to the wharf.[202]

†*September 18, 1844; Wednesday.*

> William W. Phelps took the Oath of office as Registrar of Deeds for the City of Nauvoo and filed his bond with Surety according to ordinance.
> **Sept[embe]r 18, 1844. Willard Richards Recorder**
>
> Jonathan C. Wright took the Oath of office as Marshall for the City of Nauvoo and filed his bond with Surety according to his appointment.
> **Sept[embe]r 18, 1844. Willard Richards, Recorder**

‡‡*October 12, 1844; Saturday.*[203] Regular Session, 20 Min[utes] Past 10 A.M, Daniel Spencer Mayor. [The] Meeting [was] opened by prayer by Geo[rge] W. Harris.

J[onathan] H. Hales [said][:] I would like to make a remark or two. I was reelected Assessor & Collector of taxes for the year 1844 but on account of sickness I have not commenced yet, and seeing that the Twelve [Apostles] wishes Me to go away perhaps it would be as well for another to be appointed. It was the unanimous voice of the Council that he continue his office ^as assessor & collector^ until he is going away and resigns his office.

W[illiam] W. Phelps then arose and read a petition from bro W[illia]m Clayton concerning Charles Warner the City Auctioneer.

---

[202]The Record of Proceedings repeats the appointments of Jonathan C. Wright as assessor, collector, and marshall; William W. Phelps as Recorder of Deeds; Daniel Spencer, Orson Spencer, and John Taylor as a committee to confer with the Church trustees; Hiram Kimball and Edmund D. Woolley as a committee to settle with the owners of the *Nauvoo Expositor*; and George A. Smith as a councilman replacing Daniel Spencer. The Proceedings also repeat the report of Hiram Kimball about the Higbees and Foster; the ordinance concerning the Register of Deeds; and the payment of a dollar per day to assessors and collectors, all dated and signed by the mayor and recorder.

[203]See also *History of Church*, 7:310.

[It was] moved & Sec[onde]d that Charles Warner be discontinued from his office.[204] [It was] moved & Sec[onde]d that John D Parker[205] be elected as City Auctioneer.

W[illiam] W. Phelps [said][:] I would just remark that the City Scrip should be stopt if any provisions could be made[,] for there was [more printed] to the amount of $8[00] or $900 dollars issued the other day, and it would be a good plan if any ~~pro~~ Means could be made to redeem what has gone out. Resolved by the City Council of the City of Nauvoo that the Treasurer be instructed ^not^ to issue any More City Scrip unless an order [was received] from the City Council, which was carried.

[It was] moved & sec[onde]d that the Marshall pro Tem go and bring the high Policeman J[onathan] Dunham & W[illia]m Clayton the Treasurer forthwith, which was carried. [It was] moved & Se[conde]d that the foregoing Motion be reconsidered, which was carried. Mov[e]d & Sec[onde]d that the financial committee be instructed to instruct Col[onel] Dunham concerning the city Scrip, which was carried.

Council[or] Phelps arose & read an Ordinance concerning Spirituous Liquors – [It was] moved & Sec[onde]d that the Bill be read a Second time. Moved & Sec[onde]d by Ald[erman] [Gustavus] Hills that an Amendment be Made to the Sec[on]d Sect[ion] of the ordinance, which was carried unanimously. [It was] moved, sec[onde]d & carried that the Bill be read again.

Coun[cillor] [Orson] Pratt [said][:] I think it is very indefinite that they pay a fine to the amount assessed on the licence. [It was] moved & Sec[onde]d & carried that an amendment be made on the Second Section that ^instead of 200 to 400 that^ they be fined from $25 to $400 dollars.

An Ordinance concerning
Spirituous Liquors and other purposes.

Sect. 1. Be it ordained by the city Council of the City of Nauvoo, that before any persons shall sell, or dispose of any spirituous or intoxicating drink by a less quantity than one gallon in

---

[204]Warner was fired once before, on December 16, 1843 (reinstated on December 21), for not giving the city its portion of the auctions' proceeds.

[205]John Davis Parker was born in Saratoga, New York, in 1799. He was baptized in 1832. He died in 1891.

this City, he or they shall first obtain a license from the Mayors Court, for which shall be paid down ^in specie^ for the use of the City, not less than 200 nor more than 400 hundred dollars, (& issuing fees) for one Year.

Sect. 2nd. And be it further ordained that if any person shall sell or give away, or dispose of to be drank in this City in less quantity than one gallon any Spirituous or intoxicating drink or liquors ^~~except in cases of sickness~~^ ~~without first obtaining such~~ [without a] license[,] they shall pay a fine ^for each and every offence^ of not less than 25 and not more than 400 hundred dollars to be tried before the Mayor.

Sect. 3. And be it further ordained that all ordinances or parts of ordinances of private grants ~~repugnant to the intent and meaning of this ordinance~~ concerning Spirituous & other liquors, are hereby repealed.

Sect. 4. And be it further ordained that if any person shall be convicted, before the Mayor, of drunkenness in this City he, she or they shall be fined twenty dollars. – This fine may be paid in labor upon the public streets or other public works of this city at the discretion of the Mayor.

No. 1[206] This ordinance to be in ~~full~~ force from & after its passage.

**Passed Oct[ober] 12. Daniel Spencer, Mayor. Willard Richards Recorder.**

‡[It was] motioned and carried that the City be responsible for the amount which the committee appointed to settle for the Nauvoo Expositor [agreed to][,] in which they gave Daniel Spencer & Edward Hunter and others note[s] of[:] 100.00 to Leonard Soby [and] one other note of 513.75 to Charles Ivins[,] also two other notes, one for 30.00 and the other for 81.25 to Charles Ivins[,] all together amounting to 725.00.[207]

---

[206]“No. 1” evidently refers to a contemplated revision that is either lost or was abandoned. In any case, the ordinance appears twice in the Record of Proceedings, crossed out on Oct. 12, 1844, and again, with revised wording, on Nov. 9.

[207]There is a version of this on a loose sheet that lacks dollar amounts, saying only “that the City be responsible for the amount which the committee [that was] appointed to settle for the Nauvoo expositor [agreed upon].”

[It was] motioned and carried that the Bill be allowed and the Mayor be instructed and authorized to give the City obligations for the same borrowed from Julia Ann Van Orden,[208] amounting to 75.00. [It was] motioned and carried that this meeting adjourn until the next general Session.

†Charles Warner, the City Auctioneer not having made any returns of Sales and duties to the City Treasurer[,] he was discontinued from his Office and John D. Parker was elected in his stead. **October 12, 1844. Willard Richards Recorder.**[209]

An Ordinance concerning
the duties of the Clerk of the Mayor's Court

Section 1. Be it ordained by the City Council of the City of Nauvoo that the Clerk of the Mayor's Court, shall issue process when required; shall adjourn cases from time to time in the absence of the Mayor; shall affix the seal of the Corporation of said City, to such papers and certificates as the law may require; shall take bonds and recognizances from persons bound to keep the peace; shall perform such other duties as a Mayor's Clerk may of right do, and be governed in his fees for services, according to the ordinance concerning fees.

[208]Julia Ann Haight Van Orden was a forty-year-old widow with six children, who had come to Nauvoo with her husband in 1843 with considerable savings. She was born in Windham, New York, in 1805 and married William Van Orden in 1827. Twelve years later, they converted to Mormonism. William died in July 1844. She married John Bernhisel in the spring of 1845, after which he took six other wives in Nauvoo. She apparently separated from him in 1851 and died in 1865 in Provo (Dell Van Orden, "William and Julia Ann Van Orden Timeline," *Van Orden Family*, www.vanordenfamily.org).

[209]The Record of Proceedings repeats some resolutions already quoted from other sources and omitted here to avoid redundancies. There is also a crossed-out version of the "Ordinance concerning Spiritous Liquors" with a marginal note reading, "Repealed Nov[embe]r 9th 1844," omitted from the current presentation. Someone may want to prepare a critical edition of the minutes at some future point, but that goes beyond the scope of the current project.

Section 2. All resolutions or parts of ordinances relating to the Clerk of the Mayor's Court are hereby repealed.
**Passed Oct[obe]r 12, 1844. Daniel Spencer Mayor**

*November 1, 1844; Friday.*

John D. Parker took the Oath of office as City Auctioneer and filed his bond with two Sureties for the faithful performance of his duty.
**Nov[embe]r 1, 1844. Willard Richards Recorder.**

‡‡*November 9, 1844; Saturday.* Regular Session. [Present][:] D[aniel] Spencer Mayor[;] Coun[cillors] O[rson] Pratt[,] Geo[rge] A. Smith[,] John Taylor[,] W[illiam] W. Phelps[,] [and] Brigham Young[;] [Aldermen] O[rson] Spencer[,] Hiram Kimball[,] Gus[tavus] Hills[,] Geo[rge] W. Harris[,] D[aniel] H. Wells[,] [and] W[illia]m Marks[;] [and] J[onathan] C. Wright Marshall[.]

[The] Meeting opened [with] prayer by W[illiam] W. Phelps. Coun[cillor] Geo[rge] A. Smith was sworn in by W[illiam] W. Phelps – A Bill was presented ^to the City Coun[cil] of the City of Nauvoo ~~by a Petition~~ signed by 103 of the citizens^ to open Warsaw Street from Parley St. South to the River – Mov[e]d Sec[onded] & Carried that it be referred to the committee of Streets –

W[inslow] Farr – spoke relative to additional ~~ground~~ land [being added] to the burying ground. [It was] mov[e]d sec[onded] & carried that it be referred to the committee of public grounds. [It was] mo[ved] & sec[onded] & carried that Geo[rge] A. Smith be chairman pertaining to the Committee of Public Grounds [and] mov[e]d [and] sec[onded] ~~carried~~ that Sam[ue]l Bennett['s] place be filled up pertaining to public grounds – which was carried. [It was] mov[ed] [and] sec[onded] ~~carried~~ that Coun[cillor] O[rson] Pratt be put in his stead – which was carried unanimously –

[It was] moved [and] sec[onded] that Ald[erman] [William] Marks be instructed to appear before us and gave us a statement in regard to the burying ground, which was carried. [A] Bill was presented signed by 5 of the citizens that Hodge^h^kiss [Hotchkiss] Street be opened one block West of Warsaw St[reet]. [It was] mov[ed] – sec[onded] – that it be referred to the committee of public grounds which was carried –

[It was] mov[ed] [and] sec[onde]d – that Ald[erman] Marks confer with the committee of public grounds relative to the burying ground & relate the [results of the] same to the council – which was carried. Coun[cillor] Young moved & Sec[onded] that the Bill be called ~~for~~ up again & reconsidered by the Council – relative [to] opening Warsaw Street to the River – which was carried – Coun[cillor] [Brigham] Young – arose & ~~th~~ said that he would propose that a select committee be appointed to go and see and locate the street which would be the best to open. [It was] mov[ed and] sec[onded]d that B[righam] Young – Orson Pratt – [and] H[eber] C. Kimball be the committee to go and see which will be the best street to be opened South to the River –

Coun[cillor] Geo[rge] A. Smith – arose and said that our Committee ha[d] [already had a] Conference with Alderman Marks relative to the burying ground – He says that the lots are all sold and that some of them are paid for and others is not. – He also said that he was instructed to fence it in by the proceeds which he Might receive by the sales[210] – also he further remarked if it was necessary he would give us a statement of all the sales & money rec[orde]d & what is due &c &c. [It was] mov[ed] [and] sec[onde]d – that the street remain for the present one Rod & 2 [feet][211] – which was carried –

Two Bills was presented by D[aniel] H. Wells to the am[oun]t of $43.43 c[en]ts due to W[illiam] H. Rollosson. Mov[ed] – sec[onded] that it be referred to the com[mittee] – of claims which was carried [and] reported [as] allowed.

[A] Bill [was] presented by D[aniel] H. Wells to the am[oun]t of $37 dollars due S. M. Marr[212] – Mov[ed] [and] sec[onded] that it be referred to the com[mittee] of claims which was carried [and] reported [as] allowed. [A] Bill [was] present[ed] by A[lbert] P. Rockwood to the am[oun]t of ~~21~~ $15 doll[ar]s [and] 69 c[en]ts[,] allowed. [It was] mov[ed] [and] sec[onded] – that it be referred to the com[mittee] of claims which was carried [and] reported [as] allowed.

---

[210]See the minutes of January 30, 1843.

[211]A normal street was three rods wide, according to the "Laws and Ordinances" of January 30, 1843 (see chapter 3). The road through the graveyard was not intended to handle traffic.

[212]Mr. Marr owned the "New Brick Store" on Knight Street (see his ad in the *Nauvoo Expositor*).

Be it ordained by the City Council of the City of Nauvoo that all ~~Laws~~ Ordinances or parts of ~~laws~~ ordinances in relation to Swine are hereby repealed – [A] Bill [was] presented by Bro[ther] Green to the amount of $228.82 dollars [and] cents due to John P. Green (deceased). [It was] mov[ed] [and] sec[onded] that it be referred to the com[mittee] of claims which was carried ([and] reported [as] allowed). [It was] mov[ed] [and] sec[onded] – that W[illiam] W. Phelps be added to the Com[mittee] of claims which was carried.[213]

‡Co[uncillor] W[illiam] W. Phelps presented a bill amounting to $10 due to Joseph W. Coolidge[214] which was referred to the Committee of Claims and by them allowed. [It was] motioned and carried that the bill pass, relative to having a Slaughter house in the City of Nauvoo. Adjourned for one hour – Nov[embe]r 9th, 1844.

[The] adjourned meeting met pursuant to the adjournment. [It was] motioned and seconded that the ordinance relative to Spirituous Liquors ~~pass~~, with the amendment by Co[uncillor] Orson Pratt pass, which was carried. Motioned and seconded that the 1st. Sec[tion] be stricken out which was carried. Motioned and seconded that an amendment be made to the 2nd Sect[ion] & carried. Motioned and carried that the Bill do now pass.

[It was] motioned and carried that the Marshall give receipts for the taxes marked Paid in the assessment book of John P. Green – and keep an account of the same. Motioned and carried that Co[uncillor] Orson Pratt, George A. Smith, and W[illiam] W. Phelps be a select committee in drawing up an Ordinance[.] Motioned that we adjourn to the next regular Session – Carried.

---

[213]The rough-book version of the minutes for November 9 repeats almost verbatim what is found in the loose sheets, with a few variations: Charles C. Rich is said to be one of the 101 (rather than 103) individuals petitioning to extend Warsaw Street. The petition to extend Hodgkiss Street is identified as having been made by "Hosea Stout and four others" rather than by "five citizens." Albert Rockwood's bill is "referred to the committee of claims, and ... by them allowed," while the amount "due to John P. Green (the deceased Marshall)," after being "referred to the committee of claims," was "allowed."

[214]Joseph Wellington Coolidge was born in Bangor, Maine, in 1814. He moved to Illinois in 1839. In Nauvoo he was a member of the Council of Fifty and served as administrator to Joseph Smith's estate. He died in 1871.

†George A. Smith received his Oath of Office, and took his Seat as a Councillor of the City.

**November 9th 1844. Willard Richards, Recorder**[215]

An Ordinance concerning Swine

Section 1. Be it ordained by the City Council of the City of Nauvoo that all ordinances, or parts of ordinances, in relation to Swine are hereby repealed.

~~November 9th 1844. Daniel Spencer Mayor. Willard Richards Recorder.~~ [Marginal note:] hog law was not repealed – error –

An Ordinance concerning a Slaughter house in Nauvoo

Section 1. Be it ordained by the City Council of the City of Nauvoo that Newel K. Whitney and George Miller are hereby authorized to use the barn and yard of P[arley] P. Pratt, for the purpose of slaughtering cattle, hogs and other animals for supplying the Temple hands and the City with Meat, until the first of April next.

Section 2. This ordinance to be in force from and after its passage.

**Passed November 9th 1844. Daniel Spencer Mayor. Willard Richards, Recorder.**

An Ordinance concerning
Spirituous Liquors and other purposes

Section 1. Be it ordained by the City Council of the City of Nauvoo, that if any person shall sell or give away or dispose of, to be drunk in this City, in less quantities than one gallon, any Spirituous or intoxicating drink or liquors, except in cases of sickness, they shall pay a fine for each and every offence, of not less than twenty five, and not more than four hundred dollars, to be tried before the Mayor.

Section 2. And be it further ordained that all ordinances, or parts of ordinances, or private grants concerning spirituous and other liquors, are hereby repealed.[216]

Section 3. And be it further ordained that if any person shall

[215]Many of these resolutions and ordinances are also extant in their earlier forms.

[216]Previously Joseph Smith was the only one who had a private liquor

be convicted before the Mayor, of drunkenness in this City, he she or they shall be fined twenty dollars: – This fine may be paid in labor upon the public Streets or other public works of this City, at the discretion of the Mayor.

This ordinance to be in force from and after its passage.

**Passed November 9th 1844. Daniel Spencer Mayor. Willard Richards Recorder**

Motioned and carried that the Marshall give receipts for the taxes marked Paid in the assessment book of John P. Green the late Assessor and Collector, and that he keep an account of the same.

**November 9th 1844. Willard Richards Recorder**

*November 17, 1844; Sunday.*

Allowed W[illiam] H. Rollaston his bills amounting to forty three dollars and forty three cents.

**November 17th 1844. Daniel Spencer Mayor. Willard Richards, Recorder**

*December 9, 1844; Monday.*

Thomas Bullock was appointed Deputy Recorder, of the City of Nauvoo and took the Oath of office.[217]

**December 9th 1844. Willard Richards Recorder.**

*December 10, 1844; Tuesday.*

Jonathan C. Wright took the Oath of Office as Assessor and Collector for the Fourth Ward in the City of Nauvoo and filed his bond with Surety for the faithful performance of his duty.

**December 10th 1844. Willard Richards Recorder. by Thomas Bullock, Deputy.**

---

license. See the discussion of this issue in the minutes of the January 13, 1844, meeting.

[217]"Elder Willard Richards, city recorder, opened office in his new house, and appointed Thomas Bullock his deputy. Thomas commenced putting the city records in order, which had been neglected some four months in consequence of Brother Willard's inability through sickness" (*History of Church,* 7:324).

‡*December 14, 1844; Saturday.* [At] 20 min[utes] past 10, [in a] Regular Session, [the] Names of [the] Members [were] called [and it was found that] a Quorum [was] present. Prayer by Brigham Young.

Councillor Orson Hyde read a letter ~~from~~ to the Representative – A[lmon] Babbit.[218] In answer to his letter, Ald[erman] Orson Spencer spoke on the behalf of retaining our present Charter and not to give up a good Charter because others whine – The Legislature gave us a Charter to make any law not repugnant to the Constitution – and we ought to keep it.[219]

Co[uncillor] [John] Taylor said we have not transgressed any law – We have done no wrong – If we had, there is a tribunal to bring us before – Let us hang on to the Charter – If they take away our rights they shall have the glory of it – and shew to the world that there is no faith in the Legislature.

Co[uncillor] G[eorge] A. Smith [said he] has similar feelings. I never would consent to let it be altered in the least. The Habeas Corpus ha[d] saved Joseph [Smith several times] – and we may want it to save ourselves – If one Charter cannot be defended – another cannot – If they do repeal it – let it be to their own disgrace – The letter [from Assemblyman Babbitt should] be dispensed with –

~~Motioned and carried that the ordinance relating to Swine passed last Session be stricken out~~ [A] Letter from Recorder Willard Richards [was] read and accepted. [It was] moved and seconded that Mr. ^Thomas^ Bullock be our Clerk for the time being. Mr Bull-

---

[218]Babbitt, the city's representative in the Illinois General Assembly (elected August 1844), wrote a letter outlining the "anticipated" attempt to repeal "the chartered rights of the city" (ibid., 325). He was born in October 1813 in Massachusetts, studied to become an attorney in Cincinnati, and converted to Mormonism in Ohio in the early 1830s. The Church sent him to Springfield in 1839 to represent the Church in discussions with members of the Illinois legislature. In 1841 he was sent back to Kirtland, Ohio, where he became president of the stake. In 1844 he represented the owners of the *Nauvoo Expositor* in its suit against the city. In Utah he was appointed territorial secretary and proceeded to clash with Governor Brigham Young. Babbitt was killed, presumably by Indians, in April 1856 in Wyoming while traveling to Washington, D.C. (Andrew Jenson, *LDS Biographical Encyclopedia,* 4 vols. [Salt Lake City: Andrew Jenson Historical Co., 1901-1936], 1:284; *History of Church,* 3:346; Leonard, *Nauvoo,* 465-66).

[219]For some time the Illinois Legislature had been discussing repealing the Nauvoo Charter, but it now had the votes to make it happen.

ock was sworn in as Deputy Recorder of the city of Nauvoo. [It was] moved and seconded that the alteration in Marr & Rollasons bills be made as reduced. Moved and seconded that the bill of J[ohn] P. Green be referred to the Committee of claims. D[itt]o[,] d[itt]o that Ald[erman] Orson Spencer be added to the Committee on claims for the time being. D[itt]o[,] d[itt]o that the Petition of Stephen Markham and two others for opening a Street across Block 69 be made by an ordinance.

[The council] passed [an] "Ordinance to locate an Alley on Block 69 and other Alleys or Lanes[.]" [The] ["]Ordinance incorporating the Seventies Library and Institute Association"[220] [was] read [the] 1st. time[,] 2nd. time by [its] Title – [and] 3rd time. Co[uncillor] Orson Pratt spoke on the subject – Co[uncillor] Taylor followed shewing that as the State gave us powers as large as the State – we have power to give [the] same to this Institute – Co[uncillor] Heber C. Kimball considers that we have power to give to this Institute as far as [the] right is given to us – Let us give [the] right one to another – Shall we curtail ourselves because the Legislature wants to curtail us[?]

Co[uncillor] Phelps said the Charter includes a grant to a College which goes further than this – We have power to legislate for the benefit & convenience of this City – If we pass a law for the enlightning of the human family[,] we do not go against any law – and especially the Constitution of the U[nited] States – or of this State. This bill is for the diffusion of Useful knowledge throughout all the world – Intelligence is the life of liberty – Every exertion shall be made to find out Intelligence – We shew good; that there is no evil in the thing –

Ald[erman] [Daniel H.] Wells [agreed that] there is no limit given to the power of the Charter – I am in favor of the diffusion of Knowledge – Ald[derman] Orson Spencer differed from Ald[erman] Wells in [his interpretation of] the power of the Charter. We have passed an Act to record our Deeds here instead of going 18 miles – It is for

[220]The council seems to be setting up a challenge of some kind to the county or state government. Notice how apprehensive the councilmen are about the legality of this move, giving the impression that more is at stake than just a library. In fact, the city already had the Nauvoo Library and Literary Institute, created in January 1844, which was loaning books and sponsoring lectures, so there would seem to be little need for a second library (Leonard, *Nauvoo,* 197). See below for the full ordinance.

our convenience – and he went into his views of the power of the Charter. But I think the Charter now before us is too liberal and I may vote against it.

Ald[erman] Harris had leave to withdraw to go to the [Nauvoo Stake] High Council. Co[uncillor] Taylor shewed the illiberality of the people of Illinois towards us, since the Charter was given us – and [he said that] no man can shew that he has been injured by this City Council. Co[uncillor] Brigham Young asked who was going to be injured by granting this Charter and spoke his feelings on the subject – Co[uncillor] G[eorge] A. Smith said we want this Council to grant us the Charter. The University has been a failure – If the Council can make a University – it can make a Library.

Co[uncillor] Phelps spoke. – Taylor spoke. Orson Pratt read the Sec[tion] of the Charter relating to the University[221] – and shewed that it came within the jurisdiction of this Council –Passed[,] [with a] No [vote from] Ald[erman] Wells. Co[uncillor] Brigham Young wants it to be recorded that Ald[erman] Wells voted against it "because the City Council has no authority to grant it." Ald[erman] Wells replied – [The council was] satisfied by the Title. [The council] adjourned for one hour, [it being] Dec[ember] 14, 1844.

[The] Meeting [was] opened pursuant to adjournment. [The] Petition of Samuel Bent and 21 others for permission to Newel Knight to make a dam in the Mississippi [was considered]. Co[uncillor] Taylor rose to object to the petition and to shew that an ordinance had been granted to the late Joseph Smith for the purpose – and took a review of the whole – and shewed that to grant this petition would be out of place –

Co[uncillor] Phelps stated that the Ordinance to Joseph Smith [for a dam] was [already] drawn up, and suited [to] Joseph Smith['s] [successors][.] [He] read the same – [The] Mayor said this Council has no right to operate [in that area] – for [the property has] already [been] transferred to the Successors of Joseph Smith. [It was decided to let the] Petition lie on the table.[222]

---

[221]See the Nauvoo Charter, Section 24.

[222]As quoted below, the city council passed an ordinance to amend the December 8, 1843, "Ordinance to Erect a Dam in the Mississippi River," in which "the Successors of Joseph Smith mentioned in said Ordinance are those who succeed him in the Office of Trustee in Trust in the Church of

[The] Petition of Benj[ami]n Warrington & 4 others to open [the] st[reet] east of Speers St[reet] from Parley to Young [was] granted. [The]Bill of A[lanson] Ripley [for] $5.00 for surveying Speers St[reet] [was] referred to the Committee on claims – They reported [that they had] nothing to do with it. [The] Bill of J[onathan] K. Hale [for] 48.25 for surveying & assessing ditt]o[,] d[itt]o report[,] [which was] allowed[.]

[The] Bill of Grubb & Ritchie [for] 57.81 for Liquor &c to [the] Nauvoo Legion [will] be referred to Col[onel] [Jonathan] Dunham & [Charles C.] Rich. [The] Bill [of] Hiram Kimball [for] 40.80 for Salted Beef [will] be ref[erre]d to the committee on claims (bill allowed for 30.60.) [It was] moved and seconded that the Trustees in Trust be indemnified in their claims on the City. Carried. Moved and seconded that the Treasurer audit the acc[oun]ts presented to him by the Trustees in Trust and give them receipts for the same[.] Carried. [The] Bill concerning Swine [was] read [the] 1st. time[,] 2nd time[,] [and] laid on the table. An Ordinance to amend an Ordinance [originally] passed [on] Dec[embe]r 8, 1843, passed.

[It was] motioned and seconded that the Committee on Public Grounds have further time allowed to report on the burying ground also in connection with the Old Burying Ground and be instructed to find out the boundary of the old burying ground and to make [the] same [appear] decent by fencing it out – Carried. Motioned and seconded that the Mayor fill up [the] Vacancies of Trustees & Registrar in Nauvoo University[.] [The] Mayor appointed Mr. John Taylor Registrar; ~~Trustees~~ Regents Daniel H. Wells, N[ewel] K. Whitney, William Marks[,] Geo[rge] Miller, Brigham Young[,] Amasa Lyman, John T. Barnett, Charles C Rich, Heber C. Kimball, ^Prof[essor]^ Orson Pratt[,] Orson Hyde, Willard Richards, Daniel Spencer, Gustavus Hills, George A. Smith[,] Jonathan H. Hale, Reynolds Cahoon, Parley P. Pratt, Jonathan C. Wright, Phinehas Richards, Edward Hunter, Franklin Richards,[223] & James M. Monroe[.][224]

---

Jesus Christ of Latter Day Saints," though without naming who those successors would be (*Nauvoo Neighbor Extra,* Dec. 9, 1843).

[223]Franklin Dewey Richards was born in 1821 in Richmond, Massachusetts. He was baptized in 1838 and moved to Missouri and later Illinois. He was subsequently called to join the Quorum of Twelve Apostles. He died in Utah in 1899.

[224]James M. Monroe was born in 1822 in Erie, Pennsylvania. He was

[It was] moved and seconded that the Treasurer give orders to the Councillors to the amount of their ~~taxes~~ dues. Carried. [The] Council [will] adjourn till [the] next regular Session. The municipal Court is the proper place for the persons to appeal to – Co[uncillor] Spencer read the report of the Committee. Adjourned for one hour.

[At] 5 P.M. [the] Council met pursuant to the adjournment – when the Preamble and Resolutions were again read. A Resolution was discussed respecting [the] Warsaw Signal and other papers, by Co[uncillor]s Taylor, Phelps[,] and Young – Co[uncillor] Young moved that the ~~Com~~ report of the Committee be accepted – & [this] carried. Co[uncillor] Young moved that Ald[erman] Orson Spencer ^& Dr. [Willard] Richards^ be requested to draw out Resolutions for the people. [The council] adjourned until [the] next regular session.[225]

†An Ordinance to locate an
Alley on Block 69 and other Alleys or Lanes

Section 1. Be it ordained by the City Council of the City of Nauvoo that there be an Alley located through Block 69 two rods wide, on the North side of the Original Stock Road, running East and West, and where the Road is now located, where it is now fenced and to be called Chase Alley.

Section 2. And be it also ordained that also all lanes or alleys that have been opened through Blocks by the consent of the Owners of Land or otherwise shall not be closed up, without the consent of all the Owners on each side.

This ordinance to be in force from and after its passage.

**Passed December 14th 1844. Daniel Spencer Mayor. Willard Richards Recorder**

An Ordinance incorporating the
Seventies Library and Institute Association

Section 1. Be it ordained by the City Council of the City of Nauvoo, that Brigham Young, Joseph Young, George A. Smith,

---

converted in Utica, New York, and served as a school teacher for Joseph Smith's and Brigham Young's children in Nauvoo.

[225]The Record of Proceedings repeats the appointment of Thomas Bullock as a clerk, adjustments in the amounts due Rollasson and Marr, and the addition of Orson Spencer to the committee studying Marshal Green's bill, all eliminated from the current presentation.

Levi W. Hancock and such others as may be associated with them, are hereby incorporated, to be known by the name of the Seventies Library and Institute Association, with perpetual succession and shall have all corporate powers, to sue and be sued, to plead and be impleaded, to defend and be defended, to purchase, hold, sell, or lease estate real or personal to any amount, to have a common seal which they may alter or renew at pleasure; and shall have exercise and enjoy, all powers, rights and privileges which appertain to like corporate bodies.

Section 2. That the Capital Stock of said Association shall amount to $10,000 which may be increased to any amount by a vote of a majority of the Stockholders present, at a meeting called for that purpose by the President of the Association, who shall give at least one month's notice thereof; which Capital Stock shall be divided into shares of five dollars each.

Section 3. That the books of the Association shall be opened for subscription on the 20th day of December A.D. 1844; and when two hundred dollars shall have been subscribed, the Stockholders shall elect a board of seven Trustees, who shall elect one of their number President of the Association, to hold their office during good behavior, [and] said board of Trustees shall constitute the law making department of said Association, with full power and authority to make ordain establish and execute all such laws and ordinances, as they may deem necessary for the benefit, government and regulation of said association, not repugnant to the Constitution of the United States, or the Constitution of this State.

Section 4. That the Board of Trustees shall have power to appoint a Librarian Registrar and such other officers as may be necessary, to prescribe their duties, and remove them from office at pleasure.

Section 5. That the Board of Trustees shall have power to require of all officers appointed in pursuance of this act, Bonds with such penalty and security as may be deemed expedient, for the faithful performance of their respective duties; and also to require of all officers appointed as aforesaid to take an oath for the faithful performance of the duties of their respective offices

Section 6 That the President of the Association, shall have power to fill all vacancies in the board of Trustees, that may occur from the absence of any member by appointment; a Majority of whom shall form a Quorum to do business.

Section 7 That in case of the death, removal, resignation, or neglect to serve, of any one or more of the Trustees, their place shall be filled by vote of a majority of the Stockholders present, at a meeting called for that purpose, upon a notice of at least four weeks by the President of the Association; and in case of the neglect or refusal of the President to give such notice, the duty of giving notice shall devolve upon a majority of the Trustees.

Section 8 That it shall be the duty of the Librarian, under the direction of the President, to receive in payment for Stock, all useful Books, Maps, Charts, Globes, Models, and Scientific Instruments, also paintings, engravings, sculptures, and all other useful and curious specimens of the arts and sciences, also all kinds of Natural Curiosities and antiquities.

Section 9 That the Board of Trustees shall provide for the erection of all Buildings Observatories, &c, that they may deem necessary for the benefit of the Association.

Section 10 That each member of the Association shall be entitled to one vote for each share which he may actually hold and shall be allowed to vote by proxy.

Section 11 This Ordinance to be in force from and after its passage.

**Passed Dec[embe]r 14, 1844. Daniel Spencer Mayor. Willard Richards, Recorder**[226]

An Ordinance to amend an Ordinance
entitled an Ordinance to erect a Dam in the Mississippi River
and for other purposes Passed Dec[embe]r 8, 1843.

Be it ordained by the City Council of the City of Nauvoo that the Successors of Joseph Smith mentioned in said Ordinance are those who succeed him in the Office of Trustee in Trust in the Church of Jesus Christ of Latter Day Saints.

**Passed Dec[embe]r 14, 1844. Daniel Spencer Mayor. Willard Richards Recorder**

---

[226]The rough minute book has almost identical recitals of the petition to extend the street beyond Spear Street, the claim of Jonathan Hale, the indemnity for the new trustees-in-trust, the audit of the accounts, and the decision to inform the councilmen of their dues.

A[lbert] P. Rockwood filed his Bond as Assessor and Collector in 1[st] Ward Aug[us]t 20th. Daniel Hendrix filed his bond as Assessor and Collector in 2nd Ward Aug[us]t 20. Jonathan H. Hale filed his bond as Assessor and Collector in 3rd Ward Aug[us]t 30. Willard Richards Recorder

## 5.

# "Truth ... Like a Wedge" 1845

‡*January 11, 1845; Saturday.*[1] [In the] Regular Session, [at] 2 [minutes] past 10, [the] names of [the] members [were] called[.] [There was] not a Quorum present. [The] Marshall was sent after absent members [at] 3 [minutes] to 11 [o'clock]. [After] a quorum [was] present[,] [a] prayer [was given] by Co[uncillor] [John] Taylor. [The] Minutes were read and ^[the] co[uncillors] were^ satisfied that the Minutes [should] remain as they are –

[A] Petition of Brigham Young for the Nauvoo Ferry – [was to] be referred to the Committee of Finance – [A] Letter of W[illard] Richards Recorder [was to] be referred to the Committee on Municipal Laws. Co[uncillor] Taylor wished the Taxes to be called in the year for which they are assessed. Co[uncillor] [William W.] Phelps moved that Orson Pratt fill Orson Hydes place this day on the committees.

[A] Petition of Hosea Stout and 26 others [of the police force was submitted] for one half of the penalties recovered against parties for breaking the ordinances of the city. Ald[erman] [George W.] Harris, [said] there is an ordinance already to that effect.[2] Co[uncillor]

---

[1]The *History of the Church of Jesus Christ of Latter-day Saints,* 7 vols. (Salt Lake City: Deseret News, 1902-12), 7:351, devotes two sentences to this meeting: "City council met and transacted much business. Passed an ordinance authorizing and licensing Brigham Young to run a ferry across the Mississippi at Nauvoo in place of Joseph Smith, martyred."

[2]The minutes do not record an ordinance giving the police a percent-

Phelps stated that the Police are for the protection of property. Ald[erman] [Daniel H.] Wells moved [that it] be referred to the Com[mittee] on Police and [that] Co[uncillor] B[righam] Young [be] added to the Com[mittee][.]

[The] Bill of Dan[ie]l Hendrix [for] 71.44 [was] ref[erre]d to the Com[mittee] on Claims – [and the] bill allowed – [The] Claim of A[lbert] P. Rockwood [for] 18.69 [was] allowed instead of [the bill for] 15.69 previously allowed[.] [The new] bill [was] allowed. [The] Claim of Arthur Boscow [for] 2.50 [was] refered to the Com[mittee] on Claims – [The] Co[mmittee] on Claims [said it will] have nothing to do with it – [The] report was allowed.

[The] Report of [Charles C.] Rich & [Jonathan] Dunham on Grubb & Richie's bill was read[.][3] Ald[erman] Wells moved that it be accepted – and [this] carried. [The] Bill of G. Williams for 4.04 [should] be ref[erre]d to the Com[mittee] on Claims – [The] Com[mittee] reported [that it was] allowed – and [the request was] granted.

Ald[erman] G[eorge] A. Smith stated that the Committee on Burying Grounds – wish[es] an ordinance for the removal of Durphy Street to the West – The burying ground is in the middle of the Street[.] It will take a Street 2 rods wide out of one lot – and a little on the opposite side – [The committee] wish[es] a Street to go round on the W[est] and S[outh] side of it –

[It was] moved & seconded that [a cross-street be added] before you come to the burying ground. Ald[erman] Wells enquired if there was not sufficient land reserved without going on other prop-

---

age of the fines. On July 13, 1844, the City Recorder informed the council that there was no provision at all for compensating the police. Although the council talked about this periodically throughout 1844, the councilmen seemed reluctant to give the police an incentive for writing more fines. They were also reluctant to interfere with what they saw as the prerogative of the Church president who had organized the police, drawing on men who had been Missouri Danites, to serve the interests of the Church. Later in the month when the city loses its charter (January 29, 1845), the police are organized into "deacons quorums" of ten each, headed by "bishop" Stephen Markham (D. Michael Quinn, *The Mormon Hierarchy: Origins of Power* [Salt Lake City: Signature Books and Smith Research Associates, 1994], 116-17, 152, 177, 180, 181, 649, 651; Glen M. Leonard, *Nauvoo: A Place of Peace, A People of Promise* [Salt Lake City: Deseret Book, 2002], 110-11, 469-70).

[3]Grubb and Richie's was a Nauvoo store.

erty – ~~Ald[erman]~~ Co[uncillor] G[eorge] A. Smith said half an acre was reserved – but we shall have to be at some expence in crowding on other persons property – and shewed its situation. Ald[erman] Harris spoke – Co[uncillor] Taylor [said] the Council [should] have power to alter Streets at pleasure – This Land is principally Church property – We had better take some definite action. That road looks to me like Sacrilege.

~~Ald[erman]~~ Co[uncillor] G[eorge] A. Smith – moved that an Ordinance be drawn out – [This was] not seconded. Ald[erman] Harris moved that a Committee go and examine the Records of the Deeds – [This was] not seconded. Co[uncillor] B[righam] Young [said] it is proper for an Ordinance to be drawn out – and not to [allow people to] drive over the graves – It is no use to enquire into Titles, but shun the burying ground for the time being – But [he would] draw up an ordinance – for the time being ^to^ go round [and] no action [is] required till [that] Ordinance is made –

An Ordinance in relation to the ferry across the Mississippi River [was] read [the] 1st. time 2 time – 3 time [and the] Bill passed – [All were] satisfied with the Title. An Ordinance concerning the burying ground on Durphy Street [was] read [the] 1st. time, 2 time, 3 time – and [everyone was] satisfied by the Title – Ald[erman] G[eorge] A. Smith moved that the Supervisor of Streets be empowered to use ~~delinquent~~ street labor in fencing the burying ground – Ald[erman] Wells [said that] as the City is enterprising – the Supervisor should get the Street labor & do it – Ald[erman] Harris [said] if your Honor opens the Street you are authorised to fence the ground – Ald[erman] G[eorge] A. Smith [said] we should fence all round, and have no partnership – Dont make any jungling business.[4] [It was] moved and seconded that the Supervisor fence the burying ground with delinquent Street labor [and a] subscription from the people – [The] motion [was then] withdrawn –

Mr. [James] Sloan wished to speak, and [was] allowed – [He said] [:] I was sent to Ireland by the Church – An order was made after my departure [to fill my office], and I consider that it is my right to be re-instated [as City Recorder] – I think I have been faithful – I am

---

[4]*Jungling* used to refer to setting up camp together in primitive conditions (*Shorter Oxford English Dictionary* [Oxford: Oxford University Press, 2002], s.v. "jungle").

now destitute of a situation – I had the burthen of the [Church] business at the commencement [of my term], and I hope I shall now be re-instated[5] – Co[uncillor] Young [said] its true he went to the Old Countries – [He was] C[ity] Recorder – &c. There will be a new election and ^it is^ for them to decide –

[Brigham Young continued, saying that] with regard to [who should fill] it – Brother [Willard] Richards has been appointed [and] we must reject him [in order] to take in brother Sloan – ~~if~~ I have labored, and got enough to pay my taxes – and a many have labored for nothing – We have to borrow money almost weekly – I have always attended but never charge[d] any thing. I have [an] objection to [Sloan] for Recorder of Licences – A man could not get a Licence without paying him 25 cents – He record[ed] [that] G[eorge] A. Smith "did not pay for his Licence – "If there was a ~~Licence~~ place where he could get a penny he wanted it. It is not worth while turning Br[other] Richards out, to take in Br[other] Sloan. Br[other] Richards gets his pay by Hook or by Crook as he could get it – If the feathers are picked of us, we dont want the down taken of us. I want to see men act from generous principles.

Mr. Sloan replied, that he went according to council – and I now claim to be re-instated – The charges cannot be substantiated against me – Let it be laid before the congregation, and I venture to say ~~he~~ I will be re-instated. I received the fees that was allowed by the City Council, and no more – I have right and truth on my side and [I] shall continue [to speak] it boldly. Co[uncillor] [Orson] Pratt [said] there is no such thing as being re-instated City Recorder – If a man is absent – another is elected [by the city council][,] and [he] read the resolution of [the council] appointing W[illard] Richards Recorder – We cannot turn [away] our present City Recorder without some fault [of his] – Co[uncillor] Orson Spencer [said the] Recorder is appointed by the City Council, and it would be a burlesque to appoint [Sloan] City Recorder now –

Co[uncillor] Young – ~~he~~ says Br[other] Sloan misunderstands the matter – I want him elected one of the City Council – for he always talked more than any three other [men on the] Council, when he was Clerk – I want to raise up the City, and not to sink it – I would

[5]James Sloan was sent on a mission to Ireland on May 11, 1843. When he left, Willard Richards was put in his place on the council.

just as soon send him [on] another mission. He is as smart a man as I am – Br[other] Sloan wants Br[other] Richards dropt, in order to step in – He is eternally for the picayune – He is always seeking office – Co[uncillor] Pratt moved that Mr. Sloan's petition be rejected [and this] carried.

An Ordinance to repeal an ordinance concerning the City Attorney &c [was] read 1 time [and then a] 2[nd] time[.] Co[uncillor] Phelps said [that] not long since it was considered best to reduce the City officer's salary – We want to curtail the expenses and live in harmony – Co[uncillor] Young [said][:] I conclude it is a needless expense – It is merely a salary to keep him on hand – Bro[ther] [George P.] Stiles [said][:] I am glad – At the time I received the appointment there was a press of business – I expected that when it was done away[,] that the Salary would be dropt – I never had an eye for the emoluments – I feel just as honorable as if I remained the City Att[orne]y.[6] [The ordinance was] read [a] 3[rd] time [and the] Bill pass[ed]. [All were] satisfied with the Title.

Orson Spencer reported ^on the petition of the police^ that the Informant [should be given] half of [any] fine & drew up an Ordinance [called] An Ordinance concerning fines. [It was] motioned and seconded that the Committee be discharged from their duties. Carried. [The] Bill [was] read [the] 1st. time[,] 2 time by its Title[,] [and a] 3rd time d[itt]o. [The] Bill pass[ed] – [all were] satisfied with the Title.[7] ~~Co[uncillor] Orson Pratt~~ John Taylor [said that] an election is wanted for a fresh council [to deal with these questions]. Ald[erman] G[eorge] A. Smith [said] there is [already] an ordinance on the subject.[8] Co[uncillor] Phelps read a section on the duties of the Police-

---

[6]It is interesting that the city attorney is referred to as "Brother Stiles" since he was excommunicated in December 1843, although he was retained as the city attorney. It is not clear if the council primarily wanted to eliminate his office or to get rid of him. In either case, he would receive a federal appointment ten years later to be one of the Utah territorial judges. Known to be a thorn in Brigham Young's side, Stiles's office in Utah will be ransacked with Young's approval (see, e.g., Eugene E. Campbell, *Establishing Zion: The Mormon Church in the American West, 1847-1869* [Salt Lake City: Signature Books, 1988], 221, 229-30).

[7]See below. The council limits the revenue sharing to fines involving alcohol and gives half the income to informers and half to the city–nothing directly to the police.

[8]Every time the issue of compensating the police is raised, someone

men [and added that] it may be necessary for them to have some [additional] printed authority. Ald[erman] Wells reported favorably on the petition of Willard Richards – and it was moved that the Committee be discharged. An Ordinance to amend the ordinance concerning the revenue for a specific purpose passed [on] Oct[ober] 31, 1842, [was] read 1, 2 & 3 time[s] [and] passed by its Title – and [the council was] satisfied with the Title.[9]

Co[uncillor] Taylor moved that we dissolve into a Committee of the whole to take into consideration the Elections of the Judges [to supervise the upcoming voting] – and [the motion] carried. Ald[erman] G[eorge] A. Smith moved that the election for City Officers [mayor, aldermen, councilmen] [should] be held in one place[.] [This] carried. Co[uncillor] Young moved that it be held in the ~~Music~~ Concert hall[10] ~~or near there~~ – carried. Ald[erman] G[eorge] A. Smith nominated Elijah Fordham, Hosea Stout, and Jonathan H. Hale [as election judges] – [and the motion] carried. John Taylor Chairman reported on the above [question of the election] – and the report of the Committee was accepted. ~~the nom~~

[It was] moved and seconded that the ~~nomination of the Committee be accepted~~ Bill pass – "An Ordinance for the discretionary enlargement of the No. [number] of the Policemen[,]" [which was] read 1 time, [a] 2[nd] time by title, [and a] 3[rd] d[itt]o. [The] Bill pass[ed], [all being] satisfied with the Title. [It was further agreed to] call the people together on Tuesday at 1 oclock. Co[uncillor] Young[:] Let all agree upon the right thing, and then let it be done.[11] An ~~act~~ ordinance for the fencing of the old Burying ground [was] read 1 time, 2 time[s], [and a] 3rd time. [The] Bill pass[ed] – [all] satisfied by the Title –

Co[uncillor] Young [said] we have long been desirous to put an end to all iniquity – and more so now – Our enemies are going

---

says there must be an ordinance covering it. Each time they realize there isn't such an ordinance, they nevertheless end up doing nothing about it.

[9]This has to do with property taxes. See below.

[10]The "Music Hall, also called the Concert Hall," was just nearing completion (Leonard, *Nauvoo,* 192).

[11]Three days earlier, Church leaders had met to decide who would run for office. At the public meeting announced here, Church members endorsed the slate of candidates–one person per office–and the city would vote unanimously for the candidates on February 3 (ibid., 469).

into a regular system of stealing[12] – Let the City Council draw up resolutions – print them – and send them to our friends – [It was] moved that Daniel H. Wells, John Taylor, Ald[erma]n ^Orson^ Spencer – Brigham Young – the Mayor Daniel Spencer – ^W[illiam] W. Phelps, Geo[rge] A. Smith^ and Orson Pratt be a Committee to draft the resolutions to deliver to the people. The motion was [then] rescinded.

The Mayor [is] instructed to call the Council together at the Recorder's Office on Monday at 10 A.M. [The council will stand] adjourned until [Monday] morning at 10 a.m. at the Recorders office to meet in [a] committee of the whole.

‡‡[In the] Regular Session, January 11, 1845 10 A.M.[,] the Bill of Daniel Hendrix of 71.44 for assessing & collecting in [the] 2[nd] Ward – was allowed. The claim of A[lbert] P. Rockwood for 3.00 which was deducted on Nov[embe]r 9, 1844 – [was] allowed. The Bill of G. Williams for 4.04 for Leather was allowed.[13] The claim of Arthur Boscow for 2.50 was [disallowed and the committee] reported [it had] "nothing to do with it."[14]

**Willard Richards — Recorder — by Thomas Bullock — Deputy**

†Allowed [the store of] Grub and Ritchie twenty five dollars and cost[s][,] also an order on the Nauvoo Legion for five dollars as per report of [the] Committee.[15]

**January 11, 1845. Daniel Spencer Mayor. Willard Richards Recorder.**

---

[12]Theft remained a problem. One LDS resident, Sarah Scott, wrote to her mother on February 6, 1845: "Stealing has been carried on to an alarming extent in and about Nauvoo last fall and this winter. They first began stealing from the dissenters and raised the cry that the dissenters did it themselves to bring persecution on the Church, but after a while a few of the good Mormon souls were caught in it; three have been taken to Carthage Jail, and more will likely follow" (qtd. in George F. Partridge, ed., "The Death of a Mormon Dictator: Letters of Massachusetts Mormons, 1843-1848," *New England Quarterly* 9 [Dec. 1936]: 583, 603).

[13]This appears in the Record of Proceedings with the additional information that the expense was incurred "in June last."

[14]These minutes repeat the intension to have Fordham, Hale, and Stout stage the elections at the Concert Hall, also the rejection of James Sloan's petition, omitted here.

[15]The Proceedings also include the bills of Hendrix and Rockwood, deleted here to avoid repetition.

An Ordinance in
relation to a ferry across the Mississippi River

Section 1. Be it ordained by the City Council of the City of Nauvoo, that Brigham Young is authorized and licensed to keep a ferry across the Mississippi River at the City of Nauvoo in place of Joseph Smith martyr'd under the same privileges and restrictions and regulations specified in an Ordinance entitled an Ordinance to establish a ferry across the Mississippi River at the City of Nauvoo passed June 1st 1843.

Section 2. This Ordinance to be in force from and after its passage.

**Passed January 11, 1845. Daniel Spencer Mayor. Willard Richards, Recorder.**

An Ordinance concerning
the burying Ground on Durphy Street

Section 1. Be it ordained by the City Council of the City of Nauvoo, that Durphy Street be shut up where it goes through the Grave Yard, and that the Street instead of going through the Grave Yard be opened on the south side of the grave yard running West from its present location to the extreme West side of the said Burying Ground, thence north to the north side of the said Grave Yard, thence East to the old location of the Street.

Section 2. And be it further ordained that the Street shall be three rods wide.

Section 3. This ordinance to be in force from and after its passage.

**Passed January 11, 1845. Daniel Spencer Mayor. Willard Richards Recorder.**

An Ordinance for the fencing of the old Burying Ground

Section 1. Be it ordained by the City Council of the City of Nauvoo that the Supervisor of Streets is hereby authorized and instructed to appropriate a sufficient portion of the delinquent Road Labor, to fence the old Burying Ground, the fence to be at the discretion of the Mayor.

Section 2. This ordinance to be in force from and after its passage.

**Passed January 11, 1845. Daniel Spencer Mayor. Willard Richards, Recorder.**

An Ordinance to repeal an Ordinance concerning the City Attorney & his duties

Section 1. Be it ordained by the City Council of the City of Nauvoo, that the ordinance concerning the City Attorney and his duties passed June 8, 1844, is hereby repealed.

**Passed January 11, 1845. Daniel Spencer Mayor. Willard Richards, Recorder**

An Ordinance concerning Fines

Section 1. Be it ordained by the City Council of the City of Nauvoo That all fines which may lawfully accrue hereafter for the violation of the first section of an Ordinance entitled an Ordinance concerning Spirituous Liquors and other purposes shall be awarded one half to the Complainant and the remaining half of the fine to be paid to the Corporation of the City of Nauvoo, all ordinances to the contrary notwithstanding.

Section 2. This ordinance to be in force from and after its passage.

**Passed January 11, 1845. Daniel Spencer Mayor. Willard Richards, Recorder**

An Ordinance to amend the Ordinance concerning the Revenue [originally] passed Oct[obe]r 31, 1842 for a specific purpose

Section 1. That the time for the Sale of the City lots and lands for taxes for the year 1844 be and the same is hereby deferred from the first Monday of December 1st to the first Monday in February 1845 for adjudication by the Municipal Court.

Section 2. That if any one is dissatisfied with the Assessment[,] he or they so dissatisfied shall have an opportunity of making his plea on the same before the Municipal Court on the first Monday of February 1845.

Section 3. This Ordinance to be in force from and after its passage, any other Ordinance to the contrary notwithstanding.

**Passed January 11, 1845. Daniel Spencer Mayor. Willard Richards, Recorder.**

An Ordinance for the discretionary enlargement of the Number of Police men

Section 1. Be it ordained by the City Council of the City of Nauvoo, That the Mayor of said city is hereby authorized to enroll on the list of City Police any number of men at his discretion not exceeding five hundred, provided the service of such Policemen shall not be chargable to this City.

**Passed January 11, 1845. Daniel Spencer Mayor. Willard Richards, Recorder**

It was motioned and carried that the Election for One Mayor, four Aldermen and nine Councillors be held in one place only – and that place the Concert Hall, and also that Elijah Fordham, Hosea Stout and Jonathan H. Hale be the Judges of the said Election.

**Passed January 11, 1845. Daniel Spencer Mayor. Willard Richards, Recorder.**

‡*January 13, 1845; Monday.*[16] [At] 10 A.M. [the] Adjourned Session [reconvened as a] Committee of the whole – [The] Mayor [was] in the chair. [The] Names of [the] Members [were] called – A Quorum [was] present – [The] prayer [was given] by W[illiam] W. Phelps. [The] Minutes were dispensed with –

[It was] moved and seconded that Ald[erman] [Daniel H.] Wells[,] Ald[erman] [Orson] Spencer[,] Co[uncillor] Phelps, Co[uncillor] Pratt, [and] Co[uncillor] Taylor be a committee to draft Resolutions[17] – Co[uncillor] Spencer wanted the truth to drive like a wedge – and to commence with the declaration of extermination which was threatened by our enemies. Co[uncillor] Phelps thinks it best [for the Church leadership] to be where they cannot be hindered. Co[uncillor] Taylor wants to put a stop to every iniquity – and to let every thing be clearly shewn.

Ald[erman] Wells knows of two or three instances where property has been stolen by ~~the old citizens~~ ^~~persons out of remote from the city~~^ anti mormons remote from the City and then instead of being brought to punishment – left the State in a certain N[umber]

---

[16]See also *History of Church,* 7:352-54.

[17]Taylor explained: "I was appointed one of a committee to draft resolutions pertaining to the impositions practiced by the Anti-Mormons, and to take precautionary measures to prevent thefts" (Dean C. Jessee, ed., *John Taylor Nauvoo Journal* [Provo: Grandin Book, 1996], 26). From the context, it seems the committee was also charged with responding to outside accusations against the city and its inhabitants.

of days. [The] Mayor – spoke in regard to some persons who were dissatisfied with their lands being advertized for sale for taxes – on account of a law that has been passed by the Legislature. Ald[erman] Wells[:] It had better be brought up before the Municipal Court – and for them to advise the City Council to act – and so shew that the Municipal Court obeys the State Laws.[18]

†The voice of Nauvoo[19] Proceedings of the City Council
Preamble

It is with feelings of deep and inexpressible regret, that we learn that the Inhabitants of various parts of this State are seeking to accumulate all the real and supposed crimes of the whole community [of Hancock County] for the secret or ostensible purpose of raising a tide of influence against the Mormon community [in order] that [they] shall sweep [the Mormons] into irrecoverable ruin. This course of conduct, originating with our mortal enemies and gathering in its wake other men that would [otherwise] revolt at the idea of lending a hand to oppress a long abused people that are struggling against foes within and foes without, is at the present almost insupportable to our feelings. – We have scarcely laid by our mourning weeds[20] for murdered

---

[18]The Illinois legislature passed a law that appears for the first time in the *1845 Revised Statutes* prohibiting individuals from contesting a tax sale without clear title to their land (Merritt Starr and Russell H. Curtis, eds., *Annotated Statutes of the State of Illinois,* 2nd ed. [Chicago: Callaghan and Company, 1896], 3:3498). This was important in Nauvoo because the land was mostly still owned by Isaac Galland, Horace Hotchkiss, and others who had sold it on credit to Sidney Rigdon's son-in-law, George W. Robinson, acting for the LDS Church, and the Church had sold lots to individuals without actually owning the deeds. Galland and Hotchkiss eventually decided to accept Church members' abandoned property in Missouri and on the east coast in exchange for their Nauvoo property. As historian Robert Bruce Flanders wrote, "The Hotchkiss partners faced a dilemma. Their Nauvoo property was returning them virtually nothing, but they were still legally obligated to pay the taxes since they held the deeds," and the property values and associated taxes were appreciating (*Nauvoo: Kingdom on the Mississippi* [Urbana: University of Illinois, 1965], 27-30, 34-38, 41-42, 55, 126, 128-30, 134-35, 171-75).

[19]Published in *Times and Seasons,* Jan. 15, 1845, 773-74.

[20]A *weed* was originally an article of clothing, especially "an upper garment"; by the nineteenth century it was "used only in the plural, *weeds,* for the mourning apparel of a female; as a widow's *weeds*" (Noah Webster, *An*

men [Joseph and Hyrum Smith], whom we promptly surrendered up to the State of Illinois for an equitable trial – And now we see in embryo, another campaign to spill yet more blood, and effect an other extermination and massacre. We sought to rid our City of Counterfeiters and blacklegs. These together with our foes without and within, had established a printing press of unparalleled rancor and malignity.[21] But our efforts to obtain freedom from such vicious monsters cost us much tribulation and precious blood.

The impunity thus far granted the murderers by the Senate and other authorities of the State of Illinois, has emboldened them and their apologists to set on foot a series of other exciting causes that they hope will either destroy this community, or prevent their criminals from being brought to punishment. We have not so much fear that our enemies will succeed in their fiendish designs against us, as we have that the peace and good order of the people of this State will be disturbed, and fearful anarchy and bloody misrule will ensue among those who listen to and countenance the fell designs of those who are stealing from quiet citizens of the State and palming upon them a spurious and false currency, and charging to the Mormons their own crimes. If they shall succeed, the Citizens will be involved in continual larcenies, and neighborhood broils and crimes, the end of which cannot now be foreseen. We deprecate such evils and calamities because we desire the good of all mankind; as the gratuitous labors of the greater portion of our Citizens in spreading truth throughout the world under much poverty and suffering abundantly proves.

As for us, our course is fixed, and while we are peaceable and loyal to the constitution and laws of our country, and are ever willing to join hands with the honest, virtuous, and patriotic in suppressing crime and punishing criminals, we will leave our enemies to judge, whether it would not be better to make Nauvoo one universal burying ground, before we suffer ourselves to be driven from our hard earned and lawful homes, by such high handed oppression, and it may yet become a question to be

---

*American Dictionary of the English Language* [New York: S. Converse, 1828], s.v., "weed").

[21]This refers to the *Nauvoo Expositor.*

decided by the community, whether the Mormons will, after having witnessed their best men murdered without redress, quietly and patiently, suffer their enemies to wrench from them the last shreds of their constitutional rights; and whether they will not make their City one great Sepulchre, rather than be the humble devotees at the shrine of mobocracy. But for the satisfaction of all concerned, we reiterate in the following resolutions, sentiments that we have always expressed in all places as occasions demanded:

*Resolved,* that the greater part of the thefts which have been complained of, are not in our opinion, true in fact, but have ben *trumped up* by inimical persons, in order to cover their aggressive doings, with plausibility, and entice honest and unwary citizens to unite with them in the same uncompromising hostility against this people.

*Resolved.* That we defy the world to substantiate a single instance, where we have concealed criminals, or screened them from justice; but, on the contrary, always have been, and now are, extremely anxious that they should be ferretted out and brought to justice; and to this end would esteem it a favor, that if any person should lose property or have good and sufficient reason to suspect any place of containing apparatus for making bogus or counterfeit money, that such person would follow up, trace out, and make diligent search, for all such property and apparatus, and if they can trace it into this City, we pledge ourselves to assist them legally, to the extent of our abilities in so laudable an undertaking.

*Resolved.* That it is our opinion that very many scoundrels, such as thieves, robbers, bogus makers, counterfeiters and murderers, have been induced from reports published in the Warsaw Signal, to flock into this County in order to carry on their evil practices, knowing that it would be immediately charged upon the Mormons, and thereby they escape – and although we think that the reports of thefts have been very much exaggerated, yet we know from dear bought experience that such things do exist, and further we doubt not there may be some such characters prowling in and about our City.

*Resolved,* That we are extremely anxious to ferret out and bring to justice, all such persons, if any, that are within the limits of our City, and for this purpose we have authorized our Mayor to enlarge the Police, to any number, not exceeding five hundred, and we also pledge ourselves to double our diligence, and call upon our Citizens to assist in ridding our city and country of all such infamous characters.

**Done, in Council, this 13th day of January 1845. D[aniel] Spencer, Mayor. W[illard] Richards, Recorder.**

*February 7, 1845; Friday.*[22] The Poll book for the City of Nauvoo of February 3rd 1845 being returned to the Recorder's office according to Ordinance[,] the Recorder called to his assistance Aldermen George W. Harris and William Marks and broke the Seal of said book wherein it was duly recorded that Orson Spencer had eight hundred and forty five vote[s] for Mayor, Daniel Spencer, Newel K. Whitney & Charles C Rich had each eight hundred and forty five votes for Aldermen – and George W. Harris had eight hundred and forty four votes for Alderman – and Samuel Bent, William W. Phelps, George Miller, Edward Hunter, Phinehas Richards, David Fulmer[,] Jonathan C. Wright, and James Sloan had each eight hundred and forty five votes for Counsellor, and John Pack had eight hundred and forty four votes for Counsellor[.] There were no scattering votes.[23] Due

---

[22]John Taylor recorded on January 14, 1845, that he "attended a meeting at the stand at 2 o'clock, to read preamble and resolutions, and to nominate members for the City Council" (Jessee, *John Taylor Nauvoo Journal,* 31-34). Hosea Stout added that "the Twelve ... declined serving in any capacity in the City Council" because they were preoccupied with Church matters (qtd. in Juanita Brooks, ed., *On the Mormon Frontier: The Diary of Hosea Stout,* 2 vols. [Salt Lake City: University of Utah Press, 1964], 1:14-16).

Fifteen days later, on January 29, the Illinois legislature repealed the Nauvoo Charter, leaving the city without authority to hold elections, enforce ordinances, or punish crime (36). The council met on January 30 to draft a letter to John Quincy Adams, Stephen Douglas, Andrew Jackson, Daniel Webster, and others asking their advice: "Believing you to be a man of erudition, and of legal attainments, we have thought it advisable to address you on the subject, asking for your opinion as to the most expedient course to be taken." Hosea Stout wrote that the meeting was held at the Masonic Hall at 2:00 p.m. and that it involved the "Authorities of the City & Church" (1:18).

[23]This was a way of saying that the results were not close. To be *scattered* was to be "not united; divided among many, as *scattering votes*" (Webster, *American Dictionary,* s.v. "scattering"). It was also a polite way of saying that the election was rigged since there was only one candidate per office and

notice of the election to the above named individuals was ~~duly~~ written sealed and laid upon the Recorder's table. February 7th 1845. Willard Richards Recorder

Due notice of the Election for Orson Spencer for Mayor, Daniel Spencer, George W. Harris, Newel K. Whitney and Charles C. Rich for Aldermen is made out under seal of [the city] Corporation and filed in the Post Office directed to George W. Habeker Esq[ui]re[,]Clerk of the County Commissioners C[our]t and through him to the Secretary of State on February 7th, 1845. Willard Richards Recorder[.]

[The] City Council assembled as usual in their Regular Session and upon hearing of the Report of the Recorder as on page 233 and that a majority of the Councillors had received their Oath of Office[,] the council decided that the Election was legal and that the new members were qualified to [sit] in the new council, and [the outgoing members] gave room to the Councillors elect by vacating their seats. Willard Richards Recorder.

‡*February 8, 1845; Saturday.* 2 past 10 A.M. – [The] Names of [the] members [were] called, [and it was found that] a Quorum [was] present – [The] prayer [was offered] by Ald[erman] G[eorge] W. Harris – [The] Minutes of [the] last meeting [were] read and accepted – A discussion took place on the subject of swearing in the new Council – G[eorge] A. Smith motioned that the 2 Councils sit together till noon – [It was] carried – & then withdrawn.

Ald[erman] [Daniel H.] Wells, spoke on the Election – Some illegality may have taken place – It must be approved by this Council before they can take their Seats – [It was] moved and seconded that we hear the Report of our Recorder – and he read same – " " [that] it be accepted – and [the motion] carried –

Ald[erman] Orson Spencer [said] we are satisfied of the Election, and of the Council having taken their Oath of office – Ald[erman] Wells moved "that we ~~approve~~ accept of the Election, and of the new members" and that we request the old Council to remain during the day as a matter of courtesy. [The] Recorder said there is business on

---

all of the candidates had been pre-screened by the Church and pitched to the membership before any votes were cast. It was a "sustaining vote" rather than a democratic electoral contest.

this table, that none but the old Council can attend to – [The] Mayor suggests that an action be taken on it –

Ald[erman] Wells said this is the Regular Session – & if the Old Council accept of the New Council, they (the new Council) must do that business – Co[uncillor] [Brigham] Young spoke of his time as an old Co[uncillor] being expired – Co[uncillor] G[eorge] Miller [said] the Old Aldermen must necessarily act, until the new ones are fully authorized – Co[uncillor] Phelps replied – Ald[erman] Harris [said] the old Ald[ermen] need no new Commission. G[eorge] Miller [repeated that] the old ones must act until the new ones are qualified – Co[uncillor] [John] Taylor [said] the Council is complete as there is a majority without the Old [councilmen] – Co[uncillor] Phelps spoke, [and] Young requested to know if we are not dissolved [and if] there is no more Old Council – & the new Council must do what they please – Co[uncillor] Miller moved that we invite [the old council] to stay with us this day – Ald[erman] Harris [said] it falls on the Old Mayor to ask the new one to take his seat –

Co[uncillor] [Jonathan C.] Wright[:] I understand it requires a Commission from the Gov[erno]r before he can act – I consider the new Mayor cannot act until he receives his authority. Co[uncillor] Miller [said he] dissents from the Ex. Co[uncillor] Young in regard to a new mayor – If I conceive aright the City Charter – we are a disorganized body without a head – and the Old Mayor will have to act until the new one is qualified & I renew my motion that the Old Co[uncillors] be invited to remain –

Co[uncillor] Young moved that the Old Co[uncil] be dissolved – Co[uncillor] [Phineas] Richards[:] If I understand it the Old Mayor & Ald[ermen] must act, until the new ones receive their commission to act, but the Councillors – when they take their Oath of Office – they can act – Co[uncillor] Phelps [said] it only requires a majority of the Council to act – & I move that we invite the Old Councillors to remain with us – Co[uncillor] [Orson] Pratt [said] the Mayor has a right to sit without a commission – Co[uncillor] Young said we [will] all appear to be wanting to talk – I am satisfied that the old Co[uncil] is dissolved [when] the new roll was called – Orson Spencer moved "that Dan[ie]l Spencer continue to hold his seat until the New Council call[s] upon the new Mayor to take his Seat" – seconded and carried –

Co[uncillor] Miller moved "that we invite the old council to sit with us this day[,]" [which] carried – " that we appoint a Committee to wait on them & seat them[,] [which] carried – " that G[eorge] W. Harris, Orson Spencer & Phinehas Richards be the Committee[,] [upon which] they made the request [that the old council stay][.] The report [was] accepted & carried – Ex Co[uncillor] Young returned thanks & they took their Seats again. [The council] moved & seconded that we appoint Willard Richards to be the Recorder – and [this was] carried – d[itt]o d[itt]o A[lbert] P. Rockwood to be the Marshall[,] [which] carried. Orson Spencer spoke on the [fact that it would be] proper [to allow several other] officers to continue – [It was] moved and seconded that we appoint W[illiam] W. Phelps [to] be Registrar of Deeds[.] D[itt]o " " " W[illia]m Clayton City Treasurer d[itt]o.[24]

Co[uncillor] Phelps read [the] report of the Supervisor of Streets. Ex Co[uncillor] Young [said] it will be necessary for the City Co[uncil] to have an active standing police – [also] that there may be a Supervisor [of streets] in each Ward to a good advantage – I suggest this for your consideration[.] Co[uncillor] Phelps [said] if we have a Supervisor in each Ward we can have advantage taken for benefit, it will [also] be a good thing to have one or two Constables in each Ward – Co[uncillor] Young [said] it feels [wrong][25] for some men not to have a Street to his own house, and yet have to work out ^his street labor^ in another Ward –

Ald[erman] D[aniel] Spencer said the Supervisor of Streets had been instructed to work out [the volunteer labor] on Streets most used – Ald[erman] Harris asked [the] Supervisor of Streets if he would be satisfied to have one Ward [for the whole city] – Mr. [James] Allred spoke [and said that] after Joseph's death, I have obeyed every word that the new Mayor has ordered me to do. I have done the best I could – Co[uncillor] Phelps spoke [and] suggested & motioned "that we hear the Report of the Recorder" – Ald[erman] Wells read the City Charter section[26] – & s[ai]d it wo[ul]d be best to appoint 4 Ass[istan]t Supervisors & make them Constables – [and

[24]See note 36.

[25]The word Young uses is "hard," which was idiomatic.

[26]Wells is probably quoting from Section 9 of the Nauvoo Charter which gives the city council appointment power.

we] mi[gh]t let the old Supervisor nominate them – Co[uncillor] Wright tho[ugh]t it best for the council to appoint them[.] Ald[erman] Harris [and] Co[uncillor] W[illiam] W. Phelps would like to have four Supervisors [of streets] –

Co[uncillor] Wright moved that ~~Jose~~ James Allred be Supervisor – over the 4th Ward – Co[uncillor] Miller [moved that Allred be] appointed Supervisor of Streets for the City of Nauvoo together with "three assistants[,]" [which] carried – Ald[erman] [Charles C.] Rich [said] it is for this Council to say who the men shall be – & "moved that ~~Co~~ Lorenzo Clark – Benj[ami]n Jones[27] & J[esse] P. Harmon[28] – be the 3 – [that] they are good men & are getting no pay ^for their services[.][29]^ – [The motion] carried – Ald[erman] Wells moved that D[aniel] Hendrix be one for [the] 2nd Ward – [It was] not seconded [and was] moved that the old business be disposed of –

Co[uncillor] Miller [moved that the council] "appoint 4 Constables" [and] [(]named Benj[ami]n Boyce [for the] 1st Ward), E[lijah] J. Sabine[30] [for the] 2nd " [,] Howard Egan [for the] 3nd " [,] [and] D[aniel] M Repsher [for the] 4th " [,] [which] carried. ~~"Be it ordained by the City Council of the City of Nauvoo Resolved that there be three ass[isstan]ts Supervisors appointed for the next two years"~~ Co[uncillor] [James] Sloan [said] I recollect a former time when there were certain persons appointed. It was fully discussed. Co[uncillor] Richards replied – Co[uncillor] Phelps [said] the officers are appointed – We can put the Ordinance first in the Ordinance book. Ald[erman] Wells moved that the appoint[ment] of 3 Assistant Supervisors be reconsidered – & that the men hold the two offices [of street supervisor and constable] – Co[uncillor] Miller spoke –

Co[uncillor] Young [said] if a man takes charge of a Ward – he

---

[27]Benjamin Jones was born in 1797 in Delaware, New York, and baptized in 1832. He lived in Nauvoo's 3rd Ward neighborhood. He died in 1875.

[28]Jesse Pierce Harmon was born in 1795 in Rupert, Vermont. He was baptized in 1838. He lived in Nauvoo's 4th Ward neighborhood. He died in 1877.

[29]Ultimately these four men will be given double duty as street supervisors and fire wardens while four others will receive appointments as ward constables.

[30]Elijah Jefferson Sabin was born in 1806 in Dutchess County, New York. He was residing in Nauvoo by 1843.

will get some remuneration & he may gain a little from his office – It was my idea to have different persons appointed[,] [so] the Ordinance is just right to my mind – Ald[erman] Wells replied – Co[uncillor] Young [said] I dont believe in a Constable or Marshall's ~~be~~ being idle for one hour – to sit in his house until some one comes to tell him he is wanted – They ought to search out the very [suspicious] characters & have their eyes about them – An Ordinance creating Assistant Supervisors [was] read 1 time – [a] 2[nd] time by Title – [a] 3[rd] time [and the] bill pass[ed][.] [The council was] satisfied with the Title.

Mr. Allred spoke of the way he conducted his business – I had three City Wards[.] [I] worked in [a week] 3 days[.] My bill has been 63.00 of a year[,] the highest [of anyone] – Co[uncillor] Phelps replied[.] [The] recorder spoke[.] Co[uncillor] Young spoke[.] Allred replied[.] Harris [said] "that the People of the several Wards are not to be taken out of their own Ward into another["] – Co[uncillor] Phelps motioned "that we ~~take up the accounts~~ rescind the former vote of 3 Ass[istan]t Supervisors" as we are now drawing up an Ordinance in order to put it in the proper place[.] [This] carried. Ald[erman] Rich [reported that] we went to work & created 4 Supervisors for the different Wards – [It was] motioned & seconded that Lorenzo Clark be [the] Supervisor of 1st Ward[.] [This] carried[.] Jesse P. Harmon [for the] 2nd Ward[,] Carried[.] Benjamin Jones [for the] 3rd [ward][,] carried[.] Co[uncillor] Miller Spoke to [approve the suggestion of] appoint[ing] the men for the object of giving them some remuneration for their labors for the City. Adjourned for one hour. 1 o clock PM.

[At] 2 oclock P.M. [the council] met pursuant to adjournment – [The] names of [the] members [were] called – A quorum [was] present[.] [The] standing committees [were] made out, and accepted – Co[uncillor] Wright [asked][,] will the unfinished business now in my hands have to be transferred to the new Marshall, I wish to know – I [probably] have no choice – Co[uncillor] Phelps moved that Orson Spencer be appointed in the place of the Committees that Daniel Spencer is now in. Co[uncillor] Phelps spoke on the Marshall's business – & moved "that the accounts ^of the old Council^ be referred to the Committee on claims[,]" [which] carried – [It was] motioned that Orson Spencer & Edw[ar]d Hunter fill the Committee on claims this afternoon. [It was also] motioned that the fine against Orson Hyde be remitted[,] [which] carried.

[The] Recorder spoke on his bill [for reimbursement] that would be allowed him according to the Ordinance of the City[,] [saying][:] I have left out all [subsidiary] accounts – The whole amount has cost me 50.00 to carry out the business [of the council][.] It has always been my object to save expense to the City – He also submitted the Clerks Report of dues, to the Municipal Court[,] [of which] there now remains due 188.45¾ – to the Court[.] W[illiam] W. Phelps ~~repeals~~ relinquished his amount due to him from the Court. [It was] motioned and ~~carried~~ seconded that James Sloan be Notary Public[,] [which] carried[. ] D[itt]o [that] Stephen Markham be Market Master[,] [which] carried[;] d[itt]o [that] H[enry] G. Sherwood [be] City Surveyor[;] ... D[itt]o [that] Daniel Carns [be] Flour Inspector[;] ... D[itt]o Benj[ami]n Boyce ~~Lorenzo Clark~~ [and] E[lijah] J. Sabine Fire Wardens 1st Ward[;] ... [D[itt]o ~~Jesse P. Harmon~~ " 2nd [Ward] [;] d[itt]o Howard Egan " 3rd [Ward] [;] d[itt]o D[aniel] M. Repsher " 4th [Ward][;] ... ~~John D. Lee Collector of 4th Ward rescinded~~[;] d[itt]o Theodore Turley Sealer of Weights & Measures ...[31]

~~Co[uncilor] Wright enquired why a Collector was appointed in my dis[trict][.] If there is no cause it will throw me out of a situation~~ Co[uncillor] Phelps presented a petition from Benj[amin] Aber[32] & 17 others for the remitting of a fine for selling Spirituous Liquors (against Rufus Beach[33]). [The] Mayor spoke upon the fine, and gave an account of the circumstances [involving Beach's extended family] – & recommended that it be remitted – Co[uncillor] Phelps said Rufus Beach came voluntarily & ~~fined himself~~ confessed [a lapse in] judgment [on the part of his relatives] – He s[ai]d he intended strictly to abide the ordinances of the city – Co[uncillor] Miller remarked

---

[31]The ellipses replace "do" for "d[itt]o."

[32]Benjamin Aber was born in Mendham, New Jersey, in 1790. He lived in Nauvoo as early as 1841 where he received a patriarchal blessing in 1843 and his temple endowment in 1845.

[33]Rufus Beach was born in Roxbury, Connecticut, in 1795 and was baptized in Michigan in 1839. In 1841 he moved to the Nauvoo area and became the president of one of the Seventies quorums. Not a trouble-maker, he would soon be asked to stay in Nauvoo and represent the Church as a real estate agent. For his devotion, he was allowed three additional wives in 1846. For a short time he sympathized with the Strangites. He died in 1850.

& proposed that [the] Co[unci]l take immediate action on it – & referred it the Com[mittee] of the whole house[,] [and the motion] carried –

Ald[erman] Rich [said] I do not know if it has passed all the regular course[s] – It is a hard case to be fined under the circumstances. There are other men also fined [and] we have got to have the whole difficulty brought before us at once. Co[uncillor] Phelps [said] I am acquainted with the whole facts of the case – Pulaski Cahoon has let the day pass so that he cannot carry it to the Municipal Court – This Court is the only place that can remit the fine – Mr. Beach labours under difficulties – Ald[erman] Harris [said] Br[other] Beach actually undergoes grievances – If he means to do right, he ought not to be lashed for his refractory family – [and] moved "that Br[other] Beach's fine be wholly remitted[.]" Carried[.] Phelps replied – I have no doubt W[illia]m Marks will try to get his remitted[.] I have no doubt we shall ^have^ some trouble with it[.] Co[uncillor] Orson Spencer[:] I agree with the remitting of this fine – If he cannot control his family[,] put it away[.] Co[uncillor] Wright spoke on the subject – There is no parallel case to this[.] Ald[erman] Rich replied[.]

[A] Petition of Hosea Stout & others to open Munson St. from Fullmer St. [was] granted. [A] Petition [from] G[eorge] A. Smith & D[aniel] H. Wells – to abate taxes not laid out in City Lots – ~~put~~ [was approved, the taxes] abated.[34] Ald[erman] Rich spoke in full on the above petition – ~~& the~~ [A] Petition of James Alred for 35 [dollars for several] days labor [was considered][.] [It was] motioned "that he suspend collecting for the old debts until [he is] ordered to collect by the Mayor[,]" [which] carried[,] and [the council] referred his ~~pay~~ bill to [the] Committee on claims[,] [which] allowed his claim [of] 35.00 [and his] report [was] accepted[.]

Co[uncillor] Richards motioned that ^the name of^ Warsaw St. be changed. [This was soon] withdrawn[.] Ald[erman] Rich replied [that] there is no way of bounding land ~~by~~ but by the names of Streets – & I should be sorry for the people to lose any thing by it – [The] Committee on Claims found the Recorders accounts very cor-

---

[34]The Record of Proceedings states the proposal more explicitly that "the tax on lands in the city of Nauvoo, and not laid out in City lots, and which have not been paid for the 1843 and 1844 [tax years] may be abated."

rect – and [the] report [was] favorable – [It was found] that he dont get paid for [all] his duties – and allowed 75.00 for extra services. Co[uncillor] Phelps moved that the Committee be discharged from any further duties – ^d[itt]o [that] the Report be accepted[,] [which] carried[.]^ Carried that the clerk be instructed to draw on the Treasury for the amount.

[A] Bill of J[onathan] H. Hale [was presented] for 11.10 [and] moved that it be allowed. [The] Clerk [was] ordered to ~~his~~ issue his Certificate on the Treasury for the amount in the Disbursement book [for] all except [the] Marr & Rollasons bills. Co[uncillor] Phelps read an ordinance concerning Steam Boats [which was] passed [on] Dec[ember] 16, 1843[.] Ald[erman] Rich nominated John D. Lee [to be wharf master][,] [which] carried – and to have 50 cents [of] each dollar [collected][,] as last year[,] [which] carried[.][35] [It was] moved and seconded that Jesse P. Harmon be [the] Pound master[36] – Co[uncillor] Sloan [said] there was an order to restrain the Treasurer from issuing City Scrip – & moved that the Wharf master make out his report. Co[uncillor] Phelps moved that the Treasurer make out his report at our next Regular session[,] [which] carried. [The] Recorder read his report of Finance – and Ald[erman] Harris moved its acceptance & [the motion] carried –

Co[uncillor] Richards spoke about Bro[ther] Horner [the] Flour Inspector & was replied to by [the] Mayor. D[itt]o [regarding] young men horse racing &c in the Public Streets – Orson Spencer moved that an Ordinance be drawn out – Co[uncillor] Miller spoke about a committee being appointed to revise all the City Ordinances – Co[uncillor] Phelps said that a committee was appointed for that purpose [and] we have a tolerable pretty good set of laws now – It may be necessary for us to make some little thing of this sort – It is a great desideratum for us to get together the Ordinances – and it will be a great benefit to the City[,] [for] Strangers and all persons[.]

An Ordinance to prevent horse racing ~~in the Streets~~ [was] read

---

[35]A summary in the Record of Proceedings states this more clearly: "John D. Lee was elected Wharf master for the Current year and allowed the same per centage for taxes collected of Steam Vessels as were allowed for the year 1844."

[36]Originally called the poundkeeper (June 11, 1842), this was the animal control officer.

1st[,] [then a] 2[nd] [time] by the Title[,] [and a] 3[rd] time [and the] bill pass[ed] – [all were] satisfied with Title. Co[uncillor] Phelps spoke on the subject – Ald[erman] Rich [said] it is a great curse to have too much law – Ald[erman] Orson Spencer followed – Co[uncillor] Miller suggested an alteration in the wording of the Ordinance – Co[uncillor] Phelps stated the case of Keegan – [A] Bill ~~for~~ of N[ewel] K. Knight [for] 2.00 for [a] meal for the Police [was] allowed –

~~Co[uncillor]~~ Richards spoke – [The] Recorder spoke[,] [saying] it is wisdom for me to do what I am going to do[.] I simply resign the office of Recorder and ~~appoint~~ nominate Thomas Bullock Recorder – ^The Recorder Elect [was] nominated[,]^ ~~and~~ Dr. Willard Richards ~~be Deputy to Mr Bullock~~ ^to be his Clerk – and both [motions] carried – ^ Dr. Richards spoke that it is the wisdom of God that this Motion was made – and my endeavors will always be for the good of this City – Co[uncillor] Wright spoke about some labor having been done on the Streets[.] Orson Spencer followed. [The council] adjourned till [the] next Regular Session –

†The new Council proceeded to business by electing Daniel Spencer Mayor [and] President of the Council until the Mayor elect should be qualified.[37] Willard Richards was re-elected Recorder of the City – The Standing Committees were appointed by the Mayor as follows.[38]

| of Ways and Means | of Police | of Improvements |
|---|---|---|
| James Sloan | Phineas Richards | David Fulmer |
| George W. Harris | Charles C. Rich | George Miller |
| Phineas Richards | John Pack | John Pack |
| of Municipal laws | of claims | of Public Grounds |
| W[illiam] W. Phelps | Jonathan C. Wright | Charles C. Rich |

[37]This was an interesting sleight-of-hand that showed how uncertain the city fathers were about their status after the Nauvoo Charter was revoked. The old mayor used his authority to appoint the newly elected mayor to his post, then the new mayor delegated his positions to the old mayor, hoping the governor would certify the election but knowing he probably would not. A judge would certainly see through this ruse, but instead of drafting a city charter with less sweeping authority, the mayors chose to run in circles like cats chasing their tails.

[38]The committees comprise newly elected councilmen. The old councilmen thought they could appoint whomever they chose to committee assignments and thereby legitimize the recent sham election.

| | | |
|---|---|---|
| Jonathan C. Wright | Samuel Bent | George W. Harris |
| Daniel Spencer | David Fulmer | Edward Hunter |
| | | |
| of unfinished business | of Public works | of Elections |
| Samuel Bent | Edward Hunter | George Miller |
| Newel K. Whitney | William W. Phelps | Phineas Richards |
| James Sloan | Daniel Spencer | Jonathan C. Wright |

of Finance
Edward Hunter, Daniel Spencer, William W. Phelps

The following officers were then Elected by the Council[:] W[illia]m Clayton[,] City Treasurer[;] A[lbert] P. Rockwood[,] Marshall[;] W[illiam] W. Phelps[,] Registrar of Deeds[;] Benj[ami]n Boyce[,] Constable 1st Ward[;] E[lijah] J. Sabine[,] [Constable] 2nd Ward[;] Howard Egan[,] [Constable] 3rd Ward[;] D[aniel] M. Repsher[,] [Constable] 4th Ward[;] James Allred[,] Supervisor of Streets[.]

An Ordinance creating Assisting Supervisors

Section 1. Be it ordained by the City Council of the City of Nauvoo that there be three Assistant Supervisors appointed in the same manner as the Supervisor is now appointed to act in their respective Wards.

Section 2. It shall be the duty of the Assistant Supervisors to act under the direction of the Supervisor and qualify in the same manner as the Supervisors qualify.

**Passed February 8, 1845. Daniel Spencer Mayor**

Lorenzo Clark[39] [was] appointed Assistant Supervisor of the 1st Ward[,] Jesse P. Harmon [of the] 2nd Ward, [and] Benjamin Jones [of the] 3rd Ward. The Recorder presented his Report of the Finance[s] of the City so far as can be gathered from the Records of the City Council and Municipal Court and the same were reported to the Committee of Claims and while this was under consideration the following officers were appointed[,] viz James Sloan[,] Notary Public[;] Stephen Markham[,] Market Master[;] Henry G. Sherwood[,] City Surveyor[;] Daniel Carns[,] Flour Inspector[;] Theodore Turley[,]

[39]Lorenzo Clark was born in 1806 in Grafton, New Hampshire. He was baptized in 1837. He assisted the Saints in relocating from Missouri. He died in 1901.

Sealer of Weights and Measures[;] Benjamin Boyce[,] Fire Warden 1st Ward[;] E[lijah] J. Sabine[,] [Fire Warden] 2nd [Ward][;] Howard Egan[,] [Fire Warden] 3rd [Ward][;] D[aniel] M. Repsher[,] [Fire Warden] 4th [Ward][,] February 8th 1845.

[The council] granted the Petition of Hosea Stout and Forty four others for the opening of Munson Street West of Fullmer Street[.][40] [A] Petition of James Allred for pay for 35 days labor at 1.00 per day [was] granted[.] [The] Committee on Claims reported the Recorders accounts were correct, and that he [should] be allowed seventy five dollars for extra services – which Report was accepted – and the Recorder was instructed to draw on the Treasury for the several items due the Members of the Council, and fees of the Municipal Court as named in said Report – also for all Bills in the Disbursement Book except [for] Marr & Rollasons.[41] It was ordered by the Council that the Treasurer be requested to make his report at their next Regular Session. February 8, 1845.

An Ordinance to prevent Horse racing and for other purposes

Section 1. Be it ordained by the City Council of the City of Nauvoo that any person or persons running a horse or horses within the limits of the Corporation of the City of Nauvoo, or otherwise riding or driving any horse or horses or any other animal or animals within the limits of this City so as to endanger the safety of any person or property may be fined by the Mayors Court in any sum not exceeding one hundred dollars by due process of law. Passed February 8, 1845.

| | | |
|---|---|---|
| Allowed J[onathan] H. Hale as Judge of Election & Stationery[42] | .60 | 2.10 |
| [Allowed] Hosea Stout [election judge] | | 1.50 |
| [Allowed] Samuel Bent [election judge] | | 1.50 |

[40]There are some repetitions, deleted here, about voiding the fine levied against Rufus Beach, suspending taxes for land that had not yet been surveyed, and suspending the collection of fines.

[41]More repetitions, dispensed with here, include Lee being appointed wharf master and Harmon the pound master.

[42]A repetition, deleted here, mentions reimbursements to Newel Knight for a police meal and to Jonathan Hale for election supplies, the latter having been crossed out.

| | | |
|---|---|---|
| [Allowed] Ransom Shepherd [preparing poll book, election clerk] | 1.50 | 3.00 |
| [Allowed] David Candland[43] [preparing poll book, election clerk] | 1.50 | 3.00 |
| | | $11.10 |

The City Council of the City of Nauvoo, at their Regular Session on February 8, 1845[,] allowed the following sums to the following named persons for their services, and have ordered the same to be paid out of any money in the Treasury not otherwise appropriated, to wit –

| | *City Council* | *Municipal court* | *Together* | *Fines* | *Now due* | *Fine* |
|---|---|---|---|---|---|---|
| Orson Pratt | 5.00 | 5.00 | | | 1.00 | * |
| William W. Phelps | 5.00 | 2.32 | 7.32 | | 7.32 | |
| Heber C. Kimball | 1.00 | | 1.00 | | 1.00 | |
| Benjamin Warrington | | | | 2.00 | | 2.00 |
| George A. Smith | 3.00 | 5.00 | 8.00 | | 8.00 | |
| Brigham Young | 5.00 | | 5.00 | | 5.00 | |
| Orson Spencer | 1.00 | 12.22 | 16.22 | | 16.22 | |
| Daniel H. Wells | 1.00 | 2.65 | 3.65 | 1.50 | 2.15 | |
| George W. Harris | 4.00 | 17.12 | 21.12 | | 21.12 | |
| Samuel Bennett | | 7.91 | 7.91 | 3.60 | 4.91 | |
| William Marks | | 10.75 | 10.75 | .50 | 10.25 | |
| Newel K. Whitney | 2.00 | 11.58 | 13.38 | | 13.38 | |
| Gustavus Hills | 2.00 | 11.54 | 13.54 | | 13.54 | |
| Hiram Kimball | 3.00 | .50 | 3.90 | .50 | 3.40 | |
| Aaron Johnson | 2.50 | | 2.50 | | 2.50 | |
| Elias Smith | | 2.40 | 2.40 | | 2.40 | |
| Daniel Spencer Mayor | 50.00 | 1.50 | 51.00 | | 51.00 | |
| John P Green Marshall | 1.00 | 14.07½ | 15.07½ | | 15.07½ | |
| Jonathan C. Wright d[itt]o | 4.00 | 2.50 | 6.50 | | 6.50 | |
| Willard Richards Recorder | 50.00 | | | | | |
| D[itt]o extra services | 75.00 | 18.73 | 145.73 | | 143.73 | |
| ~~Joseph Smith Chief Justice~~** | | | | | | |

[43]David Candland was born in Highgate, England, in 1819. He was baptized in England in 1841 and moved to Nauvoo in 1842. He died in 1902.

| | | | | | | |
|---|---|---|---|---|---|---|
| James Sloan | | 5.70 | | | 5.70 | |
| Horace S. Eldridge | | 7.50 | | | 7.50 | |
| Dimic B Hunintgton | | 2.95 | | | 2.95 | |
| John D. Parker | 5.07 | | | 5.07 | | |
| | 217.57 | 153.79½ | 371.29½ | 7.60 | 361.79½ | 2.00 |
| Witnesses fees – see next page | 15.50 | | | | 15.50 | |
| | | | | | 377.29½ | |

* Resigned 4.00 on August 10, 1844

** no order issued for

xxx

Witnesses names

| | | | |
|---|---|---|---|
| William Fry | 50 | Robert Clift | 50 |
| Elisha Hoopes | 50 | A[ugustus] A. Farnham | 50 |
| Ezekiel Kelly | 50 | J[oseph] A. Kelting | 50 |
| John D. Parker | 50 | – | |
| William Matthews | 50 | Augustus Stafford | 50 |
| Elbert L. Fry | 50 | Cyrus Canfield | 50 |
| Ichabod Gifford | 50 | John Gleason | 50 |
| Joel S. Miles | 50 | O[rrin] P. Rockwell | 50 |
| Andrew Lytle | 50 | John Hughes | 50 |
| John Lytle | 50 | Joseph Dalton | 50 |
| J[ohn] P. Greene | 50 | W[illia]m Clayton | 50 |
| – | | James Goff | 50 |
| – | | Leonard Soby | 50 |
| Theodore Turley | 50 | John T. McEwan | 50 |
| J[oseph] R. Wakefield | 50 | Addison Everett | 50 |
| James Jackson | 50 | James Jackson | 50 |
| John Kay | 50 | Aaron Johnson | 50 |

Total Witnesses fees 15.50[44]

---

[44]The Record of Proceedings has a duplicate notation, deleted here, about Willard Richards resigning his office as City Recorder to Thomas Bullock, followed by another prose narrative of the meeting under the heading, "Doings of the City Council, Regular Session, February 8, 1845." It includes the ordinance creating assistant street supervisors, which is presented here (see below) because it was not in the first draft of the minutes.

An Ordinance ~~concerning~~ creating Assistant Supervisors

Section 1. Be it ordained by the City Council of the City of Nauvoo that there be three Assistant Supervisors appointed in the same manner as the Supervisor is now appointed to act in their respective Wards.

Section 2. It shall be the duty of the Assistant Supervisors to act under the direction of the Supervisor and qualify in the same manner as the Supervisors qualify.

**Passed February 8, 1845. Daniel Spencer Mayor. Willard Richards Recorder.**

‡*March 8, 1845; Saturday.*[45] [A] Regular Session [was held at] 20 min[utes] p[ast] 10. [The council] met pursuant to adjournment[.] [The] names of [the] members [were] called [and] a minority [was] present. On motion of Co[uncillor] W[illiam] W. Phelps [the council] adjourned to [the] next regular Session and the Marshall [was] to notify the members to attend[.] [This was] seconded [and] carried[.] [The council] adjourned to [the] next Regular Session.

[45]This was evidently the last meeting of the Nauvoo City Council.

# Minutes of the Stake High Council

# 6.

# "The Business of Said Church" 1839

‡*October 6, 1839; Sunday.*[1] This day the first Conference of Elders and members of the Church of Jesus Christ of Latter Day Saints commenced[2] – at which there was elected an High Council for this Stake of Zion[3] the names of which are as follows – viz Samuel Bent – Henry G Sherwood – George W Harris – Alph[e]us Cutler – Newel Knight

[1]cf. Fred C. Collier, *The Nauvoo High Council Minute Book of the Church of Jesus Christ of Latter-day Saints* (Hanna, UT: Collier's Publishing Co., 2005), a 214-page publication that begins with volume 2 of the high council books, starting with the minutes of March 8, 1840. Book 1 was recently discovered at the LDS Church History Library and Archives, bound with the Oliver Cowdery Sketch Book of 1836, and begins five months prior to what Collier calls book 1. See also Joseph Smith, *History of the Church of Jesus Christ of Latter-day Saints*, 7 vols. (Salt Lake City: Deseret News, 1902-12) 4:12-13.

[2]That is, the first general conference held since the Church moved to Commerce (later Nauvoo), Illinois.

[3]The Commerce Stake was organized a day earlier with William Marks as president, but without any counselors being appointed to serve with him. "The stake included the newly platted Nauvoo, the incorporated town of Commerce, and the region extending into the farmland to the east" (Glen M. Leonard, *Nauvoo: A Place of Peace, a People of Promise* (Salt Lake City: Deseret Book, 2002), 93.

– Thomas Grover – Lewis D Wilson[,] David Fulmer – David Dort – Seymor Brunson[,] William Hunt[i]ngton[,] & Charles C Rich.

> Let it be hereby understood that the following pages[4] herewith in this Book be and is appropriated to recording the minutes and proceedings of the High Council in and for the Church of Jesus Christ [of] Latter day Saints at Nauvoo Ill[inoi]s – ordered by Said council. H[enry] G Sherwood

‡‡*October 20, 1839; Sunday.*[5] [The] High Council ^of the Church of Jesus Christ of Latter day Saints^ organized this 20th Oct[ober] 1839 [met] to decide on the case of Harlow Redfield[6] according to the decision ^& vote^ of the last conference of said Church. No charge [was] prefered against ~~Br[other] Redfield~~ Bro[ther] Redfield[,] [who] confessed an imprudence of conduct but had no evil intention and wished forgiveness – It was Motioned & voted to forgive & return him to his former standing & fellowship in the said Church – Motioned & voted and published in Times & Seasons that Br[other] R[edfield] [would] take a transcript of the minutes [to prove that he had been reinstated].[7]

---

[4]The minutes have a nonsensical redundancy, "next 2," before "following pages," deleted here.

[5]See also *History of Church*, 16.

[6]Levi Harlow Redfield was born in 1801 in New Haven, Connecticut. He was baptized in 1831 and died in 1866. He was charged with having plundered Joseph Smith's house in Missouri while Smith was imprisoned. When Redfield was exonerated he asked for a certificate to prove his innocence. See his letter to the editor, *Deseret News*, Mar. 16, 1854, 3 (and thank you to H. Michael Marquardt for drawing my attention to it).

[7]This was published in *Times and Seasons*, Jan. 1840, 47-48: "It is proper to say that at our conference [of] October inst[ant] that a species of accusation appeared against Elder Harlow Redfield, insomuch that he was suspended and required to answer to the High Council at this place. In compliance therewith, he this day appeared when no charge came against him, nor was it found proper that any should come. Therefore the council restored to him full fellowship, and all official standing[,] the same as if no such suspension had taken place."

A separate entry for this day's minutes, forming the basis of the *Times and Seasons* announcement, noted that "the case of Elder H[arlow] Redfield – against whom certain accusations were brought at our last Conference – in consequence of which he was suspended and his case refered to the H[igh] C[ouncil] for decision – ... [and against whom] no charge was

[It was] Motioned & voted that this High Council ~~discountenance~~ ^disfellowship^ any person of said Church that shall ferry or carry over the river people or freight – to injury of the ferry. [It was] Motion[ed] & vot[e]d that the horse boat[8] be repaired out of the sale of Church land. [It was] voted that Br[other] Daniel C. Davis[9] be Capt[ain] of said boat for the ensuing year. Voted that J[oseph] Smith Jun be exempt from rec[ei]v[in]g Commers & goers of company into his house as formerly & voted that the same be published &c accompanied [by the clerk's signature].[10]

Motioned &c that this council ~~disapprove of~~ ^~~& discoutenance~~ disfellowship^ any [members] of the Churches ^that^ knowin[g]ly suffer any of their animals to destroy the crops of any whether in or out of the Church & publish M[inutes] [in the *Times*] & [*Seasons*][.][11] [It was] voted that this Council be adjourned untill tomorrow at 3

---

brought ... nor did any implication appear against him ^nor do we believe that any charge could be[.]^ He ~~made~~ volunteered [a] confession of certain inadvertent imprudent [but] no[t] evil[-]meaning acts that he greatly sorrowed for – and asked for Giveness for so doing – This Council voted that Elder R[edfield] – be forgiven ~~for so doing~~ and restored to his former official State & standing & to be [in] full fellowship the same as if no evil insinuations had ever been brought against [him] – and that he take a transcript of these proceedings to be signed by the Cl[er]k of said Council."

[8]The horse ferry, *Iowa Twins*, was described by observers as "a primitive flatboat propelled by two horses, one on each side, working a treadmill. They [the horses] furnished the power to turn the wheels and propel the boat" (Leonard, *Nauvoo*, 151).

[9]Daniel Coon Davis was born in Petersburg, New York, in February 1804. Not to be confused with Amos Davis who owned a successful Nauvoo store, Daniel will famously transport Joseph Smith across the river from Iowa in 1844 so Smith can submit to arrest. Davis became a captain in the Mormon Battalion during the War with Mexico in 1846. He settled in Farmington, Utah, and had the honor of Davis County being named after him. He died at Fort Kearny, Nebraska, while traveling east in June 1850 (Andrew Jenson, *LDS Biographical Encyclopedia*, 4 vols. [Salt Lake City: Andrew Jenson Historical Co., 1901-1936], 4:741).

[10]This is clarified in the bound minutes: "Voted ^that^ Joseph Smith Jun and his family be exempt from receiving in furt[h]er such a crow[d]ed throng of visitors as have formerly thronged his house and that the same be published in the Times & Seasons."

[11]An entry in the minutes book stipulates "that this resolution be publish[ed] in the Times and Seasons" to warn animal owners of ecclesiastical sanctions stemming from neglect.

o'clock PM at the shop of D[imick] Huntington. H[enry] G Sherwood Cl[er]k. Minutes read & approved.

*October 21, 1839; Monday.*[12] [The] High council met according to ~~appointment~~ adjournment of the 20th Inst[ant] Oct[ober] 21st 1839 – 1st. Shall Joseph Smith Jun go to Washing[ton, D.C.] or not[13] – Answer[:] It is voted as follows viz 5 voted to have him go – and 2 voted for him not to go – viz Samuel Bent – H[enry] G Sherwood – David Dort – Newel Knight & Seymour Brunson are the 5 who voted to have him go – and Geo[rge] W. Harris & W[illia]m Huntington Sen voted for him not to go.

2nd. Shall J[oseph] Smith Jun have a recommend – Answer[:] He shall have a ~~recommend~~ ^one^[14] 3rd. Who shall be a clerk to attend to the land business &c as Joseph Smith Jun may need – Answer[:] James Mulhulland[15] – shall be clerk. 4th. Who shall be a general Treasurer for the Church[.] Answer[:] Joseph Smith: shall be Treasurer. 5th. Who shall be sub-Treasurer – Answer – James Mulholland – 6th. Who shall be the persons to shew contracts & sell Lots – Answer[:] Henry G. Sherwood –

7. Who shall apportion & prize the Lots – Answer[:] H[enry] G Sherwood – & to lay it before J[oseph] Smith Jun & Hiram Smith. 8th. Who shall assist H[enry] G. S[herwood] in prizing the Lots for their approval – Ans[wer] – J[oseph] Smith Jun & Hiram Smith.

9. " what shall be the standard price on the Lots for the three ensuing months – Ans[wer][:] from $200 to $800. 10. When ^& where^ shall the high council meet periodically[?] Ans[wer] – Every

---

[12]See also *History of Church*, 4:16-17.

[13]This referred to Joseph Smith's traveling to Washington, D.C., with affidavits to prove that the Saints were victims of persecution in Missouri. The Mormon delegates left for Washington on October 29, 1839. Neither Congress nor the president offered help. Martin Van Buren reportedly said, "If I do anything, I shall come in contact with the whole state of Missouri." The Mormons were advised to seek redress in the Missouri courts. See Marvin S. Hill, *Quest for Refuge: The Mormon Flight from American Pluralism* (Salt Lake City: Signature Books, 1989), 101.

[14]By "recommend" was meant an official letter of introduction.

[15]James Mulholland was born in 1804 in Ireland. After leaving Missouri, he was appointed clerk for land contracts in Nauvoo. He clerked for the Church until his death in 1839.

Sabbath evening at early candle lighting at the shop of D[imick] Huntington.

11th. ~~Voted that the office in red stone front [Sidney] Rigdons be fixed for and appropriated to the use of a store~~ 12. What price p[e]r month shall be give[n] D[aniel] C Davis while in serv^ice^ as ferry man – ans[wer] – $30 p[e]r Month – It is voted that D[aniel] C Davis shall have power to employ help & other expenses for [the ferry].[16]

Voted that these proceedings be published in the Times & Seasons[17] – Voted that ~~the ferry~~ ^~~should~~^ D[aniel] C Davis pay all ferry monies into the hands of the Treasurer every week viz on Saturday also to keep a bill of Ferriage & make Monthly returns of it to the high council –

The above minutes is a true copy of the decisions made by the high Council of the Church of J[esus] C[hrist] of L[atter] D[ay] Saints appointed ^by said Church^ to transact the business of said Church. Moved to [be] adjourned until next Sabbath evening at D[imick] Huntington.

*October 27, 1839; Sunday.*[18] [The] High Council of the Church of J[esus] C[hrist of] Latter day Saints met according to adjournment [on] Oct[ober] 27th 1839[.] Joseph Smith Jun informed the council that the wages of the Clerk must ^be^ considered – [The issue] was [considered] – and was voted that J[ames] Mulholland be Cl[er]k and that his wages be $30 – p[e]r Month during his service as Clerk[.] [It was]Voted that the resolution of the last meeting of this council respecting the red Store be erased & discontinued – ^& that [Stephen] Markham supply the place^.

Voted that this council ^& Treasurer^ pay to V[inson] Knights $150 – for the portion of ferry owned on the same side at Montrose [Iowa] as p[e]r charter. Voted that Sister Emmy [Smith][19] be the per-

---

[16]Notice that there is not a clear division between secular and religious responsibilities, the high council discussing the very same topics the city council discussed.

[17]The proceedings were never published.

[18]See also *History of Church*, 4:17-18.

[19]Emma Hale Smith was born in Harmony, Pennsylvania, in 1804. She married Joseph Smith in 1827 and moved with him to Illinois in 1839. She was appointed president of the Female Relief Society of Nauvoo in 1842.

son to select hymns [and] compile and publish a Hym book for the use of the Church[20] and that a letter be written to Brigham Young at New York informing him of the same and not to publish the Hymns taken from Commerce by him. [21] [It was] voted that this council assist in the expence of publishing a Hymn Book – as also in publishing the Times & Seasons –

Motioned & voted that ^this^ Meeting be ^~~at early candle light~~^ adjourned until tomorrow evening ^at early candle light^ [at] the house of J[oseph] Smith Jun.[22] H[enry] G Sherwood.

‡*October 28, 1839; Monday.*[23] [The council] voted to build a house of Stone at upper Commerce to be used for boarding – Voted to request Elder [Oliver] Granger to assist with funds to print the hymn book[.] Resolved that Samuel Bent[,] Davison Hibbard & David Dort be trustees for ^the^ use of building the Stone School house now in contemplation – that they circulate Subscriptions to raise funds and pay over ~~to~~ the same to the building Committy of Said house and that Jabez Durfy & A[l]pheus Cutler be the architects, and building Committy for s[ai]d house to furnish a bill of articles or materials and the probable expense of the Same –

Resolved to forthwith finish the office of J[oseph] Smith, Jun and

---

She remained in Illinois after her husband's death, in 1847 marrying Lewis Bidamon. She died in 1879.

[20]In a revelation to Joseph Smith in July 1830, Emma Smith was told: "And it shall be given thee, also, to a make a selection of sacred hymns ... which is pleasing unto me, to be had in my church" (D&C 25:11). Her first hymnal was *A Collection of Sacred Hymns* (Kirtland: F. G. Williams & Co, 1835). A second edition, referenced here, would appear similarly as *A Collection of Sacred Hymns* (Nauvoo: E. Robinson, 1841). The first collection contained ninety hymns, while the Nauvoo version totaled three hundred and three.

[21]Brigham Young was on his way to England to serve a mission with other apostles and would have been in New York by now had it not been for illness, which delayed his arrival several weeks. He arrived in the city in late January 1840 and stayed a little more than a month. On March 7 he and Heber C. Kimball boarded the *Patrick Henry* to cross the ocean. See Leonard J. Arrington, *Brigham Young: American Moses* (New York: Alfred Knopf, 1985), 73-78.

[22]See also *History of Church*, 4:18.

[23]See ibid.

that A[lanson] Ripley occupy it for the present – Voted ^that^ the recommends drawn by Elder [Henry G.] Sherwood, recommending constituting and appointing Joseph Smith Jun Sidney Rigdon & Elias Higby delegates for the Church to importune the president and Congress of the U[nited] S[tates] for redress &c ~~the Said reccommend~~ be Signed by this Council – Copied by H[enry] G Sherwood[.]

*December 1, 1839; Sunday.*[24] [The] High Council of ^the Church^ of Jesus Christ of Latter day saints met at Elder O[liver] Grangers[25] Sunday evening Dec[embe]r 1st 1839. 1st. Motioned & 2dd that Hirum Smith, Geo[rge] W Harris, & Oliver Granger be a Committee to cause a petition to go to the Legislatur[e] to discontinue certain parts of the City of Nauvoo – and also of Commerce [and] all other needful acts & alterations in relation to the afore said cities.

2nd. Voted that Hirum Smith be appointed to furnish with the needful maps & plots for the alteration of the Cities named in the first motion. 3rd. Voted that ~~E~~ ^S[eymour]^ Brunson be appointed to circulate a petition for subscribers as named in the ~~the~~ first motion.

4th. Motioned & voted that Bishop E[dward] Partridge[26] be a person [to] be appointed to draft a piece to be published in Times

---

[24]See also *History of Church*, 4:39. Hosea Stout wrote: "Before I commence recording, I would just mention that there is no minutes to be found for the month of Nov[ember] 1839. Which thing was laid before the High Council, on the ninth day of October 1841. When ... it was found that there were some minutes lost ... the Council gave me orders to proceed without them, that the recording might not be longer retarded. But, however, before I commence, I will State, that among [the resolutions] that are now missing is the one appointing Randolph Alexander a Clerk of the said High Council; also an ac[coun]t Book No 1. Minutes of the High Council of Nauvoo Illinois appointing Alpheus Cutler and Jabez Durfee to build the Stone School House which was to be done ^by them^ for Sixteen hundred dollars; Should the aforesaid lost minutes ever be found they will be inserted in the record and a reference made to them on the margin. Oct[ober] the 10th 1841. Hosea Stout Clerk."

[25]Oliver Granger was born in Phelps, New York, in 1794. He converted to Mormonism in the early 1830s. He moved to Nauvoo, Illinois, in 1839, where he served as the Church's land agent. He died in 1841.

[26]Edward Partridge was born in Pittsfield, Massachusetts, in 1793. He was baptized in New York in 1830, was named the Church's first bishop in 1831, and was appointed a bishop in Nauvoo in 1839. He died in 1840.

& Seasons informing our brethren ^in^ the west that it is improper to remove from the west to locate in Kirtland Ohio & such as [those who] do [so] will be disfellowshipped by this Council.[27]

5th. Voted that V[inson] Knight, A[lanson] Ripley,[28] & H[enry] G Sherwood be a committee to assist the Committee named in the first Motion. 6th. Voted that the Subscription for monies &c subscribed at Oct[ober] Conference be put into the care of V[inson] Knight and that he report to this Council of all that he shall receive on said Subscriptions.[29]

---

[27]This letter, published in the *Times and Seasons*, Dec. 1839, 29, reads, in part:

> We have heard it rumoured abroad, that some at least, and probably many, are making their calculation to remove back to Kirtland next season.
>
> Now brethren, this being the case, we advise you to abandon such an idea; yea we warn you, in the name of the Lord, not to remove back there, unless you are counseled so to do by the first Presidency, and the high council of Nauvoo. We do not wish by this to take your agency from you; but we feel to be plain, and pointed in our advice for we wish to do our duty, that your sins may not be found in our skirts. ...
>
> There are those who profess to be saints who are too apt to murmur, and find fault, when any advice is given, which comes in opposition to their feelings, even when they, themselves, ask for counsel; much more so when council is given unasked for, which does not agree with their notion of things; but brethren, we hope for better things from the most of you; we trust that you desire counsel, from time to time, and that you will cheerfully conform to it, whenever you receive it from a proper source.

The sin-stained-skirt idea comes from Jeremiah 2:34, where "also in thy skirts is found the blood of the souls of the poor innocents." Jeremiah threatens to lift sinners' skirts above their heads to expose their private parts (13:22, 26). However, the formulation in this letter, where someone else's sins are what stains one's own skirts is an extrapolation that nevertheless occurs elsewhere in LDS writings. As just one example, Wilford Woodruff hopes that "the skirts of the Elders of Israel may be clean before all men" (*Journal of Discourses*, 26 vols. [Liverpool: F. D. & S. W. Richards, 1855-1886], 18:115).

[28]Alanson Ripley was born in 1798 in New York. He participated in the Zion's Camp march on Missouri in 1834 and, as a surveyor, helped map Daviess County, Missouri. He was a bishop in Iowa from 1839 to 1841. In Nauvoo he was appointed City Surveyor. He did not immigrate to Utah. He died in Morgan, Illinois, in 1880.

[29]At the general conference of the Church on Sunday, October 6, 1839, Lyman Wight spoke "of raising funds by contribution" to pay "for the lands

7th. Voted that this Council Sustain Vinson Knights in cutting & providing 500 cords of steam boat wood. [The] Minutes [were] read and approved [and the] Meeting [was] adjourned untill Sabbath the 8th Inst[ant] at ~~2 Oct[ober]~~ Oliver Grangers at 2 o'clock PM –

‡‡*December 8, 1839; Sunday.*[30] [The] High Council of [the Church of] J[esus] C[hrist of] – L[atter] D[ay] Saints met according to adjournment at Elder Grangers Dec[embe]r 8th 1839. 1st. [The council] Motion[ed] & voted that the Bishop be instructed to secure the cow belonging to Sister Orson Pratt [Sarah Marinda Bates Pratt] & that it be kept for her use when needed at this place viz, Nauvoo.

2nd. Voted that Whereas Elder Tho[ma]s Grover made known certain embarrassments of his for having signed to obtain monies for the redemption of certain goods & furniture – and to more fully understand investigate or adjust it, it is agreed to suspend its investigation for the present.

3rd. Voted that the three Trustees appointed for ^the^ build[ing of] the School house[31] be delegated to obtain ~~funds at~~ the credit of the Church ^funds^ to complete the building thereof. 4th. Voted that the address [sermon] presented to warn our brethren against returning to Kirtland be accepted & ~~adopted~~ published in the Times & Seasons –

5th. Voted that the Cl[er]k of this council give a recommend to Elder Oliver Olney[32] stating his good Stan[d]ing & fellowship in this Church as an Elder. 6th. voted to adjourn. Minutes approved &c. 7. Voted that Elder O[liver] Granger ~~procum~~ ^procure^ a butcher [to] provide a place for ^to^ raise or hang up Beaves [beef] [and] agree on the price &c for ^[the] butcher [for]^ a beef or hog.

---

which had been contracted for," meaning the lands that would comprise the city of Nauvoo and environs (*Times and Seasons* Dec. 1839, 31). The land was purchased from Isaac Galland, John Gillet, Horace Hotchkiss, Smith Tuttle, Hugh White, and William White (Leonard, *Nauvoo*, 55-58).

[30]See also *History of Church*, 4:44-45.

[31]That is, Samuel Bent, Davison Hibbard, and David Dort. See the earlier entry for October 28.

[32]Oliver Olney was born in Eastford, Connecticut, in 1796. He was excommunicated in 1842 after claiming to be a prophet. He published an anti-Mormon exposé in St. Louis in 1845.

Copy of power [of attorney] to Cha[rle]s Rich: The Church of Jesus Christ of Latter day Saints – By their high council at Nauvoo Ill[inois] – ~~hereby constitute and appoint~~ By thes[e] presents do constitute and appoint Elder Charles Rich their agent with power in their Name and for the use of said Church to ask for ~~of~~ and receive of W[illia]m Thompson[,] W[illia]m Johnson or any other person or persons any and all sum or sums of money or monies that may be obtained in payment or in part payment for Town Lots or a Lot in the town of Nauvoo Ill[inois] – and for the same to rece[ip]t and secure as their agents for all such funds as fully as they[,] the Church[,] or their council could do were they personally present at the doing thereof. Done by order of the high council aforesaid this 8th day of Dec[embe]r 1839. Signed H[enry] G Sherwood Cl[er]k.

*December 15, 1839; Sunday.*[33] [The] High Council of the Church of Jesus Christ [of] Latter day Saints met at Elder O[liver] Granger ^at Nauvoo Ill[inois]^ – Dec[ember]r 15th 1839. H[enry] G Sherwood Cl[er]k pro tem.[34] 1st. [A] Motion [was made] ^that^ the Committee for building the School house be delegated to obtain a loan of $200 for a ^length of^ time at their discretion.

2nd. Voted that Bishop [Vinson] Knights provide in his own way and use his own Judgment in providing for the families of Joseph [Smith] – Sidney [Rigdon] – [and Orrin] Porter Rockwell[35] during their absence to Washington.

3rd. Voted that ^whereas^ Elder Sherwood being appointed to setle for the Church the Estate of Elder [James] Mulholland Deceased[36] – it is now voted that the Settlement aforesaid be suspended for the present – but that Elder Sherwood be hereby autho-

---

[33]See also *History of Church*, 4:46.

[34]The Latin *pro tempore* means "for the time being," in other words, a temporary appointment.

[35]Orrin Porter Rockwell was born in Belchertown, Massachusetts, in 1813. He was a childhood friend of Joseph Smith and was one of the first converts to Mormonism. He was accused, and later acquitted, of the 1842 assassination attempt on former Missouri Governor Lilburn Boggs. He died in 1878.

[36]Mulholland, age thirty-five, died on November 3, 1839. On this same date, the high council "voted that debts contracted for building [Mulholland's] house be settled" (*History of Church*, 4:46).

rized to pay such ~~as~~ debts as have accrued for services done on the house of Elder Mulholland and to Elder [Elijah] Abel[37] for making his coffin.

4th. Voted that Bro[ther]s [John C.] Annis[38] & [Squire] Bosier[39] & [George] Edmunds[40] be approbated in building a water Mill adjoined to this city plot viz Nauvoo. [The] Minutes [were] read and approved. – Meeting adjourned to our next ~~anuel~~ ^regular^ Meeting. H[enry] G Sherwood Clerk.

*December 22, 1839; Sunday.* [The] High Council of the Church of Jesus Christ ~~Jes~~ of latter day Saints Met at Elder Grangers Dec[embe]r 22nd 1839. 1st. Voted that Bishop [Vinson] Knight have the dictating & laying out of the Subscription of brother [Benjamin] Bently to be appropriated to the use of Sister O[rson] Pratt for her support. Meeting adjourned until our Next regular meeting, viz. 29th Inst. H[enry] G Sherwood.

‡*December 26, 1839; Thursday.* The High Council of the Church of Jesus Christ of Latter Day Saints of Nauvoo Illinois met at O[liver]

---

[37]Elijah Abel may have been born a slave in Maryland in 1810. He was baptized into the LDS Church in 1832 and shortly afterward was probably ordained an elder. In 1836 he made his way to Kirtland, Ohio, and received a renewed elder's license. In Nauvoo he was a mortician. He died in 1884.

[38]John C. Annis was born in May 1785 in Thetford, Vermont. In his late twenties, he served in the War of 1812. He later moved to Cincinnati and became a boat builder. He was a member of Zion's Camp in Missouri, where he was ordained a Seventy, and in Illinois he operated a lumber mill in the southwest part of the city. He died of cholera in Winter Quarters, Nebraska, in June 1849 ("John Closson Annis and the Early Mormon Church," *Annis Family Association*, www.facebook.com).

[39]Squire Bosier was born in 1792 in Kentucky and fought in the War of 1812. He helped settle LaGrange, Missouri, where he converted to Mormonism in 1836. He was one of the first Mormons to migrate to Commerce, Illinois, and here he is being authorized to build a saw mill to facilitate the construction of homes. He died in Washington Territory in 1853 ("Biographical Registers," *BYU Studies*, www.byustudies.edu).

[40]George Edmunds was born in 1822 in New York. In Nauvoo he worked in Almon Babbitt's law office (Gregory F. Knight, ed., "Journal of Thomas Bullock," *BYU Studies* 31 [1991]: 60). Dennis Rowley refers to him as one of the old settlers of Commerce ("The Mormon Experience in the Wisconsin Pineries," *BYU Studies* 32 [1992]: 165).

Granger's. 1st. Voted that the money which Seymour Brunson received, by donation, be handed over to Hiram Smith for the benefit of the brethren at the City of Washington [D.C.]

2nd. Voted that a letter by the authority of the High Council at this place, be written and directed to John P. Green, in Quincy informing him that a complaint has been made against him for detaining money put into his hands for the benefit of the Printing Office – The aforesaid letter was written by Elder H[enry] G Sherwood.

3rd. Voted that Seymour Brunson be a Committee-man to ^obtain a^ loan ^of^ certain monies to the amount of two thousand six hundred dollars, if possible. – 4th. A charge [was] prefer[r]ed against Eliphas Marsh and wife, by Nathan ^K^ Knight, for circulating slanderous reports against himself and wife. – 5th. Voted that two only shall speak on the present case who were Samuel Bent and George W. Harris[.] The ~~charge was~~ parties went into an examination of the charge, which charge was partially sustained and after the pleadings were over the parties were reconciled and the charge settled without a vote of the Council. –

6th. Voted that all persons are discou[n]tenanced ^by^ this Council, who detains monies in their hands, which is for the be[n]efit of the printing office. – This should have been [illegible] the 3rd article but was omit[t]ed through mistake[.] 7th. Voted that the Council adjourn. – Henry G. Sherwood Cl[er]k[.] Recorded on the 15th day of October A.D. 1841. By Hosea Stout Clerk. –[41]

‡‡*December 29, 1839; Sunday.*[42] [The] High Council of the Church of Jesus Christ [of] Latter-Day Saints Met at Elder O[liver] Grangers Dec[embe]r 29th 1839. 1st. Motion that Elder Granger be tolerated in using any Monies that shall come into his possession to enable him to pay $400 that he obtained from Brother [Hugh] Herrinshaw for the use of our brethren at Washington – provided that Br[other] Herrinshaw does not take lands or a Lot in payment for the Monies so borrowed by Br[other] Granger.

2. Voted that Elder A[lpheus] Cutler be appointed & authorized

---

[41]The original minutes were taken by Henry G. Sherwood in 1839 and copied into book 1 by Hosea Stout in 1841.

[42]See also *History of Church*, 4:49.

to purchase for the Church a certain piece or parcel of Government Land situated near this City viz Nauvoo. Voted that Brother Charles Rich go and see Brother [William] Casper for the purpose of borrowing Monies of him – also that Elder ^Cutler^ be appointed to give all the assistance to obtain P[ayment] in his power. Voted that Brother C[harles] Rich shall have a certificate given him[,] authorizing him to obtain the above named monies. Voted that Brother C[harles] Rich be authorised in [a] P[ayment] Certificate to use the names of the High Council if [it] shall be considered necessary to the amount of $500.00 or under. Voted that Bishop Partridge be apointed to write a letter to be published in [the] next periodical on the gathering of the Saints to this place. Voted that the Editors of the periodical be ~~notified~~ ^directed^ to insert in their next periodical that 10,000 copies of the hym Books [are to] ^be printed^ also that [the] Book of Mormon [will] be printed in this place under the inspection of the Presedency as soon as monies can [be] raised to defray the expense[,] giv[e]n by the direction of the High Council at Nauvoo.[43]

> The Church of Jesus Christ of Latter day Saints, By their high Council at Nauvoo Ill[inois] who the said Church have chosen and appointed to transact certain business for them[,] the Said Church do hereby and by these presents nominate constitute and appoint Elder Charles C Rich an Agent for the use and benefit of the said Church to use an Effort to obtain ^& loan^ a sum of money not exceeding five hundred dollars[.] And the better to satisfy him her or them for the payment of said Money so loaned he – the said Charles C Rich ~~has~~ is hereby authorised to use ~~any or~~ the ^Name or^ names of any or all of the said Councellors either Collectively or individually ~~to~~ as Security for the payment thereof – ~~Done by order of the said Council at Nauvoo Ill[inois] Dec[embe]r 30th 1839~~ which is to be fully [legal] and as binding as if each and ev[e]ry of such councillor had been personally present at the doing thereof and had have affixed his own signature to said obligation. Done by order and vote of the aforesaid High Council at Nauvoo Ill[inois] Decem[ber] 29th 1839.

[43]This notice appeared in the *Times and Seasons* Dec. 1839, 25: "*Resolved,* That Ten thousand copies of a Hymn Book, be printed; also that the Book of Mormon be re-printed in this place, under the inspection of the Presidency, as soon as monies can be raised to defray the expenses."

*December 30, 1839; Monday.*[44] The High Council of the Church [of] Jesus of Latter day Saints met on the 30th Dec[embe]r 1839 ~~at~~ in Nauvoo[.][45] Voted that commities be appointed for the purpose of transacting the business relative to the request of our Brethren in ~~at~~ Washington City. Voted that Br[other] [Alanson] Ripley be commity man to transact business on the other side [of] the River on the present affair.[46] Voted that Brother Semer Brunson ^& C[harles] C. Rich^ be commity m[e]n to transact the business in Quincy and the regions roundabout on the present occasion.[47]

Voted that Brother [Zenas H.] Gurley[48] be [the] commity man

---

[44]See also ibid.

[45]The first sentence includes the following gibberish: "~~Voted when the High shall~~ have ~~convened that each takes~~ his seat in ~~order according as he shall~~ have been appoin~~ted or numbered~~[,]" deleted here.

[46]In 1839, a new stake—Zarahemla—was created in Iowa with Alanson Ripley as an area bishop. As such, Ripley was in charge of all Church business transacted in Iowa. The "present affair" was procuring funds and obtaining land.

[47]Rich's authority in these financial matters was specified at the end of the High Council minutes under the heading, "Norvoo Dec[embe]r 30th 1839":

> Know all men by these presents that Charles C. Rich is hereby fully authorized by the High Council at Nauvoo Collectively or individualy to make a loan of Monies not to excede the Sum of five hundred Dollars [for] which [this] Council stands as surety for P[aper] Money to any person or persons of whom the loan may be made [in] P[aper] Monies and expressly for the benefit of the church and poor saints of the Church of Jesus Christ of latter day Saints.
>
> This certificate does fully authorize and empow[e]r Charles C Rich to assign or affix any or all the Names of the High Council to any bond or note as it may be ^required^ at his hand as surety to any person or persons for monies to the amount of five hundred Dollars or any sum under [that amount] done by consent and resolve of the High Council at Norvoo.

According to his biographer, "Rich negotiated several loans during that period and was also named to a committee to contract for the building of homes for wives of apostles who had been sent to England as missionaries" (Leonard G. Arrington, *Charles C. Rich: Mormon General and Western Frontiersman* [Provo: BYU Press, 1974], 68-69).

[48]Zenas Hovey Gurley was born in Bridgewater, New York, in 1801. He was baptized in 1838 in Williamsburg, Ontario. He later served as an apostle in the Reorganized Church of Jesus Christ of Latter Day Saints

to transact our business at McComb [Illinois].[49] Voted that President H[yrum] Smith, Bishop [Edward] Partridge and Bishop [Vinson] Knights, be Councilors to instruct the Brethren ^coming to this place^ relative to the present affair. (Minutes recorded on the 18th day of Oct[ober], 1841, on Book No. 1, Pages 39 and 40 By Hosea Stout Clerk.[)]

---

and died in 1871 in Joy Station, Illinois, on his way home from a speaking engagement.

[49]McComb, in McDonough County, Illinois, was home to a small Mormon congregation (branch).

# 7.
# "According to Church Laws" 1840

‡*January 5, 1840; Sunday.* The High Council of the Church of Jesus Christ of Latter Day Saints of Nauvoo[,] Illinois[,] met in Council. 1st. Voted that Elder O[liver] Granger and Stephen Markham be appointed committy-men to Settle a difficulty that seems to exist between Elders Wandle Mace, Reynolds Cahoon, and Brother George W. Rogers and [to] report the Same to the High Council of the Church of Jesus Christ of Latter Day Saints in Nauvoo Illinois. Adjourned till 12th I[n]st[ant]. Recorded on the 9th day of January 1842. –By Hosea Stout Clerk.[1]

*January 8, 1840; Wednesday.*[2] The High Council of the Church of Jesus Christ of Latter Day Saints met in Nauvoo[,] Illinois. – 1st. Voted that we make a mortguage on lands in Iowa Teritory to Brother Isaac Davis for money loaned[.][3] Also a note of [promise] hand Signed by

---

[1]The minutes were probably taken by clerk Randolph Alexander, copied later in 1840 by Henry Sherwood, and recopied in 1842 by Hosea Stout, as were the minutes for the other meetings presented here through March 1, 1840.

[2]See Joseph Smith, *History of the Church of Jesus Christ of Latter-day Saints*, 7 vols. (Salt Lake City: Deseret News, 1902-1912), 4:75.

[3]Isaac Davis was born in 1783 in Pilesgrove, New Jersey. He died in 1847 in Winter Quarters, Nebraska.

the High Council of the Church of Jesus Christ of Latter Day Saints at Nauvoo Illinois to be presented to the effect [of] the above loan (if needful)[.] Furthurmore[,] a delegate [is] to be sent to Br[other] Davis with the mortguage and note to effect [the] Said loan. –

2nd. Voted that there be a letter, immediately, written to Br[other] Seymoure Brunson at Springfield [Illinois] authorising and directing him to make loans of all monies possible for the relief of the poor Saints. – 3rd. Voted that Brother Oliver Olney [should] be appointed and authorised to receive such subscriptions as Bisshop [Vinson] Knights holds in his hand. –4th. Voted that Bishop Knights be directed to deliver over Such subscriptions to Br[other] Olney.– 5th. Voted that the eighteen dollars obtained by Br[other] Zenos H. Gurley be given into the hands of Elder Henry G. Sherwood. –

6th. Voted that Thomas Grover be [the] committy-man to transact buisness in this place and round-about relative to the present occasion. –7th. Voted that each one of the committy-men have an extract or copy of the letters from our Brethren in ~~Washington~~ Congress. – 8. Voted that Edward Partridge be appointed to draft an instrument of writing authorising each committy-man to obtain monies for the relief and benefit of the Church of Jesus Christ. –

9th. Voted that H[enry] G. Sherwood be appointed to make every discovery possible of all such persons as has been tresspassing on the Church by cutting certain timbers wrongfully and unjustly and to bring all Such before the authorities of the Church. Adjourned. Recorded on the 9th day of January 1842. By Hosea Stout Clerk. –

*January 12, 1840; Sunday.* The High Council of the Church of Jesus Christ of Latter Day Saints of Nauvoo met at O[liver] Granger's.[4] 1st.

---

[4]The council met in Granger's home from the council's founding in 1839 until mid-1840 when Granger was called on a mission to Kirtland. Since there were no public buildings in Nauvoo, meetings of all types, including Church services were held in private homes, rented warehouses, and taverns. In fact, there would never be churches (and few schools) in Nauvoo during the Mormon period, the public gatherings were limited to the Masonic Hall (1844), Music Hall (1845), and Seventies Hall (1844). In mid-1844 the council would begin meeting in Joseph Smith's office in his log house, now called "the homestead" (Glen M. Leonard, *Nauvoo: A Place of Peace, a People of Promise* [Salt Lake City: Deseret Book, 2002], 195, 197, 204; George W. Givens, *In Old Nauvoo: Everyday Life in the City of Joseph* [Salt

A Charge has been prefered against George W. Harris by Br[other]s [John C.] Annis and [David M.] Fuller which Charge is posponed for trial till Brother Joseph Smith jr shall be present.[5] – 2nd. The above Charge is dropped by Br[other] Fuller[,] the amount of money being paid, by the voice of the Council and charged to Joseph Smith Jr[,] and the parties reconciled to each other. –

3rd. A memmorial to go before Congress by a delagate, after (it was) asigned by the brethren[,] was read – the sending [of the] said memmorial and delagate was disapproved by the Council. – Adjourned. – Recorded on the 12 day of January 1842 By Hosea Stout Clerk. –

‡‡*January 19, 1840; Sunday.*[6] [The] High Council of the Church of Jesus Christ Latter day Saints of Nauvoo Met at Elder [Oliver] Grangers [on] Jan[uar]y 19th 1840.

Elder Charles C Rich reported that he had obtained a loan of five hundred Dollars of Isaac Davis on Mortgaged security of ~~Life~~ ^Lands^ ^~~for life~~ by Elder O[liver] Granger for Six months^ as directed in former Meetings of this Council [of] (S[ai]d Church[)][.] It is voted [that] the expence of recording said Morgage be paid by the ^S[ai]d Church^ ~~voted the~~ Whereas a note of five hundred Dollars was made by this Council –It is this day done by vote [and] it is burned –also certain credentials authorizing Elder Rich to loan

Lake City: Deseret Book, 1990], 3-4, 6-7, 15-16; cf. the reminiscence of Jane Snyder Richards in Carol Cornwall Madsen, *In Their Own Words: Women and the Story of Nauvoo* [Salt Lake City: Deseret Book, 1994], 171, who forty years later remembered a church or school on every corner).

[5]Joseph Smith left Nauvoo for Washington, D. C., on October 29, 1839, in company with Sidney Rigdon, Elias Higbee, and Orrin Porter Rockwell to seek redress for the losses that Church members suffered in Missouri. They arrived on November 28, visited the following day with President Martin Van Buren (who said he could do nothing for the Mormons due to political considerations), and met with Illinois Congressmen to arrange the presentation of their case, which included 678 petitions. Smith left for Philadelphia on December 21 and was still there at the time of this high council meeting. He returned to Washington at the end of January and stayed about two more weeks. In March the Senate Judiciary Committee rejected the Mormon case (see Richard L. Bushman, *Joseph Smith: Rough Stone Rolling* [New York: Knopf, 2005], 391-98).

[6]See also *History of Church*, 4:76.

monies are also returned & burned by order of this Council. It is voted that the above named $500 be placed in the hands of Elder Grangers to be disposed of by ^the^ Council of Pres[iden]t Hiram Smith according to the intention for which it was obtained –

[It was] voted that a City Lot in Nauvoo be donated to Br[other] James Hendricks[7] & ~~voted~~ that a Comty [Committee] of 3, viz C[harles] C Rich[,] Thomas Grover & Tarlton Lewis be appointed ~~the~~ ^a^ Committee to build a house for James Hendricks on the aforesaid Lot.[8] [It was]voted that a City Lot in Nauvoo be donated to Father Joseph Knight,[9] and that the same Comty [Committee] that is appointed to build a house for James Hendricks be also a Committee to build one for Father Knights – immediately after having buil[t] J[ames] Hendricks house. H[enry] G Sherwood Clerk pro [tem].

‡*February 2, 1840; Sunday.* The High Council of the Church of Jesus Christ of Latter Day Saints of Nauvoo met at O[liver] Grangers. –

1st. The case of Brother Francis G. Bishop[10] was taken up and reconsidered (which case had been appealed from the Seventies) who hitherto had been suspended by a decision of the Quorum of seventies. 2nd. Voted that two only speak on the present case pending[,] who were Samuel Bent & David Dort. – 3rd. Voted ^that^ the former suspension be null and void & considered illegal with regard to F[rancis] G Bishop, because he was a High Priest – that he be restored & placed immediately under the care of the High Priest-hood – that this be published in the "Times & Seasons" and that he have a

---

[7]James Hendricks was born in 1808 in Franklin, Kentucky. He was baptized in 1836 and moved to Nauvoo in 1839. He died in 1870.

[8]Hendricks had a house constructed for him because "he had been crippled in the battle of Crooked River, where Brother David Patton, and Brother Carter were killed" (Mosiah Lyman Hancock, "Autobiography of Mosiah Lyman Hancock," in *New Mormon Studies: A Comprehensive Resource Library,* CD-ROM [San Francisco: Smith Research Associates, 1998]).

[9]Joseph Knight Sr. was born in Worcester, Massachusetts, in 1772. He was one of the first members of the Church, having been baptized on June 28, 1830. He moved to Nauvoo in 1839 and died in 1847 on his way west.

[10]Francis Gladden Bishop was born in 1809 in Livonia, New York. He was baptized in July 1832 and ordained an elder. Given to spiritual manifestations and unorthodox doctrinal teachings, he is excommunicated by the high council on March 11, 1842, then rejoins the LDS Church in Utah shortly before his death in 1864.

certificate to that amount, to be written by H[enry] G. Sherwood.[11] –

4th. Vote[d] that the money which is in the hands of Alpheus Cutler be delivered over in the hands of this Council & to be in the care of Samuel Bent for the purpose of liquidating certain debts, in part, viz: at Washington $50-00[;] to ~~John~~ D[aniel] C. Davis $20.00[;] for lumber $100.00, [and] the remainder for the disposal of the High Council. – 5th. Voted that Alpheus Cutler & Samuel Bent be permitted & authorised to make a loan of certain money not to exceed Sixteen dollars for the benefit of the Church. Adjourned till 2 o'clock 9th Inst[ant]. Recorded on the 29th day of January A.D. 1842. –By Hosea Stout Clerk. –

*February 9, 1840; Sunday.* The High Council of the Church of Jesus Christ of Latter Day Saints of Nauvoo met in council at O[liver] Grangers. – 1st. Voted that this Council receive Sixteen dollars 12½ cents of John A. Hicks & pay the same over to Br[other] John Slingerland to be paid again to J[ohn] A. Hicks on the Sixth ^day^ of ^April^ proximo[.][12] Adjourned. Recorded on the 29th day of January A.D. 1842. By Hosea Stout Clerk. –

‡‡*February 23, 1840; Sunday.*[13] [The] High Council ^of Nauvoo^ Met [on] Feb[ruar]y 23rd 1840 at O[liver] Grangers.

[It was] voted that Elder Sherwood pay $5 – to Br[other] [Joseph] Fisher[.][14] ~~Br[other] [Samuel] Bent~~ Br[other] O[liver] Granger reported that Elder Bent had paid five dollars to him on Account [of] D[aniel] C Davis – also $3.57 for Br[other] [John] Slingerland – which with $16.12½ rec[eive]d heretofore of Elder [John A.] Hicks,[15]

---

[11]Bishop could not prove his ordination as a high priest and on April 6, 1840, was formally returned to the quorum of the Seventies. See *Times and* Seasons, April 1840, 92.

[12]Meaning "of next month" (*Shorter Oxford English Dictionary* [Oxford: Oxford University Press, 2002], s.v. "proximo").

[13]See also *History of Church,* 4:88.

[14]Joseph A. Fisher was born in 1801 in Pennsylvania. He was baptized in 1836. He immigrated to Utah in 1850, where he built and ran saw mills. He died in 1867.

[15]John A. Hicks was born in 1810 in New York. He was appointed by revelation to head the elders quorum in Nauvoo in early 1841. He was later excommunicated.

has been paid to Br[other] Slingerland and endorsed on S[idney] Rigdon's & G[eorge] Robinson's[16] note[,] it being $20.00.[17]

*March 1, 1840; Sunday.* The High Council of the Church of Jesus Christ of Latter day Saints met in Council at O[liver] Grangers[,] Nauvoo Ill[inois][,] Hancock County[,] March 1st 1840. [It was] voted that the charge prefered against Br[other] R[andolph] Alexander[18] ^by B[rother] [William] Law^ be laid over till the next Council so that the parties may have a chance to ^settle^ their own difficulties according [to] the Church laws.[19] [It was] voted that Br[other] [John] Lawson[20] have a rehearing on the case between him and Br[other] [Harlow] Redfield and that Br[other] Lawson have the chance to personally appear before this Counsel and the case fairly investigated. [It was] voted [that] Br[other] [Thomas S.] Edwards[21] [be given] the chance to have his case brought ~~the~~ before this Council & investigated.[22]

---

16George W. Robinson was born in 1814 in Pawlet, Vermont. He was appointed Church Recorder in 1837. A son-in-law of Sidney Rigdon, he became the first postmaster of Nauvoo in 1839 and helped to establish the Nauvoo Agricultural and Manufacturing Association in 1841. He later left the Church and died in 1878.

17The *History of Church* (4:88) explains: "The High Council of Nauvoo voted, that the notes given into the hands of Bishop [Edward] Partridge, by certain individuals, as consecrations for building the Lord's House in Far West [Missouri], be returned to the same [individuals] by him."

18Randolph Alexander was born in 1802 in Union, South Carolina. He converted to Mormonism in 1836 in Tennessee saying "the people of the present day made him think of a pen of hogs" and "the priests would feed them" anything and they would "swallow it down." He lived in Quincy, Illinois, during the years 1837-1839 before moving to Nauvoo, where he became a high council clerk in 1840. He died in 1879 in Utah Territory.

19In the bound minutes under this date, recorded by Hosea Stout on February 1, 1842, Stout noted that the decision to give the men a chance to settle this dispute among themselves was based "upon the advice of President Joseph Smith jr." Having just returned from Washington, D. C., Smith began attending high council meetings regularly in March 1840 (Leonard, *Nauvoo*, 94).

20John Lawson was born in Argyle, New York, in 1805. He was the leader of a Mormon branch at Ramus, Illinois, in 1841. A decade later he was living in Manti, Utah, and died in 1884.

21Thomas S. Edwards was born in 1796 in Rutherford County, North Carolina. He was residing in Nauvoo by 1842.

22The *Times and Seasons* reported a month later on April 6, 1840, p.

[It was] voted [that] Br[other] Isom have a Lot given or granted him ^in Nauvoo Ill[inois][,] H[ancock] County^ in full judgment of certain orders that were ^given^ in the hands of Bishop [Edward] Partridge [and] now in the hands of the High [Council] to the amount of $100-00 Dollars.

[It was] voted that [Edward] Partridge ~~should~~ ^do^ and have given into the hands of the Presidency certain notes and ~~receipts~~ orders ^& receipts^ [that] he has formally held. Adjourned till 2 o'clock [on the] 8th Inst[ant].

‡*March 8, 1840; Sunday.* The High Council of the Church of Jesus Christ of Latter Day Saints of Nauvoo[,] Illinois[,] met in council at the house of O[liver] Grangers [on] March 8th 1840. It was voted that the Council accept of the resignation of Randolph Alexander as Clerk of the Said Council.[23] [It was] voted that Hosea Stout act as Clerk Pro. Tem.[24] A charge was prefered against David W. Rogers,[25] by Joseph Smith jr., for unchristian-like conduct and was referred to George W. Harris, David Dort and Thomas Grover, who was to take up a labor with him.[26]

---

92: "Elder John Lawson then came forward and stated, that in consequence of some difficulty existing in the branch of the church where he resided, respecting the word of wisdom [dietary strictures] the church had withdrawn their fellowship from, him & Bro[ther] Thomas S. Edwards. After hearing the statements; it was resolved, that John Lawson and Thomas S. Edwards be restored to fellowship."

[23]In a second set of minutes under this date, recorded by Hosea Stout on February 7, 1842, Stout said that Alexander desired to resign his position as clerk of the high council "in consequence of the weakness of his eyes." However, Alexander was charged with misconduct seven days earlier so his stated reason might be similar to a politician's need to "spend more time with my family."

[24]Meaning, for the time being.

[25]David White Rogers was born in Morristown, New Hampshire, in 1787. He was baptized in 1837 and helped to relocate the Saints to Nauvoo. He resided in Montrose, Iowa. He died in 1881.

[26]Rogers was accused of "compiling an Hymn Book, and selling it as the one selected and published by sister Emma Smith; for writing a letter to N[ew] Y[ork] having reflections in it on elder John P. Green, and derogatory to his character, and likewise for administering medicine, which had a bad effect" (*Times and Seasons*, April 1840, 92). Rogers's hymnal was published as *A Collection of Sacred Hymns for the Church of the Latter Day Saints,*

A letter directed to Edward Partridge, from John Whitmer,[27] of Caldwell County Missouri, containing proposals concerning a mortgage on certain lands held by Edward Partridge, in Caldwell County Missouri, was presented by Joseph Smith jr., for the advice of the Council, where upon it was voted that he (E[dward] Partridge) should not accept of said proposals. [It was] voted that Peter Hawes be appointed to negotiate a loan of one thousand dollars, to be paid to William White,[28] on certain lands.

[It was] voted that the Council purchase the horses, waggon & harness of George W. Harris and that the horses are purchased for the purpose of the ferry boat and that the waggon and harness be for the use of President Joseph Smith jr. and that George W. Harris be assisted to pay a debt of twenty-five dollars to Amos Davis,[29] if he can not otherwise pay it himself[,] and that thirty dollars be ~~eases~~ canceled which he owes to President Joseph Smith Jr. Adjourned. Recorded on book No. 1 Pages 49 & 50. Hosea Stout Cl[er]k. Hosea Stout Clerk Pro-Tem.[30]

*March 15, 1840; Sunday.*[31] The High Council of the Church of Jesus Christ of Latter Day Saints of Nauvoo[,] Illinois[,] met in Council at the house of O[liver] Grangers [on] March 15[,] 1840[.] The charge against David W. Rogers was voted [on][,] that it be laid over till the 29 March. [It was]voted that a committee of three be appointed to superintend the affairs of the ferry. [It was] voted that the above com-

---

*Selected and Published by David W. Rogers* (New York: C. Vinten, printer, 1838), identifying it as his own, not as Emma Smith's.

[27]John Whitmer was born in Pennsylvania in 1802. He was one of the first converts to the Church as well as one of the Eight Witnesses to the Book of Mormon. He served as a scribe to Joseph Smith, then as Church Historian from 1831. He left the Church in 1838 and died in 1878.

[28]William White was a non-Mormon and one of Commerce's original settlers. In 1839 he sold 80 acres of land to the Church near Commerce.

[29]Amos Davis was born in Hopkinton, New Hampshire, in 1813. He moved to Commerce, Illinois, in the fall of 1836. By 1838, he had opened a general store there and in 1839 was made postmaster. He was baptized into the Mormon faith in 1840. He died in 1872.

[30]The minutes for this date are the first entry for book 2 of bound minutes. The original minutes are not known to exist.

[31]See also *History of Church,* 4:95.

mittee consist of the first Presidency of the Church.[32] Adjourned. Hosea Stout Clerk Pro-Tem. Recorded on book No 1. page 50. Hosea Stout Cl[er]k.

*March 16, 1840; Monday.*[33] The High Council of the Church of Jesus Christ of Latter Day Saints of Nauvoo[,] Illinois[,] met in Council at the house of Joseph Smith jr. Prayer by Hyrum Smith. Resolution 1st. That a letter be directed to Elias Higbee, [in] Washington [D.C.], approving of the measures which he is now taking.[34]

Resolution 2nd. That [the following be added to a witness list][:] Alonson Ripley, Seymour Brunson, Charles C. Rich, Francis M. Higbee, Stephen Markham, Henry G. Sherwood, Lyman Wright, Thomas Grover, King Follett,[35] Tarlton Lewis, Amanda Smith, Isaac Laney,[36] Sister Merrick, Edward Partridge, Lyman Leonard,[37] Samuel Bent, Parley P. Pratt, Chapman Duncan,[38] Porter Rockwell, Thorrett [Thorit] Parsons,[39] Smith Humphrey, John M. Burke,[40] Harvey Redfield,

---

[32]At this time, the First Presidency consisted of Joseph Smith and his two counselors, Sidney Rigdon and Hyrum Smith.

[33]See also *History of Church*, 96.

[34]The letter may be read in ibid., 96-98.

[35]King Follett was born in Winchester, New Hampshire, in 1788. He joined the Church in Ohio in 1831 and served as a Hancock County, Illinois, constable. However, he died in 1844 in an accident while digging a well in Nauvoo. His funeral sermon was delivered by Joseph Smith and included significant new doctrines, which has kept the "King Follett discourse" famous to the present day.

[36]Isaac Laney was born in 1815 in Simpson, Kentucky. He was baptized in 1838 before moving to Haun's Mill and was one of the survivors of the massacre there. He died in 1873.

[37]Lyman Leonard was born in 1793 in Springfield, Massachusetts. He was baptized in Ohio in 1832 and later came to reside in Nauvoo's 4th Ward neighborhood. He died in 1877.

[38]Chapman Duncan was born in Bath, New Hampshire, in 1812. He was baptized in December 1832 in Independence, Missouri. He later moved to Nauvoo and, in 1848, to Utah. He died in 1900.

[39]Thoret Parsons was born in 1802 in Northumberland, New York. He converted to Mormonism and joined the Saints in Missouri, then Illinois. After Joseph Smith's death, he followed James Strang rather than Brigham Young. He died in Wisconsin in 1863.

[40]John Matthias Burk was born in 1793 in Fairfield, New York. An early settler of Kirtland, Ohio, where he converted to Mormonism, he later

Erastus Snow,[41] George A. Smith, Ellis E[a]mes, Olive E[a]mes, William Seely,[42] Rebecca Judd, William Chaplin, Dr Isaac Galland,[43] Heber C. Kimball, Ira S. Miles, Alma Smith,[44] Elias Smith, Oliver Olney, Zebediah Robinson, Sidney Rigdon, Hyrum Smith[.] Resolution 3rd. That the above names be accepted by the High Council and sent to Elias Higbee in Washington, that he may order subpoenas for said persons.[45] Resolution 4 – That Robert B. Thom[p]son write the above named letter to Elias Higbee at Washington. Adjourned. Al[a]nson Ripley[46] Clerk Pro-Tem. Recorded on book No. 1 Pages 51 & 52. H[osea] Stout Cl[er]k.

---

became a member of Iowa's high council, which met in Elijah Fordham's log cabin. Burk died in 1853 in Ogden, Utah.

41Erastus Snow was born in 1818 in St. Johnsbury, Vermont. He joined the Church in 1833 in Vermont, moved to Quincy, Illinois, in 1839, and later that same year relocated to Montrose, Iowa, and was appointed to the Iowa high council. After migrating to Utah in the 1840s, he was called to the Quorum of Twelve Apostles. He died in 1888.

42William Stewart Seely was born in 1812 in Ontario, Canada. He was baptized in 1838 after being converted by John Taylor. He moved to Nauvoo in 1846, crossed the Great Plains with the main body of Saints, and died in Utah in 1896.

43Isaac Galland was born in Kanesville, Ohio, in 1791. He joined the Church in July 1839 in Commerce, Illinois, after selling over 20,000 acres of land to the Saints in and around Commerce. He served a mission with Hyrum Smith to collect funds for the Nauvoo temple. In 1842 he withdrew from the Church, traveled to California in 1853, and died there in 1858.

44Alma Lamoni Smith was born in Ohio a year after the LDS Church was founded. He was only seven years old in 1838 when he was wounded at Haun's Mill in Missouri. He was baptized in 1841, immigrated to Utah in 1850, and served three missions to Hawaii in 1856-1858, 1864-1865, and 1874-1875, twice as mission president. He died while traveling home from Hawaii in 1876. His father, Warren, was killed at Haun's Mill. His mother, Amanda Barnes, remarried a man whose name was also Warren Smith and served on the Nauvoo police force. The second Warren Smith died in 1887.

45The Church wanted these men and women to be used as witnesses before Congress in "the Latter-day Saints *versus* the State of Missouri, for redress of grievances" (*History of Church,* 4:96).

46Alanson Ripley was born in 1798 in Livonia, New York. He was a member of Zion's Camp in 1834 and was called as a bishop in Iowa Territory in 1839, serving for two years before his appointment as a Nauvoo surveyor. He died in Morgan, Illinois, in 1880.

‡‡*March 22, 1840; Sunday.* The High Council of the Church of Jesus Christ of Latter Day Saints of Nauvoo[,] Illinois[,] met at the house of O[liver] Grangers [on] March 22nd.

[It was] voted that Br[other] Sherwood continue the management of the house of Br[other] [James] Mulhol[la]n[d] and that he procure the same for the use of his wife as soon as he can conveniently.[47]

[It was] voted that the money held by B[rother] Bent, ~~be reserved belonging to B[rother] Wirick~~ be reserved and paid over to Murry Seman[48] when directed.[49] [It was] voted that [Alpheus] Cutler & [Jabez] Durfee[,][50] ^the^ committe of the School house[,] be settled with as to the funds put in their hands for ^the building^ [of the] said house immediately.[51] Adjourned. Hosea Stout Clerk Pro. tem.

*March 29, 1840; Sunday.* The High Council of the Church of Jesus Christ of Latter Day Saints, of Nauvoo[,] Ill[inois][,] met at the house of O[liver] Grangers [on] March the 29th. [It was] voted that C[harles]

---

[47]This entry was given some clarity by clerk Hosea Stout in minutes book 2: "Voted That Henry G. Sherwood continue as manager of the house, formerly owned by James Mulholand deceased, and that he procure the same for the use of his Widow as soon as practi[ca]ble."

[48]Daniel Murray Seaman wanted to leave Nauvoo due to his wife's failing health. She would die the next year in New York, after which Daniel would remarry and eventually have a total of sixteen children by two wives. He will then follow James Strang to Wisconsin (John T. Nevill, "King Strang Had Great Influence on Life of David Murray Seaman," *Evening News*, Sault Ste. Marie, MI, July 23, 1953, available at the *Seaman Family History Page*, www.seamanfamily.net).

[49]Hosea Stout noted in the bound minutes that the amount of money in question was forty-eight dollars.

[50]Jabez Durfee was born in 1791 in Newport, Rhode Island. He served as a carpenter on the Nauvoo temple and died in 1867.

[51]This is significant as one of only two or three school houses in Nauvoo, perhaps the only one built of something more permanent than logs, apparently of fieldstones. As Nauvoo historian George W. Givens writes, "the records indicate" that classes were held in at least eight locations: "the Seventies Hall, the house of John Kempton, ... over Joseph Smith's store, and in the Masonic Hall," as well as at "the corner of Knight and James streets" and "on the corner of Hibbard and Fulmer Streets," probably in private residences. There are also explicit references to "a schoolhouse on Warsaw Street" and a "schoolhouse [at Parley Street] on the hill" (*Old Nauvoo*, 241-42). The Stone School House was completed in 1841 (see the minutes for May 17, 1841) and is referred to simply as "the school house."

C. Rich answer a letter from Daniel ^Bliss^ relative to his moving to Ohio and that he be refered to the council given in the Times & Seasons on that subject[52] and that if he goes back he does it ~~on~~ without the influence of the Council.

The Charge against D[avid] W. Rogers ^~~by J[ohn] P. Green~~^ was brought up. [It was] voted that his case should not be investigated. [It was] voted that the Council accept of S[amuel] B. Bent paying Murry Seman twenty dollars and that they receive his receipt for the same. [It was] voted that the money held by S[amuel] B. Bent amounting to 28 dollars[,] and ~~also~~ 10 dollars from A[lpheus] Cutler, and also 5 dollars from H[enry] G. Sherwood be paid over to Murry Seman on demand and take his receipt for the same. Adjourned. Hosea Stout Clerk Pro. tem.

It was voted that the Clerk ^(Hosea Stout)^ keep a record of all the minutes ~~anded to~~ wrote by him and that H[enry] G. Sherwood compile all the minutes of this Council up to ~~the time~~ his time of writing (H[osea] Stout).[53]

‡*April 6, 1840; Monday.* The High Council of the Church of Jesus Christ of Latter Day Saints of Nauvoo Illinois met in council at the Stand of the General Conference,[54] April 6th 1840. John Carroll made application to the Council for them to discharge a debt due him from the Church, amounting to fifty-two dollars and twenty-five cents. He also stated that he wished to have it off-set against ^a debt^ due Jacob Gates,[55] from him, of about the same amount. Whereupon

---

52The advice, penned by Henry Sherwood and published in the newspaper, was to remain in Nauvoo and avoid the temptation to return to Kirtland (*Times and Seasons,* Dec. 1839, 29).

53A partial sentence at the beginning of this paragraph, "from Cutler & Sherwood when it can be obtained no one appearing against him," has been deleted here for being indecipherable, although it probably had reference to the money Alpheus Cutler and Henry Sherwood owed Murray Seaman.

54The conference was held in Nauvoo from Monday, April 6, through Wednesday, April 8, and the minutes appeared in the *Times and Seasons,* Apr. 1940, 91-95. It was held at the outdoor stage, which was about a quarter mile northeast of the temple lot. The "stand" is sometimes confused with the "grove," but it was west of the temple site (Leonard, *Nauvoo,* 204).

55Jacob Gates was born in 1811 in St. Johnsbury, Vermont. He was baptized in 1833 and moved to Nauvoo in 1839. He died in 1892.

it was voted that Samuel Bent, should see Jacob Gates and make arrangements, with him to that effect provided he would accede to it. Recorded on book No 1. page 54 by H[osea] Stout Clerk. Hosea Stout clerk Pro. tem. Adjourned.

‡‡*April 12, 1840; Sunday.* The High Council of Church of Jesus Christ of Latter Day Saints Met in Council at the house of J[oseph] Smith jun. [on] April 12th 1840. A charge was prefered against S. A[lanson] Ripley by Alvey Keller[56] for taking nails from his lot[.] The charge was withdrawn. ~~Voted that O[liver] Granger be forgiven for his transgressions.~~ [It was] voted that H[yrum] Smith go with O[liver] Granger to transact buisness in the East. [It was] voted that J[oseph] Smith jr. make nessessary credential[s] for O[liver] Granger & H[yrum] Smith in their buisness transaction in the east.[57]

*April 19, 1840; Sunday.* The High Council of the Church of Jesus Christ of Latter Day Saints of Nauvoo[,] Ill[inois][,] met in Council at the house of John ^~~Law~~^ Law's [on] April ~~22~~ 19th 1840. [It was]voted that ~~Hyrum Smith~~ the house of which Hyrum Smith now lives in be reserved for him. – [It was]voted that Jabes Durfee make a bill of items of all the expenses which he has been to on the School house[.] ~~voted R~~ A charge was prefered against J[ohn] P. Green [by] J[ohn] Hicks for slanderously accusing [Hicks] of lying. [It was] voted that the trial be put off two weeks. ~~Are~~ [It was] voted that J[ohn] P Green make a report of his committyship while in Quincy as touching debts involving on him and other matters at the next council.

[It was] voted that a horse be procured for Br[other] Parrish by Bishop [Vinson] Knight. [It was] voted that the council meet at 2

---

[56]Alvah Keller was born in 1809 in Cherry Valley, New York. He was baptized in 1835 and moved to Missouri. He settled in Nauvoo in 1840. He died in 1885.

[57]Hyrum Smith and Oliver Granger were sent to beg for patience from real estate agents Isaac Galland and Horace Hotchkiss when the Church defaulted on its loans. See, e. g., Joseph Smith to Oliver Granger, May 4, 1841, in *Personal Writings of Joseph Smith*, ed. Dean C. Jessee (Salt Lake City: Deseret Book, 1984), 493-94. Galland lived in Kirtland, Ohio, and Hotchkiss in New Haven, Connecticut. Granger was also told to resolve the Church's ambiguous real estate holdings in Kirtland, which the church had abandoned and now wanted to re-claim.

o'clock on every Saturday at Joseph Smith jr['s] office. Adjourned. Hosea Stout Clerk Pro tem.

*April 25, 1840; Saturday.* John P. Green made a report of his committyship while in Quincy as touching debts ~~and~~ involving on him and other matters as follows:

> Quincy May 1839[.] To save the Committee of the Church at Quincy from being Sued, I in person became responsible to Dr. H. Rogers for the sum of forty seven [dollars] and seventy-five cents for ferrying the poor accross the Mississippi river. Also to Dr. R. N. Ralstone for the sum of fifteen dollars and eighty seven cents for house rent for women whose lawful protectors were shut up or driven from their aid.
>
> The former is now paid by myself. The latter remains to be paid and it rests on my ~~shoul~~ shoulders. I do pray the ~~counsel~~ councelors to consider the ~~matter~~ above & repay the above amount to me if they can in righteousness.

That there was also seventeen dollars ~~J[ohn] P. Green~~ and fifty cents involving on him due to Edward Partridge from the said committy at Quincy and Far West[,] [it was] voted that the Council set the above report aside for the present. ^anno^ mundi anno domini[58] [It was] voted that Thomas Grover be appointed to make inquiry as to the property of the committies of Quincy and Far-West [Missouri] and see to having it applied to liquidating the ^S[ai]d^ debts & involving on John P. Green and Edward Partridge. Adjourned. H[osea] Stout Clerk.

*May 2, 1840; Saturday.* The High Council of the Church of Jesus Christ of Latter Day Saints of Nauvoo[,] Ill[inois][,] met in council at the house of William Law's. [It was] voted that the rails[59] formerly belonging to the ~~Cl~~ City plot[60] shall be applied as Bishop [Alanson] Ripley and President Joseph Smith jr. shall see proper and also that

---

[58]Latin: "year of the world, year of the Lord."

[59] By "rails" was meant "timber ... inserted in upright posts for fencing" (Noah Webster, *An American Dictionary of the English Language* [New Haven: S. Converse, 1828], s.v. "rails").

[60]A *plot* could refer to the "site or situation of a town or city," although this usage was archaic in the nineteenth century (*Shorter Oxford English Dictionary*, s.v., "plot").

those who have unlawfully taken any of the above rails shall restore the same or render a recompence for the same to the satisfaction of Bishop Ripley & President Joseph Smith jr.

In as much as H[enry] G. Sherwood[,] C[harles] C. Rich and D[imick] Huntin[g]ton have been appointed a committee to ~~bus~~ contract for the building of the houses of ^some wives^ of the Twelve and that the building of said houses be paid in town lots[,] it was voted that the same committee shall contract for the ploughing and fencing of the lots and that the labor be paid also in lots.[61]

The charge against John Hicks by John P. Green presented April 19th was brought up and (3) Lewis D. Wilson, (4) Alpheus Cutler, (5) D[avid] Fulmer, (6) G[eorge] W. Harris, (7) T[homas] Grover, [and] (8) S[eymour] Brunson, were appointed to speak on the case[.] Objections were made ^by J[ohn] Hicks^ to Thomas Grover acting [as a prosecutor] on the case[.] [It was] voted that he act [in that capacity].[62] [It was] voted that [Hicks] confess to J[ohn] P. Green for assailing his character And that [Hicks] publish a peace in the Times & Seasons stating that he ^wrongfully^ accused [Green] of [stealing a horse][,] being in consequence of a different arrangement ^made^ by the parties ^unknown to^ [who were] donating ^J[ohn] P Green^ the horse and that [Hicks] is sorry for it[,] Where upon he acceded to the said decision.[63]

---

[61]At this time, nine of the twelve apostles were serving proselytizing missions in England: Orson Hyde, Heber C. Kimball, Orson Pratt, Parley P. Pratt, Willard Richards, George A. Smith, John Taylor, Wilford Woodruff, and Brigham Young. Because of the generally unpaid nature of their work, they were unable to support their wives, whom the Church tried to aid. For general studies of the Twelve's missionary work, see Richard L. Jensen and Malcolm Thorpe, *Mormons in Early Victorian Britain* (Salt Lake City: University of Utah Press, 1989); James B. Allen, Ronald K. Esplin, and David J. Whittaker, *Men with a Mission, 1837-1841: The Quorum of the Twelve Apostles in the British Isles* (Salt Lake City: Deseret Book, 1992).

[62]On February 17, 1834, Joseph Smith received a revelation on procedures for the high council, requiring that one-half of the council should speak in behalf of the defendant: "The councilors appointed to speak before the council are to present the case, after the evidence is examined, in its true light before the council; and every man is to speak according to equity and justice. Those councilors who draw even numbers, that is, 2, 4, 6, 8, 10, and 12, are the individuals who are to stand up in behalf of the accused, and prevent insult and injustice" (D&C 102:15-17).

[63]This piece was never published.

‡*June 12, 1840; Friday.* The High Council of the Church of Jesus Christ of Latter Day Saints of Nauvoo[,] Illinois[,] met in council at the Office of Joseph Smith jr. It was resolved that the Council procure goods from William Law's Store, not exceeding fifty dollars, for the relief of Alpheus Cutler, that he may be enabled to carry on the building of the School house. Rec[orde]d on Book No 1 Page 60. Adjourned. H[osea] Stout. Hosea Stout Clerk Pro tem.

*June 20, 1840; Saturday.* The High Council of the Church of Jesus Christ of Latter day Saints of Nauvoo[,] Illinois[,] met in council at [the] Office of Joseph Smith jr. A memorial was presented from President Joseph Smith jr. praying that the Council would relieve him from the temporalities of the ^Church^, which he necessarily had to engage in, in order that a location might be effected for the gathering of the Saints[.] [Also] that he felt it his duty to engage, more particularly, in the spiritual welfare of the Saints; and, also, to the translating of the Egyptian Records[64] – the Bible[65] – and wait upon the Lord for such revelation as may be suited to the condition and circumstances of the Church.

That, in order, to relieve him from the anxiety and troubles necessarily attendant on business transaction they would appoint some one to take charge of the City Plot and attend to the business transactions which have heretofore rested upon him. That when he is relieved from such temporal duties he would have no means of support whatever and requested that some one might be appointed to see that all his necessary wants are provided for, as well as, sufficient means or appropriations for a Clerk or clerks which he may require to aid him in his important work[.]

The Council relieved President Joseph Smith jr. according to the request of the memorial and appointed Henry G. Sherwood to take charge of the City Plot and act as Clerk in that buisness and also to attend to the disposing of the remaining lots and the buisness

[64]In July 1835, Joseph Smith acquired, on behalf of the Church, four mummies and two Egyptian scrolls from a traveling dealer in antiquities. He believed that the scrolls contained the writings of Joseph and Abraham from the Bible. According to one eyewitness: "This record is beautifully written on papyrus with black, and ... red ink or paint, in perfect preservation" (*Latter Day Saints Messenger and Advocate*, Dec. 1835, 234).

[65]Joseph Smith was re-writing portions of the Bible.

transactions which have heretofore rested upon him. Al[a]nson Ripley was appointed steward to see that all the necessary wants of the First Presidency be supplied, as well as to provide sufficient means or appropriations for a Clerk or clerks to aid President Joseph Smith jr. in his important work.

Henry G. Sherwood, for and in behalf of the Church prefered a charge against Ebenezer A. Black for a course of fraudulent proceedings and conduct by him practised, on said Church[,] relative to a town lot and lots in Nauvoo commencing in falsehood[,] continuing in error and eventuating in unchristian-like conduct, done and conducted within the last twelve months. Whereupon [councillors] Nos. 9 [Vinson Knight], 10 [William D. Huntington], 11 [Charles C. Rich], and 12 [Alanson Ripley] were appointed to Speak on the case.[66] The charge was sustained after which it was decided that Ebenezer A. Black should stand ^expelled^ from the society of the Church until he makes a satisfactory confession and restored all the damages which he has caused to be done by his unchristian-like ~~&c~~ con~~duc~~t &c.

Resolved, that Henry G. Sherwood, Al[a]nson Ripley and Vin[son] Knight be appointed to visit George W. Robinson for the purpose of inquiry and examination into the affairs of the Galland purchase[67] and also of the Church Records[,] and make a report of the same to the High Council. Adjourned. Hosea Stout Clerk pro tem.

*June 27, 1840; Saturday.*[68] The High Council of the Church of Jesus Christ of Latter Day Saints of Nauvoo[,] Illinois[,] met in Council at the office of J[oseph] Smith jr. [It was] resolved –that the minutes of the Last Council be always read at the beginning of the next [meeting], by the Clerk, that the chain of buisness may be more easily come at & error in the records detected.

President Josep[h] Smith jr. sent in his veto, by Al[a]nson Ripl[e]y, to the proceedings of the Council relative to the memorial pre-

---

[66]Hosea Stout identified these four high council members by their names when he reproduced the minutes for this date.

[67]Isaac Galland had sold the Saints forty-seven acres in Illinois and an additional 14,500 acres in Iowa. The Iowa land, known as the Half-Breed Tract, had uncertain ownership.

[68]See also *History of Church,* 4:141.

sented at the last Council (of June 20)[.] The Council laid it over for a rehearing on Friday next, (July 3rd) at 1 o'clock, when the council would meet again. Adjourned. Hosea Stout Clerk pro tem.

*July 3, 1840; Friday.*[69] The High Council of the Church of Jesus Christ of Latter Day Saints of Nauvoo Illinois met in Council at the Office of Joseph Smith jr. The subject of the memorial of President Joseph Smith jr was again brough[t] up, for a rehearing, according to the decision of the Last council (June 27) when the following resolutions were entered into.

> 1st. Resolved – That we feel perfectly satisfied with the course taken by Joseph Smith Jr and feel a disposition as far as it is in our power to ~~asist~~ assist him, so as to relieve him from the temporalities of the ^Church^ in order that he may devote his time more particularly to the spiritualities of the same, believing [that] by so doing we shall promote the good of the whole church. But as he (Joseph Smith jr.) is held responsible for the payment of the City plot, and knowing no way to relieve him from that responsibility at present, we would request of him to act as treasurer for the city plot and [be the person] to whom those persons whom we may appoint to make sales of Lots and attend to the business affairs of the Church may at all times be responsible and make true and correct returns of all their proceedings as well as to account for all monies, properties &c. which may come unto their hands.
>
> [It is] therefore resolved – That Elder Henry G Sherwood act as clerk for the same. That Bishop Al[a]nson Ripley be appointed to provide for the wants of the Presidency and make such appropriations to them and to the clerk or clerks which they may require. Resolved – that the funds of the City plot shall not be take[n] to provide for the presidency of clerks, but that the Bishops be instructed to raise funds from other sources to meet the calls made on him. And that all monies received for lots shall be deposited in the hands of the treasurer to liquidate the debts of the City plot.
>
> [It is] resolved that the Clerk shall have a stipulated sum for his servises for transacting the business of the city plot and that he receive the sum of <u>twenty-six</u> dollars p[e]r month for his said servises. Resolved – That the remaining items of buisness relative to

---

[69]See also ibid., 144-45.

the memorial before the council shall be laid over to be taken up again at the next Council. Adjourned.[70] Hosea Stout Clerk Pro tem.

*July 11, 1840; Saturday.*[71] The High Council for the Church of Jesus Christ of Latter Day Saints of Nauvoo[,] Illinois[,] met in council at the Office of Joseph Smith jr. President Joseph Smith jr gave as a precedent and rule for the Council and ordered it to be recorded and established, That the Council should try no case without both parties being present[,] or having had an opportunity to be present, neither should they hear one parties complaint before his case is brought up for trial, neither should they suffer the character of any one to be exposed before the Council without the person being present and ready to defend him or herself[,] that the minds of the councellors be not prejudiced for or against any one whose case they may, possibly, have to act upon. Adjourned. Hosea Stout Clerk pro tem.

*July 17, 1840; Friday.*[72] The High Council of the Church of Jesus Christ of Latter Day Saints of Nauvoo[,] Illinois[,] met in council at the Office of Joseph Smith jr. By the nomination of Joseph Smith jr.[,] it was Resolved –that Samuel Bent and George W. Harris be appointed to go on a mission to procure money to be applied to the purpose of printing certain books.[73] Adjourned. Hosea Stout Clerk Pro tem.

---

[70]The *History of Church,* 4:145, reports a different scribe for this meeting, Robert B. Thompson, and an additional resolution: "The resolutions of the Crooked Creek Branch of the 2nd inst., were taken into consideration by President Joseph Smith, Jun., and it was thought proper to establish a Stake on Crooked Creek, agreeably to the request of said Branch, and a letter was written to the brethren to that effect." Crooked Creek was about twenty miles east of Nauvoo and eight miles east of Carthage and would soon be renamed Ramus (now Webster).

[71]See also ibid., 4:154.

[72]See also ibid., 161.

[73]Harris and Bent were "authorized agents of the Church of Jesus Christ of Latter-day Saints, being appointed by the First Presidency and High Council of said Church to visit the branches of the Church in the east, or wherever they may be led in the providence of God, to obtain donations and subscriptions for the purpose of printing the Book of Mormon, Doctrine and Covenants, hymn-books, [and] the new translation of the Scriptures. They are likewise instructed and authorized to procure loans

*July 25, 1840; Saturday.* The High Council of the Church of Jesus Christ of Latter Day Saints of Nauvoo[,] Illinois[,] met in Council at the Office of Joseph Smith jr. [It was] resolved – That Henry G. Sherwood be appointed to procure a horse, saddle, bridle and other necessaries for the use of John Tanner[74] as soon as he can consistently [leave on his mission to New York][.]

Letter[s] of Recommendation for Samuel Bent and George W. Harris, for their mission to procure money for printing purposes[,] were presented to the Council by R[obert] B. Thompson, which were approved of and signed by the members of the Council. Samuel Bent nominated Elias Higbee[,] and George W. Harris nominated John P. Green to fill their seats in the Council during their absence while on their mission to procure money for the aforenamed purposes[,] which was accepted by the Council. Adjourned. Hosea Stout Clerk Pro tem.

*August 8, 1840; Saturday.* The High Council of the Church of Jesus Christ of Latter Day Saints of Nauvoo[,] Illinois[,] met in Council at the Office of Joseph Smith jr. The Council appointed Alpheus Cutler [as] President of the High Council during the absence of Samuel Bent.

Elder H[enry] G. Sherwood[,] in behalf of the Church[,] prefered a charge against Elder Moses Martin[75] for reporting certain slanderous reports against Elders S[eymour] Brunson and A[masa] Lyman and others – stating that a gang of Gadianton robers[76] were in the Church and countenanced[,] together with certain slanderous and unchristian-like expressions[,] insinuations &c derogatory [lan-

---

in behalf of the Church, for carrying into operation the above and other important works necessary to the well being of said Church" (ibid., 164).

[74]John Tanner was born in Hopkinton, Rhode Island, in 1778. He was baptized in New York after missionaries miraculously healed his leg in 1832. In the Mormon War with Missouri in 1838, he was severely wounded. He moved to Montrose, Iowa, in 1840 and died in 1850.

[75]Moses Martin was born in 1812 in Grafton, New Hampshire. He was a member of Zion's Camp and served on a high council in Missouri before moving to Nauvoo in 1839. He died in 1899 in San Bernardino.

[76]Sherwood references a secret society in the Book of Mormon whose leader had expertise in "the secret work of murder and robbery" (Hel. 1-2), which implies a dangerous conspiracy.

guage as] to the character of certain brethren &c. &c.[,] whereupon [councillors] Nos. 1 [Elias Higbee], 2 [David Dort], 3 [Alpheus Cutler] and 4 [David Fulmer][77] were appointed to speak on the case. The charge was sustained after which it was decided that he should stand expelled from the Church untill he should make a satisfactory confession. After which decision he made a satisfactory confession and was received again into fellowship. Adjourned. Hosea Stout Clerk pro tem.

*August 17, 1840; Monday.*[78] The High Council of the Church of Jesus Christ of Latter Day Saints of Nauvoo[,] Illinois[,] met in council at the office of Joseph Smith jr. together with the First Presidency of the Church and the High Council of Iowa Territory.

The following charges were prefered against Elijah Fordham[79] by John Patten for unchristian conduct, to wit; Firstly, For libelous[,] slanderous[,] and infamous reports in the High Council of the Church of Latter Day Saints at Montrose [Iowa], against John Patten's character; charging said Patten of being guilty of lieing, Theft, burglary[,] and attempt to murder[,] and [that it was] done in the spirit of malevolence and high toned wickedness. Secondly, For having told a positive lie.

Thirdly[,] for affirming to things which he did not know in a Court of Justice[,] thereby perjuring himself in making the following statements, to wit:

> 1stly[,] that said Patten's garden was on Mr Coleman's [land][.] Claim 2ndly[,] that he never saw the garden. 3rdly[,] that the damage done by destroying said garden did not amount to five dollars. 4thly[,] that rails delivered were worth from one dollar to one dollar and a quarter and one dollar and a half, and 5thly, that every person in Montrose knew that Coleman had not relinquished his claim to the land on which said Patten's garden was situated.

Fourthly, for being privy to [David W.] Rogers taking [Patten's]

---

77 Hosea Stout later identified these four high council members.

78 See also *History of Church,* 4:180.

79 Elijah Fordham was born in New York City in 1798. He was baptized prior to 1834 and marched in Zion's Camp. He was healed by Joseph Smith in Nauvoo in 1839, immigrated to Utah in 1850, and died in 1879.

rails and destroying [his] garden[.] Fifthly, for justifying Rogers for so doing and approving of the act or Rogers conduct. Sixthly, for embezeling Rogers property to prevent the payment of Roger's debts. Seventhly[,] for having made false statements about Rogers pill nostrums,[80] saying that they had had the effect in his family last fall and winter [and] set forth by said Rogers, to wit; that he[,] the said Rogers[,] had used them twenty years and they had never failed of effecting a complete and radical cure; when it is a well known fact that Fordham and his family were sick nigh unto death during the fall and winter: thus endeavoring to vindicate the conduct of Rogers in palming his deception on [the] community.

Eightly[,] for acting [in] an unrighteous and unholy part in the High Council, and because I opposed his course he sought for evil against me, to slander and defame my character[,] destroy my influence and drive me from ^my^ seat in the council[.] [In hoping] that the council might enter immediately into the ~~conservation~~ consecration law, which he publickly declared was the determination of the High Council, [he said] I alone opposed their proceedings and had spoken against the proceedings of the High Council in public [by] stating that the council of the First Presidency was contrary to the proceedings of the High Council and that President Hyrum Smith was vested with the authority of the First Presidency in the absence of the other two Presidents[.] [Which he] contended, was not so: and I was charged with weakening or deminishing the influence of the High Council by Speaking in public against the proceedings of that quorum, which was the first charge made against me to drive me from the council, and was followed by others, such as playing the violin for a negro ball; suffering my daughter to go to balls;[81] and then followed the slanderous and vile charges ~~charges~~ first mentioned in this catalogue of crime and misdemeanors[.] And when President John Smith told him it was his duty to take up a labor with me, he replied, I was not worthy of his notice, of which I wish to convince

---

[80]The term "nostrum" referred to medicines with secret ingredients.

[81]According to George Givens, "dancing had been a controversial issue [since] Kirtland, where thirty-one brethren and sisters had been disfellowshipped" for dancing. In Nauvoo, there was a generational difference of opinion about the propriety of dancing, young people staging parties that included both dancing and kissing (*Old Nauvoo*, 158-60).

him to the contrary. After the evidence was heard Presidents John Smith, William Marks, Hyrum Smith, ^&^ Joseph Smith jr spoke on the case after which the parties were reconciled without calling a vote of the Councils.[82] Adjourned. Hosea Stout Clerk pro tem.

*August 22, 1840; Saturday.* The High Council of the Church of Jesus Christ of Latter Day Saints of Nauvoo[,] Illinois[,] met in Council at the office of Joseph Smith junior. A charge was prefered against Br[other]s Ourbough & Waggoner for grossly slandering the Presidency of this Church[;] [and] having laboured with them[,] yet they repent not[,] neither turn from the evil. [The charge was made] by John Zundel[.][83] The charge was confessed on the part of the accused and they, persisting in their own course, were expelled from the Church.

By a motion of a committee, of ^the^ singers of Nauvoo, who were sent to the council for that purpose[,] the Council decided that Benjamin S. Wilber should act as chorister or leader of the singers of Nauvoo until further directions from the High Council.[84] Resolved –That William Marks and Peter Hawes be appointed to procure provisions and other means necessary for the building of the school House. Adjourned. Hosea Stout Clerk. pro tem.

*August 29, 1840; Saturday.* The High Council of the Church of Jesus

---

[82]According to the *History of Church,* 4:180, Joseph Smith "addressed the Council at some length, showing the situation of the contending parties, that there was in reality no cause of difference; that they had better be reconciled without an action, or vote of the Council, and henceforth live as brethren, and never more mention their former difficulties. They settled accordingly."

[83]Johannes Zundel was born in 1792 in Germany. In 1831 he married Ann Christina Lautenschlager in Pennsylvania, and the two had thirteen children together. He resided in Nauvoo's 3rd Ward neighborhood. He died in 1852 in Salt Lake City.

[84]This is apparently a reference to a choral group later directed by Gustavus Hills, a music teacher. According to Glen Leonard, "Hills applauded the progress of [the] choral group in late 1841 for its progress in smoothing" out "varied musical and cultural backgrounds into an orderly whole." (Leonard, *Nauvoo,* 192). Four years later they were still performing, in one instance at the Mansion House for a party the *Nauvoo Neighbor* praised for its sophistication (Givens, *Old Nauvoo,* 160-61).

Christ of Latter Day Saints of Nauvoo[,] Ill[inois][,] met in council at the Office of Joseph Smith jr.

A charge was prefered against Elder Hirum Dayton[85] by Noah Packard for [not paying a debt][,] forfeiting his word[,] and for other unchristian-like conduct. [Councillors] Numbers five [David Fulmer] and six [George W. Harris][86] were appointed to speak on the case. The charge was sustained after which the Council decided that the parties should abide by the last contract, about which their difficulty arose, and that Noah Packard pay Hirum Dayton fourteen dollars and fifty cents as soon as he can consistently. ~~The parties acceded to the decision of the Council and were reconciled to each other.~~ The debt however [was] not to be binding upon him but left to his own conscience whether he ought to pay it or not. The parties acceded to the decision of the Council and were reconciled to each other. Adjourned. Hosea Stout Clerk pro tem.

*September 5, 1840; Saturday.*[87] The High Council of the Church of Jesus Christ of Latter day Saints of Nauvoo[,] Illinois[,] met in Council at the office of Joseph Smith jr. [It was] Resolved that Austin Cowles be appointed a member of the High Council of the Church of Jesus Christ, of Nauvoo[,] Illinois, to fill the vacancy occasioned by ^the death of^ Semour Brunson.[88]

A charge was prefered against Almon Babitt[89] by Joseph Smith jr[,] predicated upon the authority of two letters, one of the letter[s] from Thomas Burdoc,[90] [and] the other from Levi Richards and

---

[85]Hiram Dayton was born in 1798 in New York. He was living near Kirtland, Ohio, when he was baptized in 1832. He served as the president of the twelfth quorum of elders in Nauvoo. After he crossed the prairies and settled in Utah, he died there in 1881.

[86]Hosea Stout later identified these four high council members.

[87]See also *History of Church,* 4:187-88.

[88]Brunson died a few weeks earlier on August 10 at the home of Joseph Smith. He had become sick while herding cattle in July.

[89]Almon Babbit was born in Massachusetts in 1813. He was probably baptized in 1833 since he marched with Zion's Camp the next year. In 1835 he was ordained a Seventy by Joseph Smith. He later became a high priest. He practiced law, often in defense of the Church. He was a signatory to the treaty surrendering Nauvoo. He immigrated to Utah by 1855 and died in 1856.

[90]Burdick was born in New York in 1795. He served as bishop of Kirt-

Oliver Granger, accusing him (Almon Babbit) with the following charges, to wit; 1st. For stating that Joseph Smith jr had extravagantly purchased three suits of cloth[e]s while he was at Washington [D.C.][,] and that Sidney Rigdon had purchased four suits at the same place, besides dresses an[d] cloth[e]s for their families in profusion.

2nd. For having stated that Joseph Smith jr.[,] Sidney Rigdon[,] and Elias Higbee had Stated that they were worth $100,000 each while they were at Washington and that Joseph Smith jr had repeated the same statement while at Philadelphia[,] and for stating that Oliver Granger had stated that he also was worth as ^much as^ they[,] that is[,] $100,000. 3rd. For holding secret Council in the Lord's house in Kirtland[,] [Ohio], and for locking the doors of the house for the purpose of prohibiting certain brethren, in good standing in the Church, from being in the council and thereby depriving them the use of the house.[91] Numbers seven [Thomas Grover] and eight [Austin Cowles][92] were appointed to speak on the case. [The] council adjourned till ~~th~~ the 6th of Sept[ember] at 2 o'clock.

---

land, and in 1846 he moved with the Church to Kanesville, Iowa, where he stayed until 1852 and then immigrated to Utah. Lingering only a few years, he soon moved farther west to San Bernardino and then Los Angeles, where he died in 1877.

[91]In July 1840, Joseph Smith wrote a letter to Oliver Granger discussing this charge: "I am sorry to be informed not only in your letter, but from other respectable sources, of the strange conduct pursued in Kirtland by Elder Almon W. Babbitt. I am indeed surprised that a man having the experience which Brother Babbitt has had, should take any steps whatever, calculated to destroy the confidence of the brethren in the Presidency or any of the authorities of the Church. ... It was something new to me when I heard there had been secret meetings held in the Lord's House, and that some of my friends–faithful brethren–men enjoying the confidence of the Church, should be locked out. Such proceedings are not calculated to promote union, or peace, but to engender strife; and will be a curse instead of a blessing. ... If Brother Babbitt and the other brethren wish to reform the Church, and come out and make a stand against sin and speculation, &c., they must use other weapons than lies, or their object can never be effected; and their labors will be given to the house of the stranger, rather than to the House of the Lord" (in Dean C. Jessee, ed., *Personal Writings of Joseph Smith,* rev. ed. [Salt Lake City: Deseret Book, 2002], 512-14).

[92] Hosea Stout later identified these four high council members.

*September 6, 1840; Sunday.*[93] Council met according to adjournment when the evidences ~~were~~ ^were^ all heard on the case pending[,] after which the charge was withdrawn by Joseph Smith jr.[94] Adjourned. Hosea Stout Cl[er]k pro tem.

*October 10, 1840; Saturday.*[95] The High Council of the Church of Jesus Christ of Latter Day Saints of Nauvoo[,] Illinois[,] met in council at the Office of Joseph Smith jr.

A charge was prefered against Oliver Walker[96] by David Fulmer for reporting certain slanderous stories of a fallacious and calumінating nature [that were] calculated to stigmatize and raise a persecution against the Church and individuals in it[,] in this place – and for a variety of unchristian-like conduct &c. [Councillors] Numbers seven [Thomas Grover] and eight [Austin Cowles] were appointed to speak on the case.[97] Oliver Walker plead that he was not prepared to meet the charge, it being too indefinite and he not having notice previous to his leaving home. The council then adjourned until the next day at 4 O'clock, when the case was to be again taken up.

---

[93]See also *History of Church,* 4:188.

[94]Ibid., 4:188, records this meeting in greater detail: "Council adjourned till the 6th September, at 2 o'clock, when Council met according to adjournment, the evidences were all heard on the case pending, and the councilors closed on both sides. The parties spoke at length, after which, Joseph Smith withdrew the charge, and both parties were reconciled to each other, things being adjusted to their satisfaction." Though Babbitt seemed repentant, he was disfellowshiped less than a month later. According to the *Times and Seasons*, October 15, 1841, 577, "Br[other] Hyrum Smith made remarks disapprobatory of the course pursued by some Elders, in withstanding the efforts of the Presidency to gather the saints, and in enticing them to stop in places not appointed for the gathering; particularly the conduct of Elder Almon Babbitt of Kirtland. Br[other]s Lyman Wight and Henry Miller having travelled in places where Br[other] A[lmon] Babbitt had been in his journeying eastward from his visit to Nauvoo testified that he had in many places taught doctrine contrary to the revelations of God and detrimental to the interest of the Church. Moved, seconded and carried that Elder Almon Babbitt be disfellowshiped by the conference as an Elder till such time as he shall make satisfaction."

[95]See also *History of Church,* 4:219.

[96]Oliver Walker was born in 1782 in New York. He was baptized in 1835 and died in 1843 in Nauvoo of cholera. His widow married Brigham Young.

[97] Hosea Stout later identified these four high council members.

*October 11, 1840; Sunday.*[98] The Council met persuant to adjournment when the charge against Oliver Walker was taken up[.] The plaintiff ~~prosed~~ proposed withdrawing the original charge and prefering another more definite [one], which was acceded to on the part of the defendant and sanctioned by the Council[,] after which the charge was withdrawn and the following charge was preferred[:]

> To the High Council in and for the Church of Jesus Christ of Latter Day Saints at Nauvoo[,] Illinois. For and in behalf of the said Church I hereby prefer a charge against Elder Oliver Walker for several different offences herein after set forth, as said to be by him done, performed, said and committed – as also various duties omitted &c. all of which were done at different times, periods, places and seasons subsequent to Sept[ember] 1st 1838 – To wit: For a general course of procedure, of acts, ^doings^ and words and suggestions by him[,] the said Elder Oliver Walker, done[,] performed, said, spoke[n], hinted at and suggested: both directly and indirectly and as being calculated to be derogatory to the character of the heads and leaders of the church and extremely injurious and hurtful to the upbuilding, welfare, being and advancement of the same, viz: For fleeing from, quiting[,] and deserting the society, ranks and needs of his brethren in times of difficulty, with and [in] danger from their enemies "the mob" – restraining from the use of his brethren his influence[,] efforts[,] and needful assistence, at such times of need, as also for joining with and strengthening the hands, will, evil persuits[,] and designs of the mob and Gentile enemies of the Church. By expressions[,] hints[,] and suggestions of a wavering and dubious nature respecting the faith and order of the Church and of the professed calling[,] qualifications[,] proceedings &c. of Joseph Smith jr. as a seer[,] prophet[,] and one called to bring to light the fulness of the Gospel &c. in the last days –Likewise for advancing ideas, [and] notions of opinions that the different orders or sects – viz; Methodists and others could[,] by a persuit in their faith order and persuits as readily obtain every Celestial attainment and gospel advantage as they could by embracing and persuing the system brought forth by Joseph Smith jr in these last days, and moreover for suggesting within the last six months at Alton – Nauvoo, intermediate and adjacent places that in the church at Nauvoo there did exist [a] set of pilferers, who

[98]See also *History of Church,* 4:219-20.

> were actually thieving, robing, plundering, taking and unlawfully carrying away from Missouri certain goods and chattles, wares and property and that the act and acts of such supposed thieving &c. was fostered and conducted by the knowledge and approbation of the heads & leaders of the church, viz; by the Presidency and High Council; all of which items set forth as aforesaid together with any and all corroberating acts, doings, hints, expressions and suggestions in any way belonging to or connected with any or all of the aforesaid accusations [that] he[,] the said Oliver Walker[,] is hereby notified to prepare to defend in said trial. Dated Oct[ober] 11th 1840[,] Nauvoo. David Fulmer.[99]

After this second charge was prefered, he[,] the said Elder Oliver Walker[,] plead that he was not prepared to defend himself, when the trial was adjourned, according to his own choice, untill the next April conference. Adjourned. Hosea Stout Clerk pro tem.

*October 17, 1840; Saturday.* The High Council of the Church of Jesus Christ of Latter Day Saints of Nauvoo[,] Illinois[,] met in Council at the office of J[oseph] Smith jr.

---

[99]A second complaint against Oliver Walker reads:

> Truman P Richards witnesseth that he heard Oliver Walker say & report that ~~from~~ ^what [he] he~~ard~~^ heard the brethren at Nauvoo say [was] that there was much thieving done by many of the Church – and that the heads of it were knowing to it – viz the presidency & High Council & particularly br[other] Fulmer told him ^that^ the brethren were Justified in getting all that they could from Missouri – that it was only getting what was their own and not stealing – and that br[other] Fulmer told him that if he had the power to do it he would take every cent of property in Missouri – He also heard br[other] Joseph preach & in it say as much [as] if it was not wrong – but rather encouraged the brethren to think it was not wrong to take property from the Missourians[.] He reported that Joseph had been drunk and in transgression in so much that Elder [Sidney] Rigdon had written to Joseph a letter of reproof – and that Joseph had assailed the character of Elder Rigdon in public – and that br[other] Joseph and Elder Rigdon were on terms of discord or hard feelings towards each other. Dated Oct[ober] 6, 1840. Truman P Richards ("Truman Richards Testimony vs Oliver Walker," in Nauvoo Stake High Council Court Papers, 1839-1844, *Selected Collections: From the Archives of the Church of Jesus Christ of Latter-day Saint*, 74 discs (Salt Lake City: Intellectual Reserve, 2002), 1:19.

A charge was prefered against William Gregory by H[enry] G. Sherwood in consequence of the circulation of various reports purporting to have originated by and come from and circulated by him[,] the said William Gregory: to wit; that he had spread abroad certain slanderous reports and insinuations that go to carry an idea that much pilfering, pillaging, plundering, stealing &c. is practised by members of said Church and that such practise is known to and tolerated by the heads and leaders of the church (or certain of them)[,] and that the appointment of a committee to detect such nominal or all real thefts &c. was an appointment calculated in its nature to smother and cover up and blind the minds of the more honest of the said Church – Moreover for pretending that such accursed pilfering party or part thereof had stolen his oxen[,] when in fact[,] his oxen were where he left them and not stolen, and for suspicion that he himself[,] ~~other~~ either alone or in company[,] are in ^the^ like pilfering practise as is said that he accused others of – and that he spreads such slanders to blind the honest and smother his own thefts &c.[,] for and in behalf of said church[,][100] dated Nauvoo[,] 14th Oct[ober] 1840.

The trial of the above charge was adjourned untill next Saturday. Neither of the parties being ready for trial[.] Resolved – That the trustees of the School house be instructed to settle with the building committee of the same on Wednesday next the 21st inst[ant]. Adjourned. Hosea Stout Clerk pro tem.

*October 24, 1840; Saturday.* The High Council of the Church of Jesus Christ of Latter Day Saints of Nauvoo[,] Illinois[,] met in council at the office of Joseph Smith jr. Resolved – That Elias Higbee be appointed president pro tem. of the High Council, to fill the place of President Alpheus Cutler, resigned.

The charge against William Gregory, prefered, Oct[ober] 17th. was brought up for trial according to adjournment. [Councillors] Numbers seven (Thomas Grover) and eight (Austin Cowles) were appointed to speak on the case. The defendant plead not guilty. The

---

[100]The original complaint ("H. G. Sherwood charge vs. William Gregory," Nauvoo Stake High Council Court Papers, 1839-1844) lacks the phrase, "for and in behalf of said church," which probably means Sherwood filed the complaint for the Church, although it makes one wonder whether the offence was revealing secrets rather than telling gossip.

evidences ~~wer~~ were then heared. The charge was sustained and after the pleadings were over, he, the defendant, made a humble confession to the satisfaction of the Council and ~~the plantiff~~ also to the satisfaction of the plantiff. Adjourned. Hosea Stout Clerk pro tem.

*October 31, 1840; Saturday.* The High Council of the Church of Jesus Christ of Latter Day Saints, of Nauvoo[,] Illinois, met in council at the office of J[oseph]. Smith jr. A charge was prefered against John Huntsman[101] by Henry G. Sherwood, for and in behalf of the Church, For knowingly, willfully, wrongfully and unlawfully[,] by craft and fallacious tales and acts[,] interupteing[,] breaking up and destroying certain bargains and bargaining which I was about to complete for the use and benefit of the said Church and the better locating certain brethren to build up the town of Nauvoo. viz. brothers [James] Allred and [John D.] Parker and others[.] Dated October 16th 1840. The plantiff plead not guilty.

[Councillors] Numbers 9 (Newel Knight) and 10 (William Huntington) were appointed to speak on the case. When the evidences were give[n][,] the charge was sustained[,] after which it was decided that ~~that~~ Alpheus Cutler and Elias Higbee be appointed to receive propositions of satisfaction, from the defendant relative to the injury which the church has received by his interference in the aforenamed bargains &c. mentioned in the foregoing charge. Adjourned. Hosea Stout Clerk pro tem.

*November 7, 1840; Saturday.* [The High] Council met persuant to adjournment at the Office of Joseph Smith jr. [It was] Resolved That Charles C. Rich have the avails of a certain waggon, sufficient, to enable him to pay a note of hand, given by himself and others, for, and in behalf of the Church, due six month[s] after date, payable to Philip C. Quick, given July 9th 1839 amounting to about forty dollars. Adjourned. Hosea Stout[,] Clerk pro tem.

*November 28, 1840; Saturday.* The High Council of the Church of

[101]John Huntsman was born in 1814 in Indiana. After his wife, Deborah Snyder, died in 1839, he married Rozanne Leavitt in 1841 in Nauvoo. They resided in Nauvoo's 2nd Ward neighborhood. He died in 1849 in the Mormon town of Mt. Pisgah, Iowa.

Jesus Christ of Latter Day Saints of Nauvoo[,] Illinois[,] met in Council at the office of Joseph Smith jr. Resolved —That Hosea Stout be appointed Clerk of the High Council of Nauvoo[,] Illinois.

William Huntington prefered a charge against Robert D. Foster[102] as follows: "Firstly, for slandering the authorities of the Church. Secondly, for lying, profane swearing[,] and individual abuse[,] and for other unchristian-like conduct. Dated Nauvoo, Nov[ember] 20th 1840.["] The defendant plead not guilty. [Councillors] Numbers 11 (Charles C. Rich) and 12 (Henry G Sherwood) were appointed to speak on the case. ^After^ the evidences were partly given[,] the trial was adjourned untill the 12th day of December next. Adjourned. Hosea Stout. Clerk.

*December 12, 1840; Saturday.* The High Council of the Church of Jesus Christ of Latter Day Saints of Nauvoo[,] Illinois[,] met in council at the Office of Joseph Smith [on] December the 12th 1840. The charge against Robert D. Foster, presented November the 28th 1840, was again brought up for trial, according to previous adjournment.

The council proceeded to ^the^ examination of the ~~witness~~ witnesses until 12 o'clock[,] when the council adjourned one hour [later][,] after which the Council met and ~~and~~ again proceeded to the examination of the witnesses until dark and then adjourned until the next day (December the 13th) at 10. o'clock.

*December 13, 1840; Sunday.* The High Council met according to adjournment and again proceeded to the examination of the witnesses[.] At one o'clock the Council ~~the council~~ adjourned one hour[,] after which the Council met according to adjournment and again proceeded to the further examination of the witnesses until about dark[,]when all of the witnesses [having] be[en] examined[,] the Council was adjourned until December the 20th 1840.

---

[102]Robert D. Foster was born in Braunston, England, in 1811. He was baptized in 1839 and helped the Saints petition Congress for redress from Missouri persecutions by going to Washington, D.C., and drafting a document for the Senate Committee of the Judiciary. In Nauvoo, he served as a regent of the university, a member of the Agricultural and Manufacturing Association, and surgeon-in-chief of the Nauvoo Legion. He was excommunicated in April 1844, after which he helped publish the *Nauvoo Expositor.* He died in Illinois in 1878.

*December 20, 1840; Sunday.*[103] The [High] Council met again according to previous adjournment at the house of Joseph Smith jr. to decide the charge against R[obert] D. Foster[.] The case was submited to the [First] Presidency by mutual consent of the parties without making pleas on either side. The Presidency decided that he (R[obert] D. Foster) should be acquited of the charges brought against him which was voted unanimously by the Council. Adjourned. Hosea Stout. Cl[er]k.

---

[103]See also *History of Church,* 4:250.

# 8.

# "Acting in Their Proper Places" 1841

‡*February 6, 1841; Saturday.* The High Council of the Church of Jesus Christ of Latter Day Saints of Nauvoo Illinois met in Council at the office of Joseph Smith [on] February the 6th 1841. The Council appointed Aaron Johnson, in conformity to a revelation previously given to that effect, to the office of High Councellor, in the place of Austin Cowles, to fill the place of Seymour Brunson[,] deceased.[1]

A charge was prefered against, John P. Green, by Jacob Ulrich,

[1]Joseph Smith received a revelation on January 19, 1841: "I give unto you a High Council, for the corner stone of Zion; Viz., Samuel Bent, Henry G. Sherwood, George W. Harris, Charles C. Rich, Thomas Grover, Newel Knight, David Dort, [Lewis] Dunbar Wilson, (Seymour Brunson I have taken unto myself, no man taketh his Priesthood, but another may be appointed unto the same Priesthood in his stead; and verily I say unto you, let my servant Aaron Johnson be ordained unto this calling in his stead), David Fullmer, Alpheus Cutler, William Huntington" (D&C 124:132).

The difference between priesthood and priesthood office was still developing in the Church at the time. Members also had the idea that the priesthood hierarchy on earth would continue statically forever in heaven. John Taylor commented on this in an 1881 sermon: "If the priesthood administers in time and in eternity, and if quorums of this kind are organized upon the earth, and this priesthood is not taken away, but continued with them in the heavens, we do not wish, I think, to break up the order of the priesthood upon the earth; and it would seem to be necessary that these principles of perpetuity or continuity should be held sacred among us" (John Taylor, *The Gospel Kingdom: Selections from the Writings and Dis-*

for abuse for lent money, which [Green] lent him[,] and not redeeming it according to promise; and for unchristian-like conduct towards [Ulrich]. The defendant plead not guilty. [Councillors] Numbers 1 (Elias Higbee), 2 (David Dort), 3 (Lewis D. Wilson), 4 (Noah Packard pro-tem for Alpheus Cutler), 5 (David Fulmer), and 6 (Samuel H. Smith pro tem, for John P. Green) were appointed to speak on the case.

The President decided that the defendant should give his note to the plaintiff for the money due him[,] with this understanding, between the parties[:] That he, the plaintiff should not oppress or cause him, the defendant, to be oppressed, until he, the defendant, is able, in the Providence of God, to pay the plaintiff the sum due him. That if he, the plantiff[,] does oppress or cause ~~to be oppressed~~ him, the defendant, to be oppressed contrary to the above decision, he, the plaintiff, shall be guilty of unchristian-like conduct, and subject to be tried, for the same, before the High Council. Which decision was sanctioned by the Council. The Council adjourned [for] one hour.

The Council met again according to adjournment, when the following charges ^were prefered by W[illia]m Niswanger[2] and B[enjamin] L. Clapp^,[3] viz. January 26th 1841[:] We prefer a charge against ^Elder Theodore Turley.^[4] 1 – For unchristian conduct while

---

*courses of John Taylor,* ed. G. Homer Durham [Salt Lake City: Bookcraft, 1943], 184-85).

[2]William Niswanger was born in Maryland in 1805. He and his wife converted to Mormonism about 1836 and moved to Missouri. By October 1840 he was operating a limestone quarry, soon called the Temple Stone Quarry, in Nauvoo. He was a major in the Nauvoo Legion. He moved to Winter Quarters in 1848, to Utah in 1851, and then to the California gold fields on assignment from Brigham Young. In the 1860s they moved back to Missouri, where he died in 1882 ("William Niswanger: A Convert to Mormonism," *NisNews,* www.wapping.com/nisnews).

[3]Benjamin Lynn Clapp was born in 1814 in West Huntsville, Alabama. He was baptized in June 1835 and was residing in Nauvoo in 1842. He fought in the Battle of Crooked River in Missouri and tried to free Joseph Smith after his arrest in Dixon, Illinois, in 1843. In 1859 he was excommunicated. He died in 1860 in California.

[4]Theodore Turley was born in 1801 in Birmingham, England. He immigrated to Canada where he was baptized in 1837. He joined the Saints in Kirtland and later moved to Missouri and Nauvoo. He followed the main body of the Church to Utah, where he died in 1871.

on the sea [and][5] for romping and kissing the females and dancing. 2 – For sleeping with two females coming up the Lakes and on the road to Dixons ferry. 3 – For not settling with the brethren for what money he received of them, and taking the lumber from the boat without leave. 4 – For threatening the brethren that Brother Joseph [Smith] would not hear any thing that they would not tell him about[,] for he was of the same spirit and signified the same Priesthood[,] signifying if they told him he would not hear [believe] them.[6]

The defendant pled not guilty. [Councillors] Numbers 7 (Thomas Grover), 8 (Aaron Johnson), 9 (Newel Knight), 10 (William Huntington), 11 (Charles C. Rich), [and] 12 (Henry G. Sherwood) were appointed to speak on the case. The charges were sustained. After which the President[7] decided that [Turley], the defendant, in order to retain his fellowship, should acknowledge, both before the Council, and also, to a publick congregation, that he had acted unwisely, unjustly, imprudently, and unbecoming, and that he had set a bad example before his brethren and sisters as he was coming over from Europe.

The Council sanctioned the President's decision. Elder Theadore Turly then made a confession to the satisfaction of the Council, and stated that he would rejoice in the opportunity of making the like confession before the publick. Adjourned. Hosea Stout Clerk.

---

[5]Turley had served a mission in England in 1839-40 and presided over a shipload of 200 Saints gathering to Nauvoo.

[6]The original of this complaint says Turley was guilty of "unchristian Conducke while on the sea for Tamping and kising the female & dancing" and claims he "laid with two Women." It says he took "lumber from the Boat without Leaf." It also says, more understandably, that if they told Joseph Smith anything contrary to what Turley said, "he wod not believ them." The complaint was witnessed by John Ben Bow, Jane Ben Bow, Thomas Jenkins, James Hill, John Risard, Richard Slater, Mary Wald, Sharlet Jenkins, Robert Tilor, Saly Cole, and John Parry Cope ("William Niswanger + Benjn. L. Clapp vs. Theodore Turley, January 26th 1841," Nauvoo Stake High Council Court Papers, 1839-1844, *Selected Collections: From the Archives of the Church of Jesus Christ of Latter-day Saints,* 74 discs [Salt Lake City: Intellectual Reserve, 2002], 2:19).

[7]It is unclear if this refers to Joseph Smith or to William Marks, president of the Nauvoo Stake. See Gary James Bergera, "'Illicit Intercourse': Plural Marriage, and the Nauvoo Stake High Council, 1840-1844," *John Whitmer Historical Journal* 23 (2003): 63.

*March 30, 1841; Tuesday.* The High Council of the ~~Chu~~ Church of Jesus Christ of Latter Day Saints of Nauvoo Illinois met in Council at the office of Joseph Smith. President William Marks informed the Council that he had made choice of Elders Austin Cowles and Charles C. Rich for his Councellors[,] after which he proceeded to ordain them.

A charge was then prefered against ^Alonson^ Brown by B[enjamin] S. Wilber as follows. "I hereby prefer a charge against Alonson Brown on the former rumor of his having robbed or stolen, unlawfully, from ~~from~~ the same Church or others in the region hereabouts. Nauvoo Ill[inoi]s[,] March 24, 1841[.] B[enjamin] S. Wilber["]

President Marks informed the Council that he should not ~~sit~~ preside as he was a witness in the case. He then appointed his Councellors to preside without him. The defendant pled not guilty[.] [Councillors] Nos. 1[,] (Elias Higbee) 2, (Harvey Omstead pro tem) 3, (Lewis D. Wilson), and 4 (Alpheus Cutler) were appointed to speak on the case. The evidences were then given. The charge was, partially, ~~sustain~~ sustained and after the parties had spoken the Presidents decided that, as he had confessed (which he did to Br[other] Marks & others previously) and repented, he should be forgiven and held in fellowship. The Council sanctioned them in their decision. Adjourned. Hosea Stout Clerk.

*April 6, 1841; Tuesday.* The General Conference of the Church of Jesus Christ of Latter Day Saints met, according to previous adjournment, near the place where the Temple of God is to be built[8] at which ~~time~~ on the 7th inst[ant] The Conference appointed Elder James Allred [as] a member of the High Council of Nauvoo to fill the vacancy existing by the death of David Dort[,][9] and also appointed Leonard Soby a member of said Council to fill the ~~va~~ vacancy of Charles C. Rich who had been, previously, chosen one of President Mark's Councellors. After which appointments of the Conference, at

---

[8]On January 19, 1841, Joseph Smith received a revelation (D&C 124) that the Church was to build a temple in Nauvoo in which would be performed ordinances and baptisms for the dead. It was during this general conference that the corner stone for the temple was laid. For details of the ceremony, see *Times and Seasons*, Apr. 15, 1841, 380-83.

[9]Dort died on March 10, 1841.

intermission ~~for~~ at 12 o'clock, the High Councils of Nauvoo and Iowa met ^near the Conference ground^ in Council, according to the instructions of the conference, ~~to~~ to transact certain buisness then ~~to~~ necessary to be done. The Councils first proceeded to ordain Elders James Allred & Leonard Soby to the office of High Councellors of Nauvoo, according to the appointment of the General Conference[.] The Councils next proceeded to approve or disapprove of certain men [for offices] who had been objected [to] as unfit for the offices hereafter named, by the ^Quorums of the^ General Conference.

Elder John A. Hicks, President of the Elders quorum of Nauvoo, was first taken up for consideration. Objections were made to him relative to a trial which had been between him and Elder John P. Greene, which trial was had before the High Council of Nauvoo [on] May the 2nd 1840. Some were dissatisfied with him thinking that he had not abided the decision of that Council. But however[,] after the matter had ~~been~~ been explained and the subject discussed at some length[,] he was approved by a majority.

Bishop Al[a]nson Ripley was next taken into consideration[.] Objections were made to him for his drinking and immoral habits which necessarily follows[,] and his abusing his brethren while under the influence of ~~Li~~ Liquor. His situation and character was discussed at considerable length. After which he was approved by a majority.[10] John E. Page,[11] one of the Twelve, was next take[n] ~~into~~ ^into^ consideration. Objections were made to him for having written certain abusive letters, [in]criminating certain individuals, wrongfully[.] After his case had been spoken on, at considerable length, he was unanimously approved.

Noah Packard, Senior, one of the Councellors for the Presi-

---

[10]The *Times and Seasons*, Apr. 15, 1841, 388, reported Ripley's status differently: "The quorums reported, that they had investigated the conduct of the persons who had been objected to, and that they had rejected Alanson Ripley and James Foster. ... Resolved, that as Alanson Ripley, has not appeared to answer the charges prefered against him, that his bishoprick be taken from him."

[11]John Edward Page was born in Trenton, New York, in 1799. He was baptized in 1833. He was ordained a member of the Quorum of the Twelve Apostles in 1838 and moved to Warsaw, Illinois, the next year. He was next called to accompany Orson Hyde in 1840 on a mission to the Middle East, but he chose not to go. He was excommunicated in 1846 and died in 1867 in Illinois.

dent of the High Priest's quorum, was next taken into consideration. Objections were made to him for his rash and ignorant expressions, which was, however, soon reconciled. He was approved. James Foster,[12] one of the Presidents of the quorums of the seventies, was next taken into consideration. Objections were made to him, for his lack of faith and stability in the Gospel; and dishonesty in his temporal deal[ings] with his brethren. He was unanimously disapproved.[13] Newel K. Whitney, Bishop[,] was next taken into consideration. He was unanimously approved. Adjourned. Hosea Stout, Clerk.

*May 17, 1841; Monday.* The High Council of the Church of Jesus Christ of Latter Day Saints of Nauvoo Illinois met in Council at the office of Joseph Smith. Samuel Bent, having returned home from his mission to the East, took his seat in the High Council. He then stated that he wished to ascertain the present condition of the Council relative to the building of the stone School house; and come to an understanding of what had been done while he had been absent, and also, [to] make some arrangements to relieve the Council from the responsibility of all debts and obligations in which the Council was now involved.

The Council next proceeded to ascertain what amount was due to different ones, or who had claims on the Council for means furnished, or work done &c on the School house; but as all the claims could not be made out at present, it was laid over to be taken up again at the next Council [meeting]. On motion[,] a committee was appointed, <u>to make arrangements,</u> ^or ascertain on what conditions a title could be had to the lot^, <u>to secure a title</u> to the land on which the Stone School House now stand[s], who were to make a report of the same at the next Council [meeting]. On motion[,] Samuel Bent and Alpheus Cutler were appointed to be that Committee. On

---

[12]James Foster was born in 1775. He was baptized before 1834 and was a member of Zion's Camp. He was expelled from Missouri in 1839 and moved to Nauvoo. He was tried for impropriety in 1841 in Nauvoo and acquitted. He later moved to Jacksonville, Illinois, where he died in 1841.

[13]Later in the conference, Foster was reconciled: "Leave was then given for Elder James Foster, to make a few remarks to the quorums respecting the charges prefered against him; after speaking; on motion [it was] resolved, that James Foster continue his standing in the church" (*Times and Seasons*, Apr. 15, 1841, 388).

motion [the] Council adjourned untill next Friday the 21st inst[ant] at 5 o'clock P.M. Hosea Stout Clerk.

*May 21, 1841; Friday.* The High Council met persuant to adjournment and[,] there not being members enough to form a quorum[,] they adjourned until next Friday [the] 28th of May at 2 o'clock P.M. Hosea Stout Clerk.

*May 28, 1841; Friday.* The High Council met persuant to adjournment at the office of Joseph Smith. The subject of the Stone School House was again taken up and, on motion of H[enry] G. Sherwood[,] the Report, of the Committee, to ascertain on what conditions a title could be ~~had~~ obtained, for the lot of land on which the Stone School House now stands, was called for which was carried unanimous; Samuel Bent, of the committee[,] reported that a title of the lot could be obtained for one thousand dollars; one hundred of which was to be paid down or in a short time and the remainder to be paid ^in 18 anual payments^

Ebenezer A. Black appeared before the Council and, by permission, stated that as it had been a long time since he had been expelled, by this body, from the Church, that he wished to know if there were any means by which he could be restored and what those means were.[14] There were several remarks made by different ones of the Council on the subject of his trial, after which he was called upon to make his confession[,] which he did to the satisfaction of the Council and according to the requisitions of the Council when he was expelled from the Church; when on motion it was Resolved – that he (E[benezer] A. Black) be received again into the Church by the waters of baptism.[15]

El[der] Thomas Grover stated that[,] as he was going on a mission to the South to preach the gospel[,] that he wished a letter of recommendation from the Council[,] which on motion was, unanimously granted. He then informed the Council that he had selected Ronalds [Reynolds] Cahoon to fill his seat in the Council, as Coun-

---

[14]See the minutes for June 20, 1840.

[15]Notice that the council often expels someone and then restores them to full fellowship all in the same meeting, but in this case the passage of time seems to be a variable that prompts the council to require rebaptism.

cellor pro tem, while he was on his mission[,] which was sanctioned unanimously by the Council. Adjourned. Sine die.[16] Hosea Stout Clerk.

*July 4, 1841; Sunday.* The High Council of the Church of Jesus Christ of Latter Day Saints of Nauvoo Illinois met in Council at the office of Joseph Smith. A charge dated May the 1st 1841[,] prefered by S[imeon] J. Comfort[17] against Shermon Gilbert[18] for unchristian like conduct[,] was taken up[,] which charge had been appealed, from the Bishop's court of Mount Hope, by Shermon Gilbert.[19]

---

[16]The Latin for "without day" means an adjournment to an unspecified future day.

[17]Simeon J. Comfort was born about 1817 in Ohio. He was ordained an elder in 1839 and became clerk of the Columbus ward in Adams County. He thereafter helped settle Harris Grove, Iowa, and stayed two years, 1853-55, before moving to Dow City, Iowa, and becoming an attorney. He died there in June 1890 (H. H. McKenney, "Pioneer Histories of Harris Grove, 1851-1861," *Iowa GenWeb Project*, www.iagenweb.org).

[18]Sherman Gilbert was fist councilor in the Mt. Hope Stake presidency in nearby Adams County. He was baptized prior to 1836, when he appears in the historical record as the recipient of an LDS ministerial license in Kirtland, Ohio. He participated in the Zion's Camp march on Missouri. He was in the Nauvoo area by October 1840 when he was appointed to the stake presidency.

[19]Comfort accused the member of the stake presidency, Gilbert, of having appropriated timber that Peter Wimmer had cut and for defaulting on a debt to an unnamed widow who was now "in Distress." It is not clear who the widow was or what connection she had to the lumber. In any case, the bishop's court ruled against Gilbert, but he had "refuse[d] to abide the Decision and refuse[d] to make satisfaction." The bishop gave him a deadline that came and went without action from Gilbert, who then appealed to the high council in Nauvoo, which was the Church's highest court and had appellate authority (D&C 102:27). The request read: "Brethren of the High Counsel[,] I wish that you would give Br Gilbert a hearing[.] Yours in the Knew & everlasting covenant[.] D. A. Miller Bishop of Mount Hope."

An affidavit from Levi Graybill and eight women (Mary Grable, Mary Smith, Juliana Graybill, Susan Comfort, Patience Smith, Hannah Smith, Susan Ann Winegar, and Elizabeth Wimmer) stated that "on the first of May at a bishops court, when S. J. Comfort preferred a charge against Sherman Gilbert, [Gilbert] said he was glad that he had a court in this place [Mt. Hope], and it was a court of Justice, and he would abide the decision of the court: we also testify that Sherman Gilbert did not abid[e] the decision of the court[,] which was to make satisfaction to Peter Wimmer

President William Marks Stated that the charge was too indefinite and required ^of^ the plantiff (S. J. Comfort) that he should specify the items of his charge, which he did as follows: to wit: 1st. For disfellowshiping Peter Wimmer[20] without giving any reason why. 2nd. For bringing up things against him (P[eter] Wimmer) which he was unable to prove[,] which were of more than two years standing. 3rd. For taking timber which Peter Wimmer had cut on paten[t] land[21] contrary to his (P[eter] Wimmer['s]) orders, and 4th. For telling falshood. The defendant plead not guilty. Two [councillors] were then appointed to speak on a side who were (5) David Fulmer[,] (6) Harvey Ormstead pro tem.[,] (7) Reynolds Cahoon[,] [and] (8) Aaron Johnson. An investigation was then went into – The first item of the charge was Sustained after which it was decided by the Presidents and Council that the defendant (Shermon Gilbert) should acknowledge to the Church at Mount Hope that he had done wrong and acted unwisely in withdrawing the hand of fellowship from Peter Wimmer as he had [done so] without bringing a charge against him or bringing him to trial. Adjourned Sine die. Hosea Stout Clerk.

*September 21, 1841; Tuesday.* The High Council of the Church of Jesus Christ of Latter Day Saints of Nauvoo Illinois met in Council, according to previous appointment by President William Marks, at

---

and the church for timber he had taken from Peter Wimmer[.]" Gilbert made a counter-charge against Wimmer "for neglecting to attend [Church] meeting[s]" and said Wimmer had put "his hands in his daughters bosom" and other acts "derogatory to the character of a man of God!" which Wimmer denied ("S. J. Comfort vs. Charge of Sherman Gilbert, Appealed from Bishop of Mount Hope," Nauvoo Stake High Council Court Papers, 2:19).

[20]Peter Wimmer was born in 1782 in Germany. Soon after he was baptized in New Jersey in 1831, he moved to Ohio, and while there he participated in the Church's paramilitary march (Zion's Camp) against Missouri opponents. He then settled in Missouri for a time, then in Nauvoo. When Nauvoo collapsed, he traveled west to Springville, Utah, where he died in 1864 (Bob Leonard, "Peter Wimmer," in *Conquerors of the West: Stalwart Mormon Pioneers,* ed. Florence C. Youngberg [Salt Lake City: Sons of Utah Pioneers, 1999], 4:2745). Peter L. Wimmer, who was one of the discoverers of gold at Sutter's Mill, may have been Peter Wimmer's son.

[21]Patented land was former public property for which the U.S. General Land Office had transferred the title to a homesteader. The complaint against Gilbert included the amount of wood taken: "Length of the tree or from the stump to the stoke 60 ft."

the Committee house for the Temple. Pres[ident] W[illiam] Marks[,] not being well[,] did not attend.

President Austin Cowles Stated that as the High Council was unpleasantly situated in relation to its being inthraled with debts &c. which had devolved upon it in a time when it was under the necessity of transacting temporal buisness, for the Church, for the want of the proper authority being organized and prepared to transact the same[,] and that the Council had met to devise some measures to relieve itself from all such inthralments and all other buisness which did not belong to it &c. After which there were remarks made by others of the Council on the subject of the debts and responsibilities of the High Council[,] showing reasons why the Council should be relieved from the same and explaining the causes and circumstances which first brought it to act in temporal things &c. After which it was voted that the Council adjourn to meet tomorrow at 3 o'clock at the same place and that ^the papers of^ all debts and temporal buisness be brought and laid before the Council to be prepared to ~~transact~~ ^transfer^ the same to the First Presidency to be put into the hands of the proper authorities to which they belong. Adjourned ^till tomorrow at 2 o'clock^. Hosea Stout Clerk.

*September 22, 1841; Wednesday.* The High Council of the Church of Jesus Christ of Latter Day Saints of Nauvoo Illinois met in Council[,] according to previous adjournment of the 21st inst[ant]. 1st. George W. Harris, having returned home from his mission[,] took his seat in the Council.

2nd. The subject of the debts ~~of the det~~ ^and^ enthrallments of the High Council was taken up. An examination of the accounts &c. of the Stone School House, and other temporal buisness was ~~went~~ ^gone^ into, according to the decision of the last Council; but as the notes and accounts was not made out in a proper manner to show the situation of affairs it was decided that the Trustees and building Committee for the Stone School House make a report of all the debts and Credits of the same to be acted upon at the meeting of the next high Council.

3d. The following preamble and resolution was then presented by the Clerk, which was unanimously received[:] Whereas this High Council, in times past, had of necessity and by the advice and instruction of the First Presidency, [assumed authority] to transact buisness of a temporal nature, for the Church ^&^ thereby involve itself with debts and other temporal burthens which, under other circumstances, would not have devolved upon it and as the proper authorities, to which such temporalities belongs are now organized and acting in their proper places, therefore, ~~best~~ be i[t] Resolved that this High Council are prepared to transfer all debts and temporal buisness, and that all buisness of a temporal nature be and the same are in readiness to be transfered to the proper authorities.

4. Alpheus Cutler stated that as he was going to the Pineries[22] the ensuing winter [and] that he had appointed Elias Higbee [as a] Councellor pro tem. in his place during his absence. 5. Adjourned to meet on the 9th day of Oct[ober] proximo. Hosea Stout, Clerk.

*October 9, 1841; Saturday.* The High Council of the Church of Jesus Christ of Latter Day Saints of Nauvoo Illinois met in Council near the office of Joseph Smith. 1st. The Committee ^& Trustees^ for the Stone School House presented the buisness affairs of the same[,] showing the situation thereof.

2nd. Henry G. Sherwood stated ^that^ whereas he had been appointed by the General Conference of the Church, to go on a mission to New Orleans to preach the gospel, that he desired a letter of recommendation from the Council showing his good fellowship and standing in the Church. 3rd. On motion of Thomas Grover[,] it was voted ^that^ the Clerk write a letter of recommendation for Elder Sherwood according to his request. 4th. Elder Sherwood then informed the Council that he had made [a] choice of Elder Daniel Carns to act as Councellor pro-tem. during his absence on said mission. Adjourned sine die. Hosea Stout Clerk.

---

[22]This was a camp the Church owned in Wisconsin where it harvested lumber. A Mormon colony formed in the area, mostly composed of men who had been called on missions to cut and prepare wood for Nauvoo buildings.

## 9.

# "Evil Practices and Pursuits" 1842

‡*January 18, 1842; Tuesday.* The High Council of the Church of Jesus Christ of Latter Day [Saints] of Nauvoo Illinois met in council at the office of Elder Hyrum Smith. 1st. President William Marks stated that the object of the meeting of the Council was to take into consideration the affairs of the Church – to set in order all things relative to their duty as Councellors – to call on the Bishops and see if they call the Lesser Priest-hood together[1] – if they do their duty – if the Priests visit from house to house – if there was no malice – no hardness – no difficulty in the Church – that he wished to have them make a record of all who do their duty – who keep the word of wisdom[2] &c[.] He recommended that the Bishops adopt such measures

[1]The lesser priesthood refers to the Aaronic priesthood, or priesthood of Aaron. During Joseph Smith's time, holders of the Aaronic priesthood could baptize but not confer the gift of the Holy Ghost. They were asked to "assist the elder[s] if occasion requires" and "visit the house of each member, exhorting them to pray vocally and in secret, and attend to all family duties" (1835 Doctrine and Covenants, 2:10). In Utah, the responsibility to visit Church members at home would become systematized as "block teaching," later renamed "ward teaching" and then "home teaching" (D. Michael Quinn, *The Mormon Hierarchy: Origins of Power* [Salt Lake City: Signature Books and Smith Research Associates, 1994], 639).

[2]The Word of Wisdom, a revelation given to Joseph Smith in 1833 (D&C 89), recommends temperance in the use of tobacco, alcohol, and "hot drinks," later defined as tea and coffee. For more, see Paul H. Peter-

as would be most practicable and useful ~~for th~~ to bring about such an order of things – that their reports be brought before the High Council[,] that they may have a knowledge of their proceedings and the situation of the Church.

2. Elder G[eorge] W. Harris said he wished to have Br[other] Hyrum Smith[3] inform the Council whether, if the Bishops should refuse to appear before ^the Council^ at their request, they had authority to deal with them for such refusal or not. 3d. Hyrum Smith said they had power to do so – that they were subject to the High Council – He said he had been anxious a long time to see the officers of the Church take hold and stand in the office of their calling and do their duty – that the Council should call ^on^ the Presidents of the Lesser Priest-hood to attend the Council & receive instruction – and that he would meet with them if they would notify him of their meetings. That it was necessary for them to go from house to house – to his house –and to every house and see that every family [has] done their duty –that he knew that there was more than one hundred families in town who did not attend to family prayer – because of weakness, dubiety[4], and darkness which prevented them – that every ordained member was a Wa[t]chman on the wall[5] – if they did not set proper examples they must be put away and others put in their place – that a record should be kept, by the Lesser Priest-hood, and a list of names taken of all the members and given to the Church Clerk to be put on record – that [a] letter of recommendation should be given to the Church Clerk – that he might keep a record of all the members of all who ~~come~~ ^move^ in – of all who are excommunicated and all who die – that their names should be given him by the

---

son, "An Historical Analysis of the Word of Wisdom," M.A. thesis, Brigham Young University, 1972.

[3]A revelation of January 19, 1841, appointed Hyrum Smith to be a councilor to Joseph Smith in place of Oliver Cowdery, who had left the Church (D&C 124:91, 95). It seems that one of his responsibilities was to be a liaison to the high council. Since his father's death in September 1840, he was also the Church Patriarch.

[4]*Dubiety* meant "doubtfulness," although the word was "little used" in the nineteenth century (Noah Webster, *An American Dictionary of the English Language* [New Haven: S. Converse, 1828], s.v. "dubiety").

[5]"I have set watchmen upon they walls, O Jerusalem, which shall never hold their peace day nor night" (Isa. 62:6).

Sexton[6] thus keeping a ready source of knowledge of the situation of the Church – that he always wanted such an order of things [and] had not spared to ~~them~~ ^teach^ those who would not hearken [that they] should be severed off – all things were done by the faith of the people of God – that he wanted all men continually to do good – that ^a^ strict rule was the best you could take – never to turn from the way which you know to be right. He then spoke at length against the practice of Elders baptising persons into the Church, who had been cut off by regular authorities, without them making any satisfaction or showing fruits of repentance &c.

4th. On motion of Pr[esiden]t W[illiam] Marks – that the Presidents of each quorum meet with the ^High Council^ and First Presidency & receive general instruction, [it was decided to do so] on Friday next at this place. 5. Bishop ^V[inson]^ Knight reported that the Lesser Priesthood had been doing their duty – had a list of names for last year – [and] thinks they are willing to do their duty &c. 6. Pres[iden]t Marks spoke on the subject of helping the poor. 7. B[isho]p V[inson] Knight then g[a]ve some account of the situation of the poor – that means were ~~exaus~~ exhausted for their relief &c.

8. Elder Hiram Smith [said] there was a general want of action in the Church – that he wanted every one to start anew – he knew not of a resolution in all the [priesthood] quorums to stop iniquity – that they were not luke-warm but ^cold^ – he spoke against the practice of the Seventies giving [ministerial] license[s] to their Elders – that if they did[,] the Elders & all the other quorums might also – that all license[s] should come ^by order of^ ~~from~~ the General Conference[,] signed by the Church Clerk – that the pay for the license would enable him to record names &c.[,] which occupied his time for which he got nothing[7] – that the Twelve would aid in anything they

---

[6]A sexton was a Church employee who kept up the church grounds, rang the bells, and dug graves for deceased members.

[7]In the fall of 1841, Hyrum had defaulted on a loan of $2,250 from Halstead and Haines Company in Ohio (Robert Bruce Flanders, *Nauvoo: Kingdom on the Mississippi* [Urbana: University of Illinois, 1975], 166). Hyrum's principal source of revenue was the dollar he charged per patriarchal blessing, plus "ten cents for each 100 words" to transcribe it. This was noted by Hubert Howe Bancroft in his *History of Utah, 1540-1886* (San Francisco: The History Company, 1889), Appendix 15, based on documents and interviews.

were set about for the good of the Church – ~~that Br[other] Joseph [Smith] does not sanction the practice of granting license by the Seventies~~.

9. Samuel H. Smith spoke[,] showing reasons why the Church Clerk should have pay for his servises. 10. Pres[iden]t C[harles] C. Rich spoke in favor of the same thing – he objects to the practice of the Seventies granting license[s]. [He] said [Seventies] President Joseph Young informed him that President Joseph Smith gave him authority to grant license[s]. He was in favor of the teaching, which had been advanced –

11. Elder Hyrum Smith – thought it was a penurious disposition which caused such a grant of license to be applied for – he knows Br[other] Joseph never give any authority, but by importunity. 12. Elder David Fulmer spoke on the same subject. 13. Bishop V[inson] Knight spoke in favor of the general Conference only giving license[s] – 14. Elder Daniel Carns –thinks if the subject of the license was laid before the Seventies [that] they would submit to the will of the Council. 15. – Others spoke on the subject – in favor of license[s] coming from general Conference[.]

16. President Marks spoke against the Brethren sueing each other, and wished to have a piece written and published in the "Times & Seasons" – [He] recommended a committee to be appointed to draft said piece – to have it examined by the Council. 17. Others spoke in favor of the same thing – 18. On motion – Elias Higbee, David Fulmer, and Hosea Stout were appointed [as] that committee. 19. Pres[iden]t Austin Cowles spoke against suing each other – showed the evil resulting from a want of confidence in each other – Adjourned till Friday evening the 21st inst[ant] at 6 o'clock at this place. Hosea Stout Clerk.

*January 21, 1842; Friday.*[8] The High Council of the Church of Jesus Christ of Latter Day Saints of Nauvoo Illinois met in Council at the Office of Elder Hyrum Smith. The Presidents of the different Quorums were present. 1st. Pres[iden]t W[illiam] Marks stated the object of the meeting of the Council. 2nd. Elder Hyrum Smith spoke showing the proper order of things[.] [He] spoke, at length, on the word

---

[8]See also Joseph Smith, *History of the Church of Jesus Christ of Latter-day Saints,*7 vols. (Salt Lake City: Deseret News, 1902-12) 4:501.

of wisdom, the necessity of obeying it, [and] how it had been trifled with – the temporal danger in not obeying and the blessings in obeying it.

3rd. Pres[iden]t Joseph Young spoke[,] stating the reasons why the Quorums of Seventies had granted license[s] – that he applied to Pres[iden]t Joseph Smith for permission upon the solicitations of the Quorums – that their reasons for so doing were because license[s] could not be obtained from the Church Clerk – that he [Young] had no motive in it but to do right. 4th. Pres[iden]t Josiah Butterfield testified to the truth of what Pres[iden]t Young had stated. 5th. The Council was satisfied with the explanations of Pres[iden]t Young.

6. Sam[ue]l H. Smith spoke about certain difficulties which existed among the rulers of the Stake at Mount Hope [in Adams County, Illinois] – 7th. It was thought best to write them[,] citing them to appear before this Council to give an account of their conduct. 8th. E[lder] Hiram Smith was appointed to write said letter. 9th. Adjourned to meet next Friday at 6 o'clock at this place [and] also for the President of [the] Quorums to meet also[,] that there might be an opportunity for all to speak their minds &c. Hosea Stout Clerk.

*January 28, 1842; Friday.*[9] The High Council of the Church of Jesus Christ of Latter day Saints of Nauvoo met in council at the office of Elder Hyrum Smith. 1st. The committee appointed ^on the 18th inst[ant]^ to draft a piece to be published in the "Times & Seasons" [and] submitted the same to the consideration of the Council, who accepted ^~~of~~ signed^ the same.[10] Adjourned till the 4th of Feb[ruary] next at this place at 6 o'clock. Hosea Stout Clerk.

---

[9]See also ibid., 504-05.

[10]The document they signed began:

Dear Brethren,

As watchmen upon the walls of Zion, we feel it our duty to stir up your minds, by way of remembrance, of things which we conceive to be of the utmost importance to the saints. While we rejoice at the health and prosperity of the saints, and the good feeling which seems to prevail among us generally, and the willingness to aid in the building of the 'House of the Lord,' we are grieved at the conduct of some, who seem to have forgotten the purpose for which they have gathered. Instead of promoting union, [they] appear to be engaged in

*February 4, 1842; Friday.* The High Council of the Church of Jesus Christ of Latter Day Saints of Nauvoo Illinois met at Elder Hyrum Smith's office. 1st. A charge was prefered against Pres[iden]t Isaac Morley[11] ^of the Lima [Illinois] Branch^ by James Durffe,[12] for unchristian-like conduct. First[,] for refusing to pay his honest debts. Second[,] for suffering one brother to slander anothers character in a public congregation – Third & lastly[,] for saying that he had nothing against Brother James Durfee, then in a few moments raised up and called for a vote of the Branch for a disfellowship [of Durfee] and sanctioned it &c. Two were appointed to speak on each side[,] viz (9) Joshua Smith pro tem.[,] (10) William Huntington[,] (11) Leonard Soby[,] [and] (12) Daniel Cairns.

---

> sowing strifes and animosities among their brethren, spreading evil reports; brother going to law with brother, for trivial causes, which we consider a great evil, and altogether unjustifiable, except in extreme cases, and then not before the world. ..." (*Times and Seasons*, Feb. 15, 1842, 699-700).

The epistle asserts that "saints are to judge angels" (1 Cor. 6:3) and that "saints," meaning Church members, should therefore be considered competent judges of each other as well and not turn to secular courts for resolution of difficulties. Apostle Orson Pratt would pick up this theme in 1854, saying that "the Saints are ... to judge angels. Why? Because [the Saints] are superior ... they will rule over the angels, or in other words, the angels will be subject to them" (*Journal of Discourses,* ed. George D. Watt, 26 vols. [Liverpool: Franklin D. Richards, 1854-1886], 1:65). But by 1874 Pratt had decided that the Saints will judge only the "fallen angels" (*Journal of Discourses,* 17:185).

[11]Isaac Morley was born in Montague, Massachusetts, in March 1786. He moved to Ohio when he was in his twenties and served in the War of 1812 as a captain in the Ohio Militia. He was baptized in November 1830. The next year, he became a member of the Church's presiding bishopric under Edward Partridge; he later became a Church patriarch. He served missions to Missouri in 1831 and New England in 1835. For a time, he lived in Independence, Missouri. In 1839 he founded Morley's Settlement, near Nauvoo, and was called to be its bishop, then president of the Lima (Illinois) Stake the next year. In Utah he was asked to lead the first settlers to Sanpete Valley in 1849. He was a member of the territorial legislature from 1851 through 1855. He died in Fairview, Utah, in June 1865 ("People of the Time," *The Joseph Smith Papers,* josephsmithpapers.org).

[12]James Durfee (also Durphy) was born in 1798 in Fulton County, New York. He was baptized in Palmyra, New York, in or before 1831 and ordained an elder in 1833. He helped lead the charge against the Missouri militia camped at Crooked River in 1838. He died in 1844 in Nauvoo.

2nd. The plaintiff pled for an adjournment of the trial for the want of evidence sufficient to sustain his charge. After the subject had been discussed it was decided that he should not have an adjournment[,] after which the parties went into trial. After some letters had been read which were written as testimony in favor of the Plaintiff[,] it appeared that he had been disfellowshipped some time previously by the Lima Branch[,] whereupon Pres[iden]t Marks decided that the charge [should] be quashed as he was not a member of the Church; but informed the plaintiff that he could appeal from the decision of the Lima Branch to the High Council.

3. The Plaintiff then appealed ^from^ the decision of the Lima Branch[.] The minutes and charge of said trial [in which Durfee was disfellowshipped] was handed in by the Clerk of the Branch, as follows:

> January the 23rd 1842. 1st. Question by Father Morley directed to James Durfee asking him the reason why he had not [at]tended meeting for the last five months[.] [His] Reason – because he could not fellowship the authorities of the Lima Branch. Question Second [was posed, and it was decided to disfellowship Durfee] for continually bringing up difficulties which had been settled[.] Also the authorities called on him four or five weeks previous to his giving the above answer and reason[,] ~~to come~~ [and he was asked] by the Lesser Priesthood to come and give an account of himself – he also ^has^ manifested a contentious spirit ever since he has been here – His case was called – [and] no satisfaction [was] given [by Durfee][.] It was then motioned seconded, & caried that he should be disfellowshipped and his name erased from the church roll by the unanimous voice of the Branch[.]

The parties then went to trial [and] the speakers above named were to speak – the evidence was then heard – the charges were sustained after the parties had spoken[.] President Marks, previous to giving his decision, exhorted them mutually ^to^ settle the difficulty & all former hardness and henceforth walk together in meekness & brotherly love – Both parties readily acquiessed with the admonitions of the President and were reconciled.

4th. It was then voted that James Durfee be restored to his former standing & fellowship. Adjourned till tomorrow ev[en]ing at 6 o'clock at this place. Hosea Stout, Clerk.

*February 5, 1842; Saturday.*[13] The High Council met according to adjournment last evening. 1st. The case of Daniel Wood, (who had been silence[ed] from preaching by Presidents Joseph Smith and Brygum [Brigham] Young[)] from a complaint against him for teaching false doctrine[,][14] ^with privilege to appear before this council for a hearing[,]^ was taken into consideration. He produced evidence to testify that he did not teach false doctrine[15] – but was a faithful minister[,] and it appearing that he had been put down by those who had prejudices and hardness against him[,] it was decided that he be restored to his ~~to his~~ former official standing in the Church. Adjourned. Hosea Stout, Clerk.

*March 11, 1842; Friday.*[16] The High Council of the Church of Jesus Christ of Latter Day Saints of Nauvoo Illinois met in council at the Office of Pres[iden]t H[yrum] Smith. Council adjourned to the House of Pres[iden]t Joseph Smith.

1st. A charge was prefered against Elder F[rancis] G. Bishop by R[eynolds] Cahoon[,] First for setting himself up as a prophet and revelator to the Church[,] [and] Second for an improper course of conduct in meetings.[17] He pl[e]ad not guilty – two were then

---

[13]See also *History of Church,* 4:514.

[14]Joseph Smith had silenced Wood on January 23, 1842, for teaching that "the Church ought to unsheath the sword" (ibid., 501).

[15]Wood produced affidavits signed by other Church members testifying that they had never heard Wood preach anything other than what the stake president and others had preached, that Wood had not said "the saints were fire[-]fan[n]ing for war at Nauvoo," and that he had not claimed Joseph Smith said "the sword is unsheathed and never should be sheathed until his enimies were all destroyed." However, the witnesses were certain they had heard William Draper, an elder, say he was glad he had "taught the brethren to fight." In addition, they had heard "Bishop Turner while treating on the subject of war say that he longed to see the time come when he could take the sword in hand and fight" (affidavits found in Nauvoo Stake High Council Court Papers, 1839-1844, *Selected Collections from the Archives of The Church of Jesus Christ of Latter-day Saints* [Salt Lake City: Intellectual Reserve, 2002], 1:19).

In Utah, the town of Draper would be named after William Draper. Born in Canada in 1807, Draper was baptized in 1833, served as a bishop in Winter Quarters, and died in Sanpete County in 1886.

[16]See also *History of Church,* 4:550.

[17]The original complaint reads: "Nauvoo[,] March the 7th 1842[.] To

appointed to speak on each side[,] namely[,] (1) S[amuel] Bent[,] (2) James Allred[,] (3) L[ewis] D. Wilson[,] (4) and E[lias] Higbee. The charge was sustained after which it was decided that ~~the~~ he be expelled from the Church by the unanimous vote of the Council.[18] Adjourned to meet at Pres[iden]t Hyrum Smith's office on Thursday the 17th inst[ant] at 2 o'clock P.M. Hosea Stout Clerk.

*March 17, 1842; Thursday.*[19] The High Council of the Church of Jesus Christ of Latter Day Saints of Nauvoo Illinois met at the office of President Hyrum Smith. 1st. A charge was prefered against Elder Oliver Olney by Elder J[ohn] C. Bennett for improper conduct – for setting himself up as a prophet & revelator in the Church. 2nd. Two were appointed to speak on each side[,] namely (5) David Fulmer[,] (6) G[eorge] W Harris[,] (7) Thomas Grover[,] (8) & Aaron Johnson. [He] plead not guilty. The charges were sustained and unanimously decided by the Council that the hand of fellowship be withdrawn from him. His license was then demanded[,] which he consented to give up.[20]

---

the High Council of the Church of Jesus Christ of Latter day Saints[,] greeting[.] I prefer a charge against Gladden Bishop for improper conduct[:] First[,] for setting himself up as a prophet and Revelator to the Church – Secondly[,] for an improper course of conduct in meetings. R[eynolds] Cuhoon / Complaint" ("R. Cahoon vs. A. G. Bishop," Nauvoo Stake High Council Court Papers, *Selected Collections*, 1:19).

[18]Bishop was on trial for having "published or taught certain 'revelations' and doctrines not consistent with the Doctrine and Covenants of the Church." According to *History of Church*, 4:550, his revelations "appeared to be the extreme of folly, nonsense, absurdity, falsehood and bombastic egotism – so much so as to keep the Saints laughing, when not overcome by sorrow and shame."

[19]See ibid., 552.

[20]It was reported of Olney in the *Times and Seasons*, Apr. 1, 1842, 747-78: "Mr. Olney has also been tried by the high council and disfellowshiped because he would not have his writings tested by the word of God; evidently proving that he loves darkness rather than light because his deeds are evil." A later issue of the *Times and Seasons*, Feb. 1, 1843, 89, explained that Olney had claimed to have "seen and conversed with the ancients of days." Olney was born in 1796 in Eastford, Connecticut, and moved to Kirtland, Ohio, where he married a daughter of John and Elsa Johnson in 1820. He converted to Mormonism, along with others in the Kirtland area, in the early 1830s, became president of the teachers quorum, and was ordained a Sev-

3. A charge was prefered against John Jamison by Phillip Ballard,[21] Presiding Elder of the Union Branch. 1st. For teaching that the Church was driven from Missouri for stealing. 2nd. For not complying with the decision of the Union branch. 3rd. For saying that he was acquited (ie. acquited by this council of Pres[ident] H[yrum] Smith from the decision of the Union Branch) and for other ~~improper~~ unchristian like conduct[.] 4th. The defendant was not present[,] but it appear[ed] from testimony that he had been legally notified and had neglected to appear[,] [so] the council proceeded to trial. One [councilman] w[as] appointed to speak on each side[,] namely (^9^[)] N[ewel] Knight [and] (10) William Huntington. The charges were sustained. [The council] decided that the hand of fellowship [should] be withdrawn from him.

5th A charge was prefered against Elder William Wirick by Presiding Elder Phillip Ballard of the Union Branch for 1st. [saying] no man could know that this work was true without God or an angel should appear to him & tell him. 2nd. That no man could know any thing by the Holy Ghost together with other unchristian doctrines & conduct.

[The] defendant acknowledged to some of the charges after which [the council] went into trial [and] 2 [were] appointed to speak on each side, viz. L[eonard] Soby, Daniel Cairns, Samuel Bent & James Allred. It appeared from the testimony ~~that~~ and his confession that the charge was true but he was willing to submit his doctrine [to] the decision of the council[,] therefore after they decided that he was wrong he agreed to renounce it and he was restored to full fellowship. Adjourned till 25 inst[ant] at 2 o'clock at the same place. Hosea Stout Clerk.

*March 25, 1842; Friday.* [The High] Council met according to adjournment at the office of Pres[iden]t Hyrum Smith. A charge

enty in 1836. He moved to Missouri, where he endured hardships with the rest of the Church in 1838, then moved to Illinois only to have his wife die in 1841. In 1843 he published an anti-Mormon pamphlet, *The Absurdities of Mormonism Portrayed,* and another in 1845, *Spiritual Wifery at Nauvoo Exposed,* and died the same year.

[21]Phillip Ballard was born in Madison, Kentucky, in 1802. He was baptized in 1838 and moved to Nauvoo in 1840, where he helped many Saints relocate from Missouri. He died in 1868.

was prefered against Jane Price by Mercy R. Thompson[22] for taking certain articles of property ~~from belon~~ belonging to her from her house without her consent or knowledge and converting the same to her own use. Secondly[,] for denying that she has ever taken any such articles of property & for unchristian-like conduct.[23] Plead not guilty. Two were appointed to speak on each side[,] viz (3) L[ewis] D. Wilson (4) E[lias] Higbee (5) D[avid] Fulmer (6) G[eorge] W. Harris. The charges were not fully sustained. Decided that she be acquited. Adjourned till the 7th of April next at 4 o'clock at this place. Hosea Stout[,] C[ler]k.

*April 7, 1842; Thursday.* [The High] Council met according to adjournment ^[for a case] appealed by I[saac] Furgerson[,] [who had falsely accused Elihu Allen[24] of stealing a horse][.] ~~Appealed from the Freedom branch~~^ [The guilty] charge [was] appealled from the Freedom Branch[,] Adams County[,] Illinois. [The original] charge prefered against ~~Isaac Fugerson~~ ^Elihu Allen^ by ~~Elisha Allen~~ ^Isaac Furgerson^ charg[ed] him ^(Allen)^ with being a horse thief[,] and [now Ferguson] said that he ^(Furgerson)^ could prove it and that he [Allen][25] dared him to put him up for it. Isaac Furgerson was present. Elihu Allen was not ~~present~~ present on account of sickness in his

---

[22]Mercy Rachel Thompson was born in June 1807 in Bedfordshire, England. She was baptized in 1836 by Parley P. Pratt. Her sister, Mary Fielding, married Hyrum Smith, and in 1843 she too became a plural wife of Hyrum. She died in Salt Lake City in 1893.

[23]The charge of unchristian-like conduct was added for emphasis, something like charging a gangster with tax fraud. On first glance, one might assume it meant being judgmental or legalistic, but in the context of a Church court that definition would not be possible. In a now out-of-print but once influential encyclopedic work, *Mormon Doctrine,* Apostle Bruce R. McConkie stated that "in a general sense, unchristian-like conduct means any course of action inharmonious with the high standards of the gospel. It includes dishonesty, cruelty to wives and children, drunkenness, and criminal offenses of all sorts. Specifically, and according to common usage, it is an expression [that] refer[s] to adultery or some other gross form of sex immorality, the commission of which warrants excommunication from the true Christian Church" (*Mormon Doctrine* [Salt Lake City: Deseret Book, 1966], 812).

[24]Elihu Marcellus Allen was born in Cambridge, New York, in 1791. He was baptized before 1837 and died in 1850.

[25]The minutes say "Furgerson" here, but "Allen" seems to be intended.

family[,] as appeared from testimony[.][26] The case was adjourned till the 8th of May proximo at 4 o'clock P.M. at this place. Adjourned till the 15d inst[ant] – Hosea Stout Clerk.

*April 22, 1842; Friday.* [The High] Council met according to adjournment. 1st. Some of the councillors stated the reasons why they had been absent from the meeting of the high Council.

2. [A] charge [was] appealed [that originated in] the Quorum of the Seventies [as] Benjamin L. Clapp v[ersu]s Jesse Turpin[.] [It was] appealed by Elder Jesse Turpin.[27] Minutes of the trial by the Quorum of Seventies 2d. June 6th 1841 charge[d]:

> To the Council of the Seventies. I prefer a charge against Elder Jesse Turpin for the crime of adultery having married another man's wife, [that of] Benjamin L Clapp. Elder Batsore [was] called as a witness, [but] his testimony was only circumstancial evidence. [It was] voted to withdraw fellowship from Elder Jesse Turpin untill he makes satisfaction to the Quorum and the same be made public through the medium of the "Times & Seasons" A[lbert] P. Rockwood Cl[er]k[28]

---

[26]The original bishop's court was held on January 24, 1842, at which Ferguson elicited testimony from David Foote and others. In his defense, Allen wanted to call his son to testify, but his son was disqualified when he "acknowledged that he has not enrolled his name in any branch of this church since he left M[issouri]." Even so, the court decided that "Brother Fergerson has failed in our view in proving Br[other] Allen to be guilty of horse steeling and that Br[other] Fergerson shall make a publick acknowledgement before the Church that he has [w]rongfully accused Br[other] Allen and has uttered hard saings against him and that he shall thus make satisfaction to him and the Church" ("Fergerson vs. Allen[,] To be tried the 7th day of April 1842[.] Appealed from Freedom Branch 1842," Nauvoo High Council Court Papers, *Selected Collections* 1:19).

[27]Besides appealing to the high council, Turpin had written a letter to LDS Apostle Wilford Woodruff "wishing to [ap]peal his case to the Twelve for a rehearing as he had been Cut off from the Church" (in *Wilford Woodruff's Journal, 1833-1898,* ed. Scott G. Kenney, 9 vols. [Midvale, UT: Signature Books, 1983-85], 2:133).

[28]The seventies quorum withdrew fellowship from Turpin in August 1841. A notice in the *Times and Seasons,* Aug. 16, 1841, 514, stated: "The Saints are informed that the quorum of the Seventies have withdrawn their fellowship from Elder Jesse Turpin, until he make satisfaction, to said quorum for his conduct."

Objections were made to the charge coming before the Council [when] he had not been cut off legally by the Seventies[,] there being only one witness and his testimony circumstantial[.] On motion decided that ^the^ case come to trial. One [each] were appointed to speak on each side, viz; (7) T[homas] Grover [and] (8) A[aron] Johnson[29] –There were no evidences given which would give any reason to believe that he had been guilty of the charge. On motion [it was] decided that he be restored to his former fellowship & official standing in the Church[30]

3. [The] council adjourned to the house of Pres[iden]t W[illiam] Marks – 4. The case of William Hall was taken up – He stated that he had been cut off from the church by a branch of the ~~Church~~ Church in Michigan – that he was not satisfied to remain as he was – that he had endeavored to obtain the minutes of his trial[,] which they refused to give[,] nor did they make any record of his trial at the time he was cut off – that he had come before the Council to know what to do – that he wanted to be restored to his former standing &c if it could be so [and] if not[,] he was ready to come into the church again by the door – that he thought he had been cut off wrongfully but was willing to submit to the decision of the Council &c. Several of the councillors spoke in favor of ^his^ being restored when on motion, it was Resolved, that he be restored to his former standing and Official capacity in the Church and that ^the^ Clerk give him a certificate of the same.

5. On motion [it was] resolved that the High Council meet every Saturday at 4 o'clock at Pres[iden]t Hyrum Smith's office when other meetings &c. do not ~~interfere~~ prevent – 6. On motion[,] [the meeting was] adjourned till Saturday the 30th inst[ant] at Pres[iden]t H[yrum] Smith's Office. Hosea Stout Clerk.

*April 30, 1842; Saturday.* [The High] Council met according to adjournment. 1. Elder Henry G. Sherwood, having returned home from his mission to New Orleans, again took his seat in the High Council.

[29]Johnson was also marked as being high councilman number 9, a contradiction that has been eliminated from the current presentation.

[30]The result of the trial was published in the *Times and Seasons*, May 1, 1842, 771: "Elder Jessee Turpin has been before the High Councill of the City of Nauvoo, and is proven clear of the charges prefered against him; restored to full fellowship, and to his former standing in his quorum."

2. On motion Resolved – that a piece be published in the "Times & Seasons" disapprobating the conduct of certain brethren who had moved to Nauvoo from Springfield without paying their debts &c[,] in conformity to a request from Judge Adams & others in Springfield Illinois who wished advice from the Council on that subject[,] as such conduct was creating a dissatisfaction in that ~~part~~ part of the country.

3rd. On motion Resolved – That Pres[iden]ts William Marks, Austin Cowles & Charles C. Rich be the Committee to draft the piece aforesaid. 4th. On Motion Resolved – That the Council [be] adjourned till the 8th of May next at 4 o'clock at this place. Hosea Stout Clerk.

*May 8, 1842; Sunday.* [The High] Council met according to adjournment. 1. [A] charge [was] appealed from the branch at Pleasant Vale, Ebenezer Brown[31] vs. Daniel Wood[,][32] [who was] charge[d] for Lying. ^[It was] appealed by Daniel Wood^ Two were appointed to speak on each side namely – (9) N[ewel] Knight[,] (10) W[illiam] Huntington[,] (11) L[eonard] Soby[,] [and] (12) James Brown pro-tem. [Wood] plead not guilty. The ~~case~~ ^witnesses^ was examined on both sides and from their testimony it appeared that there had been difficulties & hardness in that branch of the Church, they being divided into parties, contending about points of doctrines[,] slandering one another, [and] stiring up animosities & confusion, from which things grew [into] the above charge against Br[other] Daniel Wood[;] and neither party yielding[,] Br[other] Wood was brought before ^the^ branch of the Church and was disfellowshipped[,] and [he] appealed to this Council. The charge was not sustained. Pres[iden]t Hiram Smith spoke at length on the subject, showing the situation of that ^branch^ and decided that both parties should from henceforth drop all party feelings & animosities and live together in fellow-ship and brotherly love and never more mention their past difficulties among themselves[,] and called upon the Council to sanc-

---

[31]Ebenezer Brown was born in 1805 in Salisbury, New York. He was baptized in 1835 in Pennsylvania. By 1840 he was living in Nauvoo. In 1846 he joined the Mormon Battalion. He died in 1878 in Draper, Utah.

[32]Daniel Wood was born in Duchess County, New York, in 1800. He was baptized in 1833. He lived with the Saints in Ohio, Missouri, and Illinois, and immigrated to Utah in 1848. He died in 1892 in Woods Cross, Utah.

tion it[,] which was done unanimously[.] The parties acceded to the decision and was all reconciled together.

2nd. On motion of Pr[esident] W[illiam] Marks it was Resolved ~~the~~ That the authorities of the stake at Pleasant Vale be desolved and the stake discontinued and the members of that branch be attached to the Church of Nauvoo. 3. Adjourned till tomorrow at 8 o clock at President William Marks. Hosea Stout[,] Clerk.

*May 9, 1842; Monday.* [The High] Council met according to adjournment. 1. The charge [preferred] against Elihu Allen by Isaac Furgerson of the 7th of April last was taken up[.] Three were appointed to speak on each side[,] viz (1) C[harles] C. Rich pro tem[,] (2) S[ylvester] B. Stoddard pro tem[,] (3) L[ewis] D. Wilson[,] (4) Joshua Smith pro tem[,] (5) Stephen Markham pro tem[,] and (6) G[eorge] W. Harris. The circumstances of the former trial was related by the defendant [at] the request of the Council after which the witnesses were called upon on both sides. The plaintiff failed to prove the charge. On motion of Pres[iden]t Austin Cowles[,] [it was] resolved that the defendant be acquitted[.] The parties were reconciled to each other and agreed to lay aside all hardness, and live together in fellowship. [The council] adjourned till Friday the 20th inst[ant] at 4 o'clock at H[yrum] Smith's office. Hosea Stout Clerk.

*May 20, 1842; Friday.* [The High] Council met according to adjournment[.] The committee appointed on the 30th of April last to draft a piece to be published in the Times & Seasons submitted the same to the Council. On motion [it was] resolved that the said piece be accepted by the Council & published in the "Times & Seasons."[33] Adjourned till tomorrow at 12 o'clock at this place. Hosea Stout Clerk.

*May 21, 1842; Saturday.*[34] [The] names of the members of the High

---

[33]This was printed in the *Times and* Seasons, June 1, 1842, 809-10, and read, in part: "Finally, brethren, as it is reported unto us that there be some who have not done that which is lawful and right, but have designedly done injury to their neighbor, or creditor by fraud, or otherwise thinking to find protection with us in such iniquity: let all such be warned, and certified, that with them we have no fellowship when known to be such, until all reasonable measures are taken to make just restitution to those unjustly injured."

[34]See also *History of Church*, 5:15.

Council: William Marks[,] President of the Council[,] [with] Austin Cowles [and] Charles C. Rich[,] President's Councillers[.]

| | |
|---|---|
| 1 Samuel Bent | 7 Thomas Grover |
| 2 James Allred | 8 Aaron Johnson |
| 3 Lewis D. Wilson | 9 Newel Knight |
| 4 Alpheus Cutler | 10 William Huntington Sr |
| 5 David Fulmer | 11 Leonard Soby |
| 6 George W. Harris | 12 Henry G. Sherwood |
| | Hosea Stout Clerk |

[The High] Council met at the ~~Store of Joseph Smith~~ ^Lodgs Room[35]^. 1. [A] charge [was] [preferred] against Chancy L Higbee by George Miller for unchaste and un-virtuous conduct with the widow [Sarah] Miller[36] and others. [He] plead not guilty. Two were appointed to speak on each side[,] viz – (6) George W. Harris[,] (7) Tho[ma]s Grover[,] (8) Aaron Johnson[,] [and] (9) Newel Knight. The defendant Plead for an adjournment, as he was not ready for trial for the want of his evidence. The council decided that his reasons were not sufficient for an adjournment and proceeded to trial.

Three witness[es] testified that he had seduced [several women] and at different times [had] been guilty of unchaste and unvirtuous conduct with them and taught the doctrine that it was right to

---

[35]The lodge room was Joseph Smith's general business office above his mercantile store. It was also called the assembly room and council chamber and was "the place where most of the business of the city and Church is transacted" (ibid., 119). Preceding the location, but deleted here, the minutes incorrectly reported the date as "May 20th 1842."

[36]Sarah Searcy Miller was born in North Carolina in March 1815. Her family moved to Illinois in 1830. She married James J. Miller the next year, while her brother, William, married one of her husband's sisters. Sarah and James converted to Mormonism and in 1840 moved to Nauvoo where James died the next year at age 31. Sarah was 26. She married John Thorp in December 1842, but the high council discovered that he had an estranged wife and disallowed the marriage. Sarah therefore married John Bleazard in November 1843 (see chap. 9, note 36). Five years later, John Bleazard would marry Sarah's daughter, Mary Jane, as a plural wife. The family immigrated in 1850 to Utah, where John acquired a third wife the next year, then another fifteen years later. After the family helped settle Las Vegas, Sarah divorced John and married George Pectol. They lived in Washington, Utah, five miles northeast of St. George, and she died there in March 1889 ("Wife #3: Sarah Searcy Miller," *John Hopwood Bleazard*, www.johnhopwoodbleazard.com).

have free intercourse with women if it was kept secret &c and also taught that Joseph Smith autherised him to practise these things &c.[37] On motion of President Hyrum Smith [it was] Resolved – That he (Chancy Higbee) be expelled from the Church and the same be made publick through the medium of the "Times and Seasons."[38]

2nd. [A] charge [was preferred] against Robert D. Foster by Nathan K. Knight[39] for unchristian-like conduct in not being willing to ^settle^ with me honorably for work that my Son did for him[,] and for a ten dollar ^bill^ that he had of my son which said bill ^was^ counterfeit but he refused to give it up and my son was deprived of the privilege of taking it back and exchanging it where he got it. [Foster] plead not guilty[.] One [each] were appointed to speak on each side[,] viz. (11) Leonard Soby and (12) Joshua Smith ^pro tem^. The charge was not sustained[.] On motion [it was] Resolved – That [Foster] be acquite[d], after which the parties were reconciled. Adjourned till saturday the 28th at President Hyrum Smith's office at 1 o'clock. Hosea Stout Clerk.

*May 24, 1842; Tuesday.* The High Council met according to appointment at the Lodge Room. 1st. The testimony of Mrs Sarah Miller[40]

---

[37]Days earlier, on May 17, 1842, Higbee had signed an affidavit saying "he never knew said Smith to countenance any improper conduct whatever, either in public or in private, and that [Smith] never did teach [Higbee] in private or public that an illicit intercourse with females was under any circumstances justifiable" (in "Affidavits Contained in John C. Bennett's Letters," *The Wasp,* Aug. 31, 1842). This is the first of over twenty cases the high council will adjudicate over the next few months stemming, in part, from Joseph Smith's introduction of plural marriage. For more on this, see Gary James Bergera, "'Illicit Intercourse,' Plural Marriage, and the Nauvoo Stake High Council, 1840-1844," *John Whitmer Historical Journal* 23 (2003): 59-90.

[38]This was never published.

[39]Nathan Kinsman Knight was born in 1802 in Lamoille, Vermont. He was wounded in the Mormon War in Missouri in 1838. He lived to be seventy-two.

[40]Sarah Miller's statement, dated May 24, 1842, appeared in the *Nauvoo Neighbor* on May 29, 1844. In the following transcription, words added in italics come from the original, a photocopy of which exists in the Valeen Tippetts Avery Papers at Utah State University:

> Some two or three weeks since, in consequence of brother Joseph Smith's teachings to the singers, I began to be alarmed concerning myself, and certain teachings which I had received from Chauncey L.

and Miss Margaret [Nyman][41] and Matilda Neyman[42] were taken relative to the charges ~~of~~ ^against^ Chancy Higbee and others showing the manner of iniquity practised by them upon female virtue & the un-hallowed means by which they accomplished their desires. Adjourned till tomorrow at 12 o'clock. H[osea] Stout.

*May 25, 1842; Wednesday.* The [High] Council met according to adjournment[.] 1st. [A] charge [was preferred] against John Haddon by H[enry] G. Sherwood for unlawfully detaining from Harriet Parker,[43] her house and premises. Done in her behalf[,] the defen-

---

Higbee, and questioned him (Higbee) about his teaching, for I was pretty well persuaded, from Joseph's public teachings, that Chauncey had been telling falsehoods; but Chauncey said that Joseph now taught as he did through necessity, on account of the prejudices of the people ... When he first came to my house soon after the special conference this spring, *darwin chase was with him.* Chauncey commenced joking [with] me about my getting married, and wanted to know how long it had been since my husband died, and soon removed his seat near me; and began his seducing insinuations by saying it was no harm to have sexual intercourse with women if they would keep it to themselves, ... I told him I did not believe it, and had heard no such teaching from Joseph, [neither personally] nor from the stand, but that it was wicked to commit adultery, &c. Chauncey said that did not mean single women, but married women ... When he come again, *William Smith come with him & told me that the doctrine which Chancy Higby had taught me was true.* I still had doubts, I told him I understood he, (Higbee,) had recently been [re]baptized, and that Joseph, when he confirmed him, told him to quit all his iniquitous practices, – Chauncey said it was not for such things that he was [re]baptized ... Chauncey Higbee said it would never be known. I told him it might be told in bringing forth [a child]. Chauncey said there was no danger, and that Dr. Bennet understood it, and would come and take it away ..."

[41]Margaret J. Nyman stated that in March 1842, Chauncey "came to my mother's house, early one evening, and proposed a walk to a spelling school. My sister Matilda, and myself accompanied him; but, changing our design on the way, we stopped at Mrs. Fuller's: During the evening's interview, he ... proposed that I should yield to his desires, and indulge in sexual intercourse with him." She concluded by saying, "I heartily repent before God, asking the forgiveness of my brethren" (ibid.).

[42]Like Sarah Miller, Matilda Nyman said Chauncey brought someone with him "who affirmed that such intercourse was tolerated by the heads of the Church" (ibid.).

[43]Harriet Parker was thirty-six years old. Nothing more is known of her.

dant did not appear. The charge was fully sustained. On motion [it was] resolved that he be disfellowshipped until he make satisfaction to H[enry] G. Sherwood and restore the house to Harriet Parker.

2. [A] Charge [was preferred] against Mrs. Catherine Warren by George Miller for unchaste and unvirtuous conduct with John C. Bennett[44] and others. The defendant confessed to the charge and g[a]ve the names of several other [men][45] who had been guilty of having unlawful intercourse with her[,] stating that they taught the doctrine that it was right to have free intercourse with women and that the heads of the Church also taught and practised it[,] which things caused her to be led away thinking it to be right but becoming convinced that it was not right[,] and learning that the heads of the church did not believe of [the] practice [of] such things[,] she was willing to confess her sins and did repent before God for what she had done and desired earnestly that the Council would forgive her and covenanted that she would hence forth do so no more.[46] After

[44]When Bennett resigned as mayor on May 17, 1842, the reasons were kept confidential. After testimony was solicited against him by the high council, Joseph Smith threatened to "publish him in the paper," but Bennett begged "for his mother's sake" that they keep the details private. The testimony against him would not be published in full until 1844 (Flanders, *Nauvoo,* 264).

[45]These included Darwin Chase, Lyman O. Littlefield, Joel S. Miles, and George W. Thatcher.

[46]Excerpts from Catherine Warren's statement published in the *Nauvoo Neighbor* on May 29, 1844, emphasize Chauncey Higbee's venality and downplay Bennett's seduction: "I have had an unlawful connexion with Chauncey L. Higbee [who] taught the same doctrine as was taught by J[ohn] C. Bennet[,] [saying] that Joseph Smith taught and practiced those things. But [Higbee] stated that he did not have it [directly] from Joseph, but he had his information from Dr. John C. Bennet. He, Chauncey L. Higbee, has gained his object about five or six times. Chauncey L. Higbee also made propositions to keep me with food, if I would submit to his desires."

From her full affidavit, we have: "Nearly a year ago I became acquainted with John C. Bennett, [and] after visiting twice and on the third time he proposed unlawful intercourse, being about one week after [our] first acquaintance." If she became "pregnant[,] he said he would attend to that. I understood that he would give medicine to prevent it." She learned from him that he was involved with "Mrs Shindle[,] now living beyond Ramus, and also with the two Miss Nymans." Catherine admitted to having sex with Chauney Higbee, Joel S. Miles, and George Thatcher (Valeen Tippetts Avery Papers).

which she was restored to fellowship by the unanimous vote of the Council. 3. On motion [the] Council ^adjourned^ till ~~tomorrow~~ Friday the 27th ins[tant] at 12 o'clock at this place. Hosea Stout Clerk.

*May 27, 1842; Friday.* [The High] Council met according to adjournment. 1st. [A] charge [was preferred] against Lyman O Littlefield[47] by Geo[rge] Miller for improper and unvirtuous conduct and for teaching false doctrine. [He] plead not Guilty[.] Two were appointed to speak on each side[,] viz. (1) Sam[ue]l Bent[,] (2) James Allred[,] (3) Lewis D. Wilson[,] and (4) Wilford Woodruff[.][48] The charge was sustained. On motion [it was] Resolved – That he be disfellowshipped untill he make satisfaction to this Council.

2. [A] charge [was preferred] against Darwin Chace[49] by Geo[rge] Miller for improper and unvirtuous conduct and for teaching false doctrine. Plead not guilty[.] Two were appointed to speak on the case[:] Viz. (5) David Fulmer and George W. Harris. The defendant plead for an adjournment for the want of evidence[.] On motion [it was] resolved – That this case be adjourned till tomorrow at 1 o'clock at this place.

---

47Lyman O. Littlefield was born in 1819 in Verona, New York. At age thirteen, he was one of the youngest members of Zion's Camp. He resided in Nauvoo's 4th Ward, and died in Utah in 1893.

48Wilford Woodruff wrote, "The first Presidency The Twelve & High Council & virtuous part of the Church are making an exhertion abo[u]t these days to clense the Church from Adulterors fornicators & evil persons for their are such persons crept into our midst. The high council have held a number of meeting[s] of late & their researches have disclosed much iniquity & a number [have] been Cut off from the church. I met with the High Council to day on the trial of L[yman] O. Littlefield[,] Joel S Miles & Darwin Chase. The two former were cut of[f] for Adultery & the case of D[arwin] Chase was put of[f] till tomorrow" (Scott G. Kenney, *Wilford Woodruff's Journal, 1833-1898,* 9 vols. [Midvale, UT: Signature Books, 1983-85], 2:177).

49Darwin J. Chase was born in 1816 in Ellisburgh, New York. He was baptized in 1831 and ordained a Seventy in Missouri in 1838. After spending time in Nauvoo and then Winter Quarters, he settled in California in 1849 and became postmaster of the small mining town, Mud Springs (El Dorado), in the Sierra Nevadas southwest of Lake Tahoe. He volunteered during the Civil War to help protect the overland mail route at Ft. Douglas in Utah and participated in the 1863 Bear River Massacre, in which he was killed. He is buried in the Ft. Douglas Cemetery.

3rd. [A] charge [was preferred] against Joel S. Miles[50] by George Miller for improper and unvirtuous conduct and for teaching false doctrine. [He] plead not guilty. Two were apointed to speak on the case – Viz. (7) Tho[ma]s Grover and (8) Aaron Johnson. The charge was fully sustained[.] On motion [it was] resolved that he be disfellowshiped[.] ~~until~~ Adjourned till tomorrow at 1 o'clock at this place.[51] Hosea Stout Clerk.

*May 28, 1842; Saturday.*[52] [The High] Council met according to adjournment. 1st. [A] charge [was preferred] against Justis Morse[53] by George Miller for unchaste and unvirtuous conduct with the daughter of the Widow Neyman &c &c ~~Charge was sustained The defendant did not apear before the Council but upon being cited to apear before the Council he ordered his name to be struck off of the Church Book as he did not wish to stand a trial~~ Two were appointed to speak on the case[,] viz – (9) Newel Knight and (10) William Huntington. [The] charge was sustained On Motion of President Austin Cowles – Resolved – That he (the defendant) be disfellowshiped.

2nd. The Charge against Darwin Chace (of the 27th inst[ant]) was taken up according to adjournment. [The] charge [was] not sustained[.] The President decided that he should be restored to full fellowship ~~which was carried by a majority of 8 to 4. After which the case spoken on by different ones of the Council to show further light on the subject and showing reasons why they did not secede to the Presidents decisions. The President again called on the council to sanction his decision which was done unanimously~~ ^which was carried unanimously^. On motion adjourned till Saturday the 4th of June at [blank] o'clock at Hiram Smith's office. Hosea Stout Clerk.

[50]Joel S. Miles had been a Danite in Missouri (Quinn, *Hierarchy: Origins,* 483) and was a constable in Nauvoo. He was one of Joseph Smith's bodyguards in 1841 when Smith went to court in Monmouth, Illinois.

[51]Testimony was evidently taken from the following persons: Caroline Butler, Maria Champlin, William Champlin, Ellen Edwards, Mary Hardman, and Melinda Lewis. See the photocopies of the originals of their statements in the Valeen Tippetts Avery Papers.

[52]See also *History of Church,* 5:21.

[53]Justice Morse was born in 1809 in Hampshire, Massachusetts. He was baptized in 1833 and became a Danite in Missouri. He later converted to the RLDS Church. He died in 1887.

*June 10, 1842; Friday.* [The High] Council met according to previous adjournment at the Lodge. 1st. President Marks informed the Council that Br[other] Grover was going on a mission to the State of New York and requested the council to grant a letter of recommendation for him, which was granted unanimously. 2nd. Elder Grover then nominated Elder Daniel Carn to fill his seat in the Council during his absence on the aforesaid ^mission^ which was sanctioned by the Council unanimously.

3rd. [A] charge [was preferred] against Amanda Smith by Ira S. Miles[54] for unchristian-like conduct[,] in stating that my wife, Mary K. Miles, has had too frequent intercourse with Joseph McCall, at my house, at different times and other places[,] thereby insinuating that she (that is my wife) is guilty of adultery with said Joseph McCall – One [each] were appointed to speak on each side[,] namely (11) Leonard Soby [and] (12) Henry G. Sherwood. The defendant Plead not Guilty of the charge. (Adjourned to Pr[esident] H[yrum] Smith's office). The charge was investigated in full. The charge was sustained[.][55] [The council] decided that she was to blame for not ~~taking the gospel~~ proceeding in a lawful manner by taking the Gospel rule; but spoke of it to others and that she should make this acknowledgement to the Council. This confession [by] Sister Smith [was] made. [She] said she was very sorry she had not taken the gospel steps.

A vote was taken of the council to know if they were satisfied with the acknowledgement of Sister Smith[,] which was unanimous that they were & would still hold her in fellowship in the Church – Adjourned till the 18th of June at Hyrum Smith['s] office at 4 o'clock. Hosea Stout Clerk.

---

[54]Apparently a rough character, Ira Simonds Miles, born in 1809 in Vermont, was active in the Mormon War in Missouri in 1838 and was a bodyguard to Joseph Smith in 1841. In 1843 he received a fine from the City of Nauvoo for swearing; the next year he served a mission to the Church's lumber mills in Michigan. After arriving in the Salt Lake Valley in 1847, he agreed to guide members of the Mormon Battalion returning to Iowa from the War with Mexico through the territories. He died in 1878. Aside from the fact that Mary was born in 1812 in Portage, Ohio, nothing more is known of his wife.

[55]In other words, Amanda was guilty of spreading false rumors. Mary was innocent.

*June 18, 1842; Saturday.* [The High] Council met according to adjournment and adjourned till the 25th inst[ant] at this place at 4 o'clock. Hosea Stout Clerk.

*June 25, 1842; Saturday.* [The High] Council met according to adjournment. Adjourned till Saturday the 2nd of July 1842 – at this place at 4 o'clock. Hosea Stout Clerk.

*July 2, 1842; Saturday.* [The High] Council met according to adjournment. Adjourned till Tuesday the 5th of July 1842 – Hosea Stout Clerk.

*July 5, 1842; Tuesday.* [The High] Council met according to adjournment[.] Adjourned to the house of Aaron Johnson – 1. Charge[s] [were preferred] against Hamilton Savage by Elijah Wilson. Apealled by Hamilton Savage from the Bear Creek Branch of the Church[.] Charge First[,] for running away and leaving a slander on the Branch of the Church[.] Second – for lying[.] 3. For taking away that which ~~did~~ ^was^ not his own[,] agreeable to contract[.] The decision of the Bear Creek Branch was that the charge was sustained and that he be disfellowshiped untill he make satisfaction –

The parties were Called on who said they were ready for trial. 2 ~~One~~ [councilmen] were apointed to speak on each side[,] namely[,] (1) Samuel Bent[,] (2) James Allred[,] (3) Lewis D. Wilson[,][and] (4) Erastus Bingham pro tem. for Elias Higbee. The charge was not sustained. [The council] decided that he be acquited of the charge and restored to fellowship. Adjourned till Saturday the 16th inst[ant] at 4 o'clock at H[yrum] Smith's office. Hosea Stout Clerk.

*July 16, 1842; Saturday.* [The High] Council met according to adjournment. Adjourned till tomorrow at 6 o'clock at this place. Hosea Stout Clerk.

*July 17, 1842; Sunday.* [The High] Council met according to adjournment and adjourned till tomorrow evening at 5 o clock at this place. Hosea Stout Clerk.

*July 24, 1842; Sunday.* [The High] Council met according to adjournment – adjourned till the 30th inst[ant] at this place. Hosea Stout Clerk.

*July 30, 1842; Saturday.* [The High] Council met according to adjournment. Elder Alpheus Cutler having returned home from the Pineries[,] again took his seat in the Council. Adjourned till Saturday the 5th of August 1842 at this place at 2 o'clock P.M. Hosea Stout Clerk.

*August 5, 1842; Friday.* [The High] Council met according to adjournment. Adjourned till 2 o'clock to morrow at this place. Hosea Stout Clerk.

*August 13, 1842; Saturday.* [The High] Council met according to appointment. Adjourned till the 20th inst[ant][.] H[osea] Stout Clerk.

*August 20, 1842; Saturday.*[56] [The High] Council met according to adjournments. John Hodson appeared before the Council and made satisfaction according to the decision of the Council and was restored to full fellowship in the Church.

2. [It was] Resolved that the City of Nauvoo be divided into ten wards, according to the division made by the "Temple Committee" and that there be a Bishop appointed over each ward, and, also that other Bishops ~~be~~ be appointed over such districts immediately out of the City and adjoining thereto as shall be considered necessary[.]

3rd. Resolved that Samuel H Smith be appointed Bishop in the place of Bishop Vinson Knight[,] dec[eased][.] Also that Tarlton Lewis be appointed Bishop of the 4th Ward[,] John Murdock[57] of the 5th Ward[,] Daniel Cairn of the 6th Ward[,] Jacob Foutz[58] of the 8th

---

[56]See also *History of Church,* 5:119-20.

[57]John Murdock was born in Kortright, New York, in 1792. After converting to Mormonism in 1830 in Ohio, he filled a mission to Michigan and soon thereafter participated in Zion's March. His wife died giving birth to twins (Joseph and Julia), which were adopted by Joseph and Emma Smith. John served as a bishop in Nauvoo in 1842 and served a mission to Australia in 1851. He died in 1871 in Beaver, Utah.

[58]Jacob Foutz was born in 1800 in Franklin, Pennsylvania. After his baptism in 1834, he moved to Haun's Mill, Missouri, and was injured in the massacre. He moved his family to Quincy, Illinois, in 1839 and Nauvoo in 1841, the same year he was called on a mission to Pennsylvania. They left Nauvoo in 1846 for Garden Grove, Iowa, then traveled to the Salt Lake Valley in 1847 where he became bishop of the New Fort Ward at what is now Pioneer Park. His wife, Margaret, gave birth to her twelfth child that same year. In February the next year, Jacob died of a stroke at 47 years old (Steven

Ward[,] Jonathan H Hale[59] of the 9th Ward[,] Hezekiah Peck[60] of the 11th Ward[,] Daniel Evans of the d[i]strict south of the City called the 11th ward[,] Israel Calkins[61] of the d[i]strict East of the City and South of Young street[,] [and] William W. Spencer[62] of the d[i]strict East of the City and North of Young street. Adjourned till tomorrow at 4 o'clock at this place. Hosea Stout Cl[er]k[.]

*August 21, 1842; Sunday.* [The High] Council met according to adjournment. 1. President Hyrum Smith informed the Council that

Russell Jensen, "Bishop Jacob Foutz Sr.: A Legacy of Faith," *Hoopes Genealogy,* sites.google.com/site/jeffreyhoopes/).

[59]Jonathan Harriman Hale was born in 1800 in Groveland, Massachusetts. He was baptized in 1834 and moved to Kirtland two years later and was ordained a Seventy, after which he served missions to Maine and New York. He participated in Zion's Camp in Missouri in 1834. In 1839 he leased a farm twenty miles east of Quincy. The next year he moved to Nauvoo and became a city assessor and tax collector, as well as an officer in the Nauvoo Legion. He served a mission to Kentucky that year, then traveled to Maine in 1844 to campaign for Joseph Smith's presidential bid. Hale died of malaria two years later in Council Bluffs, Iowa, at 46 years of age ("Jonathan Harriman Hale and Olive Boynton," *Family Legacy,* www.nickiedee.com/hammond).

[60]Hezekiah Peck was born in Guilford, Vermont, in 1782. He was baptized in New York in 1830. In 1831 he immigrated to Missouri. By 1840 he was in Nauvoo where he became a counselor in the priests' quorum and, of course, a bishop. He died in Missouri in 1850 ("People of the Time," *Joseph Smith Papers,* josephsmithpapers.org).

[61]Israel Calkins was born in September 1801 in Hartsford, New York, and was baptized in 1836. He received a patriarchal blessing and was issued an LDS ministerial license that year, and the next year he was appointed to the Kirtland High Council. He took his family to Missouri, where he experienced deprivation, later signing a petition for compensation of losses. After serving as a bishop in Nauvoo, he traveled to Utah and helped settle the farming town of Nephi. He died in August 1863 in Payson, Utah.

[62]William W. Spencer was born in 1808 in Delaware County, New Hampshire. He was ordained an elder and issued a ministerial license in 1836 in Kirtland, Ohio, and served a mission to the eastern states. After his Nauvoo period, he volunteered with the Mormon Battalion for its march to Mexico. Returning from the war in 1847, he was with the group of soldiers who discovered the remains of the Donner Party and disposed of the bodies. Along the way he was kicked by a mule and sustained a broken arm and other injuries. He lived for a time in Bountiful, Utah, but after going blind moved to live with his son in Missouri, where he died in 1892.

Samuel H. Smith could not take upon him the office of Bishop as appointed on the 20th inst[ant]. 2. Tarlton Lewis, John Murdock, Jacob Foutz, Jonathan H. Hale[,] Hezekiah Peck, David Evans, and Israel Calkins were ordained to the office of Bishop according to their several appointments[,] who all accepted of their offices. Adjourned till next Satterday at 4 o'clock at this place. Hosea Stout Cl[er]k

*August 27, 1842; Saturday.* [The High] Council met according to Adjournment. Adjourned till [the] 3rd of Sept[ember] next at 4 o'clock at this place. H[osea] Stout Clerk.

*September 3, 1842; Saturday.* [The High] Council met according to adjournment. A Charge was prefered against Gustavius Hills by Elisha Everett[,] one of the teachers of the Church[,] for illicit intercourse with a certain woman by the name of Mary Clift by which she is with child[,] and for teaching the said Mary Clift ~~that~~ that the heads of the Church practised such conduct & that the time would come when men would have more wives than one &c.

Mary Clift did not appear & upon vote it was adjourned untill 4 o'clock P.M. tomorrow[.] Samuel Bent[,] David Fulmer[,] Elisha Everett[,] & Gustavius Hills were to go to her house at 8 o'clock tomorrow morning and take Alderman Spencer to take her depositions and so that the trial might take place according to adjournment to morrow.

*September 4, 1842; Sunday.* [The High] Council met according to adjournment. Joshua Smith being absent[,] Elias Higbee was appointed in his place. The case of Gustavius Hills was called. President A[ustin] Cowles spoke by way of address to the council upon the subject. The affidavit of Mary Clift, dated 29th Aug[ust] 1842 as also one of Sept[ember] 4th 1842 were read.[63]

---

[63]Mary Clift was born in June 1815 in Gloucestershire, England. In 1844 she would marry Theodore Turley as a plural wife, with the approval of Joseph Smith (see George D. Smith, *Nauvoo Polygamy: "... But We Called It Celestial Marriage"* [Salt Lake City: Signature Books, 2008], 348-50). Mary would die in March 1850 in Salt Lake City. But on August 29 and September 4, 1842, Mary said:

> Hancock county, State of Illinois. Personally appeared before me Orson Spencer, one of the Alderman of the City and [an] acting justice in afores[ai]d county, Mary Clift, an unmarried woman of said county,

Esther Smith[64] gave evidence that [the] defendant told her it was lawful for people to have illicit intercourse if they only held their peac[e] & that ~~the time would~~ it was agreeable to the practice of some of the leading men or heads of the Church. It took place the Thursday before the Choir was dismissed in the upper part of Town near the Bluff at 9 o'clock in the evening – She was going home & he offered & went to accompany her and this took place upon the way

---

and made solemn oath that she was pregnant with a child which, if born alive, may be a bastard and that Gustavus Hills was the father of such child. The Said Gustavus Hills[,] about 4 or 5 weeks since[,] requested deponent to remove to Columbus (Adams county) until after her confinement and he would assist her with support as far as his means would permit; and that such ilicit conduct was practiced by the heads of the Church and that the time would come when men would have more wives than one, and he wished that time would come. Subscribed and sworn to before me this 29th day of August A.D. 1847. Orson Spencer, Alderman of the city of Nauvoo. In presence of Elisha Averett, Proxcy Keller, Sophia Beals (Journal History of the Church of Jesus Christ of Latter-day Saints, Church History Library and Archives, Salt Lake City).

Hancock Co[unty] State of Illinois Sept[ember] 4th 1842[.] Deponent saith that in the month of January 1842 near the middle of the month on the way between the House of [REDACTED] Br[other] [REDACTED] said [REDACTED] did hold illicit and carnal connexion with her [REDACTED] and that he had frequently used seducing efforts privious to that time. Said [REDACTED] in a late visit of 4 or 5 weeks since desird further connexion with deponent at that time & hoped they would yet have comfort together. Said [REDACTED] proposed several times to give [REDACTED] some medicine or drug to carry it off or cause an abortion. Said [REDACTED] told Deponent that he was intimate with another woman in town besides his wife & that the authorities of the Church countenanced and practiced illicit connexion with women & said there was no harm in [such] things provided they kept it secret. [Signature REDACTED] In presence of Elisha Averett[,] Samuel Bent[,] David Fullmer[.] Sworn to & subscribed before me Orson Spencer ("Affidavit of [REDACTED] Sept. 4th 1842," Nauvoo Stake High Council Court Papers, *Selected* Collections 1:19; the publisher of *Selected Collections* blacks out the names in ecclesiastical court transcripts).

[64]Esther Victoria Smith was born in 1810 in Stockholm, New York. In 1832 she married Amos Botsford Fuller, a young man from her home town who was her same age. They were baptized in Kirtland, Ohio, in 1836, and later resided in Nauvoo's 1st Ward neighborhood. He died in 1853 in Des Moines, Iowa, and she died three years later in Salt Lake City.

– She further testified that Mary Clift joined the Choir at Br[other] Joseph Smiths.

[Gustavus Hills] then produced a paper containing questions [he] put to & answers given by Mary Clift this morning after her deposition was taken by alderman Spencer[,] which went, together with aforesaid depositions, to prove his guilt[.] Several ~~with~~ witnesses were afterwards called upon in his behalf but none gave any evidence that he was inocent.[65]

The Councillors then spoke according to order[,] who were four in all[,] viz (5) David Fulmer[,] (6) G[eorge] W. Harris[,] (7) Simeon Carter pro tem for T[homas] Grover[,] (8) and A[aron] Johnson. Br[other] Everett & Hills then spoke[,] after which Pres[iden]t Cowles & Rich gave their judgment in which the entire council concurred by vote[,] that is[,] by disfellowshiping Gustavius Hills.

A matter in dispute[66] between Alexander Stanley & others and Br[other] Pierce, concerning a piece of land, was refered to the council & afterwards handed over to Pres[iden]t Marks, Ja[me]s Allred, Alpheus Cutler, G[eorge] W. Harris & A[aron] Johnson as arbitrators who were to try the case on Tuesday next ^to hear & decide the case that day[,]^ a bond to be previously entered into by the parties[.] The bond [was] to be executed by all parties on Monday next – [the] said arbitrators are to ~~and decide~~ [finish on] Sept[ember] 3rd 1842.

On application of J[ohn] M. Powers[67] to have a hearing of his

---

[65]Hills's questioning of Clift is dated "Hancock [County] State of Illinois Sept[ember] 4th 1842." He asked her when she stayed overnight at his house, to which she answered, "Near the middle of Jan[uar]y." She said she accompanied him home on three successive nights from the "singing schools" he taught, where she must have been a student. "The first two nights [she] slept [in bed] with [his] wife [and] the next night with [the] children."

"Q[uestion][:] Where & when did I talk of pluralty of wives? [Answer][:] At your house after you seduced me."

"Did I offer you medicine for abortion before you asked for it[?] [Answer][:] You did offer it."

"Did we have illicit connexion more than once[?] [Answer][:] no."

"Deponent saith that the night of their connexion ... was a cold windy night" ("Nauvoo Stake High Council Court Papers, 1839-1844").

[66]This is preceded by the words, "The two following articles should have been inserted on page 9 See omission," deleted here for irrelevance.

[67]John Milton Powers was born in 1815 in Ohio. He joined the LDS Church and was ordained a Seventy, after which he served a mission in Ohio. Nothing else is known of him.

appeal from the Bishops (Millers) decision which has lain over, or that he be reinstated in as much as the hand of fellowship has been with drawn from him, it was decided that the former decision stand confirmed[.] Sept[ember] 3rd 1842.

The minutes of the 3 & 4th of Sept[ember] were taken by Elder James Sloan. Adjourned till next Saturday at 4 oclock at this place. Hosea Stout Cl[er]k

*September 10, 1842; Saturday.* [The High] Council met according to adjournment. Ezra Hayes[68] came before the Council and made some confession [and] was forgiven[,] after which he was ordained an Elder – Lewis Muetze was also ordained an Elder[,] as he desired to return to Germany to preach the gospel. Councellor Samuel Bent appointed E[lias] Higbee to fill his place in the High Council during his absence on a mission. Adjourned for one week at same time & place. Hosea Stout Clerk.

*September 17, 1842; Saturday.* [The High] Council met according to adjournment. First[,] Truman Gilbert presented a Recommend from the Kirtland Branch[,] Ohio[,] and was ordained an Elder according to his request[.] Charles Greenwood requested an ordination [and] he was recommended by L[eonard] Soby[.] He was ordained[.]

Henry G. Sherwood, G[eorge] W. Harris & Hosea Stout were appointed a committee to go & see Br[other] E[benezer] Robinson ^former Clerk^ for the purpose of getting a book from him which had the Proceedings of General Conferences of the Church [and of the] High Council of ~~Kirtland ohio~~ Clay County[,] ~~M[iss]o[uri]~~ [including] Far West[,] M[iss]o[uri]. Adjourned for one week to the same time & place. Hosea Stout Clerk.

*September 24, 1842; Saturday.* [The High] Council did not meet because of a general parade of the Nauvoo Legion.[69]

---

[68]Ezra Hayes had been disfellowshipped in October 1839 "for teaching doctrine injurious to the church" (*Times and Seasons,* Dec. 1839, p. 31). He was born in 1799 in Ohio and died in May 1844 in Nauvoo.

[69]According to *History of Church,* 5:165, the troops were reviewed by General William Law, while Stephen Markham was promoted to the rank of colonel. Historians Richard E. Bennett, Susan Easton Black, and Donald Q.

*October 1, 1842; Saturday.* [The High] Council met according to adjournment. The committee appointed on the 17th inst[ant] to see E[benezer] Robinson made their report that he was ready to deliver up said book at any time that the papers could be arranged[,] which had not been recorded.

On motion [it was] resolved that Hosea Stout be appointed to assist E[benezer] Robinson in arra[ng]ing said papers in order of date and that he be authorized to receive the record with all the papers pertaining there to. Also that he be appointed to record all the proceedings of the Church & High Councils which are not on record in said book. (The latest proceedings on record is dated December 7th 1837.) And also that he be retained [and excused] from going on a mission to preach the Gospel which had previously been appointed to him by a Special Conference of the Church[.] Tarlton Lewis[,] Bishop of the 4th Ward[,] made his report according to the instructions of the Council[,] which were accepted. Adjourned ~~till~~ for one week at the same time & place. Hosea Stout Clerk.

*October 8, 1842; Saturday.* [The High] Council met acording to adjournment, [but there was] no Buisness[.] Adjourned one week at the same time and place. Hosea Stout Clerk.

*October 15, 1842; Saturday.* [The High] Council met according to adjournment. Present A[ustin] Cowles Pr[esident][,] (1) E[lias] Higbee[,] ~~(2)~~ (3) L[ewis] D. Wilson[,] (5) D[avid] Fulmer[,] (6) G[eorge] W. Harris[,] (8) A[aron] Johnson[,] (10) W[illiam] Huntington[,] (11) Leonard Soby[,] (12) H[enry] G Sherwood[,] James Sloan pro tem. Prayer by D[avid] Fulmer.

John Murdock[,] Bishop of the 5th Ward[,] made his report and stated that he had chosen Joseph Fielding[70] and John Lowry[,] High

---

Cannon comment that the soldiers "dressed in their finest, many in uniforms like those of the Regular Army, and proudly displayed their wide array of weaponry. They marched in time to the drums of their own band and followed the orders of their elected leaders to spruce up, stand erect, or about-face. On parade, the soldiers exhibited a training component sure to impress and entertain onlookers" (*The Nauvoo Legion in Illinois: A History of the Mormon Militia, 1841-1846* (Norman, OK: Arthur H. Clark, 2010), 182-83).

[70]Joseph Fielding was born in Bedfordshire, England, in 1797. He immigrated to Canada in 1832 and converted to Mormonism four years

Priests[,] for his two Councellors[.] His report was accepted by the Council. Adjourned one week, to the same time and place. Hosea Stout Clerk.

*October 22, 1842; Saturday.* The High Council met according to adjournment. Present, Austin Cowles, President, 1. Elias Higbee pro tem[,] 2. James Allred[,] 3. Lewis D. Wilson[,] 4. Alpheus Cutler[,] 5. W[illia]m Felshaw pro tem[,] 6. Geo[rge] W. Harris[,] 7. Isaac Higbee pro tem.[,] 8. Aaron Johnson[,] 9. James Sloan pro tem.[,] 10. W[illia]m Huntington[,] 11. Leonard Soby[,] [and] 12. Shadrach Roundy pro tem.

[A] charg[e] [by] Allen Talley [was preferred] against Benjamin Boydston. 1st. For imprudent conduct towards Br[other] John Turpins wife – 2nd. For insulting and abusing and striking Br[other] L[ibeus] T. Coons[71] in his own house. 3. For being of a contentious make – 4th. For misrepresenting or of telling falsehoods. 5th. For wanting Br[other] D[avid] M. Gamet[72] to carry a challenge to Br[other] L[ibeus] T. Coons, to meet him at his own time or place, with sticks, Swords, guns, or fist[s] and scull, and if he was not satisfied, there knock it out.[73] [The] defendant confessed to the charges

---

later. In 1837 he accompanied apostles Heber C. Kimball and Orson Hyde, along with Willard Richards and three Canadian converts as the first mission to Britain. He stayed there until 1841. From 1838-1840 he served as president of the mission after Kimball and Hyde returned to America. While in England, he married Hannah Greenwood in 1838. Their first child, Ellen, was born in Preston in February 1841. That year the family moved to Nauvoo. There he married Mary Ann Peak (ca. 1845) and two other women on unknown dates. He arrived in the Salt Lake Valley in 1848 and died there in 1863.

[71]Libeus Thaddeus Coons was born in 1811 in Plymouth, New York, and was baptized into the LDS Church in 1832. In Nauvoo he served as a body guard to Joseph Smith. He died in 1872.

[72]David Mallory Gamet was born in 1812 in Ostego, New York. He was baptized in 1835 and was residing in Nauvoo by 1837. He died in 1882.

[73]The original complaint mentions "unchristion and Immoral Conduct" toward the Turpins, including "imprudent conduct towards" John Turpin's wife and for "insulting and abusing and striking" John "in his own house," also for challenging Coons "to meet swords at his own time or place" or to meet "with sticks or guns or fist[s]," the names, of course, having been redacted from the DVD that contains a scan of this source (case of Allen Talley vs. Benjamin Boydston, Nauvoo Stake High Council Court

except the 3rd and 4th[.] [He] said he did not think he was contentious or guilty of misrepresentation or falsehood, and that he was willing to make satisfaction for every thing which he had done amiss.

Both parties expressed an anxiety to be reconciled [and] put an end to their difficulties. After talking over the affair before the Council[,] the parties were all reconciled together without the council having to act upon it. Adjourned as usual. H[osea] Stout[,] Cl[er]k.

*October 29, 1842; Saturday.* [The] Council met according to adjournment. Present [were] William Marks Pres[iden]t[,] 1 Samuel Bent[,] 2 James Allred, 3 L[ewis] D. Wilson[,] 4 Alpheus Cutler[,] 5 David Fulmer[,] 6 G[eorge] W. Harris[,] 7 Shadrick Roundy pro tem[,] 8 Aaron Johnson[,] 9 Newel Knight[,] 10 W[illiam] Huntington Sr.[,] 11 Leonard Soby[,] 12 – Samuel Bent having returned home from his mission again took his seat in the Council.

John Hammons made a report of Bishop Evans' of the 11th ward and informed the Council that himself and Elder Phillip Ballard had been made choice of by Bishop Evans for his Councellors which was accepted. Isaac Higbee[,] Bishop of the 1, 2 & 3 wards made his report and was accepted[.] On Motion of L[ewis] D. Wilson[,] Shadrack Roundy was appointed to fill the vacancy of Tho[ma]s Grover during his absence on a mission.

John Hammond presented the following petition from a part of the Union Branch of the 11th Ward[,] which [the council] voted that it be laid over untill Pres[iden]t Hiram Smith return home[:]

> October 18th 1842[.] To the Honorable President Joseph Smith and High Councilors of the Church of Jesus Christ of Latter Day Saints at the City of Nauvoo[:] We the undersigned subscribers, members of the aforesaid Church belonging to the Union branch [at] Golden's point,[74] do petition your most honorable body, with President Smith also, to grant unto us the privilege of organizing a new, or in other words, set us off into a new branch, including all who live in the following boundry, to wit: Beginning at the Missis-

---

Papers, *Selected Collections* 1:19. The names have been redacted from this document on the DVD).

[74]Golden's Point was six miles south of Nauvoo (Glen M. Leonard, *Nauvoo: A Place of Peace, a People of Promise* [Salt Lake City: Deseret Book, 2002], 601).

sippi river so as to include ~~J Manfests~~ Br[other] Luce and running East so as to include J. Manfest's place, continuing Easterly so as to include John Egbert[75] and Joseph Curtis, thence South 4 miles[,] thence West to the Mississippi so as to include the brethren at Montabello[,] thence North to the beginning.

We the undersigned petitioners, praying for favor of the most Honorable an[d] dignified High Councillors at Nauvoo, do hereby certify that this arrangement would be greatly to our advantage & convenience, wherefore, we subscribe ourselves Your humble petitioners and obedient servants.

We forward our petition by one of Bishop Evans' Councillors, John Hammond.

A large number of Brothers and Sister[s] had signed the above petition. Adjourned ~~till~~ as usual. H[osea] Stout Clerk.

*November 5, 1842; Saturday.* [The High] Council met as usual. No business[.] Adjourned till next Saturday at this place at 2 o'clock. H[osea] Stout Cl[er]k.

*November 12, 1842; Saturday.* [The High] Council met according to adjournment & adjourned till next Saturday at this place at 1 o'clock P.M. Hosea Stout Clerk.

*November 19, 1842; Saturday.* [The High] Council met according to adjournment. Present, 1. Samuel Bent[76] Pres[iden]t[,] 2 James Allred[,] 3 Peter Hawes pro tem.[,] 4 Alpheus Cutler[,] 5 David Fulmer[,] 6 G[eorge] W. Harris, 7 Shadrach Roundy[,] 8 Aaron Johnson[,] 9 Newel Knight[,] 10 W[illiam] Huntington Sr.[,] 11 Leonard Soby[,] 12 H[enry] G. Sherwood[,] [and] Prayer by David Fulmer.

[A] charge [by] William Marks [was preferred] against Windsor P. Lyon[:][77] "To the High Council of Jesus Christ of Latter Day

---

[75]John Egbert was born in 1778 on Staten Island, New York. He was baptized in 1833 in Indiana and died in 1873.

[76]There is an asterisk next to Bent's name with the note, "Rob[er]t Stone for S[amuel] Bent."

[77]Windsor P. Lyon was born in February 1809 in Orwell, Vermont. He was baptized in 1832 in New York. He owned an apothecary and dentist office in Nauvoo and was an officer in the Nauvoo Legion. His wife, Sylvia P.

Saints, I prefer a charge against Windsor P. Lyon for instituting a suit at Law against me on the 4th of November, and for other acts derogatory to the character of a christian. Nauvoo[,] Nov[ember] 7th 1842. William Marks, Complainant"[78]

[The] defendant said that the suit was instituted by him, in another man's name, therefore, [he] did not think he was in fault &c. Two were appointed to speak on the case, viz. (9) [Newell] Knight and (10) [William] Huntington. The Charge was fully sustained. The president then decided that, unless he ~~repent~~ humble himself and repent, the hand of fellowship be with drawn from him, which decision was unanimously sanctioned by the Councillors.

Alpheus Cutler informed the Council that Presidents Joseph & Hyrum Smith wished the Council to grant the petition of a part of the Union Branch of Oct[ober] the 18th inst[ant][.] Inasmuch as it was their desire[,] when [presented] on motion[,] it was Resolved, that the Petition be granted. Adjourned till Saturday the 26th at 2 o'clock P.M. at this place. Hosea Stout Clerk.

*November 26, 1842; Saturday.* [The High] Council met according to adjournment at Hirum's office. Voted that, whereas there is evil practices and persuits among some who profess to be saints of God among us, that Elder Henry G. Sherwood be appointed as an Aterney for this Council or in other words that he ~~seek~~ ^ferret^ out all such evil disposed persons and bring them ~~to~~ before this Council to be dealt with according to the Church rules and regulations. And also unanimously, Resolved – that this Council will sustain Elder Sherwood in ferreting out such iniquity in righteousness.

Voted that Hosea Stout be appointed to ascertain the boundrys

---

Sessions, whom he married in 1838, also married Joseph Smith in February 1842 in a case of Mormon polyandry (Todd Compton, "A Trajectory of Plurality: An Overview of Joseph Smith's Thirty-three Plural Wives," *Dialogue: A Journal of Mormon Thought* 29 [Summer 1996]: 23-30). Although Windsor would be disfellowshipped as a result of challenging the stake president in a civil court, he will be rebaptized in 1846 and soon thereafter take a plural wife, Susan Gee. He died of consumption in January 1849 in Iowa City.

[78]Marks's original complaint of March 7 was "for instuteing a suit at Law against me on the forth of November instant." In lighter ink, written sideways, appears this: "Two to speak on aside" ("W. Marks v.s. W. Payson," Nauvoo Stake High Council Court Papers, *Selected Collections* 1:19).

of the ^ten^ different ward[s] of this City, that the Bishopric may be more perfectly set in order, and make [a] report at the next Council. Adjourned till next Wednesday the 30th inst[ant] at 2 o'clock at the house of Pres[iden]t Marks. H[osea] Stout, Clerk.

*November 30, 1842; Wednesday.* [The High] Council met according to adjournment but did not do any business in consequence of the sitting of the Municipal Court which necessarily called away some of the Councellors.[79] Adjourned till next Sunday at 1 o'clock at Hyrum's office.

*December 4, 1842; Sunday.*[80] [The High] Council met according to adjournment. The report of the ~~different co~~ boundries of the different wards were made as follows:

> All that part of the City of Nauvoo, lying North of Mulholland street (which runs from West to East) is divided into five Wards, which (wards) are bounded on the West by the Mississippi river and on the East by the City boundry line[.] The First Ward is bounded on the North by the City boundry line and on the South by Brattle Street. The Second Ward is bounded on the North by Brattle Street or the first Ward, and on the South by Carlos Street of the 3rd Ward. The Third Ward is bounded on the North by Carlos Street, or on the 2nd Ward, and on the South by Joseph Street or the Fourth Ward[.] The Fourth Ward is bounded on the North by Joseph Street (or the Third Ward) and on the South by Cutler Street, or the Fifth Ward. The Fifth Ward is bounded on the North by Cutler Street, or the Fourth Ward, and on the South by Mulholland Street.
>
> All that part of the City of Nauvoo, lying South of Mulholland Street, is divided into five Wards, which constitute the, Sixth, Seventh, Eighth, Ninth, and Tenth Wards, Which are bounded on the South by the Mississippi River and the City boundry line, and on the North by Mulholland Street. The Sixth Ward is bounded on

[79]Nauvoo was one of three cities in Illinois that had a municipal court—the other two being Chicago and Alton—presided over by the mayor and aldermen. The dual religious and municipal roles of the city's leaders were what alarmed outsiders (see Leonard, *Nauvoo*, 103).

[80]See also *History of Church*, 5:199-200.

> the West by the Mississippi river, and on the East by Main Street, or the Seventh Ward. The Seventh Ward is bounded on the West by Main Street, or the Sixth Ward, and on the East by Durfee Street of the Eighth Ward. The Eighth Ward is bounded on the West by Durfee Street or the Seventh Ward, and on the East by Robinson Street or the Ninth Ward. The Ninth Ward is bounded on the West by Robinson Street, or the Eighth Ward and on the East by Green Street, or the Tenth Ward. The Tenth Ward is bounded on the West by Green Street, or the Ninth Ward, and on the East by the City Boundry line.

[It was] Resolved that Bishop [Newel K.] Whitney have the Seventh Ward alloted to him. Bishop Isaac Higbee Made report of his Wards which was accepted. Also Bishop Hezekiah Peck of the Tenth Ward ~~made~~ in his report by President Charles C. Rich[,] which was accepted. Adjourned till next Sabbath at two o'clock at this place. Hosea Stout Clerk.

*December 11, 1842; Sunday.* [The High] Council met according to adjournment. Bishop Johnathan H. Hale of the ninth Ward made a very large and elegant report of the situation and standing of his ward[,] which was accepted. [The council] adjourned till next Sabbath at 2 o'clock at this place. Hosea Stout Clerk.

*December 18, 1842; Sunday.* [The High] Council met according to adjournment. No buisness. Adjourned till next Sabbath, it being Christmas day, at 2 o'clock at this place. Hosea Stout Clerk.

*December 25, 1842; Sunday.* [The] Council met according to adjournment. No buisness. Adjourned till [the] next Sabbath at 2 o'clock at this place. Hosea Stout, Clerk.

# 10.

# "Teachings by Presidents Hiram Smith and William Marks" 1843

‡*January 1, 1843; Sunday.* [The High] Council met acording to adjo[urnmen]t. No buisness. Adjourned till next Sabbath at 2 o'clock at this place.

*January 8, 1843; Sunday.* [The High] Council met according to adjournment and adjourned to the House of Councellor Aaron Johnson's. [The council] resolved that ~~the Clerk write~~ a piece be published in the "Times & Seasons" stating that William & Alford Young[1] has been restored to fellowship (they having been disfellowshiped by

[1]William Young was born in 1806 in Smith County, Tennessee. He was baptized in 1840. He and his brother Alford organized a branch in Putnam County, where they claimed "to be empowered with ten supernatural gifts, nine of them are contained in the 12th chapter of 1st Corinthians–[including] raising the dead." They also allegedly engaged in exorcisms which caused "a trembling, twitching, falling down and wallowing in the mud; others would snort like wild beasts, bark as dogs, run through the creek, pretending to sing and speak in tongues, crying prophecy, prophecy; others would lie in a swoon for several hours, and springing to their feet again, state that the spirit had commanded them to chastise certain characters who were present, and would then fall upon them with all their strength as though they were to be exterminated in reality" (*Times and Seasons,* June 15, 1842, 819-20).

Joseph Smith upon the complaint of John D. Lee[2] and others &c[)] and that the Clerk shall prepare the piece and make [a] report thereof at the next Council. [It was] resolved that the Council meet every Sabbath at Aaron Johnson's house at 2 o'clock P.M. Adjourned accordingly. Hosea Stout Clerk.

*January 15, 1843, Sunday.* [The High] Council met according to adjournment. Present[:] William Marks, President, (1) S[amuel] Bent[,] (2) J[ames] Allred[,] (3) Reuben Hadlock pro tem.[,] (4) A[lpheus] Cutler[,] (5) D[avid] Fulmer[,] (6) G[eorge] W. Harris[,] (7) T[homas] Grover[,] (8) A[aron] Johnson[,] (9) N[ewel] Knight[,] (10) W[illiam] Huntington[,] (11) L[eonard] Soby[,] [and] (12) Elias Higbee pro tem. Prayer by Pres[iden]t W[illiam] Marks.

[A] Charge [by] Benjamin Kempton[3] [was preferred] against Jacob Gates, apealed from the Bishop's court of the [Nauvoo] ninth ward, as follows:

> Appealed by Jacob Gates.
>
> Appeal. To the Bishop and Council of the ninth Ward. I hereby prefer a charge against Jacob Gates, for taking an unchristian-like way in wronging or trying to wrong me out of about $5 which is my just due. Benjamin Kempton. Nauvoo[,] Dec[ember] 28th 1842. I hereby certify that the above is a true copy of a charge prefered before me and sustained. Nauvoo, Jan[uar]y 11th 1843. Johnathan H. Hale[,] Bishop in the ninth Ward in the City of Nauvoo.

Two were appointed to speak on the case[,] viz. Leonard Soby and Elias Higbee. After the case had been investigated at some length ^&^ the pleadings were over, the President decided that the charge

---

[2]John Doyle Lee was born in 1812 in Randolph, Illinois. Three years after his 1837 baptism, he moved to Nauvoo and became a major in the Nauvoo Legion, a recorder for the Seventies Quorum, an agent for the *Nauvoo Neighbor,* a collector for temple donations, the Masonic librarian, and later wharf master. In Utah he was implicated in the Mountain Meadows Massacre and executed for this in 1877.

[3]Benjamin Kempton was born in Bangor, Maine, in December 1814. In 1836 he moved to Kirtland, Ohio, and after being ordained an elder that year, he became a founding member of the Kirtland Safety Society bank. In 1843 he served a mission back to Ohio. When he returned to Nauvoo in 1844, he died there in March of "consumption" (tuberculosis) at age twenty-nine (*Nauvoo Neighbor,* Mar. 6, 1844, p. 3).

was not sustained – which was sanctioned unanimously by the Councellors.[4]

The piece written by the Clerk as Resolved by the last council was then read, & accepted.[5] Adjourned till next Saturday the 21st at 9 o'clock at ~~this place~~ ^Hirums office^ to attend to special buisness. Hosea Stout Clerk.

*January 21, 1843; Saturday.* [The High] Council met according to adjournment [at] Hyrum Smiths[,] William Marks & Charles C Rich, Presidents. The Council was organized as follows: Samuel Bent No 1[,] James Allred No 2[,] Lewis D. Wilson No 3[,] A[lpheus] Cutler No 4[,] D[avid] Fulmer No 5.[,] G[eorge] W. Harris 6[,] Thomas Grover No 7[,] Aaron Johnson No 8[,] Zebedee Coultrin No 9[,] W[illiam] Huntington No. 10[,] Leonard Soby No 11[,][and] Joshua Smith pro tem 12. Prayer by President Marks.

Henry H. Wilson[6] appeared before the Council and desired to know, whether, in the present condition, it would be wisdom, and also if it would be justifiable by the laws of God and man, for him to unite himself in matrimony, or not, as he had a living wife. It appeared from the evidence adduced that his wife was a very contentious, disobedient and ungovernable woman and that she would not submit to good order, or abide [by] his council and altogether refused to live with [him] and that they had been apart for the last five years[,] and many other things which was unbecoming &c. After which it was decided by Presidents Hyrum Smith and William Marks, that if he feels himself justified and can sustain himself against the laws of the land – that he is clear as far as they were concerned (ie,

---

[4]In other words, where Gates had been found guilty by the bishop's court, that decision was overturned by the high council.

[5]The notice stated that "whereas fellowship has been withdrawn from Br[other]s William and Alfred Young for teaching false and erroneous doctrine &c. in Tennessee, as published in the Times & Seasons of June 15th 1842, this is to inform the Saints abroad, that they have made satisfaction to the High Council of the Church of Jesus Christ at Nauvoo, and are restored to their former standing and fellowship in the church; and we recommend them to all with whom their lots may be cast" (*Times and Seasons,* Jan. 15, 1843, 80).

[6]Henry Hardy Wilson was born in 1803 in Milton, Vermont, and was baptized in 1836 in Kirtland, Ohio. He resided in Nauvoo's 3rd Ward neighborhood. He died in 1878.

the jurisdiction of the High Council) and was at liberty to marry again on the aforesaid conditions.

The following charge was then presented[:]

> Nauvoo[,] January 16th 1843. You Enoch King and Mary[7] your wife are hereby notified to appear before the High Council of this Stake on next Saturday, the 21st inst[ant] at 9 o'clock in the morning, to answer to charges prefered against you, for living in adultery, and unchristian-like conduct[.] Done by order of William Marks, President of the High Council.

The trial of the above case was adjourned [at] one o'clock P.M. for the want of the proper evidence as neither party was ready for trial.

Henry G Sherwood took his seat in [the] Council. The following charge was then read,

> Nauvoo[,] January 17th, 1843. You, Henry Cook,[8] are requested to appear before the High Council of this Stake, on Saturday next, at 9 o'clock, on said day, at Hyrum Smith's office, to answer, as far as fellowship is concerned, to a charge for unchristian like conduct, for selling your wife &c &c. Done by order of President Marks. President of the High Council[.]

[The] defendant said he was innocent of the charge. Two were appointed to speak on the case, viz; Samuel Bent and James Allred.

Upon examination of the case, it appeared, from evidence, that

---

[7]Enoch Marvin King was born in May 1821 in Bloomfield, New York, fifteen miles from Palmyra. His wife, Mary Bigg Ware, was born in 1816 in England. In a stunning example of lack of etiquette, William Clayton reported back to England after her arrival in Nauvoo in 1840 that she had "grown so very fat that all her best dresses are very much too little. ... She is indeed a fat lump." She married Enoch in March 1841 and had ten children. In 1848 Enoch took a plural wife in Iowa, and they arrived in the Salt Lake Valley in 1849. Four years later Enoch was excommunicated for not paying tithing (see the minutes for February 11, 1843, below for the resolution of the adultery charge). He died in Layton, Utah, in 1895. Mary died in 1911 (Ruby King Hart, "History of Mary Ware and Enoch Marvin King," *Enoch Marvin King: Our Bennett/Simpson Roots,* enouchmarvinking.wordpress.com).

[8]Henry Lyman Cook was born in 1803 in Kingsbury, New York. He was baptized in 1837 and died in 1869. He married Mary Hoag in June 1842, but they later divorced in 1843.

Cook had lost his wife not long since and was left with three children[,] and being in destitute circumstances, and not in a condition to keep house, thought that he had best get married again and advised with some of his friends who also thought it best if he could get a suitable companion. Not long afterwards, upon a short acquaintance, and the recommendation of ^some of^ his friends[,] he got married to Mary[.] Not long after this he found that she was in the habit of traveling about of nights when there was no need of it &c. and that she ~~was~~ would shamefully misuse his children & set bad examples before them, use very indecent language to them &c [and] also would abuse ~~him~~ & insult him without a cause and entirely refuse to be subject to him or be under his control, boasting that she would not be governed by no man and threaten[ed] to use violence on him and his children[,] and that she would go off and say she would leave him, but come back again and many such like improprieties, and that he had ~~use~~ remonstrated against such proceedings with as much patience as could be expected under such circumstances[,] and used every method to bring her to her duty that he thought would avail any thing with her[,] and afterwards that he had whiped her pretty severly (which was his own testimony)[,] thinking that might bring her to her duty. [He said] that he did not sell her but something had been said about it which was under stood as a joke by himself and the witnesses[,] but the party making the offer held it as a bargain & so did she. It also appeared that he had formerly been a civil upright man who desired to live in peace and good order, all of which was abundantly proven.

President Hyrum Smith spoke at some length on the subject, and, after giving Cook a very appropriate and severe reprimand for ~~using the rod~~ whipping his wife, he thought that Cook had acted as well as could be expected under his circumstances and decided that he should be acquited. The vote was then put to the council by Pres[iden]t Mark[s] and carried unanimously.

The Council adjourned [for] a few minutes and again met, after which the charge against Enoch King and [his] wife was adjourned till next Saturday at 9 o'clock A.M.

The following charge was then read:

> Nauvoo[,] January 17th 1843[.] You[,] John Thorp and widow, Sarah Miller, said ^now^ to be the wife of John Thorp, are each of you

> hereby notified to appear before the High Council of ^this^ Stake, on Saturday next at 9 o'clock in the morning at Hyrum Smith's office to answer, as far as fellowship is concerned, to a charge prefered against you for living in adultery and unchristian-like conduct. Done by order of President Marks, President of the High Council.

Two were appointed to speak on the case[,] viz[.] (3) L[ewis] D. Wilson and (4) A[lpheus] Cutler. Upon examination of the case it appeared that Thorp and Sarah Miller got married ^on the 6th of Dec[ember] last^ and that Thorp had another living wife now in this City, who was also at the trial, but he did not appear and sent word that he asked the Council no odds. Another reason which he had given ^for not coming^ was th[at] he was afraid that he would be arrested by the civil law and sent to the penitentiary for Bigamy, which was a proof of his guilt.

As for Sarah Miller, she plead ignorance[,] saying she did not know but she had a right to marry him[,] that Thorp used many arguments to induce her to have him and finely convinced her that it was right[,] and also that Dr [Robert] Foster & others had used their influence to bring it about &c. &c. Much was said on the Subject and the charge being sustained in the fullest sense, it was decided by Pres[iden]t H[yrum] Smith & [William] Marks that they both be cut off from the Church[,] which decision was sanctioned unanimously by the Council.

[A] Charge [was preferred] against John C. Annis for performing the matrimonial ceremony between John Wells ^Taylor^ and Mary Cook[,] wife of Henry Cook, who was living. It appeared that Mary Cook had left her husband[,] and [that] her and Wells got married under the plea that he had bought her of Cook for her weight in cat-fish and that Annis had married them[,] which thing he frankly confessed, and stated that he had found out since [and] he had no right to do it, and his reasons for it &c[.] He manifested a spirit of deep repentance and remorse for what he had done, and was willing to make any satisfaction which would be required &c. ~~which wa~~ President Hyrum Smith spoke at some length on the subject and reprimanded Annis for what he had done, without understanding his duty &c and then decided that he should be acquitted[,] which was sanctioned by the Council unanimously.

The following charge was then read[:]

Nauvoo[,] January 21st 1843. [A] charge [was preferred] against Thomas Prouse, and Charity Thorp, now ~~the wife~~ ^living with Prouse,^[9] for the crime of adultery and other unchristian-like conduct. Done by order of the High Council.

Upon examination of the case it appeared that Prouse and Mrs Thorp was married on the 22nd day [of] Dec[ember] last. That she had previously to this came to his house to work for him, as he had lost his wife, and he had ascertain[ed] that she had some difficulty with her husband and that they did not live together and that he did not provide for her as he should &c.[,] and that he became more & more attached to her the more he became acquainted, and also his children became ~~acquainted~~ attached to her and did not want her to leave their house[,] and often solicited him to marry her which at last he did.

His reasons in justification of himself was that Thorp abused her and did not provide for her[,] and because of the attachment of his children to her and more especially after Thorp had got married to Sarah Miller &c[,][10] all this was ~~the~~ [based on the] statement of the parties and [was] strengthened by other testimony – President Hyrum Smith spoke at [the council] upon the subject[,] showing the iniquity of their conduct[,] that they were living in adultery[.] ~~and that was the only way for them to~~ He then decided that they both be disfellowshiped, which was sanctioned by the Council unanimously[.] [The] Council then adjourned till next saturday at 9 o'clock ^at this place^ when the other buisness now before the council would be taken up. Hosea Stout Clerk.

‡‡*January 28, 1843; Saturday.* Henry H. Wilson[11] applied for an ordination – After remarks[,] it was by the Council vote[d] to ordain him an Elder ^this vote [was] seconded by the council^ [The] Coun-

---

[9]The minutes repeat the name "Prouse" here.

[10]It will be remembered that Charity's husband, John Thorp, married Sarah Searcy Miller in December 1832 without first divorcing Charity (see chapter 9, note 36).

[11]Henry Hardy Wilson was born in May 1803 in Milton, Vermont. Baptized in Ohio in 1836, he moved four years later to Nauvoo, where he met and married Frances Kelly of Tennessee. They immigrated to Utah and died in St. George, she in 1871 and he in 1878.

cillors [were] present[,] viz[:] Sam[ue]l Bent – [Lewis] D Wilson[,] D[avid] Fulmer, T[homas] Grover – N[ewel] Knight – L[eonard] Soby – Joshua James Allred[,] A[lpheus] Cutler – G[eorge] W Harris[,] A[aron] Johnson – W[illia]m Huntington [and] Isaac Higby [were the] Councillors present – organized &c.

[A] Charge [was preferred] against W[illia]m Wilsey for pronouncing a marriage ceremony.[12] [The] Defe[ndant] plead guilty & sorrow – Francis Boggs[13] [presented] Evidence [and] spoke in favor of [the] Def[endan]ts character[.] Pres[iden]t H[yrum] Smith thought that [the] Defe[ndant] had done wrong – but believed that he had [done so] through debility of body & mind [and may have] done more [wrong] than right but that he might be forgiven. Pres[iden]t W[illiam] Marks – cautioned against future acts of the kind – that Elders should be cautious & wise in [the] future – and that [the] Def[endant] be acquitted – which was done by vote of the Council.

[A] Charge [was preferred] against – [John] Blizzard[14] & Mrs [Betsy] Pool[15] for living in adultery – Br[other]s D[avid] Fulmer [5] & G[eorge] W Harris [6, were] speakers – in the trial witn[ess] Thomas Miller [gave] Evidence [and] said that Mrs Pool has a husband who she left in England[,] viz[.] Mr [Daniel] Pool[16] [and] that

---

[12]This was the marriage of Thomas Prouse and Charity Thorp, both of whom were disfellowshipped on January 21.

[13]Francis Boggs was born in May 1807 in Belmont, Ohio and was baptized in 1841 in Nauvoo. He was part of the pioneer company that first entered the Salt Lake Valley in 1847 and went on to help settle Las Vegas. He died in 1889 in southern Utah. He had been a member of the Utah legislature. By occupation, he had been a carpenter (Andrew Jenson, *LDS Biographical Ecyclopedia*, 4 vols. [Salt Lake City: Jenson Historical Company, 1901-1936], 3:322).

[14]John Hopwood Bleazard was married to Sarah Ann Newell and had six children. Sarah was from Yorkshire, England, where she was born in February 1801. She married John in about 1819. She died in Nauvoo in January 1846.

[15]Elizabeth "Betsy" Miller Poole was born in November 1805 in Dublin and converted to Mormonism in 1838, immigrating to Nauvoo two years later with her three children but without her husband. She married John Bleazard in 1840 on an island in the middle of the Mississippi River near Nauvoo. She died in Nauvoo in October 1843 (Joan Bleazard Thomas, "Early Life of John Hopwood Bleazard, 1803 to 1840" *John Hopwood Bleazard*, www.johnhopwoodbleazard.com).

[16]Daniel Poole was Elizabeth Poole's English husband, born in Middle-

he & she had difficulties – yet not ^very^ serious or very uncommon – not on account of any adultery[.] [The] parties [had] separated – not divorced. Ann Booth[17] – said that Mr Pool wished to continue to live with her – Mary Hardman said that Mr Pool did not like to [live] with his wife – [but] loved & respected her – and that she sought occasion to have him speak evil against her to enable her to quit him – and that they parted with [good feelings and] affectionately when she left England[.] Elder D[avid] Wilding says he never gave any advice for her to marry – or to leave her husband – [and] believes she had no right to ^marry[.]^ Rob[er]t Williams[18] said [the same of] Pool & his wife.

[John] Blizzard said he asked advice of B[righam] Young who would not give [him] leave to marry[.] [Brigham said that] if he married it must be for himself[.] G[ustavus] Hills[,] Esq. said to Blizard that he thought it [was] lawful to Marry Mrs Pools – that Hills [had] asked Josephs[19] opinion and said that Joseph directed that Blizzard & Mrs Pools [should] be married[.] [It was] by Hills [that Bleazard was] married to ~~Mrs Pool~~ ^her^.

Gustaves Hills – [gave] Evidence [and] said Blizzard [had] asked his opinion respecting Marrying Mrs Pool[.] [Hills] answered that it was wrong [to ask him] in th[at] B[lizzard had already] employed Hill to ask Josephs advice[.] Josephs advice was to marry[.] Mrs Pools letter to Joseph accused her husband ^Mr Pool^ of ill usage[.] Hills pronounced the ceremony of B[lizzard] & Mrs Pool on [an] Island [in the river]. Mrs Pool says that Mr Pool was cross and used her roughly[.] Whenever she was pregnant[,] viz [he] beat her – [he] never beat her only when pregnant – until they both joined the Church –after which he was more cross – but did not beat her.

Coun[se]lors [David] Fulmer & [George W.] Harris spoke on it – then Pres[iden]t H[yrum] Smith spoke and stated that he advised her

wich, Cheshire, in December 1800. Daniel died in Leftwich, Cheshire, in March 1876.

[17]Ann Booth was baptized in 1839 in Manchester, England, before she immigrated to Nauvoo.

[18]Robert Williams was born in 1815 in London. In 1838 he was baptized in Manchester, left for America in 1841, and arrived in Nauvoo in 1842. He later worked in St. Louis as a tailor but returned to Nauvoo. He died in 1882.

[19]That is, Joseph Smith's opinion.

not to marry unless ~~the~~ ^she^ was divorced from her husband – and [said it] would be wrong &c but gave it as his opinion that they now live in adultery and that they cannot be retained in fellowship[.] The Council was then called on[,] who Sanctioned the same – [and the defendants] were accordingly cut off.[20]

[The council] adjourned 30 minutes [and] met again pursuant to adjournment[.] [A] charge [was preferred] against Enoch King and Mary Eagleton for adultery[,] as [h]ad [been brought] before [the council previously][,] ~~parties~~ ^or [when the] Def[endan]ts^ plead for an adjournment – which was adjourned for two weeks from this day at 2 Oclock PM.

[A] charge [was preferred] against James Reed[21] and Mary Powell for adultery[:]

> To the High Council of the Church of Jesus Christ of Latter day Saints[,] I hereby prefer a charge [against] James Reed and Mary Powell for an act of adultery by being ^living^ together – Jan[uar]y 28 1843 by C[harles] C. Rich.

[The] parties [were] present. Tho[ma]s Evens[,] [giving] Evidence[,] says that Mrs Powell['s] Husband lived in pursuit of illicit conduct with females[.] [He] knew he tried to marry another woman[.] Charlott Arthur[,] [for] Evidence[,] sais that Mrs Powells husband was of [a] bad character[.] [The] separation [has been] 3 years [since] last June[,] since he left Mrs Powell.

James Reed said that Mr Powell was about to get married. Mary Powell Said that Mr Powell was endeavoring to get married [and] denied [having] been married to [her][.] [But] she [had] a certificate of the marriage[.] Powell refused to support her (Mrs Powell) and [admitted] that he was living in adultery with another woman[.] The] parties [were] acquitted and held in fellowship[.] [The] Council agreed to it.

[Henry] Cooks wife – viz[.] the cat fish woman[,] and [John] Wells[,] who said he had bought her – their case [was] brought up [and opinions] formed [from the] minutes t[a]k[en] as evidence and both [were] expelled from the Church by the Council. [The coun-

---

[20]Not to worry, the council changes its mind on February 4, below, and the defendants are reinstated in the Church.

[21]James Reed was married in Nauvoo on December 26, 1842.

cil] adjourned until Next Saturday at one Oclock PM at this place – when & where the case of Albert Clements and his wife will be called upon. H[enry] G. Sherwood[,] Cl[er]k protem.

‡*February 4, 1843; Saturday.* [The High Council] Met according to adjournment at Hyrum Smith's office. 1[.] William Marks & Charles C. Rich Presiding[,] [the following] Counsellors [were] present[:] (1) Thomas Carico pro tem.[,] (2) [James] Allred[,] (3) [Lewis D.] Wilson[,] ~~(4)~~ 5 ~~Fulmer (5)~~ (4) [Alpheus] Cutler[,] (5) [David] Fulmer[,] (6) [George] Harris[,] (7) [Thomas] Grover[,] (8) [Aaron] Johnson[,] (9) [Newel] Knight[,] (10) Eli Norton pro tem[,] (11) [Leonard] Soby[,] (12) Joseph Kingsberry pro tem.

The case of John Blazzard and Mrs Pool was again take[n] up for a rehearsing as they wished to adduce additional testimony, when it appeared that ~~the former husband of~~ Mr Pool was an adulterous man by the evidence. After which it was decided that they be again admitted to fellowship by baptism.

The following charges were then read[,] viz[:]

> To the High Council of the Church of Jesus Christ of Latter Day Saints at Nauvoo, I prefer the following charges against Albert Clements[22] & wife. For unchristian-like conduct in not abiding the decision of the Bishop's Court which they [had originally] agreed to do – and for family difficulties. February 4th 1843. Winslow Farr.

Two were to speak on [each] side[,] viz[.] (9) ^N[ewel]^ Knight[,] (10) ^G[eorge] W.^ Harris in the place of Norton[,] (11) L[eonard] Soby[,] and (12) [Joseph] Kingsberry. The charge was decided to be illegal as it did not come as an appeal from the Bishops' Court and was rejected by the Council unanimously.

After which, as the difficulties lay between Br[other] Clements and his wife, and not from any hardness &c on the part of Bro[ther] Farr, the parties (ie. Clements & his wife), agreed to submit all their ^difficulties^ to the decision of the High Council and abide their

---

[22]Albert Clements was born in 1801 in Fort Ann, New York. He was baptized in 1832 and moved to Ohio the next year to participate in Zion's Camp a year after that. After Joseph Smith's assassination in 1844, Albert followed Sidney Rigdon for nearly a decade before moving to Utah in 1852. He died in Springville in 1888.

advise, which if they did not do they were to be no longer members of the Church. The case was then investigated at length[,] and it appearing that the grounds of difference between them were that Sister Clements was not willing to abide the advice of her husband ~~in the~~ in some of his views in his temporal concerns &c. The Council decided that it was her duty to be in subjection to her husband according to the Scriptures & also, gave him some instruction relative to his duty towards his wife. Adjourned till next Saturday at 10 oclock A.M. Hosea Stout Clerk.

*February 11, 1843; Saturday.* [The High] Council met according to adjournment, [William] Marks & [Charles C.] Rich Presiding. [Councilors present:] (1) Peter Haws pro tem.[,] (2) [James] Allred[,] (3) [Lewis D.] Wilson[,] (4) Abraham Parmer pro tem[,] (5) [David] Fulmer[,] (6) Eli Norton pro tem[,] (7) [Thomas] Grover[,] (8) [Aaron] Johnson[,] (9) [Newel] Knight[,] (10) [William] Huntington[,] (11) [Leonard] Soby[,] [and] (12) Charles Snow pro. Tem[.] [The] prayer [was offered] by [Thomas] Grover.

[A] charge [was heard] vs. Noble Rogers[23] and [his] wife[.] (No. 1.) Plead not guilty[.] One [councilman] on [each] side [was appointed][,] viz[:] [Peter] Hawes & [James] Allred. Nothing [was] sustained vs. Noble Rogers. The charge vs. his wife was sustained. [It was] decided ^by the Pres[iden]t^ that the hand of fellowship be withdrawn from her untill she make satisfaction. She then made satisfaction which was accepted – without a vote of the council on the Pres[iden]t['s] decision.[24]

---

[23]Noble Rogers was born in August 1799 in Bethlehem, Connecticut. In 1825 he and his brother Noah moved to Ohio. After Noble was baptized in 1837, he followed instructions to move to Missouri with his wife, Mary Bates Rogers, even though she declined to join the LDS Church herself. Later, when they got situated in Nauvoo, Noble signed the petition the Church sent to Washington asking for compensation for losses in the Mormon War. He adapted well to Nauvoo society, joining the Masonic lodge, for instance. But when the apostles removed to Utah, he and his family stayed in the Midwest. He died in Buffalo, Kansas, in 1880 (Douglas S. Pike, "Noah and Edna Hollister Rogers and Family," mightmalls.com/mission/Noah).

[24] The original complaint accused Noble and his wife of falsely accusing Nancy and Joseph Gilbert of stealing "wood and corn" from them ("Truman Gilbert vs. N. Rogers and Wife no. 1," Nauvoo Stake High Council Court Papers, 1839-1844, *Selected Collections from the Archives of The*

[The] Council adjourned one hour and convened accordingly[.] Again David Winding took the place of James Allred during the remainder of this session of the Council. The case of E[noch] King and [his] wife was again taken up for trial[.] They were acquited unanimously ~~acquited~~ by the Council in [the] ~~committee~~ ^council^ of the whole. Adj[ourne]d till next Saturday at 9 o'clock A.M.

‡‡*February 18, 1843; Saturday.* [The High Council] met according to adjournment at the Lodge Room. [Present:] H[yrum] Smith, W[illiam] Marks & C[harles] C. Rich Presiding [and] Councellors present (1) John Snider pro tem[,] (2) [James] Allred[,] (3) [Lewis] Wilson[,] (4) [Alpheus] Cutler[,] (5) [David] Fulmer[,] (6) [George W.] Harris[,] 7 [Thomas] Grover[,] (8) [Aaron] Johnson[,] (9) [Newel] Knight[,] (10) [William] Huntington[,] (11) [Leonard] Soby[,] [and] (12) Isaac Higbee protem. Prayer by President H[yrum] Smith.

[A] charge [was preferred] against Josiah Ells[25] [and then] appealed by Ells from the decision of the Elders Quorum at Laharpe Branch: viz.[:]

> LaHarpe[,] January 24th 1843. Br[other] Josiah Ells. Sir, the following charges are prefered against you before the Elders Quorum in the Branch of the Church of Jesus Christ of Latter Day Saints in this place to wit[,] [you are] charge[d] 1st. For killing two hogs in ^the^ woods about [the] 15th of November last ~~not~~ which were not his[.] Charge 2nd. [regarding what occurred] on or about the first [of] January [of the] present month[,] that the said Josiah Ells did kill or cause to be killed one of Dr Coulston's hogs without said Coulston's knowledge, and converting it to his own use. Charge 3rd. For Lying about a settlement with James Dunn for some oats

---

*Church of Jesus Christ of Latter-day Saints* [Salt Lake City: Intellectual Reserve, 2002], 1:19).

[25]In England in 1805, Josiah Ells was born, and by the time he immigrated to Philadelphia in 1831, he had become a preacher in the Methodist denomination. He was baptized into the Mormon Church in Pennsylvania in 1838, thereafter moving to Nauvoo, where he became a lieutenant colonel in the Nauvoo Legion. He was disfellowshipped in 1844 and gravitated to William Law's reform movement, then to Sidney Rigdon's Church, following Rigdon to Pittsburgh in 1850. In 1865 Ells was ordained an apostle in the RLDS Church. He died in West Virginia in 1885 ("People of the Time," *The Joseph Smith Papers,* josephsmithpapers.org).

and calling him an old lying hypocrite[.] Charge 4th. For taking Br[other] Griffith's potatoes contrary to the stipulated agreement, to the injury of the said Griffith. Charge 5th. For fraudulently obtaining one hundred and twenty dollars from Br[other] Huddleston. January 23rd 1843. Echeem Holden[,] Daniel P Barnes[,] Cornelius Cox[26]

It was decided by said Quorum that he be disfellowshiped. Two were appointed to speak on [each] side[,] viz[:] (3) [Lewis] Wilson[,] (4) [Alpheus] Cutler[,] (5) [David] Fulmer[,] and (6) [George W.] Harris. The charges were not sustained. [It was] decided by President Hyrum Smith that he be acquitted[,] which was sanctioned by the Council. Adjourned till tomorrow at 9 o'clock A.M. at this place. Hosea Stout Clerk –

‡*February 19, 1843; Sunday.*[27] The [high] council met according to adjournment at the Lodge Room. Presidents Joseph & Hyrum Smith, William Marks & Charles C. Rich presiding[,] [the following] Councellors [were] present[:] (1) John Snider pro tem[,] (2) [James] Allred[,] (3) [Lewis] Wilson[,] (4) [Alpheus] Cutler[,] (5) [David] Fulmer[,] (6) [George W.] Harris[,] (7) [Thomas] Grover[,] (8) [Aaron] Johnson[,] (9) [Newel] Knight[,] (10) [William] Huntington[,] (11) [Leonard] Soby[,] [and] (12) Isaac Higbee pro tem. Prayer by Alpheus Cutler.

The case of Wilson Law and U[riah] C[hittenden] Nickerson[28] was brought up. Wherein a charge was prefered against Wilson Law by U[riah] C[hittenden] Nickerson and also a charge against Nickerson by Law. There being charges prefered by both parties against each other[,] the Council decided that they should go into an investi-

---

[26]The original complaint is addressed to "Iasiah Ells" and mentions the "Elders quar [quorum]" and Ira "Caulson." It is signed by "Jehuin Holden, David Barnes, and Cornelius Case" (Nauvoo Stake High Council Court Papers, 1:19).

[27]See also Joseph Smith, *History of the Church of Jesus Christ of Latter-day Saints*, 7 vols. (Salt Lake City: Deseret News, 1902-12), 5:280.

[28]Uriah Chittendon Hatch Nickerson was born in 1810 in Windsor, Vermont. He was baptized in April 1833 and moved to Nauvoo about ten years later and died there in 1844. For more on this particular incident, see Richard P. Howard, ed., *Memoirs of President Joseph Smith III, 1832-1914* (Independence, MO: Herald House, 1979), 14-15.

gation of all their difficulties on both sides of the question, both parties to bring up all matters of grievances against each other which was also according to the wish of the parties. U[riah] C[hittenden] Nickerson to be plaintiff. One [of the councilmen] were appointed to speak on [each] side viz. (7) [Thomas] Grover and (8) [Aaron] Johnson.

There were a great many witnesses on both sides and a very long trial ensued which lasted from 9 o'clock A.M. till midnight.[29] The essential grounds of difficulty was concerning the title to some of the islands in the Mississippi River[,] both parties supposing they had a good right to the same island or a part of an island. The matter was as follows[:] There had been a decree, in the Court of Chancery in Iowa Territory, to sell the said island as a part of the "half breed" track of land and Nickerson put in money with Arthur Morrison[30] to buy his claim, who was to bid it off for him & make a deed to Nickerson, which he did not do but sold the island to Br[other]s Law & did not reserve the claim for Nickerson which he had purchased with Nickersons money[,] neither did he let Br[other]s Law know the situation of Nickerson's Claim. Neither party knew the situation of the others claim and each ^party^ supposed the other to be trespassing on his claim: Moreover there was a Law in the Territory of Iowa which guaranteed to each actual settler his claim on certain conditions by which law Nickerson had a good title to his claim.

President Joseph Smith spoke at length on the subject[,] clearly showing the situation of the affair, and what was the true nature of the titles to the islands.[31] That they did not belong to the "Half Breed tract" and also that the Court of Chancery had no right to sell them. That they were refused lands [property with no title] which the government did not see fit to do anything with[,] consequently were free [for settlers to] plunder or belonged to the actual setler &c. although, as they were to be sold, it was best that the brethren buy

---

[29]Joseph Smith's diary records the council lasting from "9 A.M. to 1 P.M.," although he may have meant 1 a.m. (Scott H. Faulring, ed., *An American Prophet's Record: The Diaries and Journals of Joseph Smith* [Salt Lake City: Signature Books and Smith Research Associates, 1989], 306).

[30]Arthur Morrison was a non-Mormon merchant who had lived among the Mormons in Missouri and followed them to Nauvoo. In 1841 he ran unsuccessfully for a position on the city council.

[31]Smith said he "explained the laws of the U[nited] S[tates and] the laws of Iowa and Illinois" (Faulring, *American Prophet's Record,* 306).

them to avoid any difficulty with those out of the Church, who might buy them &c

As the matter ~~appointed~~ appeared to be whether Law should give Nickerson a title to his claim according to the money he put in or not (i.e) a title from that Court of Chancery such as he had, that [by] taking the situation of the islands into consideration and the nature of their titles, he [was able to] g[i]ve the following decision[:] Let Br[other]s Laws deed what they feel that they can conscientiously do to Nickerson & let Nickerson say that he will [accept a] receipt [for] it and strike hands and be friends hence forth.

Both parties agreed to the decision and shook hands in friendship[,] which decision was sanctioned by the Council. Adj[ourne]d till ~~next~~ the 25th inst[ant][.] H[osea] Stout Clerk.

*February 25, 1843; Saturday.* [The] Minutes of the High Council of the Church of Jesus Christ of Latter Day Saints of Nauvoo[,] Hancock County, Illinois, from the 25th of February 1843. [The] Names of the Members of the High Council of Nauvoo[,] Ill[inois]: William Marks[,] President of Council[,] [with] Austin Cowles [and] Charles C. Rich[,] [the] President's Councellors[.] [The] Names of the High Councellors[,] viz[:] Samuel Bent No 1[,] James Allred No. 2[,] Lewis D. Wilson No 3, Alpheus Cutler No 4[,] David Fulmer No 5[,] George W. Harris No 6[,] Thomas Grover No 7[,] Aaron Johnson No 8[,] Newel Knight No 9[,] William Huntington Sr. 10[,] Leonard Soby No 11[,] [and] Henry G. Sherwood No. 12[.] Hosea Stout[,] Clerk of Council.

[The] Council met according to adjournment at Law's Store in Nauvoo, William Marks and Charles C. Rich Presiding[.] [The] Council [members] pres[e]nt [were][:] (1) Eli Norton, pro tem.[,] (2) [James] Allred[,] (3) [Lewis] Wilson[,] (4) [Alpheus] Cutler[,] (5) [David] Fulmer[,] (6) [George] Harris[,] (7) [Thomas] Grover[,] (8) [Aaron] Johnson [,] (9) [Newel] Knight[,] (10) [William] Huntington[,] (11) David Evans pro tem[,] [and] (12) Tarlton Lewis pro tem. Prayer by President Rich.

The following case was then taken into consideration[,] which had been appealled from the Court of Bishop Isaac Higbee by W[illiam] Edwards[32] to wit:

[32]William Edwards was born in 1810 in Herefordshire, England. He

> The copy of a charge prefered before me, and was acted upon on the 12th of February 1843. We, the Teachers of the Church of Jesus Christ of Latter Day Saints, prefer a charge against Sister Parker, the wife of Joseph [D.] Parker, and William Edwards, and wife, for refusing to settle a difficulty that now exists between them. Signed[,] F. W. Huntsman [and] Samuel Eggleston[.][33] Dated Feb[ruary] the 19th 1843. When the parties appeared for trial[,] J. W. Huntsman [indicated] the particulars of the difficulty[,] [and] said that sister Parker said she saw a pig killed and [that someone] took [it] into Br[other] Edward's house[,] which circumstance Br[other] and Sister Edwards denied. After hearing the testimony it was my decision that Br[other] and Sister Edwards be no longer members of the Church. Isaac Higbee, Bishop.

[It was] Decided that one speak on [each] side to wit: (9) [Newell] Knight & (10) [William] Huntington. After hearing the evidence it was the Decision of President Marks that the charge was not sustained by the Council unanimously.[34] [The] Council adjourned half an hour and convened accordingly[.]

The ^following^ case was then taken up which had been appealed from the Court of Bishop Johnathan H. Hale, by Chandler Holbrook[35] to wit:

---

was present in Missouri during the troubles there. He died in Salt Lake City in 1883.

[33]Samuel Eggleston was born in 1804 in Marcellus, New York, and was a tanner by trade. In 1827 he married Lurania Powers Burgess, with whom he had eight children. A year after their 1841 conversion to the LDS Church, they moved to Nauvoo. Beginning in 1846 they spent five years in Winter Quarters, Nebraska, then moved across the river to the east to Council Bluffs, where Samuel served as a justice of the peace for ten years. He also became the postmaster both there and, for two years, in nearby Crescent City. In 1862 they made the trek to Utah, settling in Ogden. Samuel became both a bishop and a patriarch. He died in 1884 (Karen Eggleston Stark, "Samuel Eggleston," *Family Tree Maker Online*, genealogy.com).

[34]This apparently implies that the Edwardses were reinstated as members of the Church.

[35]Chandler Holbrook was born in September 1807 in Florence, New York, and married Eunice Dunning in June 1831. They were baptized in 1833. A year later they moved to Kirtland, Ohio, and he left for Missouri with Zion's Camp. His wife and infant daughter soon joined him in Missouri, where the couple's next two children were born. They would have two more children in Nauvoo and two in Utah. They immigrated to Utah

Nauvoo City[,] February 10th 1843[.] To the Bishop of the Ninth Ward, Johnathan H Hale and his Councellors. Sirs[:] I prefer a charge against Charles Shumway,[36] for not paying the first consideration of a note, or what is now due of a note given January or February 1842, for borrowed money, which was to be paid [in] the Spring following. Given by Charles Shumway, and the note was given up to Charles Shumway and Joseph Holbrook's note was given for the principal & interest of said note that is given up, under consideration that Charles Shumway should pay the note that J[oseph] Holbrook gave, if he received the money first[,] which he agreed to do at that time. And he has received money since but has refused to pay [the] said note. Chandler Holbrook[.]

This is to certify that the within charge was tried before the Bishop's Court of the 9th Ward of the City of Nauvoo and not sustained. February 11th 1843[.]

[It was] voted that one speak on [each] side to wit: (11) David [Evan]s pro tem. [and] (12) Tarlton Lewis pro tem. The Council in committee of the whole decided the charge was not sustained, unanimously. [The] Council adjourned till next Saturday at or near this place at 10 o'clock A.M.

*March 4, 1843; Saturday.* [The High] Council met according to adjournment at [William] Law's store in Nauvoo, William Marks Presiding. [The following] Councel[or]s [were] present[:] (1) [Samuel] Bent[,] (2) [James] Allred[,] (3) [Lewis D.] Wilson[,] (4) [Alpheus] Cutler, (5) [David] Fulmer[,] (6) [George W.] Harris[,] (7) [Thomas]

---

in 1848 and settled in Fillmore, where Chandler died in September 1889, his wife a year later (Tom L. Day, "Chandler Holbrook," *Genealogy Project,* mydayfamily.net).

36Charles Shumway was born in August 1806 in Oxford, Massachusetts. After he married Julia Ann Hooker in 1832, they moved to Illinois. In 1841 they were baptized into the LDS Church and moved downriver to Nauvoo. He became a member of the Nauvoo police force. When the Saints were run out of Nauvoo in February 1846, the Shumways were among the first to cross the Mississippi River to the west, but Julia Ann died that same year in Winter Quarters. Charles and his son went on to be part of the pioneer company that first entered the Salt Lake Valley in 1847 and later settled Manti, Utah. Charles filled missions to Canada and New England. He died in southern Utah in May 1898 ("Pioneer Families," *Central Utah Pioneer Heritage Association,* pioneerheritagecenter.org).

Grover[,] (8) [Aaron] Johnson[,] (9) [Newel] Knight[,] (10) [William] Huntington[,] (11) [Leonard] Soby[,] [and] (12) Eli Norton pro tem. [A] prayer [was given] by Pres[iden]t Marks.

Thomas Woolsey[37] [entered] against Job Green[38] [the following] charge[:]

> To the High Council of the Church of Latter Day Saints at Nauvoo. February 23rd 1843. I prefer the following charge against Job Green for unchristian like conduct. For this that he made an attempt to go to be[d] [with] two young females and acted otherwise very imprudently at the time[.] [Signed,] Thomas Woolsey.[39]

[Job Green] Plead not guilty[.] One [councilman] was appointed to speak on [each] side to wit: (1) [Samuel] Bent and (2) [James] Allred. After the evidence was heard[,] there being but one witness which went to establish the most important item[,] it was decided that the charge was not sustained[,] which was sanctioned by the Council unanimously.

[The] Council adjourned [for] a few minutes and met [again] accordingly[.] [The meeting was] adjourned to the Lodge Room[.] Edman Durfee[40] [entered] against James Durfee [the following] Charge[:]

> To the High Council of the Church of Jesus Christ of Latter Day

---

[37]Thomas Woolsey was born in November 1805 in Fishing Creek, Kentucky. He was baptized in 1834 in Illinois and moved to Nauvoo around 1841 to work on the temple. He enlisted in the Mormon Battalion in February 1846 and arrived in Utah in 1852. He had seven wives. He died in January 1897 in Sanpete County (Wilford Whitaker, "Full Pioneer Story: Thomas Woolsey," *Sons of Utah Pioneers,* suplibrary.org/stories).

[38]Job Edward Green was born in May 1812 in Grafton, New Hampshire. He was baptized in 1838 in New York. He died in May 1876 in Mt. Pleasant, Utah.

[39]The original complaint says he "made an attempt to go to bed to two young females" ("[REDACTED] vs. [REDACTED]," Nauvoo Stake High Council Court Papers, *Selected Collections,* 1:19).

[40]Edmond Durfee was born in October 1788 in Rhode Island. He and his wife, Magdalena Pickle, were baptized in early 1831 in Ohio. After escaping persecution in Missouri in the late 1830s, they moved to Morley's Settlement near Nauvoo. In September 1845, a mob attacked the town and set the buildings on fire. Edmond and others moved their families to Nauvoo for safety and then went back to harvest crops, whereupon Edmond was shot and killed.

> Saints at Nauvoo. I hereby prefer the following Charges against James Durfee to wit: 1st attempting to defraud me ^out^ of the land that I now live upon. 2nd For stating that I had used my influence to prejudice the minds of the Church against him. 3 For bringing up old difficulties that had been settled. 4th For treating the authorities of the branch with contempt at Lima. Edman Durfee.

[The] Defendant plead not guilty[,] whereupon two [high councilmen] were appointed to speak on [each] side[,] viz.[:] (3 L[ewis] D. Wilson[,] (4) A[lpheus] Cutler[,] (5) D[avid] Fulmer[,] (6) and G[eorge] W. Harris. President Charles C. Rich took his seat in [the] Council. After the evidence was heard on the part of the prosecution, the Council adjourned until tomorrow morning at 9 o'clock. Hosea Stout, Clerk.

*March 5, 1843; Sunday.* [The High] Council met according to adjournment at the Lodge Room. Prayer by Newel Knight. The buisness before the Council [from] the day before was taken up on the part of the defence, after which President [Charles C.] Rich spoke showing the reasons why James Durfee should make Edman Durfee safe in the title of his lands; and the nature of the difficulty &c. President [William] Marks then decided that Edman ^Durfee^ should make satisfaction, for all things which he had said or done, against James Durfee, which was unchristian-like and that he also make satisfaction, or pay, James Durfee for his portion of the expence, which James Durfee has been at in procuring a title to the land[,] that James Durfee make or secure a right and title to the land to Edman Durfee, or satisfy him for his improvements on or before the 15th day of April next ~~that~~ ^~~or~~ or^ the hand of fellowship ^must^ be withdrawn from them[.] Also if James Durfee has placed the land beyond his control so that he can not make a title or satisfaction, he must be cut off[,] and that Elder Isaac Morley be appointed to inform the Council whether James Durfee complies with the decision or not within the time specified. The decision was sanctioned by the Council.

Edman Durfee then made satisfaction for all ^that^ he had said or done amiss and agreed to ^abide^ [by] the decision of the Council[,] after which James Durfee made satisfactory acknowledgements and also agreed to abide the decision. [The] Council adjourned till next Saturday at 9 o'clock A.M. Hosea Stout, Clerk.

*March 11, 1843; Saturday.* [The High] Council met according to adjournment at [William] Law's Store. [The] Council [were] all present except T[homas] Grover & H[enry] G. Sherwood[.] Zebedee Coultrin & Eli Norton was apointed in their place[.] Prayer by Samuel Bent. The buisness before the Council was adjourned till the 19th of this month at 9 o'clock A.M. [The] Council adjourned till next Saturday at 9 o'clock A.M.

*March 18, 1843; Saturday.* [The High] Council met according to adjournment at the Lodge Room. [The] Prayer [was offered] by James Allred, William Marks & C[harles] C. Rich Presiding. All the Council [were] present. The buisness before the Council was adjourned till tomorrow at 1 o'clock P.M. at this place. [The] Council adjourned till tomorrow (19th inst[ant]) at this place at 9 o'clock. Hosea Stout, Clerk.

*March 19, 1843; Sunday.* [The High] Council met according to adjournment at the Lodge Room, W[illiam] Marks & C[harles] C. Rich Presiding. All the Council [was] present. Prayer by L[ewis] D. Wilson. A complaint was made against Ezra Haynes by Daniel Avery[41] for preaching false doctrine and other improper conduct in Ohio, where he thought he was doing much injury. [The] Council adjourned till 1 o'clock and met accordingly.

Daniel Shearer [preferred a charge] against Peletiah Brown.[42] A number of charges was prefered against Br[other] Brown for teaching false doctrine and for speaking against the character of Br[other]

---

[41]Daniel Avery was born in July 1798 in Oswego, New York. He joined the LDS Church and participated in the Mormon War in Missouri. In 1840 he became president of the elders quorum in Iowa. When Joseph Smith was killed, he followed James Strang to Voree, Wisconsin, and died in October 1851 in Illinois.

[42]This charge against Brown was responded to by Joseph Smith at general conference the next month on April 8, 1843. Smith said that "Elder Pelatiah Brown ... was hauled up for trial before the High Council. I did not like the old man being called up for erring in doctrine. It looks too much like the Methodist, and not like the Latter-day Saints. Methodists have creeds which a man must believe or be asked out of their church. I want the liberty of thinking and believing as I please. It feels so good not to be trammelled. It does not prove that a man is not a good man because he errs in doctrine" (*History of Church,* 5:340-41).

Shearer while he was on a mission. The charges were mostly acknowledged by Br[other] Brown except for speacking against Bro[ther] Shearer to his injury. Two were appointed to speak on [each] side, viz: (7) T[homas] Grover[,] (8) A[aron] Johnson[,] (9) N[ewel] Knight[,] [and] (10) & W[illiam] Huntington.

The charge was not sustained. President Marks Decided that they should strike hands in friendship, and begin anew, and bury all their former difficulties and hardness. which ^decision^ the parties readily complied with before having to call a vote of the council. [The] Council adjourned till Saturday at 9 o'clock A.M. H[osea] Stout, Clerk.

*March 25, 1843; Saturday.*[43] [The High] Council met according to adjournment at Pres[iden]t H[yrum] Smith's office, Pres[iden]t W[illiam] Marks Presiding[.] [Those of the] Council present [were]: (1) Edmand Harris[,] (2) [James] Allred[,] (3) David Evans pro tem.[,] (4) [Alpheus] Cutler[,] (5) [David] Fulmer[,] (6) [George W.] Harris[,] (7) [Thomas] Grover[,] (8) [Aaron] Johnson[,] (9) [Newel] Knight[,] (10) [William] Huntington[,] (11) [Leonard] Soby[,] [and] (12) [Henry G.] Sherwood[.]

Lewis D. Wilson [preferred a charge] against Osmon M Duel.[44] Charge[:]

> February the 11th 1843. To the High Council of the Church of Jesus Christ of Latter Day Saints. I hereby prefer the following charges against Osmon M. Duel, to wit: 1st. For forfeiting his contract with Thomas Grover in Missouri concerning a piece of land. 2nd. For forfeiting his contract in Nauvoo in refusing to pay borrowed money, and for refusing to pay for beef and hogs that he bought of T[homas] Grover. 3. For swearing to a lie in a lawsuit

---

[43]See also *History of Church,* 5:311-12.

[44]Osmyn Merrit Duel was born in 1802 in Galaway, New York. He joined the LDS Church in 1832 and left the Church during the Kirtland apostasy of 1837-1838, but returned to endure the final troubles in Missouri. During the Nauvoo period, he filled a mission to New York. He moved to Utah in 1847 and helped settle Centerville, where he died in January 1889. Although he had four wives, he was unable to produce any children (John Wyatt, "Our Ancestor Contributions to the Church," *Saxton History,* issuu.com/solomonsaxton).

> between Nathaniel Whiting & T[homas] Grover in not telling the whole truth. L[ewis] D. Wilson.[45]

After some remarks on the nature of the case Br[other] Grover was released from the Council during this trial, at his own request, as being concerned in the trial & Elder Alexander Williams took his seat for the time being. As there was much matter of difficulty between Br[other] Duel and Br[other] Grover[,] the Council decided that the whole difficulty [should] be brought up before the Council on both sides[,] that all matter of grievances might be settled between Br[other] Duel and Br[other] Grover and that Br[other] Wilson remain as plaintiff.

Br[other] Duel said as the ^whole^ difficulty was to be brought up on both sides that he was not ready for trial. The trial was then adjourned until one week from tomorrow (2nd April) at 10 o'clock A.M. Br[other] Wilson & Br[other] Grover then took their seats in the Council[.] Br[other] Bent also took his seat in the Council[.]

William B. Simmons [preferred a charge] against Benjamin Hoyt, appealed from Bishop Evans' Court of the 11th Ward by Benjamin Hoyt, as follows:

> Charges [were] prefered by William B. Simmons,[46] in behalf of the Church against Br[other] Hoyt. For accusing certain persons of being witches or wizzards and endeavoring to cure such as he said was bewitched, by art, and meddleing with those things unlawfully. March 9th 1843. William B. Simmons.
>
> The decision of the Court is that Br[other] Hoyt cease to call certain characters witches or wizzards; and that he cease to work with the rod he calls a divining rod[47] and that he cease to burn a board or boards to heal the sick by art ~~that of heating a board~~

---

[45]This issue had been brought to the attention of the high council on February 11, 1843. The original complaint was against "Osmon M Dull" ("Wilson vs. Duel," Nauvoo Stake High Council Court Papers, *Selected Collections,* 1:19).

[46]William Burt Simmons was born in April 1799 in Westmoreland, New Hampshire. He was baptized in 1836 in Ontario, Canada. He moved to Nauvoo in 1841. After moving to Utah, he died in Morgan County in August 1866.

[47]A divining rod was a wand that, when asked questions, either moved, implying an answer in the affirmative, or not, implying a negation (D.

~~before the fire, to heal the sick by art~~ March 11th 1843[.] David Evans[,] Bishop.

[The] Defendant plead not guilty [and] two were appointed to speak on the case, to wit: (11) L[eonard] Soby and (12) H[enry] G. Sherwood[.] President Hyrum Smith took his seat in Council. After the investigation President Hyrum Smith Decided that the Council confirm the decision of the Bishops Court[,] which was voted by the Council unanimously. [The] Council adjourned till next Saturday at 9 o'clock A.M. Hosea Stout, Clerk.

*April 1, 1843; Saturday.* [The High] Council met according to adjournment at the Lodge Room, W[illiam] Marks & C[harles] C. Rich Presiding. [The] Council [was] all present. Elder [Henry G.] Sherwood was released from the Council and ~~Zebedee Coultrin~~ Graham Coultrin took his place ~~during this trial~~. [The] prayer [was offered] by David Fulmer. Isaac Allred [preferred a charge] against Jordan P. Hendrixson.[48] Charge:

> February the 24th 1843[.] To the High Council of the Church of Jesus Christ at Nauvoo[,] Illinois. I prefer the following charges against Jordan P. Hendrixson. First, that he married a second woman when his first wife was living, from which he was not released by the laws of God or of man[,] consequently [he] committed adultery. Second, that he told the second woman before he was married to her and also others that he had a bill of divorcement from his wife. Third, For abusing & neglecting her and not admin-

---

Michael Quinn, *Early Mormonism and the Magic World View* [Salt Lake City: Signature Books, 1987], 30).

[48]Jordan P. Hendrickson was born in 1809 in Kentucky. He married Mary Ann Taylor in November 1839 near Nauvoo as her second husband, her first marriage in Missouri in 1834 having lasted one month before her sweetheart died of cholera. Then Mary Ann herself died after three years in Nauvoo, in September 1842, at the age of twenty-four. The existing records show Jordan marrying Frances Kelly six months later, but in fact there must have been some overlap in the marriages, Hendrickson courting Kelly while Taylor was dying. Jordan and Kelly eventually moved to the Mormon settlements in the San Luis Valley in Colorado where many of the Southern Saints located (see "Mary Ann Taylor," *The Joseph Taylor Sr. Family Association,* www.taylorassociation.org; Shari Humpherys Frank, "Family History of the Joseph Taylor Jr. and Sarah Best Family," www.familyorigins.com).

istering to the wants of the second woman while she was on her death bed. Fourth For slandering the character & speaking evil of her since dead. Isaac Allred.[49]

[The] Defendant plead not guilty; whereupon two were appointed to speak on the case, to wit. (1) Samuel Bent & (2) James Allred. When the evidence was nearly all heard[,] the Council adjourned to the Office of H[yrum] Smith.

President W[illiam] Marks decided that, as the ~~matter~~ case now presents itself, it was his feelings to continue him in the Churc[h], that if he did not observe the advice of this Council he would do something ^else^ to [merit] cut[ting] him[self] off before long (that he did not feel that Mr Hendrixson had done what he had wilfully). The decision was not sustained by the Council. There was then remarks made by several ~~remarks~~ of the Councellors explaining the reasons ~~that~~ why they did not concur with the Presidents decision. The vote was put whether there ^was^ new light elicited sufficient to warrant a new hearing, which was carried by a majority of one[,] that there was. The Councellors then all spoke on the case, at some length giving their views on the subject, when on motion it was Voted that he be cut off from the Church. [The] Council adjourned till tomorrow at 10 o'clock A.M. Hosea Stout, Clerk.

*April 2, 1843; Sunday.* [The High] Council met according to adjournment at the Lodge Room, W[illiam] Marks & C[harles] C. Rich Presiding. [The] Councillors present [were][:] (1) [Samuel] Bent[,] (2) [James] Allred[,] (3) Zebedee Coultrin pro tem[,] (4) Elias Higbee pro tem.[,] (5) [David] Fulmer[,] (6) [George W.] Harris[,] (7) Peter Haws protem.[,] (8) [Aaron] Johnson[,] (9) [Newel] Knight[,] (10) [William] Huntington[,] (11) [Leonard] Soby[,] [and] (12) [Henry G.] Sherwood. [The] Defendant[50] plead not guilty. Two [high councilmen] were then appointed to speak on [each] side, to wit: (3) Coultrin[,] (4) Higbee[,] (5) Fulmer[,] and (6) Harris. After the evidences was given there was much said on both sides of the subject[,] after which President Rich spoke showing the necessity of a reconcilia-

---

[49]See also "[REDACTED] vs. [REDACTED], 1843 April 1st" Nauvoo Stake High Council Court Papers, *Selected Collections,* 1:19.

[50]Unidentified.

tion among all parties aggrieved[,] that the difficulties might all be settled without a decision of the Council[.] The parties then agreed to drop all former difficulties & hardness and bury them forever. [The] Council adjourned till Friday the 14th inst[ant] at 9 o'clock A.M. Hosea Stout, Clerk.

*April 14, 1843; Friday.* [The High] Council met according to adjournment at A[lexander] Mills[51] Masonic Hall [Hotel], W[illiam] Marks & C[harles] C. Rich presiding. Present[:] (1) [Samuel] Bent[,] (2) [James] Allred[,] (3) [Lewis D.] Wilson[,] (4) [Alpheus] Cutler[,] (5) [David] Fulmer[,] (6) [George W.] Harris[,] (7) [Thomas] Grover[,] (8) [Aaron] Johnson[,] (9) Numan G. Blodgett pro tem[,] (10) Philo Dibble pro tem. [,] (11) Zebedee Coultrin pro tem[,] [and] (12) [Henry G.] Sherwood. Prayer by Thomas Grover.

Graham Coultrin [preferred a charge] against Anson Mathews and wife[.]Charge[:]

> To the High Council in and for the Church of Jesus Christ of Latter Day Saints, I hereby prefer a charge against Anson Matthews & Elizabeth Matthews[,] his wife[,] for unchristian like conduct[.] Specification 1st. For a failure in refusing to perform according to contract respecting the sale of a piece of land by him sold to me.
>
> Specification 2nd. For transfering his property in a way to enable him to bid defiance to the result and force of law to compel him to abide the aforesaid contract[,] thereby wronging me out of my just due to the same[,] and for lying &c. Nauvoo[,] March 20th 1843. Graham Coultrin.[52]

---

[51]The Masonic Hall Hotel and Tavern must have been next to the city's emerging Masonic temple. Mills was a forty-two-year-old British immigrant who had sustained losses in the Mormon War in Missouri and became a member of the Nauvoo police and corporal in the Nauvoo Legion. He should not to be confused with a twenty-seven-year-old Irish tinsmith of the same name who helped construct the Nauvoo temple.

[52]The Matthewses had been summoned by letter: "Brother Anson Mathews[,] You and your wife are requested to appear before the Council on Saturday of the first day of April at Brother Hirams Office at ten oclock AM to answer to the within charges[.] William Marks President." For some reason, the case was postponed half a month beyond the originally scheduled time.

The disagreement was over whether the Matthewses would transfer

1st Defendant ^Br[other] Matthews^[53] admitted the first Specification and denied the rest. [The council] decided that Br[other] Matthews be tried separate from his wife and that one [councilman] speak on [each] side, to wit: (7) [Thomas] Grover and (8) [Aaron] Johnson. After the evidence was heard the Council adj[ourne]d one hour and met accordingly. [The] charge was sustained in substance.

[It was] Decided by President Marks that Br[other] Matthews use his utmost endeavors to make Br[other] Coultrin a title to the ^land^ according to the Bond – that if he (Mathews) cannot make a title he must make satisfaction to Br[other] Coultrin for the damage which he will sustain in the failure[,] also that Mathews make an endorsement on the Bond which Coultrin holds against him of satisfaction for the payment thereof and give up the notes he holds against Coultrin (which has been paid)[,] and that when Coultrin get[s] a deed he shall pay Matthews ten (10) dollars and that if Br[other] Mathews does not comply with the above decision[,] that he be disfellowshiped. Br[other] Mathews gave up the notes & endorsed the Bond & as aforesaid and agreed to abide the decision.[54] Adjourned till 2

---

a parcel of land to Coultrin in exchange for building materials (Coultrin's assertion) or a completed house (the Matthewses' assertion). Laborer George Rals wrote that he, "with another hand[,] did haul building timber two days," upon which Coultrin allegedly defaulted "by leaveing the Building and goeing on with work for Brother Markum and others" on another project, rather than "performing according to agreement with Father Mathews."

The defendants kept Coultrin's promissory notes and wanted payment in cash, as outlined in the "Defendants Plea & Specifications." Where the Matthewses had expected to have a house suitable to live in by November 5, 1841, Coultrin had produced only the basement by that date. Coultrin hurriedly added a top floor but it was "bad work" and one of the walls collapsed. Therefore, the defendants transferred Coultrin's notes to someone else, but not, they said, with the intent to ruin him ("Graham Coltrin vs. Anson Matthews in High Council April 14th 1843," Nauvoo Stake High Council Court Papers, *Selected Collections,* 1:19).

[53]For some reason, the minutes have the number "12" next to Matthews's name, deleted here.

[54]To the contrary, Matthews stated that he was "dissatisfyed with the verdict rendered by the Afore said Council and do Solisit and appeal before the first Presidency for a rehering." He asserted that at the time of the trial, he "did not fuly understand the Charges preferred against me and consequently was not prepared with competent Witness's to defend My Case." He said he was "deprived" of the benefit of a key witness because the council

weeks (28th inst[ant]) from to day at 9 o'clock A.M. Hosea Stout[,] Clerk.

*April 28, 1843; Friday.* [The High] Council met according to adjournment at J[oseph] Smith's store up stairs, [William] Marks & [Charles C.] Rich presiding[.] Present[:] (1) [Samuel] Bent[,] (2) [James] Allred[,] (3) [Lewis D.] Wilson[,] (4) [David] Fulmer[,] (5) [Alpheus] Cutler[,] (6) [George W.] Harris[,] (7) [Thomas] Grover[,] (8) Sidney Roberts pro tem ^[because of] Johnson being released^[,] (9) Dan[ie]l Shearer pro tem.[,] (10) [William] Huntington[,] (11) [Leonard] Soby[,] [and] (12) Lorenzo Snow pro tem[.] [The] prayer [was offered] by Aaron Johnson.

H[enry] G. Sherwood [preferred a charge] against Peter Forey. Charge[:]

> To the High Council of the Church of Jesus Christ of Latter Day Saints at Nauvoo[,] Illinois[,] April 12th 1843. I hereby prefer a charge against Peter Forey as follows: 1st. For refusing the reasonable renumeration to my wife[,] my daughter Jane, and family that justice and gratitude require for their Labor and attendance on him and his daughter when [they were] sick and living in my house [during] AD 1841.
>
> 2nd. Also for seeming to smuggle and secrete his property[,] apparently to evade a visible means in him to pay any or all the just due as aforesaid.
>
> 3rd. Also for ungenerous and ungrateful sarcastic and slanderous epithets by him made respecting my family. H[enry] G. Sherwood.

The defendant plead that as his witness[es] were not here he was not ready for trial[,] whereupon the trial was adjourned until the 12th of May next at 9 o'clock. [The] Council then adjourned untill the same time. Hosea Stout[,] Clerk.

---

moved the hearing "from the appointed Place of Holding forth" without informing him. Further, "the Plantif" had given "a partial and unjust testimony denying positive facts which I am able to prove in another tribunal" ("Defendants Plea and Specifications," Nauvoo Stake High Council Court Papers, *Selected Collections,* 1:19). The First Presidency heard the appeal and ruled on April 30 that "the charges against [Matthews] are not sustained" (*History of Church,* 5:371-72).

*May 12, 1843; Friday.* [The High] Council met according to adjournment and adjourned till the 19th instant at 9 o'clock A.M. Hosea Stout[,] Clerk.

*May 19, 1843; Friday.* [The High] Council met according to adjournment at Pres[iden]t [William] Marks house and adjourned till the 27th instant at 9 o'clock A.M. Hosea Stout[,] Clerk.

*May 20, 1843; Saturday.* [The High] Council met by appointment[.] A trial was had [but] the minutes was mislaid.

*May 27, 1843; Saturday.* [The High] Council met according to adj[ournmen]t at H[yrum] Smiths office. The case between [Henry] Sherwood & [Peter] Forey was adj[ourne]d till next Saturday at 1 o'clock. H[osea] Stout[,] Clerk.

*June 1, 1843; Thursday.* [The High] Council met at H[yrum] Smith's office according to ~~adj~~ appointment, prayer by [William] Huntington. Jesse Hichcock[55] appeared before the Council and desired to know if there was any way that he could make satisfaction and be restored to the Church. Which, for the want of proper testimony his case was adj[ourne]d untill it could [be] procured. H[osea] Stout[,] Clerk.

*June 2, 1843; Friday.* [The High] Council met at H[yrum] Smith's office according to adj[ournmen]t, W[illiam] Marks Presiding. Present[:] (1) [Samuel] Bent[,] (2) [James] Allred[,] (3) Asa Smith pro tem[,] (4) [Alpheus] Cutler[,] (5) [David] Fulmer[,] (6) [George W.] Harris[,] (7) [Thomas] Grover[,] (8) Alburn Allen pro tem.[,] (9) [Newel] Knight[,] (10) [William] Huntington [,] (11) [Leonard] Soby[,] [and] (12) Bushrod W. Wilson pro tem. Prayer by Leonard Soby.

The case between [Henry G.] Sherwood and [Peter] Forey was

[55]Jesse Hitchcock was born in North Carolina in August 1801 and moved to Missouri before 1821 when he and Mary Polly Hopper got married. They were baptized ten years later, and in 1833 he was appointed to the Missouri high council. For a time in 1836 he served as Joseph Smith's scribe. He was asked, while in Nauvoo, to advertise why Nauvoo had challenged arrest warrants from Missouri. Hitchcock died in 1848 in Mt. Pisgah, Iowa. See the minutes for June 17, 1843, for the resolution of his case.

taken up.[56] Two [high councilmen] were appointed to speak on [each] side, to wit: (11) [Leonard] Soby, (12) B[ushrod] W. Wilson pro tem. (1) [Samuel] Bent[,] and (2) [James] Allred. The charge was sustained[.] President Marks decided that the hand of fellowship [should] be withdrawn from the defendant, which was voted unanimously by the Council. Adj[ourne]d till two weeks from to day at one o'clock P.M. H[osea] Stout[,] C[ler]k

*June 17, 1843; Saturday.* [The High] Council met at H[yrum] Smith's office according to adj[ournmen]t, prayer by President [William] Marks. The case of Jesse Hitchcock was taken up and after an investigation of the case it was decided that, as the matter now presented itself, he could not be restored to fellowship and that the Clerk inform him of the decision of the Council, by letter. Adj[ourne]d [for] 2 weeks. H[osea] Stout[,] Cl[er]k

*July 1, 1843; Saturday.* [The High] Council met at [the] Nauvoo Seminary[57] and adj[ourne]d till the 8th inst[ant] at 2 o'clock P.M. H[osea] Stout[,] Cl[er]k.

*July 8, 1843; Saturday.* [The High] Council met according to adj[ournmen]t and adj[ourne]d [un]till next Saturday the 15th inst[ant] at 2 o'clock. H[osea] Stout.

*July 15, 1843; Saturday.* [The High] Council met according to adj[ournmen]t at the Nauvoo Seminary, Pres[iden]t [William] Marks Presiding[,] prayer by Pres[iden]t A[ustin] Cowles. Adj[ourne]d [un]till next Saturday the 22nd inst[ant] at 2 o'clock P.M. H[osea] Stout[,] Clerk.

*July 22, 1843; Saturday.* [The High] Council met according to adj[ournmen]t at the Nauvoo Seminary, William Marks Presiding. Pres-

---

[56]Sherwood submitted a bill totaling nearly thirty dollars he felt Forey owed him (Sherwood vs. Forey," Nauvoo Stake High Council Court Papers, *Selected Collections,* 1:19).

[57]The Nauvoo Seminary was a private elementary school that met in the second story of the Red Brick Store. In Nauvoo, school typically lasted "only a few weeks" (George W. Givens, *In Old Nauvoo: Everyday Life in the City of Joseph* [Salt Lake City: Deseret Books, 1990], 240-41).

ent[:] (1) [Samuel] Bent[,] (2) [James] Allred[,] (3) Joshua Smith pro tem.[,] (4) Tarlton Lewis pro tem.[,] (5) [David] Fulmer, (6) [George W.] Harris[,] (7) [Thomas] Grover[,] ~~(8) George W. Grouse pro tem~~ (8) [Aaron] Johnson[,] (9) George W. Crouse pro tem.[,] (10) [William] Huntington[,] (11) [Leonard] Soby[,] [and] (12) Erastus Derby. Israel Bowen [preferred a charge] against Elizabeth Rowe. Charge[:]

> Nauvoo[,] July the 15th 1843[.] To the High Council of the Church of Jesus Christ ~~of~~ I hereby prefer a charge against Elizabeth Rowe, for unchristian-like conduct having been caught in bed with a man not her husband at two different times. Israel Bowen.

[The] defendant plead not guilty. Two [high councilmen] were appointed to speak on [each] sid[e], to wit: (3) [Joshua] Smith, (4) [Tarlton] Lewis[,] (5) [David] Fulmer[,] [and] (6) [George W.] Harris. The charge was sustained. President Marks decided that the hand of fellowship be withdrawn from her, which was unanimously sanctioned by the Council. Adj[ourne]d [un]till next Saturday the 29th at 2 o'clock P.M. Hosea Stout[,] Clerk.

*July 29, 1843; Saturday.* [The High] Council met according to adj[ournmen]t at H[yrum] Smith's office, W[illiam] Marks & A[ustin] Cowles Presiding. Present[:] (1) [Samuel] Bent[,] (2) [James] Allred[,] (3) [Lewis D.] Wilson[,] (4) [Alpheus] Cutler[,] (5) [David] Fulmer[,] (6) [George W.] Harris[,] (7) [Thomas] Grover[,] (8) [Aaron] Johnson[,] (9) Robert Stone pro tem.[,] (10) [William] Huntington[,] (11) [Leonard] Soby[,] [and] (12) Benjamin S. Wilber pro tem. [The] pray[er] [was uttered] by [James] Allred. [The] Case of Betsy Dean [was considered][:]

> North Canaan May 23rd 1843[,] Connecticut[:] To the honorable High Council at Nauvoo. The undersigned desires to State that she was not notified of the withdrawing of the hand of fellowship from her, by the Saints in North Canaan and likewise that she was cut from the Church without her knowledge or receiving any notification of such proceeding from Elder Gibson Smith[,] Presiding Elder of this branch, which took place [a] full two years since, and would likewise state, she was not aware but what she was in the kingdom of God untill this day.
>
> For particulars [we] would refer you to Elders [Wilford] Wood-

> ruff, J[onathan] H. Hale & J. H. Holmes, who would give you every information relative to her case, and likewise to Elder B[enjamin] S. Wilber[,] President of the Conference held this day at the house of Brother Francis Benedick[.] Witness[,] James G. Willie Clerk of the meeting. Betsy Dean

It was decided that she be reinstated in the Church and that she be notified by letter of the same[,] and that David Fulmer & Hosea Stout be appointed to write to her[,] and also that they inform the Branch at ^North^ Canaan that they are advised by the High Council to move to Nauvo[o], if they wish to save themselves.[58]

Addison Pratt[59] ^by E[rastus] H Derby – his Agent^ [preferred a charge] against Buckly Anderson.[60] [An] appeal [was] led by Buckly Anderson, to wit,

---

[58]This counsel to relocate to Nauvoo was in reference to the Church-wide gathering then in progress. British members, who were converted when the first mission opened there in 1837, started emigrating in 1841. By 1843, Church leaders were serious enough to instigate disciplinary action against slackers, and a conference in New York voted to cut off "any Elder who taught doctrine contrary to the spirit of gathering" (Glen M. Leonard, *Nauvoo: A Place of Peace, a People of Promise* (Salt Lake City: Deseret Book, 2002), 85.

[59]Addison Pratt was born in 1802 in Winchester, New Hampshire, and baptized into the LDS Church in 1835. In 1843 he was ordained a Seventy in Nauvoo and was soon called on a mission to Hawaii, traveling to the Pacific by way of a whaling ship launched from New Bedford, Massachusetts, in October. Although Pratt never reached Hawaii, he spent three years in Tahiti, then served as the presiding Church officer in San Francisco for a short time on his way to Utah–also witnessing the discovery of gold at Sutter's Mill. Arriving in Salt Lake City for the first time in 1848, Addison was called on yet another mission to Tahiti, this time with his wife, Louisa Barnes. But when the missionaries were evicted from the Society Islands in 1852, the Pratts started for Utah but paused in California, where Addison refused an entreaty from the leadership to practice polygamy. This led to a separation from Louisa, who supported the idea. Addison died in 1872 in Anaheim, Louisa in Beaver, Utah, seven years later (Andrew Jenson, *LDS Biographical Encyclopedia,* 4 vols. [Salt Lake City: Jenson Historical Company, 1901-1936], 3:698; see also S. George Ellsworth, ed., *The Journals of Addison Pratt* [Salt Lake City: University of Utah Press, 1990]; Ellsworth, ed., *The History of Louisa Barnes Pratt: Being the Autobiography of a Mormon Missionary Widow and Pioneer* [Logan: Utah State University Press, 1998]).

[60]Buckley Burnham Anderson was born in January 1819 in Berlin, Ohio, the twin of Blakley B. Anderson. In 1834 Buckley's family converted

> May the 14th 1843[.] A charge was prefered before me against Buckly Anderson by Adison Pratt for unchristian-like conduct in depriving him of his rights. [On] May the 17th the parties met for trial and the charge [was] sustained and [it was] decided that Buckley Anderson give possession of a lot which Addison Pratt claimed or be disfellowshiped. Isaac Higbee, Bishop.

One [high councilman] was appointed to speak on [each] side, viz: (7) [Thomas] Grover and (8) [Aaron] Johnson. [It was] decided by Pres[iden]t Marks that the Council sustain the decision of the Bishops' Court[,] which was unanimously sanctioned by the Council[.] [The council] adjourned till next Saturday the 5th of August at 2 o'clock P.M. Closed in Prayer by Pres[iden]t Cowles. Hosea Stout[,] Clerk.

*August 5, 1843; Saturday.* [The High] Council met according to adjournment at Hiram's office. [There was] no buisness before the Council[.] Adjourned till next Saturday the 12th at 2 o'clock P.M. Hosea Stout[,] Clerk.

*August 12, 1843; Saturday.* [The High] Council met according to adj[ournmen]t at H[yrum] Smith's office. No buisness before the Council. Teaching by Pres[iden]ts Hiram Smith & William Marks.[61]

---

to Mormonism and followed the Saints to Ohio and Missouri, while his future wife's family made the same peregrinations. He and Sally Marie Cutler met and married in 1837 in Missouri. He was eighteen and she was nineteen. They would eventually have thirteen children together. After the fall of Nauvoo, the Andersons followed Alpheus Cutler, Sally Marie's father, to Manti, Iowa, where he led a schismatic group of Mormons. After Father Cutler's death, the Andersons moved to Minnesota, then back to Missouri in 1888. Buckley died in Lebeck, near Joplin, in 1895 ("Buckley Burnham Anderson," *Anderson Clan,* anderson-clan.com).

[61]At this meeting, Hyrum Smith taught his brother Joseph's doctrine of plural marriage, as confirmed by statements by those in attendance. Austin Cowles, who rejected the doctrine and joined William Law's Reformed Church the following year, stated in the *Nauvoo Expositor* on June 7, 1844, that Hyrum Smith "read the said revelation in the said Council" and that it was these "heresies" that "determined me to leave the office of first counsellor to the president of the Church at Nauvoo, inasmuch as I dared not teach or administer such laws."

Four former high councilmen signed affidavits to that effect in 1869: David Fulmer (June 15), Thomas Grover (July 6), James Allred (October 2 and Aaron Johnson (October 2). Fulmer stated to notary public James

Adj[ourne]d till next Saturday at 2 o'clock P.M. Hosea Stout, Clerk.[62]

*August 19, 1843; Saturday.* [The High] Council met according to adj[ournmen]t at Hirams office, W[illiam] Marks & [Austin A.] Cowles Presiding. Present[:] (1) [Samuel] Bent[,] ~~(2) [James] Allred (3) [Lewis D.] Wilson (4) [Alpheus] Cutler (5) [David] Fulmer (6) [George W.]~~

---

Jack on June 15, 1860, that at the meeting in question, Lewis Wilson "made enquiry in relation to the Subject of a plurality of wives as there were rumors afloat respecting it, and he was 'Satisfied there was something in those rumors, and he wanted to know what it was.' Upon which the said Hyrum Smith Stepped across the road to his residence and Soon returned, bringing with him a copy of the revelation on Celestial Marriage given to Joseph Smith July twelfth A.D. 1843[,] and read the Same to the High Council and bore testimony to its truth."

Grover's statement to James Jack on July 6, 1869, was that "Hyrum Smith reasoned upon said Revelation for about an hour, clearly explaining the same, and then enjoined it upon said Council, to receive and acknowledge the same, or they would be damned." He said that William Marks, Austin Cowles, and Leonard Soby rejected it. Allred, who appeared before L. John Nuttal to make his statement two months later on October 2, 1869, emphasized that Marks, Cowles and Soby were "the only members of the Council present who voted against the Revelation and the Testimony of Hyrum." After these affidavits had been prepared, Johnson read them and confirmed to Nuttall on October 2 that they were all "true and correct," according to his memory. Allred, Fulmer, Grover, and Johnson then signed a joint letter dated October 10, stating essentially the same thing. All of these are available at the LDS Church History Library and Archives, as well as the 1883 statement by Leonard Soby to Justice J. W. Roberts that in August 1843, Hyrum Smith

> presented to said Council the Revelation on polygamy enjoining its observance and declaring it came from God; unto which a large majority of the Council agreed and assented, believing it to be of a celestial order[,] though no vote was taken upon it, for the reason that the voice of the prophet in such matters was understood by us to [be] the voice of God to the church, and that said revelation was presented to said Council as before stated, as coming from Joseph Smith the prophet of the Lord, and was received by us as other revelations had been.

On January 11, 1886, a letter from Grover in the *Deseret News* recapitulated the event, Grover mentioning that "from that time forward there was a very strong division in the High Council. These three men [Cowles, Marks, Soby] greatly diminished in spirit[,] day after day, so that there was a great difference in the line of their conduct, which was perceivable to every member that kept the faith."

[62]Stout later explained why the minutes for this meeting were abbre-

~~Harris (7) [Thomas] Grover (8)~~ (2) Daniel S. Miles pro tem[,] (3) [Lewis D.] Wilson[,] (4) Andrew Lameraux[,] (5) [David] Fulmer[,] (6) [George W.] Harris[,] (7) [Thomas] Grover[,] (8) [Aaron] Johnson[,] (9) [Newel] Knight[,] (10) [William] Huntington[,] (11) [Leonard] Soby[,] [and] (12) Rob[er]t Stone. Prayer by G[eorge] W. Harris. Samuel T. Winegar [preferred a charge] against James Rollins.[63] Charge[:]

> August 12th 1843. To the High Council of the Church of Jesus Christ of Latter Day Saints. I hereby prefer a charge against James Rollins for taking my wheat which grew on the land which he sold to Br[other] Elisha Turner. Samuel T Winegar.

[The] Defendant plead not guilty. Two [high councilmen] were appointed to speak on [each] side, viz: (9) Knight, (10) Huntington[,] (11) Soby[,] and 12 Rob[er]t Stone. The defendant objected to Andrew Lameraux sitting on the Council on the grounds that he had given his ~~opinion again~~ judgement against him previously[,] after which Rob[er]t Stone took the place of A[ndrew] Lameraux and Hosea Stout took the place of R[obert] Stone. The charge was sustained [and] decided by President Marks that the defendant pay the plaintiff the amount of wheat taken[,] which appeared to be about five or six bushels, in a reasonable time[,] say[,] two months, or be disfellowshiped, which was unanimously sanctioned by the Council. Adj[ourne]d [un]till next Saturday the 26th at 2 o'clock P.M. Hosea Stout, Clerk.

*August 26, 1843; Saturday.* [The High] Council met according to adj[ournmen]t. No buisness [was brought] before the Council. [The meeting was] adj[ourne]d [un]till next friday the 1st of Sept[ember] at 10 o'clock AM. H[osea] Stout, Clerk.

---

viated: "At that very time I had another appoint[ment] to meet, and was excused by the council, supposing [the revelation] would be filed there and come into my hands as clerk [and] I could then peruse it at my leasure. When I returned the Council had adjourned, and [Hyrum] had gone, taking the revelation with him. But I saw several of the counsellors, who informed me as to the purport of the revelation, which corresponded to what is published and [is] now in the book of Doctrine and Covenants [as Section 132]" (Stout to Joseph F. Smith, July 24, 1883, qtd. in H. Michael Marquardt, *The Rise of Mormonism, 1816-1844* [Longwood, FL: Xulon Press, 2005], 618-19]).

[63]James Rollins was born in 1798 in Dublin, New Hampshire. He was residing in Nauvoo at least by 1844. He followed the Church west to Utah and died in 1880 in Nephi. Nothing more is known of him.

*September 1, 1843; Friday.*[64] [The High] Council met according to adj[ournmen]t at the Stand near the Temple, W[illiam] Marks Presiding. [The] Councillors present [were][:] (1) [Samuel] Bent[,] (2) [William] Huntington in the place of [James] Allred, who was sick[,] (3) [Lewis] Wilson[,] (4) [Alpheus] Cutler[,] (5) [David] Fulmer[,] (6) [George] Harris[,] (7) [Thomas] Grover[,] (8) [Aaron] Johnson[,] (9) [Newel] Knight[,] (10) Duncan McArthur pro tem.[,] (11) [Leonard] Soby[,] [and] (12) [Henry G.] Sherwood. Prayer by David Fulmer. ~~On motion of Tho[ma]s Grover there were appointed to speak on a side viz Bent (2) Huntington (3) Wilson (4) Cutler (5) Fulmer (6) Harris.~~ The following charges were then prefered to wit[:]

> To the Honorable High Council of the Church of Jesus Christ of Latter Day Saints. A[ustin] Cowles[,] against George J. Adams[,] prefers the following charges, to wit – In general, for unchristian conduct. Specific Charges. 1st. For adultery[.] 2nd. For Breach of covenant. 3rd. For lying[.] 4th. For Slandering. 5th. For putting the stumbling block of his iniquity before his face and raising an image of jealousy and causing people to worship it.

Br[other] Cowles explained the nature of the charges &c. [The] Defendant plead not guilty and read a document from the first Presidency and objected to any thing being brought up previous to the date thereof.

[It was] Decided by the Council that nothing should be brought against Br[other] Adams previous to the 5th of June (the date of the aforesaid document as all things previous thereto had been settled before the First Presidency and the Twelve[)].[65] On motion of Tho[ma]s Grover three were appointed to speak on [each] side to wit: (1) [Samuel] Bent[,] (2) [William] Huntington[,] (3) [Lewis D.] Wilson[,] (4) [Alpheus] Cutler[,] (5) [David] Fulmer[,] [and] (6) [George W.] Harris.

---

[64]See also *History of Church,* 6:2.

[65]Adams returned from a mission to England, reportedly with "a wife and child ... even though he had a family already in Nauvoo." He was excommunicated and reinstated. For more on this, see Irene M. Bates, "William Smith, 1811-93: Problematic Patriarch," *Dialogue: A Journal of Mormon Thought* 16 (Summer 1983): 18-19; and Scott G Kenney, ed., *Wilford Woodruff's Journal, 1833-1898,* 9 vols. [Midvale, UT: Signature Books, 1983-85], 2:236.

After some witnesses had been called[,] the Council adjourned one hour and met according to adj[ournmen]t. The charge was not sustained. [It was] decided by the President that the hand of fellowship be still extended to Br[other] Adams. Adj[ourne]d [un]till next Thursday the 7th at 2 o'clock P.M. Hosea Stout, Clerk.

*September 7, 1843; Thursday.* [The High] Council met according to adj[ournmen]t at Pres[iden]t [William] Mark's house, W[illiam] Marks & A[ustin] Cowles presiding[,] [with] all the Councellors present. On motion of President Marks [the council] Resolved[:] That a committee of three be appointed to draft a piece to be published in the "Times & Seasons" stating that Br[other] George J. Adams has been brought before the High Council and that he had been honorably acquitted and Hosea Stout, Samuel Bent and H[enry] G. Sherwood [are to] be that committee. The committee then withdrew a short time and made the following report which was accepted[:]

> To whom it may concern. This is to certify that Elder George J. Adams has been honorably acquitted by the High Council in Nauvoo, from all charges heretofore prefered against him from any and all sources; and is hereby recommended as a faithful laborer in the Church of Jesus Christ of Latter Day Saints, and a servant of the Lord that is entitled to the gratitude, confidence, liberality and clemency of the saints and honorable men in all the world.[66]

Adj[ourne]d [un]till next Thursday the 14th at 2 o'clock P.M. Hosea Stout[,] Clerk.

*September 14, 1843; Thursday.* [The High] Council met according to adj[ournmen]t at President [William] Mark's house. [The council] resolved that the clerk be authorized to deliver the book, containing the record of the High Council &c in Missouri, to Elder Willard Richards, for his use, for the time being, while he is writing the history of the Church.[67] Adj[ourne]d [un]till next Saturday the 23rd inst[ant] at 2 o'clock P.M.[68] Hosea Stout, Clerk.

---

[66]See also the Aug. 15, 1843, edition of the *Times and Seasons*, p. 303, which despite its date was published in September.

[67]Richards was appointed Church Historian in July.

[68]Another case heard on this date, not recorded in the minutes, was

*September 23, 1843; Saturday.* [The High] Council met according to Adj[ournmen]t at Hyrum Smith's office. President Austin Cowles resigned his seat in the Council[69] as Councillor to President [William] Marks[,] which was accepted by the Council. Adj[ourne]d till next Friday the 29th at 2 o'clock P.M. Hosea Stout[,] Clerk.

*September 29, 1843; Friday.* [The High] Council met according to adj[ournmen]t at the house of President W[illiam] Marks. No buisness. Adj[ourne]d [un]till Saturday the 14th of Oct[ober] at 2 o'clock P.M. H[osea] Stout[,] Clerk.

*October 14, 1843; Saturday.* [The High] Council met according to adj[ournmen]t at President Hyrum's office. All [were] present except [Samuel] Bent & [Henry] Sherwood. John M. Powers, who had been disfellowshiped by the Council on the 3rd of Sept[ember] 1842, on an appeal from Bishop [George] Miller's Court, and has since been rebaptized by the consent of President Marks, appeared before the Council and wished to be ordained[,] which was on motion decided that he be ordained to the office of an Elder, which was done under the hands of Councellors David Fulmer & Leonard Soby. [The]

---

that of George Black v. J. T. Eason "for speaking aga[i]nst the a[u]tharitys of the Church." Eason responded in a letter to the high council that Black had "never come to ... talk with me about [this] charge face to face as Paul advises in such cases." He said:

I do not consider that I have injured any person, either in property, person or private character; neither do I wish to injure any person or be injured myself, — I consider the best plan will be to drop the matter just where it stands. If my name is on your books as a member of your church, you will please drop it, and consider me as such no longer. I respect and love a great number of this people, and I ... hope therefore that I will not be charged with being a mobocrat because I have withdrawn from the church. ... I hope therefore I shall be permitted to withdraw quietly (J. T. Eason, letter dated Sept. 13, 1844, Nauvoo Stake High Council Court Papers, *Selected Collections,* 1:19).

The high council voted that he be "expelled from this church" and a notice be placed in the newspaper to that effect.

[69]According to a contemporary, Cowles was "far more outspoken and energetic in his opposition to that doctrine [plural marriage] than almost any other man in Nauvoo" and felt he could not continue as a counselor in the stake presidency due to that doctrine (qtd. in Robert Bruce Flanders, *Nauvoo: Kingdom on the Mississippi* [Urbana: University of Illinois Press, 1965], 273).

Council adj[ourne]d [un]till two weeks from today [on] the 28th of Oct[ober][.] Hosea Stout[,] Clerk.

*October 28, 1843; Saturday.* [The High] Council met according to adj[ournmen]t at H[yrum] Smith's office, W[illiam] Marks & C[harles] C. Rich presiding. Present[:] (1) [Samuel] Bent, (2) [James] Allred, (3) D[imick] B. Huntington ^pro tem^[,] (4) Jos[eph] M. Cole pro tem[,] (5) [David] Fulmer[,] (6) [George W.] Harris[,] (7) [Thomas] Grover[,] (8) [Aaron] Johnson[,] (9) [Newel] Knight[,] (10) [William] Huntington[,] (11) [Leonard] Soby[,] [and] (12) [Henry G.] Sherwood. Prayer by David Fulmer.

Bushrod Wilson [preferred a charge] against Livsy A Brady.[70] Charge[:]

> Oct[ober] the 23rds 1843[.] To the President of the High Council of the City of Nauvoo. I do hereby prefer a charge against Livsy A Brady for refusing to make deeds for certain Lots of Land between himself and myself and Betsy Foot when the money was tendered in full of all dues on said land. Bushrod W. Wilson.

The defendant plead that the conditions of the bond for said deeds were not complied with. [The council] decided that one [high councilman] speak on [each] side: viz; (7) [Thomas] Grover and (8) [Aaron] Johnson.

[It was] decided by the Presidents that the defendant give the deeds claimed according to the bond for the same when all the money is paid which is his due, which decision was unanimously sanctioned by the council, after which the parties agreed to abide the decision. Adj[ourne]d [un]till next Saturday the 4th of November. Hosea Stout[,] Clerk.

*November 4, 1843; Saturday.* [The High] Council met according to adj[ournmen]t at J[oseph] Smith's store [with] W[illiam] Marks & C[harles] C. Rich Presiding. Present[:] (1) [Samuel] Bent[,] (2) [James]

---

[70]Lindsey Anderson Brady was born in June 1811 in Lincoln, Kentucky. He married Elizabeth Hendrickson in 1831. Four years later they were baptized. In 1839 they were living in Far West, Missouri, where their second child was born. Their fourth child, Tranquilla, was born in Nauvoo in 1846 and their fifth, Sarah, in Fort Union, Utah, in 1852. Lindsey died in June 1885 in Fairview, Utah.

Allred[,] (3) Samuel Williams pro tem.[,] ~~(4) [David] Fulmer (5) Cut~~ (4) [Alpheus] Cutler[,] (5) [David] Fulmer[,] (6) [George W.] Harris[,] (7) Joseph M. Cole pro tem[,] (8) [Aaron] Johnson[,] (9) [Newel] Knight[,] (10) [William] Huntington[,] (11) [Leonard] Soby[,] [and] (12) [Henry G.] Sherwood. Prayer by Aaron Johnson.

Alfonzo Young[71] [preferred a charge] against John Workman.[72] Charge[:]

> To William Marks President of the High Council, I prefer a charge against John Workman for ill treatment, for refusing to ^pay^ me what he owed me, when he had the money and could have done so: and I had informed him of the destitute situation of my sick family. I also charge him with making false statements to my injury. October 20th 1843.[73] A[lfonzo] Young[.]

[The] Defendant plead not guilty. Two [high councilmen] were then appointed to speak on the case, viz. (9) [Newel] Knight and (10) [William] Huntington. After the trial was partly investigated the parties agreed to leave their difficulties to Presidents Marks and Rich and abide their advice. Adj[ourne]d till next Saturday the 11th at 2 o'clock P.M. Hosea Stout[,] Clerk.

*November 11, 1843; Saturday.* [The High] Council met according to adj[ournmen]t at President J[oseph] Smith's store, W[illiam] Marks & C[harles] C. Rich presiding. Br[other] Benjamin Vickery was recommended by Councellor [Leonard] Soby to the Council to be ordained to the office of an Elder. [The council] decided that he be ordained which was done under the hands of Councellors Soby and

---

[71]Alphonzo Young was born in September 1805 in Smith County, Tennessee. Baptized in May 1841, he served a mission to Tennessee with John D. Lee the next year. When the Twelve left the Midwest in 1847, he stayed in Iowa, eventually joining the Reorganized LDS Church.

[72]John Workman was born in 1789 in Cumberland, Maryland. He married Lydia Bilyeu in Tennessee in 1809 and was baptized thirty years later in the same state. He died in April 1855 in Salt Lake City. He and his wife had thirteen children who grew to adulthood and seven who did not.

[73]The original complaint included a list of potential witnesses: "Levi Stuart, A[braham] O. Smoot, A[lphonzo] Young [himself, presumably], Samuel B. Frost, Hosea Stout, and D[imick] B. Huntington" ("A Young vs. J Workman," Nauvoo Stake High Council Court Papers, *Selected Collections,* 1:19).

Sherwood. [The] Council adj[ourne]d [un]till next Saturday on the 18th inst[ant] at 2 o'clock P.M. Hosea Stout[,] Clerk.

‡‡*November 18, 1843; Saturday.* The High Council Met this 17th [sic] day of Nov[ember] 1843 agreeably to adjournment[.] [The] Council opened with prayer by Brother [Thomas] Grover. Present[:] President William Marks and President Charles C Rich [and] Brothers [Samuel] Williams[,] [James] Allred[,] [Daniel] Carn[,] [Alpheus] Cutler[,] [David] Fullmore[,] [George W.] Harris[,] [Thomas] Grover[,] [Aaron] Johnson[,] [Newel] Knight[,] [William] Huntington[,] [Leonard] Soby[,] [and] [Henry] Sherwood.

Appeared [before the council] Sister Mahala Overton[74] vs James Carroll. Brother ^Soby was^ appointed Council for ~~defendant~~ complainant, and brother Sherwood appointed Council for Defendant. The parties Mutually agreed to leave their difference to appraisers to say what the defendant should pay to the plaintiff[.] Brothers Soby and Sherwood were appointed said Appraisers. The defendant proposed to pay said appraisement in provisions such as he shall receive for his labour, to which the complainant agreed –

The president then called up the case of Quartes S. Sparks,[75] against whom a charge had been prefered by Sidney Roberts.[76] The parties being ready[,] the council proceeded to ^the^ trial by appoint-

---

[74]Mahala Ann Overton was a survivor of the Haun's Mill Massacre. She joined the Female Relief Society in June 1842 over the objection of some members, but the reason for the opposition is unknown. In Nauvoo she married Jacob Morris in December 1843, Joseph A. Kelting performing the ceremony.

[75]Quartus Strong Sparks was born in October 1820 in Northhampton, Massachusetts. He converted to Mormonism and was instrumental in establishing the LDS Church on Long Island. In 1846 he and his wife sailed with the ship *Brooklyn* to San Francisco, where they lived until 1853, then moved to the Mormon outpost of San Bernardino. Quartus practiced law there. In 1855 his wife, Mary Holland Hamilton, gave birth to their fourth child, and the same year divorced Quartus to marry Charles Wesley Wandell of Beaver, Utah. Quartus remarried soon thereafter and would marry twice more after that before he died in San Bernardino in August 1891 (Paul E. Sparks, "Quartus Strong Sparks, Mormon Teacher and Preacher," *The Sparks Family Association Online,* www.sparksfamilyassn.org).

[76]The charge was "Seducing and getting a Sister with Child ... and other unchristian like conduct" (Charge dated Oct. 25, 1843, Nauvoo Stake High Council Court Papers, *Selected Collections,* 1:19).

ing Brother Williams and Carn speakers for the complainant and Brothers Allred and Cutler Speakers for [the] Defendant.

Mary Aber[,] the Subject of the complaint[,] with a child in her arms[,] testified that the said Sparks is the father of said Child and that it was got by seduction and force [and] that she resisted him until 3 o'clock at night, when he got the advantage and acomplished his purpose. Brother [J. G.] Devine testified that at a conference held in the East[,] said Sparks stated in his presence that he would not be tried at that conference but would either marry Mary Abor or be tried at Nauvoo –

Sister Howantes Stated that Mary Abor [was] neglected [by] or appeared to be neglected by Said Sparks, on her passage from New York to Nauvoo. Brother Norris stated that he was acquainted with said Mary Aber and had been from her infancy and that she had always borne a good character from her infancy to the present time and that he had never known or heard anything against her character until this fault. Brother Divine Stated that he was acquainted with said Mary in the city of New York and that she bore a good character –

Brother Wandall Stated that ["]there were enough of good victuals to eat which Mary Might have had if she had come to me or my wife or brother Sparks and asked for the key which unlocked the chest in which the provisions were locked.["] He [(]Wandle[)] felt hurt and angry at Mary and [felt] a great sympathy for Sparks, on account of the sympathy which the passengers had for Mary in consequence of her talking[,] and the many questions that was asked her by the passengers – that he could not tell whether her talking was not caused by leading questions from passengers or not. Sister Wandall Stated in substance the same as her husband that she believed Sparks showed a willingness to provide necessaries for, and make her (Mary Aber) comfortable on the passage.

Sister Robanks Stated that When she first came in company with Mary Aber on the passage [that] she felt much prejudiced against her in consequence of iniquity and that she kept from her and slighted her until she saw her weeping and that repeatedly her sympathy was awakened in her favor[.] She afterwards conversed some with her; [she] do[es] not recollect all that was said, and has tried to forget what was said – She believed her to have been weeping in consequence of her want of food; [she] believes her to have been neglected by Sparks – that Mary Abers conduct was Christian-like on the passage.

Quarties S. Sparks, Stated that he did not neglect her (Mary) on the passage, that he did tell her when arriving at Nauvoo that she must now Shirk for herself[;] that he had done all by bringing her up to Nauvoo that was required of him by God or man. A letter was introduced and read as testimony written by J[o]siah L Deforrest which is hereunto attached[.] See letter Signed [by] Josiah L Deforrest[77] – also a letter introduced and read as testimony written by Susan Gourman, which is also attached; see letter Signed Susan Gourman.[78]

Mary Aber Stated that the crime was committed in a house where the family were unbelievers[,] that in consequence she did not cry out, for the sake of the Church[,] he being a Mormon Elder [and] knowing they would report the same against the Elders of the Church – that for the sake of the reproach it would bring upon the Church she went to Brooklin and hid herself up there until the child was born and remained so five weeks after, before it was known to any one of the Church and that she left there for Nauvoo, unbeknown to her parents and friends – that when she was about landing at Nauvoo [and] he (Sparks) said she must now shirk for herself[,] that she was at the house of Mr. Thomas, and had gone to bed when Sparks came to the house and came to her bed and persisted in his

---

[77]DeForest said in his letter to Aber that "Quartiez S. Sparks told me on board of the Steam Boat Amaranth" on October 12, 1843, that on May 30, 1842, she had entered his bedroom "when he wuz going to bed" and that he "took you upon his knee and felt of you in a verry insolent manner" and then left, but that when he returned "you wuz there still [a]nd that you had got undressed and ... you c[a]n guess the rest" (Josiah L. DeForest, letter dated Oct. 30, 1843, Nauvoo Stake High Council Court Papers, *Selected Collections,* 1:19).

As a matter of detail, the steamship *Amaranth* carried English emigrants from the harbor in New Orleans north to Nauvoo. For instance, Thomas Bullock and his wife rode the *Amaranth* in May 1843 when they emigrated from England (Jerald F. Simon, "Thomas Bullock as an Early Mormon Historian," *BYU Studies* 30 [Winter 1990]: 72). The *Amaranth* was also featured in the Samuel Clemens story, "The Steamboat Race."

[78]Gourman wrote that Sparks had admitted the child was his, had "owned the child in my hearing on bo[a]rd of the c[a]n[a]l Boat Bunker hill." The *Bunker Hill* was a barge that carried freight from Pittsburgh to Erie (Letter of Susan Gourman, Nauvoo Stake High Council Court Papers, *Selected Collections,* 1:19).

attempts until 3 oclock. She had got up when he got the advantage of her and threw her on the bed and succeeded in accomplishing his purposes.

Sparks [testified]. [He] stated that he had gone to bed when Mary Aber came into his room and sat down[.] After a while he got up and went and sat down by her and put his arm around her neck and took other liberties with her[.] They then arose and walked across the floor once or twice and then he threw her on the bed and then went out of the room to avoid her; and give her ^a^ chance to go away; but when he returned he found her still laying on the bed[,] when he could no longer resist, but had intercourse with her once and once only – that he did not seduce her but she seduced him – It was a unanimous vote by the High Council that the hand [of fellowship be withdrawn from Sparks].[79]

‡*November 25, 1843; Saturday.*[80] [The High] Council met according to adj[ournmen]t in the upper room of J[oseph] Smith's Store. Prayer by Br[other] [William] Huntington, W[illiam] Marks & C[harles] C. Rich Presiding. Council [members] all present.

Francis Fox [preferred a charge] against Thomas Richardson.[81] Charg[e][:]

> To William Marks President of the High Council, in the Church of Jesus Christ of Latter day Saints, I, Francis Fox, do prefer a charge against Elder Thomas Richardson, to wit: 1st. For demanding my licence unlawfully. 2nd. For also demanding and taking the licence of other Brethren in a clandestine manner &c &c in Chicago[,] Cook County[,] Ill[inois] in the month of February 1842. City of Nauvoo[,] Nov[ember] 15th 1843. Francis Fox Elder.

One [high councilman each] were appointed to speak on [either] side[,] viz[:] (5) [David] Fulmer and (6) [George W.] Harris. The mat-

---

[79]The version in the bound minutes has the bracketed insertion given here.

[80]See also *History of Church,* 6:81.

[81]Thomas Richardson was born in 1804 in Wigan, Lancashire, England. He converted to Mormonism sometime before 1840, the year he was called from Manchester to proselytize in Herefordshire. He was residing in Nauvoo by 1845 and joined the Mormon Battalion in the War with Mexico the next year. He died in Cache Valley in November 1886.

ter of difficulty appeared to be in relation to the manner of organizing a branch of the Church in Chicag[o], and some ordinations which took place. [It was] Decided by the President that the ordinations were legal and that Elder Richardson had not [the] right to demand their licence[,] which [decision] was unanimously sanctioned by the Council.

The case of Elisha Hoops[82] was next brought up on the complaint by letter from Pike C[ounty][,] Ill[inois][,] for getting drunk and using bad language[,] which thing he confessed, and asked forgiveness but thought that he did not use bad language[.][83] ~~asked~~ President Marks give him some instructions which he accepte[d], [and] he was continued in the Church.

Joseph Smith [preferred a charge] against [William Henry] Harrison Sagars. Charge[:]

> Nauvoo City[,] November 21st 1843. Brother Marks[.] Dear Sir, I hereby prefer the following charges against Elder Harrison Sagars, namely: 1st. For trying to seduce a young girl, living at his house[,] by the name of Phebe Madison.[84] 2nd. For using my name in a

[82]Elisha Thomas Hoops was born in 1813 in Fairview, Pennsylvania. He was baptized in 1834 and received an LDS ministerial license in 1837. He eventually settled in Beaver, Utah. He is most remembered for his testimony in the Mountain Meadows Massacre trials, in which he claimed he saw the ill-fated immigrants poison Indian water sources. He died in 1887.

[83]The letter of October 27, 1843, from Pittsfield, signed by "Wiley B. Corbith, [illegible] Burton, Thomas Benton, and Ephraim Roberts," stated that "a certin Elder Elisha Hoops has bin hear and went into pitsfield and got drunk[.] I went and talked to him and he [said] ... if I Reported him to the high Council that I had better prefer a charge aganst brother Joseph [Smith] for he got drunk and rode into broth[er] davises house with his horse[.] ... [I] leve it to you[r] good judgment what to do with him" (Nauvoo Stake High Council Court Papers, 1:19; for more on Joseph Smith being "intoxicated" and "running horses" until he "turned over a buggy and broke it up," see Stan Larson and Samuel J. Passey, eds., *The William E. McLellin Papers, 1854-1880* [Salt Lake City: Signature Books, 2007], 512-13).

[84]Phoebe Madison was Sagers's sister-in-law, who lived with Sagers and his wife, Lucinda. Rumors circulated that Joseph Smith sanctioned a sexual relationship between Sagers and his wife's sister, and in fact, Sagers would be allowed to marry the sister in a polygamous ceremony a month later. He would also take another three wives in Nauvoo and five more in Utah (George D. Smith, *Nauvoo Polygamy: "... But We Called It Celestial Marriage* [Salt Lake City: Signature Books, 2008], 346-47, 617-18).

> blasphemous[85] manner, by saying that I tolerated such things in which thing he is guilty of lying &c &c. Joseph Smith.

The defendant plead not guilty. One [high councilman each] were appointed to speak on [either] side, viz. (7) [Thomas] Grover and (8) [Aaron] Johnson[.] The charge was not sustained, but it appeared that he had taught false doctrine which was corrected by President Joseph Smith,[86] and the defendant was continued in the church.[87] [The] Council adj[ourne]d [un]till Saturday the 9th day of Dec[ember] next at 2 o'clock P.M. Hosea Stout[,] Clerk.

‡‡*December 9, 1843; Saturday.* The High Council met this 9th day of Dec[ember] 1843 agreeably to adjournment at the house of President William Marks. Present[:] Presidents William Marks & Charles Rich[.] Present [of the] Councelmen[:] James Allred[,] Jacob Syffrt, George W. Harris[,] Aaron Johnson[,] Hugh Herringshaw[,] Joseph M Cole[,] ~~Levi H Hancock~~ ^Samuel Bent^[,] Lewis D Wilson[,] David Fulmer[,] Abraham O Smoot[,] Newell Knight[,] [and] Leonard Sobey.

[The] Council opened with Prayer by Brother Knight. [The] Case [of] Brother Albert Gregory[88] vs Charles Wandall [was presented]. Brother H[ugh] Herrenshaw [was] appointed council for [the] defendant. Brother Knight [was] appointed council for [the] plaintiff. Charges prefered were[,] 1st. Unchristian conduct towards certain colored brethren by leaving them at Cleavland in Ohio – after hav-

---

[85]Notice the misuse of "blasphemous" where he probably means "slanderous."

[86]Wilford Woodruff recorded that he was "called in the evening to a Council with the Twelve. When I arived at Joseph Smith's Store I found the High Council sitting on a case of Harrison Sagers for some improper Conduct or other towards some female. At the close President Joseph Smith made an address upon the subject [and said no one had] ... any license from him to commit adultery[,] fornication or any such thing" (Kenney, *Wilford Woodruff's Journal,* 2:328).

[87]A contemporary account of Sagers's trial appeared in the *Warsaw Signal,* Mar. 20, 1844, under the pseudonym, "Traveler." The observer said the room was "crowded to excess" with curious onlookers.

[88]Albert Gregory was born in September 1802 in Norwalk, Connecticut. He was ordained an elder in May 1843, married Elizabeth Tuttle in 1828 and Charlotte Ann Stillwell in 1852, and fathered one child that is known of. He died of cholera in May 1855 in Atchison, Kansas, returning home from a mission. Nothing more is known of him.

ing engaged to conduct them to Nauvoo. Charged 2d. A violation of his word in not using his endeavours to deliver their effects at Nauvoo according to promise.

The charges against Brother Charles Wandall were not sustained. He was therefore honorably acquitted[.] Signed this 9th day of Dec[ember] 1843, Joseph M. Cole Clerk pro tem. The council adjourned to Saturday the 16th at 2 oclock P.M. at the same place.

*December 16, 1843; Saturday.* The [High] Council Met agreeably to adjournment at the store of Joseph Smiths this 16th day of Dec[ember] 1843. There being no business before the Council[,] it adjourned until Saturday the 23d inst[ant] at ~~the same place~~ two oclock P.M. at the same place. Signed J[oseph] M. Cole[,] Cl[er]k pro Tem.

*December 23, 1843; Saturday.* [The High] Council met according to adjournment at the residence of Pres[iden]t W[illiam] Marks. No buisness [was presented] before the council[.] [It] adjourned till next Saturday the 30th [of] Dec[ember] 1843. H[osea] Stout[,] Clerk.

‡*December 30, 1843; Saturday.* [The High] Council met according to adjournment at the residence of President [William] Marks. Present[:] William Marks, Pres[iden]t[,] (1) [Samuel] Bent[,] (2) [James] Allred[,] (3) [Lewis D.] Wilson[,] (4) Joseph Mount pro tem[,] (5) [David] Fulmer[,] (6) [George W.] Harris[,] (7) [Thomas] Grover[,] (8) [Aaron] Johnson[,] (9) Sidney Roberts pro tem[,] (10) [William] Huntington[,] (11) [Leonard] Soby[,] [and] (12) Howard Corey pro tem. [A] prayer [was offered and a few matters] taken up, [after] which [the meeting] was adjourned till next Saturday.

The case of Sidney A Knowlton[89] against Benjamin Willis was next taken up, which adjourned till next Saturday. An appealed case was next taken which was appealled from the Bishop of the Sixth ward, to wit:

Nauvoo Dec[ember] 20th 1843[.] A trial took place before me, on

[89]Sidney Algernon Knowlton was born in May 1793 in Ashford, Connecticut. He married Harriet Burnham in 1816 and had ten children with her. He began selling land in Hancock County, Illinois, in 1836 and joined the LDS Church there in 1840. Nine years later he traveled to Utah. He died in Utah in April 1863.

> the 8th day of Sept[ember] 1843 between Isaac Higbee plaintiff and Amos Lour Defendant. The charges were sustained by Isaac Higbee and the hand of fellowship withdrawn from Amos Lour, untill he will pay five dollars and twelve and a half cents to the said plaintiff in ten days. Daniel Carn B[isho]p 6[th] W[ard] Nauvoo.[90]

One [high councilman each] were appointed to speak on [either] side, viz: (11) [Leonard] Soby and (12) [Howard] Coray. The charge was sustained. [The council] decided that the defendant pay the plaintiff five dollars or be disfellowshiped[.] Adjourned till next Saturday the sixth inst[ant] at one o'clock P.M. Howard Coray[,] Clerk pro tem.

[90]The charge against Lour and the high council assignments to Soby and Corey are also found in loose minutes.

# 11.

# "Deceived by His Specious Pretenses" 1844

‡*January 6, 1844; Saturday.* [The High] Council met according to adjourn[men]t at the residence of President [William] Marks. Present[:] Marks & [Charles] Rich[,] Presiding[.][Councilors present][:] (1) [Samuel] Bent[,] (2) [James] Allred[,] (3) [Lewis D.] Wilson[,] (4) [Alpheus] Cutler[,] (5) [David] Fulmer[,] (6) [George] Harris[,] (7) [Thomas] Grover[,] (8) [Aaron] Johnson (9) (8) Samuel William pro tem.[,] (9) [Newel] Knight[,] (10) [William] Huntington[,] (11) [Leonard] Soby[,] [and] (12) [Henry G.] Sherwood. Prayer by Leonard Soby. Sidney A. Knowlton [preferred a charge] against Benjamin Willis[.] Charge[:]

> To the Honorable High Council of Nauvoo. I prefer the following charges against Benjamin Willis, viz: First[,] for neglecting or refusing to comply with his contract with me in a farm which I rented [to] him, and left it on my hands late in the Season by which I sustained considerable damage. Second[,] for [my] coming to Nauvoo with my team to move [him] to my ~~house~~ place according to his request, he having previously sent [for] me, and then being disappointed by his refusing to move, [the] damage to me being greater as it was in the time of planting. Third, for suing me at law without giving me any notice of so doing. Nauvoo City[,] Dec[ember] 23rd 1843. S[idney] A. Knowlton.[1]

---

[1]Sidney Algernon Knowlton was born in Ashford, Connecticut, in 1793. He married Harriet Burham in 1816 and, in 1835, after living several years in Pennsylvania, Kentucky, and Ohio, moved to Bear Creek in

[The] defendant plead not guilty. Two were appointed to speak on the case, viz: (1) [Samuel] Bent and (2) [James] Allred. On motion George Snider took the place of Thomas Grover during the above trial. The charge was sustained. ~~Decided that~~ The parties then agreed to leave the matter to refferees to say how much the plaintiff had been damaged. Adjourned till next Saturdy[,] [one] week at one o'clock P.M. (the 20th). Hosea Stout[,] Cl[er]k[.]

*January 20, 1844; Sunday.* [The High] Council met according to adj[ournmen]t at the residence of President [William] Marks. No buisness [was presented] before the council. [We] adjourned till next Saturday (the 27th) at one o'clock P.M. Hosea Stout Clerk.

*January 27, 1844; Saturday.* [The High] Council met according to adjournment at the residence of President William Marks. No buisness [was presented] before the council. [The council] adjourned till next Saturday (the 3rd of Feb[ruary]) at one o'clock P.M. Hosea Stout, Clerk.

‡‡*February 3, 1844; Saturday.*[2] [The High] Council met at [the house of] P[resident] [William] Marks. [We] read [a portion of the previous council] minutes[,] [made some ammendments], and approved C[harles] Rich, [David] Fulmer[,] [George] Harris & [Hosea] Stout [as a] committee [to write an article for the *Times and Seasons*].[3]

---

Hancock County, Illinois. There he became known as a "scientific farmer." He came to the aid of the Mormons when they were settling in Commerce (Nauvoo) after fleeing Missouri in 1839. A former follower of Alexander Campbell, Knowlton and his family were baptized into the LDS Church in 1840. Beginning in November 1842, he served a six-month mission to Pennsylvania with his son-in-law, Howard Coray. He immigrated to Utah in 1849, where he married several plural wives beginning in 1855 and died in 1863.

[2]See also Joseph Smith, *History of the Church of Jesus Christ of Latter-day Saints*, 7 vols. (Salt Lake City: Deseret News, 1902-1912), 6:195.

[3]The information in brackets comes from the minutes book under this date, recorded by Stout. The March 1, 1844, issue of the *Times and Seasons* (pp. 458-59) carried the announcement, signed by the stake presidency and high council:

> BELOVED BRETHREN: – Realizing as we do, the importance of the work in which we are engaged, we deem it expedient to lay before you such matters from time to time, as in our opinion, will be beneficial to

‡*February 17, 1844; Saturday.*[4] [The] High Council met according to adjournment at the residence of President William Marks, William Marks and Charles C. Rich Presiding. Councillors present[:] (1) S[amuel] Bent[,] (2) J[ames] Allred[,] (3) L[ewis] D. Wilson[,] (4) ^A[lpheus]^ Cutler[,] (5) D[avid] Fulmer[,] (6) George W. Harris[,] (7) Tho[ma]s Grover[,] (8) Richard D. Sprαugue ^pro tem.[,]^ (9) Joseph M. Cole pro tem[,] (10) W[illiam] Huntington[,] (11) L[eonard] Soby[,] & (12) H[enry] G. Sherwood. Prayer by Pres[iden]t Charles C. Rich.

~~President Marks then informed the Council that a difficulty had been~~ A difficulty from the members of the Highland branch[5] was laid before the Council by president Marks, and after some remarks by the Council it was laid over and Councillors Samuel Bent and Alpheus Cutler were appointed to go and visit [the] said branch and settle the difficulty and make such organizations as they might consider best calculated for the good of the branch.

James Newberry[6] [preferred a charge] against Warren Smith. Charge[:]

Nauvoo[,] February 3rd 1844. To the High Council of the Church

---

the saints ... We would remind our brethren, the elders, who have at sundry times been sent forth as flaming heralds: ... we [the high council] have had our mission to remain at Nauvoo, and to participate with the saints in the blessings of poverty, if such it may be called, [and] ... our time has been spent in endeavoring to settle difficulties ... Individuals have been brought before us, charged with high crimes in the violation of the laws of heaven, on whom much patient exertion in the labors of love have by us been bestowed, to reclaim them from the error and evil of their doings. We regret to have it to say, that in some instances ... we have (reluctantly) been compelled to sever them from the church as withered branches. ... We would ... remind the elders that it is improper for them to re-baptize any such expelled persons ... and that [to baptize such a person] will subject [the baptizing elders] to censure, and bring them to trial before a proper tribunal of the church. We therefore, hope for the future, that certain officious, forward feeling elders will be more prudent in such cases hereafter. We remain yours in the bonds of the new and everlasting covenant.

[4]See also *History of Church*, 6:220.

[5]The Highland Branch was southeast of Warsaw.

[6]James Newberry was born in 1791 in Warwick, New York. He was integral in helping the Saints leave Missouri. He later jointed the Reorganized Church of Jesus Christ of Latter Day Saints and died in 1884.

> of Jesus Christ[.] I hereby prefer a charge against Warren Smith for unchristian like conduct. 1st. In exacting more of me than is his just due[;] 2nd. For breaking his promise by withholding from me a deed of a certain piece or lot of land which I have paid him for according to agreement. James Newberry.

Councillor [Samuel] Bent observed that he thought that this difficulty could be settled without bringing it before the Council; upon which by consent of [the] parties it was left to Councellors Sam[ue]l Bent and Alpheus Cutler to settle it and after a short absence they returned and reported that they had settled the matter to the satisfaction of the parties.

The committee appointed on the 3rd inst[ant] [to draft a notice for the newspaper] reported[,] ^to^ which ~~were~~ there was some amendments propose[d] by the Council[,] and the Committee [was] give[n] to the next meeting to report again and Henry G Sherwood [was] added to the committee[.]

The case of Orlando D. Hovey[7] against Levi Nickerson[8] was next brought up and the defendant not being present[,] it was adjourned till next meeting of the Council and Councillor Thomas Grover was appointed to ^try and^ effect a settlement between the parties before the time. [The council] adjourned till two weeks from to day at one o'clock P.M. (the 2nd of March). Hosea Stout, Clerk.

*March 2, 1844; Saturday.* [The] High Council met according to adjournment at the ~~residence~~ ^upper room^ of President ~~Marks~~ Joseph Smith's Store[.] Prayer by James Allred, W[illiam] Marks & C[harles] C. Rich Presiding. Councillors Present: (1) [Samuel] Bent[,] (2) [James] Allred[,] (3) [Lewis] Wilson[,] (4) [Alpheus] Cutler[,] (5) [David] Fulmer[,] (6) [George W.] Harris[,] (7) [Thomas] Grover[,]

---

[7]Orlando Dana Hovey was born in 1809 in Middlesex, Massachusetts. He lived in Quincy, Illinois, 1839-1843, then moved to Nauvoo. A practitioner of Thompsonian medicine, he helped care for many Saints after their expulsion from Missouri. When he immigrated to Salt Lake City, he lived in the Nineteenth Ward. He died there in 1890.

[8]Levi Stillman Nickerson was born in 1814 in Springville, Pennsylvania. He was baptized in 1833 and ordained a Seventy in Kirtland, Ohio, in 1835. In 1838-1839 he helped to move the Saints from Missouri. He also visited Joseph Smith and others confined at Liberty Jail. He took part in the Battle of Nauvoo. Three years after crossing the plains to Utah, he died in 1853.

(8) absent[,] (9) [Newel] Knight[,] (10) [William] Huntington[,] (11) [Leonard] Soby[,] [and] (12) [Henry G.] Sherwood.

Councillors Alpheus Cutler and Samuel Bent made a report of their proceeding with the Highland Branch acording to ~~their~~ their appointment on the 17th of February last, as follows.

> Wednesday[,] February 21st 1844. 11 o'clock A.M. A conference of the Highland Branch met at the School House. After hearing a discourse from Samuel Bent and Alpheus Cutler, upon family union and brotherly love, the members of said branch unanimously covenanted to bury all former difficulties, and reorganize said branch. Moved and carried unanimously that Benjamin Gardner[9] should be president, and Ally D. Boren Clerk. Conference adjourned at 3 o'clock P.M.

Which report was accepted by the council.

The case of O[rlando] D. Hovey against L[evi] Nickerson was adjourned till next Saturday at one o'clock P.M. An appealed case was then brought forward from the Bishop's Court of the 9th Ward as follows:

> Nauvoo[,] January 24th 1844[.] A true copy of a charge prefered by James Brinkerhoff[10] against James Pace.[11]

---

[9]Benjamin Gardner was born in August 1800 in Johnstown, New York. His parents were among the first to settle in Erie County, Pennsylvania, where Benjamin married Electa Lamport in 1822. They couple had ten children. Three years after being baptized in 1840, the family moved to an area outside of Nauvoo near Morley's Settlement. Non-Mormon neighbors burned their house and crops in 1845, whereupon they took refuge in Nauvoo. They followed the exodus west as far as Bentonsport, Iowa, where they farmed for six years, arriving in Utah in 1852. They settled near Ogden. He died in July 1875 and his wife in August 1890 (Mary Elizabeth Williams Gardner, "Biography of Benjamin Gardner," *Rootsweb,* ancestry.com).

[10]James Brinkerhoff was born in Semprenius, New York, in May 1816. He and his first wife were baptized in 1842 and moved to Nauvoo. He was called the same year to serve a mission to Ohio. After returning, they lived a few years in the city. In Utah, they helped settle Centerville in northern Utah, then St. George in southern Utah fifteen years later. He died in March 1875 in Glendale, near St. George, leaving behind three wives and some twenty-five children (Mattie B. Fish, "A Story of the Life of James Brinkerhoff Sr.," www.shaweb.net).

[11]James Pace was born in June 1811 in Murfreesboro, Tennessee. He

> To the Bishop ^and his council^ of the ninth ward, I hereby prefer the following charge against James Pace[:] For recommending a horse[,] [by which he] sold [to] me [a] different [kind of animal] from what he [said it] was and [he] thereby deceived me. James Brinkerhoff. Nauvoo[,] February 3rd 1844. The above charge was tried before the said Bishop and Council and the charge [was] not sustained. Jonathan H. Hale Bishop of the 9th Ward.

[Upon] which [the meeting] was adjourned till next Saturday at one o'clock P.M.[12] and [the council said] that the parties were to leave the matter to two disinterested men who were to try and settle their difficulty previous to that time.

The Committee appointed on the 3rd [of] Feb[ruary] reported again[,] which was accepted with one amendment. Adjourned till next Saturday at one o'clock P.M. Hosea Stout[,] Clerk.

*March 9, 1844; Saturday.* [The] High Council met according to adjournment at the residence of President William Marks. Councillor W[illiam] Huntington informed the Council that the difficulty between James Brinkerhoff and James Pace, as presented [at the] last meeting of the Council was settled. The rest of the buisness before the Council was laid over. Adjourned till ~~next~~ Saturday the 23rd day of March. Hosea Stout[,] Clerk.

*March 23, 1844; Saturday.* [The] High Council met according to adjournment at the residence of Pres[iden]t W[illiam] Marks. No buisness. [The council] adjourned till next Saturday the 30th at 1 o'clock P.M. Hosea Stout[,] Clerk.

*March 30, 1844; Saturday.* [The] High Council met according to adj[ournmen]t at the residence of President [William] Marks. No buis-

---

was baptized in 1839 in Shelby, Illinois, and soon moved to Nauvoo, where he became a member of the police force. He served a political mission to campaign for Joseph Smith in Arkansas in 1844. In July 1846 he was called by Brigham Young to serve in the Mormon Battalion. As an officer, he was entitled to a servant, so he enlisted his son, William, to accompany him. The Utah town of Payson was named after this father-and-son team. James died in Thatcher, Arizona, in 1888.

[12]In other words, the bishop's court had ruled against Brinkerhoff, and now the high council was postponing consideration of the case.

ness. Adj[ourne]d [un]till Saturday the 20th day of April next. Hosea Stout[,] Clerk.

*April 13, 1844; Saturday.*[13] [The] High Council met according to previous notice at the residence of President [William] Marks. Prayer by Councillor Samuel Bent, Presidents W[illiam] Marks & C[harles] C. Rich Presiding. Councillors present[:] (1) [Samuel] Bent[,] (2) [James] Allred[,] (3) L[ewis] D. Wilson[,] (4) [Alpheus] Cutler[,] (5) [David] Fulmer[,] (6) [George] Harris[,] (7) J[ames] G. Devine pro tem.[,] (8) [Aaron] Johnson[,] (9) [Newel] Knight[,] (10) [William] Huntington[,] (11) [Leonard] Soby[,] [and] (12) [Henry G.] Sherwood. George Morris[14] [preferred a charge] against Jacob Shoemaker.[15] Charge[:]

> To the High Council of the Church of Jesus Christ, I prefer the following charges against Jacob Shoemaker. 1st. For borrowing my axe and breaking it and not making it good again. 2nd. For laying violent hands on me in my own house, and using harsh and abusive language in threatening to whip me, and chargeing me with stealing my axe from his shop. Nauvoo City[,] April 11th 1844. George Morris.

The defendant plead not guilty[,] whereupon one [high councilman each] were appointed to speak on [either] side[,] to wit[:] (3) L[ewis] D. Wilson on the part of the plaintiff and (4) A[lpheus] Cutler on the part of the defendant. The Council then adjourned to the upper room of Joseph Smith's brick store. The charge was sustained. [It was] decided by President Marks that the hand of fellowship be with drawn from the defendant untill he make good the damages

---

[13]See also *History of Church,* 6:333.

[14]George Vernon Morris was born in 1816 in Cheshire, England, and was baptized in Manchester, England, in 1841. The next year he immigrated to Nauvoo, where he helped build the temple and served as a temple guard. When the city was threatened by insurgents in 1846, he helped defend it, personally disarming Chauncey Higbee of his rifle. He immigrated to Utah in 1848 and died in 1897 ("Autobiography of George Morris," typescript, Special Collections, Brigham Young University).

[15]Jacob Shoemaker was born in 1798 in Cumberland County, Pennsylvania. He owned a blacksmith shop in Nauvoo. He was called to proselytize in Pennsylvania in 1844. For the resolution of his case, see the minutes for May 18, 1844, below.

done [to] the plaintiff by breaking his axe and also [to] make satisfaction for abusing him.

The Council then adjourned a few moments & met [again] according to [the terms of the] adjournment. Isaac Higbee took the place of William Huntington who was absent. Lucinda Sagars [preferred a charge] against [William Henry] Harrison Sagars. Charge[:]

> To the Presidency and the Twelve. Inasmuch as you have declared officially that you will deal with all persons who teach or have taught the abominable doctrine of Spiritual wive[s], this is to notify you that Harrison Sagars is guilty of ~~that~~ said sin, which thing can be proven by credible witnesses, and if he is not chastized for it by the church the laws of the land will be enforced against him.
>
> H[arrison] Sagars left his family in December last[,] since which time he has not provided for them in any way whatever. The cause of the innocent demand action immediately and you are the ones to take the matter in hand. Lucinda Sagars.
>
> Brother Harrison Sagars,
> Dear sir[:] As this complaint has been handed over to the High Council by the First Presidency to act upon, you are requested to appear before [the] Council on Saturday the 13th inst[ant] at my house at 2 o'clock P.M. to answer the ~~within~~ ^above^ charges. Nauvoo City[,] April 10th 1844. William Marks President of said Council.[16]

[The] Defendant plead not guilty. Two were appointed to speak on [each] side to wit[:] (5) D[avid] Fulmer & (7) J[ames] G. Divine on the part of the plaintiff and (6) G[eorge] W. Harris and (8) A[aron] Johnson on the part of the defendant.

[It was] decided that ^as^ the first part of the charge had been brought before the Council before (on the 25th of Nov[ember] 1843)[17] and he [being] tried on it; that the Council had no right to deal with

---

[16]A scan of the original document can be seen at the Nauvoo Stake High Council Court Papers, 1839-1844, *Selected Collections from the Archives of the Church of Jesus Christ of Latter-day Saints,* 74 DVDs (Salt Lake City: Intellectual Reserve, 2002), 1:19.

[17]The minutes here advise the reader to also "see page 21" of the high council minute book.

him on that item. And that the second part was not sustained and therefore that he should remain in the Church.[18] Adjourned till the 27th inst[ant] at one o'clock P.M. Hosea Stout[,] Clerk.

*April 27, 1844; Saturday.* [The] High Council met according to adjournment at the residence of President [William] Marks. No buisness. Adjourned till the 4th day of May proximo at one o'clock P.M. Hosea Stout[,] Clerk.

*May 4, 1844; Saturday.* [The] High Council met according to adjournment in th[e] upper room of Jos[eph] Smith's Brick Store. Councillor Samuel Bent informed the Council that as he was going to be absent on a mission for some time that he had chosen Brother Shadrach Roundy to act in his place in the Council during his absence, which

---

[18]Notice that the action against Sagers is driven by his wife, while the high council remains surprisingly lackadaisical in its response to alleged adultery. It appears that they knew Sagers had been given permission to take his sister-in-law as a second wife. If so, considering that the revelation required a man receive his first wife's permission, the high council was complicit in the transgression (D&C 132:61; but cf. vv. 64-65).

A document in the LDS Church History Library and Archives titled "Trial of Harrison Sagar[s] defendant and his wife Lucinda Sagars" states that

> Ja[me]s Hadlock – says that he heard the defendant teach the doctrine of spiritual wives, and that he said he believed it to be the order of God[.] It was before he had his trial before this council, that [the] def[endan]t said his whole salvation ~~wd?~~ rested on having 2 certain Girls to wit[,] [seventeen-year-old] Amanda Higbee and [twenty-five-year-old] Phebe Madison[,] and that was the way [he and his first wife] came to part[.] ... They seperated last fall ...
>
> P. Wells testifies [he heard James] Hadlock [speak about the] ... spiritual wife doctrine ... last fall [but] ... thought it was all a joke. Mrs Hadlock says def[endan]t taught[the] spiritual wife doctrine ... He frequently comes to see his child [and says] ... that he must get an old woman to get young women for him ... [The] def[endan]t and wife parted by agreement on the 8th of Dec[ember] ... His wife said [the] def[endan]t and his mother all was whores ...
>
> [It was] decided that as the first part of the charge had been brought up before the Council before (on the 25 Nov[ember] 1843) and he [was] tried on it[,] that the Council had no right to deal with him on that item, and that the second part was not sustained and therefore that he should remain in the Church (Nauvoo Stake High Council Court Papers, *Selected Collections*, 1:19).

was sanctioned by the Council. Adjourned till next Saturday the 11th inst[ant], at [blank] o'clock P.M. Hosea Stout[,] Clerk.

*May 11, 1844; Saturday.* [The] High Council met according to adjournment at [blank]

‡‡*May 18, 1844; Saturday.*[19] [The] High Council met agreably to adjournment on the 18th day of May 1844[.]Present[:] Shadrich Roundy acting President[,] J[ohn] D Parker[,] Joshua Smith[,] Newel Knight[,] Leonard Knight[,] J[oseph] M. Cole[,] George W. Harris[,] James Alread[,] Rob[er]t Stone[,] Alva L Tippets[,] A[aron] Johnson[,] William Huntington Sen[,] [and] H[enry] G Sherwood.

President Harris presented a Statement[20] made by George Morris that Jacob Shoemaker has made full satisfaction for charges heretofore brought before this Council – [It was] resolved unanimously that the said Jacob Shoemaker be ^fully^ Restored to the Church of Latter day Saints. [It was also] resolved on motion of H[enry] G. Sherwood that Peter I Forey be Received to fellowship in said Church.

On a letter Received from F[ields] B. Jacaway[21] from New Orleans[,] Acting president of a conference held in that place whereby Samuel C Brown[22] was there cut off or disfellowshipped from said Conference[,] his case was brot before the council and as there were not any legal ~~council~~ charge[s] for trial[,] [the council] prefered the

---

[19]See also *History of Church,* 6:398.

[20]The minutes say "a Statement of on made by," the "of on" having been deleted here.

[21]Fields Bruce Jacaway was born in Upper Alton, Madison County, Illinois. In 1843 he served a mission to Ohio, and the following year he became branch president in New Orleans. In 1845 or 1846 he went to Clay County, Missouri, and was killed in a duel, although an alternative narrative claims he hung himself.

[22]A few years earlier, in 1842, Samuel C. Brown, feeling he was doing his part to promote the Church, began publishing a newspaper called the *Mormon Expositor.* The minutes of a Church conference held in New York on October 19, 1842, noted: "Resolved, That in the judgment of this conference, the publication of a paper called the 'Mormon Expositor,' published at Baltimore, by elder Samuel C. Brown, is detrimental to the cause of the church of Christ, and that the clerk be instructed to transmit to the quorum of the Twelve, at Nauvoo, stating our disapprobation with the reason, and a file of the paper" (*Times and Seasons,* Apr. 15, 1843, p. 175).

case [to be] carried over sine die – The case of Brothers J[onah] R. Ball,[23] and W[illia]m Gribble[24] [was] bro[ugh]t on [before the council][.] Newell Knight [was appointed] Council for J[onah] R. Ball [and] W[illia]m Huntington [was appointed] for W[illia]m Gribble.

A[lvin] L Tippits [provided] Testimony as one of the arbitrators [and] W[illia]m Huntington [also provided] Testimony as one of the arbitrators[.] [They] stated as arbitrators in a case between them (the said Ball and Gribble, that William Gribble did agree to and consented to perform on his part a decision made by the said arbitrators) [that in being] questioned by both parties[,] [the defendant] answer[ed] the same. Edethia M Anderson Testifies, she knew of no title to have been offered to Brother Ball, by William Gribble. William Huntington & W[illia]m Gribble Testif[ied] that the said Gribble agreed to give a quit claim <u>deed</u> and [that] the occupant at the same time agread to give to J[onah] R. Ball emmediate possession.

J[ohn] D Parker stated that both parties agreed to abide the descision of the arbitrators but there always seemd to be a misunderstanding between each of the others intention as there was a neighbourhood difficulty between them. A[lvin] L Tippits states that on the first day of April W[illia]m Gribble called upon him (said witness) and they together called upon J[onah] R. Ball and said Gribble[,] then on his part[,] offered to fulfill on his part in full the descession previously made by the arbitrators in their litigation, but that J[onah] R. Ball replied that he was not well and[,] his Attorney not being present at the time[,] he should defer it to another time – [It

[23] Jonah R. Ball was born in 1803. When he met Joseph Smith in the 1840s, he found him to be "familiar in conversation, easy & unassuming," and said that when the prophet preached, "the way he unfolds the scriptures is beyond calculation or controversy." He died of consumption (tuberculosis) in Nauvoo in April 1845 (*Nauvoo Neighbor,* Apr. 23, 1845, p. 3).

[24] William Gribble was born in August 1817 in Perth, Ontario, but was living in Utica, New York, when he and his wife converted to Mormonism in 1837. They moved to Kirtland, Ohio, the next year, then to Springfield, Illinois, for a few years until they moved to Nauvoo in 1841. William was part of the shadow government in Nauvoo called the Council of Fifty, and he served a political mission in 1844 to Michigan. In 1846 he joined the Mormon Battalion. In Utah he lived in Ogden, Payson, Ephraim, and Gunnison; he died of appendicitis in October 1866 on a trip to Nephi (Kimberly Teichert Parker, "William Gribble and Elizabeth Brunell Whiting," *Heritage Past,* www.heritagepast.com).

was] decided unanimously that the hand of fellowship be withdrawn from J[onah] R Ball for refusing to abide the decision of the Arbitrators in the above named controversy.

[It was] resolved that James Blakesly[,][25] Frances M Higbee, Charles ~~Higbee~~ Ivans[,][26] and Austin Cowles be cut off from the Church for apostatizing.[27] George W Harris[,] Pres[iden]t pro Tem. Joseph M Cole[,] Cl[er]k pro Tem.

*June 1, 1844; Saturday.* The High Council of the Church of Latter-day Saints met at the Seventies Hall[28] agreeably to adjournment on the 1st of June 1844 at 2 o clock P.M. Present[:] William Marks President[,] Counsellors George W. Harris[,] James Allread[,] Alpheas Cutler[,] William Huntington[,] Peter Haws in place [of] Sal Bent[,] Henry G. Sherwood[,] Lewis D. Wilson[,] William C. Perry in place

---

[25]James Blakesly was born in 1802 in Milton, Vermont. He was baptized in 1833. He subsequently served a mission to Bastard, Ontario, in 1837 and to the Isle of Man in 1840. He was excommunicated from the LDS Church in May 1844, joined Sidney Rigdon's Church, and then affiliated with James Strang's denomination until he was excommunicated for heresy in 1851. In 1859, Blakesly was baptized into the RLDS Church. He died in 1866.

[26]Charles Ivins was born in Cream Ridge, New Jersey, in April 1799 and converted to Mormonism in New Jersey, moving to Nauvoo in 1841 and three years later to Iowa, where he joined with the dissenters against Joseph Smith. He later became a bishop in William Law's Church. Willard Richards claimed that Ivins "aided and abetted" the mob that killed Joseph Smith. Ivins died in Burlington, Iowa, in January 1875.

[27]On May 10, 1844, a "Prospectus of the Nauvoo Expositor" appeared on the streets under the names William Law, Wilson Law, Charles Ivins, Francis M. Higbee, Chauncey L. Higbee, Robert D. Foster and Charles A. Foster. It was known that James Blakesly and Austin Cowles were also involved with the attempt to create an opposition newspaper. The prospectus called for the repeal of the Nauvoo Charter and asked citizens "to oppose, with uncompromising hostility, any union of church and state"–as well as to display "unmitigated disobedience to political revelations" and to resist the "gross moral imperfections" being propagated, in presumed reference to polygamy.

[28]The Seventies Hall was completed six months earlier in December 1844, its primary function being to host teaching sessions for prospective missionaries and allow them an opportunity to practice preaching from a pulpit (Glen M. Leonard, *Nauvoo: A Place of Peace, a People of Promise* [Salt Lake City: Deseret Book, 2002], 500).

of Leonard Sobey[,] D[avid] Fullmore[,] Aaron Johnson[,] Robert Stone [(]in place of Tho[ma]s Grover[)][,] [and] Newell Knight[.]

Prayer by President William Marks – Voted unanimously on Motion of William Marks that Joseph M. Cole be and is hereby appointed Clerk of the High Council – Case 1st. Complaint brought by James Ivins against Alphonzo Green[29] for damages done by said Greens horses to J[ames] Ivins' grass field[30] – By advice of President Marks[,] the parties agreed to submit their differences to arbitrators and proceeded to choose said arbitrators – J[ames] Ivins chose Josiah Ells, and A[lphonzo] Green chose brother Gates[.] These two were to choose the third person[,] by whose descision the parties agreed to abide[.]

Case 2d. Moses Daily[31] vs. Conference of Highland Branch. At a conference of the Highland Branch on the 3rd day of May 1844[,] Moses Daily was cut off from said Branch, from which said Daily took an appeal before this Council. H[enry] W. Miller[32] stated that Daily

---

[29]Alphonso Green was born in July 1810 in Brookfield, New York. He was baptized in 1840. The next year, he and his wife moved to Nauvoo. They later followed the migration to Utah and settled in American Fork, establishing a farm and hotel there. Ironically, considering the current context, he died in American Fork in August 1875 when he was kicked by a horse.

[30]The original complaint was "against Brother Alphonzo Green for Suffering his horses (or if not his horses[,] he has them in his charge) to run at large and destroy my grass that I have kept expressly for the purpose of making hay, which I have notified him from time to time that they were trespassing on my lot, which he would promise to take care of them and not let them damage me any more[,] but his word [is something] he appears to pay no regard to ("Complaint of James Ivins vs. Alphonso Green, May 28, 1844," Nauvoo Stake High Council Court Papers, *Selected Collections,* 1:19).

[31]Moses Daley was born in Wallkill, New York, in 1794. He was baptized by 1832 and became a land agent in Kirtland, Ohio, then settled in Adam-ondi-ahman, Missouri. He crossed the Great Plains in 1848, then moved on from Utah to San Bernardino in 1851. He remained in California until he died in Riverside in 1865.

[32]Henry William Miller was born in May 1807 in Lexington, New York. He moved to Illinois around 1827 and was baptized there in 1839. He settled in Nauvoo and worked in Wisconsin gathering timber for the Nauvoo House and Nauvoo temple in 1841-1842. In 1846 he moved his family to Kanesville, Iowa, then he made the trek to Utah in 1852 and raised crops in Farmington before bringing his family west. He was elected to the territorial legislature, served a mission to the Indians, and in the 1860s led five

refused to be tried by said conference in consequence of the difficulty then before the conference having been submitted to arbitrators by whose descision he was willing [to] abide[.] H[iram] Kimball testified to the same in substance – John W. Archey Testified in substance the same as the other two and further said that the ~~other~~ said Conference withdrew the hand of fellowship from said Daily by reason of his having refused to be tried by said Conference – H[enry] W. Miller stated that said Daily and Br[o]t[her] Wilkins both agreed to abide the descision of the above name[d] arbitrators; said Miller was one of the arbitrators.

Michael Stoken sai[d] that he was one of the arbitrators as above named by H[enry] W. Miller [and] that Daily refused to be tried by said conference for several reasons; first[,] they had no right to try him but he would submit to a trial before the high Priest Quorum. 2d. That he had not the proper witnesses and 3d. That he had agreed to submit his said difference to arbitrators – Kenedy states the same in substance as Stoken. The case was duly sumed up by Counsellor Sobey o[n] the part of Moses Daily and Counselor Sherwood for the Conference[.] [It was] decided by a unanimous vote of this council that the descision of the highland Conference against Moses Daily be reversed and said Daily be restored to a standing in the Church –

On motion of George W. Harris [it was] resolved that John Scott[33] and Younger Green[34] be cut off from this church for Apostacy[.] [In the] case of Samuel C. Brown vs [the] Branch at New Orleans, fellowship having been withdrawn from Samuel C. Brown by a conference held at New Orleans on the 14th day of January

---

wagon trains to Utah. He helped settle southern Utah. In 1885 he died at his son's home in Farmington.

[33]John Scott was born in May 1811 in Armagh, Ireland. In 1819 his family immigrated to Quebec, then moved to Trafalgar, Ontario. He married Elizabeth Menary in 1836, and both joined the LDS Church and moved to Kirtland two years later. In Nauvoo, John became a body guard to Joseph Smith, a member of the Nauvoo Legion, and a Seventy. He objected to plural marriage at first but he ultimately followed the prophet's counsel and took two plural wives. The four of them, with their children, traveled to Utah in 1848 to settle in Mill Creek. In 1857 he served a mission to Ireland. He died in Salt Lake City in 1876 (Sarah M. Scott Walker, "A Sketch of the Life of John Scott," www.brufordscottreynolds.org).

[34]Younger Green was an associate of William Law. He became a counselor in Law's Church. Nothing else is known of him.

1844[,] from which descision said Brown took an appeal to this council[,] [it was] resolved that this council sustain the descision of the New Orleans Conference against said Samuel C. Brown[.][35]

*June 15, 1844; Saturday.* [The] High Council Met agreeably to adjournment at the Seventies hall on the 15th of June 1844 at 2 oclock P.M. Present William Marks President [and] Councellors Shadrach Roundy[,] James Allread[,] Lewis D. Willson[,] Alpheus Cutler[,] Josiah Smith for George W Harris[,] D[avid] Fullmore[,] Aaron Johnson[,] Edmund Fisher [for] [Thomas] Grover[,] William Huntington[,] Ezra Parrish [for] [Newel] Knight[,] Leonard Sobey[,] [and] Henry G. Sherwood[.]

Case 1st. L[ibeus] T. Coons[36] vs. Joseph Pennock. ~~David M. Gamet~~ S[hadrack] Roundy [was appointed] counsellor for L[ibeus] T. Coons [and] Ja[me]s Allred Councellor for Joseph Pennock. L[ibeus] T. Coons made some introductory remarks upon the charges preferred against Penncok which were Lying, dishonesty, [and] rude contempt. L[ibeus] T. Coons introduced some affidavits which were not received by the Council – David M Gamet, stated that if the branch would give him [(]Joseph Pennock[)] three days time he could bring witnesses to impeach ~~witnesses~~ the Testimony of the two Binghams. The time was granted and at the next meeting Joseph Pennock denied having asked for an adjournment on the account of witnesses.

Daniel E. Loveland states the same things as D[avid] M Gamet. Charles Webb[37] stated that J[oseph] Pennock said he thought he

[35]The minutes are signed by "William Marks[,] President[;] Joseph M. Cole[,] Clerk." See also Donald Q. Cannon and Lyndon W. Cook, eds., *Far West Record: Minutes of the Church of Jesus Christ of Latter-day Saints, 1830-1844* (Salt Lake City: Deseret Book, 1983), 227-28.

[36]Libeus Thaddeus Coons (he went by "LT") was born in 1807 in Plymouth, New York, and was a doctor. He converted to Mormonism early on, in 1832, and participated in Zion's Camp in 1834. The next year, he was called as one of the original members of the First Quorum of Seventy. In Nauvoo he was one of Joseph Smith's body guards. In 1846 he moved to Iowa and helped found the town of Bethlehem (East Plattsmouth) and was the LDS bishop there. In 1854 he immigrated to Utah, where he died in Richfield in 1872 (William O. Lewis III, "Libeus T. (Thaddeus) Coons," www.gapages.com).

[37]Charles Young Webb was born in May 1819 in New York. When he was baptized in 1843, he was living in Iowa, where he was also ordained a

could produce witnesses that would impeach the Binghams, that he [(]Pennock[)] did not deny asking for an adjournment – At this stage of the proceedings[,] for the want of Witnesses and by an agreement of the parties[,] the case was adjourned till Saturday[,] two weeks from today at 2 oclock P.M.[38]

Case 2d. Ethan Pettit[39] vs. Elder David Bennett.[40] For want of certain witnesses the case[,] togeather with the council[,] [is to] be adjourned till next Saturday at ~~2 oclock P.M.~~ June 22d at 2 oclock P.M. J[oseph] M Cole[,] Cl[er]k[41]

‡‡*August 31, 1844; Saturday.*[42] The High Council met this 31st day of Aug[us]t 1844 agreeably to adjournment. Present[:] President William Marks, [Samuel] Bent, [Newel] Knight[,] [and] [Leonard] Soby. [A] Charge [had been] presented June 1 [18]44 against Elder David Bennet of Nashville[,] Lee Co[unty][,][43] I[owa] T[erritory][,] [and]

---

Seventy. In 1846 his first of three plural wives was a seventeen-year-old girl, while he was twenty-seven. Later that year, his first wife died, although he was already on his way to Mexico with the Mormon Battalion. After the war, he settled in southern Utah in 1850, where his remaining three wives bore him some thirteen children from 1851 to 1870. His fourth wife was fifteen years old when they married and he was thirty-six. He seems to have died in October 1900 in Tennessee ("Spickler and Rockwood Genealogy," *Rootsweb*, www.ancestry.com).

[38]The next time the case is mentioned is on April 19, 1845, when the scribe recorded that the parties resolved the disagreement privately and withdrew the charge.

[39]Ethan Petit was born in February 1810 on Long Island. Baptized in 1840, and having lived in Nauvoo for six years, the Church leaders asked him to travel to the southern states to assist the members preparing to travel west. He died in 1884 in Salt Lake City.

[40]David Bennett was born in 1801 in New York and was baptized in 1832. He was present during the Missouri troubles and was beaten up in Jackson County in 1832; he was also present at the Haun's Mill Massacre. He immigrated to Utah in 1850 and died at Mt. Pleasant three years later.

[41]See Cannon and Cook, *Far West Record,* 229-30.

[42]This is the first meeting of the high council after the murders of Joseph and Hyrum Smith on June 27.

[43]The original complaint was for "unchristian like conduct in not complying with his contract which he had previously sworn to do verry much to the damage of the complainant[.] 2nd for shewing his utter contempt to the council of Brethren which were selected and put on oath to settle the difficulty between them[,] such Bret[h]ern being selected by himself

was this day brought forward when William J. Bennet stated that in a difficulty between Elder David Bennet and Ethan Pettet the two chose Referees to settle their difficulties[.] [He] said [the] Refferees were William J. Bennet,[44] Moses Martin, William Vannosdale, Cyrus H Wheelock[,][45] and James Whaley[,] who [had] proceeded to investigate their difficulties and found that David Bennet was indebted to Ethan Pettet two hundred and some odd dollars.

The said refferees then proceeded ~~and~~ ^to^ appraise the property of said Bennet as had been agreed by the parties, where there was a difference in opinions of the Refferees ~~at that time~~, ^about the price of property^. It was unanimously postponed for that time, but a part of said refferees feeling themselves bound to appraise said property by the Oath they had taken before a Magistrate notified the others to meet for that purpose at a certain time when three of them met accordingly and appraised the same and rendered their report of the same, as presented to the honorable High Council. [The] said Report was shown to said D[avid] Bennet who said that it was all illegal and that he would have nothing to do with it – he would not even hear the report[,] [according to] W[illia]m J. Bennett.

The three appraisers were James Whaley[,] C[yrus] H Wheelock[,] and W[illia]m J. Bennet. Moses Martin stated [his approval] as regards [to] the proceedings[,] [even though he acknowledged] dif-

---

and the complainant[.] Third for using abusive and unbecoming language accompanied with threats and imprecations" (Nauvoo High Council Court Papers, *Selected Collections*, 1:19).

[44]William J. Bennett was born in 1790 in Prince Edward, Virginia. His family moved to Tennessee, then left the South to farm in Shelbyville, Illinois, in 1829. In 1831 he heard Hyrum Smith and William McLellin preach and was convinced by their message. He was baptized in 1835; his wife was baptized four years later, upon which they moved to Nauvoo and were initiated into the Church's temple rites in February 1846. Although they headed west with the rest of the Saints, William was murdered on the banks of the Des Moines River in Iowa on October 30. The reason is unknown. His family continued to Utah in 1851 and settled in Payson.

[45]Cyrus Hubbard Wheelock was born in February 1813 in Henderson, New York, and was baptized in 1839. He famously smuggled a six-shooter pistol to Joseph Smith in jail in Carthage in 1844, which Joseph used to defend himself the day he was murdered. The Wheelocks immigrated to Utah in 1853 and settled in Sanpete County, where he wrote the hymn "Ye Elders of Israel." Wheelock served missions to Vermont, England, and the Midwest. He died in Mt. Pleasant in October 1894.

ferences [in the] debt [owed] from Bennet to Petet[t][,] the same stating the precise debt to be $228.50 cents but [that he] differs from W[illiam] J Bennet by saying the refferees agreed to disagree at the first time of attempting to appraise D[avid] Bennet's property and signed a verdict to that effect – and do not know of a postponment for another appraisal[,] [according to] Moses Martin.

*September 7, 1844; Saturday.* [The] High Council [met] Sep[tember] 7 1844. E[lde]r S[amuel] Bent offered a motion that all withdraw except the Councilors after which E[lde]r Bent called upon E[lde]r [William] Huntington to state the business. E[lde]r W[illiam] Huntington said the business he had was that he felt to make an objection to bro[ther] [Leonard] Soby's sitting as councillor in consequence of his saying that [Sidney] Rigdon was president.[46]

E[lde]r Soby said it was like a thunderstorm to him. He wondered why bro[ther] [William] Clayton[47] was invited this morning and now why he should be appointed clerk. He would like to know what you mean. ["]Has there been any charges brought against me – Am I to be cut off contrary to the practice[?] I challenge this council to show where I have committed an immoral act. What have I done that I should be treated this way[?] I don't want to commit myself [to secrecy] – [You say] I must be made a sacrifice [to] all in secret – [to a policy] concocted in secret[.] If you feel disposed to sacrifice me – if you feel disposed to reject me, do it.["]

E[lde]r Bent said he was aware that bro[ther] Huntington was

---

[46]Soby thought that as a surviving member of the First Presidency, Rigdon held authority superior to that of the high council and that he could not be judged by it. This rankled some of the high councilmen. In the context of the tussle for leadership, with the Quorum of Twelve stepping forward to claim preeminence, the high council thought Soby's position was at least undiplomatic.

[47]William Clayton was born in Penwortham, England, in 1814. He was one of the first Mormon converts in England in 1837. The very next year, he was named to the mission presidency. He immigrated to America in 1840 and settled in Nauvoo to become a secretary to Joseph Smith, Nauvoo City treasurer, and temple recorder. He was one of the pioneer company that arrived in the Salt Lake Valley in 1847; he also invented the wagon odometer to measure the daily mileage. He had ten wives. As a lyricist, he is best remembered for his words to "Come, Come, Ye Saints." He died in Salt Lake City in 1879 ("Biographical Registers," *BYU Studies,* byustudies.byu.edu).

going to reject bro[ther] Soby and thats why he wished the council alone. It was out of regard to his feeling. The brethren thought it was best to be alone. E[lde]r Soby again replied that his objections was not against [what] the brethren put out[,] but against bro[ther] Clayton being called in to be clerk. ["]Has any brother come to labor with me[?] I have no objections to [an] investigation. All I want is [that] the same measure I have measured to others should be measured unto me[,] and [with] the measure you mete to me[,] [you] shall be measured[,] [the same] to you. I say it in the name of the Lord Jesus.["]

Pres[ident] [Charles C.] Rich said that he considered this move to be a course designed to save brother Soby and not destroy him. Bro[ther] Huntington had objections and this is the place where it should be investigated while we are by ourselves. There has been no feelings but to save each other and we should not suffer prejudice to rise in our hearts. If there is any thing wrong it is our privilege to have it investigated. As to bro[ther] Clayton being here for clerk it was voted by the Council.

Bro[ther] Huntington said he had talked on the subject with bro[ther] Soby and he said that when he had talked in secret his language had been misconstrued. It is a time of great interest to the church[.] There are many [claimants] rising up and calling [us] up. It is ["]lo here & lo there["] [in] no less than five branches – I have found that your house is a house of resort for Pres[ident] Rigdon – I dont think it is right. I think Pres[ident] Rigdons course is got up by the devil. ~~and~~ No man on earth[,] I believe[,] has any idea of killing Pres[ident] [William] Marks. Your house is a place of resort for those who are seeking to uproot the kingdom. I have good feeling towards you so far as you go right. The authority is in the twelve.[48]

E[lde]r Soby said there has always been good feelings. ["]A few days ago our private clerk was turned out of the room in a case of more importance than mine. I[t] must be brought up [that in this instance][,] the clerk must write down all I say without a moment warning. Is that christian like[?] Did bro[ther] Huntington advise me

---

48This determination to follow the Twelve had come only within the past month when Brigham Young and Sidney Rigdon alternately spoke to a Church gathering, stating their respective claims to be the rightful successor to Joseph Smith (Richard S. Van Wagoner, "The Making of a Mormon Myth: The 1844 Transfiguration of Brigham Young," *Dialogue: A Journal of Mormon Thought* 28 [Winter 1995]: 1-24).

[of what to expect?] – I thought so little of our discourse I have not thought of it. The remarks I ~~then~~ made ^in this upper room^ are as firm now as they was then.[49] I said I believed E[lde]r Rigdon was the man, I still believe it – Why was I not cut off then[?] Bro[ther] Bent could ha[ve] as easily consulted me as to bring bro[ther] W[illia]m Clayton to write down all I say.[50] It seems to be for my destruction – I dont want to injure this place, the twelve or any man – I have not had a bad heart – I prayed and got the highest degree of evidence I could – Bro[ther] Hyrum [Smith] told me I was not to blame. Bro[ther] Joseph [Smith] did not curse me as has been supposed. Why not give me another week to give me a chance to act my feelings out[?] – I have not expressed my feelings untill within a day or two.["]

E[lde]r Bent said to bro[ther] Soby[:] ["]This is the place where we should express our feelings["] – He asked bro[ther] Soby to tell his feelings about E[lde]r Rigdon – Soby said he did not want to be judged in haste[.] ["]Dont ask me questions here to condemn myself.["] E[lde]r Bent said he was willing that S[oby] should have time. The question he wanted to ask was, did he acknowledge E[lde]r Rigdon to preside or the Twelve[?]

E[lde]r G[eorge] W Harris moved that the charges be written out and presented for trial at a future meeting. This was objected to by several. S[oby] said he would not answer any questions to day. E[lde]r [Alpheus] Cutler said the charges can be made out in a few minutes. Soby has took a course for his own injury. Had the other clerk been here he would have been rejected. This charge is brought up by the authority of the Twelve, and if brother Soby is not with the Twelve he is no longer a counseller here. E[lde]r Rigdon has no authority to lead this church.

---

[49]Soby is probably referring to an altercation involving Orson Hyde, Brigham Young, Sidney Rigdon, and himself on September 3, 1844, when Young and Hyde questioned Rigdon and Soby about meetings in which they had ordained individuals "prophets, priests, and kings." See Richard Van Wagoner, *Sidney Rigdon: A Portrait of Religious Excess* (Salt Lake City: Signature Books, 1994), 354.

[50]William Clayton misdates the meeting to September 6 and says nothing about the fact that he was brought in behind Soby's back, saying only that Sobey "spouted hard" when questioned (George D. Smith, ed., *An Intimate Chronicle: The Journals of William Clayton* [Salt Lake City: Signature Books, 1991], 148.)

E[lde]r [Henry G.] Sherwood said brother Sobys objection to the clerk was of no use [because] at the time he refers to we had no need of a clerk. Another objection [was] at the time we had a private council – he says he had the same feelings and [asked] why did we not cut him off then – It would have been moonshine[51] untill there was a proper organization. He referred to Sobys objections against the clerk. ["]The position you have taken[,] bro[ther] Soby[,] has gone against you – And I have objections to setting in Council with you untill this is settled – We set in council to judge of matters in the Church and I want all to be in the same faith. I think bro[ther] Soby is disqualified from being a counciller["] –

E[lde]r Soby said he had no man to defend him. ["]I can answer his objections – but there is no one to defend me. Has there been no defence in other cases[?] This thing has been concocted by the Twelve – therefore my doom is fixed [and] my die is cast. Who could make a speech without there being some objections[?] You do not expect me to be infallible.["] E[lde]r Marks proposed that he withdraw, but [Thomas] Grover objected untill he had answered certain questions.

E[lde]r Rich said this council[,] if it is any thing[,] it is the council of God to judge matters pertaining to the Kingdom of God. If there are things in the Council which are wrong we are not fit to do business. Bro[ther] Soby has been ordained by E[lde]r Rigdon and is going away and [they] are using an influence against this place[.] We object to holding on to any one who are taking this course. We want to take a course to save ourselves – and this is the reason why we want bro[ther] Soby to come out and answer the charges.

Soby said he felt sorry that he should cause this body to be so impure – He came to this place and would not enter into any traffick with men [in a way that would compromise his principles][,] that he might keep himself pure. ["]If I err it is in doctrine – I have not made bogus[52] or committed adultery[,] but because I err in doctrine I must be given to the buffetings of Satan. I am in your hands – do with me as you please. The Quorum of the Twelve have made a decision against me (corrected)[.] The intimation is strong. Will you destroy

---

[51]The word "moonshine," in the context used above, meant "a matter of no consequence or of indifference" (Noah Webster, *American Dictionary of the English Language* [New York: S. Converse, 1828], s.v. "moonshine").

[52]That is, counterfeit money.

me[?] I am an innocent man before God. Because I esteem that man and you do not[,] am I to be sacrificed[?] – I believe this to be the High Council of God and I am one of its members. I stand high in authority and must not have the chance of a common member. I hold this is the council of God but we may make a wrong decision.["]

Bro[ther] Grover called upon the chair for order – & insisted that bro[ther] Soby shall answer questions. Bro[ther] [David] Fullmer said this is a meeting of inquiry – Bro[ther] Grover said the council has been insulted forty times and the chairman has taken no notice of it. [Soby] admitted that this was the High Council of God – And if he will not answer questions it is the option of the church to cut him off.

E[lde]r Cutler said, ["]This council is resolved not to sit in council to try our fellow men[,] [with] one of us following one and another following another. We have decreed never to turn [our] back upon the Twelve and when a man does it I will not fellowship with him. Nobody acused you of adultery or bogus making. There is no compulsions but you cant travail the road you have done and I [remain on the same] council with you. When we see you running astray we shall not come to you to know if we shall have a clerk.["]

Soby said[:] ["]It seems this council has been a merciful council[,] but not so with me. What if I have gone astray[?] – Am I not to be heard[?] It will be your turn sometime. I never had any difficulty with those brethren, and that I should be treated so. Go [after] it[,] go [after] it[,] go [after] it with a rush, [but] I am innocent[.] [Even so][,] there is no use keeping me here.["]

E[lde]r Harris renewed his motion which was again objected to[.] E[lde]r Harris still thought he ought to have till Monday or Tuesday. E[lde]r Grover said he should have any time only now. ["]E[lde]r Rigdon has been here for three or four weeks.[53] I ha[ve] known that this council did not believe Sidneys revelations except he and bro[ther] Marks – He has been initiated into some high rank – deep in Rigdons instructions.["][54]

---

[53]Rigdon had been sent to Pittsburgh by Joseph Smith to establish residency in another state since he was Smith's running mate for the U.S. presidency, also to build up the Church there. He had not run away, as Brigham Young and others insinuated. Like the Twelve, who were also away at the time, Rigdon rushed back to Nauvoo when he heard of the assassinations (Van Wagoner, "Making of a Mormon Myth," 3-4).

[54]According to *History of Church,* 7:268, by the time the meeting had

*September 8, 1844; Sunday.*[55] [The] Congregation[56] [was] brought to order by Brigham Young at ¼ past ten oclock[.] After singing[57] & prayer by Elder Orson Hyde, Br[other] Young said[:]

> I will now call upon the congregation [and] will attend to the subject which is now before us. Police.[58] I will now lay before the congregation [the issue as] well [as I can]. Some are for Paul, some for Cephas, and there are a great many for Christ; & I will now Say

---

adjourned, "Leonard Soby was disfellowshipped by the high council for following Elder [Sidney] Rigdon." A few days beforehand, Clayton had written regarding those in sympathy with Ridgon: "Every one of his followers as far as I can learn are ordained prophets and immediately receive the same spirit Elder Rigdon is of. In the evening the Twelve and a few others of us met at Elder Youngs and offered up prayers for our preservation and the preservation of the church, and that the Lord would bind up the dissenters that they may not have power to injure the honest in heart." See also Smith, *An Intimate Chronicle*, 148.

55See *History of Church,* 7:268-69 and transcription in D. Michael Quinn Papers, Special Collections, Beinecke Rare Book and Manuscript Library, Yale University, New Haven, Connecticut.

56This session of the High Council was convened at the meeting ground in Nauvoo to allow spectators to observe the consideration of charges against Sidney Rigdon. Although it is nominally considered to be a high council meeting, the members of the Quorum of the Twelve present take over and conduct the meeting and offer the testimony against Rigdon. The members of the Twelve present on the stand are Orson Hyde, Heber C. Kimball, Amasa Lyman, Orson Pratt, Parley P. Pratt, George A. Smith, John Taylor, and Brigham Young. They are accompanied by William Marks, stake president; Charles C. Rich, counselor; and high councilmen James Allred, Samuel Bent, Alpheus Cutler, David Fullmer, Thomas Grover, George W. Harris, Aaron Johnson, Henry G. Sherwood, and Lewis D. Wilson. The three members who were absent were replaced by Ezra T. Benson, Reynolds Cahoon, and Asahel Smith. The proceedings were published as "Trial of Elder Rigdon," *Times and Seasons*, Sept. 15, Oct. 1, 15, 1844, pp. 685-87, 660-67, 685-87.

57The singing was performed by a choir, which sang both before and after Hyde's prayer.

58Young said, "I will first make a request that the police will attend to the instructions given them by the Mayor [Orson Spencer] this morning, and that is, to see that there is perfect order on the outside of the congregation. We are not afraid of disturbance here, but there is generally some disposed to talk on the outside, which prevents those from hearing who are near them, and we wish all to hear what is said from the stand" (*Times and Seasons,* Sept. 15, 1844, 647).

there is some for Bro[ther] Joseph & Hyrum [Smith] & the Book of Mormon & revelations & for the building of the temple & some for [James] Emmet[59] & Some for Sidney Rigdon & there will be some for the Twelve – for I will say now that those who are for Bro[ther] Joseph & Hyrum, the book of Mormon & doctrine & covenants & building up of the temple are for the Twelve [and] this will be considered one party & those that are for Sidney Rigdon [–] I want them to be just as honest as what they are in their Secret Combinations[60] & boldly Manifest the Same when they shall be called upon, also those who are for Lyman Wight[,] let them do likewise.

Now to our organization this morning according to the Book of Doctrine & covenants, with the high council [and] with Bishop [Newel K.] Whitney as their head[,] who is one of the oldest bishops in the church, the high council was organized in Kirkland [Ohio][61] & their are many of them here to day & they can sit in

[59]James Emmett was born in Boone County, Kentucky, in February 1803. He and his wife were baptized in Illinois in 1831. Six years later he was briefly disfellowshipped, but by 1841 he was serving on the Iowa high council. By 1843 he was employed as a Nauvoo policeman and as one of Joseph Smith's twelve body guards. After Joseph Smith's murder in 1844, Emmett led a group of followers to Camp Vermillion in South Dakota. Most of his group eventually migrated down to Utah, but Emmett remained aloof. After settling in California in 1849, he died there in December 1853 (Donald Q. Cannon, Richard O. Cowan, and Arnold K. Garr, *Encyclopedia of Latter-day Saint History* [Salt Lake City: Deseret Book, 2001).

[60]This was a rhetorical slur, "secret combinations" being a Book of Mormon term for criminal alliances. Ironically, any secret meetings in Nauvoo were attended jointly by both Young and Rigdon. They were both members of the Masonic lodge, both members of the Council of Fifty that had crowned Joseph Smith "King, Priest, and Ruler over Israel on the Earth," and both participants in temple ceremonies where individuals had been ordained "kings and priests, queens and priestesses." For the sake of argument, if Rigdon were the rightful heir, he would not need Young's permission any more than Young thought he needed Rigdon's permission to engage in clandestine deliberations and rituals. See Michael W. Homer, "The Mormon Temple Endowment in Nauvoo, Illinois," *Dialogue: A Journal of Mormon Thought* 27 (Fall 1994): 33-34; D. Michael Quinn, *The Mormon Hierarchy: Origins of Power* (Salt Lake City: Signature Books, 1994), 124, 128, 137, 140, 229, 534.

[61]The first stake high council was established in Kirtland, Ohio, on February 17, 1834. It was presided over by a stake presidency consisting of Joseph Smith, Sidney Rigdon, and Frederick G. Williams. Its members were Jared Carter, John S. Carter, Joseph Coe, Oliver Cowdery, Martin Har-

judgement against any of the first presidency.[62] So we this Morning will sit in judgment on the case of Sidney Rigdon. Again[,] he is a Man that I esteem very much indeed for this eleven years past & I have watch[ed] over him with my gun upon my shoulder to guard him from the enemies & he is a man that I do love.

Sidney Rigdon has sent [word] up here to inform us that he is unwell & cannot attend this morning, but I can tell you that they [Rigdon's followers] have had a council this morning already & I dare say he is just as much unwell as I was & that he had plenty of time to send up & let us know if he wished us to defer this case until [the] future & he has not [done so] & I think he has had plenty of time[,] for we gave him notice on Tuesday evening last[63]

---

ris, Orson Hyde, John Johnson, Luke Johnson, John Smith, Joseph Smith Sr., Samuel H. Smith, and Sylvester Smith. Its purpose was "settling important difficulties which might arise in the Church, which could not be settled by the Church or the Bishop's council to the satisfaction of the parties" (*History of Church,* 2:28). In other words, it was a court of last resort.

[62]The Doctrine and Covenants specifies that "inasmuch as a President of the High Priesthood shall transgress, he shall be had in remembrance before the common council of the church, who shall be assisted by twelve counselors of the High Priesthood" (107:82). By citing this, Young seems to acknowledge that Rigdon has retained his position as a member of the First Presidency with authority over all of them. The scripture may remind readers that as originally conceived, there was to have been one high council for the entire Church, commonly referred to as the "standing high council" as opposed to the Quorum of Twelve, which was called the "traveling high council" and was subordinate to the First Presidency.

That hierarchical order will be turned on its head and forever changed after this meeting–something that was perhaps inevitable as a result of Church growth. Already there had been a proliferation of stakes and standing high councils. "The Twelve [Apostles]," Joseph Smith had said at about the time of their creation in 1835, "will have no right to go into Zion, or any of its stakes, and there undertake to regulate the affairs thereof, where there is a standing high council" (*History of Church,* 2:220). For more on this, see Quinn, *Mormon Hierarchy: Origins,* 65; Van Wagoner, *Sidney Rigdon,* 166; Edwin Brown Firmage and Richard Collin Mangrum, *Zion in the Courts: A Legal History of the Church of Jesus Christ of Latter-day Saints, 1830-1900* (Urbana: University of Illinois Press, 1988), 35; Gregory A. Prince, *Power from on High: The Development of Mormon Priesthood* (Salt Lake City: Signature Books, 1995), 48, 61-62; B. H. Roberts, *New Witnesses for God,* 3 vols. (Salt Lake City: LDS Church, 1911), 1:343; James E. Talmage, *The Articles of Faith* (Salt Lake City: LDS Church, 1899), 215.

[63]William Clayton recorded: "Last evening the Twelve and some others met together with Elder Rigdon to investigate his course. He came out

> & we also heard that [Rigdon and others] had a Meeting on the same evening & were ordaining some to be prophets[,] Seers & Revelators & some to [be] Kings & Priests & I asked Elder Orson Hyde if he would go down & see Elder Rigdon & see if it was really the case that such conduct was going on. Accordingly Orson Hyde & myself went down to see Bro[ther] Rigdon & I had to ask many a question before I could [get] any definite answer from him & asked him if it was the case if they had a Meeting & [were] ordaining men to such & such office & he asked Bro[ther] [Leonard] Soby if they had a Meeting last night & they looked at each other & after much ado they said they guessed they had, after which we asked Elder Rigdon if he would wish to have the twelve in council in his house that night.[64]

Orson Hyde [followed Brigham Young with the following remarks]:

> I have not had the opportunity before until this morning [to consider this matter][,] for [I was not available] at the time of the death of the Prophet [Joseph Smith] & Patriarch [Hyrum Smith][,]

---

full against the Twelve and said he would not be controlled by them. They asked him for his license, and he [said if he had to give it up][,] he would ... expose all the works of the secret chambers and all the iniquities of the church. The Twelve withdrew fellowship from him and James Emmett" (Smith, *Intimate Chronicle,* 147-48). George A. Smith recorded that Rigdon "was angry and said he would expose the councillors of the Church and publish all he knew" (Diary, September 3, 1844, LDS Church History Library and Archives).

[64]Historian Andrew Ehat wrote that at the meeting in question, "Sidney said his authority was greater that than of the Twelve. He claimed to have [had] many visions and revelations." By ordaining "prophets, priests, and kings in secret meetings," this "implied [that] he had higher authority than any [other] man in the Church" ("Joseph Smith's Introduction of Temple Ordinances and the 1844 Mormon Succession Question," M.A. thesis, Brigham Young University, 1982, 214-15).

The *Times and Seasons*, Sept. 15, 1844, 649, explained that "eight of the Twelve together with bishop Whitney, went to elder Rigdon's," then met at Willard Richards's house to decide how to proceed. "A committee of three was chosen, who went over and demanded [Rigdon's] license, but he refused to give it up, at the same time saying, 'I did not receive it from you, neither shall I give it up to you.'" They therefore published a notice in the newspaper that they would try him for his membership at the meeting ground on September 8. The Twelve were only to be "witnesses in this trial, and not judges."

[at] which time I was [in the] state of Connecticut & went to Boston where I found Elder Young to get the twelve all together[.] Consequently I sent a letter to Elder Rigdon & John E. Page & requested them to come to Nauvoo & [to be] where slumbered the ashes of our Murdered brethren[,] & we came home as quick as we could & to our astonishment Bro[ther] Rigdon was here after receiving the letter from us, but we saw there was a great anxiety to hurry business & matters in this place.

Now if Bro[ther] Rigdon had got a revelation from his God that he was designated to be the President or guardian of this people[,] I think he would not have been in such a great hurry as to get the business over[,] for it was his desire & intention to get the matters all over & settled before the Twelve came[,] for if these men came here he was sure he would not accomplish his designs. Again there is a quorum here in this place that can test all the revelations before they can go forth to the public according to the order of our beloved Bro[ther] Joseph.[65] Again when Elder Rigdon came to this place[,] did he go to this quorum or call this quorum together & lay before them his revelations that he stated he had rece[ive]d? No! He did no such thing! But he wanted to get all these important subject[s] and matter[s] hurried on & get it settled before the Twelve comes here.

Again we ~~called~~ the Twelve sent & requested Bro[ther] Rigdon to meet us in council but we could never get him to attend our councils. Consequently we went to see him [to ask] of him if he had got any Keys higher than the twelve in authority & he ans[wered] no! He said he had no jurisdiction over us – but[,] said

---

[65] Hyde is referring to the Quorum of the Anointed, or Holy Order, not to the Quorum of the Twelve. In the published account of the trial, this is made clear:

> There is a way by which all revelations purporting to be from God through any man can be tested. Brother Joseph gave us the plan[.] Says he, when all the quorums are assembled and organized in order, let the revelation be presented to the quorums[.] If it pass one[,] let it go to another, and if it pass that, to another, and so on until it has passed all the quorums; and if it pass the whole without running against a snag, you may know it is of God. But if it runs against a snag, then says he, it wants enquiring into: you must see to it. It is known to some who are present that there is a quorum organized where revelation can be tested. Brother Joseph said, let no revelation go to the people until it has been tested [t]here (*Times and Seasons*, Sept. 15, 1844, 649-50).

> he[,] there will be many churches built up, for there will be one here & another there. When Bro[ther] B[righam] Young said to him th[at] it will not be the church of Christ[,] for where there is a Kingdom divided against itself [it] cannot stand, & he claimed no jurisdiction over the twelve.

After which a testimony was read to the congregation but the man did not wish his name to be made know[n][,] but if it is necessary[,] [he said][,] you can call out my name & I will answer to it.[66]

[Then Orson Hyde continued][,] [saying]:] When we asked Elder Rigdon to give up his license he would not do it, because he said he did not get [it] from us. Now for example if I was abroad & saw an Elder in transgression & I requested his licences to be given up, [I would expect to receive it][.] But now[,] said E[lder] Rig[don][,] ["]Since you have done this & demanded my licence I will consider it my duty & [will] publish it in the public prints & there is a scourge &c which awaits this people for I will write the history of this people since they came to Nauvoo of all their iniquity & midnight abominations.["][67] To which Elder Hyde stated ["]I have just got the secrets of your heart & it is all we wanted & I did not have to get at it before but we have all counted the cost and our lives are ready to be laid down for the cause of God, in which we are engaged.["] But Elder Rigdon said ["]as much if you do so[,] I will turn traitor & publish all your iniquities[.]["][68]

---

[66]Presumably in the interest of expediting the process, Hyde read aloud from several prepared testimonies by individuals who were present in the crowd and "ready to testify to the same before the congregation if it [was] necessary." The man who requested anonymity said that Rigdon told him his intent was to "divide the people" and take those who would follow him "and let the remainder follow the Twelve" (ibid., 650).

[67]Rigdon is likely referring to polygamy. Joseph Smith had proposed to Nancy Rigdon, Sidney's nineteen-year-old daughter, in April 1842, and Sidney thought this kind of libertinism was what put Joseph and Hyrum "into the power of their enemies and was the immediate cause of their death[s]" (George D. Smith, *Nauvoo Polygamy: "... But We Called it Celestial Marriage"* (Salt Lake City: Signature Books, 2008), 147-54, 440-41).

[68]In the published version, Hyde said Rigdon later admitted he had been "angry and did not mean" what he said. "But I would ask this congregation," Hyde continued, "can a man say what is not in his heart? I say he cannot." Hyde blamed Rigdon for the Mormon War in Missouri, saying no one had been as provocative than Rigdon when he spoke at Far West

[Elder Hyde continued][:]

For about the space of 2 or 3 months before the martyrdom of our prophet & Pat[riarch] of the church of God[,] when we were in council together[,] [at the time] when Bro[ther] Joseph carried us through all the ordinances of the house of God[,] now says he (Joseph) ["]Upon your shoulders [(]the Twelve[)] the burden of this church rests & you must ~~turn~~ round up your shoulders to the same[,] for the Lord is going to let me rest a little while.["] Again when Joseph Smith was [a] speaker [in our meetings][,] when [he said this repeatedly][,] [why] did he not say Hyrum [?] ["The spirit knew that Hyrum would be taken with him, and hence he did not mention his name; Elder Rigdon's name was not mentioned, although he was here all the time"][.][69]

P[arley] P. Pratt –

I rise up to bear my testimony before the Bishop & the high council[.] I was well acquainted with Bro[ther] Sidney Rigdon before this church was organized & it is now near 15 or 16 years since & I was the man that first carried the tidings of this gospel & I was witness to his coming into this Kingdom[.][70] When I arrived i[n] this place I went to shake hands together with a few others & as he was shaken hands at the same time I said that is just what we wanted & I invited him to attend a council of the few of the twelve

---

on July the Fourth, 1838: "He was the cause of our troubles in Missouri, and although Brother Joseph tried to restrain him, he would take his own course, and if he goes to exposing the secrets of this church, as he says, the world will throw him down and trample him under their feet" (*Times and Seasons*, Sept. 15, 1844, 650). In the speech referred to, Rigdon prophesied that Mormons would "exterminate" their Missouri neighbors ("It shall be between us and them a war of extermination, for we will follow them till the last drop of their blood is spilled or else they will have to exterminate us."). This infuriated Governor Lilburn W. Boggs, who three months later ordered the Mormons to leave or face "extermination" (Heman C. Smith and Joseph Smith III, *History of the Reorganized Church of Jesus Christ of Latter Day Saints*, 4 vols. [Independence, MO: Herald House, 1951], 2:165).

[69]The quoted sentence comes from the *Times and Seasons*, Sept. 15, 1844, 651.

[70]Parley P. Pratt had been a member of Rigdon's Reformed Baptist Congregation in Mentor, Ohio. When Pratt converted to Mormonism in 1830, he sought out Rigdon and introduced him to the Book of Mormon. Rigdon was baptized in November of that year.

that was here in this city at the time to meet at Bro[ther] [John] Taylors as he was lying at the time with his wounds.[71] I called at Elder Rigdon the next Morning at 8 oclock to get him down along with us to reason & council together with the few of the twelve that was here so that we could get each others feelings upon the subject which was before us. But he said he was engaged with some person being in the house at the time & we could not get Elder Rigdon to any of our councils to see what was best to be do[n]e for this people but there seemed to be a great anxiety with him to get matters settled.

[We] consequently called a meeting of the church on Tuesday, when I was determined if it were to be the case I would go up to the stand & close the meeting in the name of the Lord until the twelve would return home[.] This was previous to the Thursday when the Twelve was here. Consequently the meeting was pos[t]poned until Thursday w[h]e[n] [the] business was hurried over & [I] asked Elder Rigdon [if he would not agree] that there was no use of [saying we would be] choosing a President or guardian [next week] & he said [if that was what I thought][,] I was mistake[n] for it was only to be a prayer Meeting & [to] p[o]ur out our souls in supplication to God & consequently I told [this to] the people [who] came enquiring of me ["]Was it to be a business meeting or a prayer meeting[?]["] to which I said that Elder Rigdon said it was to be a prayer meeting & afterwards I heard that he had contradicted himself three differ[en]t times & it was give[n] out on the Sunday ~~following~~ previous by President Marks that Elder Rigdon requested a full meeting of the church on Thursday[—] first for the people to choose their guardian[,] & if it had been so & the twelve [had not] got here, I for one would have come up to the stand & dismiss[ed] the people in the name of the Lord.

Consequent[ly] I was called upon by the rest of the twelve to go down to Elder Rigdon on Tuesday evening concerning ordaining men to such unheard offices in our organization[,] for he neither ordained them unto the quorums of the high Priests or the Seventies, Elders, Priests, Teachers or Deacons, & last Sunday when he was upon the stand he told us he had told all of his revelation[s]

---

[71]John Taylor was with Joseph Smith at his death and was himself shot five times in the jail cell. He was laid up for months as his wounds healed (*History of Church,* 7:104-05). Sometimes the meetings were held in his house to facilitate his attendance.

which he received at Pittsburgh but on Tuesday next we received a great deal more of it.

Now I want the council & the Bishop & the Clerks which is here to take notice of what I am going to say – for I charge him with false revelations & visions & in telling lies in the Name of the Lord! I know it is the case. Now said I to Elder Rigdon[,] that [regarding] the battle of which you prophecy that will take place in Pittsburgh & you at the top, now if the God has sent me in these last days I tell you that this battle will not take place at the place of which you state it will & I oppose it in all shapes & manners.

Elders Orson Hyde, Amasa Lyman & Myself were appointed to go & demand the licence of Elder Rigdon when he began to state what Elder Hyde stated. But there is sum more of the revelations & visions which [he] had in Pittsburgh. [He said he was] sitting laughing at the conduct of the twelve in cutting him off from the church. He said that we were fulfilling the very revelation which he had[,] for it was revealed unto him that the twelve would do what you have done this evening & [he has] been sitting laughing at it to see it fulfilled.

Now you will remember that last Sunday he had nothing but blessings in his head for us, but when Bro[ther] Hyde [s]aid that he had found out the bottom of his heart[,] then Rigdon began to say that he would not publish[,] for to [do so would be to] bring iniquity upon this people. We the twelve have not said go to the prairies of Dieuchiene[72] or like [James] Emmet[t] gather together into secrets chambers & let the temple alone[.] [We have said to] pay [your tithing] & receive your endowments for yourselves & your dead according to the admonition of our beloved prophet Joseph Smith & get that temple finished as soon as possible. Now concerning the revelation of Sidney – it is a peice of lies – hatched up to destroy this people.

O[rson] Hyde said he had got up to relate a story[:] ["]Now in the days of Solomon two women went to bed together & each of them

[72]Prairie du Chien, Wisconsin, is about 200 miles northwest of Nauvoo and sixty miles south of where the Black River, which led to the Church's lumber mills ("pineries"), meets the Mississippi River. At the time, Apostle Lyman Wight and Bishop George Miller were there to investigate whether to establish a Church colony in Wisconsin, but they would soon reject Young outright and take a faction of the Church to Texas (Flanders, *Nauvoo,* 289).

had a child & one of the women lay upon her child & it died[.] ["As soon as she discovered this, she took her own dead child and placed it by the side of the mother of the living child, and took the living child to herself. When the mother of the living child awoke in the morning, ... she found it was not her child."[73]] That [is] the story I wanted to tell.["]

Amasa Lyman[:]

> After the much as has been said already by Bro[ther]s Young, Hyde, & Pratt, & I can say no mor[e] but that it is all true & I may say I have seen most of it with my eyes & heard with my ears. Now we want this people to [be] at [one] in wisdom when they are called upon & state whether they will sustain the Twelve & uphold them or will they follow Sidney Rigdon & choose him for there president & let the Twelve go away some other way. Now what has Elder Rigdon done to build up the church of God within the last four or five years ago[,] while there is some of my brethren [here who] has travelled through all the states & in Europe & away to Palestine[74] while he at the same time he was asleep & while he was awake he would sit in the corner smoking his pip[e] or drinking his liquor. Now this is the man that the god of heave[n] has give[n] this wonderful revelation & not one of the twelve has received it[,] nor President Marks who has been here all the time. Again there is a revelation from Appenoose[75] stateing that Elder Rigdon was to take the charge of this people & John C. Ben[n]ett was to take his (Sidney Rigdon's) place.
>
> Again I have no doubt when the decision of this people is carried to him he will say that he was sitting laughing at the proceedings of the church for it was just fulfilling some more of the revelation which he had in Pittsburgh, that he knew before he came

---

[73]Hyde went on to say, drawing from 1 Kings 3:16-2, that the two mothers went to King Solomon, both claiming the child was theirs, and the king suggested cutting the baby in half to share it equally, at which the true mother forfeited her interest in the child rather than see it sacrificed. "Elder Rigdon says let the child be divided, ... and I believe if the great God would speak from heaven this morning, he would say to the Twelve, you are the mother, (or rather the father) of the living child, and the church shall not be divided" (*Times and Seasons*, Sept. 14, 1844, 654).

[74]Orson Hyde served a short mission to Palestine in 1840 to pray on the Mount of Olives (*History of Church,* 4:454-60).

[75]Appanoose Township, like Nauvoo, was located in Hancock County.

here that the people would reject him & that it would just filfil one important passage in the scripture v[i]z "that the stone which the builders rejected, would become the head of the cor[n]er," to carry out the idea that he was some great one – & no person has ever heard of Sidney Rigdon receiving any revelation this four or five years, but now when he Sidney [is] in a manner cursing God saying that he had suffered too much that he was in Jail & also was poor in Missouri[.] & while at the same time Bro[ther] B[righam] Young did not say anything about being in prison[,] neither did Parley P. Pratt[,] [but] was in [prison a] good while long[e]r than what [Rigdon] was & yet this is the man [Rigdon] that has so much of the spirit & receive[s] revelation & [a] vision which had in it the destruction of the body of the church of Christ[,] & his preaching has been that all along [he was] for a division of this body[.]

He [Lyman] then related [from] 1832 about a revelation he (Sidney) had received & Joseph told him it was from the devil & that he would be give[n] into the hands of the devil to be buffeted [and] demanded his [two] licence[s][,] for said he (Joseph) the less power you have[,] the devil will have the less power over you. He gave up his licence[s] & Bishop Whitney has them to this day (to which Bishop Whitney said that was a fact,) and according to the testimony of his ownself (Sidney Rigdon) that the devil pulled him out of his bed three times by his heels & he was buffetted & tormented by his (Satanic Majesty) the devil for the space of three or four months. Now when we went down & demanded his licence he said he would publish all the history of this people & their iniquities but if it is [to be so][,] [no wonder "he was in a wonderful hurry to bet back to Pittsburgh][.]"[76]

W[illiam] W. Phelps –

It becomes necessary[,] as it is a matter of great consequence[,] [to become] acquainted with all the fact[s][.] Only the last evening we [have seen] the council of the twelve [assemble the relevant evidence]. When I heard that ~~Josep~~ Sidney was coming from Pittsburgh I thought that their was something wrong but [that was] before I [had] read a revelation which I hold now in my hands. I

[76]Lyman added: "Brother Joseph has said at different times, that if elder Rigdon was to lead the church twelve months, he would lead them to the devil. When he attempted to lead the people in Kirtland, it was to lead them to the devil" (*Times and Seasons*, Oct. 1, 1844, 660).

am tolerable acquainted with the revelation – The twelve are the High travelling council & they are the men who comes in next after the first Presidency no matter wither there was two or three presiding. Now w[h]ether will you follow one man or will you follow the twelve whom you the other day choose & to abide by their council[,] [involves this question] again, [which is] what did you all gather together to Zion [for][?] It was to build up a holy city & a temple.

[He] then read a revelation give[n] on the 19th [of] Nov[ember] 1833 concerning Elder Rigdon.[77] [He continued][:]

If I had time[,] I would say some more concerning this Man. I would make a few remarks but enough has been said for I have went to see Sidney & he has told me two different stories.[78] I say then that his revelations that has [been] give[n] upon this stand to this people [are for you to consider][.] I say [this to] anyone that has the spirit of God in them, but that they could judge for themselves[,] for the Lord God said that he would make them Ju[d]ges in the last days. I want to know if there is any person here to day that will [follow Sidney Rigdon and thus] barter & give away that which they have received & go down to perdition where there is weeping & wailing & gnashing of teeth where they shall be given up to the Judge [of perdition].

H[eber] C. Kimball.

I have set here & heard my brethren speak & [can say] that I have been in their councils & [know] what they have stated is correct[,]

[77]The revelation, which is addressed to "Brother Sidney," says Rigdon is "like unto an ass" and that in order to learn "his master's will," he needs "the stroke of the rod." Although it predicts that Rigdon will eventually be lifted "up out of deep mire," it does not leave an entirely positive impression (Dean C. Jessee, Mark Ashurst-McGee, and Richard L. Jensen, *The Joseph Smith Papers: Journals* [Salt Lake City: Church Historian's Press, 2008], 1:19).

[78]These "two stories" were that Rigdon "said he wanted to form an intimacy with the Twelve, but he has never taken one step to do it, but has in every instance endeavored to shun them. The devil has blinded his eyes, and he has endeavored to blind the minds of the people against those revelations that have been our guide since we came into this church" (*Times and Seasons*, Oct. 1, 1844, 663).

[and] although I was not among the three of the committee that went to see Elder Rigdon[,] but I was with them both before & after & he has been in but few councils for this three years aback only when brother ~~brother~~ Phelps brought him to the council this spring. I know all the ordinances that he received on his head & I know what we ~~I~~ have received. You all remember that when there were some thousands gathered together when Joseph threw him off his shoulders & would not have him any more as his councillor but he said if you (the Church) will have him you may, but I never will, but Hyrum said [we should] have a little mercy upon him to which Bro[ther] Joseph replied ["]if you will have him you take him upon your own responsibility for I never will["] & here is the man [(]pointing to Amasa Lyman[)] who was ordained & [was to be] put in the place of Sidney Rigdon as councillor to Joseph.[79]

---

[79]A significant portion of Kimball's remarks were omitted from the minutes. They are important, both in their criticisms of Rigdon and his followers and in addressing Rigdon's diminished relationship with Joseph Smith:

> Elder Rigdon is a man I have always respected as a man, but I have not respected his course for more than five years past. – Brethren, I have known his course and was aware of it all the while. When I have gone abroad to preach and have returned again, I would not have the privilege of sleeping, before Brother Joseph would call us to council; and there is not a thing of importance which was ever done, but Brother Joseph counselled with us. Elder Rigdon after he came from Pittsburgh never attended council only when he could not avoid it.
>
> He has no authority only what he receives from the church. If he was one with us, why was he not in our councils? He was not in the council pertaining to the High Priesthood until just before he started for Pittsburgh. Brother Phelps was the means of bringing him in, but he has not got the same authority as others; there are more than thirty men who have got [second anointings and have] higher authority than he has. Elder Rigdon has intimated that if we opposed him we should have a mob on us. – Brethren, if I have to be martyred for the truth, amen to it! If I have to go as Joseph and Hyrum did, it will be a short work.
>
> Elder Rigdon has not been in good standing as a counsellor to Brother Joseph for some years. Brother Joseph shook him off at the conference a year ago, he said he would carry him no more; if the church wanted to carry him they might, but he [Joseph] should not. Joseph said, he [Rigdon] had no more authority in his office as counsellor. Elder Amasa Lyman was appointed in his stead, and all the power and authority and blessings which Elder Rigdon ever had, was put on the head of Brother Amasa. Brother Hyrum plead to have

B[other] Brigham Young –

Now if Bro[ther] Sidney Rigdon will publish our iniquities[,] we will publish his[.] [And] what is his [but] the revelations & visions in a secret chamber in Pittsburgh[?] But he will just be like John C. Ben[n]ett [and] others who have left this church, he will just publish li[e]s, for if he has the keys of conquest & [there is] still iniquity going on & [he does] not publish & purge & cast it away, [it would be a sin][.] I wonder who is here that has seen men make bogus money or any of my brethren [of] the twelve or in passing counterfeit money, & if I could believe what the prophet said[,] [that] the spirit[,] power & authority [that] was taken from Elder Rigdon was conferred upon Amasa Lyman[,] he is here & he is not making any great fuss, but he is at our side & is as one with us [with] heart in hand & I likewise requested Elder Rigdon to be as one with us.

[Brigham Young] then read some testimonies [against those who were associating with Rigdon] & gave these individuals into the hands of the devil to be buffetted – which was sanctioned by the congregation with a hearty Amen.[80]

---

Elder Rigdon restored, he said try him a little longer, try him another year; Brother Joseph would not receive him again but shook him off.

The church voted to try him again, and it was the church that received him and not Brother Joseph. If Elder Rigdon was in good standing, why has he not been with Bro[ther] Joseph in all his councils. He has not acted as a councillor in Bro[ther] Joseph's councils for five years, but the Twelve have, they have never forsaken him. Now when Bro[ther] Joseph is gone, he [Rigdon] comes and sets us aside. I have handled with my hands, and have heard with my ears, the things of eternal reality, but I never betrayed Bro[ther] Joseph.

Brethren, as it was in the days of Moses, so it is now. When Moses went into the Holy of Holies, he pulled off his shoes; Bro[ther] Joseph has passed behind the vail and he pulled off his shoes, and some one else puts them on, until he passes [beyond] the vail to Bro[ther] Joseph. President Young is our president, and our head, and he puts the shoes on first. If Brother Hyrum had remained here, he would have put them on – Hyrum is gone with Joseph and is still his counsellor. The Twelve have received the keys of the kingdom and as long as there is one of them left, he [Smith] will hold them in preference to any one else. I wish the people would hear and be wise, and those who have been upholding Brother Sidney, would turn about before they go into everlasting despair (ibid., 663-64).

[80]Young's published remarks were more colorful and mocking than

[Nauvoo Stake] President [William] Marks[:]

I feel disposed to speak in favor of Elder Rigdon & I will take up the opposite side & I have always been a friend to Elder Rigdon & I suppose there is many here that loves him too & it has been a long time since I have been [asked to defend someone as] the president of the [high] council & I feel for a few moments to take his side[.] I do [not] wish to do what is wrong. Nor I do not wish to uphold any lies or [be involved] in any thing that is wrong – but I will endeavor to do justice to him. There has been many [faults] & a great many crimes that has been alleged against that man [in the past] & as there are many of you here today [who] know that none of the charges were [ever] sustained against him & if there was no [additional] charges against him [than] that[,] that there was no use of bringing the[m] up again at this time but [we should only] bring up the charges preferred against him at the present time.[81]

---

the summary in the minutes, making William Marks's defense of Rigdon all the more courageous:

> Brother Sidney says, "if we go to opposing him he will tell all of our secrets!" but I would say, oh dont, Brother Sidney! dont tell our secrets, oh dont! But if he tells of our secrets, we will tell of his – tit for tat. He has had long visions in Pittsburgh revealing to him wonderful iniquity amongst the saints. Now, if he knows of so much iniquity, and has got such wonderful power, why dont he purge it out? He professes to have got "the keys of David." Wonderful power, and revelations, and he will publish our iniquity! Oh dear, Brother Sidney, dont publish our iniquity! Now dont! John C. Bennett said in his exposure, he knew all of Brother Joseph's secrets, and he would publish them. Joseph H. Jackson, says he has published all Joseph's secrets, but nobody believes their tales, because they lie! And if Sidney Rigdon undertakes to publish all of our secrets, as he says, he will lie the first jump he takes. If Sidney Rigdon knew of all this iniquity why did he not publish it sooner?
>
> If there is so much iniquity in this church, as you talk of, Elder Rigdon, and you have known of it so long, you are a black hearted wretch because you have not published it sooner. If there is not this iniquity you talk of, you are a blackhearted wretch, for endeavoring to bring a mob upon us and murder innocent men, women and children! Any man that says the Twelve are bogus makers, or adulterers, or wicked men, is a liar; and all who say such things shall have the fate of liars, where there is weeping and gnashing of teeth. Who is there that has seen us do such things? No man (ibid., 664).

[81]Rigdon had previously been accused of corresponding with "John C. Bennett, with Ex-Governor Carlin, and with the Missourians" and of dem-

I have heard Joseph [Smith] Say a short time before [Sidney] left to go to Pittsburgh that Sidney was all right & that he had nothing against [h]im & that he had blessed him & that he was going to Pittsburgh to build up a Kingdom unto himself. Again Sister Emma [Smith] at the same time had peculiar feelings against Sidney Rigdon but afterwards confessed that she had no hard feelings against him. The twelve know & the high council know that this quorum should [n]ever be laid down & thrown away. Again I have laid on hands myself along with Joseph Smith some where about Two years ago & that at the time he (Sidney) was ordained to be a prophet, seer translator & revelator & if he held that power & authority at that time he still holds the same for I have [no reason to suspect][,] nor do [I] know[,] that he is guilty of any crimes, & th[erefore] he should still remain as a member of this council.[82]

I have searched diligent & if I know I am honest before God[,] [then I know] that there should always be a first presidency over this people (This is My idea) to receive revelations through Joseph & from him to this people & to lead the Church. If I am right[,] I feel that this quorum (the first presidency) should continue[,] but if I a[m] wrong I wish to be corrected – The idea [about] the twelve[,] that I had had concerning them[,] was [that they were] to be the travelling high council to go to all the Nations of the earth & to build up the Kingdom [in] all the wor[l]d, & it is my opi[ni]on that if this is to be done I think it is enough for twelve men to do.

---

onstrating "a treacherous character" in "endeavoring to defraud the innocent" (*Times and Seasons,* Sept. 15, 1843, 329-30). The new accusations were that he had prophesied that the temple would never be built, that Nauvoo would be overthrown, and that God would reject the Saints. In addition, the Twelve were unhappy that he, as someone who had not yet received his second anointing, was administering the temple endowment (Van Wagoner, *Sidney Rigdon,* 352-55).

[82]Marks added: "As respects his not presenting his vision or revelation before the first quorum [Quorum of the Anointed], I can say, that Elder Rigdon did not know that this order was introduced. Brother Joseph told us that he, for the future whenever there was a revelation to be presented to the church[,] he should first present it to that quorum, and then if it passed the first quorum, it should be presented to the church. But Brother Rigdon did not know this, for he was only just brought into the quorum before he left to go to Pittsburg" (*Times and Seasons,* Oct. 1, 1844, 665). Rigdon received his endowment on May 11, 1844 (Devery S. Anderson and Gary James Bergera, *Joseph Smith's Quorum of the Anointed, 1842-1845: A Documentary History* [Salt Lake City: Signature Books, 2005], xxxix-xliii).

I have had a long acquaintance[83] with Bro[ther] Sidney & if the congregation feels to sever him from the body I am will[ing] to go by the Majority of the church[.] I feel to go with it, but perhaps through a long acquaintance my mind may be prejudiced against [this], but I may be wrong for I am unqualified to say that he is guilty of any crimes & if he is guilty I do not know, & I do not know of any other man this day that has the same power to receive revelations as Sidney Rigdon[,] as he has been ordained to be a prophet unto this people, & if he is cut off from the body this day I wish to see the man if there is any that has the same power as he (Elder Rigdon).[84]

Bro[ther] Young said that[:]

Sidney had done as much [as was needed to show his unworthiness] when he arrived from Missouri[;] he had done as much as would sever any man from the priesthood[,] for he said that Jesus Christ[,] that [t]he [man] Jesus[,] was a blamed fool & that he [Sidney] would not go to hell if all the people would go to hell along with [him] & that he would have the riches of the earth & when he came here he wanted to go back to Kirkland where the[re] was fine rods & plent[y] of peaches & apples & the reason why he was ordained to be a prophet & seer was in consequence of his continually whining [about his "sufferings"] & it was to save him if possible & keep here in Nauvoo & Bro[ther] Hyrum plead mightily on his (Sydney['s]) behalf that Joseph would try him once more ["bless him – hold on to him, for I believe he will yet straighten out"], & when he went away to Pittsburg Joseph blessed him, but what was it for, it was to see if he would do good, but has he done any good[?] No! and they have prophecied that the temple will [not] be finished & that this church will go to the devil.[85]

---

[83]The minutes repeat the words "I have had," deleted here.

[84]Marks also commented that "men [have] been ordained prophets, priests, and kings, but I have never heard of any one being ordained a seer and revelator, ... and if he is cut off, who will we have to obtain revelations? ... If there is a man ordained to lead this people, I do not know it. I dont believe there are sufficient revelations given to lead this people, and I am fully of the belief that this people cannot build up the kingdom except it is done by revelation" (*Times and Seasons*, Oct. 1, 1844, 666).

[85]The bracketed items in quote marks are from the published version. Brigham Young predicted that if the high council retained Rigdon, "you

Bro[ther] John Taylor[:]

I wish to say a few more words as my testimony & that there has been as much said against him ~~that~~ so as to criminate. I know that the twelve are his friends & they have solicited h[im] (Sydney) to unite & be with the twelve & to hold & build up the Kingdom of God, but has he, No! & has he fulfilled the Mission he got from Joseph to go to Pittsburgh & to take no other person with him[?] No! But he has held secret meetings & [has been] ordaining men to the offices of Prophets, Priests & Kings, illegal[ly] and without authority, & yet at the same time while he himself does not hold the office of a Prophet, Priest, or King,[86] & ~~can~~ is it reasonable that a Priest can ordain an Elder & an Elder an High Preist, No! & he is in possession of the same spirit which hurled the devil & those who we[r]e with him from heave[n] down to perdition[.] This is an important subject[,] this[,] & there cannot be enough said about it. I will tell you whom I look upon as the murder[er] of Joseph & Hyrum. I do not hold the men who loaded & fired the guns & killed the prophet & patriarch as much [responsible] as those who were the instigators, never the less they are Murderers but I blame W[illia]m & Wilson Laws, the [Robert D. and Charles] Fosters & [Chauncey and Francis M.] Higbees as the Murderers [o]f Joseph & Hyrum Smith, having said so much upon this subject I feel satisfied.

O[rson] Hyde.

I would say to this people that Bro[ther] Marks said [he did not know] if there was any one ordained to the office of a Prophet[.] I would say to this people that when Joseph [was "in one of their councils," he "told the Twelve that he had given them all the keys and ordinances which had been committed to him"].[87]

---

will soon have John C. Bennett here, with the Laws and Fosters and all the murderous clan." Rigdon was "liable to be deceived, and has already been deceived" (ibid., 666-67).

[86]Although Rigdon had been endowed, he had not received the so-called "fullness of the priesthood." The second anointing "would have made Rigdon a prophet, priest, king, and god in the flesh." The reluctance to advance Rigdon, according to historian Richard Van Wagoner, was "probably because Smith could not win him over to polygamy" (*Sidney Rigdon*, 353).

[87]The bracketed words in quotation marks come from the published version of the trial. At this point, the congregation called for the matter to

Bishop [Newell K.] Whitney.

> I call the attention of the high council & as I could give a history of Bro[ther] Rigdon for about the last twenty years past[,] I de[em] it unnecessary & [will say] that I have been acquainted with him & I tell you I never put much confidence in his revelations[,] for I have heard Bro[ther] Joseph ~~say unto~~ rebuke him time & time again for speaking in the name of the Lord & [it] has been stated Joseph took him in council along with four others & told him to give up his licences for he would go into the hands of Satan & he [Satan] will handle you as one does another. I feel that Elder Rigdon came here with a bad spirit & as he calls it a Revelation & think[s] that the less we have to do with the source from when it came[,] the less we have to do with it[,] the better, & I think that he wants to scatter this people & [is planning on] taking them away from this place instead of a gathering & [is not planning on] building up the house of our God & he has preached lies here on the stand[,] for what he preached here the first day & [in] another [sermon] the second day [was false][,] & I feel to sustain the twelve in taking fellowship from him & I feel to do so [now] & if this meets the decision of this council let them signify the same by standing up.

[It was] moved by Elder Phelps that Sydney Rigdon be cut off from the Church & delivered over to the buffettings of Satan until he repents. It has now passed the high council unanimously. Then it was proposed to the congregation & seconded when it was carried unanimously as above. [It was] motioned by Elder Phelps that all those who hold up their hands to support [Sidney] Rigdon as Prophet & Revelator to this people be withdraw[n] from fellowship until they be tried before the high council.[88]

[It was] motioned by O[rson] Hyde & second by Elder Phelps that fellowship be withdraw[n] [from Samuel James] until he makes full sat-

be settled, and "President Young without further ceremony submitted the case to Bishop Whitney and the High Council" (*Times and Seasons,* Oct. 15, 1844, 686).

[88]The published version mentions that before the congregation voted, "President Young arose and requested the congregation to place themselves so that they could see all who voted. We want to know who goes for Sidney and who are for the Twelve." After the vote, "Elder Young arose and," for good measure, "delivered Sidney Rigdon over to the buffetings of Satan, in the name of the Lord, and all the people said, amen" (ibid.).

isfaction to this people.[89] [It was] motioned & seconded that whereas Jared Carter[90] had gon[e] from this place without council ["on some mission, contrary to council, under the new revelation"][91][,] that he [be informed] we [are] withdrawing [fellowship] from him until he return & make satisfaction. [It was] motioned by Amasa Lyman & seconded that Samuel Bennet[92] be cut off from the church ["for having received a false ordination"]. [It was] also motioned & sec[onde]d that Bro[ther] Soby be cut off from the church ["for the same cause"].[93]

---

[89]After the vote to excommunicate Rigdon, there followed a series of suggestions to summarily excommunicate other members by simple acclamation. Hyde wanted James Emmett and Zachariah Wilson to be removed from the rolls "until they repent," but "at the request of Elder Young the motion was withdrawn." It was not yet certain whether Emmett was a rival to Young, although notice from note 63 that William Clayton thought the Twelve had already disfranchised Emmett. In any case, things would not go so well for Samuel James, whom Hyde said had been asked by Young to preach a funeral sermon, and what he preached was "any thing but a funeral sermon." When he was through with the eulogy, Hyde said, he added that if Brigham Young wanted something better, "he might preach it himself." It was therefore "moved that Samuel James be disfellowshipped from the church. The vote was unanimous" (ibid., 686-87).

[90]Jared Carter was born in Benson, Vermont, in June 1801. He was baptized in 1831 and moved to Ohio, where he was ordained a priest and demonstrated a healing gift. He served a mission to the eastern states. On his return, he was named to the Kirtland High Council. After moving to Missouri, he served on the Far West High Council, where he also participated in the assaults on neighbors by the Danites. He became disaffected in Nauvoo when Joseph Smith prevented him from taking a plural wife. In September 1846 Carter joined William Marks in escorting the Smith family north on a steamboat to Fulton to wait until it was safe enough to return to Nauvoo. Carter then traveled on to Chicago and died three years later in July 1849 in DeKalb, west of Chicago.

[91]The quoted words in brackets come from the published version in the *Times and Seasons*, Oct. 15, 1844, 687. Originally, members were encouraged to act on personal revelation. "If ye have desires to serve God, ye are called to work," the revelation stated (D&C 4:3). But by the Nauvoo period, it became impractical to allow people to act on individual impulse.

[92]Samuel Bennett was born in England in 1810. After serving as the presiding elder in Cincinnati, Ohio, in 1840, he became an alderman and associate justice of the municipal court in Nauvoo. He was among the conspirators who were arrested for destroying the *Nauvoo Expositor*. He left the Saints after Joseph Smith's death and associated with groups led by James Strang and Sidney Rigdon.

[93]"The vote was unanimous" (*Times and Seasons*, Oct. 15, 1844, 687).

[It was] m[oved] & sec[onde]d by Brigham Young, [that] George Movey be cut off from the church. [It was] moved & sec[onde[d that Jos[eph] H. Newton be cut off fro[m] the church. [It was] moved & sec[onde]d that John A Forgeus[94] be cut off.[95] [It was] moved & seconded that we get an expression from Bro[ther] Marks if he is in approval of this days proceedings.[96] [It was] moved & seconded that the Meeting be dismissed which was carried.[97] [It was] moved & seconded that the Minutes of this day be published.

*September 10, 1844; Tuesday.* [The] High Council of Nauvoo met Sept[ember] 10th 1844. Councellor [Samuel] Bent nominated Elder Ezra Benson for councillor to fill the vacancy of Leonard Soby – dismissed[.] All the council spoke in the case of Elder Benson & approbated him[.] He was called on to Speak & did so[.] [He] accepted the appointment and was ordained a Councellor. It was motioned to dismiss the present clerk, viz. Elder [Joseph M.] Coles – after remarks being made by the Council[.] It was voted to dismiss him – It was voted that William Clayton be the clerk of said Council.

The faith, principle and pursuit of Elder [William] Marks was called up – when it was found that he imbibed a notion different from the apostles or council – and was voted that the Council (in future)

---

[94]John A. Forgeus was born in 1809 in Pennsylvania. He was baptized in 1840 and immediately contributed $200 toward a third printing of the Book of Mormon. He served two missions and ran unsuccessfully for Nauvoo City Recorder. After his excommunication, he became president of Rigdon's Quorum of the Twelve. In 1862 John and his wife joined the RLDS Church and settled in Little Sioux, Iowa. A local history claims he was irascible and one day got into a fistfight with a neighbor, both of whom "were cripples, the former using crutches, while the latter could scarcely get beyond a respectable walk." Forgeus was also tarred and feathered and reportedly "loudly objected" to the way the tar was removed by well-meaning neighbors wielding knives and the "careless manner in which these instruments were used on certain parts of his person" (Joe H. Smith, *History of Harrison County, Iowa* [Des Moines: Iowa Printing, 1888], 300-01).

[95]In both instances, the vote was unanimous (*Times and Seasons,* Oct. 15, 1844, 687).

[96]Marks was in attendance. He "arose and said he was willing to be satisfied with the action of the church on the case" (ibid.).

[97]The meeting ended at 4:00 p.m., with a prayer by William W. Phelps (ibid.).

do business without him at their head.[98] [The] Councel adjourned until Saturday next at 2 o'clock, P.M. at the 70's hall. H[enry] G Sherwood[,] cl[er]k protem. N[ota] B[ene][:] [The council] voted that Elder H[enry] G Sherwood acquaint Elder Marks of the proceedings – and obtain from him the papers[,] Book[,][99] Pen[,] &c.

‡*September 21, 1844; Saturday.* The High Council of the Church of Jesus Christ of Latter-Day Saints met in the Seventies' Hall according to adjournment at 2 o'clock P.M. and opened by prayer[.] The case of [Ethan] Pettit. vs. [David] Bennett was taken up but as the accused was not present, the trial was postponed until Oct[ober] 5th at 9 o'clock A.M. [The council] voted to adjourn and meet in the Seventies' Hall [on] Oct. 5th 1844 at 9 o'clock A.M. C[alvin] C. Pendleton[,] Cl[er]k.

*October 5, 1844; Saturday.* The High Council of the Church of Jesus Christ of Latter Day Saints met this day in the Seventie's Hall at 9 o'clock A.M. and proceeded to an organization [of the seating]. Councellors Present[:] Sam[ue]l Bent[,] Cha[rle]s C. Rich (in Place of Lewis D. Wilson)[,] David Fulmer[,] Tho[ma]s S. Gates (in place of Tho[ma]s Grover)[,] Newell Knight[,] Ezra T. Benson[,] Ja[me]s Allred[,] Alpheus Cutler[,] Geo[rge] W. Harris[,] Aaron Johnson[,] Simeon A. Dunn (in place of W[illia]m Huntington)[,] [and] Henry G. Sherwood.

The Case of [Ethan] Pettit, vs. [David] Bennett was laid over until some subsequent time in consequence of sickness on the part of Brother Bennett. [The council] voted that in appealed cases from a Bishop's Court, when the parties do not present themselves at the time specified[,] they consider the Bishops decision in force, and will take no further notice of the case.

An appealed case from Bishop John Murdock's Court of E. M. Wight (vs) Almira Babbit[100] was brought before the Council. [The]

---

[98]Marks seems to be absent from this meeting, maybe because he was asked to absent himself from it. Four weeks later on October 7, 1844, he was rejected as Nauvoo Stake president because he sympathized with Rigdon. He will be replaced by John Smith, the uncle of the slain prophet (Leonard, *Nauvoo*, 441).

[99]This would probably be the bound minute book.

[100]Almira Castle Babbitt was born in February 1810 in Pompey, New

Charges prefered were: failing to fulfil agreements; and abuse. [It was] voted by the Council that one on [each] side shall speak[.] Ezra T. Benson [was appointed] Counsellor for [the] Complainant, H[enry] G. Sherwood [appointed] Counsellor for the Accused. After some deliberation on the part of the council for the parties; and some feeling and suitable remarks by Pres[iden]t Sam[ue]l Bent, Alpheus Cutler and Newell Knight, [it was] decided by a unanimous voice of the Council, that the parties retain their membership, and that they go home and settle their difficulties between themselves, and live in peace forever after. [The council] voted to adjourn ~~and meet in the Hall of the Seventies~~ ^till next Saturday at one oclock^ P.M. to meet in this Hall. C[alvin] C. Pendleton[,] Clerk.

*October 12, 1844; Saturday.* The High Council of the Church of Jesus Christ of Latter Day Saints met in the Hall of the Seventies agreeably to adjournment, and organized for business. Councellors Present[:] Sam[ue]l Bent, Lewis D. Wilson[,] David Fulmer[,] Andrew A. Timmons in place of Tho[ma]s Grover, Ja[me]s Carroll in place of Newell Knight, Ezra T. Benson, Ja[me]s Allred[,] Isaac Allred in place of A[lpheus] Cutler[,] George W. Harris[,] Aaron Johnson[,] W[illia]m Huntington[,] [and] Henry G. Sherwood[,] Cha[rle]s C. Rich acting President.

[The first] Subject for investigation [was] an appealed case from Bishop Isaac Higbee's Court of Harvy Olmsted, vs. Arthur Morrison. [The] Charge prefered was fraud in settleing accounts. [It was] voted that one [high councilman] on [each] side shall speak. Sam[ue]l Bent [was assigned to be] Counsellor for [the] Complainant, [and] Ja[me]s Allred Counsellor for the Accused.

After some little consultation, [it was] voted, by the Council that the parties at variance make [a] choice of referees to investigate and settle their difficulties, and their decisions shall be abided, or the one refusing to abide such decisions shall be disfellowshipped, and [unless][101] A[rthur] Morrison abide such decision as they [(]the referees[)] shall make, he shall be disfellowshipped by the Church. H[arvey] Olmstead chose Ja[me]s Carroll, [and] Arthur Morrison

---

York. She married Lorin Whiting Babbitt and had five children. She was baptized sometime prior to 1836 and died in Nauvoo in August 1845.

[101]The minutes say "in case" Morrison agreed with the referees.

chose Henry Snider, and they jointly made choice of E[dwin] D. Wooley.[102] ~~Pres~~ [The council] voted to adjourn until next Saturday to meet in this Hall at one o'clock P.M. C[alvin] C. Pendleton[,] Clerk.

*October 19, 1844; Saturday.* The High Council of the Church of Jesus Christ of Latter-Day Saints met at one o'clock in the Hall of the Seventies (~~owing to repairs being made in the First Presidency's Hall~~[103] ^according to adjournment.^ Present of the Council[:] Sam[uel] l Bent[,] Lewis D. Wilson[,] David Fulmer[,] Tho[ma]s Grover[,] Newel Knight[,] Ezra T. Benson[,] Ja[me]s Allred[,] Geo[rge] W. Harris[,] [and] W[illia]m Huntington. No business being brought before the Council, ~~Res~~ [we] ^voted^ to adjourn until next Saturday at one o'clock P.M. C[alvin] C. Pendleton[,] Cl[er]k.

*October 26, 1844; Saturday.* The High Council of the Church of Jesus Christ of Latter-Day Saints met at the usual place of meeting according to adjournment, but as no business was presented for investigation, adjourned till next Saturday at one o'clock P.M. to meet in the Hall of the Seventies. C[alvin] C. Pendleton[,] Cl[er]k.

*November 2, 1844; Saturday.* The High Council of the Church of Jesus Christ of Latter-Day Saints, met in the Seventies Hall pursuant to adjournment; no business being brought before said Council, ~~Resolved~~ [it was] ^voted^ to adjourn till next Saturday at 1 o'clock P.M. C[alvin] C. Pendleton[,] Cl[er]k.

*November 9, 1844; Saturday.* The High Council of the Church of Jesus Christ of Latter-Day Saints, met in the ^Seventie's^ Hall ~~of the First Presidency~~ pursuant to adjournment, but no ^business^ being brought before said Council ~~Resolved~~ [it was] ^voted^ to adjourn

---

[102] Edwin Dilworth Woolley was born in West Chester, Pennsylvania, in June 1807, converted to Mormonism in 1837, and moved to Illinois in 1839. In Utah he became Brigham Young's business manager, a territorial legislator, and a founder of the Deseret Telegraph Company. He was a longtime bishop in Salt Lake City, where he died in October 1881.

[103] The new clerk will mistakenly call the Seventies Hall the "First Presidency's Hall" three times before avoiding the mistake (see the minutes for Nov. 9, 16).

until next Saturday, to meet in this Hall at one o'clock P.M. C[alvin] C. Pendleton[,] Cl[er]k

*November 16, 1844; Saturday.* The High Council of the Church of Jesus Christ of Latter-Day Saints, met this day in the ~~First Presidencys~~ ^Seventies^ Hall, according to adjournment, and opened by prayer from Councellor Lewis D. Wilson. George W. Harris, and David Fulmer were ~~then~~ appointed a Committee to visit Elder Amos B. Tomlinson[104] and demand his License in consequence of[105] ^apostacy.^ &c.[106] [The council] ~~Resolved~~ ^voted^ to adjourn till next Saturday at one o'clock Afternoon. Calvin C. Pendleton[,] Cl[er]k

*November 23, 1844; Saturday.* The High Council of the Church of Jesus Christ of Latter-Day Saints met in the Seventie's Hall pursuant to adjournment and adjourned to the dwelling house of President Brigham Young, and opened the Counsel for business by prayer from broth[er] David Fulmer.

It was then moved by Counsellor [George W.] Harris and seconded by brother Thomas Grover, that Ebenezer Robinson[107] &

---

[104]Amos B. Tomlinson was born in April 1808 in Newtown, Connecticut, if the person listed at *FamilySearch* (www.familysearch.org) is the right Amos B. Tomlinson. He was living in Nauvoo by 1842, and in 1843 he filled a mission to Connecticut. After having his ministerial license revoked, he followed Rigdon to Pennsylvania and became a president of the Seventy in the Church of Christ. He participated in the idealistic communal society there, investing "all [his] worldly wealth in Rigdon's visions of New Jerusalem" and then losing it all, according to Van Wagoner, *Sidney Rigdon,* 388. Tomlinson apparently died in August 1877.

[105]The clerk wrote and then struck out the following: "his holding to and advocating false doctrines, such as this: 'the Twelve are out of their place, having usurped the authority of the First Presidency.'"

[106]At this point, Pendleton wrote and then struck the following: "Some appropriate remarks were then made by Councellors Fulmer, Allred, Bent, Harris, Huntington, and Grover; respecting punctuality of attendance on the part of the Council, and a perfect union of feeling and concert of action in all their transactions as a Quorum, also respecting the Law of tithing and the necessity of strict punctuality on the part of the saints in paying and receiving credit for the same."

[107]Ebenezer Robinson was a prominent member of the LDS Church who had been clerk of the Missouri high council and long-time editor of the *Times and Seasons.* He was born in Floyd, New York, in May 1816. He

Wife be cut off from the Church for apostacy; ^(and notice of the same to be given in the Times & Seasons[)][,]^ [which] carried unanimously. The License of A[mos] B. Tomlinson was then presented by brother Aaron Johnson, when it was motioned by Councellor D[avid] Fulmer & seconded by brother T[homas] Grover that he (A[mos] B. Tomlinson) be cut off from the church in consequence of apostacy; and notice to be given as above directed. Carried unanimously.[108]

[It was] ~~Resolved~~ ^voted^ that James Ivins, W[illia]m Marks and wife; Dr Josiah Ells,[109] Ephraim S. Green,[110] and W[illia]m Stanley, receive a written notice from the clerk of the Council to meet said Council in the Seventie's Hall on next Saturday, at ten o'clock A.M. [The council] ~~Resolved~~ ^voted^ on motion that Councellor Ezra T. Benson receive a letter of recommendation ^from the Council^ to the Eastern Churches; and carried unanimously. [It was] ~~Resolved~~ ^voted^ that Phineas Richards, fill the place of Ezra T. Benson (as a councellor) during his absence. [The council] also ~~Resolved that this~~

---

worked at the *Utica Observer* and *Ohio Star* before he moved to Kirtland, Ohio, in May 1835, and was baptized by Joseph Smith. Robinson served missions to New York and Ohio. On moving to Illinois in 1839, he worked at the *Quincy Whig* and was elected a justice of the peace. He produced editions of the Book of Mormon and the Doctrine and Covenants. After the action taken against him, he followed Sidney Rigdon to Pennsylvania and published the *Messenger and Advocate of the Church of Christ.* He later joined the RLDS Church, only to eventually associate with David Whitmer's Church of Christ, editing *The Return.* Robinson died in Davis City, Iowa, in March 1891 ("People of the Time," *The Joseph Smith Papers,* josephsmithpapers.org; see also the minutes for Sept. 17, Oct. 1, 1842, herein).

[108]This appeared in the *Times and Seasons,* Dec. 1, 1844, 734: "Resolved, by the High Council that Amos B. Tomlinson, Ebenezer Robinson and wife, be cut off from the church of Jesus Christ of Latter day Saints, for apostasy."

[109]Josiah Ells was born in Lewes, England, in 1806. He came to America and settled, first in Philadelphia, and then in New Jersey, where he was baptized in 1838. He moved to Nauvoo in 1840 and served in the Nauvoo Legion as a lieutenant-colonel. After his disfellowshipment in 1844, he joined Sidney Rigdon's Church of Christ and was called to the apostleship. He later joined the RLDS Church, becoming an apostle there as well. He died in Colorado in 1885.

[110]Ephraim S. Green was born in March 1807 in Rodman, New York, and was baptized in 1841. Five years later he joined the Mormon Battalion. Genealogical records show that he may have had as many as five wives. He died in October 1874.

~~Council~~ ^voted to^ adjourn until next Saturday at ten of the clock ^A.M.^ to meet in the Seventie's Hall. C[alvin] C. Pendleton[,] Cl[er]k

Note. A letter was also written to Bishop Joseph L. Heywood[111] of Quincy; with instructions to Elder Trueman Wait[112] to return to Nauvoo and make satisfaction to the Church (if possible) in relation to reports in circulation respecting him; with a request of Brother Heywood to send such inteligence respecting the conduct of Elder Wait, as were in his power.

*November 30, 1844; Saturday.* The High Council of the Church of Jesus Christ of Latter-Day Saints, met in the Seventie's Hall according to adjournment, and opened by prayer from Father John Smith,[113] President of the Stake – who, with Gen[era]l Cha[rle]s C. Rich – one of his Councellors – acted in concert with President ^S[amuel] Bent^ in Presiding. ~~(Counsellors, all came)~~ The minutes of the previous

---

[111]Joseph Leland Heywood was born in August 1815 in Grafton, Massachusetts. He was a merchant in Quincy when Mormons arrived in 1839. He and his wife were baptized in 1842 but did not move to Nauvoo until 1845. They immigrated to Utah three years later. Heywood married three more wives. He became the Salt Lake City postmaster and bishop of the 17th Ward. Later he worked as a highway surveyor and was appointed a U.S. marshal. He died in October 1910 in Panguitch (Florence C. Youngberg, *Conquerors of the West: Stalwart Mormon Pioneers* [Salt Lake City: Agreka Books and Sons of Utah Pioneers, 1999], 2:1091-93).

[112]Truman Wait was born in 1810 in Vermont. In 1833 he was baptized by Hyrum Smith, served a mission in the eastern states, and met and married a recent convert, Sarah Hodges–all in the same year. In 1837 he and his wife were among the first to settle the town of Far West, Missouri. They were living in Nauvoo by 1842. When the main branch of the Church moved west in 1846, Truman and his wife moved to St. Louis. He died there in 1847. His wife converted to the RLDS Church and died in Lamoni, Iowa, in 1895 (*Saints' Herald,* Nov. 27, 1895, 772, qtd. at "Sarah Hodges Wait Lucky: First House in Far West," www.farwesthistory.com).

[113]John Smith was born in July 1781 in Hillsborough, New Hampshire. He was baptized by his nephew, Joseph Smith Jr., in 1832 and moved to Kirtland the next year to become president of the Kirtland High Council. After serving a mission to the eastern states, he was appointed a counselor in the LDS First Presidency. Oddly, he simultaneously was called to be president of the Kirtland Stake, then of the Adam-ondi-Ahman stake, the Iowa Stake, and Nauvoo Stake until released from the First Presidency in 1844. He became a patriarch that year but would not become the Church Patriarch until 1849. He died in Salt Lake City in May 1854.

meeting were then read and approved. [It was] moved by Pres[iden]t Bent and seconded by D[avid] Fulmer, and carried unanimously, that the Council proceed to question those individuals who were cited (by vote of the previous meeting), relative to their faith &c., as the Council was not yet full.

Elder W[illia]m Marks arose and stated that he had never spoken against the Council or Church, but thought there had been some hasty moves made, but wished to do the thing that was right: did not think of apostatizing, but wished to carry out every righteous principle. – [There] were things practiced in our midst that were not right, such as stealing and the like which had been a trouble to him, [he] thought some had treated him with coldness and neglect &c. – Wished to sustain the Church. As respect[ing] the present organization, he was willing to conform to, and abide by it.

Were his present feelings to be with the Church[?] [He] did not wish to leave the Church, nor did he wish to crowd himself into the society of those who did not want him with them; [he] had heard many threats and hard speeches concerning him [and] was willing for the brethren to do with him as they saw fit and he would abide by it. [He] had the best of feelings towards those that treated him well, but there were those who were continually telling foul lies about him, and stealing every thing ^from him^ they could lay their hands upon. His mind had been in an unsettled state respecting how the church should be organized, but since its present organization, [he] was, and ever had been satisfied with it.[114] [It was] moved by H[enry] G. Sherwood, and seconded by David Fulmer, that brother Marks have our fellowship, and that we give him our heart and hand for his Spiritual and Temporal welfare. Carried without a dissenting vote.

Dr. Ells was then called upon[,] who stated that he had ever feared God from his youth up: [He] had thought & still thought that the right of Presidency was perpetua[l].[115] – [He] was not fully satisfied that the present organization of the church was exactly right, or not – [but he] was willing to sustain the twelve in their stations, as they formerly stood (ie) as Apostles. His feelings were now towards

---

[114]There is a notation here that this is "Page 10" of the minute book, deleted here for lack of relevance.

[115]In other words, once a member of the First Presidency, always a member of the presidency until an individual's death.

Elder Rigdon, but [he] was not willing to risk his salvation upon Sidney Rigdon[,] the "Twelve" or any other men. [He] thought Rigdon had the right of Presidency and should so think until he had more knowledge upon the subject. – [He] had prayed earnestly to God to know what was right and if he had suffered him to be led astray, he was willing to take it so. [He] had no predilection for Elder Rigdon, but though[t] from the Revelations in [the] Book of Covenants [that] he was to be Pres[iden]t & had been so apointed.

Elder Orson Hyde then made some very appropriate and pointed remarks relative to the organization of the Church, the course of Elder Rigdon and others; and also of the appointment of the Twelve by Brother Joseph on the 23d of March last, to ~~stand in~~ their present office, that on them the responsibility of bearing of the Kingdom rested, and tho' they had many difficulties to encounter, they must "Round up their shoulders and bear it like men of God and not be bluffed off by any man," which statements were sanctioned by Councellor A[lpheus] Cutler. Brother Hyde also prophesied ~~of~~ that the influence and prosperity of those who go from this place without council, would be taken from them.

Elder John Taylor also made some very instructive remarks on the same subject. No testimony, nor argument, seemed to satisfy Dr. E[lls][.] [The council] ~~Resolved~~ ^voted^ unanimously that ~~Dr. Ells~~ Dr Josiah Ells be disfellowshipped from the church until he shall reform in principles of faith, and notice hereof ~~Resolved that notice~~ be given in the "Times and Season."[116]

Ephraim S. Green was then called upon, who [s]eemed to manifest a desire to act in conformity to the rules of the church, and the wishes of the authorities of the same. But owing to some matter of consideration between him and Elder Hyde, his case was laid over for the present.

Other[s] cited were not present, as it was difficult or impossible for them to attend. A letter from Bishop [Joseph L.] Heywood of Quincy respecting Elder Trueman Wait was then read by the clerk. Elder Wait being present made some remarks denying reports against him. Elder O[rson] Hyde reported unfavorably against him – [He]

---

[116]The *Times and Seasons* explained that "the hand of christian fellowship was this day withdrawn from Dr. Josiah Ells, until he shall reform in principles of faith" (Dec. 1, 1844, 734).

had frequently seen him in the grogshops, and considered his conduct very unworthy. [The council] ~~Resolved~~ ^voted^ upon motion of President John Smith & the sanction of Councellor Harris, that Elder Waits licence be taken from him and he stand as a private member.

By request of Elder H[eber] C. Kimball, the case of J[onah] R Ball was brought up. Elder Kimball seemed to ~~think~~ [feel] compassionate [toward] his situation, and was of the opinion that he had been willing to do by brother [William] Gribble as he had agreed, and wished him restore[d] to fellowship if found worthy. After some consultation, [it was] moved by Councellor [K]night and seconded by Brother Cutler that J[onah] R. Ball be received into the church by baptism and ordained to his former standing and authority. [It was] carried unanimously. [It was then] ~~Resolved~~ ^voted^ to adjourn till next Saturd^a^y at one o'clock P.M. to meet in the Seventie's Hall. C[alvin] C. Pendleton, Clerk.

Note Councellor A[lpheus] Cutler arose and stated that Elder S[idney] Rigdon came to him on the morning that he arrived in Nauvoo (from Pittsburg), and saluted him very cordially ~~and~~ Stated his joy to see him and told him that he (Cutler) was to ~~become~~ be a great man in the Kingdom; and Elder W[illia]m Marks also said to him that he himself, was to be head Patriarch over the whole Church.[117] Elder Cutler also remarked that he felt bound to sustain the Twelve, and all the Quorums in the Church with its present organization, for [it was] on [this] that his salvation depended, and asked Elder Marks if he could take him by the hand as a brother and go with him ^in^ these matters. Elder Marks frankly said yes, Heart and Hand. N.B. The Council was full.

*December 7, 1844; Saturday.* The High Council of the Church of Jesus Christ of Latter Day Saints met in the Seventies Hall at one o'clock P.M. pursuant to adjournment and opened by prayer from Elder George W. Harris. ~~The Minutes of the~~ Councellors Present[:] Samuel Bent, James Allred[,] Lewis D. Wilson[,] David Fulmer[,] Thomas Grover[,] Newel Knight[,] Phineas Richards in place of ~~Elisha~~ ^Ezra^

---

[117]Here is how William Clayton interpreted this: "Brother [Alpheus] Cutler said that in the council yesterday he drew out from [William] Marks that Sidney Rigdon was to be president and Marks Patriarch" (Smith, *Intimate Chronicle,* 141).

T. Benson[,] Alpheus Cutler[,] George W. Harris[,] Aaron Johnson[,] William Huntington[,] [and] Henry G. Sherwood[.] Also present, of First Presidency, George A. Smith, and Amasa Lyman. The minutes of the previous meeting were read and approved.

President Bent arose and stated to the Council that during the present week he had presented a written article from the "Twelve" to Elder W[illia]m Marks to sign, thereby confirming to them his declarations on last Saturday ^before the Council viz.^ to acknowledge ^and uphold^ the Twelve and all the Quorums of the Church of Jesus Christ [a]s in its present organization, and thereby show to all, his renunciation of Sidney Rigdon and his claims; but he ~~full belief in~~ would not sign it. He then returned the paper to Pres[iden]t Orson Hyde who ~~struck off a~~ drew up an other article leaving out the most objectionable clause to him: (viz the acknowledgeing the authority of the Twelve,) and again presented it to Elder Marks but he utterly refused to sign it, and said he would sign no paper and did not want his name to go abroad.

Pres[ident] A[masa] Lyman then remarked, that as Elder Marks had been sustained in fellowship by [the] High Council ^by his acknowledgement^; the Twelve also wished to be satisfied of his present feelings: and thought it proper to write a manifesto to ~~present to~~ [for] Elder Marks ^to sign^ that he might show or acknowledge that he had been deceived by ~~by~~ Sidney Rigdon and that in so doing his name and influence abroad should not be used against this Church.

Pres[iden]t Geo[rge] A. Smith confirmed Elder Lyman's statements, and said that as Elder Marks had had more influence abroad than Elder Rigdon and his name was used to the injury of the Church, they wished his acknowledgements to uphold the Twelve and all the authorities of this Church in its present organization, and his renunciation of S[idney] Rigdon; to be published, that his name might cease to wield an influence against us. After much deliberation, [it was] unanimously ~~Resolved~~ ^voted^ ~~on notice~~ that Elder Marks be cited for trial before this Council, in the Seventie's Hall on Mon[day] the 9th inst[ant] at ten o'clock AM. for refusing to comply with the Covenant made by him ~~to face~~ [to the] said Council on last Saturday, viz to sustain the Twelve and all the Quorums of the Church; and also ~~Reas~~ ^voted^ that his wife be notified to attend with him, said inteligence to [be] given by the Clerk.

[It was] ~~Resolved~~ ^voted^ that Sister Hannah Ells be notified by the clerk to attend the Council at the time and place above specified, as ~~evidence in the case for trial~~ [a] witness in matters to come before the Council. [It was] ~~resolved~~ ^voted^ to adjourn till Monday next at ten o'clock A.M. to meet in the Seventie's Hall. C[alvin] C. Pendleton[,] Cl[er]k

*December 9, 1844; Monday.* The High Council of the Church of Jesus Christ of Latter Day Saints met in the Seventies Hall pursuant to adjournment, and opened by prayer from Brother Tho[ma]s Grover. Presidents Orson Hyde, John Smith & Cha[rle]s C. Rich sat with the council. Councellors Present[:] Sam[ue]l Bent[,] Lewis D. Wilson[,] David Fulmer[,] Tho[ma]s Grover[,] Newell Knight, Phineas Richards[,] ~~in place of E[zra] T. Benson~~ Ja[me]s Allred[,] Alpheus Cutler[,] Geo[rge] W. Harris[,] Aaron Johnson[,] W[illia]m Huntington[,] [and] H[enry] G. Sherwood.

1stly. [It was] ~~resolved~~ ^voted^ by the Council, that ^Elder^ Samuel C. Brown deliver up his licence, which he refused to do. 2dly. [It was] ~~Resolved~~ ^voted^ that the said Sam[ue]l C. Brown be cut off from the Church of Jesus Christ of Latter-Day Saints, ~~and~~ for refusing to comply with the requisitions of said Council, and notice of the same be given in the "Times and Seasons."[118] Elder W[illia]m Marks was present, who after some consultation, signed the following article. (from the "Twelve."[)]

> After mature and candid deliberation, I am fully ~~factorily~~ and satisfactorily convinced that Mr Sidney Rigdon's claim to the presidency of the church of Jesus Christ of Latter-Day Saints [is] not founded in truth. I have been deceived by his specious pretences, and now feel to warn every one over whom I may have any influence to beware of him and his pretended visions and revelations. The Twelve are the proper ~~authorities~~ ^persons^ to lead the Church[.]*
> Nauvoo Dec[ember] 9th 1844. William Marks

*Note[:] This clause acknowledging the authority of the "Twelve"

---

[118]"Resolved, by the High Council that Elder Samuel C. Brown be cut off from the church of Jesus Christ of Latter day Saints, for refusing to comply with the requisitions of said council" (*Times and Seasons,* Dec. 15, 1844, 782).

was a voluntary addition of Elder Marks. C[alvin] C. P[endleton]. [The] Council ~~Resolved~~ ^Voted^ to adjourn till next Saturday at one o'clock P.M. C[alvin] C. Pendleton[,] Cl[er]k

*December 14, 1844; Saturday.* The High Council of the Church of Jesus Christ of Latter Day Saints met in the Seventie's Hall according to adjournment, and opened by prayer from Brother Aaron Johnson. After mutual conversation upon principles of salvation, [it was] voted that all the decisions of this council, be made with uplifted hands. ~~Voted to adjourn till next Saturday at one o'clock P.M. C[alvin] C. Pendleton Cl[er]k.~~

Councellors Present[:] Sam[ue]l Bent[,] Lewis D. Wilson[,] David Fulmer[,] Tho[ma]s Grover[,] Ja[me]s Allred[,] Alpheus Cutler[,] Geo[rge] W. Harris[,] Aaron Johnson[,] W[illia]m Huntington[,] Phineas Richards ~~in place of E[zra] T. Benson~~[,] [and] H[enry] G. Sherwood. ~~Good~~ Cha[rle]s C. Rich [was] presiding in concert with Pres[iden]t Bent[.] [The council] voted to adjourn till next Saturday at one o'clock P.M. C[alvin] C. Pendleton[,] Cl[er]k

*December 21, 1844; Saturday.* The High Council of the Church of Jesus Christ of Latter Day Saints, met in Council in the Seventie's Hall at the hour appointed and opened by prayer from councellor Newell N [K]night. Councellors Present[:] Samuel Bent[,] Lewis D. Wilson[,] David Fulmer[,] Thomas Grover[,] Newell Knight[,] Phineas Richards ~~for E[zra] T. Benson~~, Ja[me]s Allred[,] P[hilip] H. Buzzard in place of Alpheus Cutler, Geo[rge] W. Harris[,] Aaron Johnson[,] W[illia]m Huntington[,] [and] H[enry] G. Sherwood. ~~Ja[me]s. Allred~~ Presidents Orson Hyde and Cha[rle]s C. Rich sat with President S[amuel] Bent in presiding over the Council.

The case before the council, was an appeal from the branch of the Church in Nashville, I[owa] T[erritory] of W[illia]m R. Orton[119]

---

[119]William Reed Orton was born in March 1802 in Breson, North Carolina, and he and his wife, Rebecca Huey, had ten children. In 1835 they were baptized and moved to Missouri for a time, then back to Illinois. He and his family moved to Provo in 1852, but twelve years later they converted to the RLDS Church and moved to Tabor, Iowa, where he died in June 1891 and she four years later ("William Reed Orton," *Pioneer Family Heritage Society*, pioneer-family-heritage.org).

vs. Samuel P. Hoyt.[120] [The] Charge prefered was unchristian like conduct in refusing to pay a just demand. [The council] voted that two on [each] side shall speak upon the case, viz. Lewis D. Wilson & David Fulmer, councellors for Plaintiff[,] and Geo[rge] W. Harris & P[hilip] H. Buzzard, councellors for [the] Defendant.

The Charge was not sustained on the grounds that Elder Hoyt had not been ^fully^ empowered to settle demands against the estate of one Mr Wright deceased, [the] said demand being ^against^ that estate, some portion of which was log[g]ed in the hand of Brother Hoyt. [It was] moved by Pres[iden]t O[rson] Hyde, seconded by Brother T[homas] Grover and carried by a unanimous vote, that Brother S[amuel] P. Hoyt, shall loan $11.25 cents to Brother W[illia]m R. Orton without interest, until he shall receiv[e] legal authority to settle demands against said Estate.

Pres[iden]t O[rson] Hyde asked Elder Hoyt, if he would covenant to the Council, to pay the demand of brother Orton's, (it being $11.25) to him (Orton) as soon as empowered so to do, to which he readily covenanted. [It was] voted unanimously that Elder Sam[ue]l P. Hoyt be restored to the fellowship of the church, also voted to adjourn to the dwelling house of H[enry] G. Sherwood, to meet on Saturday next at one o'clock P.M. C[alvin] C. Pendleton[,] Clerk.

*December 28, 1844; Saturday.* The High Council of the Church of Jesus Christ of Latter Day Saints, met at the dwelling house of Councellor H[enry] G. Sherwood. [The meeting was] opened by prayer from Councellor W[illia]m Huntington and organized for business. Councellors Present[:] Sam[ue]l Bent[,] Lewis D. Wilson[,] David Fulmer[,] Tho[ma]s Grover[,] Newell Knight[,] Phineas Richards ~~for E[zra] T. Benson~~[,] Ja[me]s Allred[,] Jacob Morris in place of A[lpheus] Cut-

---

[120]Samuel Pierce Hoyt was born in November 1807 in Chester, New Hampshire. He married Emily Smith in 1834; they had one child. She was baptized in 1836 and he converted a year or two later. They lived in Missouri for a time, then in Iowa across from Nauvoo, where he was engaged in supplying steamboats with wood. He served a mission to Massachusetts, then moved to Utah in 1851 and helped settle Fillmore. His plural wife, Emma Burbidge, gave birth to twelve children. In 1861 Samuel built a gristmill near Coalville and founded Hoytsville, where he died in August 1889 (Lyman C. Pedersen Jr., "Samuel Pierce Hoyt and His Home on the Weber," *Utah Historical Quarterly* 33 [Spring 1965]: 99-108).

ler, Geo[rge] W. Harris[,] Aaron Johnson[,] W[illia]m Huntington[,] [and] H[enry] G. Sherwood[,] [with] President Cha[rle]s C. Rich ~~Chairman~~ ^Presiding.^[121]

Charges were prefered by Elder Myron Higley[122] ^~~and Homer Hoyt~~^ against Elder Daniel Botsford and Nancy his wife, for sundry ^committed in ~~the~~^ unchristian like conduct, such as ^N[ew] York^ fraud, falsehoods, opposition to the principle of Gathering &c. whereupon it was unanimously, voted, firstly, that Elder Daniel Botsford and Nancy his wife be cut off from the Church, and published in the "Times and Seasons."[123] Secondly[,] that Councellor H[enry] G. Sherwood, edit said matter for publication. Voted to adjourn till next Saturday, to meet at one o'clock P.M. in the Seventie's Hall. C[alvin] C. Pendleton[,] Clerk.

---

[121]The clerk wrote the following and then struck it out: "Voted Unanimously that Samuel Music has no fellowship with the church, and that notice hereof be given in the 'Times and Seasons.'"

[122]Myron Spencer Higley was born in December 1801 in Bridgewater, Connecticut. In 1826 he married Pricilla Eberson, with whom he had eleven children. They were baptized in 1839, then moved to Leeds, Canada. By 1842, when he was called on a mission to New York, they were living in Iowa. Ten years later they immigrated to Utah, settling at the mouth of Weber Canyon, then in Hooper, where Myron died in 1887.

[123]"BEWARE OF IMPOSTERS. Daniel Botsford and Nancy his wife, who left Nauvoo about June last, are by the High Council expelled from the church of Jesus Christ of Latter-Day Saints, at Nauvoo, on complaint of their improper and erroneous efforts and course of doings to unlawfully obtain a sustenance from certain kind and hospitable members of said church, in some of the eastern branches, together with reporting certain slanderous tales respecting the leaders and church at Nauvoo" (*Times and Seasons,* Jan. 15, 1845, 778).

# 12.
# "Opened for Business"
# 1845

‡*January 4, 1845; Saturday.* The High Council of the Church of Jesus Christ of Latter Day Saints, met at the Seventies' Hall according to appointment, and from thence convened at the dwelling house of ^Coun[cilo]r^ H[enry] G. Sherwood and opened by prayer from Brother Phineas Richards. Councellors Present[:] Samuel Bent[,] Lewis D. Wilson[,] David Fulmer[,] Tho[ma]s Grover[,] Newel Knight[,] Phineas Richards ~~for E[zra] T. Benson~~[,] Ja[me]s Allred[,] Alpheus Cutler[,] Geo[rge] W. Harris[,] W[illia]m Huntington[,] [and] H[enry] G. Sherwood[,] [and] Presidents John Smith and Cha[rle]s C. Rich presiding[1] with President Bent.

[The council] voted that H[enry] G. Sherwood be a committee to inform Brother Christopher Murkley[2] to meet in the dwelling house

---

[1]At the end of the previous year, John Smith replaced William Marks as president of the Nauvoo Stake and retained Charles C. Rich as one of his two counselors. In mid-1845, Smith will choose John Edmundson as his second counselor.

[2]Christopher Merkley was born in Williamsburg, Ontario, in Dec. 1808. He and his wife were baptized in 1837 and moved to Missouri, then Illinois; he would later serve several missions back to Canada. Good with horses, he became a member of the cavalry regiment of the Nauvoo Legion. He contributed a team to help excavate the foundation for the Nauvoo temple and he operated a ferry across the Missouri River during his stay in Council Bluffs. In 1849 he traveled to Utah with "two wagons, a span of French horses, one yoke of oxen, and various other animals." He participated in

of President John Smith on Tues[da]y evening next, in order to settle a difficulty existing between him and Brother Sam[ue]l Music, before Pres[iden]t John Smith[,] W[illia]m Huntington, & H[enry] G. Sherwood.

Councellor Sherwood then read an article touching the case of Dan[ie]l and Nancy Botsford, which was approved. [The council] voted to adjourn till next Saturday at ^this house to meet at^ one o'clock P.M. Dismissed [with] Prayer from Pres[iden]t John Smith. Calvin C. Pendleton[,] Clerk.

*January 11, 1845; Saturday.* The High Council of the Church of Jesus Christ of Latter Day Saints, convened at the dwelling of Councellor H[enry] G. Sherwood agreeably to adjournment and opened by prayer from Councellor P[hineas] Richards. Councellors Present[:] Sam[ue]l Bent[,] Lewis D. Wilson[,] David Fulmer[,] Tho[ma]s Grover[,] Newel Knight[,] Phineas Richards ~~for E[zra] T. Benson~~[,] Ja[me]s Allred[,] Geo[rge] W. Harris[,] Aaron Johnson[,] W[illia]m Huntington[,] [and] H[enry] G. Sherwood[,] [with] Pres[iden]t Cha[rle]s C. Rich ~~Chairman~~ ^Presiding^.

Councellors H[enry] G. Sherwood ~~and W[illia]m Huntington~~ reported concerning the meeting on Tues[da]y evening at Pres[iden]t John Smith's, holden in behalf of Christopher Murkley and Sam[ue]l Musick; and stated that brother Murkley appeared willing to comply with every thing within the bounds of reason; but that brother Musick was obstinate, and unyielding in the extreme, which was ^corroborated by Brother Huntington[.]^ [The council] voted to lay the matter over till next Saturday. [The council also] voted to adjourn till next Saturday at ten o'clock A.M. ~~in this House~~, to meet in the dwelling of H[enry] G. Sherwood. Dismissed by prayer from Pres[iden]t Cha[rle]s C. Rich. C[alvin] C. Pendleton, Clerk.

*January 18, 1845; Saturday.* The High Council of the Church of Jesus Christ of Latter Day Saints met in the dwelling of Councellor H[enry] G. Sherwood pursuant to adjournment, and opened by prayer from Pres[iden]t Sam[ue]l Bent. Councellors Present[:] Sam[ue]l Bent,

---

several skirmishes with Indians before his death in 1893 in Salt Lake City (Paul Brown, "Christopher Merkley," *Three Rivers: Hudson, Mohawk, Schoharie,* www.threeriversHMS.com/merkley.htm).

Lewis D. Wilson[,] David Fulmer[,] Thomas Grover, Ja[me]s Allred, Alpheus Cutler (present at the latter part of the meeting)[,] Geo[rge] W. Harris[,] Aaron Johnson[,] Phineas Richards for E[zra] T. Benson, [and] Henry G. Sherwood[,] ~~Phineas~~ Pres[iden]t John Smith Presiding.

[The council] voted that Elder Samuel Music be cut off from the Church of Jesus Christ of Latter Day Saints, for theft, striking brother Christopher M[e]rkley with a sword, and contempt of Council and Church authority, and notice hereof be given in the "Times and Seasons." [The council also] voted that Councellor Sherwood draft an article for publication, touching the case of Sam[ue]l Music.[3]

[It was] voted that the Council do not receive the charges of Dan[ie]l Avery[4] against Ebenezer Richardson[5]; and that Brother Avery be refered to the Seventies, for an investigation of the last charge, (viz.,) that he is not a regular member of the Church.[6] [The

[3]This was not published.

[4]Avery claimed that Richardson had helped Missouri officials abduct Avery's son, Philander. In late December 1843, Philander swore an affidavit saying that Richardson had led him to Warsaw "by false pretenses," where Philander was seized, bound, and taken across the river, a bowie-knife held to his throat, until he confessed that he had stolen a horse and colt from Joseph McCoy of Missouri and that his father had helped hide the horses (Joseph Smith, *History of the Church of Jesus Christ of Latter-Day Saints,* 7 vols. [Salt Lake City: Deseret News, 1902-12], 6:122).

[5]Ebenezer Clawson Richardson was born in August 1815 in Dryden, New York, and married Angeline King in 1833. The next year, the couple converted to the LDS Church and moved to Kirtland. He was shot in the chest during the Haun's Mill Massacre in Missouri. In 1843 he married a polygamous wife, Polly Ann Child, Joseph Smith officiating. He took a third wife, Phoebe Wooster Child (his second wife's sister), in 1848, and his three wives gave birth to twenty-nine children. The expanding family settled at Brigham's Fort, north of Ogden, where Ebenezer became a deputy sheriff. He served a mission to South Africa in 1857. On his return, he married another wife who bore him five children and then left him. He went to California to do mining work and was hit in the head by a rock and died a month later in September 1874 in Plain City, Utah (David A. Blocher, "Family of Legends (and the Unknown)," *Rootsweb,* ancestry.com).

[6]It seems that the reason Richardson helped officials arrest Philander Avery, might have been not because Richardson was sympathetic with mobsters, as some Church members probably assumed, but because Avery was guilty. By raising a question of jurisdiction, the high council was able to avoid that issue.

council] voted [to] adjourn till next Saturday at one o'clock P.M. to meet at Brother H[enry] G. Sherwood's. Closing prayer by Pres[iden]t John Smith. C[alvin] C. Pendleton[,] Clerk.

*January 25, 1845; Saturday.* The High Council of the Church of Jesus Christ of Latter-Day Saints met at Henry G. Sherwoods according to adjournment and opened by prayer from Councellor Ja[me]s Allred. Councellors Present[:] Sam[ue]l Bent[,] Lewis D. Wilson[,] David Fulmer[,] Newel Knight[,] Phineas Richards[,] Ja[me]s Allred[,] Alpheus Cutler[,] George W. Harris[,] Aaron Johnson[,] [and] William Huntington[.] Presidents John Smith and Cha[rle]s C. Rich Presiding.*

A Charge [was] prefered against Jonathan T. Packer[7] and Widow Mortley, (for unchristian-like conduct in not settleing a difficulty between them,) by Nathan W. Packer and W[illia]m Thompson; [it] was rec[orde]d to be acted upon on Saturday ~~the first day of Feb[ruar]y~~ ^next.^ [The] said case is an appeal from the Court of D[avid] Evans. Bishop, holden on the 21st of Dec[embe]r 1844. [It was] voted to adjourn till next Saturday at ten o'clock A.M. to meet in this house. Closing prayer by Pres[iden]t John Smith. Calvin C. Pendleton[,] Cl[er]k[.]

*Note. All the previous minutes of the Council which had not been read, were read and approved.

*February 1, 1845; Saturday.* The High Council of the Church of Jesus Christ of Latter Day Saints met according to adjournment at Councellor H[enry] G. Sherwoods and opened by prayer from Councellor Lewis D. Wilson. The minutes of the previous meeting were read and approved.

The case to be acted upon, was pos[t]poned ~~by permission~~ in consequence of the Plaintiff's inability to procure an essential witness. [The council] voted that said case be laid over for action, on Saturday the 15th i[n]st[ant] at one o'clock P.M. ~~The~~ Councellors Present[:] Sam[ue]l Bent[,] Lewis D. Wilson[,] David Fulmer[,] Tho[ma]s Grover, Ja[me]s Allred[,] Alpheus Cutler[,] Geo[rge] W. Harris[,] Newel

---

[7]Jonathan Taylor Packer was born in 1817 in Perry, Ohio. He was baptized in 1836. After coming to Utah, he settled in Garfield County and was ordained president of the Cannonville Branch in 1876. He served in that capacity until 1880 and died in 1889 in Safford, Arizona.

Knight[,] Phineas Richards[,] [and] William Huntington. [The council] voted to adjourn till two weeks from to day at one o'clock to meet at Councellor Sherwood's. Closing prayer by President Cha[rle]s C. Rich. C[alvin] C. Pendleton[,] [clerk].

*February 15, 1845; Saturday.* The High Council of the Church of Jesus Christ of Latter-Day Saints met according to adjournment, at Councellor Henry G. Sherwood's and opened by prayer from Councellor Alpheus Cutler. The minutes of the previous meeting were read and approved. Councellors Present[:] Samuel Bent[,] Lewis D. Wilson[,] David Fulmer[,] Thomas Grover[,] Newel Knight[,] Phineas Richards[,] James Allred[,] Alpheus Cutler[,] George W. Harris, Aaron Johnson[,] [and] William Huntington, Presidents John Smith and Cha[rle]s C. Rich Presiding with President Bent.

The case to be tried, (being an appeal from Bishop D[avid] Evans Court of Dec[ember] 21, 1844) was not acted upon in consequence of the parties not presenting themselves. Calvin C. Pendleton was ordained an high priest, under the hands of Presidents John Smith, Sam[ue]l Bent, and Cha[rle]s C. Rich[.] [The] closing prayer [was offered] by President John Smith. [The council] voted to adjourn till next Saturday, to meet in this house at ten o'clock A.M. C[alvin] C. Pendleton[,] Clerk.

*February 22, 1845; Saturday.*[8] The High Council of the Church of Jesus Christ of Latter Day Saints met pursuant to adjournment at councellor [Henry G.] Sherwood's and from thence removed to the Seventies Hall and opened by prayer, from councellor David Fulmer. Minutes of the previous meeting were read, and approved. Councellors Present[:] Samuel Bent, Lewis D. Wilson, David Fulmer, Thomas Grover, Newel Knight, Phineas Richards[,] James Allred[,] Alpheus Cutler[,] George W. Harris[,] Aaron Johnson[,] William Huntington[,] [and] William Snow in place of H[enry] G. Sherwood[.] By ~~the~~ a unanimous vote of the Council, Presidents Brigham Young, John Smith and Charles C. Rich presid[ed][,] with President Sam[ue]l Bent. The following Charge, prefered by Horace Burgess,[9]

---

[8]See also *History of Church,* 7:375.

[9]Horace Burgess was born in 1816 in Putnam, New York. He was baptized in 1832; four years later he became a shareholder in the Church's Kirtland

against Lester Brooks[10] was brought before the Council for investigation.

> A Charge is hereby prefered before the High Council of the Church of Jesus Christ of Latter Day Saints, against Lester Brooks[,] a member of said church for unchristian-like conduct in influencing the following persons to trade with Nelson Millet their farms in the State of Ohio, for property in this State, such as land and personal property; and also, were influenced to take said Millet's Notes, or notes for much of the property which they disposed of to said Millet, and said persons have, through the influence of said Brooks, made said trades with the said Millet; and most of the individuals have lost about all the property they had, by conveyance to said Millet. The names of the individuals defrauded, are, Zebina Smith, Hiram Picket, Daniel P. Young, Brother Willis and Hiram Foush; and said Brooks appeared to be engaged in riding about for Millet to make some of the trades for him as Agent, and I hereby state, that said Brooks had a design in defrauding said individuals, who traded with Nelson Millet. Some of them have taken Bonds from said Millet for Deeds of Land to be conveyed, lying here, and Said Brooks has misrepresented the price of ~~said~~ lands and also in regard to ^the^ titles, in relation to the above trades. Horace Burgess, Feb[ruar]y 8th 1845.

[The council] voted that two [councilmen representing each] side shall speak[:] Thomas Grover & Newel Knight, Council for Plaintiff, [and] Aaron Johnson & William Huntington, Council for Defendant. After much deliberation, and ^many^ pertinent and impressive remarks by the presidents and council, Brother Brooks was

---

Safety Society "anti-bank." He was in Missouri when the Mormons were driven out in 1839, then remained in Nauvoo until 1848. He hosted a New Year's party at the end of 1845 "in spite of the impending downfall of [the] city," according to historian James B. Allen in *Trials of Discipleship: The Story of William Clayton, a Mormon* (Urbana: University of Illinois Press, 1987), 182. Burgess headed west in 1849 but ended up dying in Winter Quarters, Nebraska.

[10]Lester Brooks was born in 1802 in Lanesboro, Massachusetts. He was baptized sometime before 1837 in Kirtland, Ohio, and moved to Missouri in 1838. He moved back to Kirtland three years later and became a counselor to President Almon Babbitt in the Kirtland Stake. In 1845 he was called to be a branch president in Ohio, although he then converted to James J. Strang's Church and served a Strangite mission to England with Book of Mormon witness Martin Harris in 1846. He died in 1878 at Buffalo, New York.

dismissed from the charges prefered, and [the council] voted unanimously to continue fellowship with him. A vote of the congregation present, approving the proceedings of the Council, was taken, which was general.[11]

[The council] voted that William Snow fill the place of Henry G. Sherwood, as a councellor, during the absence of councellor Sherwood, who is from home on Church business. Closing prayer by President Brigham Young. [The council also] voted to adjourn, and meet in this Hall on next Saturday at one o'clock P.M. C[alvin] C. Pendleton[,] Clerk.

*March 1, 1845; Saturday.*[12] The High Council of the Church of Jesus Christ of Latter Day Saints met in the Seventies Hall pursuant to adjournment[.] Councellors Present[:] Newell Knight, Phineas Richards, James Allred[,] George W. Harris[,] Aaron Johnson[,] William Huntington[,] [and] William Snow. No business was brought before the Council. [The council] voted to adjourn till Saturday next, to meet in this Hall at one o'clock P.M. C[alvin] C. Pendleton[,] Cl[er]k[.]

*March 8, 1845; Saturday.*[13] The High Council of the Church of Jesus Christ of Latter Day Saints, met in the Seventie's Hall according to adjournment and opened by prayer from Councellor George W. Harris. The minutes of the two previous meetings were read and approved. Councellors Present[:] Lewis D. Wilson[,] David Fulmer[,] Thomas Grover[,] Newel Knight[,] Phineas Richards, James Allred[,] George W. Harris[,] Aaron Johnson[,] William Huntington[,] [and] William Snow[,] Charles C. Rich Presiding. Closing prayer by the President. [The council] voted to adjourn till next Saturday, to meet in this Hall at one o'clock P.M. Calvin C. Pendleton[,] Clerk.

*March 15, 1845; Saturday.*[14] Present[:] Samuel Bent, Charles C. Rich, Albert P. Rockwood, David Fulmer, Thomas Grover, Newel Knight,

[11]The council had moved to the Seventy's Hall to accommodate the large audience, which no doubt was composed of people Brooks had allegedly defrauded. In addition, the presence of members of the Quorum of the Twelve provided an additional draw for spectators.

[12]See also *History of Church,* 7:379.

[13]See also ibid., 380.

[14]See also ibid., 383.

Phineas Richards, W[illia]m Huntington, Aaron Johnson, George W. Harris, Alpheus Cutler, James Allred and W[illia]m Snow. Also President Brigham Young, Heber C. Kimball, Orson Pratt, John Taylor, George A. Smith & John E. Page of the Quorum of the Twelve[;] N[ewel] K. Whitney and George Miller[,] Presiding Bishops[;] and W[illia]m Clayton and Daniel Carn.

Pres[iden]t Bent called upon W[illia]m Clayton to act as clerk pro tem, inasmuch as the regular clerk was sick.[15] [The] council opened by prayer from Elder O[rson] Pratt.

Pres[iden]t B[righam] Young then said[:]

> We want to take into consideration the case of Brother George J. Adams who is now present. I have objections to brother Adams' conduct, and to the course he has taken and shall tell them here.[16] First when brother Adams came home last ~~last~~ fall, I asked him if he had any money for the Temple; he said no, he handed every

---

[15]Clayton recorded: "P.M. at the High Council taking minutes. G[eorge] J. Adams had his trial. Pr[e]s[iden]ts [Brigham] Young and H[eber] C. Kimball were witnesses against him. Many hard things were proven against him which he confessed and begged for mercy[.] It was decided that he write a confession of his wickedness, and agree to be one with the Twelve and do right here after, which he agreed to. The property in his hands belonging to the Temple[,] he promised to bring and have a settlement. It was a good and interesting season and will do Adams much good" (George D. Smith, ed., *An Intimate Chronicle: The Journals of William Clayton* [Salt Lake City: Signature Books, 1991], 160).

[16]Adams had been a problem for Brigham Young and the Twelve because he believed Joseph Smith III to be the rightful successor to the martyred prophet. Following Adams's dismissal, he organized his own Church with Joseph Smith III as the intended president. The *Times and Seasons*, Apr. 15, 1845, 878, carried notice of Adams's punishment:

> THIS may certify that Elder George J. Adams has been disfellowshipped and cut off from the church of Jesus Christ of Latter day Saints. – His conduct has been such as to disgrace him in the eyes of justice and virtue, and we cannot and will not sanction a man who is guilty of such things, as we have every reason to believe that he has been[,] from the most indubitable testimony; we have for some time been unwilling to believe the foul statements made concerning him; but the nature of the testimony now adduced, compels us to believe that the statements are but too true, and that under the sacred garb of religion, he has been practising the most disgraceful and diabolical conduct. We think it just to the saints at large to make this statement. And let this be a warning to other elders, if there are any guilty of like conduct.

thing to W[illia]m Smith. Since then W[illia]m Smith has wrote and said he sent some money and some cloth by brother Adams for the Temple; we have not got it. I have also been told that brother Adams has frequently read some kind of a note before the people, which represents him as having some great authority over every body else, and also that he was appointed Joseph [Smith]'s Spokesman. I have been told that brother Adams says the Church owes him something from six hundred to one thousand dollars in money.[17] Now I want to know if brother Adams can explain these things, and whether he is satisfied to have the matter investigated before this council.

Brother Adams then went on to explain [himself] to the Council, relative to the above charges. He denied having said that he was ^appointed^ Joseph's spokesman. He explained about the Temple money, and said he was willing to meet [with] any committee this council might appoint, and settle the whole account with them. He also explained how the church owed him money.

Pres[iden]t Young then prefered some other charges relative to his conduct in the East, to which, after many remarks on both sides, Adams plead guilty and begged for mercy.

Many remarks were then made by sundry individuals, substantiating the charges, prefered by Pres[iden]t Young, each one expressing a strong desire for brother Adams' salvation.[18] After spending

[17]Brigham Young wanted Adams "to explain how the church owes him $600" and to "bring the names of those who donated money," saying other agents had collected "hundreds of dollars" without any trouble meeting their expenses, while Adams "lost $200 coming [to Nauvoo][,] but [Young] dont belive it. [Adams] told us in the fall it was $150 now it is $200" (from a typescript in D. Michael Quinn Papers, Beinecke Rare Book and Manuscript Library, Yale University, New Haven, Connecticut).

[18]Nearly everyone spoke: all seven apostles in attendance, six high councilmen, and one of the presiding bishopric. Brigham Young said he knew through personal revelation that Adams and William Smith had both married "scores" of women back east, adding that he was also "all the time receiving letters from the East giving account of your prostituting young women and ruining the churches." Adams said he had "promise[d] not to tell" about their misadventures, to which Young said he was "willing to cover all things up if [William] will go and do right and stop his boasting." Young "asked if all [in attendance] were willing to keep all that has been said here to themselves – their wives not excepted – unanimous."

Young then proceeded to conduct other business, suggesting that the

much time in investigation, the Pres[iden]t S[amuel] Bent, arose to give his mind on the case, but a motion being made that Pres[iden]t Young give the decision, Pres[iden]t Bent gave way.[19]

Pres[iden]t Young then arose and said he wanted Brother Adams to sit down and write that he had done wrong, that he asks forgiveness, and is willing henceforth to listen to council, and do right without incriminating any one else; also that the proper authorities of this Church are here, and that he is with the Twelve and will be with them to bear off this Kingdom. I want brother Adams to write this freely and confess his iniquities; a mans confession will never do him hurt unless he turns round and does wrong again.[20] Meeting adjourned, to meet in the Seventie's Hall on Saturday next at one o'clock P.M.

*March 22, 1845; Saturday.* The High Council of the Church of Jesus Christ of Latter Day Saints met in the Seventies Hall pursuant to adjournment, ~~at one oclock P.M.~~ and [then] adjourned till next Saturday at one o'clock P.M. to meet in this Hall. C[alvin] C. Pendleton[,] Clerk.

*March 29, 1845; Saturday.* The High Council of the Church of Jesus Christ of Latter Day Saints met in the Seventie's Hall according to

---

city stop construction of a planned dam and concentrate instead on the temple and Nauvoo House hotel. "The dam will bring difficulty," he said. "Will it not be better to drop it & put all forces on the gardens and the Temple[?] G[eorge] A. Smith moved that the council recommend this course. J[ohn] Taylor said he had heard that some [of the leaders] had fears the people would be dissatisifed but he did not think they would (ibid.).

[19]This is an interesting and perhaps significant concession on the part of the president of the high council in allowing the Quorum of the Twelve to make the final decision, seemingly as a matter of etiquette but nevertheless representing how far the Twelve had come in convincing the high council to submit to the Twelve.

[20]D. Michael Quinn explained that "the only one who was seriously urging the succession of Joseph Smith III in 1845 was George J. Adams. Ordained a special apostle by Joseph [Smith] and admitted as one of the original members of the Council of Fifty, Adams [was] excommunicated on 10 April 1845 for defying the Quorum of Twelve by teaching and practicing polygamy in New England" ("Joseph Smith III's 1844 Blessing and the Mormons of Utah," *Dialogue: A Journal of Mormon Thought* 15 [Summer 1982]: 82).

adjournment and opened by prayer from Councellor Huntington. The Minutes of Mar[ch] 8th ^and 22d^ were read and approved. Counsellors Present[:] Samuel Bent[,] Lewis D. Wilson[,] David Fulmer[,] Phineas Richards[,] James Allred[,] George W. Harris[,] Aaron Johnson[,] William Huntington[,] William Snow, [and] C[harles] C. Rich Presiding with President Bent. The following Charge was presented to the Council by Joseph Pennock.

> Nauvoo March 29. 1845. To the Honorable High Council of the Church of Jesus Christ in Nauvoo. I hereby prefer a charge against Elder Libeus T. Coons, John Dixon, David M. Gamett & brother Young, for contempt of a decision of the High Council pertaining to the case of L[ewis] T. Coons and J[oseph] Pennock in stating that J[oseph] Pennock had been reinstated in Nauvoo, but not in the Camp Creek Branch. Joseph Pennock

~~Closing prayer by President C[harles] C. Rich~~ [The council] voted to adjourn till Saturday the 19 day of April next to meet in this Hall at one o'clock P.M. and that the case of J[oseph] Pennock vs L[ewis] T. Coons and others as above stated be acted upon. Closing Prayer by President Rich. [Minutes] approved [by] C[alvin] C. Pendleton[,] Clerk.

*April 19, 1845; Saturday.* The High Council of the church of Jesus Christ of Latter Day Saints met according to adjournment and opened by prayer from Councellor George W. Harris. Councellors Present[:] Lewis D. Wilson[,] David Fulmer[,] Thomas Grover[,] Phineas Richards[,] Alpheus Cutler[,] James Allred[,] George W. Harris [(]pres[iden]t pro tem.)[,] Aaron Johnson[,] William Huntington[,] [and] William Snow.

The following petition [from the wife of councilman Newel Knight], ~~was~~ accompanied with a bottle of Oil[,] was presented before the Council.

> To the Honorable President and Brethren of the High Council: by request of my husband, I write you an apology ^for^ his absence; he is sick; quite confined to his bed with a severe cough and fever: he joins with me in asking you all to join in prayer for his recovery and also requests this bottle of Oil to be consecrated, for, and in

behalf of my husband, whom I love and reverence, even as Sarah did Abraham, when she honored him calling him Lord.[21] Yours with respect. Lydia Knight.[22]

The Oil was consecrated and set apart for the healing of the sick, under the hands of Councellors Harris, Cutler and Huntington, and the Council joined with Brother Harris in prayer for the recovery of Councellor [Newel] Knight.[23]

The case of Joseph Pennock (vs.) L[ewis] T. Coons and others to be acted upon today, was not brought before the Council as the case was settled and charge withdrawn. Brother Alva L. Tippets stated to the council [that something should be done about] the licentious course of conduct of one James Johnson ^and family^ of Indiana[,] according to the best of his information both from his own ~~information~~ ^observation^ and the Statements of others, but action upon the case was defered till next Saturday. [In] that [way] Bishop J[ohn] Murdock might be present[,] [as he] also was with Brother Tippets in the State aforesaid.

[The council] voted to adjourn till ~~next~~ Saturday ^May 3d^ at three o'clock P.M. in the Seventies Hall. C[alvin] C. Pendleton Clerk. [The council] voted that in naming the place of [meeting and] date

---

[21]See Gen. 18:12.

[22]Lydia Knight was born in Sutton, Massachusetts, in June 1812. Her first husband, an alcoholic, abandoned her and her baby in 1831, and she moved in with friends in Canada where she was converted by Joseph Smith and Sidney Rigdon in 1833. When she married Newel Knight in 1835, the ceremony was performed by Joseph Smith. She was among the founders of the female Relief Society. All seemed well with the family when they left Nauvoo in 1846. However, Newell died in January 1847 and left Lydia and seven children to get by as best they could. The family reached Salt Lake City in late 1850. She became a plural wife to John Dalton, whom she divorced seven years later. She remarried again, but her last husband died after three years of matrimony. They had moved to St. George to serve in the temple, and she stayed there, dying in St. George in 1884 ("Lydia Goldthwaite Bailey Knight," *Women's Manuscripts, BYU Digital Collections,* contentdm.lib.byu.edu).

[23]In Mormon teaching, when giving an individual a healing blessing, the priesthood holder performing the ordinance anoints the head with consecrated olive oil. See Jonathan A. Stapley and Kristine Wright, "The Forms and the Power: The Development of Mormon Ritual Healing to 1847," *Journal of Mormon History* 35 (Summer 2009): 42-87.

in the High Council minutes, that the Name ["]City of Joseph["] [should be] suppl[ied] [in] the place of Nauvoo. Approved.[24]

*May 3, 1845; Saturday.* The High Council of the Church of Jesus Christ of Latter Day Saints met according to adjournment and opened for business by prayer from Counsellor Tho[ma]s Grover. Councellors Present[:] Samuel Bent[,] Lewis D. Wilson[,] David Fulmer[,] Thomas Grover[,] Newel Knight[,] Phineas Richards[,] James Allred[,] Alpheus Cutler[,] George W. Harris[,] Aaron Johnson[,] William Huntington[,] [and] William Snow. [The] minutes of the two previous meetings were read and approved.

The case of James Johnson of Indiana, was again taken into consideration. Brother Alva L. Tippets stated to the Council that by a decision of Bishop John Murdock and himself, while on their Mission; the said James Johnson was cut off from the Church, whereupon it was unanimously voted that said decision remain in effect upon him (the said Johnson). [It was] voted to adjourn to meet in this Hall on Saturday, two weeks from to day at three o'clock P.M. Closing prayer by president Bent. Approved. Calvin C. Pendleton[,] Clerk.

*May 10, 1845; Saturday.* The High Council of the Church of Jesus Christ of Latter Day Saints met pursuant to adjournment, and opened by prayer from Councellor Aaron Johnson. The minutes of the previous meeting was read and approved. Counsellors Present[:] Samuel Bent[,] Lewis D. Wilson[,] David Fulmer[,] Thomas Grover[,] Newel Knight[,] Phineas Richards[,] James Allred[,] Alpheus Cutler[,] George W Harris[,] Aaron Johnson[,] William Huntington[,] [and] William Snow. No business was presented to the Council to be acted upon.[It was] voted to adjourn, to meet in this Hall on Saturday three weeks from to day at three ^o'clock^ P.M. [The] closing prayer

---

[24]Two weeks earlier, at the general conference held on April 6, Brigham Young had proposed the name change to "City of Joseph." But "the name change was more symbolic than literal," write George W. and Sylvia Givens, "since no further legal attempt was made to change the name of the city, either with the proper state officials or through the postal service" (*Five Hundred Little-Known Facts about Nauvoo* (Springville, UT: Bonneville Books, 2010), 132.

[was offered] by President Bent. [The minutes were] approved [by] C[alvin] C. Pendleton[,] Clerk.

*June 1, 1845; Sunday.* Special Meeting, City of Joseph[,] June 1st 1845. The High Council of the Church of Jesus Christ of Latter Day Saints, met this day, to act upon the case of James Braden[25] vs. Jacob Myers,[26] and the branch over which [Myers] presides, (viz) ^Mill Creek^ Freedom Branch,)[27] it being an appeal from said branch where the said Braden was expelled.[28] Counsellors Present[:] Samuel Bent[,] David Fulmer[,] Thomas Grover[,] Newel Knight[,] Phineas Richards[,] James Allred[,] Alpheus Cutler[,] George W. Harris[,] Aaron Johnson[,] William Huntington[,] [and] William Snow[,] [along with] Charles C. Rich Presiding[,] with President Bent.

A written account of Braden's trial before ^a Conference holden at^ the Freedom Branch was presented to the Council, together with the following communication from Pres[iden]t Bent, to Jacob Myers[:]

To Jacob Myers, President of the Mill Creek Branch[,] Adams

---

[25]James Braden was born in 1801 in West Bethlehem, Pennsylvania. He was baptized prior to 1833, the year Sidney Rigdon questioned the legitimacy of Braden's ordination as a priest. He received an elder's licence in 1836. From Missouri, he escaped with the other Mormon refugees who were forced to flee the state in 1839. He died in Woodpine, Iowa, in 1881.

[26]Jacob Myers was born in Pence, Pennsylvania, in August 1782. He married Sarah Elizabeth Coleman, who bore fifteen children. In 1834 they were baptized, and he was ordained an elder the next year. In Kirtland he was active in the United Firm, the Church's communal order. In Missouri he was a millwright who was wounded during the attack at Haun's Mill. He died in October 1867 and was buried in Nauvoo.

[27]The Freedom Branch in Adams County, Illinois, included Mill Creek. See the "Autobiography of Warren Foote," BYU Special Collections, 58, 60, 63 (available at "Writings of Early Latter-day Saints," *GospeLink Digital Library by Deseret Book,* gospelink.com). Foote added that "Elder James Braden was disfellowshipped [in December 1844] for dishonest dealings with his stepdaughter" (64).

[28]Braden was excommunicated on January 19, 1845, notice of which appeared in the *Times and Seasons,* Feb. 15, 1845, 806. The notice said that Braden refused to give up his license when it was demanded of him.

Co[unty][:] I hereby notify you that James Braden has made a complaint to the High Council at Nauvoo, against you and your Branch for disfellowshipping said Braden; This is to notify you to appear before said Council on Saturday the 31st day of May next at the Seventies' Hall at one o'clock to show cause why you disfellowshipped said Braden. Samuel Bent President of said Council.

N.B. Said Braden appeals from your decision upon his case, to the High Council. Brother Meyers, I desire you to strive with all the powers of your soul, to reclaim Brother Braden, and settle with difficulty with him in your Branch, and not trouble the Council with it. Yours with Respects, Samuel Bent.

The High Council decided that the branch had done right in expelling him, (the said Braden.)[29] Meeting adjourned until Saturday 7th inst[ant] at the Seventie's Hall at 3 o'clock P.M. (H[enry] G. Sherwood) Clerk Pro Tem. Approved.

*June 7, 1845; Saturday.* The High Council of the Church of Jesus Christ of Latter Day Saints, met according to adjournment, ^in the Seventie's Hall^ and opened by prayer from Counsellor Huntington, from thence convened to the dwelling of H[enry] G. Sherwood. Minutes of previous meetings [were] read and approved. Counsellors Present[:] Samuel Bent[,] David Fulmer[,] Thomas Grover[,] Newel Knight[,] Phineas Richards[,] James Allred[,] George W. Harris[,] William Huntington[,] [and] Henry G. Sherwood, who having returned from his mission filled his place in the Council. [The members] voted to adjourn, and meet in the Seventie's Hall on Saturday, two weeks from to day at three o'clock [in the] afternoon. Closing prayer by Counsellor H[enry] G. Sherwood. Approved. Calvin C. Pendleton, Clerk.

*June 21, 1845; Saturday.* The High Council of the Church of Jesus Christ of Latter-Day Saints met according to adjournment and opened by prayer from Counsellor P[hineas] Richards. [The] Minutes of the previous meeting were read and approved. No business

[29]Bent's initial impulse had been to fellowship Myers, but his opinion changed, apparently after hearing the evidence. Perhaps Myers's "dishonest dealings with his stepdaughter" proved to be something worse than one might like to assume (see note 26).

being brought before the Council[,] [therefore] a vote was taken to adjourn sine die. Counsellors Present[:] Samuel Bent[,] David Fulmer[,] Newel Knight[,] Phineas Richards[,] James Allred[,] George W. Harris[,] Aaron Johnson[,] William Huntington[,] [and] Henry G. Sherwood, Charles C. Rich presiding with Pres[iden]t Bent. Closing prayer by Pres[iden]t Rich. Approved Oct[ober] 18, 1845.

*August 9, 1845; Saturday.* The High Council of the Church of Jesus Christ of Latter Day Saints met in Council this day in the dwelling of Elder George A. Smiths'. Opened by prayer from Pres[iden]t John Smith[.] Counsellors Present[:] Samuel Bent[,] Lewis D. Wilson[,] David Fulmer[,] Thomas Grover[,] Newel Knight[,] Ezra T. Benson[,] James Allred[,] Alpheus Cutler[,] George W. Harris[,] Aaron Johnson[,] William Huntington[,] [and] Presidents John Smith and Charles C. Rich presiding with Pres[iden]t Bent.

W[illia]m Pomroy was cut off from the Church by a unanimous vote of the Council for drunkenness, profanity and for cursing the President of the Church; on the testimony of Counsellor Huntington, and Pres[iden]t John Smith. [The council] voted unanimously that Selah Lane[30] be cut off from the Church of Jesus Christ of Latter Day Saints for unchristian-like conduct, and ^that^ publication of the same be given in the "Times and Seasons" and [Nauvoo] Neighbor.[31]

---

[30]Selah Lane was born in 1800 in New York. About thirty years later, he moved to Hempstead, Long Island, and built a house the neighbors called "the temple" because of both its size and Lane's religious inclinations. Even so, he was said to be a man of "refinement and learning" who had been a ship's captain. Semi-retired, he came to operate a toll booth to Rum Point. The neighbors noticed that among the "frequent" guests at his home were Brigham Young and Wilford Woodruff. In 1849 he was asked to be a counselor in the First Presidency of William Smith's Church (Daniel M. Tredwell, *Personal Reminiscences of Men and Things on Long Island* [Brooklyn: Charles A. Ditmas, 1912], 241-42; Scott G. Kenney, *Wilford Woodruff's Journal, 1833-1898,* 9 vols. [Midvale, UT: Signature Books, 1983-1985], 1:257, 367; *Melchisedeck and Aaronic Herald,* May 1, 1849, online at www.connellodonovan.com/herald.pdf).

[31]This was not done. Lane appeared before Church leaders in New York to make a confession, saying he had been misled by William Smith. But according to the commentary in the British LDS *Millennial Star,* Nov. 20, 1846, 140-41, although "W[illia]m Smith had more sins of his own to answer for than he would be able to cancel," the Church would toler-

[The council] unanimously voted that Elder Freeman Nickerson, fill the seat of Counsellor Sherwood during his absence on a mission.[32] [The council] also voted, that the Clerk give notice to ^Brother^ Alanson Ripley[33] to appear before the Council in two weeks from to day at two o'clock P.M. [The council] voted to adjourn to the present place of meeting, untill Saturday, two weeks from to day at two o'clock [in the] afternoon. Closing prayer by Pres[iden]t Bent. Approved. C[alvin] C. Pendleton[,] Cl[er]k[.]

*August 23, 1845; Saturday.* The High Council of the Church of Jesus Christ of Latter Day Saints met according to adjournment at Elder George A. Smith's, and opened for business by prayer from Brother Isaac Morley. Counsellors Present[:] Samuel Bent[,] Lewis D. Wilson[,] David Fulmer[,] Thomas Grover[,] Newel Knight[,] Ezra T. Benson[,] James Allred[,] Alpheus Cutler[,] George W. Harris[,] Aaron Johnson[,] William Huntington[,] [and] Freeman Nickerson. Minutes of the previous meeting were read and approved.

[The council] voted that the case of Alanson Ripley [should] be laid over till the next sitting of the Council, (two weeks from to day 2 o'clock P.M.) in consequence of his absence on business for the Nau-

---

ate no "scape-goat[s]" and Lane would have to repent and be rebaptized. Everything seemed settled until Lane "threatened violence against" those who had "informed of him" and the rebaptism was canceled. He thereafter joined the Strangites and later re-associated with William Smith. "Oh happy pair!" mocked the *Millennial Star,* "the glory of thy union is like the odours that rise from a den of pole-cats, or like the perfume that ascends from a putrid carcass to invite a sumptuous feast [for] every bird whose maw can alone be satisfied with that kind of food."

[32]Sherwood had just returned from a mission and was already making preparations to leave again. Brigham Young needed a reliable and rugged man like Sherwood, a former city marshal, to go to James Emmett's colony at Vermillion on the upper Missouri River and take control of it, which Sherwood did (*History of Church,* 7:495-96).

[33]A former Nauvoo City surveyor, bishop, and one-time clerk for the high council, Alanson Ripley had once been so close to Joseph Smith that he occupied his office while Smith was away in Washington, D.C. However, Ripley was tried in 1841 for "abusing his brethren while under the influence of Liquor," for which he lost his position as bishop. Ripley was also the force behind the move to declare Robert Foster's barn a nuisance on the same day the city council heard the *Nauvoo Expositor* case. For these details, see the city council minutes for Mar. 8, 1841; June 10, 1844; and high council minutes for Oct. 21, 1839; Mar. 16, 1840; Apr. 6, 1841; also chapter 6, note 28.

voo House. The following charge was prefered ^before the Council^ against Ira L Miles:

> To the Honorable High Council of the Church of Christ at Nauvoo. I hereby prefer the following charges ~~against~~ before your body, against Ira L. Miles. Firstly: For being engaged with a Rabble, Secondly, For stealing watermellons & pulling up vines. Thirdly, For Brickbatting[34] a house and other improper conduct. Nauvoo Aug[ust] 17, 1845. Hezekiah Peck.

By vote of the Council, the preceding charge was also laid over until the next meeting of the Council, in consequence of the absence of brother Miles.

Daniel F. Botsford, (who together with his wife had been expelled from the Church) came before the Council and petitioned for a rehearing whereupon it was Unanimously decided that he have a rehearing. Said Botsford being unprepared to clear himself from charges against him, it was unanimously voted that he stand as he is, until he shall bring sufficient evidence to clear himself from existing testimony or charges, or until he make confession of his faults. Note after the setting of the Council the said Botsford and the aggrieved parties became reconciled, and together went to the Counsellors and was rec[eive]d by rebaptism[.]

[The council] voted that the clerk notify Lindzey A. Brady[35] to appear before this Council on Saturday two weeks from to day at 2 o'clock P.M. on charge of rebaptizing Jordon Hendrickson, and otherwise maltreating the Council. [The council] voted unanimously that the clerk also Notify ~~Amsa~~ Amasa Bonney[36] to ~~meet~~ appear

---

[34]A “brickbat” was a “fragment of a brick,” meant to hurt or destroy property when thrown, yet not to do major damage (Noah Webster, *An American Dictionary of the English* Language [New York: S. Converse, 1828], s.v “brick bat”).

[35]Lindsey Anderson Brady was born in June 1811 in Lincoln, Kentucky. He was baptized by Wilford Woodruff in 1835, after which he and his family moved from Kentucky to the Mormon town of Far West, Missouri, only to be kicked out of the state in 1839. They moved to Nauvoo and later continued west, arriving in Utah in 1850. He died in Fairview, Sanpete County, Utah, in June 1885.

[36]Amasa Bonney was born in Auburn, New York in 1804, and after his conversion to Mormonism he was ordained a Seventy in Kirtland in

befor said Council at the time and place above specified [to answer a] Charge [of] un ~~Ch~~ christian like conduct in the use of intoxicating drinks.

[The council] voted to adjourn, to meet in this house 2 weeks from to day at 2 o'clock P.M. President John Smith & Council[ors] (Isaac Morley and Cha[rle]s C Rich[37]) presiding with Pres[iden]t Bent. Approved. C[alvin] C. Pendleton[,] Clerk.

*September 6, 1845; Saturday.* The High Council of the Church of Jesus Christ of Latter-Day Saints met this day according to appointment in the dwelling of Elder George A. Smith and opened for business by prayer from Pres[iden]t [Samuel] Bent. Counsellors Present[:] Samuel Bent[,] Lewis D. Wilson[,] Joshua Holman in place of D[avid] Fulmer)[,] Thomas Grover[,] Newel Knight[,] Ezra T. Benson[,] James Allred[,] Alpheus Cutler[,] George W. Harris[,] Aaron Johnson[,] William Huntington[,] [and] Freeman Nickerson[,] [and] Charles C Rich Presiding with President Bent. Elder John E Page [was] also Present.

[The council] voted unanimously that Elder Joshua Holman fill the place of David Fulmer (pro tem.) Amasa Bonney (who had been cited before the Council) on the charge of drunkenness) appeared in a high state of intoxication, with a bottle in his pocket; and was soon in a state of ~~stupor~~ sleep, in the Council room, whereupon it was voted unanimously that he be cut off from the Church of Jesus Christ of Latter Day Saints, and was forthwith conducted from the room [by] Counsellors Wilson & Holman.

The following Charge, ^and communications^ ~~Dated Aug[ust] 31~~ were presented:

---

1835. He helped run the Kirtland Safety Society. In fact, he is said to have purchased seven horses from a Kirtland farmer with notes printed by the Safety Society. When the farmer realized the notes were worthless and returned to reclaim his horses, he was refused—at least according to Arthur B. Deming, *Naked Truths about Mormonism,* Apr. 1888, 3. The account might be biased, but Bonney's appearance, drunk, before the high council on September 6, 1845 (below) does little to burnish his reputation. Bonney served a mission to New York in 1843, but little else is known about him. He died in 1865.

[37]The scribe repeated the name "C. C. Rich" above the line in the original minutes.

> Nauvoo Aug[ust] 31, 1845. To the President of the High Council of the Church of Jesus Christ of Latter day Saints. I tender a complaint against David Elliot[38] for unchristian-like conduct and abuse to his wife. Signed, Joshua S. Holman.
>
> Nauvoo Aug[ust] 31, 1845. Brother David Elliot, You are hereby notified to appear before the High Council on Saturday the 6th day of Sept[ember] at 2 o'clock P.M. at George A. Smith's to answer to a charge prefered against you by Joshua S. Holman, for unchristian like conduct in abuse to your wife &c. By order of said Council[.] Samuel Bent, Pres[iden]t of s[ai]d Council.

A written request from Elders David Elliot & W[illia]m Smith for an adjournment in consequence of ill health and want of time of the part of brother Elliot ^to procure witnesses;^ was read, where upon by ^with^ consent of Brother Holman, it was unanimously voted that the case of David Elliot be laid over for the present.

The case of Elder Lindsey A. Brady was then considered[.] Elder Brady, plead ignorance of a decision of the ^High^ Council, relative to rebaptizing excommunicated members, viz that an elder or ^any^ one authorized to baptize should forfeit his membership in case of rebaptizing any excommunicated individual without due retraction or satisfaction being made to the Church, but [he] confessed his fault, asked forgiveness, and promised never to be guilty of the like offence. [The council] voted unanimously that Elder Brady be continued in fellowship.

Jordan Hendrickson being present wished a standing in the church whereupon it was unanimously voted that his case be laid over till Saturday two weeks from to day. [The council] voted unanimously that the case of Ira L. Miles be investigated ^he not presenting himself. [The council also] voted that President Rich give a decision without further ~~voted that one on a side speak Charles C. Rich Council~~

---

[38]David Elliott was born at Charleston, New York, in November 1799 and was trained as a blacksmith. He was baptized in Ithaca, New York, in 1831, the year he married Mary Cahoon. They had three children. He marched in Zion's Camp in 1834. On his return, he was ordained a Seventy. Thereafter, he and his wife moved to Missouri where she died in 1838. The next year, David moved to Springfield, Illinois, and later immigrated to Salt Lake City, where he died in December 1852 ("Biographical Registers," *BYU Studies,* byustudies.byu.edu).

~~for Plaintiff~~ investigation of the subject.^ ~~James Allred Council for Defendant~~ [The] charges [were] sustained, and ~~on motion C[harles] C. R[ich]~~ [the council] unanimously voted that Ira S. Miles be cut off from the Church of [Jesus] Christ of Latter-Day Saints.

[The council] voted that James M. Flack[39], and Francis Pullen[40] be cited by the Clerk, to appear before this Council in two weeks from today, on charge of inebriation. [The council] voted to adjourn and meet in this house on Sat[urday] two weeks from to day at two o'clock P.M. Closing prayer by Elder John E. Page. C[alvin] C. Pendleton[,] Cl[er]k[.]

*September 20, 1845; Saturday.* Owing to troubles caused by mob violence, the High Council did not meet and business pertaining to the Council was defered till some subsequent time.[41] Approved. C[alvin] C. Pendleton, Clerk.

---

[39]James M. Flack was born in 1818 in New York. It is not known when he joined the LDS Church, but he made his way to Nauvoo by 1841, when he appears as an officer in the Nauvoo Legion and as part of an expedition to Wisconsin to obtain lumber for the Nauvoo temple. In 1843 he married Irene Summer Miles, whose first husband had recently died. By September 1846 the couple can be found in Winter Quarters, Nebraska. However, Irene left James the next year to marry Sam Wheaton and move to Poor Man Gulch in Dakota Territory. Flack continued on to Utah to become one of the "Hickman Hounds," Bill Hickman's gang of gunmen who were sworn to protect Brigham Young. Where and when Flack died are unknown.

[40]Francis Pullen was born in September 1802 in Ledbury, England. In 1838 he was visited by Brigham Young and Wilford Woodruff and converted to Mormonism. Within two years Pullen was on his own proselyting mission in England. He married Martha Embrey and they had one child. By 1843 he was living in Nauvoo and working as a brick mason in partnership with Philander Colton. In Council Bluffs in 1846 he constructed a brick kiln. He is traceable the next year, making his way to Utah. He seems to have settled in American Fork, but then the documentary scent grows weak and nothing more can be found of him.

[41]Many Illinoisans had decided the Saints needed to leave the state. In September 1845, people living on the county line between Adams and Hancock Counties planned to drive out the newcomers. Conspiring to make it appear as though the Mormons had fired on them first, 300 non-Mormon men proceeded to burn Mormon farms. "Brigham Young reported on September 15 that forty-four buildings had been destroyed, with the arson continuing," as historian Robert B. Flanders wrote. "Terrified Mormons were fleeing to Nauvoo, and 134 teams and wagons were sent from the city to aid

*October 18, 1845; Saturday.*[42] The High Council of the Church of Jesus Christ of Latter-Day Saints met according to appointment and adjourned to the dwelling of President John Smith. [The] opening Prayer [was delivered] by Father [Isaac] Morley. Counsellors Present[:] Sam[ue]l Bent[,] David Fulmer[,] Newel Knight[,] Ezra T. Benson[,] James Allred[,] Alpheus Cutler[,] George W. Harris[,] [and] Aaron Johnson, [with] Father John Smith, Isaac Morley, & Charles C. Rich Presiding. [The council] voted unanimously, that Jordon Hendrickson be received into fellowship in this Church by rebaptism.

[The council] voted unanimously that the case of David Elliot be dropped, as no prosecutor appeared against him. [The council also] unanimously voted that the cases of Alanson Ripley, James M. Flack, and Francis Pullen be dropped for want of prosecutors. [The council then] voted to adjourn Sine Die. [The] closing prayer [was offered] by Counsellor Allred. [The minutes were checked and] approved [by] Calvin C. Pendleton[,] Clerk.

---

in the evacuation" (*Nauvoo: Kingdom on the Mississippi* [Urbana: University of Illinois Press, 1975], 326-27).

Two days after the high council meeting, non-Mormon citizens met in Quincy to consider options for peace, quickly becoming known as the Quincy Committee. At their recommendation, Governor Ford recruited militiamen to position themselves between the Mormons and non-Mormons as a buffer. He issued a proclamation warning outsiders not to enter Hancock County. Before long, Brigham Young promised the Quincy Committee that the Mormons would begin making preparations to leave Nauvoo. For more on this period of the city's history, see Marshall Hamilton, "From Assassination to Expulsion: Two Years of Distrust, Hostility, and Violence," in *Kingdom on the Mississippi Revisited: Nauvoo in Mormon History,* eds. Roger D. Launius and John E. Hallwas (Urbana: University of Illinois Press, 1996), 214-230.

[42]See *History of Church,* 7:482. This was evidently the last meeting of the Nauvoo High Council. To follow the operations of a sitting high council after the Nauvoo era, see Edward L. Kimball and Kenneth W. Godfrey, "Law and Order in Winter Quarters," *Journal of Mormon History* 32 (Spring 2006): 172-218.

# Appendices

# A.

# The Nauvoo Charter

*In October 1840, a year after the Latter-day Saints began to establish themselves in Nauvoo, one item of business at the Church's general conference was to appoint a committee composed of John C. Bennett, Joseph Smith, and Robert B. Thompson to draft a bill incorporating Nauvoo as a city. Two months later, on December 16, the Illinois General Assembly approved the petition and granted Nauvoo a charter, which took effect on February 1, 1841. Since 1837, when Chicago became the first town in Illinois to be granted city status, Alton, Galena, Springfield, and Quincy had followed by 1840; the Nauvoo charter was similar to the five others that had preceded it, with significant differences. First, section thirteen granted Nauvoo "such other legislative powers as are conferred on the city council of the city of Springfield," rather than specifically enumerating those powers. Second, section twenty-five provided for a military unit, the Nauvoo Legion, with powers unlimited by state laws. Third, the rules dictating the establishment, functions, and scope of the city council were precisely outlined. Another unique aspect of the charter was that it granted the city council authority not only to appoint city officers–the marshal, assessor, supervisor of streets, etc.–but also to dismiss them without cause.*

*Because of the liberal provisions of the charter, the blending of church and state, and the general controversial nature of Mormonism, with its secret, yet rumored practice of plural marriage, calls to repeal the charter by the Church's enemies came early and frequently. Measures calling for repeal were also proposed and defeated in the state legislature. Later, Joseph Smith encountered influential local enemies such as* Warsaw Signal *editor, Thomas Sharp, whose newspaper called for repeal. Mormon dissidents voiced their views in the* Nauvoo Expositor *(portions of which appear in this volume as Appendix B), where they advocated in bold letters the "UNCONDITIONAL REPEAL OF THE NAUVOO CITY CHARTER." In December 1844, six months after Joseph Smith's murder, Governor Thomas Ford acknowledged that the provisions of the charter had been "much abused," and in January 1845 the state senate voted 25-14, and the House voted 75-31, for repeal. A year later, the majority of the Saints began the exodus to the West. The charter was published by the city in 1842, and a photographic reproduction is available online at "Mormon Publications: 19th and 20th Centuries,"* BYU Digital Collections, *http:contentdm.lib.byu.edu/*

---

THE

CITY CHARTER:

LAWS, ORDINANCES, AND ACTS

OF THE

CITY COUNCIL

OF THE

CITY OF NAUVOO.

AND ALSO, THE ORDINANCES

OF THE

NAUVOO LEGION:

FROM THE COMMENCEMENT OF THE CITY TO THIS DATE.

---

NAUVOO, ILL.
PUBLISHED BY ORDER OF THE CITY COUNCIL.

**JOSEPH SMITH, Printer.**

..............

**July...1842.**

# CITY CHARTER.

---

## AN ACT TO INCORPORATE THE CITY OF NAUVOO.

SECT. 1. *Be it enacted by the People of the State of Illinois, represented in the General Assembly*, that all that district of country embraced within the following boundaries, to wit: beginning at the north-east corner of section thirty-one in township seven, north of range eight, west of the fourth principal meridian, in the county of Hancock, and running thence west to the north-west corner of said section; thence north to the Mississippi river; thence west to the middle of the main channel of the said river; thence down the middle of said channel to a point due west of the south-east corner of fractional section number twelve, in township six, north of range nine west of the fourth principal meridian; thence east to the south-east corner of said section twelve; thence north on the range line between township six north and range eight and nine west, to the south-west corner of section six, in township six, north of range eight west; thence east to the south-east corner of said section; thence north to the place of beginning; including the town plats of Commerce and Nauvoo, shall hereafter be called and known, by the name of the "CITY OF NAUVOO," and the inhabitants thereof are hereby constituted a body corporate and politic by the name aforesaid, and shall have perpetual succession, and may have, and use, a common seal, which they may change, and alter at pleasure.

SEC. 2. Whenever any tract of land, adjoining the "City of Nauvoo," shall have been laid out into town lots, and duly recorded according to law, the same shall form a part of the "City of Nauvoo."

SEC. 3. The inhabitants of said city, by the name and style aforesaid, shall have power to sue and be sued, to plead and be impleaded, defend and be defended, in all courts of law and equity, and in all actions whatsoever; to purchase, receive, and hold property, real and personal, in said city, to purchase, receive, and hold real property beyond the city for burying grounds, or for other public purposes, for the use of the inhabitants of said city; to sell, lease, convey, or dispose of property, real and personal, for the benefit of the city, to improve and protect such property, and to do all other things in relation thereto as natural persons.

SEC. 4. There shall be a City Council to consist of a Mayor, four Aldermen, and nine Councillors, who shall have the qualifications of electors of said city, and shall be chosen by the qualified voters thereof, and shall hold their offices for two years, and until their successors shall be elected and qualified. The City Council shall judge of the qualifications, elections, and returns of their own members, and a majority of them shall form a quorum to do business; but a smaller number may adjourn from day to day, and compel the attendance of absent members, under such penalties as may be prescribed by ordinance.

SEC. 5. The Mayor, Aldermen and Councillors, before entering upon the duties of their offices, shall take and subscribe an oath or affirmation that they will support the Constitution of the United States, and of this State, and that they will well and truly perform the duties of their offices to the best of their skill and abilities.

SEC. 6. On the first Monday of February next, and every two years thereafter, an election shall be held for the election of one Mayor, four Aldermen, and nine Councillors, and at the first election under the act, three judges shall be chosen *viva voce* by the electors present; the said judges shall choose two clerks, and the judges and clerks, before entering upon their duties shall take and subscribe an oath or affirmation, such as is now required by law to be taken by judges and clerks of other elections; and at all subsequent elections, the necessary number of judges and clerks shall be appointed by the City Council. At the first election so held the polls shall be opened at nine o'clock A. M. and closed at six o'clock P. M.; at the close of the polls the votes shall be counted and a statement thereof proclaimed at the front door of the house at which said election shall be held; and the clerks shall leave with each person elected, or at his usual place of residence, within five days after the election, a written notice of his election; and each person so notified shall, within ten days after the election, take the oath or affirmation herein before mentioned, a certificate of which oath shall be deposited with the Recorder, whose appointment is hereafter provided for, and be by him preserved; and all subsequent elections shall be held, conducted, and returns thereof made as may be provided for by ordinance of the City Council.

Sec. 7. All free white male inhabitants who are of the age of twenty one years, who are entitled to vote for state officers, and who shall have been actual residents of said city sixty days next preceding said election, shall be entitled to vote for city officers.

Sec. 8. The City Council shall have authority to levy and collect taxes for city purposes upon all property, real and personal, within the limits of the city, not exceeding one-half per cent. per annum, upon the assessed value thereof, and may enforce the payment of the same in any manner to be provided by ordinance, not repugnant to the Constitution of the United States, or of this State.

Sec. 9. The City Council shall have power to appoint a Recorder, Treasurer, Assessor, Marshal, Supervisor of Streets, and all such other officers as may be necessary; and to prescribe their duties and remove them from office at pleasure.

Sec. 10. The City Council shall have power to require of all officers appointed in pursuance of this act, bonds with penalty and security, for the faithful performance of their respective duties, such as may be deemed expedient; and also, to require all officers appointed as aforesaid to take an oath for the faithful performance of the duties of their respective offices.

Sec. 11. The City Council shall have power and authority to make, ordain, establish and execute, all such ordinances, not repugnant to the Constitution of the United States or of this State, as they may deem necessary for the peace, benefit, good order, regulation, convenience, and cleanliness, of said city; for the protection of property therein from destruction by fire or otherwise, and for the health, and happiness thereof; they shall have power to fill all vacancies that may happen by death, resignation, or removal, in any of the offices herein made elective; to fix and establish all the fees of the officers of said corporation not herein established; to impose such fines, not exceeding one hundred dollars for each offense, as they may deem just, for refusing to accept any office under the corporation, or for misconduct therein; to divide the city into wards; to add to the number of Aldermen and Councillors; and apportion them among the several wards, as may be most just and conducive to the interests of the city.

Sec. 12. To license, tax, and regulate auctions, merchants, retailers, grocers, hawkers, peddlers, brokers, pawn-brokers, and money-changers.

Sec. 13. The City Council shall have exclusive power within the city, by ordinance, to license, regulate, and restrain, the keeping of ferries, to regulate the police of the city; to impose fines, forfeitures, and penalties, for the breach of any ordinance, and provide for the recovery of such fines and forfeitures, and the enforcement of such penalties, and to pass such ordinances as may be necessary and proper for carrying into execution the powers specified in this act; *Provided* such ordinances are not repugnant to the Constitution of the United States, or of this State: and, in fine, to exercise such other legislative powers as are conferred on the City Council of the City of Springfield, by an act entitled "An Act to incorporate the City of Springfield," approved, February third, one thousand eight hundred and forty.

SEC. 14. All ordinances passed by the City Council shall, within one month after they shall have been passed, be published in some newspaper printed in the city, or certified copies thereof be posted up in three of the most public places in the city.

SEC. 15. All ordinances of the city may be proven by the seal of the corporation, and when printed or published in book or pamphlet form, purporting to be printed or published by authority of the corporation, the same shall be received in evidence in all courts or places without further proof.

SEC. 16. The Mayor and Aldermen shall be conservators of the peace within the limits of said city, and shall have all the powers of Justices of the Peace therein, both in civil and criminal cases, arising under the laws of the State: they shall, as Justices of the Peace, within the limits of said city, perform the same duties, be governed by the same laws, give the same bonds and security, as other Justices of the Peace, and be commissioned as Justices of the Peace in and for said city by the Governor.

SEC. 17. The Mayor shall have exclusive jurisdiction in all cases arising under the ordinances of the corporation, and shall issue such process as may be necessary to carry said ordinances into execution and effect; appeals may be had from any decision or judgment of said Mayor or Aldermen, arising under the city ordinances, to the Municipal Court, under such regulations as may be presented by ordinance; which court shall be composed of the Mayor, as Chief Justice, and the Aldermen as Associate Justices, and from the final Judgment of the Municipal Court, to the Circuit Court of Hancock county, in the same manner of appeals are taken from judgments of the Justices of the Peace; *Provided*, That the parties litigant shall have a right to a trial by a jury of twelve men, in all cases before the Municipal Court. The Municipal Court shall have power to grant writs of habeas corpus in all cases arising under the ordinances of the City Council.

SEC. 18. The Municipal Court shall sit on the first Monday of every month, and the City Council at such times and place as may be prescribed by city ordinance; special meetings of which may at any time be called by the Mayor or any two Aldermen.

SEC. 19. All process issued by the Mayor, Aldermen, or Municipal Court, shall be directed to the Marshal, and in the execution thereof he shall be governed by the same laws as are, or may be, prescribed for the direction and compensation of Constables in similar cases. The Marshal shall also perform such other duties as may be required of him under the ordinances of said city, and shall be the principal ministerial officer.

SEC. 20. It shall be the duty of the Recorder to make and keep accurate records of all ordinances made by the City Council, and of all their proceedings in their corporate capacity, which record shall at all times be open to the inspection of the electors of said city, and shall perform such other duties as may be required of him by the ordinances of the City Council, and shall serve as Clerk of the Municipal Court.

SEC. 21. When it shall be necessary to take private property for the opening, widening, or altering any public street, lane, avenue, or alley, the corporation shall make a just compensation therefor to the person whose property is so taken; and if the amount of such compensation cannot be agreed upon, the Mayor shall cause the same to be ascertained by a jury of six disinterested freeholders of the city.

SEC. 22. All jurors empanneled to enquire into the amount of benefits or damages that shall happen to the owners of property, so proposed to be taken, shall first be sworn to that effect, and shall return to the Mayor their inquest in writing, signed by each juror.

SEC. 23. In case the mayor shall at any time be guilty of a palpable omission of duty, or shall wilfully, and corruptly be guilty of oppression, mal-conduct, or partiality in the discharge of the duties of his office, he shall be liable to be indicted in the Circuit Court of Hancock county, and on conviction he shall be fined not more than two hundred dollars, and the court shall have power, on the recommendation of the jury, to add to the judgment of the court that he be removed from office.

SEC. 24. The City Council may establish and organize an Institution of learning within the limits of the city, for the teaching of the Arts, Sciences, and Learned Professions, to be called the "University of the City of Nauvoo," which institution shall be under the control and management of a Board of Trustees, consisting of a Chancellor, Registrar, and twenty-three Regents; which Board shall thereafter be a body corporate and politic, with perpetual succession by the name of the "Chancellor and Regents of the University of the City of Nauvoo," and shall have full power to pass, ordain, establish and execute all such laws and ordinances as they may consider necessary for the welfare and prosperity of said University, its officers, and students; *Provided,* That the said laws and ordinances shall not be repugnant to the Constitution of the United States, or of this State; and *Provided,* also, that the Trustees shall at all times be appointed by the City Council, and shall have all the powers and privileges for the advancement of the cause of education which appertain to the Trustees of any other College or University of this State.

SEC. 25. The City Council may organize the inhabitants of said city, subject to military duty, into a body of independent military men to be called the "Nauvoo Legion," the Court Martial of which shall be composed of the commissioned officers of said Legion, and constitute the law making department, with full powers and authority to make, ordain, establish, and execute, all such laws and ordinances as may be considered necessary for the benefit, government and regulation of said Legion; *Provided,* said Court Martial shall pass no law or act repugnant to, or inconsistent with, the Constitution of the United States, or of this State; and, *Provided,* also, that the officers of the Legion shall be commissioned by the Governor of the State. The said Legion shall perform the same amount of military duty as is now, or may be hereafter, required of the regular militia of the State, and shall be at the disposal of the Mayor in executing the laws and ordinances of the City Corporation, and the laws of the State, and at the disposal of the Governor for the public defence, and the execution of the laws of the State, or of the United States, and shall be entitled to their proportion of the public arms; and, *Provided,* also, that said Legion shall be exempt from all other military duty.

SEC. 26. The inhabitants of the "City of Nauvoo" are hereby exempted from working on any road beyond the limits of the city, and for the purpose of keeping the streets, lanes, avenues, and alleys in repair, to require of the male inhabitants of said city, over the age of twenty-one, and under fifty years, to labor on said streets, lanes, avenues, and alleys, not exceeding three days in each year; and person failing to perform such labor, when duly notified by the supervisor, shall forfeit and pay the sum of one dollar per day for each day for each day so neglected or refused.

SEC. 27. The City Council shall have power to provide for the punishment of offenders by imprisonment in the county or city jail, in all cases when such offenders shall fail or refuse to pay the fines and forfeitures, which may be recovered against them.

SEC. 28. This act is hereby declared to be a public act, and shall take effect on the first Monday of February next.

WM. L. D. EWING,
Speaker of the House of Representatives.
S. H. ANDERSON,
Speaker of the Senate.

Approved, December 16, 1840.

THO. CARLIN.

---

STATE OF ILLINOIS.
OFFICE OF SECRETARY OF STATE.

I, Stephen A. Douglas, Secretary of State, do hereby certify that the forgoing is a true and perfect copy of the enrolled law now on file in my office.

L.S.

Witness my hand, and seal of State, at Springfield, this 18th day of December, A. D. 1840,

S. A. DOUGLAS,
Secretary of State.

B.

# Prospectus and Excerpts from the *Nauvoo Expositor*

*The* Nauvoo Expositor *was a newspaper established by disaffected members of the LDS Church. On May 7, 1844, the paper's founders set up a print shop on Mulholland Street, near the rising temple, and on the 10th issued a prospectus for the publication. The prospectus was also reprinted on the last page of the premier issue. The first and only number of the paper was published on Friday, June 7, 1844–a four-page edition with a print run of 1,000 copies. It unapologetically denounced Joseph Smith's doctrine of a plurality of gods, the secret teaching and practice of plural marriage, and the theocratic nature of Mormonism in Nauvoo.*

*When the paper appeared, it was met with angry denunciations by Church and city leaders. The city council took the matter in hand and met on Saturday, June 8, and Monday, June 10, to decide how to respond. Addressing the* Expositor*'s exposé of polygamy, Joseph and Hyrum Smith played down the contents of the revelation on plural marriage and criticized the moral character of the paper's publishers. Council members finally consulted British authority on common law William Blackstone to find the paper a public nuisance. The council then passed its first libel law, and based on that law, Joseph Smith, as mayor, directed the destruction of the press, which was carried out by the city marshal and Nauvoo Legion. They threw and scattered the type outside the printing office and burned the remaining copies of the paper. The legal issues surrounding the destruction of the* Expositor *have been the subject of much debate, then and now. The controversy led to Joseph Smith's arrest, imprisonment in Carthage Jail, and ultimately his murder.*

*The* Expositor, *like many papers of the day, contained news items from other papers and even a short romantic story called "Adeline." Only the specific content that led to its destruction is provided below.*

---

## PROSPECTUS OF THE NAUVOO EXPOSITOR

The undersigned propose publishing a Journal of the above title, which will appear on Friday of each week, on an Imperial sheet, with a new Press, and materials of the best quality, and rendered worthy of the patronage of a discerning and an enlightened public.

The Expositor will be devoted to a general diffusion of useful knowledge, and its columns open for the admission of all courteous communications of a Religious, Moral, Social, Literary, or Political character, without taking a decided stand in favor of either of the great Political parties of the country. A part of its columns will be devoted to a few primary objects, which the Publishers deem of vital importance to the public welfare. Their particular locality gives them a knowledge of the many *gross abuses exercised under the pretended authorities of the Nauvoo City Charter,* by the legislative authorities of said city; and the insupportable *oppressions* of the *Ministerial powers* in carrying out the unjust, illegal, and unconstitutional ordinances of the same. The publishers, therefore, deem it a sacred duty they owe to their country and their fellow citizens, to advocate, through the columns of the Expositor, the *UNCONDITIONAL REPEAL OF THE NAUVOO CITY CHARTER*; to restrain and correct the abuses of the *Unit Power*; to ward off the Iron Rod which is held over the devoted heads of the citizens of Nauvoo and the surrounding country; to advocate unmitigated *disobedience* to *Political Revelations,* and to censure and decry gross moral imperfections wherever found, either in the Plebian, Patrician, or *self-constituted MONARCH;* to advocate the pure principles of morality, the pure principles of truth; designed not to destroy, but strengthen the main-spring of God's moral government; to advocate, *and exercise*, the freedom of speech in Nauvoo, independent of the ordinances abridging the same; to give free toleration to every man's religious sentiments, and sustain all in worshiping God according to the monitions of their consciences, as guarantied by the Constitution of our country; and to oppose, with uncompromising hostility, any *Union of Church and State,* or any preliminary step tending to the same; to sustain all, however humble, in their equal and constitutional rights, and oppose the sacrifice of the Liberty, the Property, and the Happiness of the *many* to the *pride* and *ambition* of the *few.* In a word, to give a full, candid, and succinct statement of *facts as they exist in the city of Nauvoo,* fearless of whose particular case they may apply, being governed by the laws of Editorial courtesy, and the inherent dignity which is inseparable from honorable minds; at the same time exercising their own judgment in cases of flagrant abuses, or moral delinquencies; to use such terms and names as they deem proper, when the object is of such high importance that the end will justify the means. We confidently look to an enlightened public for aid in this great and indispensable effort.

The columns of the Expositor will be open to the discussion of all matters of public interest, the productions of all correspondents being subject to the decision of the Editor alone, who shall receive or reject at his option. National questions will be in place, but no preference given to either of the political parties. The Editorial department will contain the political news of the day, proceedings of Congress, election returns, &c., &c. Room will be given for articles on Agriculture, the Mechanic Arts, Commercial transactions, &c.

The publishers bind themselves to issue the paper weekly for one year, and forward fifty-two copies to each subscriber during the year. Orders should be forwarded as soon as possible, that the publishers may know what number of copies to issue.

The publishers take pleasure in announcing to the public, that they have engaged the services of SYLVESTER EMMONS, Esq., who will have entire charge and supervision of the editorial department. From an acquaintance with the dignity of character, and literary qualifications of this gentleman, they feel assured that the Nauvoo Expositor must and will sustain a high and honorable reputation.

TERMS.

Two Dollars per annum in advance,

Two Dollars and Fifty cents at the expiration of six months,

Three Dollars at the end of the year.

Six copies will be forwarded to one address for Ten dollars in advance; Thirteen copies for Twenty Dollars, &c.

Advertising and Job Work in all their varieties, done on short notice, and upon the most satisfactory terms.

All letters and communications must be addressed to *"Charles A. Foster, Nauvoo, Illinois," post paid,* in order to insure attention.

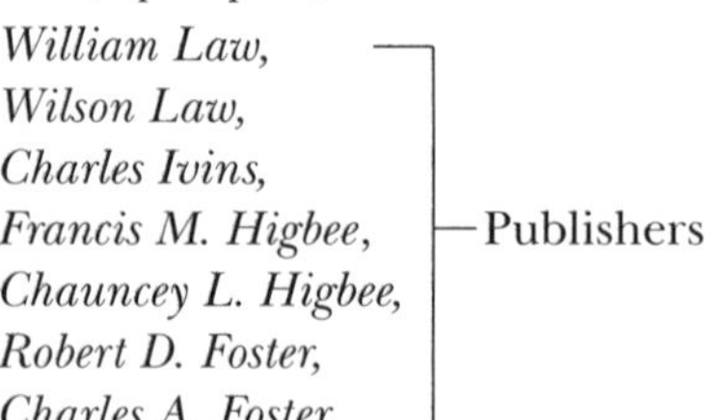

*William Law,*
*Wilson Law,*
*Charles Ivins,*
*Francis M. Higbee,* — Publishers.
*Chauncey L. Higbee,*
*Robert D. Foster,*
*Charles A. Foster.*

# EXCERPTS FROM THE *NAUVOO EXPOSITOR*

## PREAMBLE.

It is with the greatest solicitude for the salvation of the Human Family, and of our own souls, that we have this day assembled. Feign would we have slumbered, and "like the Dove that covers and conceals the arrow that is preying upon its vitals," for the sake of avoiding the furious and turbulent storm of persecution which will gather, soon to burst upon our heads, have covered and concealed that which, for a season, has been brooding among the ruins of our peace: but we rely upon the arm of Jehovah, the Supreme Arbiter of the world, to whom we this day, and upon this occasion, appeal for the rectitude of our intentions.

If that God who gave bounds to the mighty deep, and bade the ocean cease–if that God who organized the physical world, and gave infinity to space, be our front guard and our rear ward, it is futile and vain for man to raise his puny arm against us. God will inspire his ministers with courage and with understanding to consummate his purposes; and if it is necessary, he can snatch them from the fiery furnace, or the Lion's den; as he did anciently the three Hebrews from the former, and Daniel from the latter.

As for our acquaintance with the Church of Jesus Christ of Latter Day Saints, we know, no man or set of men can be more thoroughly acquainted with its rise, its organization, and its history, than we have every reason to believe we are. We all verily believe, and many of us know of a surety, that the religion of the Latter Day Saints, as originally taught by Joseph Smith, which is contained in the Old and New Testaments, Book of Covenants, and Book of Mormon, is verily true; and that the pure principles set forth in those books, are the immutable and eternal principles of Heaven, and speaks a language which, when spoken in truth and virtue, sinks deep into the heart of every honest man. – Its precepts are invigorating, and in every sense of the word, tend to dignify and ennoble man's conceptions of God and his atributes. It speaks a language which is heard amidst the roar of Artillery, as well as in the silence of midnight: it speaks a language understood by the incarcerated spirit, as well as he who is unfettered and free; yet to those who will not see, it is dark, mysterious, and secret as the grave.

We believe that all men, professing to be the ministers of God, should keep steadily in view, the honor and glory of God, the salvation of souls, and the amelioration of man's condition: and among their cardinal virtues ought to be found those of faith, hope, virtue and charity; but with Joseph Smith, and many other official characters in the Church, they are words without any meanings attached—worn as ornaments; exotics nurtured for display; virtues which, throwing aside the existence of a God, the peace, happiness, welfare, and good order of society, require that they should be preserved pure, immaculate and uncorroded.

We most solemnly and sincerely declare, God this Day being witness of the truth and sincerity of our designs and statements, that happy will it be with those who examine and scan Joseph Smith's pretensions to righteousness; and take counsel of human affairs, and of the experience of times gone by. Do not yield up tranquilly a superiority to that man which the reasonableness of past events, and the laws of our country declare to be pernicious and diabolical. We hope many items of doctrine, as now taught, some of which, however, are taught secretly, and denied openly, (which we know positively is the case,) and others publicly, considerate men will treat with contempt; for we declare them heretical and damnable in their influence, though they find many devotees. How shall he, who has drank of the poisonous draft, teach virtue? In the stead thereof, when the criminal ought to plead guilty to the court, the court is obliged to plead *guilty* to the criminal. We appeal to humanity and ask, what shall we do? Shall we lie supinely and suffer ourselves to be metamorphosed into beasts by the Syren tongue? We answer that our country and our God require that we should rectify the tree. We have called upon him to repent, and as soon as he shewed fruits meet for repentance, we stood ready to seize him by the hand of fellowship, and throw around him the mantle of protection; for it is the salvation of souls we desire, and not our own aggrandizement.

We are earnestly seeking to explode the vicious principles of Joseph Smith, and those who practice the same abominations and whoredoms; which we verily know are not accordant and consonant with the principles of Jesus Christ and the Apostles; and for that purpose, and with that end in view, with an eye single to the glory of God, we have dared to gird on the armor, and with God at our head, we most solemnly and sincerely declare that the sword of *truth* shall not depart from the thigh, nor the buckler from the arm, until we can enjoy those glorious privileges which nature's God and our country's laws have guarantied to us—freedom of speech, the liberty of the press, and the right to worship God as seemeth us good.—We are aware, however, that we are hazarding every earthly blessing, particularly property, and probably life itself, in striking this blow at tyranny and oppression: yet notwithstanding, we most solemnly declare that no man, or set of men combined, shall, with impunity, violate obligations as sacred as many which have been violated, unless reason, justice and virtue have become ashamed and sought the haunts of the grave, though our lives be the forfeiture.

Many of us have sought a reformation in the church, without a public exposition of the enormities of crimes practiced by its leaders, thinking that if they would hearken to counsel, and shew fruit meet for repentance, it would be as acceptable with God, as though they were exposed to public gaze,

"For the private path, the secret acts of men,
If noble, for the noblest of their lives."

but our petitions were treated with contempt; and in many cases the petitioner spurned from their presence, and particularly by Joseph, who would state that if he had sinned, and was guilty of the charges we would charge him with, he would not make acknowledgment, but would rather be damned; for it would detract from his dignity, and would consequently ruin and prove the overthrow of the Church. We would ask him on the other hand, if the overthrow of the Church was not inevitable, to which he often replied, that we would all go to Hell together, and convert it into a heaven, by casting the Devil out; and says he, Hell is by not means the place this world of fools suppose it to be, but on the contrary, it is quite an agreeable place: to which we would now reply, he can enjoy it he is determined not to desist from his evil ways; but as for us, and ours, we *will* serve the Lord our God!

It is absurd for men to assert that all is well, while wicked and corrupt men are seeking our destruction, by a perversion of sacred things; for all is not well, while whoredoms and all manner of abominations are practiced under the cloak of religion. Lo! the wolf is in the fold, arrayed in sheep's clothing, and is spreading death and devastation among the saints: and we say to the watchmen standing upon the walls, cry aloud and spare not, for the day of the Lord is at hand—a day cruel both with wrath and fierce anger, to lay the land desolate.

It is a notorious fact, that many females in foreign climes, and in countries to us unknown, even in the most distant regions of the Eastern hemisphere, have been induced, by the sound of the gospel, to forsake friends, and embark upon a voyage across waters that lie stretched over the greater portion of the globe, as they supposed, to glorify God, that they might thereby stand acquitted in the great day of God Almighty. But what is taught them on their arrival at this place?—They are visited by some of the Strikers, for we know not what else to call them, and are requested to hold on and be faithful, for there are great blessings awaiting the righteous; and that God has great mysteries in store for those who love the Lord, and cling to brother Joseph. They are also notified that Brother Joseph will see them soon, and reveal the mysteries of Heaven to their full understanding, which seldom fails to inspire them with new confidence in the Prophet, as well as a great anxiety to know what God has laid up in store for them, in return for the great sacrifice of father and mother, of gold and silver, which they gladly left far behind, that they might be gathered into the fold, and numbered among the chosen of God.—They are visited again, and what is the result? They are requested to meet brother Joseph, or some of the Twelve, at some insulated point, or at some particularly described place on the bank of the Mississippi, or at some room, which wears upon its front—*Positively NO admittance.* The harmless, inoffensive, and unsuspecting creatures, are so devoted to the Prophet, and the cause of Jesus Christ, that they do not dream of the deep-laid and fatal scheme which prostrates happiness, and renders death itself desireable, but they meet him, expecting to receive through him a blessing, and learn the will of the Lord concerning them, and what awaits the faithful follower of Joseph, the Apostle and Prophet of God, when in the stead thereof, they are told, after having been sworn in one of the most solemn manners, to never divulge what is revealed to them, with a penalty of death attached, that God Almighty has revealed it to him, that she should be his (Joseph's) Spiritual wife; for it was right anciently, and God will tolerate it again: but we must keep those pleasures and blessings from the world, for until there is a change in the government, we will endanger ourselves by practicing it—but we can enjoy the blessings of Jacob, David, and others, as well as to be deprived of them, if we do not expose ourselves to the law of the land. She is thunder-struck, faints, recovers, and refuses. The Prophet damns her if she rejects. She thinks of the great sacrifice and of the many thousand miles she has traveled over sea and land, that she might save her soul from pending ruin, and replies, God's will be done and not mine. The Prophet and his devotees in this way are gratified. The next step to avoid public exposition from the common course of things, they are sent away for a time, until all is well; after which they return, as from a long visit. Those whom no power or influence could seduce, except that which is wielded by some individual feigning to be a God, must realize the remarks of an able writer, when he says, "if woman's feelings are turned to ministers of sorrow, where shall she look for consolation?" Her lot is to be wooed and won; her heart is like some fortress that has been captured, sacked, abandoned, and left desolate. With her, the desire of the heart has failed—the great charm of existence is at an end; she neglects all the cheerful exercises of life, which gladen the spirits, quicken the pulses, and send the tide of life in healthful currents through the veins. Her rest is broken. The sweet refreshment of sleep is poisoned by melancholy dreams; dry sorrow drinks her blood, until her enfeebled frame sinks under the slightest external injury. Look for her after a little while, and you find friendship weeping over her untimely grave; and wondering that one who but so recently glowed with all the radiance of health and beauty, should so speedily be brought down to darkness and despair, you will be told of some wintry chill, of some casual indisposition that laid her low! But no one knows of the mental malady that previously sapped her strength, and made her so easy a pray to the spoiler. She is like some tender tree, the pride and beauty of the grove—graceful in its form, bright in its foliage, but with the worm praying at its heart; we find it withered when it should be most luxuriant. We see it drooping its branches to the earth, and shedding leaf by leaf until wasted and perished away, it falls in the stillness of the forest; and as we muse over the beautiful ruin, we strive in vain to recollect the blast or thunder-bolt that could have smitten it with decay. But no one knows the cause except the foul fiend who perpetrated the diabolical deed.

Our hearts have mourned and bled at the wretched and miserable condition of females in this place; many orphans have been the victims of misery and wretchedness, through the influence that has been exerted over them, under the cloak of religion and afterwards, in consequence of that *jealous disposition* which predominates over the minds of *some,* have been turned upon a wide world, fatherless and motherless, destitute of friends and fortune; and *robbed of that which nothing but death can restore.*

Men solace themselves by saying the facts slumber in the dark caverns of midnight. But Lo! it is sudden day, and the dark deeds of foul fiends shall be exposed from the house-tops. A departed spirit, once the resident of St. Louis, shall yet cry aloud for vengeance.

It is difficult—perhaps impossible—to describe the wretchedness of females in this place, without wounding the feelings of the benevolent, or shocking the delicacy of the refined; but the truth shall come to the world. The remedy can never be applied, unless the disease is known. The sympathy, ever anxious to relieve, cannot be felt before the misery is seen. –The charity that kindles at the tale of wo, can never act with adequate efficiency, till it is made to see the pollution and guilt of men, now buried in the death-shades of heathenism. –Shall we then, however painful the sight, shrink from the contemplation of their real state? We answer, we will not, if permitted to live. As we have before stated, it is the vicious principles of men we are determined to explode. It is not that we have any private feelings to gratify, or any private pique to settle, that has induced us to be thus plain; for we can respect and love the criminal, if there is any hope of reformation: but there is a point beyond which forbearance ceases to be a virtue.

The next important item which presents itself for our consideration, is the attempt at Political power and influence, which we verily believe to be preposterous and absurd. We believe it is inconsistent, and not in accordance with the christian religion. We do not believe that God ever raised up a Prophet to christianize a world by political schemes and intrigue. It is not the way God captivates the heart of the unbeliever; but on the contrary, by preaching truth in its own native simplicity, and in its own original purity, unadorned with anything except its own indigenous beauties. Joseph may plead he has been injured, abused, and his petitions treated with contempt by the general government, and that he only desires an influence of a political character that will warrant him redress of grievances; but we care not–the faithful followers of Jesus must bear in this age as well as Christ and the Apostles did anciently; although a frowning world may have crushed him to the dust; although unpitying friends may have passed him by; although hope, the great comforter in affliction, may have burst forth and fled from his troubled bosom; yet, in Jesus there is a balsom for every wound, and a cordial to assuage an agonized mind.

Among the many items of false doctrine that are taught the Church, is the doctrine of *many Gods,* one of the most direful in its effects that has characterized the world for many centuries. We know not what to call it other than blasphemy, for it is most unquestionably, speaking of God in an impious and irreverent manner.– It is contended that there are innumerable Gods as much above the God that presides over this universe, as he is above us; and if he varies from the law unto which he is subjected, he, with all his creatures, will be cast down as was Lucifer; thus holding forth a doctrine which is effectually calculated to sap the very foundation of our faith: and now, O Lord! shall we set still and be silent, while thy name is thus blasphemed, and thine honor, power and glory, brought into disrepute? See Isaiah c 43, v 10; 44, 6-8; 45, 5, 6, 21, 22; and book of Covenants, page 26 and 39.

In the dark ages of Popery, when bigotry, superstition, and tyranny held universal sway over the empire of reason, there was some semblance of justice in the inquisitorial deliberations, which, however, might have been dictated by prudence, or the fear of consequences: but we are no longer forced to appeal to those states that are now situated under the influence of Popery for examples of injustice, cruelty and oppression–we can appeal to the acts of the inquisitorial department organized in *Nauvoo,* by Joseph and his accomplices, for specimens of injustice of the most pernicious and diabolical character that ever stained the pages of the historian.

It was in Rome, and about the twelfth century, when Pope Innocent III, ordered father Dominic to excite the Catholic princes and people to extirpate heretics. But it is in this enlightened and intelligent nineteenth century, and in Nauvoo–a place professing to be the nucleus of the world, that Joseph Smith has established an inquisition, which, if it is suffered to exist, will prove more formidable and terrible to those who are found opposing the iniquities of Joseph and his associates, than ever the Spanish inquisition did to heretics as they termed them.

On thursday evening, the 18th of April, there was a council called, unknown to the Church, which tried, condemned, and cut off brothers Wm. Law, Wilson Law, and sister Law, (Wm's. wife,) brother R. D. Foster, and one brother Smith, with whom we are unacquainted; which we contend is contrary to the book of Doctrine and Covenants, for our law condemnest no man untill he is heard. We abhor and protest against any council or tribunal in this Church, which will not suffer the accused to stand in its midst and plead their own cause. If an Agrippa would suffer a Paul, whose eloquence surpassed, as it were, the eloquence of men, to stand before him, and plead his own cause, why should Joseph, with others, refuse to hear individuals in their own defence?–We answer, it is because the court fears the atrocity of its crimes will be exposed to public gaze. We wish thc public to thoroughly understand the nature of this court, and judge of the legality of its acts as seemeth them good.

On Monday, the 15th of April, brother R. D. Foster had a notice served on him to appear before the High Council on Saturday following, the 20th, and answer to charges preferred against him by Joseph Smith. On Saturday, while Mr. Foster was preparing to take his witnesses, 41 in number, to the council-room, that he might make good his charges against Joseph, president Marks notified him that the trial had been on Thursday evening, before the 15th, and that he was cut off from the Church; and that same council cut off the brother Laws', sister Law, and brother Smith, and all without their knowledge. They were not notified, neither did they dream of any such thing being done, for William Law had sent Joseph and some of the Twelve, special word that he desired an investigation before the Church in General Conference, on the 6th of Ap'l. The court, however, was a tribunal possessing no power to try Wm. Law, who was called by special Revelation, to stand as counsellor to the President of the Church, (Joseph,) which was twice ratified by General Conferences, assembled at Nauvoo, for Brigham Young, one of the Twelve, presided, whose duty it was not but the President of the High Council– See Book of Doctrine and Covenants, page 87.

RESOLUTIONS.

*Resolved* 1*st,* That we will not encourage the acts of any court in this church, for the trial of any of its members, which will not suffer the accused to be present and plead their own cause; we therefore declare our decided disapprobation to the course pursued last Thursday evening, (the 18th inst,) in the case of William and Wilson Law, and Mrs. William Law, and R. D. Foster, as being unjust and unauthorized by the laws of the Church, and consequently null and void; for our law judgeth no man unless he be heard; and to all those who approbate a course so unwarranted unprecedented and so unjust, we would say beware lest the unjust measure you meet to your brethren, be again meeted out to you.

*Resolved* 2*nd,* Inasmuch as we have for years borne with the individual follies and iniquities of Joseph Smith, Hyrum Smith, and many other official characters in the Church of Jesus Christ, (conceiving it a duty incumbent upon us so to bear,) and having labored with them repeatedly with all Christian love, meekness and humility, yet to no effect, feel as if forbearance has ceased to be a virtue, and hope of reformation vain; and inasmuch as they have introduced false and damnable doctrines into the Church, such as a plurality of gods above the God of this universe, and his liability to fall with all his creations; the plurality of wives, for time and eternity; the doctrine of unconditional sealing up to eternal life, against all crimes except that of sheding innocent blood, by a perversion of their priestly authority, and thereby forfeiting the holy priesthood, according to the word of Jesus: "If a man abide not in me, he is cast forth as a branch and is withered, and men gather them and cast them into the fire, and they are burned," St. John, xv. 6. "Whosoever transgresseth and abideth not in the doctrine of Christ, hath not God, he that abideth in the doctrine of Christ, hath both the Father and the Son; if there come any unto you and bring not this doctrine, receive him not into your house, neither bid him God speed, for he that bideth him God speed is a partaker of his evil deeds;" we therefore are constrained to denounce them as apostates from the pure and holy doctrines of Jesus Christ.

*Resolved 3rd,* That we disapprobate and discountenance every attempt to unite church and state; and that we further believe the effort now being made by Joseph Smith for political power and influence, is not commendable in the sight of God.

*Resolved 4th,* That the hostile *spirit* and *conduct* manifested by Joseph Smith, and many of his associates towards Missouri, and others inimical to his purposes, are decidedly at variance with the true spirit of Christianity, and should not be encouraged by any people, much less by those professing to be the ministers of the gospel of peace.

*Resolved 5th,* That while we disapprobate malicious persecutions and prosecutions, we hold that all church members are alike amenable to the laws of the land; and that we further discountenance any chicanery to screen them from the just demands of the same.

*Resolved 6th,* That we consider the religious influence exercised in financial concerns by Joseph Smith, as unjust as it is unwarranted, for the Book of Doctrine and Covenants makes it the duty of the Bishop to take charge of the financial affairs of the Church, and of all temporal matters pertaining to the same.

*Resolved 7th,* That we discountenance and disapprobate the attendance at houses of revelling and dancing; dram-shops and theatres; verily believing they have a tendency to lead from paths of virtue and holiness, to those of vice and debauchery.

*Resolved 8th,* That we look upon the pure and holy doctrines set forth in the Scriptures of Divine truth, as being the immutable doctrines of salvation; and he who abideth in them shall be saved, and he who abideth not in them can not inherit the Kingdom of Heaven.

*Resolved 9th,* That we consider the gathering in haste, and by sacrifice, to be contrary to the will of God; and that it has been taught by Joseph Smith and others for the purpose of enabling them to sell property at most exhorbitant prices, not regarding the welfare of the Church, but through their covetousness reducing those who had the means to give employment to the poor, to the necessity of seeking labor for themselves; and thus the wealth which is brought into the place is swallowed up by the one great throat, from whence there is no return, which if it had been economically disbursed amongst the whole would have rendered all comfortable.

*Resolved 10th,* That, notwithstanding our extensive acquaintance with the financial affairs of the Church, we do not know of any property which in reality belongs to the Church (except the Temple) and we therefore consider the injunction laid upon the saints compelling them to purchase property of the Trustee in trust for the Church, is a deception practiced upon them; and that we look upon the sending of special agents abroad to collect funds for the Temple and other purposes as a humbug practiced upon the saints by Joseph and others, to aggrandize themselves, as we do not believe that the monies and property so collected, have been applied as the donors expected, but have been used for speculative purposes, by Joseph, to gull the saints the better on their arrival at Nauvoo, by buying the lands in the vicinity and selling again to them at tenfold advance; and further that we verily believe the appropriations said to have been subscribed by shares for the building of the Nauvoo House to have been used by J. Smith and Lyman Wight, for other purposes, as out of the mass of stock already taken, the building is far from being finished even to the base.

*Resolved 11th,* That we consider all secret societies, and combinations under penal oaths and obligations, (professing to be organized for religious purposes,) to be anti-Christian, hypocritical and corrupt.

*Resolved 12th,* That we will not acknowledge any man as king or law-giver to the church; for Christ is our only king and law-giver.

*Resolved 13th,* That we call upon the honest in heart, in the Church, and throughout the world, to vindicate the pure doctrines of Jesus Christ, whether set forth in the Bible, Book of Mormon, or Book of Covenants; and we hereby withdraw the hand of fellowship, from all those who practice or teach doctrines contrary to the above, until they cease so to do, and show works meet for repentance.

*Resolved 14th,* That we hereby notify all those holding licences to preach the gospel, who know they are guilty of teaching the doctrine of other Gods above the God of this creation; the plurality of wives; the unconditional sealing up against all crimes, save that of shedding innocent blood; the spoiling of the gentiles, and all other doctrines, (so called) which are contrary to the laws of God, or to the laws of our country, to cease preaching, and to come and make satisfaction, and have their licences renewed.

*Resolved 15th,* That in all our controversies in defence of truth and righteousness, the weapons of our warfare are not carnal but mighty through God, to the pulling down of the strong holds of Satan; that our strifes are not against flesh, blood, nor bones; but against principalities and power against spiritual wickedness in high places and therefore we will not use carnal weapons save in our own defence.

---

## AFFIDAVITS

I hereby certify that Hyrum Smith did, (in his office) read to me a certain written document, which he said was a revelation from God, he said that he was with Joseph when it was received. He afterwards gave me the document to read, and I took it to my house, and read it, and showed it to my wife, and returned it next day. The revelation (so called) authorized certain men to have more wives than one at a time, in this world and in the world to come. It said this was the law, and commanded Joseph to enter into the law.—And also that he should administer to others. Several other items were in the revelation, supporting the above doctrines.

WM. LAW.

State of Illinois, Hancock County, } I Robert D. Foster, certify that the above certificate was sworn to before me, as true in substance, this fourth day of May A. D. 1844.

ROBERT D. FOSTER, J. P.

I certify that I read the revelation referred to in the above affidavit of my husband, it sustained in strong terms the doctrine of more wives tha[n] one at a time, in this world, and in the next, it authorized some to have to the number of ten, and set forth that those women who would not allow their husbands to have more wives than one should be under condemnation before God.

JANE LAW.

Sworn and subscribed before me this fourth day of May, A. D. 1844.

ROBERT D. FOSTER, J. P.

*To all whom it may Concern:*

For as much as the public mind hath been much agitated by a course of procedure in the Church of Jesus Christ of Latter Day Saints, by a number of persons declaring against certain doctrines and practices there-in, (among whom I am one,) it is but meet that I should give my reasons, at least in part, as a cause that hath led me to declare myself. In the latter part of the summer, 1843, the Patriarch, Hyrum Smith, did in the High Council, of which I was a member, introduce what he said was a revelation given through the Prophet; that the said Hyrum Smith did essay to read the said revelation in the said Council, that according to his reading there was contained the following doctrines; lst. the sealing up of persons to eternal life, against all sins, save that of shedding innocent blood or of consenting thereto; 2nd, the doctrine of a plurality of wives, or marrying virgins; that "David and Solomon had many wives, yet in this they sinned not save in the matter of Uriah. This revelation with other evidence, that the afore-said heresies were taught and practiced in the Church; determined me to leave the office of first counsellor to the president of the Church at Nauvoo, inasmuch as I dared not teach or administer such laws. And further deponent saith not.

AUSTIN COWLES.

State of Illinois, } ss. To all whom<br>
Hancock County, } it may concern<br>
I hereby certify that the above certificate was sworn and subscribed before me, this fourth day of May, 1844.

ROBERT D. FOSTER, J. P.

---

## INTRODUCTORY.

In greeting our patrons with the first number of the Expositor, a remark is necessary for the expression of some views, and certain principles by which we intend to be governed in our editorial duties. Many questions and surmises are made by those who suppose we will come in conflict with some of their darling schemes of self-aggrandisement. Others, more honest, desire to know whether our object is to advocate any particular religious tenets, or any favorite measures of either of the political parties of the country. To all such questions we answer in the negative. Free toleration in religious sentiments, we deem compatible with the organization of our government, and should not be abridged. On the other hand, we believe religious despotism to be incompatible with our free institutions. What we conceive to be despotism, engendered by an assumption of power in the name of religion, we shall have occasion to show hereafter. In relation to politics, whatever our own views may be upon the federal measures that now, or may, hereafter agitate the country, the Expositor will not be the exponent thereof; and all the strife and party zeal of the two great antagonistical parties for the success of their respective candidates for the Presidency, we shall remain neutral, and in an editorial capacity, inactive. Another party, however, has sprung up in our midst, the leader of which, it would seem, expects, by a flourish of Quixotic chivalry, to take, by storm, the Presidential chair, and distribute among his *faithful* supporters, the office of governor in all the different States, for the purpose, we presume, of more effectually consolidating the government. This party we may be disposed to treat with a little levity, but nothing more. As it respects the local questions which may arise in our own county, and the candidates for the legislature from this county, we reserve the right to expatiate upon the respective claims—not on account of their politics—be they whig or democrat, but on account of a combination which we believe has for its object the utter destruction of the rights of the old citizens of the county, who have borne the heat and burden of the day; who have labored hard as pioneers of the county; who have rights that should be respected by every principle of honor and good faith, and whose wishes should be consulted in the choice of officers, and not have men imposed upon them, who are obnoxious, for good and sufficient reasons. In relation to such questions, we intend to express our mind freely, as our duty dictates, regardless of consequences. If a fair and honorable course be taken by the dominant party at Nauvoo, we will have nothing to battle against; but if they do not pursue that course, we shall be prepared for the warfare. We must confess, however, if we are to judge of the future by the past, we have little to expect from that quarter: but apart from local political considerations, we have a high and more noble duty to perform. We shall spread the banner to the breeze for a radical reform in the city of Nauvoo, as the departure from moral rectitude, and the abuse of power, have become intolerable. We shall speak out, and spare not, until certain grievances are redressed or corrected; until honor, virtue, and reputation shall take their accustomed habitations, and be respected; until we teach men that no exclusive privileges can be allowed to any individual under our form of government; that the law of the land, based upon the revealed laws of heaven, are paramount to all other earthly considerations; and he who sets the laws at defiance, and evades their operation, either by direct or indirect means, pursues a course subversive of the best interests of the country, and dangerous to the well-being of the social compact. That there does exist an order of things with the systematic elements of organization in our midst—a system which, if exposed in its naked deformity, would make the virtuous mind revolt with horror; a system in the exercise of which lays prostrate all the dearest ties in our social relations—the glorious fabric upon which human happiness is based—ministers to the worst passions of our nature, and throws us back into the benighted regions of the dark ages, we have the greatest reason to believe.

The question is asked, will you bring a mob upon us? In answer to that, we assure all concerned, that we will be among the first to put down anything like an illegal force being used against any man or set of men. If any one has become amenable to the law, we wish to have him tried impartially by the laws of his country. We are among the number who believe that there is virtue and integrity enough in the administrators of the law, to bring every offender to justice, and to protect the innocent. If it is necessary to make a show of force, to execute legal process, it will create no sympathy in that case to cry out, we are mobbed. There is such a thing as persons being deceived into a false sympathy once, who, the second time, will scrutinize very closely, to know who, or which party, are the persecutors. It is not always the first man who cries out, stop thief, that is robbed. It is the upright, honest, considerate and moral precepts of any class that will be respected in this or any other enlightened age—precepts which have for their end the good of mankind, and the establishment of fundamental truths. On the other hand, paradoxical dogmas, new systems of government, new codes of morals, a new administration of the laws by ignorant, unlettered, and corrupt men, must be frowned down by every lover of his country. The well-being of society demand it at our hands. Our country, by whose laws we are protected, asks us for a manifestation of that patriotism which should inspire every American citizen—the interests of the State of Illinois require it, and as a citizen of Illinois, we intend to respond to the voice of duty, and stand the hazard of the die.

We believe that the Press should not be the medium through which the private character of any individual should be assailed, delineated, or exposed to public gaze: still, whoever acts in an official character, who sets himself up as a public teacher, and reformer of morals and religion, and as an aspirant to the highest office in the gift of the people of this glorious republic, whose institutions he publicly condemns, we assert and maintain the right of canvassing all the public acts and animadverting, with terms of the severest reproach upon all the revolutionary measures that comes to our notice, from any source. We would not be worthy of the name of an American citizen, did we stand by and see, not only the laws of the State, but the laws of the United States set at defiance, the authorities insulted, fugitives from justice fleeing for refuge, asking and receiving protection from the authorities of Nauvoo, for high crimes committed against the government of the United States, the Mayor of a petty incorporated town interposing his authority, and demanding the right of trial for the fugitive on the merits of the case, by virtue of a writ of Habeas Corpus, issued by the Municipal Court of Nauvoo. It is too gross a burlesque upon common sense—a subterfuge too low to indicate any thing but a corrupt motive.— Such acts, whether committed in a private or public capacity, will be held up to public scorn. An independent Press is bound by every sense of duty, to lay before the public every attack upon their rights: we, therefore, in the exercise of our duty, expect the support and the aid of our fellow citizens in our enterprise.

---

We hope all those who intend subscribing for the "Expositor," will forward their names as soon as possible; Editors, Postmasters, and others, to whom the Prospectus, and paper may be sent, will confer a favor upon us, by noticing, exchanging, and circulating the same, in their respective vocations, and forwarding accordingly.

In consequence of the importance of the cause in which we have engaged, and the assurances we have received from different sources, we have concluded to issue one thousand copies of the first number of the paper, that all who wish, may be supplied, and further, that none may plead ignorance of our complaints, or exonerate themselves from an interest in our behalf. We do not wish, or expect, the publication of the "Expositor" to prove a matter of pecuniary profit, neither do we believe the public will suffer it to prove a loss. It is a subject in which we are all interested, more particularly the citizens of this county, and surrounding country; the case has assumed a formidable and fearful aspect, it is not the destiny of a few that is involved in case of commotion, but that of thousands, wherein necessarily the innocent and helpless would be confounded with the criminal and guilty. We have anxiously desired, and strenuously advocated a peaceable redress of the injuries that have repeatedly been inflicted upon us, and we have now the means in our hands, through which we can peaceably and honorably effect our object. For ourselves, we are firmly resolved not to quit the field, till our efforts shall be crowned with success. And we now call upon all, who prize the liberty of speech, the liberty of the press, the right of conscience, and the sacred rights of American citizenship, to assist us in this undertaking. Let us stand up and boldly and fearlessly oppose ourselves to any and every encroachment, in whatever form it may appear, whether shaped in superstitious domination or civil usurpation. The public abroad have not been informed in relation to facts as they really existed in our midst, many have supposed that all was rumor, and having no organ through which to speak, our silence has been to them sufficient proof.

The facts have been far otherwise, we have watched with painful emotion the progress of events in this city, for some time past, until we were sick with the sight; injury upon injury has been repeated, insult has been added to insult till forbearance has ceased to be virtuous, and we now have the proud privilege, we have long wished for, of defending ourselves against their foul aggressions and aspersions and of informing the public of things as they really are. We intend to tell the whole tale and by all honorable means to bring to light and justice, those who have long fed and fattened upon the purse, the property, and the character of injured innocence; –yes, we will speak, and that too in thunder tones, to the ears of those who have thus ravaged and laid waste fond hopes, bright prospects, and virtuous principles, to gratify an unhallowed ambition. We are aware of the critical position we occupy, in view of our immediate location; but we entertain no fears, our purpose is fixed and our arm is nerved for the conflict, we stand upon our rights, and we will maintain those rights, whatever may be the consequence; let no man or set of men assail us at the peril of their lives, and we hereby give notice to all parties, that we are the last in attack, but the first and foremost in defence. We would be among the last to provoke the spirit of the public abroad unnecessarily, but we have abundant assurance, in case of emergency, that we shall be all there.

---

An individual, bearing the cognomen of Jeremiah Smith, who has evaded the officers for some time, has taken refuge in the city of Nauvoo. It appears he is a fugitive from justice for the offence of procuring four thousand dollars from the United States Treasury at the city of Washington, under false pretences. A bill of indictment was found in the District of Columbia against him, and a warrant issued for his arrest. The Marshal of Iowa Territory got intelligence of his being in this place, and procuring the necessary papers for his arrest, proceeded to this place in search of him, about three weeks ago. After making inquiry, and becoming satisfied that he was secreted in Nauvoo, under the immediate protection of the Prophet, he said to him (the Prophet,) that he was authorised to arrest the said J. Smith, for an offence committed by him against the United States government, and wished to know where he was–to which the Prophet replied, that he knew nothing about him. The Marshal said he knew he was secreted in the city, and was determined to have him; and, unless he was given up, he would have the aid of the Dragoons to find and arrest him. Joseph Smith then replied, that was not necessary; but, if the Marshal would pledge his word and honor that he should have the benefit of a city writ of Habeas Corpus, and be tried before him, he would produce the fugitive in half an hour. After some hesitancy, the Marshal agreed to do so, when the prisoner was produced in the time specified. A writ of Habeas Corpus was issued, and the prisoner taken from the Marshal and brought before the Municipal court of Nauvoo for trial. The court adjourned until thursday, the 30th ult., when he was tried, and discharged, as a matter of course. In the interval, however, application had been made to Judge Pope, of the District court of the United States for the State of Illinois, who issued his warrant, directed to the United States Marshal, who sent his deputy to make a second arrest, in the case the other officer did not succeed in taking him from the city. Smith was found by the Illinois Marshal and arrested, when it became necessary for the high corporate powers of the city again to interpose their authority. The potent writ was again issued–the prisoner taken from the Marshal–a trial had, during which, the attorneys for Smith relieved themselves of an insupportable burthen of legal knowledge, which completely overwhelmed the learned court, and resulted in the triumphant acquittal of the prisoner, with a judgement for costs against the U. States.

Now we ask if the executive and judicial authorities of Illinois deem it politic to submit to such a state of things in similar cases? Can, and will the constituted authorities of the federal government be quiescent under such circumstances, and allow the paramount laws of the Union to be set at defiance, and rendered nugatory by the action of a court, having no more than co-ordinate powers, with a common justice of the peace? If such an order of things is allowed to exist, there is every reason to believe that Nauvoo will become a sink of refuge for every offender who can carry in spoils enough to buy protection. The people of the State of Illinois will, consequently, see the necessity of repealing the charter of Nauvoo, when such abuses are practiced under it; and by virtue of said chartered authority, the right of the writ of Habeas Corpus in all cases arising under the city ordinance, to give full scope to the desired jurisdiction. The city council have passed ordinances, giving the Municipal court authority to issue the writ of Habeas Corpus in all cases when the prisoner is held in custody in Nauvoo, no matter whether the offender is committed in the State of Maine, or on the continent of Europe, the prisoner being in the city under arrest. It is gravely contended by the legal luminaries of Nauvoo, that the ordinances gives them jurisdiction, not only jurisdiction to try the validity of the writ, but to enquire into the merits of the case, and allow the prisoner to swear himself clear of the charges. If his own oath is not considered sufficient to satisfy the adverse party, plenty of witnesses are ready to swear that he is to be believed on oath, and that is to be considered sufficient by the court to put the quietus on all foreign testimony and the discharge of the prisoner follows, as a necessary consequence.

---

## JOE. SMITH – THE PRESIDENCY.

We find in the Nauvoo Neighbor of May 29th, a lengthy letter from Joseph Smith a candidate for the Presidency on his own hook, to Henry Clay, the Whig candidate for the same office. It appears to be a new rule of tactics for two rival candidates to enter into a discussion of their respective claims to that high office, just preceding an election. Smith charges Clay with shrinking from the responsibility of promising to grant whatever the Mormons might ask, if elected to the Presidency. Smith has not been troubled with any inquiries of committees as to what measures he will recommend if elected; nevertheless he has come out boldly and volunteered his views of certain measures which he is in favor of having adopted. One is for the General Government to purchase the slaves of the south and set them free, that we can understand. Another is to pass a general uniform land law, that certainly requires the spirit of interpretation to show its meaning as no explanation accompanies it. Another which no doubt will be very congenial to the candidate's nervous system, is to open all the prison doors on the country, and set the captive free. These with some other suggestions equally as enlightened, ought to be sufficient to satisfy any man that Joseph Smith is willing that his principles shall be publicly known. If however any individual voter, who has a perfect right to know a candidates principles, should not be satisfied, he may further aid his inquiries, by a reference to the record of the grand inquest of Hancock County.

Martin Van Buren is charged with non-commitalism; Henry Clay has not been the man to answer frankly the question whether he would restore to the Mormons their lands in Missouri. Joseph Smith is the only candidate now before the people whose principles are fully known; let it be remembered there are documents [of] the highest degree of evidence before the people; a committee of twenty-four, under the solemnity of their oaths, have inquired into and reported upon his claims in due form of law. Shades of Washington and Jefferson–Henry Clay the candidate of a powerful party, is now under bonds to keep the peace; Joseph Smith, the candidate of another "*powerful*" party has two indictments against him, one for fornication and adultery, another for perjury. Our readers can make their own comments.

---

We have received the last number of the "Warsaw Signal;" it is rich with anti-Mormon matter, both editorial and communicated. Among other things it contains a lengthy letter from J. H. Jackson, giving some items in relation to his connection with the "*Mormon Prophet,*" as also his reasons for the same. It will be perceived that many of the most dark and damnable crimes that ever darkened human character, which have hitherto been to the public, a matter of *rumor* and *suspicion,* are now reduced to *indisputable facts.* We have reason to believe, from our acquaintance with Mr. Jackson, and our own observation, that the statements he makes are true; and in view of these facts, we ask, in the name of heaven, where is the safety of our lives and liberties, when placed at the disposal of such heaven daring, hell deserving, God forsaken villains[?]. Our blood boils while we refer to these blood thirsty and murderous propensities of men, or rather *demons* in human shape, who, not satisfied with practising their dupes upon a credulous and superstitious people, must wreak their vengeance upon any who may dare to come in contact with them. We deplore the desperate state of things to which we are necessarily brought, but, we say to our friends, "*keep cool,*" and the *whole tale* will be told. We fully believe in bringing these iniquities and enormities to light, and let the majesty of violated law, and the voice of injured innocence and con[d]emned public opinion, speak in tones of thunder to these miscreants; but in behalf of hundreds and thousands of unoffending citizens, whose only fault is religious enthusiasm, and for the honor of our own names and reputation, let us not follow their desperado measures, and thereby dishonor ourselves in revenging our own wrongs. Let our motto be, "Last in attack, but first in defence;" and the result cannot prove otherwise than honorable and satisfactory. ...

---

## CIRCUIT COURT.

The May Term of the Circuit Court of this county closed on the 30th ult. after a session of ten days. We understand a large number of cases were disposed of, none, however of a very important character. The cases wherein Joseph Smith was a party, were transferred by a change of venue, to other courts; that of A. Sympson vs. J. Smith, for false imprisonment, to Adams County; that of F. M. Higbee vs. J. Smith, for slander, and that of C. A. Foster vs. Joseph Smith, and J. W. Coolidge for false imprisonment, and that of A. Davis vs. Joseph Smith, and J. P. Green, for trespass, were all transferred to the County of McDonough. The Grand Jury found two bills against Smith, one for perjury, and another for fornication and adultery; on the first of which Smith delivered himself up for trial, but the State not being ready, material witnesses being absent, the case was deferred to the October term.

The regular session of the Municipal Court of this City came off on Monday last. The cases of R. D. Foster, C. L. Higbee, and C. A. Foster, on appeals from the Mayor's Court, wherein they had each been fined in the sum of one hundred dollars, (for the *very enormous* offence of refusing to assist the *notorious* O. P. Rockwell, and his "*dignity*" John P. Green, in arresting a respectable and peaceable citizen, without the regular process of papers) and of A. Spencer, wherein he was fined in the same sum on a charge of assault and battery, were all taken up and gravely discussed; after the most mature deliberation, with the assistance of the *ex*tinguished City Attorney, this honorable body concluded to dismiss the suit and issue a *procedendo* to the lower court, which was accordingly done.

The cases referred to above, afford abundant reason both for complaint and comment. We intend as soon as our time will allow, to express our views freely upon this feature of Mormon usurpation; first, enact a string of ordinances contrary to reason and common sense, and then inflict the severest penalties for not observing them. ...

---

NAUVOO, June 5th, 1844.
CITIZENS OF HANCOCK COUNTY.

It is well known to all of you that the August election is fast approaching, and with it comes the great and terrible conflict. It is destined to be a day pregnant with big events; for it will be the index to the future.— Should we be defeated upon that occasion, our die is cast, and our fate is sealed; but if successful, alike may Joseph Smith, Hyrum Smith, and their devoted followers, as well as their enemies, expect that justice will be meted out. The present is portentious of the great effort that is to be made upon that occasion, by Joseph for power; Hiram Smith is already in the field as a candidate for the legislature, but will *you* support *him,* that same *Hyrum Smith* the devoted follower and brother of Joe, who feigned a revelation from God, directing the citizens of Hancock County to vote for J. P.

Hoge, in preference to Cyrus Walker, and by so doing blaspheming the name of God? Will *you*, gentlemen of Hancock County, support a man like that, who claims to move in a different sphere, a sphere entirely above you; one who will trifle with the things of God, and feign converse with the Divinity, for the sake of carrying an election? I will unhesitatingly assume to myself the responsibility of answering in the negative. I flatter myself you are not so depraved, and so blinded to your own interests, as to support a man totally ignorant of the laws of your country, and in every respect alienated from you and your interests.

In supporting *Hyrum Smith*, you, *Citizens of Hancock County*, are supporting Joseph Smith, for whom he (Hyrum) goes teeth and toe nails, for President of the United States. The question may arise here, in voting for Joseph Smith, for whom am I voting? You are voting for a man who contends all governments are to be put down and the *one* established upon its ruins. You are voting for an *enemy* to your government, hear Phelps to Joe in his affidavit before Judge King of Missouri:—"Have you come to the point to resist all law?" "I have," says Joe. You are voting for a sycophant, whose attempt for power find[s] no parallel in history. You are voting for a man who refuses to suffer criminals to be brought to justice, but in the stead thereof, rescues them from the just demands of the law, by *Habeas Corpus*. You are voting for a man who stands indicted, and who is now held to bail, for the crimes of adultery and perjury; two of the gravest crimes known to our laws. Query not then for whom you are voting, it is for one of the blackest and basest scoundrels that has appeared upon the stage of human existence since the days of Nero, and Caligula.

In supporting Hyrum Smith, then are you not supporting Joseph Smith? [M]ost assuredly; pause then my *countrymen*, and consider cooly, calmly and deliberately, what you do? Support not that man who is spreading death, devastation and ruin throughout your happy country like a tornado. Infinite are the gradations which mark this man's attempts for power, which if not checked soon, must not only shed a deleterious influence on the face of this county, but on the face of the adjoining counties. He is already proudly boasting that he is beyond your reach; and I regret to think I am under the painful necessity of admitting the fact. Is it not a shame and a disgrace, to think we have a man in our midst, who will defy the laws of our country; the *laws* which shed so gentle and nourishing an influence upon our fathers, which fostered and protected them in their old age from insult and aggression; shall we their sons, lie still and suffer *Joseph Smith* to light up the lamp of tyranny and oppression in our midst? God forbid, lest the departed spirits of our *fathers,* cry from the ground against us. Let us arise in the majesty of our strength and sweep the influence of tyrants and miscreants from the face of the land, as with the breath of heaven. The eagle that is now proudly borne to earth's remotest regions by every gale, will perch himself in the solitude of mid-night if we do not arouse from our lethargy.

It is the worst of absurdities for any individual to say there is a man in our midst who is above the reach of violated law, and not lend a helping hand; all talk and nothing more will not accomplish *that* for your country and your God, which the acts of Washington did. Then gentlemen organize *yourselves* and prepare for the dreadful conflict in August; we go with you heart and hand, in the attempt to suppress this contaminating influence which is prostrating our fairest prospects, and spreading desolation throughout our vale. Call into the field your best men under the solemn pledge to go for the unconditional repeal of the Nauvoo Charter, and you have our support; whether they be Whig or Democrat we care not; when a friend presents us with a draught of cool water, we do not stop to inquire whether it is contained in a silver vase, a golden urn or a long handled gourd. We want no base seducer, liar and perjured representative, to represent us in *Springfield,* but while Murrill represents Tennessee in Nashville, Munroe Edwards, New York, in Sing Sing, Br. Joseph may have the extreme goodness to represent Illinois in Alton, if his lawyers do not succeed in quashing the indictments found against him by the Grand Jurors of Hancock County, at the May term 1844.

FRANCIS M. HIGBEE.

# INDEX

F



G

I



J

Q



R

Y



Z